THE ROUTLEDGE COMPANION TO SMART DESIGN THINKING IN ARCHITECTURE & URBANISM FOR A SUSTAINABLE, LIVING PLANET

This comprehensive companion surveys *intelligent design thinking* in architecture and urbanism, investigates multiple facets of "smart" approaches to design thinking that augment the potentials of user experiences as well as his/her physical and mental interactions with the built environment.

Split into six paradigms, this volume looks at the theoretical and historical background of smart design, smart design methodologies and typologies, smart materials, smart design for extreme weather and climatic regions, as well as climate change issues and side effects, smart mobility, and the role of digital technologies and simulations in architectural and urban design. Often at odds with each other, this volume places emphasis on smart design for various typologies and user groups, emphasizing on advancements in form-making and implementation of technology for healthy and sustainable living environments.

Written by emerging and established architects, planners, designers, scientists, and engineers from around the globe, this will be an essential reference volume for architecture and urban design students and scholars as well as those in related fields interested in the implications, and various facets and futures of smart design.

Mitra Kanaani is a fellow of the American Institute of Architects (FAIA) and a fellow and Distinguished Professor of the Association Collegiate Schools of Architecture (DPACSA). Mitra holds a DArch, with a focus on Performative Architecture, and an MArch, with a minor in Structural Engineering, as well as a Master of Urban Planning and a BA in Musicology. She is the former chair of the NewSchool of Architecture, and an active researcher, author, and editor. She is currently on the California Architect Board, a Global Associate faculty with BIHE, and their liaison with the UIA.

THE ROUTLEDGE COMPANION TO SMART DESIGN THINKING IN ARCHITECTURE & URBANISM FOR A SUSTAINABLE, LIVING PLANET

Edited by Mitra Kanaani

Routledge
Taylor & Francis Group

LONDON AND NEW YORK

Designed cover image: Nasim Rowshan

First published 2025
by Routledge
4 Park Square, Milton Park, Abingdon, Oxon OX14 4RN

and by Routledge
605 Third Avenue, New York, NY 10158

Routledge is an imprint of the Taylor & Francis Group, an informa business

British Library Cataloguing-in-Publication Data
A catalogue record for this book is available from the British Library

ISBN: 978-1-032-46990-4 (hbk)
ISBN: 978-1-032-46997-3 (pbk)
ISBN: 978-1-003-38411-3 (ebk)

DOI: 10.4324/9781003384113

Typeset in Sabon
by codeMantra

Let us not lose sight of the fact that it was humans' intelligence and ingenuity that provided us with possibilities of further envisioning new opportunities with AI and technological manifestations.

Now, rather than competing with this creative trend, it is incumbent upon us to explore and nurture expertise in areas that complement automated processes through our creative and critical thinking abilities, toward furthering human dignity, elevating social empathy, and benefiting the sustenance and well-being of Planet Earth.

This comprehensive book of Smart Design Thinking is dedicated to all who are immersed in various fields of architecture, design, planning, engineering, sciences, and technology, deploying their expertise, dedicating their knowledge, and striving with sincere intentionality to save our endangered planet-- currently in a deep state of uncertainty...
Mitra Kanaani

CONTENTS

Contents

PREFACE

The Background of the Idea, Objectives, and the Conceptual Framework of the Publication – *Meanings and Various Domains of Smart Design Thinking*

Mitra Kanaani

In architecture and urbanism, the concept of *utopia* has often resembled a strong aspiration and yearning for an *ideally perfect* world pursued by visionary designers toward creating opportunities for progress and advancement in the design discipline. The design discipline has always been focused on the future of the world not only toward improving the quality of life and advancement in the development of the built environment, but also in addressing social and political reforms and dogmas. The resulting development of new types of *spatial entities* and urban settings with higher expectations for performative use has become the propellers for inevitable dynamic shifts in the lives of the users, and unprecedented transformation in the lifestyle of people in the communities. They have also driven innovations, advancements, and empowerment for aspiring governmental authorities around the globe.

Through the lens of utopian thinking, visionary ideas in architecture and urbanism look to possible futures that transcend the existing disillusionment currently engulfing our world. Utopian concepts have opened the door for designers to soar to new imaginative horizons. The world of architecture and the built-environment is encountering experimental attempts in design and construction of various types of self-sustained performative habitats as part of the trend toward *smart city design concepts*. Various visionary architects and urban designers, around the globe, in pursuit of experimenting ecological utopia or eco-utopian design concepts are contributing to the advancement of smart design concepts and its various means of application. In essence, the trend is rapidly accelerating toward a smart transition in *design thinking* that requires a new frame of mind and demands novel ways of living. More than ever, users of our built environment must learn to live smarter, cleaner, healthier, and more efficiently, if we intend our next generation to thrive, and if we intend them to inherit and benefit from a better quality of life on the *planet* in the near future and beyond.

The History of an Evolutionary Trend in Architecture

The 1850s second Industrial Revolution and the discovery of the approach to mass production of steel with different grades of carbon and the consequential discovery of ferroconcrete paved the path to the advent of high-rises in the twentieth century, and the current trend toward transformation to skyscrapers as the symbol of progress and advancement in various parts of the world. This evolutionary trend has charted bewildering complexity to our interconnected world, accompanying an unprecedented and fast-paced trajectory toward industrial and technological discoveries that have inevitably brought about their cultural transformations, and unique needs, as well as innovative technological opportunities. Nowadays, these needs are applied not only to tall buildings but also to various large-scope multifunctional types of occupancies including multifaceted institutional and governmental agencies, airports and specialized laboratories, and multiuse residential and commercial habitats constituting cities within the cities.

Design sophistication has brought the demand for the integration of various computer software, Internet of Things (IoT) devices, and artificial intelligence (AI) toward the development of intelligent/smart buildings. Intelligent buildings based on the demands of various typologies or building types pursue specific levels of *control* and *automation* measures that can be unique to every building type of use and occupancy. These needs relate but are not limited to design decisions related to climate control factors (including, temperature, humidity, and air circulation), as well as the needs for various innovative levels of light intensity, communication, safety, and security systems, and stability variables, which are constantly emerging and on the rise. In general, intelligent designs are about smart architectural designs with the crucial hybrid theme of how smart technology and AI will affect both our physical world and the way humans construct the symbolic world and how they see their place in their social and "natural" worlds, not just as the users but contributors to those environments.

Today's concept of smart buildings goes hand in hand with eco-friendly and human-centered green architecture, epitomizing intelligent ecological design thinking and performativity, which includes comprehensive responses to an urgent global need for environmental conservation and energy efficiency, promoting innovative technologies toward creating efficient and sustainable architectural constructs.

Smart building design, along with various development devices and the usage of sensors, has promoted advancement in the realm of innovative and new synthetic and nanotechnology of materials with amazing qualities and properties.

Efficient smart buildings are not just about added IoT and sensors, and demand integration of smart forms and design concepts. To use them efficiently, they demand a new culture of form-making and knowledge and understanding of efficient use and their proper operation.

What Is the Smart Definition as a Design Thinking Concept?

In our current evolutionary status of the world, smart and smartness, in architecture and design, have become buzzwords, signifying innovation in technological transformations. They have even become marketing tools. However, smart concepts for the design of the built environment have a noble mission. They must be considered as *design thinking tools* for the development of safer, healthier, environmentally efficient, equitable, and friendly spaces, transcending beyond showcasing the advancement of technology. As a rapidly expanding concept, "smartness" has the potential to enhance many aspects of daily life by demanding increased convenience and safety while dealing with the inevitable challenges of adapting to sophisticated intelligent systems. However, smart design is not just about automation, the IoT, AI, or robotics. As smart design expands and penetrates deeper into humanization, the psychology, and behavioral and social impacts of smart services, the act of design thinking can become more meaningful, effective, and adaptive for users. By the same token, these characteristics can also render designs that are irrelevant, non-workable, and ineffective for the users.

In this publication, six selected paradigmatic smart design categories have created the framework for its comprehensive content. The six defined paradigmatic categories offer various facets of smart strategies that inform the design of the built environments, user experiences, and the quality of life with a keen eye on sustainability and resiliency of the planet and its inhabitants. This study not only analyzes human health, experience, innovation, and creativity in design production but also investigates alternative solutions for negative psychological effects and mitigating generational trends toward alienation and isolation in our fast-expanding urban environments.

Smart Design Thinking is about designs that focus on equity, respect for diversity, tolerance, safety, and freedom of choice, as well as dignified human life for all citizens and users. It promotes beauty, innovation, and a healthy sense of physical, mental, emotional, and social well-being at all levels of living. *Smart Design Thinking* is an approach and an attitude rather than just the usage of technological tools. It needs to be adopted and introduced cohesively by all experts in various fields of design, technology, and scientific fields toward a fully integrative design methodology, at the onset of the development of the design concepts.

Smart design allows the human experience to reach its highest potential by promoting the inherent sensual and perceptual effects and tangibilities of the built environments. It allows for tangible opportunities to merge measurable and immeasurable attributes of design and promotes a sense of belonging that reduces alienation between inhabitants and the spaces they occupy.

In essence, *Smart Design Thinking* as a methodology of design thinking is about promoting convenience, safety, and well-being, through healthful and resilient urbanizations, spatial entities, and contextual settings that contribute to the sustainability of the *Planet as a Haven for its inhabitants*. By utilizing smart concepts and approaches in design thinking and form-making, and integrating innovative technologies, as tools, it is possible to support healthy generations and sustainable living environments.

This publication incorporates studies and manifestos on integrated inter-transdisciplinary smart design research that impacts our daily lives. Organized around paradigmatic[1] realms, the chapters investigate the impacts of *smart design – some of them still at their infancy level*. Papers and manifestos revolve around topics that promote human intelligence and creative achievement, sophistication in spatial constructs and innovative materiality, cognitive control, and physical well-being for healthy urbanizations and remedial actions to address major ramifications of climatic transformations and global warming. Authored by aspiring inquisitive contributors including architects, planners, designers, scientists, researchers, and engineers, various sections and articles investigate multitudes of notions of "smart design," as visionary processes, products, and design manifestos.

This book is organized around the following six Paradigmatic Categories:[1]

Paradigmatic Category 1: Various Domains of Smartness, Theoretical Discourses, and Approaches

This Paradigmatic Category initiates the discourse, alluding to the fact that the concept of *smart design thinking* in architectural design is not new. It underscores the contradictory implications of the application of smart design concepts in emerging habitats, cityscapes, and the global economy. The chapters in this paradigmatic grouping portray a critical outlook on the psychological, physical, social, and cultural impacts of digital technologies and AI on society and users' lifestyles, health, and well-being.

The chapters in this grouping offer the discourses, manifestos, and theories that analyze the impact of smart design thinking on current evolutionary issues: equity, diversity, inclusivity, social reforms, performativity, and safety. This paradigm expands and promotes architectural and utopian visions and theories that reinforce ideals promoting the development of future smart built environments, from mega-scope masterplans to individual intelligent constructs that are safe, uplifting, flourishing equitable, and healthful, as well as ecologically-friendly.

Paradigmatic Category 2: Smart Design Methodologies and Concepts for Intelligent Typologies and User Needs

This Paradigmatic Category expands on design innovations based on users' needs and architectural types, as well as specific smart methodologies, means, and approaches that constitute design intelligibility and are specific to architectural types and users. This section expands on smart design concepts, their applications for the built environment, and their impacts on the design of spaces and infrastructure. This paradigmatic realm focuses on smart specificity needs for architectural designs based on unique characteristics and qualities of contextual settings, as well as spatial performative typological requirements and users' restrictive conditions. The contextual setting can be in space, under bodies of water, or within a fully enclosed environment, in which the specificity of the user's needs in conjunction with certain physical or cognitive shortcomings, as well as physical restrictive qualities, can create specific design performativity demands. For instance, design for the blind or design for cognitive disorders necessitates certain functionalities that demand designed spaces must be charged with the capacity to address specific performative aspects of their use through smart design thinking concepts and means, for example, in *design for learning* and *design for healing*.

Paradigmatic Category 3: Smart Materiality

This Paradigmatic Category focuses on the role of fast-evolving smart materials and their impact on the process of form-making and the creation of design concepts that are free from material constraints and their advancements. Smart responsive materials undertake considerable responsibility for environmentally sensitive progressive architecture and promoting the ideals of realistic sustainable and energy-efficient built environments. By using information derived from quantum physics, nanotechnology, biology, chemistry, and AI, the chapters in this section offer progressive advancements that are currently taking place in the development of smart materials and tectonics of the built constructs. The fast-paced progressive role of imaging technology in developing various scales of super-hard super-light synthetic materials with superhuman properties is indeed a major contributor to the creation of smart spaces for the design of various typologies.

Paradigmatic Category 4: Smart Design for a Changing Climate

This Paradigmatic Category focuses on smart design solutions in defiance of Climate Change, and resiliency for regions with extreme hot, cold, or arid climates. It considers bodies of water as contextual settings for developing living environments. It also investigates the consequences of major climatic changes, such as fires, and flooding, and new approaches in bridging architecture with agriculture through urban farming, net zero, and clean energy production through artificial and natural aquatic systems, and avoidance of usage of fossil fuels to prevent environmental toxic and harmful pollutions. This section discusses unchartered territories and regions entangled with extreme climates and geographical extremities, constraints, and challenges. It reflects on recently developed technologies for smart habitats and living environments, offering smart solutions to adapt to the negative impacts of intense climates. It also champions the appreciation of good practices for climate-resilient communities and sustainable livable constructs in harmony with their natural settings.

Paradigmatic Categories 5: On Smart Design Mobility and in Defiance of Pollution

This Paradigmatic Category covers topics related to *Intelligent Mobility Systems* and their impact on the design of urban and built environments toward augmenting the space potentials within the buildings and cities – chapters include sustainable design mobility solutions and agendas that synthesize manufacturing, computing energy, and material, toward developing safer, cleaner, and more convenient means of transportations in and between future cities. This paradigm introduces eco-mobility, which prioritizes walking, cycling, public transportation, and shared light electric vehicles. It promotes travel through integrated socially inclusive and environmentally friendly options independent of privately owned vehicles. It gives priority to health, safety, low-emissions, and people-centered urban development encouraging circular and regional economies while limiting the impact of freight transport.

Articles in this section expands on future visions of short distances, long-distance mobility systems, and breaking away from cultural attachments to cars and the infrastructure that supports them. It also introduces lessons learned from developments in Space Architecture.

Paradigmatic Category 6: Simulation and Advancements in Digital Technologies and Data-Driven Smart Designs

This Paradigmatic Category focuses on the technology of design production and the impact of *Smart Design Productions* on the direction of today's design methodology. This Paradigmatic realm looks into new technology and tools utilized in architectural design focused on efficiency, sustainability, and optimization goals. It considers smart methodologies for the production and manufacturing of design constructs. Chapters in this realm reflect on creative advancement in integrative design and construction processes of smart buildings, and how new technologies inform and improve the design process and production. This final section focuses on the idea that buildings are increasingly considered smart self-sufficient structures, which are automated and networked, as intelligent machines for living.

The main goal of this publication is to help raise awareness about the critical condition of our planet concerning the profound ecological and environmental challenges it is facing.

The famous English historian Arnold Toynbee (1889–1975) in his monumental *A Study of History* refers to the fact that "…the well-being of a civilization depends on its ability to respond creatively to challenges, human and environmental"[2].

If we believe that with every challenge, there is an opportunity, smart design thinking in architecture will be a warrant for optimism in saving our planet, and its future generations of inhabitants. Smart design thinking is about the power and utopian promises of a creative design agency that has the highest capacity to transform and reshape our future.

Editor's Notes and Acknowledgments

Sadly, during the production of this massive volume, our large team of contributors and authors was faced with the major loss and sudden passing of Dr. Eduardo Macagno, former Chair and Professor of Cell/Developmental Biology and Neuroscience, and the co-founder of the Academy of Neuroscience and Architecture. I am proud that his last writing and contribution to the world of science is included in this publication, with the sincere work and co-authorship of his graduate student, Julia del Rio.

Design of the Book Cover and Notes of Appreciation

The cover illustration designed by Nasim Rowshan is a collage of concepts toward a vision of speculative design solutions and for what the prospects of the cities might be and the way we might live and work in the future. It is the creative rendition of an exploration of the kaleidoscopic implications and possibilities of kinds of visionary spatial and functional relationships that a self-sufficient multifaceted city might contain and convey.

A special note of appreciation and deep gratitude to Nasim, who was one of my talented students of the BIHE and a graduate of Yale, for her contributions to the design of the book cover. Also, a special note of appreciation to Lucy Campbell for her sincere support and collaboration in the editorial needs of the publication.

Notes

1 Paradigmatic Category refers to a prototypical classification and formation of a group of concepts and subjects that belong to a specific paradigm or field of association.
2 Bruce Mau, in the Introduction of the book *Massive Change*, under the title of: Now that we can do anything, what will we do?. Mau is referring to the main thesis of famous English historian Arnold J. Toynbee's. In his monumental publication, *A Study of History*, Toynbee declares: "The twentieth century will be chiefly remembered by future generations not as an era of political conflicts or technical innovations but as an age in which human society dared to think of the welfare of the whole human race as a practical objective."
   Toynbee, A. J.: 1957, *A Study of History*, New York: Oxford University Press. As cited in Mau, B.: 2004, *Massive Change*. New York, NY: Phaidon Press.

INTRODUCTION

The Design Imagination – Is Smart Design Enough?

Harrison Fraker

The definition and scope of 'smart design' thinking is wide ranging and emergent as evident by the diversity of the 59 essays in this first *Routledge Companion to Smart Design Thinking in Architecture & Urbanism for a Sustainable and Living Planet*. The essays do a good job of illustrating different types of 'smart design thinking', but they represent only a small sampling of smart design strategies that will be necessary to mitigate and adapt to the challenges of climate change in creating a more sustainable and living planet. In fact, a comprehensive review of such smart design strategies would take multiple 'companions' to cover the range and complexity of design considerations. Nonetheless, the smart design strategies included in the *Companion* give a revealing glimpse into the range of innovative strategies that will be necessary to respond to the existential challenges of climate change.

In an effort to help comprehend the scope and diversity of smart design thinking, the essays can be grouped into several broad categories. In the first, the concept of 'smart design' is applied to improving the **performance**[1] of the built environment and specific physical systems. Through the use of smart, wireless sensors, data analytics, and smart controllers, the operation of systems can be managed to be more efficient and more responsive to the changing conditions of their environment and the precise, multi-sensory needs of users. In the second category, 'smart design' focuses on improving the intelligence of the design process itself, specific **methodologies** by which designers search for more appropriate and effective design solutions. A third category of smart design is less about a smart technology or smart methodologies, but more about an expanded **design sensibility**, one that explores the value of integrated whole-systems design thinking in imagining entirely new system configurations; and an expanded role of the senses, not only in custom designing places for special users, but also in making more meaningful places. And finally, smart design can be applied to the **intelligent manufacturing** of building elements, previously unimagined, that can be made more sustainable.

Smart Design Performance

Using 'smart design' to improve the performance of physical systems has been at least 50 years in the making. The development of the smart, programmable thermostat, which

DOI: 10.4324/9781003384113-1

allowed homeowners to program the timing and temperature settings of their thermostat rather than adjust them manually, is an excellent early example of improving energy efficiency. The evolution in performance of smarter systems has followed the improvement and sophistication in wireless sensors, data analytics, and programmable controllers. It has become almost ubiquitous. It can be found in almost any physical device, home appliance, car operations, not to mention driverless vehicles. It has been crucial in designing buildings to become zero carbon in energy operation. By improving energy efficiency through smart management of HVAC systems, the dynamic response of building envelopes (see Kalantar/Ekeda, Mostafavi/Bao/Montejano_), and even optimizing the properties of smart programmable materials (see Tholen, Rian), the energy demand can be reduced so that the application of local renewables (solar PV and/or wind) can deliver cost-effective energy self-sufficient building operations. It extends to larger systems like the management of urban infrastructure using data analytics and Artificial Intelligence (AI) to anticipate and control system operations. Examples include water supply/storage and maintenance, storm water management, waste water treatment, traffic control, and urban services. It is used by utilities to anticipate and manage energy supply and demand, the use of storage, backup generation, and the integration of renewables (see Herr, Isaac/Casals/Carta, Toyne/Williams, Leach, Thanghavelu, Fairburn/Mohanty/Imhof, Del Campo). It is also being used to measure the moisture content of soils, which, when coordinated with weather forecasting, can deliver more efficient agricultural irrigation.

All of these are examples of 'smart design' using technical intelligence to improve the performance of discrete systems. It has been shown that 'smart design' strategies are particularly effective when the boundary of the system and the metrics of measuring performance are well defined. The question is what happens when the boundary of the design problem is expanded to include other systems that, previously, have been seen as outside the problem but could be integrated to become design resources. What this calls attention to is that 'smart design' needs to adopt a more integrated, whole-systems design sensibility, where 'smart design' captures synergies across systems, where systems are seen as interconnected (see Braham). For example, where sewage is not seen as waste, treated and dumped in the environment, but is seen as a resource that can be treated and re used for irrigation, or gray water, or even potable water; where organic waste is not just dumped or composted, but processed to create biogas for energy. The concept is captured by the analogy with the international space station's self-sufficient, closed-loop operation and thus leads to the hypothesis of a 'spaceship city' (see Cohen/Imhoff) or buildings with a 'brain' (see Arbib). Articulating this kind of expanded 'smart design' thinking holds the promise of it playing a crucial role in both mitigating and adapting to the existential threat of climate change. Many of the essays illustrate the value of integrated whole-system design thinking, by capturing the potential of previously unrecognized opportunities in creating new innovative design solutions. (See Sterry, Mueller, Cody, Besancon, Steudel, Piatek/English, Piatek, Baumeister, Linarki/Baumeister/Stevens/Burton, Dunsmore, Tomber, Young, Mahadevwala.)

Smart Design Methodologies

Recent improvements in the intelligence of the design process build on long-standing traditions in the design professions – both the practice of analyzing precedents and researching the literature on 'post-occupancy' evaluations of building types. Alan Colquhoun reminded us of the value of intelligent pre-design research in his article, 'Typology and Design

Methods' in *Perspecta 13*, where he essentially argues that good design can spring from the creative evolution and adaptation of known building types, rather than starting from scratch with a simple social/functional diagram of program elements. Intelligent (smart) pre-design research has evolved to include the creation and use of 'digital twins' not only to simulate and evaluate the performance of precedents but also to compare the performance of new design alternatives. The construction of digital twins or prototypes can also enable the smart manufacturing of building elements using 3D printing and robotics (see Neumayr, Mostafavi/Mehan/Bagher, Piroozfar/Farr, Kalantar/Borhani). Yet the biggest development in smart design methods is the exponential increase in the search power of generative AI.

Over the past few years, there has been an explosion in the development of AI architecture generator programs (18 have been recently reviewed in Construction Magazine, Aug 28, 3023). These architecture generators have special functions according to the nature of the advanced AI algorithms hidden in them, ranging from 'advanced machine learning', 'CLIP' (contrastive language-image learning pre-training), 'neural network technology', and 'deep learning'. In most cases, the search depends on mastering appropriate text-based input. For example, 'imagine': subject (building type), user, background, arch style desired (can name well-known architect), time period, site, total area, and cost. The program then visualizes multiple design options. But some programs can also begin with an image input that can be edited, renovated, and rendered. Each AI generator can be used specifically for different phases and aspects of the design process, including visualizing alternate schematic designs and/or 'ideagrams', visualizing and rendering different styles, creating pseudo-realistic images, drawing plans for analyzing energy performance and resulting carbon footprint, working with 3D modeling programs like SketchUp, Revit and Rhino to do high-quality rendering. Some programs are customized for interior design, site planning, restoration, urban design, and landscape design.

These AI design generator programs are powerful tools for exploring and developing design ideas. While they may generate unexpected, if not wildly unusual alternate solutions, even completely non-sensical proposals, exposure to them can stimulate the design imagination. Furthermore, they can be used to optimize design alternatives for different criteria, helping make more informed and smart decisions. By automating many menial drafting tasks, they free up time for creative thinking and problem solving and increase design efficiency. It is like having an expansive team of design assistants at the designer's finger tips. Nonetheless, in spite of AI's unparalleled power of search and visualization, a final design proposal (architecture or urban design) depends on the creativity, intuition, critical thinking, and decision-making of the designer.

Of course, the quality of output from AI design generators depends on the depth and efficacy of the data base being searched and mastery of the text-based or image-based input being used (not to mention the nature of the advanced AI algorithms being used). This is a challenge for 'smart design' generators because the data bases used to visualize alternative design concepts are not necessarily linked to performance data of the design problem being explored, either post-occupancy evaluations or energy performance. The data bases are primarily visual and/or scenographic. Furthermore, the metrics on performance vary from technical to social to economic to aesthetic and are not standardized (not to mention the array of data on city performance). This suggests not only the need to expand and improve the data bases, but also a multi-phase design process that first visualizes a solution and then goes through an iterative performance evaluation to arrive at an optimal solution. It also suggests the need to expand the content of the design data bases being searched to include performance metrics beyond the spatial and visual. (Some of the papers address this challenge, see Farr and Piroozfar.)

This challenge of linking spatial images to performance has been recognized by some in the industry. For example, Autodesk, which provides drafting and modeling tools for the design professions, has been working to develop a tool named 'Generative Design'. It brings the complete information on building designs, documented in their BIM (Building Information Management) data base, together with performance modeling tools (digital twins) to compare simulated performance with measured performance and user satisfaction of different designs. The tool will give designers a rich trove of information to evaluate different spatial patterns and configurations, construction materials, envelope designs, and HVAC system specifications to inform their early design explorations. It can inform the search for zero-carbon sustainable solutions. And yet, such a tool does not generate a final design solution, it provides a more intelligent and informed benchmark.

Similar tools have been developed for urban and regional planning scenarios. One example is Urban Footprint. It uses Geographic Information System (GIS) to map the physical characteristics and information sets of a city and its region, including the zoning plan, environmental and climate data, energy supply and demand, building data – use type, construction and density, census data, traffic data, commercial activity, air quality, and health data. It then proposes a menu of 36 place-types, derived from current development models with all their physical characteristics, to be used for planning future development scenarios. For example, the place types include medium density; mixed-use; walkable neighborhoods served by public transit; or low density suburban residential sprawl; commercial centers; regional malls and storage/distribution centers, to name a few. By locating different places types spatially in a city or region, it allows urban designers and planners to paint different futures, to construct different scenarios. The program then calculates the consequence and impact on traffic flow, energy demand/consumption, carbon footprint, water demand, storm water flows, sewage treatment demands, health consequence, to name a few metrics. It is a form of digital prototyping and simulation analysis; however, it does not design the place types in detail, nor does it include new place types. It just reveals estimates of measurable consequences from the spatial deployment of place types, allowing for a comparison among different scenarios (see Schumacher/Blooshan).

These two examples of 'smart design' tools illustrate how 'smart design' improves the intelligence of design research and exploration. Through the use of AI and data analytics, it can discover new patterns, expand the number of potential design solutions, anticipate new needs, and guide the intelligent management and performance of physical systems. By building digital twins, it can model and compare the performance of design alternatives, a form of digital prototyping. Furthermore, with an expanded design sensibility, using integrated whole-systems thinking, it can discover new previously unrecognized synergies across systems. When the expanded design sensibility includes an increased awareness of the role of the senses in user experience and satisfaction, it can custom design environments for users with specialized needs. (See Othon-Villegas, Zhang/Evan-Green, Bauman, Downey/Arbib, Giovannella/Roccasalva, Zisch/Stroe/Ward, Gepshtein/Proietti, Macagno/ de Rio, Gaines.)

Thus, the power of 'smart design' as portrayed in the papers is just emerging with the potential to radically improve our search for design solutions that will mitigate and adapt to the existential threat of climate change, helping create a more sustainable and livable planet. In fact, it may be essential for the survival of the planet as we know it.

Nonetheless, there are questions to be asked that are inherent in the definition of and application of 'smart design thinking'. It is particularly good at improving the efficiency of existing systems through intelligent feedback and control, but what about discovering entirely new systems or approaches that are outside or replace existing solutions? AI 'smart design' generators are particularly good at synthesizing the principles and patterns of 'best practices' and visualizing a wide range of alternative solutions. While it may discover previously unrecognized patterns in the data and expand the landscape of potential design solutions, it is limited to existing available data sets. By its own constraints, it is unable to discover entirely new solutions, 'outside the box' of known practices. So, does 'smart design', bound by its search of existing data, limit the search for new innovative and transformative design concepts?

Furthermore, smart design depends on measurable data for its comparisons, but what about the immeasurable – the emotional, the sensorial, and visceral experience of places? While it will be essential in comparing the measured performance of different approaches to climate change, can it also assist in creating places that are more meaningful? This is a complicated question because in many cases meaningful design goes beyond the measurable. Often the immeasurable qualities of a place, along with its technical performance, are why we value, fund, and maintain it. So, the question is are there emotional, sensorial, and visceral qualities of smart design strategies that are under recognized and could lead to creating more meaningful places?

By way of illustrating the immeasurable in design, it is hard to imagine that 'smart design' played any role in Peter Zumthor's creation of the Bruder Klaus Chapel. His idea of burning logs, arranged in a teepee like pyre, enclosed in a concrete box, to carve out a memorial space for a martyred patron saint is an imaginative leap of genius. It creates a powerful sensorial and evocative experience from the lingering smell of the burn, the color and texture of the concrete formed by the burned-out logs, the sparkle of minerals in the burned concrete, the mysterious top light left by the absence of the teepee's apex, and the twinkle of light coming through the concrete tie-holes. It creates a space of reverie that springs from Zumthor's imagination, informed by his embodied visceral experience of the world, not from any AI, simulations, or machine learning.

The same can be said for Louis Kahn's design of the Salk Institute. His brilliant solution to arrange the 'servant' spaces between the 'served' floors in section allows for maximum flexibility and access to all technical support. It comes from his own critical 'post occupancy' evaluation of the Richard's Medical Center, where the 'servant' spaces, arranged in plan as towers around stacked laboratory floors, forced the services to be strung across the ceilings in order to reach lab stations. While the shift to a solution in section can be described as a form of 'smart design', learning from a precedent, its source is not an application of AI or a simulation, but Kahn's own direct experience. Furthermore, while the sectional arrangement of 'servant' and 'served' spaces is an essential idea of the design, it is the clustering of the research office space, forming a cloister with views of the horizon and setting sun that captures a more poetic version of the Institute. It embodies the idea of a community with 'the power of science to explore the foundations of life'. It is this aspect of the design idea that springs from Kahn's imagination, his notion of a community of scientists, that captures our aesthetic imagination and makes the place memorable.

From these two examples, creating meaningful places depends on the creative imagination of the designer to capture special and resonant qualities that transform the experience of a place, beyond its technical performance. This springs from the experience of the designer(s), her/his/their visceral, sensorial, and embodied experience of the world. While 'smart design' can greatly enhance the intelligence of early design explorations and test the performance of alternatives, it needs to recognize and create a place in the process for the design imagination to search for and capture experiences that go beyond the measurable and touch on the emotional. From this perspective, 'smart design' is and will be critical in improving the quality of design for a sustainable and living planet, but not the whole story.

Note

1 The concept that the physical environment performs (beyond its visual construct), that it can be responsive to the needs of users, that it can be designed to perform in response to multiple concerns is foundational to the development of 'smart design thinking'. The case for a performative and responsive built environment (architecture and urbanism) is historically explained and developed in Branko Kolarevic's paper.

PROLOGUE

Architects, Smart Futures, and Climate Change

Jim Dator

This volume seeks to spur futures-orientation by architects in at least two of the most important of the many novelties of the present and immediate futures.

One area of novelty to which all architects should be responsive is the rising power and ubiquity of artificial intelligence, artificial life, robotics, autonomous entities (artilects), smart buildings in smart environments with smart materials and performative architecture – flexible, adaptive, intelligent, anticipatory, alive, and evolvable. Some architects have shown an active awareness of these novelties as they emerged over the years in progressively powerful forms and functions. But while the history of these technologies is long, their futures will be even longer, wider, and more disruptive as biomolecular processes join with and in many areas surpass electronic processes that have already marginalized if not yet eliminated all traditional physical and mechanical ways and means.

The "surprising" launch in November 2022 of ChatGPT transformed the future. Open AI's announcement casually stated, "We've trained a model called ChatGPT which interacts conversationally. The dialogue format makes it possible for ChatGPT to answer follow-up questions, admit its mistakes, challenge incorrect premises, and reject inappropriate requests" [https://openai.com/blog/chatgpt]. That modest announcement hit the attentive community with explosive power equal to the launch of Sputnik into Earth orbit in October 1957 and of the crash of Flights 11 and 175 into the Twin Towers in September 2001. In all three cases, "we" had been warned well ahead of time but ignored the warnings – while then flailing hysterically about after the events. This time, panic vacillated being certain the world had come to an end – the robots would kill us all – to asserting, NO! they weren't *really* intelligent – but they would take all our jobs! To desperately seek to decide who to blame. Thor Benson frankly stated that "artificial intelligence is arguably the most rapidly advancing technology humans have ever developed" and that "the AI era promises a flood of disinformation, deepfakes, and hallucinated 'facts.' Psychologists are only beginning to grapple with the implications." (Benson 2023). Many nations, and even the United Nations, hastily convened conferences to discuss what should be done to save humanity from our too-clever artificial creations.

There is no doubt one world ended with ChatGPT. But a new world also began as well. How much better it would have been if we had heeded warnings and prepared for and

DOI: 10.4324/9781003384113-2

ameliorated the impacts. (Dator 2020, 2022). I would seriously wonder about any architect who has not by now already joined the conversation about—and actively experimented with – the impact of AI at least on their particular sector of the profession.

The second novelty of concern to all contributors to this book is climate change, sea level rise, the disruption of patterns of seasons, rain, snow, drought, hurricanes, and the rest that have guided farmers, fishers, planners, architects, and others for the past several hundred years. Land use practices and building solutions that seemed eternal are now seen as ephemeral – indeed vanishing – and will not be replaced by a new normal but rather by increasingly uncertain, extreme, temporary, fluid processes.

The Sixth Assessment Report of the United Nations' Intergovernmental Panel on Climate Change, which has been tracking data for many decades states:

> Human activities, principally through emissions of greenhouse gases, have unequivo-cally caused global warming, with global surface temperature reaching 1.1°C above 1850–1900 in 2011–2020. Global greenhouse gas emissions have continued to increase, with unequal historical and ongoing contributions arising from unsustain-able energy use, land use and land-use change, lifestyles, and patterns of consumption and production across regions, between and within countries, and among individuals.
>
> *(IPCC 2023)*

An independent international team of bioscientists say, we are "entering uncharted territory":

> Life on planet Earth is under siege. We are now in an uncharted territory. For several decades, scientists have consistently warned of a future marked by extreme climatic conditions because of escalating global temperatures caused by ongoing human activities that release harmful greenhouse gasses into the atmosphere. Unfortunately, time is up. We are seeing the manifestation of those predictions as an alarming and unprecedented succession of climate records are broken, causing profoundly distress-ing scenes of suffering to unfold. We are entering an unfamiliar domain regarding our climate crisis, a situation no one has ever witnessed firsthand in the history of humanity.
>
> *(Ripple 2023)*

Some architects, scholars, and others have been aware of these environmental challenges for many years and endeavored to warn the rest of us, but their warnings have also been discounted, denied, and ridiculed while activities that created the dis-ruptions have increased rather than diminished in extent and impact. It is no longer possible for responsible decision-makers to deny the reality and growing omnipres-ence of climate change and its impacts, even though no one can be certain of the precise location, timing, and magnitude of the resulting novelties and how best to prepare to thrive in them. We have not yet had, and we may never have the kind of singular wake-up call of climate change that we had for AI. But the possible abrupt cessation of the globally-circulating thermohaline current that could put Europe into a sudden deep freeze while disrupting other climate patterns worldwide might be the trigger, especially since all of the few eyes attentive to the issue are on global warming and not renewed freezing. And yet, the term is, correctly, climate *change* in all directions and dimensions.

(Ditlevsen and Ditlevsen 2015)

Architects and other shapers of the built environment must endeavor to access the best current and evolving information about climate change, designing flexible forms that perpetually anticipate, accommodate, embrace, and co-evolve with these and other pressing novelties. Fortunately, a major resource for anticipating and adapting wisely to continual climate and weather uncertainty lies in cooperating with increasingly powerful artificial intelligence in designing and creating artificial, synthetic, environments fit for whatever the weather is.

Unfortunately, a major handicap to cooperation between humans and artificial intelligence and life is the existence of extremely powerful images of that relationship as portrayed in the annals and current productions of science fiction. Not only are most humans unable clearly to distinguish between what is scientifically and technologically possible from what science fiction seduces our lizard brains to perceive and desire, but also contemporary life, as well as history, is full of visionary utopias of futures that quickly become bloody dystopia for the people who have to live in them.

It is my sincere hope that the chapters in this book exhibit some of the best ideas and actions according to current knowledge and foresight regarding these and other issues that individual authors may wish to highlight. The dreams of architects have consequences well beyond the lifetime of the dreamers.

References

Benson, Thor. "Humans Aren't Mentally Ready for an AI-Saturated 'Post-Truth World'." *Wired*, June 18, 2023.

Dator, Jim. "Epilogue: Architects, Artilects, and Climate Change", in Mitra Kanaani, ed., *The Routledge Companion to Ecological Design Thinking*. Routledge, 2022, pp. 616–625.

Dator, Jim. "Towards Responsibly Anticipatory Evolvable Architecture for the Anthropocene", in Mitra Kanaani, ed., *The Routledge Companion to Paradigms of Performativity*. New York, Routledge, 2020.

Ditlevsen, Peter and Susanne Ditlevsen. "Warning of a Forthcoming Collapse of the Atlantic Meridional Overturning Circulation." *Nature Communications*, July 25, 2023. https://doi.org/10.1038/s41467-023-39810-w

IPCC, 2023. "Summary for Policymakers", in: *Climate Change 2023: Synthesis Report. Contribution of Working Groups I, II, and III to the Sixth Assessment Report of the Intergovernmental Panel on Climate Change*. Core Writing Team, H. Lee and J. Romero, eds., IPCC, Geneva, Switzerland, pp. 1–34, 2023, doi: 10.59327/IPCC/AR6-9789291691647.001

Rahmstorf, Stefan, Jason E. Box, Georg Feulner, Michael E. Mann, Alexander Robinson, Scott Rutherford, and Erik J. Schaffernicht. "Exceptional Twentieth-Century Slowdown in the Atlantic Ocean Overturning Circulation." *Nature Climate Change* 5 (2015), 475–480. https://doi.org/10.1038/nclimate2554

Ripple, William J., Christopher Wolf, Jillian W. Gregg, Johan Rockström, Thomas M. Newsome, Beverly E. Law, Luiz Marques, Timothy M. Lenton, Chi Xu, Saleemul Huq, Leon Simons, and Sir David Anthony King. "The 2023 state of the climate report: Entering uncharted territory." *BioScience*, August 30, 2023. https://doi.org/10.1093/biosci/biad080

PARADIGMATIC CATEGORY 1

Various Domains of Smartness in Design Thinking, Theoretical Discourses, and Approaches

This Paradigmatic Category initiates the discourse, alluding to the fact that the concept of *smart design thinking* in architectural design is not new. It underscores the contradictory implications of the application of smart design concepts in emerging habitats, cityscapes, and the global economy. The chapters in this paradigmatic grouping portray a critical outlook on the psychological, physical, social, and cultural impacts of digital technologies and AI on society and users' lifestyles, health, and well-being.

The chapters in this grouping offer the discourses, manifestos, and theories that analyze the impact of smart design thinking on current evolutionary issues: equity, diversity, inclusivity, social reforms, performativity, and safety. This paradigm expands and promotes architectural and utopian visions, and theories that reinforce ideals promoting the development of future smart built environments, from mega-scope masterplans to individual intelligent constructs that are safe, uplifting, flourishing equitable, and healthful, as well as ecologically-friendly.

DOI: 10.4324/9781003384113-3

1.1
EMERGING SMART DESIGN THINKING

A Utopian Futuristic Trend, and an Enduring
Theoretical Discourse, ….or an Interim Stance?

1.1.1

UNDERSTANDING THE EMERGING DOMAINS OF SMART DESIGN THINKING CONCEPTS AND INTELLIGENT DESIGN METHODOLOGIES IN ARCHITECTURE

Background, Theoretical Tenets, and Various Facets of Smart Thinking in Architectural Design and Conceptualization

Mitra Kanaani

Abstract

The meaning of the word *smart*, being perceptive, astute, and shrewd, in *smart design* connotation is widely used as a synonym for nearly everything deemed to be contemporary, and progressive, particularly involving advanced high intelligent technologies and even high-tech features and approaches.

Ironically, with regard to the background of the *Smart Design* as an approach in design thinking, it is not a new concept in the survey of the history of design and architecture. The architects of antiquity were considered well-informed skillful scientists and visionary design-builders of their time. Some remaining known masterpieces of ancient architectural heritage around the globe manifest the most sophisticated design concepts and vivid demonstration of gravitation to the pursuit of futuristic and technically challenging design thinking trajectories experimented by master builders, as resemblances of visionary and advanced design thinking manifestations of various eras of architecture.

There are many examples of smart masterpieces that can be traced throughout the history of civilization and in various transformative eras of architecture, specifically with respect to the evolutionary trend in building materials and the systems, as well as vernacular architecture. The Industrial Revolution and emergence of various grades of steel, and types of composite ferro-concrete, as well as new synthetic smart materials and their detailing techniques demonstrate a major rise in the advancement of smart buildings and sophistication in architectural design thinking. The modern movement in architecture by utilizing new materials and incorporating new systems have a vast palette of design opportunities for sophistication in design thinking and building construction.

The inaugurating chapter for this compressive publication on *smart design thinking*, by way of investigating various facets of smart strategies and approaches will focus and expand on the evolutionary background and meanings of the *Intelligent Design Thinking*, which distinguishes itself from the meaning of *Smart Design*, and *Smart Design Thinking*. The Smart Design as a methodology will analyze data-driven performative approaches and factors that are focused on utopian visionary concepts in architecture and urbanism. This chapter expands on the fact that *Intelligent Design* concepts have been accompanying social and political reforms necessitating development of new types of spatial setting needs for emerging lifestyles. By becoming the vehicle for new ways of living and thinking, *Smart Design* approaches signify progress and advancement for visionary development of the cities and the built environments.

Introduction – Background of Emerging Intelligent Design Concepts, and Smart Design Thinking

Throughout the history of architecture there are buildings that are considered as marvels, due to the sophistication in their design concept and construction. Ancient masterpiece such as Stone Henge has been operating as a giant built calendar and a clock, based on its compliance with the revolution of the sun around its built form on the daily, monthly, and seasonal basis. The scientifically selected design features and orientation of the building's facade elements were meant to demonstrate the time of the day and change of the seasons based on the formal synchrony with the revolution of the earth and its orbit around the sun (Figure 1.1.1).

Also, located in the central plateau of Iran, the ancient City of Yazd's underground network of an aqueduct system, have been acting not only as the channels for distribution of water, but also operating as the most advanced natural cooling and ventilating system. Performing not only as underground channels for the distribution of water, but the system of aqueducts were also the most advanced natural cooling and ventilating system in combination with the architecturally eye-catching wind catchers. Strategically located at the heart of the buildings' super structures, the wind catchers along with the underground network of aqua-ducts have been creating the most intelligent architectural design solution for introducing natural ventilation while simultaneously acting as the cooling system in one of the most arid and hot climatic regions of the world (Figure 1.1.2).

Another marvel of architecture is the Sheikh Baha'i Bath house in Isfahan. Throughout the Middle Ages, there were sophisticated architectural examples as marvels. With a highly sophisticated plumbing system, the Sheikh Baha'i bathhouse is another marvel in the architecture of antiquity, providing a constant flow of hot water for the bathhouse users. The entire plumbing system of the bathhouse was operated by the steady flame of a lit candle connected to the ventilation duct system of the nearby mosque's heavily used public toilets. By using a natural suction method and by burning the human-generated urine gases including methane, and sulfur oxides, as the only generated fuel, there was a constant flow of hot water for the bathhouse users all throughout its operating time (Figure 1.1.3).

Another example is the famous moving minarets of the Menar Jonban, a marvel of architecture in the historical city of Isfahan. This monument had the capacity to move sideways,

Figure 1.1.1   Stonehenge, Salisbury Plain Wilshire, England.

Credit: Jonathan-ridley-ZLDp62DrLo-unsplash.

Figure 1.1.2   Historical City of Yazd, Iran – Wind Towers.

Credit: Hasan-Almasi-Jp3OEDO4Q-8-unsplash.

Figure 1.1.3　Sheikh Bahai bath-house, Isfahan, Iran[1].

Credit: Courtesy of, Iran Front Page, CC BY 4.0 Deed | Attribution 4.0 International | Creative Commons.

back, and forth without collapse, shaking its entire structural system by way of operating a mechanical handle, without jeopardizing the integrity of the building.

The ingenious marvels of ancient architecture signify the sophistication and intelligent design thinking of their visionary designers at the time of their most primitive technological capacities and scientific capabilities. However, throughout the ages, it is interesting to follow the impact of humanity's technological, and scientific advancements combined with social reforms agendas, as the main propellers for the emergence of various architectural movements. Constant transformation in societies' needs and expectations, combined with high fascination with technology, and nanotechnology, allowing invention of innovative synthetic building materials and systems with high resilience and capacities have marked the start of a new direction and development of a movement that can be marked as the era of AI in architecture.

The entire movement has a trace in the history of architecture, with the rise of industry in the Industrial Revolution and its transformative period of mass production of steel and invention of reinforced concrete that is marked as a new chapter in the history of modern architecture for the use of industrially produced materials.

Toward the 20th century, there was a rise in the hypothetical projects of avant-garde architectural groups, such as Archigram and Green Brothers who in pursuit of creating novel technology-based design concepts, were proposing responsive, indeterminate, user-driven architectural entities as *intelligent environments*. These visionary architectural projects inherently exemplified the search for intelligent design concepts and solutions as remedies for social problems by integrating all aspects of life together within the built environment. In various design concepts such as the Walking City, Plug-in-City, and Instant City, "the design proposals included flexible and adaptive architectural ideas, pop culture images and space travel hardware." (Yiannoudes, S. IEEE 2011, Conference Proceedings)

Thus, the movement became the symbol of neo-futurist and pro-consumerist ideologies, combining architecture, technology, and society. With a tremendous amount of fascination for technology, a number of visionary architects of the time have been motivated by a self-reflecting investigation regarding the meaning of advancement and progress, while being obsessed with many facets of ecological challenges. Throughout the decades, intelligent design initiatives have endured a robust trajectory, shifting towards the development of many facets of ecotopian visions. Currently, various architectural design projects involving social reforms with focuses on environment, education, health, safety, and equity for citizens, as well as various design concepts for mitigating the challenges of climate change and promoting sustainability and the resiliency of our ailing planet and its inhabitant, are actively pursued through *Intelligent* and *Smart Design* approaches and agendas.

Smart Design Thinking Versus Intelligent Design Methodology

Smart Design Thinking and Intelligent Design approaches maintain overall analogous objectives, while conveying inherent strategic differences in their execution and practice. Intelligent Design approaches pursue concepts and goals of sustainability, human comfort, health, and safety, as well as building efficiency. Smart Design, for the most part, conveys the overall message of advancement and innovation and pursues achieving such design goals by way of usage of digital technology and AI. Considering that building in its totality consists of a multitude of systems, in a Smart Design methodology there is an opportunity for independent control of various systems of the building through technological means and AI sophistication.

In general, Intelligent Design concepts for the most part are synonymous with Green Architecture, following low-tech or eco-tech environmentally responsive goals and objectives in form-making and usage of the systems and materiality, with or without involvement of high-tech approaches and the usage of AI, advanced sensors, and or Information and Communication Technology (ICT). The main difference between the two concepts or design methodology is the degree of control and close monitoring of outputs with respect to sustainability goals, energy efficiency, automation, data analysis (for instance, with respect to human comfort), and collection of the information about experiences, connectivity of the systems, safety and security, as well as optimization. (Autodesk: Smart Building, 6/28/2024). In general, Smart buildings use technology to collect, store and use data toward a set goal for optimization. In essence, *smart designs* are *intelligent designs*, but not every intelligent design is smart!

To recognize the differences between *Intelligent and Smart Designs*, majority of the time there are a number of identifying goals that allow distinguishing them from each other:

- *Smart buildings*, for the most part focus on technologically oriented interdisciplinary goals and practices. Whereas *Intelligent buildings* pursue more holistic solutions, and focus on the outcome for safety, security, and human comfort.
- *Intelligent buildings* are designed for their adopted concepts of safety, security health and wellbeing, energy-efficiency and more, from the onset of their approach in design

thinking. Typically, *Smart buildings* in practice, are the result of adoption of certain concepts in renovation and transformation of existing buildings.

- *Intelligent buildings* utilize analytical thinking for optimizing overall performance of the building, whereas *Smart buildings* use digital technology and are focused toward achieving efficiency of certain building systems or elements.
- *Intelligent buildings* versus *Smart buildings* have different approach in collection and usage of the data. *Smart buildings* have independent data collection for each system versus *Intelligent buildings* that are designed to share data across all systems.
- *Intelligent building* has seamless and optimized systems' performance for a full automation. Whereas not all systems in Smart buildings are automated.
- *Intelligent building* has centralized systems, whereas *smart building's* various systems are individually controlled and independent from each other.
- *Intelligent building* uses people and processes toward creating a smart and efficient indoor environment, which is going beyond just the use of technology (Valle, 2022).

In general, the current *smart architectural design* is a data-driven design approach focused on developing smart buildings that involve adaptation of high- and low-intelligent systems by tapping into an array of new and evolving technologies through artificial or human intelligence, or IT automation. However, due to the fact that they both address "intelligence," there are recently seen confusion between the fields of Artificial Intelligence (AI) and Intelligent Design (ID). Considering that the fundamental goal of science is to develop designs that are practical real-world models, AI systems optimizes the performative aspects of what happens in the intelligent design experiments particularly with respect to resources and manipulates the built environment to effectively engage its users by way of complex and organized information. Intelligent design thinking involves a sophisticated data-driven approach of planning, design and construction combining architecture, engineering and technology towards developing aesthetically pleasing, performative and functionally sustainable built environments.

In discussing science's role in modeling space, time, and energy, scientists believe that we are still encountering not enough attention paid to the precise representation of nature's information that is still untapped. With regards to understanding the essential role of information in closely examined evolution theory, the authors of "Introduction to Evolutionary Informatics" discuss about fusion of results from complexity modeling and information theory allowing simplest way for both meaning and design in nature to be measured in bits and the experienced impact. However, with respect to comparison of computer and human mind their logical argument is:

"Intelligent design addresses the information observed in nature beyond that explainable by *undirected randomness*. (From the Oxford dictionary, *undirected*, meaning lacking a clear purpose or objective; and randomness, meaning, eccentricity, unpredictability, lacking a pattern or principle of organization). Artificial intelligence has historically dealt with the mimicry of human intelligence. But computer-based artificial intelligence lies far from the creative ability of the human mind. The limitations of computer creativity, as dictated by the law of conservation of information and algorithmic information theory (AIT) applied to computers, places a ceiling on creativity both in computer models of nature and human intelligence. Computers are able in principle to execute any algorithm. There is something more happening in observable nature and the human mind that has not, and probably cannot, be explained by algorithms and computers.

(Marks, Dembski, & Ewert, 2017, p. 1)

In essence, for designers, planners, and architects, the concept of *Smart Design* is synonymous with the dynamism of this era, signifying progressive creativity, contemporaneity, and modernism as well as achievement of the goals for sustainability and resiliency of the built environment. By involving highly intelligent technologies and scientific designs, there will be more opportunities to penetrate the *creativity ceiling* and offer relevant and effective built environmental design solutions that solve specific complex and critical problems.

Smart City Toward Utopian Urban Design Concepts

The concept of *smart* or *intelligent* is more effective when initiated as a system of planning and design that is charged with the capacity to provide citizens of the city with vital needs efficiently and equitably. A *smart city* as a concept resembles to be a city or a region that uses different types of electronic methods and represents itself as technologically modern. However, the usage of the word "smart" has a more progressive connotation. Nowadays, the implementation of this concept is inherently involved with the addition and adoption of innovative strategic means and methods, including high-level computer technology, sensors, hardware, and digital data storage devices for storing data or information, technological operations, and cybernetic enhancements.

Planning for Future Smart Cities

"Socially equitable cities are smart cities, and good social infrastructure triggers smart Citizenship" (Figueiredo, Krishnamurthy, Schroeder, & Torsen, 2020, p. 177)

With the utopian goal of developing future smart cities, the focus is on infrastructure that enhances efficiency, sustainability, and public safety while empowering the citizenship and well-being of residents. These goals include but are not limited to:

- Harnessing technology for the future infrastructure of the smart cities,
- Transforming urban landscape by revolutionizing infrastructure,
- Building resilient smart cities to better implement planning,
- Using sustainable solutions to pave the way for eco-friendly infrastructure,
- Involving information communication technology to manage city functions, safety, security, and the enforcement of efficient management systems,
- Connecting infrastructure and utility networks via sensors,
- Well-connected and functional layers of mobility and transportation systems,
- Strategizing for socially just and equitable cities through smart housing and citizenship (utilitiesone.com, 2023).

Planning for smart necessarily includes sustainable goals for social justice, for example, proportionally balanced improvement to safety, income, and public transportation. Strategies for the inclusion of social urbanism and human rights in the design and planning of smart cities are vital necessities for the sustainability of smart cities.

Smart cities have both positive and negative connotations in urban planning and design. Urban design scholars have yet to assertively and deeply define the meaning of the smart city and the ramifications of the insertion of new technologies. Pro-smart planners encourage the progress that new technologies can provide to solve imminent social and environmental issues. Nineteenth-century social science research methods have sparked modern urban planning, and smart city planners expect digital data to provide insights and evidence to unravel crucial urban issues. Anti-smart city planners argue that it is just a fad or an urban labeling phenomenon for marketing purposes. They contend that the smart city concept has only expedited a sense of placelessness in the city and worsened cultural gaps between various classes and societal groups.

At these early stages of the movement toward smart design concepts, the attainment of utopian societies is far beyond simply advanced utilization of technology and smart design thinking. In our comprehensive research on many facets of smart design thinking, the possibility of applying smart concepts toward developing perfect solutions for current world problems and seeking technological utopia is still a shallow analysis. By channeling smart solutions toward the urgent ecological and climatic matters of our time, we can take steps toward developing sustainable societies where utopian concepts seem to be practical solutions, and promising viable outlooks.

Intelligent Design concepts have been accompanying social and political reforms, which inevitably demand developing new types of design philosophy for spatial settings as context for new ways of living and thinking.

Philosophy of a Revolutionary Design Transformation – Toward Smart Design as a Global Interdisciplinary Solution

Buckminster Fuller ("Bucky") was one of the most influential design theoreticians and futurists of the twentieth century. In *Operating Manual for Spaceship Earth*, he explores the synergetic laws of intellectual integrity that govern the universe beyond laws made by man. Bucky depicts *Earth as a spaceship* with a limited amount and number of resources, and its human inhabitants as the astronaut crew. He portrays an image of the earth, not as a natural phenomenon, but as a construct that must be preserved for operation and sustenance. He considers this task a huge responsibility and implores the world's architects, planners, and engineers to work together harmoniously to find solutions for the preservation of the unique construct he refers to as "The Spaceship Earth!" (Fuller, 2010, p. 48, 199–120). Planet Earth, currently engulfed with a seriously stressed ecosystem, is in a state of increasing urgency for collective mitigating considerations and actions due to the severe ramifications of climate change. Bucky's "Spaceship Earth" metaphor makes meaning more than ever, urging us to seek effective solutions toward preserving our planet and its resources.

In response to the urgency of this critical era, Bucky raises the question in conjunction with the status of our surrounding *contextual setting*. In a letter to an associate, he elaborates on the need for new ways of design thinking and reflects on the e status of the world: "I am pitting a world-around, bloodless, constructive, design transformation revolution against a world-around destructive bloody revolution. The Design Science revolution can be won by all. The bloody revolution can be won by none" (Fuller, 1960, p. 10).

The fact that design is revolutionizing approaches to current annoying problems on our planet is undeniable. However, the question of effectiveness, intelligence, and speed to save our Spaceship Planet remains unanswered. In response, it makes sense to also follow what Bucky Fuller offers as blueprint schemes for the future of the planet, and prospects for humanity: "All humanity now has the option to 'make it' successfully and sustainably by virtue of our having minds and being able to employ these principles to do more with less" (Fuller, 1960, Introduction). This is what he offers with great optimism for the opportunity to create a world where the needs of 100% of humanity are addressed.

In essence, smart design thinking requires the maintenance of mindful, conscious awareness to tune into all aspects of our global context toward therapeutic and mediative design techniques. Keeping this mindset in design thinking will inevitably channel the progress toward an interdisciplinary, scientific design revolution.

Smart Design Methodology as Both Nucleus and Ingressive Merger of *Cognition* and *Action*

Smart design as a design methodology can be considered the outcome or nucleus of an application-oriented ingressive approach. Such an integrated approach utilizes two pillars of cognitive action: the purely sensual (artistic), and the purely mental (scientific). It requires design methodologies that humanize design outcomes and bring user experience to ultimate productivity by using deep research, technological insights, sophisticated design strategies, and automatic computer control. In fact, *Smart Design* is the ultimate integrated theory of design thinking as an ingressive merger of *cognition* and *action* in art and science or in more architectural thinking, and as a union of the two pillars of "*immeasurable and measurable*". The two pillars move toward a central point of action (application), in which the outcome is the *design of nature* transformed by *humankind* (Bali, Half, Polle, & Spitz, 2018, p. 14). This vision originated with the Bauhaus and was soon followed by the Ulm School of Design which trained socially minded designers to pursue modernist principles for building new democratic worlds inseparable from social impacts.

In today's terms, smart design is a data-based approach that utilizes performative design approaches involving the use of AI in problem-solving and management. This applies to both the scope of individual buildings and the entire city for the development of advanced planning of infrastructure.

Autonomic Anthropomorphic View as a Template for Smart Design and, Automation as Implicit and Explicit Objectives of Smart Design Strategies

When comparing buildings as physical entities with the functions of the human body, we can find meaningful analogies within networks of organs as systems. This comparative analysis has been shared with students of architecture for years. The make-up of the human body and its organs can be considered a highly smart construct, with a constituent coherent network of systems. In this comparative analysis, the list of building systems might include the structure or exoskeleton, the enclosure, plumbing, electrical, or lighting. As part of this analogy, the nervous system of a smart building can be viewed as similar to the *Autonomic Nervous System* of the human body. Both are required to function harmoniously within the network of their other systems, and both entail a network of sensors with external and internal sensory stimuli assisting with conscious control and functionality.

With its unsurpassable automation system, a healthy human body follows a process and operates automatically. As human-made constructs, smart buildings also use automation to optimize all necessary processes that are expected to take place internally, as well as between the building and its external contextual elements. These processes operate by way of systems, including heating, cooling, lighting, ventilation, water usage, security, transportation, and more. Now, in reference to building resiliency, it has to do with the capacity of building systems to withstand foreseeable and unforeseeable impacts of natural and man-made forces. Increasingly, this is what today's architects and engineers are urged to consider in the design performativity and development of man-made structures. Towards developing ecologically friendly spaces, with increasing expectation for buildings to be sustainable, resilient, safe, and healthy built environments, there are more requirements for the use of technology, and inevitably the need for buildings to become smarter automated constructs.

Ultimately smart architecture learns from nature and natural elements as it strives to be in harmony with its surrounding's network of interconnected ecosystems and be compatible with its natural settings.

In 2021, an AIA-published article proposed three main channels of thought to consider when in the planning phase toward strategizing the design of smart buildings.

1 Smart Design Thinking is a Green Design Approach:
    In the design of *Smart Buildings*, inherent sustainability, and green design considerations are inevitably accompanying factors in the entire design process. The issues related to the health of the occupants, indoor air quality, energy production-consumption from renewable sources, and net zero for balancing and healthy usage of the materials and their production for the reduction of environmental impacts and global warming considerations for the reduction of greenhouse gases, as well as eco-friendly materials, improved acoustics, and green roof systems are considered part of the strategy for intelligent built environments.
2 Active investigation into the usage of Smart materials:
    Encouraging the application of smart materials that with the help of nanotechnology and other approaches are engineered to become lighter, stronger, more resistive to wear and tear, and impacts and resistant to heat loss and heat gain, and overall, more friendly to the environment with reducing the level of carbon footprint while promoting the concept of "less is more."
3 Promoting certain vital design concepts of this era:
    This includes, but is not limited to, health and well-being, comfort, safety, and security of the building occupants and users, issues related to climate action ramifications, power and energy reduction, cybersecurity, resiliency, and sustainability through the usage of technology toward specific design considerations for smart building lighting, and shading devices, smart air quality monitoring and control, smart building safety features, and capacity for predictive opportunities for maintenance and security with operating indicators, optimization of the HVAC automation for the reduction of expense and consumption of energy, as well as intelligent parking operation for efficient usage of parking spaces, particularly in large scope projects. Additionally, in general, the overall concept of comfort relates to all the above-indicated design aspects affecting the ergonomics of the building design (Deltek, 2023).

Smart Design and AI in Architecture as a Maturely Coherent Internet of Things

Today's anthropomorphic autonomic concepts of smart design are augmented by both natural elements and AI. In the realm of digital networking, there is the possibility of unlimited layers of information and connectivity with any number of elements. "The Internet of Things (IoT) is a network of physical devices, machines, and other objects that use sensors and software to collect data and exchange it over the internet, enabling remote monitoring and control" (SoftwareAG, 2023, para. 1).

IoT consists of IoT devices, connectivity, an IoT platform, and the application layer.

IoT physical devices consist of any combination of objects that measure and transmit information. This can include sensors, cameras, and actuators that allow the measurement of data, including location, temperature, velocity, pressure, and vibration. Devices relay information to the IoT platform. Information flows from IoT devices to the platform, which is located on an on-premises server or the cloud. The role of the platform as the central hub is to connect everything in the IoT ecosystem. The IoT platform connects devices to the internet, manages and analyzes the data, and provides the necessary tools to build and deploy IoT applications.

Considering that architecture's goal is to serve the day-to-day needs of people, the concept of the IoT in architecture promotes linking, monitoring, regulating, and assimilating data toward obtaining an analysis that best represents the state of a building's various systematic conditions and their performances and detecting the needs of the people as users of the built environment. The IoT can be used as a means toward the development of *Smart Design* solutions. On the IoT, technology provides an opportunity for the exchange of information and finding relationships between various selected elements that are considered "things," and many layers of selected sources and systems.

Establishing clearer views of the complicated digital usage of automation technology, and AI allows the design analysts to focus on one of the key concepts of today's integrative design goals; for example, in the case of the need for the pressing important issue of "energy efficiency." The interwoven impacts and effects of large quantities of data are gathered from numerous building components, including products, construction materials, and services (including but not limited to ventilation, lighting, heating, cooling, and types of doors, windows, insulation, and more). The IoT can then process, analyze, and assess the information toward developing coherently intelligent, interdisciplinary, data- and product-based, human-centered design solutions, and efficiently planned contextual business models. Digital networking provides opportunities in the design process for the exchange of information between any number of elements and "things."

Automation technology and AI in architecture allow users of buildings and residents of the cities to experience added comfort, safety, and energy efficiency. It links, monitors, and regulates layers of data, to find solutions for architectural and urban design practices.

Smart Design Thinking, as a Noble Goal and Forward-Thinking Approach – An Integrative Design Thinking of Form and Function – Toward *Form Follows Performance*

In conclusion, let's focus on the inherent meaning of *smart design* as a process and noble humanitarian mission in architectural form-making. Considering design thinking as a balancing act of convergent and divergent analytical and intuitive processes, *Smart Design Thinking* is an integrative, prescriptive, yet descriptive, and predictive act of design that leans more on the efficacy of design outcomes and outputs. This would not be possible without the adoption of interdisciplinary and integrative design strategies, as well as technological insights that lead to efficient implementation of humanized products and services that are user-centric and empathetic to the health and well-being of our *planet*.

Smart design thinking can also be viewed as an evolved version of what Sullivan (1896) referred to as *form follows function*. It conveys the message that form and function are one, and based on the law of nature, what Sullivan meant was that function does not change so long as the form remains unchanged. However, in this age of constant change, there is a need to critically transform this concept toward a more dynamic direction. The *performative* requirements of building forms are constantly changing based on the user needs. By the same token, this famous concept can be updated to "Form Follows Performance," which supersedes the expected subjective functionality of the form-making approach, and instead pursues a more dynamic, performative, and integrative approach. Currently in architecture, this is the approach that inherently and inevitably involves *Intelligent Design* and *Smart* thinking approaches that are specific to the needs of various users, architectural types, and contextual unique characteristics. (Kanaani, 2016)

Smart design thinking is a forward-thinking approach that looks ahead to the design of the built environment and cities as they relate to economic, cultural, social, scientific, and technological trends of the time and the location, as well as the uniqueness of the architectural type and the setting.

> Smart architecture is always time-base, it reacts in differing time cycles, changing user exigencies, climatological conditions, changes of function, and social development......
> it is system-based, it relates, it is evolutionary, it is network-minded......it is natural, it speaks for itself. It learns from nature and uses it when necessary. Smart architecture sees technology not as an enemy of nature, but as a natural ally.
>
> *(Van Hinte, Neelen, Vink, & Vollaard, 2003)*

Note

1 Sheikh Bahai was one of the most outstanding scientists who lived in the Middle Ages during the Safavid period. He was known for his mastery of mathematics, architecture, and engineering. His bathhouse project is among Bahai's most outstanding works.

1.1.2

THE SMART CITY IS MORE THAN JUST TECHNOLOGY AND DATA COLLECTION

A Critical Stance

Michael Stepner

The term Smart City is used to describe the use of high-tech tools to manage cities. Increasing urbanization and diminishing resources are making these complex urban spaces increasingly difficult to manage.

But a parallel concept, the "15 Minute City," is defined as a place that enables residents to access most daily needs and amenities within a 15-minute walk from where they live. It too can be considered a Smart City.

Are these conflicting ideas? This is not a new question.

Lloyd Ruocco FAIA, one of San Diego's great mid-century modern architects, asked this question in 1960 when he founded the design and planning advocacy organization Citizens Coordinate for Century Three (C3). *"How do we make cities fit to live in?"*[1] Fifty years earlier, Daniel Burnham, the father of modern city planning, wrote *"Cities are not collections of buildings; they are living, breathing entities that shape and are shaped by the people who inhabit them."*[2]

Similar questions and similar statements have been made and asked since people came together in the very first villages.

The latest "tool" is the Smart City, the use of sophisticated technology to manage and adjust the urban landscape to the needs of inhabitants. Or is it to adjust our needs and desires to what we think technology has to offer?

A smart city is defined as an urban area that uses technology to monitor urban services and infrastructure to collect information that is used to *efficiently* manage how services are provided and used. AI urbanism is a further evolution that not only provides the data but may also provide a "story" of how the data should be used.

The word keyword in the above description is *"Efficiently."* The question that must be asked is, is it *Effective?* Does this technology and data really address the needs of the community?

Canadian Neuroscientist and Urban designer Colin Ellard (2022) in support of social connectivity and interaction has questioned the public pressure to bear on policymaking for bringing scientific evidence related to the way we live, act, and feel in the urban environments... *"how to bring scientific evidence related to how we live, act and feel in cities to bear on policy and from there to the streets themselves?"*

In 1982, author John Naisbett referred to the trend towards *"high tech-high touch"* that *having excessive high technology necessitates more need for human touch, and that there is a need for balancing between our physical world and the human sense of spiritual reality* (Naisbett, 1982).

Naisbett's concerns have become even more relevant with our increasing reliance on technology.

Another definition of a smart city with a different perspective is proposed by Amit Ray, an Indian Spiritual Master, and Civil Engineer.

A smart city is a city where humans, trees, birds, and other animals can grow with all their glories, imperfections, freedom, and creativity. They are not just cities of technology, but cities of love, life, beauty, dignity, freedom, and equality.[3]

These are values that cannot be measured, quantified, or monitored with technology. They are however critical to the well-being and quality of life of people who dwell in cities. As William Shakespeare reminds us in Coriolanus III, "What is a city, but the people: true the people are the city" (White, 2023).[4]

Are these two perspectives on what is a Smart City mutually exclusive, or can they be compatible? The design and governance of an urban community is much more than the application of data. It is about creating an environment where people can thrive. As a process, it is more subjective than objective.

In 1974, urban planners Appleyard and Lynch produced their landmark study for the San Diego California *Temporary Paradise? A look at the special landscape of the San Diego Region*. Now celebrating its 50th anniversary, this treatise is still one of the most relevant and important guides to how we think about cities. Appleyard and Lynch defined city design and outlined considerations for planning, designing, and managing cities.

City Design is not just about the physical arrangement of things to satisfy today's needs, but also to do with fundamental human values and rights, justice, freedom, control, learning, access, dignity, and creativity. City design is not the representation of environments in the image of the present order, but really about what should and could be.

(Bookey, 2023, para.1)

The values suggested by Lynch and Appleyard are what we now put under the umbrella of equity, indicating how closely tied social equity is to the design of the built environment. These qualities cannot be understood and managed on a spreadsheet.

The pandemic has not necessarily uncovered any new problems, rather it has lent a new sense of urgency to the problems we have not resolved: social justice, economic disparity, healthy urbanism, and climate change. All of these are connected and infrastructure, physical and social, are part of the solution. As Chicago artist and urban revitalizer Theaster Gates (2015) reminds us, *"Beauty is a basic service."*

While technology is a tool, it is only one part of the toolbox. The creation of smart cities still requires human judgment to determine why you want the data, what it tells us, and how to understand and apply it. We must know exactly what issues we are trying to address. We must understand, analyze, interpret, and apply the information that is collected. Most importantly, the needs, feelings, perspectives, and concerns of people must shape the use of data.

Notes

1 Ruocco made this statement in speeches and writings in the late 1950s and early 1960s as he was talking about the need for an advocacy organization and the role it should play. The quote is originally from Jane Jacobs: "There is no logic that can be superimposed on the city; people make it, and it is to them, not buildings, that we must fit our plans."
2 Concerning the "Plan of Chicago 1909" also it is a statement Burnham made in speeches before and after the publication of the Plan.
3 This is a quote Amit Ray has made in many speeches in varied forms. It appears in many discussions
4 Shakespeare borrowed the source for the plot of As You Like It from Thomas Lodge's … "What is a city, but the people; true the people are the city" (Act III …188 pages).

References

Appleyard, D. and Lynch, K. (1974). *Temporary Paradise? A Look at the Special Landscape of the San Diego Region*. A Report to The City of San Diego Planning Department. San Diego, CA, USA.

Autodesk. Smart Building: Connection, Analysis, and Optimization. www.autodesk.com/solutions/smart-building. 05/28/2024

Bali, M., Half, D. A., Polle, D. and Spitz, J. (2018). *Smart Building Design: Conception, Planning, Realization, and Operation*. Basel, Birkhauser.

Bookey. (2023). *30 Best Kevin Lynch Quotes with Image*. http://www.bookey.app/quote-author/kevin-lynch

Deltek. (November 28, 2023). *Smart Building Strategies: Three Winning Strategies for Smart Building Design*. https://www.aia.org/resource-center/three-winning-strategies-smart-building-design.

Ellard, C. (July 7, 2022). Brains, Cities, Nimbys, and Neurobollocks. *The Wandering Brain*. https://colinellard.substack.com/p/brains-cities-nimbys-and-neurobollocks.

Figueiredo, S. M., Krishnamurthy, S. and Schroeder, T. (2020). *Architecture and the Smart City*. London, Routledge.

Fuller, R. B. (1960). *Utopia or Oblivion: The Prospects for Humanity*. Ed. Snyder, J. Zurich, Germany, Lars Muller Publisher.

Fuller, R. B. (2010). *Operating Manual for Spaceship Earth*. Zurich, Germany, Lars Muller Publisher.

Gates, T. (March 2015). *How to Revive a Neighborhood: With Imagination, Beauty, and Art* [Video]. TED Conferences. https://www.ted.com/talks/theaster_gates_how_to_revive_a_neighborhood_with_imagination_beauty_and_art/transcript.

Kanaani, M. (2016). *"Performativity: the Fourth Dimension in Architectural Design."* The Routledge Companion for Architecture Design and Practice, edited by Mitra Kanaani, Routledge, Taylor & Francis Publishers, pp. 93–116.

Marks, R. J., Dembski, W. A. and Ewert, W. (2017). *Introduction to Evolutionary Informatics*. Iowa City, USA World Scientific; Singapore, Stallion Press. https://doi.org/10.1142/9789813142152_0008

Naisbett, J. (1982). *Megatrends: Ten New Directions Transforming Our Lives*. Grand Central Publishing. Published September 30, 2021. Internet Archive, by O Hall. http://archive.org: the tall office building artistically considered.

SoftwareAG. (2023). *What Is IoT? Internet of Things Challenges and Benefits*. https://www.softwareag.com/en_corporate/resources/iot/guide/internet-of-things.html.

UtilitiesOne. (November 22, 2023). *Smart Cities: The Future of Infrastructure*. https://utilitiesone.com/smart-cities-the-future-of-infrastructure.

Valle, Giovanni, (July 31, 2022) Intelligent Building vs. Smart Building:11 Differences. Innovative Technology, Builder Space-Gateway to the Building Industry.

Van Hinte, Ed., Neelen, M., Vink, J. and Vollaard, P. (2003). *Smart Architecture: The Green Challenge.* Rotterdam, 010 Publishers.

White, J. (June 23, 2023). *621 Perfect Quotes about City Lights to Brighten Your Night.* https://www.consultclarity.org/post/quotes-about-city-lights.

Yiannoudes, S. (2011). *The Archigram vision in the context of Intelligent Environments and its current potential* (PDF), IEEE Conference Proceedings (researchgate.net).

1.2

THE UNITED NATION'S SUSTAINABLE DEVELOPMENT GOALS, HOW SMART DESIGN CAN PROMOTE EQUITY AMONG THE UNDERSERVED INHABITANTS OF CITIES

Thomas Fisher

Abstract

The United Nations 17 Sustainable Development Goals (SDGs) offer a path toward achieving a more equitable and environmentally responsible future for humanity. While all the goals relate to each other, this chapter considers each goal in turn, with examples of how architects and designers have addressed each one in a wide range of projects. The chapter ends with the idea that the built environment does not just play a key role in achieving the SDGs, but also that it can serve as a metaphor for how countries and communities might reach the goals in more collaborative and creative ways.

Equity often gets confused with equality, which can lead to a lot of inequitable outcomes. Treating everyone equally overlooks the fact that we all have different capacities, abilities, and backgrounds, and so equal treatment frequently perpetuates the inequalities of the past and present. Embracing equity means recognizing the different starting points of different people – and different species – and accommodating and adjusting for those differences so that everyone has the same opportunity to achieve the best results and have the best possible future for themselves and others.

One of the most important efforts at promoting equity is the United Nations 17 Sustainable Development Goals (SDGs).[1] While two of those goals specifically address the built environment, SDG 9 and 11, all of them have implications for architecture and design. At the same time, the built environment can help make the achievement of the goals less about the collection of data and more about specific actions that individuals and communities can take to improve people's lives and ecosystems' health. The hope is that those who read this

DOI: 10.4324/9781003384113-7

Figure 1.2.1 The 17 sustainable development goals.
Credit: United Nations.

will find the motivation and inspiration to join in the vitally important work of the SDGs in making our planet and all who occupy it a more equitable place (Figure 1.2.1).

SDG 1, No Poverty

The UN notes that in 2015, "700 million people, or 10 percent of the world population, lived in extreme poverty," with the COVID-19 pandemic having pushed "an additional 71 million additional people" into that category.[2] While the elimination of poverty obviously involves public policies that provide direct assistance to impoverished people and create equitable employment opportunities for them, the built environment can aid in this effort. Buildings, for instance, can create communal resources for people to help them access the education and services they need to get out of poverty. An example is MASS Design Group's proposal for the Iftiin Peace Hub in Somalia,[3] which "will host programs dedicated to giving at-risk youth and ex-combatants in Somalia a clear pathway to employment stability and mental health support … by providing vocational training, entrepreneurship support, psychological support, and employment assistance."

The built environment can also provide direct employment opportunities, especially to women, who play such a key role in helping families and children escape poverty. The Women's Opportunity Center in Rwanda,[4] by Sharon Davis Design, helps women "learn income-generating skills," including "the manufacture of (the facilities) bricks" and "hands-on construction administration." Architecture can also provide spaces that enable people to meet their own needs, as a form of self-employment. Alejandro Aravena's "Incremental Housing" in Chile,[5] for example, provides a basic housing unit, with a kitchen, bathroom, and space for eating and sleeping, with covered outdoor space within which families can add rooms over time, literally building their generational wealth.

SDG 2, Zero Hunger

With an estimated "2 billion people… (lacking) regular access to safe, nutritious, and sufficient food in 2019,"[6] this goal may seem far removed from the built environment. And yet architecture has a lot to offer in terms of eliminating hunger. Human Habitat in Denmark[7] has designed a low-cost, easily disassembled, hydroponic greenhouse "designed as a highly efficient system with the capacity to produce two to three tones of crops a year on only 50 square meters" of land, using rainwater, recirculated in a closed loop, to grow crops and reducing the use of freshwater irrigation by as much as 85%. This system can grow, in 0.01 acres, the same amount of food as an acre of typical farmland.

Smart design can also combine ending poverty with zero hunger by providing agricultural skills training in the process of growing food. MASS Design's Food Systems Design Lab[8] "applies design thinking to the reconstruction of regional, equitable, and self-determined food systems," in projects like the Rwanda Institute for Conservation Agriculture, where students learn the most sustainable farm practices across six different agricultural enterprises. Hunger arises not because of a lack of food, per se, but because of its inequitable distribution, with many people living in food deserts. Myriad non-profits focus on the distribution of food, such as Second Harvest Heartland[9] in the US, which runs a food bank that "sources and distributes fresh food, free groceries and healthy, nutritious meals through a network of local food shelves."

SDG 3, Good Health and Well-Being

The UN says that "an additional 18 million health workers are needed, primarily in low- and lower-middle income countries."[10] The built environment has a tremendous impact on health and well-being, although most architects have focused on the design of healthcare facilities – hospitals and clinics – which typically aid people already ill. This SDG calls on us to imagine a built environment that promotes good health and helps keep people healthy.

The Destination Medical Center[11] in the US has, as its goal, making Rochester, Minnesota, "America's City for Health." As the location of one of the best hospitals in the world, the Mayo Clinic, Rochester has focused on what it takes to keep people healthy, investing in public spaces and streets that encourage physical activity, healthy eating, social interaction, and environmental responsibility. Discovery Walk, designed by Coen + Partners,[12] epitomizes that work, turning a street into a series of activity spaces for people.

Well-being involves psychological as well as physical health. Foster + Partners' Maggie's Centres,[13] such as the one in Manchester, UK, provide "a place of refuge where people affected by cancer can find emotional and practical support." The opposite of the traditional hospital setting, the center has ample daylight, access to nature, a greenhouse garden, and a variety of spaces, including a large central kitchen and communal table in which to share a meal with others. Buildings like this show how architecture can help make us all healthy, even those who are already sick.

SDG 4, Quality Education

This goal addresses the lack of any formal schooling in parts of the world, with 773 million still illiterate, with an inequitable access to education for many girls.[14] Efforts to bring education to school deserts include the work of Ove Arup & Partners, who have designed simple structures in rural areas, such as the Thnouh School in Cambodia,[15] that use local materials and construction techniques, providing work as well as education for local communities. In countries that treat girls differently than boys when it comes to education, innovations can still occur. The Kalbod Design Studio in Iran[16] has designed a "Lego African School" that can accommodate primary and secondary school children in separate, but visually connected spaces, on a variety of sites. Such low-cost, replicable models can bring education to a part of the world most in need of schools: Sub-Saharan Africa.

And even in places that have enough schools, the quality of education can always improve. The Frederiksbjerg School in Denmark by Henning Larsen[17] responds to a new Danish law requiring more physical activity during children's school day. The architects achieve that through unconventional means, such as a climbing wall ramp that children can use instead of a stair, group swings in the common spaces, and play spaces in, around, and on top of the building. It makes physical activity as not just something children do during a recess, but also as something they do between and even during classes.

SDG 5, Gender Equality

Although many countries have espoused gender equality, there remain inequities in pay, responsibility, and power between men and women throughout the world. The UN, for example, notes that women hold only 28% of management positions worldwide.[18]

One of the best ways to achieve gender equality is to give women the skills they need to participate in their economies. C-re-aid, a Belgian non-profit working in Tanzania, has done that in several projects, including their Women Community Shop and their Women's Center.[19] Such projects provide opportunities for women to learn construction skills and give women access to a tool shop, store, office, and meeting space, which can transform their lives and provide the mutual support they often need in patriarchal societies.

This applies to girls as much as women. Based on research that shows that girls have different preferences when it comes to physical activity, VEGA Landskab in Denmark[20] has designed playgrounds with spaces that accommodate the play of girls as much as boys, with spaces that allow for more cooperative and less physically rough activities.

SDG 6, Clean Water and Sanitation

The UN estimates that 2.2 billion people lack access to safely managed drinking water, and this is an area design can make a big difference.[21] Sometimes, this involves bringing water to where people most need it. Architect John Dwyer designed a "Clean Hub"[22] that provides solar-powered clean water and composting toilets, packaged within a shipping container that can be transported to wherever those services are absent (Figure 1.2.2).

Other design strategies allow people to clean water themselves. The "Life Straw"[23] filters out pollutants as people draw water from a polluted source; the "Life Sack"[24] cleans water in a bag that doubles as a grain sack; and the "Solarball2"[25] uses the sun to condense and capture clean water from a polluted origin. In places without the ability to deliver clean water, such micro-infrastructural ideas represent an important innovation.

The same is true of innovative sanitation designs. The "Crapper"[26] has a rotating aerobic drum and costs about $100 per unit; the "Sabine Schober Toilet"[27] mixes excrement with charcoal to produce soil for reforestation; and the "Diversion Toilet"[28] works without water or a sewer connection and converts waste into fertilizer or biogas.

Figure 1.2.2 The clean hub in place in New Orleans.
Credit: John Dwyer.

SDG 7, Affordable and Clean Energy

Of the over 1 billion people lacking access to electricity, most live in remote or rural locations, which makes local power generation more important.[29] Some innovations, like "Solskin"[30] which has moveable panels that follow the sun, are a high-tech solution for high-end building applications, but a community version of it could power a large number of homes. Other innovations, like "Soft House" by kva matx,[31] "can create close to 16,000 watt-hours of electricity by transforming household curtains into flexible, semi-transparent, solar collectors," with applications in even the most underserved communities. Solar textiles apply not just to curtains, but to apparel as well. Sheila Kennedy's work[32] has shown how field workers can wear solar textiles that generate power during the day for powering lights at night.

Meanwhile, the developed world continues to invent innovative ways of generating clean and affordable energy. *Gottlieb Paludan Architects* and UD Urban Design have produced the largest biofuel urban project in the world, Stockholm's Vartan Bioenergy CHP-plant,[33] by burning bio-refuse from the wood industry. Snøhetta has designed Powerhouse Brattøokaia office building in Norway[34] that generates more than twice the power than it uses with exterior walls of solar panels. Meanwhile, at the urban scale, the integration of solar, wind, and geothermal energy systems in cities continues, although 80% of it has occurred in wealthier, temperate climate countries.[35] Lowering their cost and making these systems more accessible in developing countries remains a challenge.

SDG 8, Decent Work and Economic Growth

With "22 percent of the world's youth … not engaged in either education, employment, or training," the built environment provides a lot of opportunity.[36] Youth need safe working and learning environments, with innovations like SiteCover,[37] turning building construction into an indoor activity. Young people and especially young women need job-training opportunities in construction as well. MASS Build Ltd. has worked with Deutsche Gesellschaft für Internationale Zusammenarbeit (GIZ) and Rwanda's construction industry to "train and upskill existing workers, so they are more effective on-site and more employable post-project."[38] Buildings can provide both the place and the means to do decent work.

The built environment can also drive economic growth. In a study of how architecture can fuel local economic development, Alejandra Cervantes worked with faculty at the University of Minnesota and architects at HGA to explore how the specifications of locally sourced, wood-based products and systems in a new health clinic could help revive the community's defunct wood-products industry.[39]

Architecture can also spur local economies through tourism as well as simply improving the daily lives of people and communities so that they can be as effective and productive as possible in their lives and work.[40] In a world where as Chilean architect Alejandro Aravena notes, "we will have to build a city for one million people each week for the next fifteen years," in order to handle population growth, the built environment plays a central role.[41]

SDG 9, Innovation, Industry, and Infrastructure

Nearly 3 billion people globally lack access to the Internet, many of them because of poverty, physical isolation, and/or age, representing what the United Nations has called "the new face of inequality" around the world.[42] This will require addressing a variety of needs at the same time, as the non-profit Smart North has done by placing technology centers in healthcare and social service facilities, so that the people's other needs – like housing or food insecurity and physical or mental health challenges – can be met along with their access to computers and the internet.[43] That non-profit has also developed "smart streetlights" that use the existing infrastructure in cities to deliver high-bandwidth access to the internet to every household.

Other innovations, like the development of autonomous vehicles, will not just reduce traffic injuries but also transform the physical infrastructure of cities by turning paved streets now full of cars and trucks into largely green streets, with one narrow travel lane in each direction able to handle the same amount of traffic, with pervious pavement in most of the street, and with much wider sidewalks able to accommodate pedestrians and other modes of transportation.[44] Driven vehicles took over our streets a 100 years ago and autonomous vehicles will largely give streets back to people (Figure 1.2.3).

SDG 10, Reduced Inequalities

With 20% of humanity having experienced discrimination, according to the UN, reducing inequalities might have a greater effect on more people than almost any other goal.[45] And yet, because of the breadth of the problem, it also becomes more difficult to address. The built environment can help, nevertheless.

Reducing barriers to people with physical or mental limitations is one such area. The Danish House of Disability Organizations commissioned Gottlieb Paludan Architects to design the "world's most accessible office building," involving people of various abilities to create a structure that makes it easy for those who have physical or cognitive impairments

Figure 1.2.3 Autonomous vehicles will enable us to have safer, cleaner, and quieter streets, with much more room for people.

Credit: Joseph Hang, Java Nyamjav.

to work or find their way to and through the building.[46] The goal was to prove that "equality and opposing needs do not have to collide."

Helping people who have stable living conditions is also key to reducing inequalities. In projects led by my Minnesota Design Center colleague, Emily Stover, she has worked with people we have faced eviction to come up with a number of strategies that enable them to get the help and information they need prior to being evicted, and access to financial help after eviction to get back on their feet. And she has worked with people living in adult foster care settings and their families to help them attain the best conditions and have the greatest choice in how they live and who they live with (Figure 1.2.4).

SDG 11, Sustainable Cities and Communities

Of all the SDGs, this one aligns most closely with the built environment, and yet many in the design community have argued that we need not just sustainable cities, but resilient and regenerative ones as well; not only reducing negative environmental impacts, but also creating positive ones that improve ecosystems.[47]

Regenerative design includes "biomimicry," in which the built environment functions like natural systems; "biophilic design" that brings nature into the built environment; "multi-species cities" that accommodate other species as much as humans; and "bio-urbanism" that looks at cities as inseparable parts of larger ecosystems. Efforts in this direction include the "National Park City" movement,[48] which seeks to connect people and nature more thoroughly in cities; Denmark's "Wildest Municipality" competition,[49] which recognizes the wildest ideas to re-wild cities; and the Regenesis Group in the US,[50] which

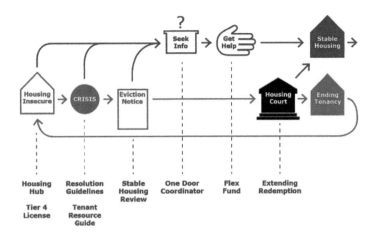

Figure 1.2.4   Emily Stover engaged people facing eviction to arrive at a number of solutions.
Credit: Emily Stover.

offers educational opportunities in regenerative design as well as consulting with communities around the world in how they might embrace more regenerative development.

One of many architectural examples is the Omega Center for Sustainable in Rhinebeck, New York, which contains an "Eco Machine" that uses natural systems to recycle its wastewater, solar collectors and a geothermal heat pump to generate its power, and materials that enable the building to have a zero-carbon footprint.[51] The goal of the Center, says its founder Skip Backus, is not just creating a "living building" but also "to help people reexamine how they relate to the world."

SDG 12, Responsible Consumption and Production

Humans remain the only species on the planet that generates landfills, full of waste that neither biodegrades nor feeds other living things. The production of so much waste should cause us all to look at our own contributions to this and at the perverse systems that make such irresponsible activity so widespread. I recently did a study with a graduate student of what it would take to design a building with no waste leaving the job site, and it turned out to be extraordinarily difficult. Wasting is easy; responsible consumption, hard.

Yet not impossible. The Lendager Group in Denmark have designed "Upcycle Studios,"[52] 20 townhouses made from "recycled concrete, repurposed double glazing windows and discarded flooring boards," and containing spaces that people can reconfigure in any number of ways to accommodate changes in their living situations. The project reduced its carbon footprint by 45% and turned 1,000 tons of waste into building materials.

The recycling of waste after a building is complete offers another way to think about responsible consumption. The condominium tower, designed by Renzo Piano Building Workshop, at 565 Broome Street in New York, diverts over 90% of the waste of its inhabitants from the landfill, with "zero-waste" rooms to sort trash into recycling bins and to donate disposed garments to local charities.[53] This reflects the goals of the "Zero Waste International Alliance," which highlights "positive alternatives to landfill and incineration and to raise community awareness of the social and economic benefits to be gained when wasted materials are regarded as resources which can create both employment and business opportunities."[54]

SDG 13, Climate Action

Of all the SDGs, this one may override all the rest, given the existential threat that rapid and dramatic climate change presents to humanity and to other species. And our response to this threat – the need to reduce greenhouse gas emissions by over 7.6% each year, according to the UN – has fallen far short, so far.[55] But those responsible for the built environment, which contributes a sizable percentage of those emissions, have begun to change practices.

IBAVI in Spain have designed a housing development that demonstrates what climate action looks like in development.[56] Using compacted sea-salt as insulation, local timber, reused doors and windows, a biomass boiler, and design strategies that involve passive heating and cooling, the architects reduced waste production during construction by 50%, CO_2 emissions during construction by 62%, water consumption by 67%, and on-going energy consumption by 75%. They also created beautiful, simple housing able to accommodate a diversity of family sizes and types.

Climate action also involves looking to natural ecosystems to help meet our needs. Turenscape's design for the Minghu Wetland Park in China transformed a river confined to a concrete channel into a wetland park that provides "storm-water management, water cleansing, and recovery of native habitats, as well as ... public space for gathering and aesthetic enjoyment."[57] Projects like this show how climate action can create better places for people as well as a better environment.

SDG 14, Life Below Water

In contrast to many of the previous goals, this one may seem the farthest afield from what designers and architects do, but that misses the direct impact that decisions above water have on life below it. And with over 3 billion people depending on marine life for their livelihoods, according to the UN, ensuring the health of plant and animal life below water is essential.[58]

Fishing nets and plastics present some of the greatest hazards to marine life, and some companies have designed products to take those things out of the waste stream. Fischer Lighting, for example, produces a line of lighting fixtures that recycles plastic made from the 640,000 tons of discarded or lost fishing nets.[59] Meanwhile, Bionic makes an industrial-strength yarn from recycled marine plastic,[60] and Ocean Plastics upcycles plastic from the ocean to replace virgin plastic in products and apparel.[61]

Architects have proposed equally large-scale uptake of ocean plastic. Belgian architect Victor Callebaut has envisioned "oceanscrapers," large underwater buildings made of 3D printed, recycled ocean plastic meant to protect marine life as well as reduce the footprint of buildings on land.[62] Less utopian, but no less compelling, is the design by Marshall Blecher and Studio Fokstrot of a series of floating islands in Copenhagen's harbor that create mini parks above water and habitat below water for marine plants and animals to thrive.[63]

SDG 15, Life on Land

With 2 billion hectares of degraded land, which also degrades the lives of over 3 billion people, according to the UN, the built environment plays an especially important role in protecting and improving the quality and quantity of habitat, not just for humans, but also for the other plant and animal species.[64]

Many architects have begun to cover the exteriors of buildings with plants, providing habitat for animals as well as shading from the sun and purification of intake air. Rollimarchini Architects and G8A Architects have designed a naturally ventilated factory in Vietnam with layers of exterior planting trays that shade and help cool the interior.[65] Architect Jean Nouvel's Quai Branly Museum in Paris has green walls, with plants serving as the outermost layer of exterior cladding.[66] And architect Stefano Boeri has created "vertical forests," high-rise buildings, with balconies containing plants and even small trees up their facades.[67]

Designers have also created structures for other species. Architecture students at the University of Buffalo have designed and built a "skyscraper for bees," with a bee hive elevated at the top of the tower and with a glass bottom so that people can watch the hive from below.[68] And Llowarch Llowarch Architects have created oak-and-mesh aviaries for ravens at the Tower of London, providing a protected place for that legendary animal.[69]

SDG 16, Peace, Justice, and Strong Institutions

The built environment has long served to protect communities from violence and war, with castles and forts, as well as to provide people with places to enact justice, in courthouses and jails. But in an era, according to the UN, in which 100 civilians are killed in armed conflicts every day, the built environment has a more challenging role to play.[70]

That can involve creating buildings that cause us to muse on the impact that armed conflict has on innocent people, whether evoking the architecture of death camps, such as architect James Ingo Freed's US Holocaust Memorial Museum Washington D.C.,[71] or using architecture to convey what violence itself feels like, such as Daniel Libeskind's Jewish Museum in Berlin.[72] Design can also create spaces whose character leads us to contemplate the number of deaths that come from war, such as Peter Eisenman's Holocaust Memorial in Berlin, with its row upon row of casket-sized blocks.[73]

At the same time, the built environment can help strengthen institutions. The meaning of that has changed in recent decades from a focus on institutional buildings per se to a focus on architecture that builds the institutional capacity of communities. The Museum of Modern Art's exhibit, "Small Scale, Big Change," reflects that shift. Featuring projects such as Francis Kéré's primary school in Burkina Faso, Estudio Teddy Cruz's Casa Familiar, and Rural Studio's $20,000 House, the exhibit showed the important role that the built environment plays in strengthening the institution of family and community.[74]

SDG 17, Partnerships for the Goals

This last goal pushes us to work together to achieve all of the previous ones. The unsustainability and inequities that pervade this planet arise, in part, from the ways in which we have fragmented the world and exploited people and resources in the process. In that sense, buildings might serve as a metaphor for the partnerships that need to happen in every sector. We cannot construct the built environments unless we work together: architect and community, designer and client, civil engineer and landscape architect, and general contractor and product company. Nothing gets built without partnerships.

The same is true politically. We cannot build a sustainable, equitable future without partnerships among countries, counties, cities, and communities. And to achieve that, we need more clarity about who are the clients and communities of peace: the people least served by the existing systems; who are the architects and engineers of peace: those most committed to working with the underserved; and who are the contractors and companies of peace: those who have the most capacity to make change happen. Smart design can promote equity among the underserved inhabitants of cities, only if we are smarter about what design has to offer.

Notes (all accessed October 20, 2023)

1 https://www.un.org/sustainabledevelopment/
2 https://www.un.org/sustainabledevelopment/
3 https://massdesigngroup.org/work/design/iftiin-peace-hub
4 https://sharondavisdesign.com/project/womens-opportunity-center-rwanda/
5 https://www.elementalchile.cl/en/
6 https://www.un.org/sustainabledevelopment/
7 https://uia2023cph.org/case-studies/impact-farm/
8 https://massdesigngroup.org/food-systems
9 https://www.2harvest.org/
10 https://www.un.org/sustainabledevelopment/
11 https://dmc.mn/
12 https://www.coenpartners.com/project/discovery-walk/
13 https://www.fosterandpartners.com/projects/maggie-s-manchester
14 https://www.un.org/sustainabledevelopment/
15 https://architizer.com/projects/thnouh-school/
16 https://architizer.com/projects/lego-african-school/
17 https://henninglarsen.com/en/projects/1200-1299/1246-frederiksbjerg-school
18 https://www.un.org/sustainabledevelopment/
19 https://architizer.com/firms/c-re-aid/
20 https://vegalandskab.dk/projekt-kategori/born-og-unge/
21 https://www.un.org/sustainabledevelopment/
22 https://johndwyerarchitecture.com/projects/cleanhub/
23 https://lifestraw.com/
24 https://inhabitat.com/life-sack-solves-drinking-water-issues-for-the-third-world/
25 https://inhabitat.com/hamster-ball-shaped-solarball-uses-the-sun-to-purify-water/solarball2/
26 https://inhabitat.com/8-toilet-designs-that-could-save-millions-of-lives-around-the-world/
    the-crapper/
27 https://inhabitat.com/8-toilet-designs-that-could-save-millions-of-lives-around-the-world/
    sabine-schober-toilet/
28 https://inhabitat.com/8-toilet-designs-that-could-save-millions-of-lives-around-the-world/
    eawag-toilet/
29 https://www.un.org/sustainabledevelopment/
30 https://www.solskin.swiss/en
31 https://inhabitat.com/solar-harvesting-textiles-energize-soft-house/
32 https://energy.mit.edu/news/getting-wrapped-up-in-solar-textiles/
33 https://www.archdaily.com/873405/vartan-bioenergy-chp-plant-ud-urban-design-ab-plus-gottlieb-
    paludan-architects
34 https://www.archdaily.com/924325/powerhouse-brattorkaia-snohetta

35 https://www.irena.org/publications/2020/Oct/Rise-of-renewables-in-cities

36 https://www.un.org/sustainabledevelopment/

37 https://sitecover.com/

38 https://www.developpp.de/en/projects-success-stories/rwanda-architecture-company-trains-workers-for-the-construction-industry

39 https://sites.google.com/umn.edu/ms-rp/projects/challenges-and-issues/just-communities#h.alonyc4js7bl

40 https://www.re-thinkingthefuture.com/architectural-community/a9917-how-architecture-helps-economic-growth/

41 https://www.sdgfund.org/pritzker-laureates-architecture-must-contribute-improve-peoples%E2%80%99-opportunities

42 https://www.un.org/sustainabledevelopment/

43 https://www.smartnorth.org/

44 https://design.umn.edu/research/centers/minnesota-design-center/projects/future-streets

45 https://www.un.org/sustainabledevelopment/

46 https://handicap.dk/huset/magasin-om-huset

47 https://bloxhub.org/news/how-do-we-make-regenerative-cities/

48 https://www.nationalparkcity.org/

49 https://dkvild.dk/english/

50 https://regenesisgroup.com/

51 https://www.eomega.org/center-sustainable-living/the-living-building

52 https://lendager.com/project/upcycle-studios/

53 https://www.cityrealty.com/nyc/market-insight/features/future-nyc/what-zero-waste-buildings-could-they-work-new-york-city/33921

54 https://zwia.org/

55 https://www.un.org/sustainabledevelopment/

56 https://www.archdaily.com/910485/life-reusing-posidonia-ibavi-instituto-balear-de-la-vivienda

57 https://www.archdaily.com/590066/minghu-wetland-park-turenscape

58 https://www.un.org/sustainabledevelopment/

59 https://issuu.com/fischer_lighting_aps/docs/051018_brochure_fischer_family

60 https://bionicyarn.com/

61 https://parley.tv/oceanplastic#re_copy-of-ocean-plastic-program

62 https://www.dezeen.com/2015/12/24/aequorea-vincent-callebaut-underwater-oceanscrapers-made-from-3d-printed-rubbish-ocean-plastic/

63 https://www.dezeen.com/2020/04/15/marshall-blecher-studio-fokstrot-floating-copenhagen-islands/

64 https://www.un.org/sustainabledevelopment/

65 https://www.dezeen.com/2022/11/01/jakob-factory-rollimarchini-g8a-architects/

66 https://architizer.com/blog/inspiration/collections/living-facades/

67 https://www.archdaily.com/777498/BOSCO-VERTICALE-STEFANO-BOERI-ARCHITETTI

68 https://www.dezeen.com/2013/05/06/skyscraper-for-bees-by-university-at-buffalo-students/

69 https://www.dezeen.com/2015/12/11/llowarch-llowarch-architects-raven-enclosure-aviary-tower-of-london-england/

70 https://www.un.org/sustainabledevelopment/

71 https://www.ushmm.org/information/press/in-memoriam/james-ingo-freed-1930-2005

72 https://www.jmberlin.de/en/libeskind-building

73 https://www.thoughtco.com/the-berlin-holocaust-memorial-by-peter-eisenman-177928

74 https://www.moma.org/interactives/exhibitions/2010/smallscalebigchange/index.html

1.3

A SMART PARADIGM FOR PARTICIPATORY URBAN DESIGN

Patrik Schumacher and Shajay Bhooshan

Abstract

This chapter describes, illustrates, and discusses the idea of a gamified online platform for the participatory planning and design of synergy clusters. It is constructed in analogy to the white papers that outline Crypto and Web 3.0 projects, i.e., it outlines a research and development programme rather than presenting results. The synergy clusters facilitated by the platform might be physical urban developments or metaverse developments. The key tasks are sufficiently analogous to merit being investigated and addressed together.

The underlying scenario here is that the described platform facilitates intended development projects that are presumed to be unencumbered by prior planning legislation. This chapter outlines a schema or 'genotype' for delivering tailored game development solutions to developers like start-up city entrepreneurs, municipal master developers, real estate developers, or metaverse platform developers. The conception of pertinent planning rules – embodied in spatial modules and their rules of combination – is a key part of the tailored game development, and so is the design of pertinent market mechanisms that create value for all participants.

Introduction

This chapter might be interpreted as proto white paper for a start-up company delivering a platform plus game-development services, or for an open-source project, evolving a game development platform which would allow cities, municipalities, developers, or would-be communities to create their own participatory urban development game. The platform is especially congenial to start-up city entrepreneurs who intend to operate a City-as-a-Service (CAAS) business model.

The development success criteria for the authors' conception of the participatory game schema focus on maximising total economic value, i.e., the total social utility generated in the process, rather than the founders' expected profit. However, the identification of a new utility enhancing methodology and tool schema is inherently opening up entrepreneurial profit opportunities that should be able to capture a part of the overall end-user value surplus that might be generated by such a tool.

The underlying idea of the envisioned Participatory Urban Development Platform (PUDP) was first explored at the Architectural Associations' Design Research Lab (AADRL) in 2001 via a project entitled 'Negotiate My Boundary', with the ambition to develop a mechanism that gives a residential block the chance to become a residential community.

> Negotiate my boundary ... incorporates the communicative power of the internet to build up a virtual community in anticipation and preparation of the real residential community. This is a crucial step that significantly lowers the threshold of personal communication and allows the self-selection and communal self-organisation to take off in the safe and non-committal virtual domain.
>
> *(Schumacher, 2006)*

The idea was picked up again by Shajay Booshan within the AADRL and developed into an ongoing, multi-year design research project (Bhooshan & Vazquez, 2020). More recently the idea was picked up as research and development (R&D) agenda within Zaha Hadid Architects (ZHA).

A key accomplishment and advantage of such a gamified participatory planning tool is that it can facilitate community building ahead of construction and thus reduces the risk of product-market fit by generating information about preferences of potential future stakeholders. A key aspect of the posited importance of community building – residential communities, creative industry clusters, or retail clusters – is the premise that the key to real estate value is the creation of co-location synergies. This is the real meaning of the mantra 'location location location'. The market here is always also a match-making market. The networking on the basis of information-rich self-exposure, typical of social media platforms, is to be brought to bear as a key feature of the community building game. Networking here implies co-location, including the opportunity of space and asset sharing between players, firmed up by token-based market transactions rather than remaining non-committal exchanges of ideas. Tokens can be used to pay down deposits that function to reserve parcels or voxels and can be traded like options or redeemed by finalising the purchase. Tokenisation – including non-fungible tokens – allows also for fractionalisation of real estate assets, thus further liquefying the markets. The possibility of selling fractions of real estate assets is a financing tool that allows passive investors to participate in anticipated downstream appreciation and revenue streams, while a single point of control over the build-out, use, or sale of the asset remains in place.

A second key ambition of the platform and gaming schema is the suggestion and facilitation of explicit collective action initiatives, as well as the facilitation of self-evolving governance structures and procedures, potentially ushering in a liquid stakeholder democracy, in conjunction with market processes. The platform would lower the inevitable transaction/governance costs and do the heavy lifting of the initial formation and provisional structuration of the would-be 'polity of the invested'.

The endgame or goal of the design participation game is global value maximisation by allowing all future stakeholders – future owners, investors, tenants, and end-users – to engage with and, in the aggregate, steer the development by trading both with the platform and with each other during the design stage. The facilitation of bi-lateral and multi-lateral space sharing agreements delivers individual and overall space utilisation efficiencies, as well as opportunities for positive spillover effects between the activities that intersect in these specifically shared spaces. Generic shared spaces, in contrast, cannot be relied upon to bring more positive than negative externalities. The same applies to the usual, often nearly random relative locations that result in the absence of the kind of information and engagement facilitated by the gaming platform proposed in this chapter: they produce more friction than synergy.

In summary, the new paradigm promises prosperity gains by introducing new markets, by expanding trading opportunities, by increasing liquidity via tokenisation, and finally via the facilitation of tailored, self-adapting urban planning and governance procedures for a liveable, prosperous, and sustainable urban environment.

Network Society: Urban Design Implications for Physical and Virtual Cities

Within contemporary post-fordist network society, the productivity of everybody depends on being plugged into professional and cultural networks that exist only in cities. What each of us is doing needs to be continuously recalibrated with what everybody else is doing, directly or indirectly. While this continuous adaptive re-calibration of economic activity is facilitated by the system of prices in the case of the ongoing output of products and services, in the R&D arena – where prices are not yet active – this requires inter-awareness via the intervisibility of R&D work and via communicative interaction. All further productivity gains depend on this, and it requires a new level of communicative density that is only available in cities. This is an important component of what economists measure as 'agglomeration economies'.

Urban economist Edward Glaeser investigated what he called innovation clusters and emphasised the proliferation of productive ideas that cities throughout history had incubated, and he observed that 'even in our age of information technology, ideas are often geographically localized' (Glaeser, 2011, location 812). As striking evidence Glaeser refers to a study that found patents exhibit a strong tendency to cite other patents that originated in geographically close proximity.

Since the neat division into work and leisure has disappeared and we feel the vital urge to remain connected to the network 24/7, it is as important for us to live in the city as it is inevitable for us to work in it. Everything piles into the centre, the more the better. This spells a new desire for an unprecedented degree of urban intensification.

The satisfaction of this demand requires new degrees of freedom for urban entrepreneurs (and their architects) who need this freedom to experiment, discover, and create the best ways to weave the new urban texture and to garner the potential synergies through new intricate programmatic juxtapositions. Only an unhampered market process can be such a discovery process and has the information processing capacity and agility to weave a viable complex urban order for this new dynamic societal context. That's why positive, physical modernist urban planning had to vanish. Planning was hence-force confined to operate negatively, by means of restricting private actors.

Productivity advantages of concentration, as hinted at above, are referred to as agglomeration economies. There are two kinds: direct economic benefits via firm-to-firm cooperation and indirect benefits of urban facility sharing. Agglomeration economies thus include transport efficiencies, wider and more diverse amenity sharing, the benefit of large labour pools enlarging the skill-base for companies, larger service markets with more variety of specialised services (long tails), increased innovation potential due to knowledge and technology spillovers within and between industries, and most importantly cooperation between complementary firms/activities allowing for specialised knowledge industry hubs.

The demand for networking, knowledge exchange, and ramifying cooperation is so great that urban concentration, business travel, and internet-based telecommunication increased simultaneously. Since 2020, accelerated by the global pandemic, remote working and tele-conferencing expanded exponentially. This experience also catapulted the old idea of 'cyberspace' or the 'metaverse' into a breathtaking take-off. We believe that the development of the metaverse will spawn creative industry clusters within virtual worlds, as a complementary (perhaps partially substitutive) development to physical urban concentration, without, however, reversing the trend of physical concentration in knowledge economy hubs. In any event, the metaverse is as much a task domain of architecture as is the city (Schumacher, 2022). The formation of effective co-location synergies will also be an important aspect of metaverse urbanism. Therefore, the envisioned PUDP discussed in this chapter is also applicable in the metaverse. The radical degrees of freedom metaverses offer as politically unencumbered true start-up cities make this new domain an ideal test case for the PUDP. Our recently launched metaverse and virtual start-up city Metrotopia (www. metrotopia.io) – aspiring to become the go-to virtual industry hub for the whole design ecosystem – affords such a test case as soon as we move into our urban expansion mode. ZHA also designed the Liberland Metaverse addressing at the web3.0 ecosystem as target audience for a creative industry hub. A catalogue of modules was developed to facilitate the fit-out of the initial multi-tenant incubator building, anticipating the development of an in-world builder empowering user-generated content (Figure 1.3.1).

The unique aspect of the Liberland Metaverse project is that its purpose is to anticipate and facilitate the physical settlement of Liberland, as well as perhaps spawning franchises elsewhere, anticipating Balaji Srinivasan's idea of a 'network state'.

With respect to both physical and virtual urban agglomerations, the intricate social and functional ordering of activities is a matter for giving space to market-based self-sorting processes, premised on a new level of informational empowerment of all market participants. PUDPs of the kind projected here offer a new mechanism for such vital self-organisation processes.

Community Creation

In advanced metropolitan societies, social networks are largely divorced from immediate locale. "Community" is increasingly becoming an unreal euphemism. Communities barely exist any longer. To the extent they still exist they linger on as an anachronism, mostly in relatively unproductive social milieux. Nobody knows their neighbours anymore. Residential co-location takes place blindly, without any prior acquaintance with, or even information about, neighbours. In our highly differentiated contemporary society, self-sorting based on generic social categories or income levels is too blunt to overcome the problem of anonymity. The design of multi-tenant houses is usually focussed on how to maximise privacy within a condition of aggregation that is seen as cost-imposed necessity rather than as welcome benefit or opportunity. Neighbours experience each other primarily as nuisance, compromising privacy. Neighbourhoods as integrated communities must remain illusory unless new social mechanisms of neighbourhood formation are devised.

Is this anonymity and disappearance of community an inevitable condition of modern life or can this trend be countered? We believe that this trend can be countered with new

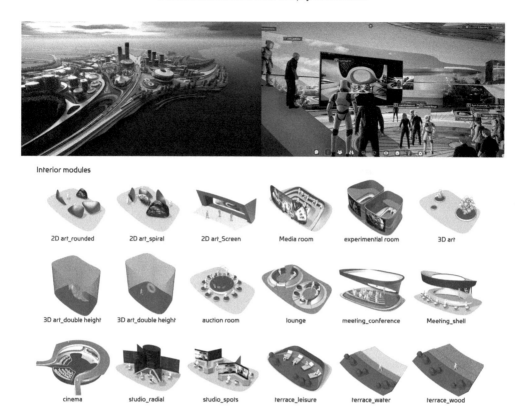

Interior modules

2D art_rounded	2D art_spiral	2D art_Screen	Media room	experimential room	3D art
3D art_double height	3D art_double height	auction room	lounge	meeting_conference	Meeting_shell
cinema	studio_radial	studio_spots	terrace_leisure	terrace_water	terrace_wood

Figure 1.3.1　Zaha Hadid Architects, Liberland Metaverse: Urban plan, an event within incubator building, catalogue of socially functional interior fit-out modules, 2020.

Source: (c) Zaha Hadid Architects.

computationally empowered social technologies. The aim here is to facilitate the creation of an urban community, comprising several subcommunities, like closely knit collaborative networks of densely co-located firms together with integrated residential communities.

Our proposed platform allows future residents to learn about each other and select each other as future neighbours and encourages potential buyers to reveal their identity and intentions to each other, both in words and via actions within a 3D gamified city building simulation. Potential buyers or tenants are making choices about locations, programme type, as well as selecting urban and architectural modules from a rich but coherently developed kit of parts. There are thus two mechanisms of personalisation at play: the self-tailoring of the apartment and the self-sorting of residents into affinity clusters. Both forms of personalisation are value enhancing.

Start-Up Cities as Paradigm Application Case

One important precondition for the application of the envisioned PUDP and for the full unfolding of its potential is the availability of sufficient degrees of freedom to allow the urban development process to be shaped by the participatory discovery process. This implies the absence of preconceived and politically predetermined urban development outcomes as usually prescribed in municipal land-use/zoning plans. This condition of freedom from political impositions prevails in the metaverse. With respect to physical cities, this condition is very rarely, if ever, realised. That's why libertarian start-up city projects present a viable scenario and context for the elaboration of an urban game platform.

Naturally, radical innovations in terms of political as well as urban rule sets are easier to pull off with a fresh start, without infringing on any pre-existing population. This is Paul Roemer's idea of new cities with new rules to opt-in (Romer, 2010, p.8), rather than trying to implement reforms with existing populations. The new problem then emerges how to get a critical mass of people to join a nascent city, how to initiate a bootstrapping dynamic. The difficulty of a start-up city is that the political space that makes the desired innovation possible is usually rather remote from existing population centres. This means that the special innovations and freedoms must be substantial enough to motivate the move to a new city far away from current metropolitan hubs.

While Roemer is no libertarian, he inspired some libertarians who, after years of sustained but largely unsuccessful political agitation, have come to the conclusion that a political shift within the advanced societies is too heavy lifting and ultimately rather unrealistic. A more realistic strategy might be, so the hypothesis of this group, to make a fresh start somewhere else, with a newly and voluntarily gathered, more entrepreneurial and less risk averse polity. In these special political zones, the unfulfilled economic promises of our technological era can take off and show the way. This is the idea of start-up cities or free private cities (Gebel, 2023).

Most recent start-up city projects are motivated by the opportunity that is opening up due to the economic paralysis witnessed in all advanced societies since 2008. This phenomenon of a decline in economic growth predates the 2008 crisis and can be attributed to the anti-competitive accumulation and entrenchment of special interest groups in mature, stable economies. The gradual growth of such interest groups or 'distributional coalitions' has been identified as a primary reason for the general long-term secular stagnation that has been witnessed in the mature Western democracies, as hypothesised, and argued for with evidence by economist/political scientist Mancur Olson (1982). The 2008 crisis did not break up these paralysing coalitions. To the contrary, since 2008 this process of political entrenchment of powerful distributional coalitions has only intensified.

Start-up cities become economically plausible to the degree to which existing cities are politically inflexible and resist innovations without which growth must stall. Innovations require the expansion of entrepreneurial degrees of freedom and are incompatible with the preponderance of politically entrenched incumbent interests. To the extent that there are sufficiently large pent up innovation potentials, new, unencumbered places that can unlock these potentials become economically viable, or at least economically plausible. To be sure, start-up cities are high-risk entrepreneurial ventures. But high-risk-high-return scenarios always attract at least some protagonists. In the case of start-up cities libertarian ideological zeal also comes into the mix, so that a veritable start-up city movement is emerging. ZHA is currently working with three such start-up city projects: Liberland (liberland.org), Praxis (cityofpraxis.com), and Honduras Prospera (honduraspropera.com).

The hypothesis is that people from all over the world, entrepreneurial people that feel stifled in our current overregulated, risk-averse societies, will come to join in these new city adventures. However, they cannot simply gather en masse as undifferentiated crowd. Cities are economic and cultural engines by way of bringing people together, but not by mixing everybody equally with everybody else. Cities bring people together in a structured way, generating co-location synergies via the process of market-based spatial self-sorting. Communicative interaction is always specific, highly selective with respect to purpose and partners, and always spatially framed and articulated. This spatial framing supports the definition of the situation, which is a precondition of all meaningful, productive communication.

Cities, via the distribution and articulation of both private and public spaces, should function as a differentiated spatial matrix for social self-sorting according to social similarity/affinity, occupation/collaboration, interests, cultural pattern, family status, etc. The resultant spatio-social order is the more functional, the more degrees of freedom are available to the process of self-organisation. This spatio-social order can then be proficiently navigated and a plentiful supply of relevant partners for desired forms of communication are easy to find, undisturbed by irrelevant crowds. This spontaneously emerging functional order is the built environment prosperity enhancing contribution to society. This ordering process has been severely curtailed by the political overregulation of the urban development process. There is no real market process here. The result is an imposed, dysfunctional pseudo-order substituting for a real, functional, vital order. Clearing away the overbearing political control is a necessary step. But we can go a step further by enhancing the market-based process of urban self-organisation by means of inventing and developing new tools, mechanisms, and processes.

Multiplayer Configurator for Honduras Prospera

At the onset of the global pandemic in early 2020, ZHA instantiated the PUDP described above for Honduras Prospera. The protagonists of Prospera were looking to catalyse the creation of an 'ideational community', initially online, with a shared communal vision and synergy potentials as described previously. The intention is to bring this online community on-land, within the Prospera jurisdiction in Roatan, Honduras. The multiplayer configurator platform that ZHA customised and licensed to Prospera can be considered a minimally sufficient product to test the hypothesis of using of a gamified platform to discover customer preferences, including co-location synergies. 'Configurators are comprised of components (the building blocks), processes (the rules, and taxonomies), a knowledge base (datasets for economic evaluation) and people (the users)' (Louth et al., 2023). For detailed description of technical and implementation specifics, consult the related paper entitled 'Configurator: A Platform for Multifamily Residential Design and Customisation'[1] by the ZHA CODE research team (Louth et al., 2023).

The PUDP is a game-engine–based interactive platform that was developed using Unreal Engine, a platform typically used to develop photorealistic video games. The PUDP or 'the architectural game' is being delivered via a standard web browser, whereby potential apartment buyers are able to login, build up their profile, and select the location of their house or apartment in a 3D grid or voxel array defined within the boundaries of the development site. Subsequently, they can build up their house or apartment by choosing from a menu of room modules and customise the interior layout of the chosen rooms via interior fit-out modules. Furthermore, they can augment their apartment by exterior add-ons such as balconies and roof-types. Most importantly, the choices each player makes are visible to other players, and players are able to invite 'friends' to 'play' the game and build something together, or at least in a coordinated way.

One of the important consequences of basing the PUDP on a real-time, photorealistic video game engine is that it improves the confidence of non-expert buyers in both the viability of the proposed novel architecture and that eventually what-you-see-is-what-you-get (WYSIWYG). The WYSIWYG aspect extends to terrain, vegetation, and climate of the site, all of which aids in improving the buyer confidence in typically a large financial transaction. Both the designers and potential end-users constantly experience the spaces within immersive communicative interactions. They can meet and discuss the project within the immersive multiplayer virtual simulation of the evolving design.

Equally importantly, the photorealism foregrounds the need for a phenomenological basis of architectural and urban form. This means that the designed and then the built architectural configurations maintain legibility in the face of versatility and complexity, thereby facilitating easy orientation and intuitive navigation.

In the first real application of the configurator on a beautiful Roatan site overlooking the waterfront, 13 prospective buyers registered their preferences and made their selections. In this case, our architectural design team subsequently had to reconcile many conflicting choices and adjust physically infeasible or difficult to engineer options. The reconciled option was subsequently engineered for construction, and the result is currently being tendered.

The price of the apartments was, in this case, not just based on their respective sizes, add-ons, and fit outs. The pricing of the space voxels was also dependent on their location in the 3D grid due to a number of considered factors: views of the ocean, exposure to summer sun, walking distance to amenities, etc. The participants in the game were further informed about the preferences and selections of the other participants. The gaming process allowed for the discovery of preferred locations within the 3D grid, e.g., bulk heads and top level positions, as well as adjacency preferences with respect to other participants as potential neighbours (Figure 1.3.2).

In practical terms, with respect to both functional and physical criteria, the proposed apartments are constituted from a 'kit of building parts' such as walls, roofs, and balconies. Furthermore, these kits of parts are assembled into pre-set space modules that can replace the voxel selections made by users in real time, via an intuitive drag & drop interface. Lastly, a shape-grammar encodes various allowed and architecturally relevant combinations of the spatial modules. The grammar ensures that allowed selections always make physical and functional sense. Each of the elements of the 'kit of parts' geometrically encodes the constraints of its physical realisation. Each selected element includes information of its production time, material and energy consumed in its production, construction costs, etc. The actual fabrication of the modules happens locally, after selections have been confirmed and committed to, in a near-site micro-factory (Figures 1.3.3 and 1.3.4).

City-As-A-Service

Agglomeration benefits of cities are by virtue of the high-frequency interaction of human producers of goods, services, culture, and knowledge in a compact footprint. Coupling this wealth creation mechanism with the increased need of accommodation for an increasing population locking for an urban life implies both densification of existing cities and the creation of new cities (Ritchie & Roser, 2018; Wheeler, Jones & Kammen, 2018; California yimby, 2021). The requirement to successfully cater for this rapid development pressure calls for low-risk sandboxes for urban experimentation. The PUDP provides a good

Figure 1.3.2   Configurator for Honduras Prospera, Roatan, Zaha Hadid Architects, 2020. A minimally sufficient instance of the Participatory Urban Development Platform deployed to aggregate occupiers of residential units and customise their layouts, before physical realisation.

Source: (c) Zaha Hadid Architects.

'simulation' environment to test both novel urban configurations that could aid the synergetic agglomeration and the architectural kit of parts that could enable its rapid physical realisation. The PUDP provides a robust platform that might become an integral tool for a CAAS business model.

One critical aspect of this whole approach is a new engagement with modularity. Modules are critical for both the participation of non-designers (developers and end-users) in the urban and architectural design process. We are building up a large catalogue of modules, both general and function-type specific. The system of models is ordered hierarchical and thus offers both integrated ready-made large space modules and the opportunity to build up space modules from smaller components, thereby gaining huge combinatorial variety. Further, all modules are set up as parametric modules, i.e., they are capable of dimensional tailoring as well as geometrical adaptation. The design of all modules is being shaped by structural and environmental engineering logics as well as by materiality and fabrication constraints. This implies that tectonism is the architectural language of choice (Schumacher, 2023).

We are currently extending the Configurator deployment for Prospera to an urban district scale. Thus, instead of multiple individual apartment buyers as players, we are elaborating our platform to cater for stakeholder representatives such as a municipal master developer representing the collective interests of the planned community, and several other developers focussed on residential, commercial, and office space real estate, respectively. Correspondingly, the spatial pre-sets now include much larger chunks, up to complete buildings, as well as different function types, i.e., not only residential but also office and commercial assets.

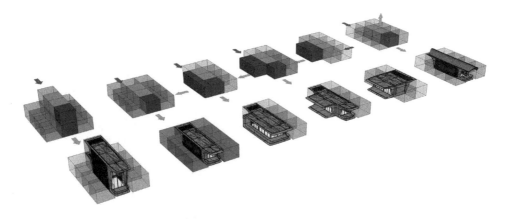

Figure 1.3.3   Zaha Hadid Architects, Beyabu Configurator & Residential Development in Roatan, Honduras, 2020. The game of substituting voxels with pre-set composite modules, and a likely outcome of the participatory design game within the Configurator, visualised within the game engine.

Source: (c) Zaha Hadid Architects.

Simulating Likely Outcomes

PUDPs are cyber-physical platforms in that they couple the virtual spatial environments with their physical counterparts. In this sense, PUDPs are the inverse of the so-called Digital Twin technologies where the virtual spaces are typically a digital recreation of spaces that already exist physically. The coupling of virtual and physical spatial environments enables the use of the virtual worlds as gamified low-risk sandbox environment for rapid experimentation and iteration within plausible physical and economic conditions. The PUDP represents potential owners or end-users as players, encodes player preferences, augmented with decision support information, to arrive at choices and trades. The game platform can be deployed virtually for many interested parties to engage with the evolving project and each other. The thus enabled stakeholder co-creation represents a 'crowdsourcing'

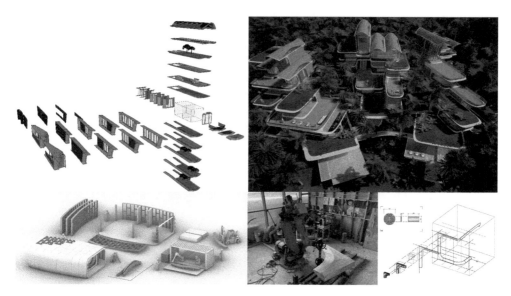

Figure 1.3.4   Kit-of-parts for Beyabu Configurator & Residential Development in Roatan, Honduras; implemented in timber via local robotic micro-factory.

Source: (c) Zaha Hadid Architects.

of value-relevant end-user knowledges. This addresses one of the key issues of the built environment development process: the high risk of malinvestment, the wasting of valuable time and resources on buildings/locations that the envisioned users might not value.

The PUDP can also be helpful without, or in advance of, engaging actual players in the development game. The game invites automated testing in a game theoretic sense. The potential outcomes of the urban game can be simulated computationally by defining a set of representative agents/players with their respective preferences and economic strategies and then see how the games would play out. Each player can be assumed to be a rational actor and proceed to simulate a sequence of most rational choices by each player at each turn. A related paper entitled 'Interactive Geometric Simulation of 4D Cities' proceeds to simulate the growth of a city based on such assumptions, specifically a game-theoretically rational land use allocation (Weber et al., 2009).

By way of such agent-based simulations, the PUDP becomes a potent tool of economic modelling and urban development exploration: different game rules can be tested as well as different player preferences and strategies. The results can then be compared with respect to a number of success metrics, as well as being intuitively appraised by expert urbanists and architects. The discovery and elaboration of optimal player strategies (in view of player preferences) can then be fed back as empowering computational support tools for the players when it comes to actual game play.

There are several related game platforms, which, although they have different purposes, inform our ongoing work on the PUDP: city and world builder games such as Sim City, Cities: Skylines and Minecraft, for educational and experimental use in urban design. There are also professional and validated planning tools that are instructive (Blackarcs, 2023; Wadell, 2023).

The Unreal Engine based VU.City platform in London, being an accepted format for official digital planning applications and approvals, bodes well for PUDP to participate in a tangible pathway to physical realisation.

Conclusion

The PUDP couples the social, exploratory, and network-effect benefits of online worlds with the effective utilisation of immersive digital twin technologies: On the one hand, such platforms provide a low risk, online environment geared towards the active, participatory incorporation of the wisdom and the often only implicit, situated knowledge of professionals and end-users. On the other hand, due to the modular approach allowing for optimisation, they provide for expedient and resource-efficient physical realisation and operation.

In summary, the principal innovations of the PUDP are:

- End-user or representative 'players' that capture the socio-economic preferences/motivations of the stakeholders of a prospective urban development, city district, or start-up city.
- High-performance, architectural system of modules (kit of parts) that can provide feedback on the economic and ecological costs of physical realisation.
- All modules are parametric (adaptive) and optimised in terms of engineering and fabrication logics and articulated in accordance with the paradigm/style of tectonism.
- Open-ended urban playing field as search space for socially optimal land-use allocations.
- Gamified multi-author design, communication, and exchange process that maximises the utilisation of the dispersed stakeholder knowledge for enhanced product-market fit via consumer co-production.
- Immersive and engaging real-time photorealistic rendering of the evolving urban configurations implied in the participants selections.
- Garnering of latent co-location synergies and facilitating space sharing efficiencies, for both physical and virtual (metaverse) industry clusters as well as urban communities.
- The platform is also an urban economics research tool affording the simulation of urban configurations that aggregate and integrate variously defined stakeholder interests/strategies.

The claim put forward here is that these innovations, presuming political green light, deliver the set of necessary and sufficient mechanisms to maximise all stakeholder/end-user interests, i.e., maximising the total social value of the invested resources, including land resources.

Furthermore, the PUDP provides a computational framework and vehicle to research and reason operationally about critical aspects of the political economy of city building with a new level of precision. PUDP is therefore not only a CASS business tool but also a tool of research and academic discourse.

End.

References

Bhooshan, S., & Vazquez, A. N. (2020). Homes, Communities and Games: Constructing Social Agency in Our Urban Futures. *Architectural Design*, 90(3), 60–65. https://doi.org/10.1002/ad.2569 Blackarcs. (2023). *Blackarcs*. Available at: https://blackarcs.org/.

California yimby. (2021). *700 Cities, One Warming Planet*. Available at: https://cayimby.org/blog/700-cities-one-warming-planet/ (Accessed 10 December 2023).

Gebel, Titus (2023). *Free Private Cities: Making Governments Compete For You*, 3rd edition, Aquila Urbis.

Glaeser, E. (2011). *Triumph of the City: How Urban Spaces Make Us Human*. Pan Macmillan.

Louth, H. D., Fragachan, C., Bhooshan, V., & Bhooshan, S. (2023). Configurator: A Platform for Multifamily Residential Design and Customisation. In Barberio, M., Colella, M., Figliola, A., & Battisti, A. (Eds.), *Architecture and Design for Industry 4.0: Theory and Practice*. Springer International Publishing.

Olson, M. (1982). *The Rise and Decline of Nations Economic Growth, Stagflation, and Social Rigidities*. Yale University Press. https://doi.org/10.12987/9780300157673.

Ritchie, H., & Roser, M. (2018). *Urbanization*. Available at: https://ourworldindata.org/urbanization (Accessed 21 March 2023).

Romer, P. (2010). Technologies, Rules, and Progress: The Case for Charter Cities, Center for Global Development. https://www.cgdev.org/sites/default/files/1423916_file_TechnologyRulesProgress_FINAL.pdf

Schumacher, P. (2006). Autopoeisis of a Residential Community. In Ram, T. V., Dekleva, A., & Steele, B. (Eds.), *Negotiate My Boundary! Mass-Customisation and Responsive Environments*. Birkhäuser.

Schumacher, P. (2022). The Metaverse as Opportunity for Architecture and Society: Design Drivers, Core Competencies. *Architectural Intelligence*, 1, 11. https://doi.org/10.1007/s44223-022-00010-z

Schumacher, P. (2023). *Tectonism: Architecture for the 21st Century*. Images Publishing.

Wadell, P. (2023). *Urbansim*. Available at: https://www.urbansim.com/ (Accessed 10 December 2023).

Weber, B., Müller, P., Wonka, P., & Gross, M. (2009). Interactive Geometric Simulation of 4D Cities. *Computer Graphics Forum*, 28(2), 481–492. https://doi.org/10.1111/j.1467–8659.2009.01387.

Wheeler, S. M., Jones, C. M., & Kammen, D. M. (2018). Carbon Footprint Planning: Quantifying Local and State Mitigation Opportunities for 700 California Cities. *Urban Planning*. PRT, 3(2), 35–51.

1.4

SMART RESPONSIVE DESIGN THINKING IN NEUROARCHITECTURE

Towards creating homeostasis balance, equitability, diversity, inclusivity, interactivity, and social performativity in the built environment

1.4.1

NEUROARCHITECTURE FOR COGNITIVE ECOLOGIES

Equitable, Diverse, and Inclusive Smart Design

Fiona Zisch

Abstract

In moving toward achieving better design through interdisciplinary paradigms and methodologies, a tradition of phenomenological and cybernetic architecture interested in cognition has evolved the promising field of Neuroarchitecture, a distinct and notable intersection of architecture and neuroscience. However, often normative and prescriptive research and practice pervade Neuroarchitecture, with a tendency to embrace generalities over particularities (equality over equity), universality and the use of technology for its supposed "objectivity" (uniformity over diversity), and a standardized human over an ecology of different humans and other living – and non-living – cognizers (exclusivity over inclusivity).

This chapter will put forward a more *wicked, transdisciplinary, and adaptive Neuroarchitecture* and suggest potentials for equitable, diverse, and inclusive research and practice. This Neuroarchitecture integrates other, for example, techno-feminist, dimensions and proposes a centrality of notions of care, kinship, and porosity in/for a world of multiplicities.

In the late 1990s, Donna Haraway, ever astute, suggested: "Technology is not neutral. We're inside of what we make, and it's inside of us. We're living in a world of connections – and it matters which ones get made and unmade" (Haraway, 1997). Much like technology, architecture is not neutral. We are inside architecture and it is inside us. Architecture, and the forms it produces, are minds externalizing and internalizing themselves in an ever-evolving spiral (Hendrix, 2012). It matters which buildings, spaces, and interactions we design, build, inhabit, and enable. It matters what we make and what we unmake. Similarly, despite scientific objectivity (Daston & Galison, 2021) which demands rigor and does not claim absolute truth but continuous interrogation and evolution of knowledge, neuroscience is not neutral. Again, it matters what we make and what we unmake.

Neuroarchitecture – where architecture and neuroscience intersect – the result of a long history of architectural interest in human experience, yet still seen as a recent emergence, is also not neutral. It is often hoped that Neuroarchitecture will provide a means of reducing human subjectivity during design and knowledge production and offer objective and unbiased solutions. However, there is value in sensible, sensitive, and informed subjectivity

DOI: 10.4324/9781003384113-10

56

in that it can enable equity over equality. Equitable approaches do not assume homogeneity but demand heterogeneity when searching for solutions to problems. Neuroarchitecture – as is often the case in design – deals with Wicked Problems (Rittel & Webber, 1972; Rittel & Webber, 1973), indeterminate, shapeshifting, and hard to solve conclusively and globally. Wicked Problems require wicked thinking, wicked methodologies, and wicked practice. Neuroarchitecture *is*, in my understanding, wicked (Zisch, 2020). It is a dynamic threshold space, a space of change; transdisciplinary, transgressive, and translational, it must allow informed and wicked subjectivity. Wickedness can mean making and unmaking, responding, adapting, and evolving in synchrony with changing circumstances. In this wicked context, rather than just ask *what Neuroarchitecture should make and unmake*, one must also ask *how Neuroarchitecture should make and unmake*.

Before making and unmaking (in) Neuroarchitecture is addressed below in a collection of thoughts, a (very) brief consideration of Neuroarchitecture as a result of architectural and scientific concerns over time is helpful. Historically, questions of human experience have been considered predominantly through, for example, phenomenological or cybernetic lenses (Murrani, 2011) and an interest in the (embodied) human brain in relation to space is not new. Coined not just as an argot, but also to appeal to a contemporary, broad audience, Neuroarchitecture is, much like other portmanteaus that include the prefix neuro-, trendy. It is trendy as in fashionable, but also as in being the outcome of a long and influential line of trends. The Age of Enlightenment heightened an awareness of the impact of architecture on mental and emotional states. The Industrial Revolution accelerated innovative design solutions in response to changing urban and work environments. Twentieth-century architecture, already informed by phenomenology and welcoming architectural cybernetics, saw, in its last years, Neuroarchitecture emerge as the explicit intersection of disciplines (Edelmann, n.d.).[1] The foundations of Neuroarchitecture, through significant technoscientific advancements, undoubtedly enabled novel approaches to architectural design addressing questions of, for example, health, well-being, or creativity. The twenty-first century has seen Neuroarchitecture mature and a shared sense of shedding previously often reductive and deterministic traps can be felt. However, there is still a long way to go before Neuroarchitecture can fully meet its intrinsic potential in addressing questions in an inclusive, equitable, and diverse manner to harness an inherent "Smartness".

Smart Design can refer both to designed artifacts and design processes being smart. This chapter offers thoughts in reference to the latter, but toward the creation of the former, by proposing a Wicked Neuroarchitecture that encourages equity, diversity, and inclusion to engender critical and adaptive Smart Design for Cognitive Ecologies – a manifold, interconnected tapestry *of and for the many*. In its integration of neuroscientific, quantitative (and qualitative in its links to psychology) data-centric approaches, Neuroarchitecture is data-based – one way of understanding Smart Design. Data-based design is often operationalized using S.M.A.R.T. principles, first introduced as *specific, measurable, assignable (sometimes termed actionable), realistic,* and *time-related* (Doran, 1981), originally a method for achieving effective management goals – somewhat transferrable to scientific and design domains. Data-based design and the use of smart principles have ostensible merit; however, they need to be considered with substantial openness and care, to allow for change and diverse contexts, not to construct all too hermetic and linear a system where initially effective frameworks no longer permit agility and adaptation. The integration of other, for example (techno)feminist, dimensions is decisive in thinking about equity and inclusivity, as well as considering notions of care and kinship in/for a world of multiplicities. The point herein is simple: to make diverse and smart Neuroarchitecture as designed output that results in more equity and inclusion in the built environment, the field of Neuroarchitecture as a transdiscipline must itself become more diverse and wicked. It must include not only different disciplines but also researchers and practitioners with diverse lived realities and diverse ways of approaching the world.

Wicked Problems: Understanding Space and Body

Space and the (Embodied) Brain

Space, comprising material substance and immaterial qualities, is a boundless and intricate composition of inhabitant-cognizers, objects, attributes, relations, and interactions; an evolving scaffold for individual and collective experience. To construct (architectural) experience – the composite of perception as world-observation through the senses and conception as world-appropriation by concepts (Gumbrecht, 2004) – the brain is continuously modulated by its environment and reflects this in neural patterns experienced as thoughts and feelings. What underlies the experience of space, what cognitive systems enable it? To cognize and allow sensible action in space, sensory input, gathered from interacting with the world, is combined to construct an internal representation, known as a cognitive map (O'Keefe & Nadel, 1978; Epstein et al., 2017; Jeffery & Zisch, 2022). The cognitive map is a neural model of spatial relationships, representing external geometry and spatial context in relation to the position, orientation, and movement of one's body. While each respective space establishes a base map, cognitive maps, when recalled, adapt, depending on the current context (Bostock et al., 1991; Poulter et al., 2015). Cognitive maps are constructed by all mammals and some technologies; humans draw upon the same foundational processes as rodents and Machine Learning Algorithms to represent and navigate space (De Cothi et al., 2022). Complementing cognitive maps, recently cognitive gists – cognitive maps stripped of perceptual details – and spatial schemas – an amalgamation of related gists that construct spatial typologies rather than space/place-specific representations – have been proposed (Farzanfar et al., 2023). Cognitive maps, gists, and schemas underlie spatial cognition, experience, and action. Many of their constructing processes parallel design methodologies and design concepts invented and employed by architects who intuitively, over time, learn to subjectively tune their strategies to specific challenges and contexts (Zisch, 2020). Cognitive maps, gists, and schemas can, in considering how to make and unmake Neuroarchitecture, serve as analogies.

Spaces and (Embodied) Brains

The brain. *Whose* brain? It makes little sense to generalize. Looking at space and its many inhabitant-cognizers, the notion of an ecology of many different inhabitant-cognizers, objects, attributes, relations, and interactions seems obvious. It then makes sense to consider specific cognizers and how they cognize space[2] before considering what and how to measure, how to analyze and make and action decisions, how to design. Cognitive ecologies, adapted from Katherine Hayles's "planetary cognitive ecology" (2017), include, as the name suggests, diverse cognizers – human animals, non-human animals, as well as technological entities. It must be noted that Neuroarchitectural research ecologies include non-human biological cognizers. Consider, for example, the many rodents we humans sacrifice to learn about spatial cognition. In view of this bittersweet, Hayles's proposal of the terms cognizers and non-cognizers aims to overcome the human/non-human binary in suggesting they operate in cognitive assemblages where the "crucial features distinguishing cognizers from noncognizers are interpretation and choice (or selection). The two are entwined because, without choice, there can be no interpretation, which requires at least two available options" (Amoore & Piotukh, 2019). While fundamental aspects of spatial cognition, such as the construction of cognitive maps, are pervasive across all cognizing mammals and some technologies, differences in how specific choices are made and interpreted arise when space and its experience are considered more widely and diversely. Spatial cognition research explores not only how general (mammalian) populations perceive, remember, and navigate the physical world, but also how individuals differ, often in relation to cultural background, age, gender, or (dis)ability (Hegarty et al., 2006; Nazareth et al., 2019; van der Ham et al., 2020; Zach & King, 2022; Corti et al., 2022; Li & King, 2019; Fernandez-Velasco & Spiers, 2023; Banker et al., 2021). Importantly, spatial cognition does not encompass the entirety of spatial experience, where cognition is complemented not only by affect and emotions but also action. This leads to questions of body politics, embodiment, and enactivism (Butnor & MacKenzie, 2022).

The architect Jonathan Tyrrell offers the twinned notions of (spatial) "sensibility" and "sense*ability*" (Tyrrell, 2023). Sensibility as appreciation and response to complex emotional influences is here met by sense*ability* as a way of emphasizing diverse needs and diverse abilities in relation to sensory perception, conceptualization, and thus experience. In considering body politics, Silvia Federici explores bodies as and through (socio-political) action to understand them as enactive and enacted processes (Federici, 2020). Sense*ability* highlights ability in relation to (en)action. In being both enactive and enacted, as well as – as radically embodied – ecological (Baggs & Chemero, 2021), space and bodies are interdependent. Understanding and designing (for) one helps understanding and designing (for) the other(s). Radically embodied, critical, inclusive Neuroarchitecture can base its work on iterative and reciprocal exploration of shifting conditions *for and of* diverse cognitive ecologies where insight not only informs and forms the design of equitable spaces for many bodies (and brains), but equitable spaces form many bodies (and brains). Therefore, in a sense, Neuroarchitecture holds political potential and responsibility for designing not only space but also bodies, by making and unmaking an evolving, experiential platform upon which all cognizers can develop, both collectively and as individuals.

Wicked Designing: Making and Unmaking Space and Bodies

Ambiguity and Uncertainty

Space and bodies are connected via an array of interdependent and intertwined sensory modalities. High-level, multi- and cross-modal input is driven by the way architecture is configured in its geometry and materiality, experienced as atmospheric expression, the interaction of "environmental qualities and human states" (Böhme, 1993). (Embodied) brains gather and process (sensory) stimuli, tune these against memories and expectations, and adapt experience in response to a respective environment and state. Depending on sensibility and sense*ability*, different atmospheric compositions, cognition, and actionabilities arise.

For (Neuro)architects, this shifting dynamic means ambiguous and uncertain parameters upon which to design space(s). Ambiguity and uncertainty are, of course, hallmarks of Wicked Problems. Ambiguity does not mean illegibility, nor does it mean solutions cannot be offered. Ambiguity arises from states of manifold, where multiplicities and diversities are not only present but invited, as are complexities, sometimes contradictions, and paradoxes. Recall Robert Venturi in "Complexity and Contradiction" (1997) discussing the both-and in architectural objects that encourage interpretation when no one state can and should be assumed. Any object experience (object as physical space, virtual space, spatial interaction) is always a question of interpretation and not tied to only one percept. From percept, a concept is encoded as an abstract memory, ready to be recalled from many other percepts, and then interpreted (Barsalou, 1999, 2005). An object and its perceptual correlates are interconnected via multiple and adaptive strands. Consider cognitive maps, gists, and schemas – shared foundations idiosyncratically and adaptively expressed in relation to specific, diverse contexts. They are always both-and, generic and idiosyncratic, adaptive in relation to who is constructing them, when and where. Interpretation in states of both-and cannot be overlooked, neither in experience nor in measurement and design of space. In design and in science, unavoidable ambiguity and uncertainty cannot be met by singular and finite Neuroarchitecture; smart, adaptive approaches based on rigorous, wicked methods of interpretation are needed. One way of meeting challenges that are manifold and shifting, and include multiplicities and diversities, is by widening scientific measurement pools, always drawing from context-specific data, as well as including more perspectives and diversifying ways of interpreting and actioning. More recently, neuroscience and architecture (at last) aim to increase diversity not only in who is studied or designed for, but equally increase diversity in who makes-unmakes science and who makes-unmakes architecture. Collaboration is vital, as is intuition (as embodied knowledge) in a diverse, shared repertoire across populations of cooperating Neuroarchitects toward an iterative, open-ended system responding to wicked challenges – inherently making and unmaking.

Collaborative, Intuitive, Iterative, Open-Ended

While not all architects – nor scientists – admit it, all operate, in some way, intuitively. Intuition is not irrational but a highly adaptive and embodied mechanism that allows flexible and tailored responses from acquired knowledge. Brains, sometimes described as operating through metaphors (Schrott & Jacobs, 2011), prognose and extrapolate from available information. They are highly capable of lateral thinking (Dingli, 2008), taking information from one domain and transfiguring it to another. Humans, in performing intuitive operations and thinking laterally, draw on external resources to augment their cognitive capacities. These include other cognizers – biological, such as other humans, and technological, such as recently Machine Learning Algorithms, where impressive achievements are being made. While transfer learning (Zhuang et al., 2020) is possible, intuitive lateral thinking in Machine Learning has not yet been achieved. However, in cooperation with human cognizers, Machine Learning cognizers augment intelligent processes toward Smart Design by supporting specific, fast, effective, and adaptive responses. An intuitive Neuroarchitecture does not solely design *for* cognitive ecologies but indeed designs *as* a cognitive ecology. Sustained, diverse collaboration of human and non-human cognizers in iterative constructions of knowledge and design processes results in more diverse output to meet different and dynamic demands. Neuroarchitecture *for and of* cognitive ecologies, dealing with uncertainties, certainly includes implicit playfulness where

> 'Play' (and its associated behavioral variability) is not purely entertainment or a luxury to be given up when things get serious. It is itself a highly adaptive mechanism for dealing with the reality that the context for behavior is always largely unknown.
>
> *(Grobstein, 1994)*

Playfully intuitive, adaptive, iterative, Neuroarchitecture's (second order) cybernetic roots become evident (Glanville, 2007). A feedback loop, Neuroarchitecture is relational and relative, transferable and dynamic, cyclically building collective intuition from/to scientific knowledge and architectural output. Done carefully, this, of course, includes ongoing reflection and critical (self)scrutiny. Critical neuroscience has emerged within the wider field of the brain sciences and acts as a reflective and scrutinizing voice (Choudhury & Slaby, 2016). Equally, architecture has a long history of self-reflection and self-critique (Hays, 1984; Frampton, 2020). As a diverse transdiscipline and open system, demanding ongoing critical discourse, allowing contradictory views and debate, Neuroarchitecture must therefore be unequivocally (self)critical and collaborative. Interpretation in debate and collaboration "requires at least two available options" (Ammore & Piotukh, 2019) – these are only possible if *at least* two perspectives exist. To engender fruitful collaboration across diverse sensibilities and sense*abilities* in domains with different methodologies and (sometimes) ideologies, kinship traversing options need to be built and nurtured.

Wicked Ecologies: Unmaking and Making Worlds

Kinship and Care

In and as an adaptive and agile cognitive ecology, it is central to foreground care in

> Everything we do to maintain, continue and repair our world so that we may live in it as well as possible. That world includes our bodies, ourselves, and our environment, all of which we seek to interweave in a complex, life-sustaining web.
>
> *(Tronto & Fisher, 1990)*

To enable designing for and working in/as a life-sustaining-*and-enhancing* web, diversity in collaboration and the value of iteration and intuition have been highlighted. Collaboration is not always easy or straightforward, especially when differences and contradictions are taken into consideration. Mutualism must be constructed. Keller Easterling references Karen Barad to emphasize the virtues of interdependence and the intertwining of elements in constructing mutualism. "Intra-action" (Barad, 2007) and entanglement in constructing mutualism are, as Easterling offers, "embodied in spatial arrangements. Focussing not only on objects in […] space but also the matrix of relationships that connects them" (Easterling, 2021). Collaborative matrices of relationships akin to cognitive maps, gists, and schemas as spatial arrangements build varied Neuroarchitectural entanglements in order to deepen exchange. These enable collaboration not solely on the basis of intermittent intersection, but as an ongoing and adaptive space to think, practice, intuit together, and, importantly, care in. To support a deeply entangled cognitive ecology that integrates care, it is useful to remember that the strength of a system is determined by the depth of its relationships (Brown, 2017). Deep connections built from simple intra-actions into cumulative, connected, spatiotemporal practices where "complex systems and patterns arise out of a multiplicity of relatively simple interactions" (Brown, 2017, p. 6) allow diverse Neuroarchitectural cognizers to both individually and collectively gather insight, think, and intuit in response to specific challenges, then make and unmake decisions together. As simple interactions amalgamate over time, complex interactions with grand impact result. Distributing responsibilities removes individual burden and results in "caring – with", a caring ecology reliant on trust and solidarity in processes of interaction (Tronto's, 2013). Building care(ful) connections for making and unmaking Neuroarchitecture becomes a distributed undertaking where "nobody [must] be kin to everything, but our kin networks can be full of attachment sites" (Haraway, 2019). Neuroarchitectural kin networks, of course, include non-biological cognizers (Hayles, 2017) that scaffold our practice, especially in consideration of Smart Design – in both of its senses. Increasingly, antidotes to conventional understandings of care that center solely around human needs are being offered to allow more ecological thinking and practice to consider the ethics, obligations, and politics of care in "more than human" (Puig de la Bellacasa, 2017) worlds infused and scaffolded by technology.

Glitchy, eXtended, Transformative

Technology is not only used to design and make Neuroarchitecture; it is increasingly – not just recently – entangled into our lived and experienced environments where it can no longer be disentangled. The term "Glitch Feminism" proposes the glitch as a way of rethinking existing techno-infused systems and structures to overcome a host of binary understandings and re-make more equitable world(s).

> In glitch feminism, we look at the notion of glitch-as-error with its genesis in the realm of the machinic and the digital and consider how it can be reapplied to inform the way we see the AFK (Away From Keyboard) world, shaping how we might participate in it toward greater agency for and by ourselves.
>
> *(Russell, 2020)*

A technological Neuroarchitecture drawing from proactively integrating glitch to shape (make, unmake, remake) worlds permits distributed, contextual agency, where "technological devices are embedded in levels of contextual meanings, apart from which they are merely 'objects'" (Ihde, 2000). Neuroarchitecture as contextually embedded and entangled with technology reminds, of course, of extended (Clark & Chalmers, 1998) or scaffolded (Sterelny, 2010) minds – cognitive ecologies. These notions have been in circulation for decades. Especially in considering a more inclusive, technological Neuroarchitecture, technology as an extension or scaffold is improving, for example, accessibility, navigation, and sensory experience. Here, above all, emphasis on Smart Design is paramount – the integration of intelligent technologies into design processes as well as into built and virtual environments as interactive architecture.[3] Technological cognizers enable biological designer-cognizers to create more customizable solutions as well as support biological inhabitant-cognizers with assistive technologies, embedded into space and worn on bodies. This includes virtual space and entangled, eXtended virtuality and physicality across the reality-virtuality continuum (Skarbez et al., 2021) in the contemporary world-as-experienced. This PolySocial Reality

(Applin & Fischer, 2013), multi-directional, multi-platform, multi-voice, is a porous, hybrid space – a polyphonous hyperspace, continuously made, unmade, and remade. Hyperspace Neuroarchitecture *of and for* diverse minds and bodies, heterogeneous cognitive ecologies, is, in the words of Brian Massumi considering cognitive maps two decades ago but still pertinent, a "hyperspace[s] of transformation" (Massumi, 2002, p. 184).

Notes

1 Gerard Edelmann suggests that neuroarchitecture as explicit intersection emerged in the 1990s
2 ... and cognize themselves; understanding their own understanding (Von Foerster, 2007), central to Neuroarchitectural discourse and aims.
3 See, for example, Michael Arbib in Chapter 1.4.3 on cybernetics, responsivity, interactivity and Stroe, Ward, and Zisch in Chapter 2.8 on healthcare technologies.

Bibliography

Amoore, L., & Piotukh, V. (2019). Interview with N. Katherine Hayles. *Theory, Culture & Society*, 36(2), 145–155.

Applin, S. A., & Fischer, M. D. (2013). Thing theory: Connecting humans to location-aware smart environments. *LAMDa'*, 13, 29.

Baggs, E., & Chemero, A. (2021). Radical embodiment in two directions. *Synthese*, 198(Suppl 9), 2175–2190.

Banker, S. M., Gu, X., Schiller, D., & Foss-Feig, J. H. (2021). Hippocampal contributions to social and cognitive deficits in autism spectrum disorder. *Trends in Neurosciences*, 44(10), 793–807.

Barad, K. (2007). *Meeting the Universe Halfway: Quantum Physics and the Entanglement of Matter and Meaning*. Durham, NC: Duke University Press.

Barsalou, L. W. (1999). Perceptual symbol systems. *Behavioral and Brain Sciences*, 22(4), 577–660.

Barsalou, L. W. (2005). Abstraction as dynamic interpretation in perceptual symbol systems. In *Building Object Categories in Developmental Time* (pp. 407–450). Psychology Press.

Böhme, G. (1993). Atmosphere as the fundamental concept of a new aesthetics. *Thesis Eleven*, 36(1), 113–126.

Bostock, E., Muller, R. U., & Kubie, J. L. (1991). Experience-dependent modifications of hippocampal place cell firing. *Hippocampus*, 1(2), 193–205.

Brown, A. M. (2017). *Emergent strategy: Shaping change, Changing Worlds*. Chico, CA: AK Press

Butnor, A., & MacKenzie, M. (2022). Enactivism and gender performativity. In McWeeny, J., Maitra, K. (eds.), *Feminist Philosophy of Mind*, 190–206.

Choudhury, S., & Slaby, J. (eds.) (2016). *Critical Neuroscience: A Handbook of the Social and Cultural Contexts of Neuroscience*. John Wiley & Sons. https://www.google.co.uk/books/edition/Critical_Neuroscience/pjFECwAAQBAJ?hl=en&gbpv=1&dq=Choudhury,+S.,+%26+Slaby,+J.+(eds.)+(2016).+Critical+Neuroscience:+A+Handbook+of+the+Social+and+Cultural+Contexts+of+Neuroscience.+John+Wiley+%26+Sons.&pg=PR8&printsec=frontcover

Clark, A., & Chalmers, D. (1998). The extended mind. *Analysis*, 58(1), 7–19.

Corti, C., Oprandi, M. C., Chevignard, M., Jansari, A., Oldrati, V., Ferrari, E., ... & Bardoni, A. (2022). Virtual-reality performance-based assessment of cognitive functions in adult patients with acquired Brain Injury: A scoping review. *Neuropsychology Review*, 32(2), 352–399.

Daston, L., & Galison, P. (2021). *Objectivity*. Princeton, NJ; Woodstock: Princeton University Press. https://www.google.co.uk/books/edition/Objectivity/TtsPEAAAQBAJ?hl=en&gbpv=0

De Cothi, W., Nyberg, N., Griesbauer, E. M., Ghanamé, C., Zisch, F., Lefort, J. M., ... & Spiers, H. J. (2022). Predictive maps in rats and humans for spatial navigation. *Current Biology*, 32(17), 3676–3689.

Dingli, S. (2008). Thinking outside the box: Edward de Bono's lateral thinking. In Tudor, R., Mark A. R., & Susan, M. (eds.), *The Routledge Companion to Creativity* (pp. 338–350). London: Routledge.

Doran, G. T. (1981). There's a SMART way to write management's goals and objectives. *Management Review*, 70(11), 35–36.

Easterling, K. (2021, 19 January). Reading mutualism: A contemplation after medium design. *Verso*. https://www.versobooks.com/blogs/4976-reading-mutualism-a-contemplation-after-medium-design (Accessed 6 November 2023).

Edelmann, G. (n.d.). *Neuroarchitecture*. https://www.youtube.com/watch?v=p1LoP9W5Qng (Accessed 6 November 2023).

Epstein, R. A., Patai, E. Z., Julian, J. B., & Spiers, H. J. (2017). The cognitive map in humans: Spatial navigation and beyond. *Nature Neuroscience*, 20(11), 1504–1513.

Farzanfar, D., Spiers, H. J., Moscovitch, M., & Rosenbaum, R. S. (2023). From cognitive maps to spatial schemas. *Nature Reviews Neuroscience*, 24(2), 63–79.

Federici, S. (2020). *Beyond the Periphery of the Skin: Rethinking, Remaking, and Reclaiming the Body in Contemporary Capitalism*. Oakland, CA: PM Press.

Fernandez-Velasco, P., & Spiers, H. J. (2023). Wayfinding across ocean and tundra: What traditional cultures teach us about navigation. *Trends in Cognitive Sciences*, 28(1), 56–71.

Frampton, K. (2020). *Modern Architecture: A Critical History (World of Art)*. London: Thames & Hudson.

Glanville, R. (2007). Try again. Fail again. Fail better: The cybernetics in design and the design in cybernetics. *Kybernetes*, 36(9/10), 1173–1206.

Grobstein, P. (1994). Variability in brain function and behavior. In Ramachandran, V. S. (ed.), *The Encyclopedia of Human Behavior* (Vol. 4, pp. 447–458). Amsterdam: Elsevier Science. https://www.google.co.uk/books/edition/Encyclopedia_of_Human_Behavior/yASuxMCuhKkC?hl=en&gbpv=0

Gumbrecht, H. U. (2004). *Production of preSence: What Meaning Cannot Convey?* Stanford, CA: Stanford University Press.

Haraway, D. (1997, February). *Wired Magazine*. https://www.wired.com/1997/02/ffharaway/ (Accessed 15 October 2023).

Haraway, D. (2019, 6 December). Making Kin: An interview with Donna Haraway (Steve Paulson interviews Donna Haraway). *LA Review of Books*. https://www.lareviewofbooks.org/article/making-kin-an-interview-with-donna-haraway/ (Accessed 5 June 2021)

Hayles, N. K. (2017). *Unthought: The Power of the Cognitive Nonconscious*. Chicago, IL: University of Chicago Press.

Hays, K. M. (1984). Critical architecture: Between culture and form. *Perspecta*, 21, 15–29.

Hegarty, M., Montello, D. R., Richardson, A. E., Ishikawa, T., & Lovelace, K. (2006). Spatial abilities at different scales: Individual differences in aptitude-test performance and spatial-layout learning. *Intelligence*, 34(2), 151–176.

Hendrix, J. (2012). Architecture as the psyche of a culture. In Paul Emmons, Jane Lomholt, John Shannon Hendrix (eds.), *The Cultural Role of Architecture: Contemporary and Historical Perspectives* (pp. 208–215). London: Routledge.

Ihde, D. (2000). Putting technology in its place. *Nature*, 404(6781), 935–935.

Jeffery, K., & Zisch, F. (2022). Spatial entities of the future: Design through the lens of neuroscience. In Mitra Kanaani (ed.), *The Routledge Companion to Ecological Design Thinking* (pp. 92–103). New York: Routledge.

Li, A. W., & King, J. (2019). Spatial memory and navigation in ageing: A systematic review of MRI and fMRI studies in healthy participants. *Neuroscience & Biobehavioral Reviews*, 103, 33–49.

Massumi, B. (2002). *Parables for the Virtual: Movement, Affect, Sensation*. Durham, NC: Duke University Press.

Murrani, S. (2011). Third way architecture: Between cybernetics and phenomenology. *Technoetic Arts*, 8(3), 267–281.

Nazareth, A., Huang, X., Voyer, D., & Newcombe, N. (2019). A meta-analysis of sex differences in human navigation skills. *Psychonomic Bulletin & Review*, 26, 1503–1528.

O'Keefe, J., & Nadel, L. (1978). *The Hippocampus as a Cognitive Map*. Oxford: Clarendon Press.

Poulter, S., Lee, S. A., & Lever, C. (2015). *Place Cells and Episodic Memory*. https://www.researchgate.net/profile/Sang-Ah-Lee/publication/273127587_Place_Cells_and_Episodic_Memory/links/559d1aaa08aece2562fc0c98/Place-Cells-and-Episodic-Memory.pdf

Puig de la Bellacasa, M. (2017). *Matters of Care: Speculative Ethics in More than Human Worlds*. Minneapolis: University of Minnesota Press.

Rittel, H. W. J., & Webber, M. M. (1972). Dilemmas in a General Theory of Planning. Working paper presented at the Institute of Urban and Regional Development, University of California, Berkeley, November 1972.

Rittel, H. W., & Webber, M. M. (1973). Dilemmas in a general theory of planning. *Policy Sciences*, 4(2), 155–169.

Russell, L. (2020). *Glitch Feminism: A Manifesto*. London: Verso.

Schrott, R., & Jacobs, A. (2011). *Gehirn und Gedicht. Wie Wir Unsere Wirklichkeiten Konstruieren*. München: Carl Hanser.

Skarbez, R., Smith, M., & Whitton, M. C. (2021). Revisiting Milgram and Kishino's reality-virtuality continuum. *Frontiers in Virtual Reality*, 2, 647997.

Sterelny, K. (2010). Minds: Extended or scaffolded? *Phenomenology and the Cognitive Sciences*, 9(4), 465–481.

Tronto, J. C. (2013). *Caring Democracy: Markets, Equality, and Justice*. New York; London NYU Press.

Tronto, J. C., & Fisher, B. (1990). Toward a feminist theory of caring. In Abel, E. K. and Nelson, M. K. (eds.), *Circles of Care: Work and Identity in Women's Lives* (pp. 35–62, p. 40). New York: State University of New York Press.

Tyrrell, J. (2023). *Sense and Senseability, Lecture, the Bartlett School of Architecture*. London: University College London.

van der Ham, I. J., Claessen, M. H., Evers, A. W., & van der Kuil, M. N. (2020). Large-scale assessment of human navigation ability across the lifespan. *Scientific Reports*, 10(1), 3299.

Venturi, R. (1977). *Complexity and Contradiction in Architecture* (Vol. 1). New York: The Museum of Modern Art.

Von Foerster, H. (2007). *Understanding Understanding: Essays on Cybernetics and Cognition*. New York: Springer Science & Business Media.

Zach, S., & King, A. (2022). Wayfinding and spatial perception among adolescents with mild intellectual disability. *Journal of Intellectual Disability Research*, 66(12), 1009–1022.

Zhuang, F., Qi, Z., Duan, K., Xi, D., Zhu, Y., Zhu, H., ... & He, Q. (2020). A comprehensive survey on transfer learning. *Proceedings of the IEEE*, 109(1), 43–76.

Zisch, F. (2020). Wicked neuroarchitecture: Reciprocity, Shapeshifting problems and a case for embodied knowledge. *Architectural Design*, 90(6), 118–127.

Zisch, F. E. (2020). *Doppelkopf Neuroarchitecture. A Wicked Threshold Space* (Doctoral dissertation, UCL, University College London).

1.4.2

SMART DESIGN FOR PROMOTING SOCIAL PERFORMATIVITY AND INTERACTIVITY OF ALL THE SENSES

Luis Othón Villegas-Solís

Abstract

The ever-evolving concept of Smart Design in architecture emphasizes creating human-centric and immersive interactive experiences. This chapter explores the expansive scenery of Smart Design by focusing on the synthesis of multisensory perception with visual, voice, tactile, cognitive, and emotional interactions in their intersection with action-oriented engagement. It aims to delve into architecture and design that enhances a "people-oriented" approach, prioritizing user experiences. This exploration will tap into social performativity to illuminate the flexible nature of Smart Design as a form of social engagement. Smart design is viewed here as fueled by the aspiration to offer users comprehensive interactions within physical spaces and between human emotions and senses. Seamlessly integrating technology, functionality, and aesthetics amplifies user engagement and satisfaction, redefining the landscape of architectural experience.

Interactive Sensorial Experience and Smart Design

In a world where human interaction with technology continues to evolve, multisensory perception has emerged as a cornerstone of understanding how we experience the world. It encompasses the traditional senses of sight, hearing, smell, taste, touch, and proprioception—the awareness of our body's position in space. Fusion of sensory inputs empowers individuals to understand their environment comprehensively. It departs from the notion that perception is solely visual, revealing a richer, subtler tapestry that underpins our interactions with the external world. Beyond passive reception, multisensory perception intersects with action-oriented engagement. The context in which a stimulus is presented profoundly influences its perception. As we interact with our surroundings, our perception adapts, and these adaptations, in turn, shape our actions. This dynamic interplay highlights

DOI: 10.4324/9781003384113-11

the inseparable relationship between perception and motor stimulation, as both merge to craft our reality of experience.

Architectural design is undergoing a significant paradigm shift, marked by the fusion of emotional engagement and technological innovation, fundamentally reshaping spatial experiences. The smart-emotional architecture combines the principles of dynamic interaction with state-of-the-art technology to craft immersive environments that can profoundly stimulate the human senses. Central to this interpretive framework are the contributions of Juhani Pallasmaa in his works "The Architecture of the Seven Senses" and "The Eyes of the Skin." Both works particularly stand as cornerstone manifestos, underscoring the pivotal role of emotions in architecture and serving as an unwavering compass for architects seeking to seamlessly incorporate multisensory dimensions into their designs.

Architectural spaces transcend the confines of visual aesthetics, accentuating the significance of senses like touch, smell, and hearing. This perspective is increasingly relevant as technology advances, providing architects with innovative tools to influence how we encounter a multisensorial experience. Integrating emotion, aesthetics, and atmosphere in the context of multisensory perception and Smart Design is crucial for creating immersive and user-centric experiences. Gernot Böhme's concept of atmosphere, as described in his work on "Atmosphäre" (1989/1999), plays a crucial role in this framework. The atmosphere serves as the bridge between the objective qualities of an environment and the sensory and emotional states of a person within said environment. From this perspective, atmosphere represents the notion that our perception of space is not solely about its physical attributes but is deeply shaped by how it makes us feel. It transcends the tangible and quantifiable design aspects, connecting with our personal, emotional, and sensory responses.

The synergy between perception and memory forms a foundational framework for interactive design. Embracing atmosphere as a crucial element of Smart Design empowers designers to create environments that intentionally elicit specific emotional and sensory responses. As individuals engage with smartly designed spaces, their interactions with screens, interfaces, and technological devices become integrated into their daily lives, thus influencing their emotional states and underscoring the connection between objective design elements and subjective human experiences. In essence, Smart Design buildings emphasize the "in-between" nature of design and new technologies where the objective and the subjective intertwine.

Haptics

We now recognize that haptic systems technology involves touch-sensitive surfaces, vibrational modalities, and force-feedback mechanisms to enable users to perceive tactile dimensions in unprecedented ways. Smart Design systems employ haptic feedback to enhance user perception and interaction by providing tactile sensations or vibrations. In the context of smart homes, haptic technology can create touch-sensitive surfaces on the floor. These surfaces can adapt and provide different textures or signals to users based on their needs. This is particularly beneficial for visually impaired users who can navigate and interact with their environment using these tactile cues. For non-visually impaired users, haptic technology can be applied in various ways, such as providing feedback during virtual reality experiences or enhancing the sensation of interacting with digital interfaces, like touchscreens, through tactile feedback.

Haptic technology adds value by offering a dynamic and adaptable tactile experience beyond static physical features. It allows for personalized interactions and enhances the overall user experience in practical and immersive scenarios. The aim is to provide a seamless and satisfying experience where the technology adapts to the user's needs and preferences, ultimately creating a multisensory interaction that is functional and enjoyable within the context of natural and architected spaces (Li et al., 2020).

The realm of Smart Design introduces a compelling narrative of adaptability within architectural environments. For instance, technology is reshaping dining experiences in smart furniture design, especially in restaurants. As exemplified by IRT Kodisoft, interactive touch tables enable waiter-independent ordering with sharp graphics and clever suggestions, streamlining the process and encouraging guests to order freely. Integration with social networks allows diners to promote the restaurant, organically offering a valuable marketing avenue. The benefits are clear: improved efficiency, enhanced customer satisfaction, and increased visibility through user-generated content. Nevertheless, some customers may prefer traditional, human-centered service, and both privacy concerns and technology costs need consideration. When implementing such innovations, weighing these potential drawbacks against the benefits is essential.

Think of smart urban furniture design, which extends well beyond mere power stations in urban settings; it encompasses furniture that collects data by sensing people's movements and interactions at public bicycle stands, bus stops, and park benches equipped with USB ports. This innovative approach integrates technology and design principles to deliver feedback, enhance user experiences, elevate public spaces' functionality, and advance ecological sustainability. Key features include solar-powered charging stations, dynamic digital displays, and robust, recyclable materials. While not exclusively haptic, these examples showcase the potential for smart urban furniture to create multisensory interactions, with haptics being one element among others that enhance the overall experience.

Tailored to suit specific urban environments, these designs adapt to local demands, offering diverse functions that enhance users' haptic experiences. Smart urban furniture solutions prioritize eco-friendly principles, following the 3R approach: reuse, reduce, and recycle, which is vital in optimizing resource allocation within cities, improving overall efficiency, and enriching user comfort through haptic interactions. These innovative designs create a functional, user-centric, and sustainable urban environment by seamlessly integrating technology, creative design, environmental consciousness, and sensory-rich urban experience (Keçecioğlu Dağlı & Özdemir Durak, 2022).

Beyond Acoustics

Sound and acoustics play a significant role in architectural design beyond simply controlling noise. The soundscape of a space can convey its identity, proportions, and function, evoking emotions ranging from intimacy to hostility. Unwanted noise is a growing concern in various settings, including restaurants, hospitals, and open-plan offices. In restaurants, excessive background noise remains a top complaint among users. In hospitals, loud noise can hinder patient recovery and increase nurses' chance of misinterpreting requests or instructions (Edelstein & Macagno, 2012), while open-plan offices frequently need help with noise distractions that affect worker productivity (Fenko & Loock, 2014).

The sensory aspects of the built environment, including sound, profoundly influence our perception, emotions, and behavior. Incorporating natural sounds, such as running water, can help mask disruptive conversations and enhance the overall ambiance of a space. Smart-designed buildings that utilize sound masking techniques can influence people's perceptions and provide relief. While promising serene environments and comfort, integrating these networks into architectural designs without compromising aesthetics remains challenging.

Implementing personalization in shared spaces requires a delicate balance between individual needs and maintaining a cohesive atmosphere. In this sense, when designing a restaurant or a bar, we are exploring the relationship between music and food and how it has yielded a body of research with varied outcomes. Some studies suggest that music influences eating habits by modulating psychological responses, such as arousal and emotions, increasing the amount of people's intake of beverages and food. Elements like the volume, genre, and tempo of music have been scrutinized as potential variables that mediate this connection. However, it is important to note that not all studies have consistently detected significant effects, suggesting that the interplay between music and food intake may be context-dependent (Cui et al., 2021).

Through the seamless integration of acoustic considerations and carefully curated soundscapes, designers have the power to amplify the influence of music on food intake. Deliberately crafted acoustics can exert control over sound diffusion and absorption, potentially reshaping how individuals perceive auditory elements, including music and rhythm, during their dining experience and how these musical beats can heighten or reduce arousal levels. Additionally, selecting materials, layout, and effective architectural isolation further fine-tune the auditory ambiance within dining spaces (Spence, 2020).

A relevant example illustrating the impact of music on consumer behavior comes from the experiment conducted by North et al. (1997, 1999). In their study, the type of music played in a supermarket influenced the wine purchase by customers. Specifically, when French music was played, most of the wine purchased was French, and when German music was played, most of the wine purchased was German. Interestingly, most customers denied that the background music influenced their choices, suggesting that these sensory cues can subtly influence our behavior without conscious awareness. This underscores the importance of meticulously integrating soundscapes and acoustics within design to create environments that foster desired behaviors and experiences.

Future research endeavors should explore the psychological and contextual dimensions and consider how Smart Design in interior spaces and architecture can be harnessed to create environments that facilitate healthier eating habits. As our understanding deepens and we integrate these elements, we may discover innovative ways to promote mindful dining and well-being through harmonious design. Combining sound and voice interaction, sensor networks, and personalized acoustics presents a promising future for enhancing user experiences. However, architects must navigate privacy concerns, and most importantly, ethical considerations are paramount as we seek to maximize the benefits while mitigating the potential drawbacks of these innovations.

Smell and Taste

The incorporation of fragrance into architectural and urban design represents an emerging field poised to revolutionize our perception and interaction with spaces, thanks to the integration of smart technology. Designers are expanding their sensory repertoire, recognizing the potential to create more engaging and health-enhancing environments while acknowledging the often-overlooked dimension of scent in the design equation.

Scents can have a profound impact on human behavior. For example, subtle citrus notes have been linked to increased cleanliness, suggesting the potential use of fragrances like aromatic flowers in public spaces to discourage littering and vandalism. Additionally, certain scents, such as lavender, have demonstrated remarkable benefits for well-being, including stress reduction, improved sleep, and enhanced recovery from illness. While the mechanisms driving these mood alterations are still being explored, theories range from cognitive priming effects to direct physiological pathways (Spence, 2020).

Within the realm of Smart Design's influence on architecture and urban planning, a subtle yet significant shift is underway, recognizing the role of scent in shaping the atmosphere and experiences within spaces. Noteworthy examples include the Barclays Center in Brooklyn, which has introduced distinctive fragrances to establish a unique olfactory identity. This trend harks back to 1913 when the Marmorhaus cinema in Berlin infused Marguerite Carré's perfume into its auditorium. Today, luxury retail brands are venturing into bespoke scent design for personalized sensory experiences (Albrecht, 2013).

Our firm, LVS-Architecture, embraced this approach in the design development of a prototype project for a nutritional products store in Mexico. Our central objective was to create a distinctive and evocative retail environment, leveraging the olfactory dimension to trigger customer memories and foster a profound sense of place and brand attachment. The core concept involved infusing the store's atmosphere with a fragrance reminiscent of our client company's top-selling beverage, exemplifying Smart Design by meticulously integrating sensory elements into the store's overall concept. Beyond its aesthetic appeal, this approach was strategically driven, with the scent serving as a cognitive trigger designed to evoke specific memories and emotions associated with the brand, thereby deepening customer loyalty. The store's design signifies the transformation of a conventional retail space into an immersive, emotionally resonant sensory experience (Figure 1.4.2.1).

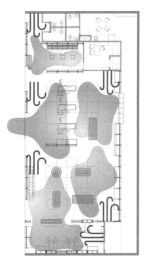

Smell difusion   CEDIS Omnilife Center Veracruz, México.

Figure 1.4.2.1 In the floor plan, a diagram indicates suggested fragrance diffusers placed at the store's entrance and rear to enhance its carefully designed aroma. Tienda Omnilife.

Source: Luis Othon Villegas-Solis. Picture by Arce Studio. Arturo González and Cecilia Gutiérrez.

In restaurants, smell plays a pivotal role in enhancing the dining experience. As exemplified by seafood, there is a subtle but critical correlation between architectural elements and the menu. The aroma of the sea can evoke a sense of freshness, but there is also a need to avoid overpowering fishy smells. Smart Design mechanisms, such as well-designed ventilation systems and air purification, can help maintain a delicate balance, ensuring that the sea's pleasant scent prevails while preventing unwanted odors from dominating the dining area.

Consider another example: grilling in a steakhouse. The aroma of grilling is undeniably important, as it contributes to the anticipation and enjoyment of the meal. However, constantly smelling the grill can become fatiguing for diners. In this scenario, introducing the scent of natural wood can be a game-changer. Smart Design mechanisms can come into play here, utilizing technology devices to diffuse natural wood scents into the restaurant. One challenge with scents is that our sense of smell can quickly adapt, and we may not notice the scent as distinctly after a few minutes. To overcome this limitation, technology devices with scent diffusers can be used. For instance, a restaurant can intermittently diffuse the natural wood scent to maintain a consistent and pleasant ambiance without overwhelming diners with the constant smell of grilling. This innovative approach embodies Smart Design principles, where the integration of sensory elements into architectural planning creates an immersive and memorable dining experience. In restaurants, the strategic use of scent, in harmony with architectural elements, not only enhances the atmosphere but also shapes diners' perceptions and overall satisfaction.

Visual Interaction

It is widely acknowledged that visual interaction is essential in shaping our experience of the built environment. However, we aim to underscore how vision can collaborate with our other senses to enhance human experience and behavior within architectural spaces. A profound understanding of how the brain processes visual information, alongside other sensory inputs, is imperative for effective architectural design.

Architects can harness the knowledge of the brain and inform their architecture and designs; let us consider the "Two Visual Systems" model, which delineates the distinction between the dorsal "How" stream, responsible for spatial awareness, movement, and action, and the ventral "What" stream, which facilitates object recognition and the perception of objects (Arbib, 2021). The dorsal and ventral stream relationships can help formulate strategies for designing spaces that align seamlessly with human behavior and navigation patterns.

Recently, we embarked on a comprehensive redesign of a supermarket's navigation path, employing deliberate strategies to transform the space and enhance the overall shopping experience. The original layout suffered from overwhelming visual clutter, resulting in a sense of confusion among shoppers. Our approach began with a thorough analysis to identify the causes of distraction and pinpoint the elements responsible for visual pollution within the space. We devised our first design strategy based on our understanding of how the dorsal stream in the brain's visual system operates. We sought to simplify the visual landscape by eliminating elements that cluttered the space and diverted attention. To achieve this, we introduced a key design element: a perimeter ribbon. This ribbon served as a unifying feature, creating a continuous visual guide along the actual walls of the supermarket (Figure 1.4.2.2).

Before

After

Figure 1.4.2.2 In the top picture, before the intervention, an excessive amount of information was visible through the advertisements, boxes, and objects on the walls. The after image presents a cleaner approach by introducing an architectural feature resembling a ribbon along the perimeter. This feature directs the user's gaze and enhances spatial cleanliness. The ribbon introduces order, rhythm, and visually organized spaces for advertisements, creating a simple pattern that mitigates the overstimulation experienced in the previous space. Supermercado HEB.

Source: Luis Othon Villegas-Solis. Picture by Arce Studio. Arturo Gonzalez and Cecilia Gutierrez.

A thoughtful selection of consistent colors complemented the introduction of this clear perimeter layout. This choice not only promoted spatial orientation but also greatly enhanced the overall viewing experience. Additionally, it helped organize advertisements, price boards, and product publicity, ensuring that they no longer overwhelmed shoppers. Simultaneously, we harnessed insights from the ventral stream of the brain's visual system. To address the need for clear differentiation of different areas within the supermarket, we designed a series of fixed elements, including canopies and structural markers. These elements served as functional markers for various supermarket departments and were pivotal in creating well-defined zones within the space.

These well-defined zones and clear pathways optimized the user experience by providing an organized and easily navigable layout. Shoppers were now guided intuitively through the supermarket, minimizing confusion and frustration. In essence, our redesign of the supermarket's navigation path harmonized the principles of the dorsal and ventral streams in the brain's visual system. By simplifying the visual landscape, organizing the space with a clear perimeter layout, and strategically placing fixed elements, we transformed a cluttered and confusing environment into one that prioritized spatial orientation, enhanced the shopping experience, and promoted ease of navigation for customers.

By integrating technology, architects can create environments that react to users' movements and preferences. This allows sensory adjustments to be made to lighting, temperature, and other environmental factors to ensure optimal comfort and experience. However, Smart Design also advocates for informed architecture, ensuring that all design decisions are based on evidence from research.

Smart Design, facilitated by technology and a profound understanding of human perception and behavior, enriches architecture by creating immersive, user-centric spaces. By leveraging insights from the dorsal and ventral streams, architects can optimize physical room layouts to enhance navigation and overall experience. Technology integration further elevates these experiences, allowing adaptive environments that respond intuitively to users' needs and preferences while connecting architecture with broader ecosystems.

Enhancing Architectural Design with Cognitive and Emotional Interaction

The highlights of how cognitive interaction, such as spatial perception, memory, and wayfinding, significantly influence how people interact with and perceive architectural environments is an insight that provides architects and designers with a solid basis for implementing cognitive interaction principles. By harmonizing with users' psychological and mental processes, this approach facilitates the creation of spaces that enhance well-being, identity, and a sense of belonging (Rapoport, 1990).

Smart Design buildings exemplify the effectiveness of cognitive interaction. For instance, smart office buildings adjust lighting, temperature, and layouts based on individual user patterns, providing a personalized and comfortable workspace. However, the extent to which these adjustments cater to individual users and the degree of user choice in these settings still need to be improved. The state of the art continues to evolve, with future challenges, including considering additional senses beyond the commonly addressed ones, such as bodily effort and thought patterns.

Cognitive interaction aligns naturally with the principles of multisensory design, enriching user experiences by engaging various senses. Among these, temperature plays a prominent role. Technology-driven temperature adjustments based on user preferences and context increase sensory engagement, enriching the overall experiential dimension. The concept of dynamic adaptation takes center stage in cognitive interaction, allowing architectural spaces to respond to contextual cues in real time. In smart homes, this could involve modifications to lighting, temperature, and security settings based on factors like occupancy and time of day, ensuring the built environment remains synchronized with evolving user needs.

Contemporary examples of the synergy between smart, emotionally responsive architecture and technology are exemplified in the design of modern retail stores. These establishments skillfully incorporate Don Norman's (2005) three levels of design—visceral, behavioral, and reflective—to evoke multifaceted responses from customers. On the visceral level, as users step inside these stores, they are greeted by subtle, authentic fragrances that trigger immediate visceral reactions and initial impressions, conveying a sense of comfort and setting the ambiance for the entire shopping journey. On the behavioral level, customers subconsciously evaluate how the store's layout and design facilitate their shopping objectives, assessing the ease with which they can navigate the space. The goal is to instill a sense of control and ensure minimal effort, ultimately elevating their satisfaction with shopping. Finally, on the reflective level, customers consciously assess the design's performance and benefits, including perceived value for money.

The evolution of retail spaces into immersive, personalized environments that captivate and engage shoppers is a testament to the successful fusion of smart technology and emotional architecture. By embracing this convergence, architectural spaces can become living canvases that sensitively respond to occupants' emotional needs, fostering richer experiences and enduring connections. As design horizons expand, the journey into smart, expressive architecture promises a new chapter of spatial storytelling, sensory engagement, and emotional resonance.

Social Performativity and Adaptability

The concept of social performativity, deeply rooted in anthropology, geography, and philosophy, illuminates the ever-evolving nature of human actions and interactions. As this concept gains prominence, its applications extend to architectural design, emphasizing user-centric methodologies and adaptability. Within this context, the integration of Smart Design principles becomes not just relevant but pivotal.

Social performativity embodies the inherent flexibility of social behaviors and functions, recognizing their susceptibility to change. This concept highlights the importance of comprehending users' evolving needs, preferences, and interactions within architecture and urbanism. In this pursuit, Richard Sennett's profound insights, particularly as elucidated in "The Craftsman" (2009), resound with a call for adaptability and responsiveness in design and underscore the innate synergy between the adaptable nature of human action and the design of environments.

Restaurants serve as examples of spaces where social performativity unfolds. Beyond mere dining establishments, they evolve into arenas for intricate social interactions, personal expression, and cultural exchange. The design of a restaurant profoundly influences these interactions, with factors such as seating arrangement, lighting, and decor setting the stage for varying levels of intimacy and social dynamics. In the end, people go to restaurants to see and be seen. Formal interactions may be encouraged in upscale establishments, while casual settings foster communal atmospheres. Here, adaptability emerges as a central part of restaurant design.

Given the social dynamics and dining habits, restaurants must be designed to accommodate diverse group sizes, preferences, and cultural norms. An adaptable design enables adjustments, promoting inclusivity across social contexts. Flexible seating arrangements, multipurpose spaces, and modular design components contribute to this adaptability. Smart Design principles further enhance the restaurant experience. Examples include digital menus, interactive table surfaces, as IRT Kodisoft mentioned, and personalized ambiance control through mobile applications, providing functional convenience and an enhanced dining experience. However, successfully integrating technology into these social spaces demands a delicate balance that enriches user experiences without detracting from the authenticity of human interactions.

While the principles of social performativity, adaptability, and Smart Design remain reliable, the challenges presented by urbanism are distinct from those of individual building design. Urban spaces demand integration on a grander scale to create harmonious, functional environments for diverse populations. The smart urban design extends to encompass intelligent traffic management, sustainable energy solutions, and interconnected public spaces, underscoring the role of technology in fostering holistic urban experiences (Kirwan & Fu, 2020).

A Multisensory Future

In architecture and design, we find ourselves on the threshold of an exhilarating transformation poised to redefine our perception, interaction with, and inhabitation of spaces. Our exploration into the evolution of architecture reveals a promising future at the intersection of multisensory engagement and Smart Design.

As we delve deeper into multisensory smart design, we recognize the profound significance of senses beyond vision. A trace of a scent can trigger memories, sound resonance can evoke emotions, and the tactile sensations of textures can forge connections. Integrating these sensory dimensions into the design process empowers us to create spaces that resonate on a deeper level. It fosters environments where individuals do not merely observe architecture but fully experience it—where the built environment becomes a symphony of sensory engagement.

However, as we venture into this future, we must strike a delicate balance. Technology should always maintain the human essence that defines the purpose of architecture. The goal is not to surrender to a world dominated by machines but to leverage technology to enrich human interaction with spaces. The seamless integration of intuitive design and technological innovation is pivotal in crafting spaces that enhance well-being, satisfaction, and connection. As we navigate this transformative landscape, we must remain attuned to the delicate equilibrium between innovation and the enduring core of human connection. By embracing the tactile intricacies of our senses and the boundless potential of Smart Design, we step into a future where architecture does not merely construct structures—it crafts experiences that elevate the human spirit.

References

Albrecht, L. (2013). *Barclays Center's "signature scent" tickles noses curiosity*. https://www.dnainfo.com/new-york/20130520/prospect-heights/barclays-centers-signature-scent-tickles-noses-curiosity

Arbib, M. A. (2021). *When brains meet buildings: A conversation between neuroscience and architecture*. Oxford University Press.

Cui, T., Xi, J., Tang, C., Song, J., He, J., & Brytek-Matera, A. (2021). The relationship between music and food intake: A systematic review and meta-analysis. *Nutrients*, 13, 2571. https://doi.org/10.3390/nu13082571.

Edelstein, E.A., & Macagno, E. (2011). Form Follows Function: Bridging Neuroscience and Architecture. In: Rassia, Stamatina Th. & Pardalos, P. M. (eds), *Sustainable Environmental Design in Architecture: Impacts on Health*, 1–13. UK, London: Springer.

Fenko, A., & Loock, C. (2014). The influence of ambient scent and music on patients' anxiety in a waiting room of a plastic surgeon. HERD (Health Environments Research and Design Journal), 7(3), 38–59. https://pubmed.ncbi.nlm.nih.gov/24782235.

Herssens, J., & Heylighen, A. (2008). Haptics and vision in architecture.

IRT Kodisoft. (2023, September 26). Smart furniture design in restaurants: Enhancing dining experiences. *IRT Restaurant*. https://itrestaurant.net/benefits

Jahandideh, F., & Tabibian, M. (2015). Smart building, a way to achieve sustainable architecture.

Keçecioğlu Dağlı, Pelin & Özdemir Durak, Manolya. (2022). Smart urban furniture as innovative landscape design elements in public spaces.

Kirwan, C. G., & Fu, Z. (2020). *Smart cities and artificial intelligence: Convergent systems for planning, design, and operations*. Elsevier.

Li, Z., Zhang, J., Li, M., Huang, J., & Wang, X. (2020). A review of smart design based on interactive experience in building systems. *Sustainability*, 12, 6760. https://doi.org/10.3390/Su12176760.

North, A. C., Hargreaves, D. J., & McKendrick, J. (1997). In-store music affects product choice. *Nature*, 390, 132.

North, A. C., Hargreaves, D. J., & McKendrick, J. (1999). The influence of in-store music on wine selections. *Journal of Applied Psychology*, 84, 271–276.

Norman, D. A. (2005). *Emotional design: Why we love (or hate) everyday things*. Basic Books.

Rapoport, A. (1990). *The meaning of the built environment: A nonverbal communication approach*. University of Arizona Press.

Sennett, R. (2009). *The craftsman*. Yale University Press.

Spence, C. (2020). Senses of place: Architectural design for the multisensory mind. Cognitive Research, 5, 46. https://doi.org/10.1186/s41235-020-00243-4.

1.4.3

NEUROMORPHIC ARCHITECTURE AT A TURNING POINT

Michael A. Arbib

Abstract

Neuromorphic architecture (NMA) is the approach to smart architecture that emphasizes that insights from neuroethology, the study of brain mechanisms underlying animal behavior, can offer strategies for the integration of the physical spaces of a building with "neural spaces" linking sensors, effectors, and the "brains" that coordinate them. As such, it overlaps the concerns of cybernetic, responsive, and interactive architecture. Key concepts include systems of systems and the body schemas of people and buildings. Applications include homeostasis, social interaction, and buildings that adapt over the long term. The turning point is occasioned by both the widespread impact of the digital ecosystems of smartphones and the internet and the dramatic increase in the capability of AI (Artificial Intelligence) systems that made headlines in 2023. It is noted that both neurorobotics and the artificial adaptive neural networks that power the learning capabilities of the new AI are neurobiologically inspired. Crucially, though, NMA will address neuroethology at a level that extracts concepts and applications for technology rather than asking the architect to master the underlying neuroscience.

Neuromorphic Architecture Is Cybernetic, Responsive, and Interactive

We consider a range of approaches that embed sensors, processors, and actuators (effectors) in the building so that the form, structure, or mood of a space can be altered in real time.

Cybernetic architecture explicitly reflects the influence of Wiener's (1948) book on *Cybernetics* and its subsequent extension from information theory, control systems, and neural networks to include the "second-order" cybernetics of human interactions. Perhaps the best-known practitioner of cybernetic architecture is Gordon Pask (Haque, 2007).

Responsive architectures are those that adapt their form, shape, or other characteristics in response to changing environmental conditions. Such responsiveness may, for example, improve the energy performance of buildings.

Interactive architecture deals with buildings that reconfigure in real time in response to people's behavior as well as the wider environment and includes forms of interaction that may be purely communicative.

DOI: 10.4324/9781003384113-12

Kolarevic and Parlac (2015) emphasize buildings whose structure can be changed dynamically. All this poses constraints on the materiality of the effectors that move steel, glass, bricks, or concrete. One of their examples was of a building that changed its shape so that wind passing around it would cause as little damage and heat loss as possible.

In the spirit of Wiener's subtitle, "Control and Communication in the Animal and the Machine," *Neuromorphic Architecture* (NMA) is that part of cybernetic architecture that explicitly seeks insights from *neuroethology*, integrating study of brains into ethology, the study of diverse animals' behaviors. We seek lessons for architecture from the observation that an animal needs an adaptable brain and a flexible body equipped with sophisticated sensors and effectors for reconfiguration of the internal and exterior milieux – and for interaction. The term *neuromorphic* does *not* imply that the building has the form of a brain; rather, it may have artificial "brains," e.g., computer implementations of artificial adaptive neural networks, that offer a variety of brain-like *functions*.

Systems of Systems

A human is both a system of systems and part of diverse *systems of systems*. Each human has a complex body with diverse subsystems linked by specialized components of the nervous system, including those involved with control of heart rate, breathing, and other homeostatic functions and those engaged in directing overall behavior in interaction with the physical and social world. As illustrated by the availability of lifts and washing machines as "intelligent" subsystems of contemporary buildings, a neuromorphic building will also be a system of systems. The challenge for NMA is to design the static and cybernetic components of a building so that they work together to serve (with the usual tradeoffs) the interests of the human occupants.

The design of WOHA's Kampung Admiralty in Singapore (WOHA & Bingham-Hall, 2015, pp. 406–425) stresses building a sense of community both for those who live there, and for the wider neighborhood. Kampung Admiralty was designed as a node within diverse systems. It is a gateway to the mass rapid transit system and guides pedestrian flow through the public spaces. The elderly residents can access lively public space, a noisy food center, a community garden and more – all within the complex.

Once we consider a building as a system of systems, we are open to a conversation about which of those subsystems may be ripe for an architectural transition to being cybernetically enabled and informed by neuroethological insights – which here extend beyond single creatures to their interaction with the social and physical environment.

Neural and Physical Spaces for Buildings

The *Umwelt* or "World" of an organism (von Uexküll, 1957/1934) may vary from species to species as a consequence of specialized body structure, receptors and effectors (sensors and actuators), and the nervous system that integrates them. A human or animal's world is defined by their *effectivities* (the range of actions at their command) and their *affordances* (the opportunities for action they can perceive). Consider, for example, a lawn as part of a creature's world. For a human, this is something to walk on or to mow, but for a mole this is a place to burrow for food and shelter. Moreover, effectivities and affordances are subject to learning.

An animal moves around in its world. For a building, we turn this inside-out: the world is inside the body, the building itself, and the "brains" of a neuromorphic building are then monitoring the activity inside (and around) the building to guide various actions.

Each building forms part of the Umwelt of the people within it. The "space" so defined within the building may differ between its various users. In an art gallery, the electrical outlets may be "invisible" to the art-goers, yet crucial to the cleaners.

NMA posits that a cybernetic building, too, has an Umwelt that includes the people within it. This will depend not only on what information the building can gather but also on what actions it can perform and what interactions it can support. New goals set the search for hitherto-neglected affordances, and these change the Umwelt – the framing of which sets new challenges for the architect. For example, electrical outlets have become a major need for travelers in airports, and the design of waiting areas is changing accordingly.

For NMA, there is no claim that the building must be human-like or have a human-like brain or human intelligence or feelings. The brains of animals, and not only their bodies, can vary greatly across species. Moreover, a neuromorphic building may have multiple "brains" dedicated to different functionalities and/or different rooms, and/or coordination among them. Thus the "brain" of a building may be akin to a network of animal brains that, strangely, may be gifted with some command of language.

Some terminology: The *neural space* encompasses not only the "brains" of the building but also their sensors. Information flow in this neural space will support the dynamic interaction of the building with its inhabitants. The *physical space* is the "body" or "fabric" of the actual building. It may thus include moveable parts that provide the effectors that the neural space is to control within an ongoing action-perception cycle.

As buildings become more neuromorphic, we may expect the neural space to no longer be considered an add-on to an otherwise-designed physical space. Rather, the design process will develop the neural space and physical space together to yield dramatically new designs – just as elevators made skyscrapers possible and changed top floors from garrets to penthouses.

The Body Schemas of People and Buildings

Head and Holmes (1911) knew of a brain lesion on the right side of the human brain that can cause the patient to neglect the left side of their body. This phenomenon was part of what motivated them to introduce the *body schema* as a neurological reality by including within that notion.

> [a]nything which participates in the conscious movement of our bodies is added to the model of ourselves and becomes part of those schema[s]: a woman's power of localization may extend to the feather of her hat.

Today, few wear feathered hats but many of us have had the experience when wearing a hat and coming to a low doorway of ducking one's head subconsciously to go through the doorway – even though without the hat one would not have done so. Tool use further demonstrates that the body schema can incorporate changed affordances and effectivities. As it is being picked up, the tool is like any other object being manipulated. But once the tool is held properly, the affordances and effectivities are now with respect to the tool, not the hand (Arbib, Bonaiuto, Jacobs, & Frey, 2009). Moreover, the body schema is not only dynamic in its assemblage but is also a learning system, adjusting the tuning of actions to available affordances and patterns of their coordination (Maravita & Iriki, 2004).

The relevance to the architect is that the inhabitant's body schema proceeding out from the body is complemented by what we might call the *environment schema*, incorporating certain affordances that the surroundings provide for our effectivities. For example, placement of windows may serve both to offer affordances for seeing what is outside the building and, with the possible help of internal lighting, help the user locate relevant affordances for action inside the building.

Recent years have seen the "invasion" of the home by electronic assistants that are connected to the internet and thus to large databases exploiting the deep learning that AI (artificial intelligence) systems may employ. They can use increasingly effective speech communication. Controllers can now monitor many of the appliances of the home and communicate by smartphone with distant humans, the current commercial realization of the Internet of Things for household products. Robotics may be even more relevant to NMA. A range of active furniture may include robots (consider robot vacuum cleaners) that act as dedicated subsystems for a building, while the building itself would act as an "inside-out" robot, or even a network of such. Design would be constrained not only by the differing roles of different rooms but also by the need to support multiple users in diverse activities and their flow between the rooms with a tradeoff in "room dynamics" between the users and the room "itself."

We may at times see all the building as external, whereas at other times we may incorporate aspects of the building into our own body schema. Driving a car offers an interesting pair of perspectives: as we approach the car and settle into the driver's seat, the car itself provides the environment for our actions. However, once we start to drive, our body schema extends to the edges of the car, and the environment is now provided by roads and the traffic on them.

The slogan *out from the body and in from the building* offers something deep for us to pursue and understand. Treating the building as a sort of inside-out robot, we learn to use a room or a building by adjusting our body schema not only to a tool in our hand but also to the complementary tool that is the changing interface with the building. We may even speak of the *body schema of the building* when, enriched by NMA, it must be able to deploy its own effectors appropriately to changes in its environment, especially in relation to the movement and inferred needs of its inhabitants. However, when parts of the building act somewhat autonomously, we may then see them as separate agents with which we interact. To take a contemporary example, if we have a garage with a door that opens automatically as we drive toward it, we are likely to view the door-system as a separate agent rather than an extension of ourselves.

Homeostasis

Homeostasis in animals refers to keeping critical bodily variables like temperature, blood sugar, and oxygenation in the range necessary for an animal's survival. One example of "exotic" homeostatic architecture may point the way to neuromorphic strategies for homeostasis in the future – yet also provide a cautionary note.

In Jean Nouvel's Institutes du Monde Arabe in Paris, one facade contains an array of panels based on the Islamic *mashrabiya* to break the direct impact of sunshine. However, Nouvel's panels were feedback systems. Hundreds of light-sensitive diaphragms regulate the amount of light that is allowed to enter the building. The effect is aesthetic as well as homeostatic:

interior spaces are dramatically modified by these changes in natural lighting, while the exterior exhibits a fluid shifting of geometric pattern. However, after a few years more and more of these apertures became locked in place, necessitating lengthy reconstruction.

This emphasizes the challenge of designing a reliable "body" for a dynamic building, whether the control network is brain-inspired or not, while the success of NMA will require coupling neural space and effector-equipped physical space together to close the loop in a physically and aesthetically satisfying way for the people who experience that building.

Social Interaction

One of the earliest explicit example of NMA was the Interactive Space "Ada" (Eng et al., 2003). It employed sensors for touch, vision, and hearing along with effectors and simple artificial neural networks to "invite" visitors to form small groups, and then play games with them. There were also conventional architectural challenges that had to be met in handling the flow of visitors through the pavilion in which Ada was housed (see Arbib, 2021, §7.3, for details of both neuromorphic and "conventional" elements). The designers even developed a computational model of "emotions" for Ada. In some sense, Ada "wanted" to interact with people – though care must be taken in using terminology that we apply to humans (Fellous & Arbib, 2005). But if NMA may find the "emotions" of buildings relevant, the real concern is with the emotions of humans who use the building. Architecture must offer satisfactions that span from basic needs to the aesthetic emotions, establishing an appropriate architectural atmosphere (Canepa, Condia, & Wynne, 2023; Tidwell, 2014).

When we consider the "social interaction" of rooms or buildings with people in or near them (as exemplified by Ada), adapting buildings to the needs of their inhabitants, inspiration comes from the discovery of *mirror neurons* (di Pellegrino, Fadiga, Fogassi, Gallese, & Rizzolatti, 1992). First discovered in macaques, these were neurons that fired only when the monkey was carrying out a specific action or recognized others acting similarly. Hypotheses about these neurons as inferred from human brain imaging (that is too coarse-grain to show the activity of individual neurons but can constrain hypotheses about them) suggests that they may aid imitation in humans (but not monkeys) by allowing one to learn from observing the actions of others (Oztop, Kawato, & Arbib, 2013) and may also support empathy by linking the actions of others to some sense of their mental states (Arbib, 2021, Chapter 5; Iacoboni, 2009). (Both skills involve much additional circuitry "beyond the mirror" to work with mirror neurons.) However, apart from humanoid robots acting as staff, neuromorphic components of a building will rarely have effectors and action repertoires akin to a human's. Thus research must go beyond shared actions as recognized by mirror neurons to neuroethological analysis of reciprocal interaction in which one animal recognizes the action of the other as the basis for continuing or modifying a course of action that can attain mutual goals or preserve one's own goals in the face of antagonistic action by the other.

Consider the (unbuilt) neuromorphic design (Arbib, 2012) of an intelligent kitchen. Many of the components of the room's "brain" were based on models of specific brain regions or guided by brain operation principles. The neural space included speech recognition, emotion recognition, event localization, and processing facial expressions. It also included recipe management – choosing the meal and selecting ingredients. Artificial neurons akin to mirror neurons tracked the manual actions of the cook, although the observed actions were not in the room's action repertoire. Rather, they were integrated with systems "beyond the mirror" to keep track of the state of preparation according to a particular recipe. Iteration with design of the physical space would, for example, re-assess the placement of the cameras and microphones to meet the needs of different users – like the reconfigurable driving seat and rearview mirror in some modern cars.

Note that, if we view a building as a system of systems in which some of the subsystems are indeed human, there is nothing in the above scenarios to preclude that humans would be in the loop when high-level decisions are being made.

Neurorobotics and Adaptive AI

If one turns to Google Scholar to search for articles on "neuromorphic architecture," one finds that almost all the articles are on the design of (portions of) computers that incorporate patterns of distributed and parallel processing in layers of artificial neurons – for example, in preprocessing visual images. Computer scientists gather ideas from neuroscientists to develop useful new technologies, while neuroscientists gain new computing tools to help them investigate brains in more detail.

For a long time, AI was dominated by a symbol-processing paradigm based on the one-instruction-at-a-time operation of serial computers. Famously, Minsky and Papert (1969) demonstrated the impracticality of a *limited* class of *Perceptrons* – a simple model (Rosenblatt, 1958) of networks of neurons that could adjust their connections on the basis of "teacher" feedback – and for some years convinced many people that networks of adaptive neurons were irrelevant to the future of AI. However, their elegant mathematics did not rule out claims for the power of adaptive neural networks with multiple layers and loops and varied activation levels rather than binary states of 0 or 1, on or off. By 2003, the basic tools were all in place for the neural network technology (Arbib, 2003, offers reviews by multiple authors) that supported developments in AI that led to the innovations that provided the capabilities of systems such as ChatGPT and DALL-E. Their amazing ability at conducting a conversation (converting text to text) and creating drawings (text to image), respectively, captured headlines in 2023 and stoked furious debates about the dangers and not just promise of AI.

Animals and humans – and hence NMA-endowed spaces – differ from ChatGPT in that their role is not simply to take a string of tokens comparable to the morphemes of a human language and produce another string of tokens but rather to guide interaction with a complex and dynamic environment which requires that they have diverse sensors and effectors. *Neurorobotics* brings us much closer to neuroethology. Prescott, Ayers, Grasso, and Verschure (2016) discuss robots inspired by a lobster following an odor trail in water and a rodent exploring its environment by "whisking" its whiskers across surfaces, while Ijspeert (2020) considers what can be learned from studies of locomotion in various creatures. Such studies enhance the vocabulary of design for buildings with dynamic physical subsystems.

In recent years, many people have come to depend on language-enabled systems like Alexa or Siri to not only interact with the web and entertainment media, but also to control a variety of household functions. This raises privacy concerns – we may accept that part of our building's computing is "out there," but for sensitive information related to our use of the building, we will want any computer records and learning patterns to be held locally and securely in separate nodes of "intelligence" in the system of systems of the building. The bad news is that computer security is under attack. The good news is that the operation and learning required within each node (such as that serving the control of heating and cooling in different spaces in response to different individual preferences) will be manageable by modest local resources that can interact with language interfaces without displaying their inner workings.

Buildings that Learn; People Who Adapt

The design of the physical space for the kitchen mentioned earlier was conventional, with addition of a few effectors and receptors coupled by a "brain" that could support the room's "social" interaction with the human users. However, even a novice cook could become frustrated by a kitchen that kept offering suggestions for cooking routines that they had by now mastered. This motivates bringing in emotion and learning as crucial themes for NMA. Someone who cooks rarely may need a lot of assistance, and even an experienced cook may find it helpful to receive timely reminders when working with a complex recipe. In either case, too much "help" can become intrusive. Two factors then enter. One is to use facial and vocal cues to recognize the emotional state of the user. Do they indicate frustration with excessive instruction or a measure of desperation in preparing the current dish? The room should be able to perform accordingly. And this leads into learning – about what the user can handle without assistance and where help is needed (and this changes over time), as well as how the user chooses to modify recipes so that the room can keep track of the user's preferences.

Stewart Brand's (1994) *How buildings learn* emphasizes what happens to a building as humans restructure it over time to meet different needs. In the present context, though, we can consider how the building itself may form an adaptive system, restructuring its "body" as its "brain" compiles more data. This takes us beyond the notion of "self-repair," inspired by biology. Animals certainly have pain receptors and can detect wounds. However, in many cases of human pain, we are unclear as to whether its cause is physical or mental, or whether there is any immediate action we can take without expert advice. It thus seems unreasonable to expect even a smart house to be able to detect all problems and ameliorate them. For minor cracks, perhaps, self-repairing materials can indeed close the "wound," but in the case of an earthquake, the damage is too great, and may indeed incapacitate the information infrastructure of the building.

"Lifelong" Building Information Models (BIMs) may come to play an important role (Dave, Buda, Nurminen, & Främling, 2018; Heidari, Peyvastehgar, & Amanzadegan, 2023) with a BIM not just keeping track of the structure of the building, but also keeping track of the operation of how well its NMA components function. The aim would be to assess not only how the building itself might change but also lessons that can be fed back into general practice. The latter certainly raise further privacy issues.

AI and the Future of NMA

Recent AI breakthroughs (as of 2023) suggest that almost everything written about AI today will be out of date in the near future. Ideas from neuroethology for use in NMA will also change drastically because neuroscience is developing massive new datasets and computing technology to analyze them. However, just as most users of AI will work with application software that hides the underlying neural networks and the computer chips that support their training and use, so will NMA address neuroethology at a level that yields systems and products for use by the architect rather than asking the architect to master the underlying findings on neural networks.

Whatever AI's siliconic successes, there will be a continued interplay between notions of AI, neuroscience, and psychology to better understand natural intelligence in humans and other animals embedded in their environments (and this applies perhaps even more tellingly to the human experience and design of buildings, not just to NMA – see Arbib, 2021). Architecture is inherently a human enterprise directed at the physical and mental (and, some would add, the aesthetic and spiritual) well-being of humans in buildings. Thus, even as AI and neuroscience expand their reach, architects must continue to learn from the humanities and, in this twenty-first century, the humanities must learn from the biological and social sciences, including their embodiment in the cognitive social neuroscience of brains in bodies interacting in the physical and social environment (Hart, 2015).

Related Studies: Arbib, Banasiak, and Othón Villegas-Solís (2022) assess, among other topics, challenges of linking NMA to the well-being of humans who live in favelas and shantytowns. Downey and Arbib (2024) discuss smart architecture for the blind. And see the chapter "Toward performative, environmentally responsive architecture" by Branko Kolarevic in this volume.

Acknowledgement: My sincere thanks to the architects Bob Condia, Bob Hart, and Luis Villegas-Solís for their illuminating comments on an earlier draft.

References

Arbib, M. A. (Ed.) (2003). *The Handbook of Brain Theory and Neural Networks,* Second Edition. Cambridge, MA: A Bradford Book/The MIT Press.

Arbib, M. A. (2012). Brains, machines and buildings: Towards a neuromorphic architecture. *Intelligent Buildings International, 4*(3), 147–168. https://doi.org/110.1080/17508975.1750201 2.17702863

Arbib, M. A. (2021). *When Brains Meet Buildings: A Conversation between Neuroscience and Architecture.* New York: Oxford University Press.Arbib, M. A., Banasiak, B., & Othón Villegas-Solís, L. (2022). Systems of systems: Architectural atmosphere, neuromorphic architecture, and the well-being of humans and ecospheres. In M. Kanaani (Ed.), *The Routledge Companion to Ecological Design Thinking: Healthful Ecotopian Visions for Architecture and Urbanism* (pp. 64–74). London: Taylor & Francis.

Arbib, M. A., Bonaiuto, J. J., Jacobs, S., & Frey, S. H. (2009). Tool use and the distalization of the end-effector. *Psychological Research, 73*(4), 441–462. https://doi.org/10.1007/s00426-009-0242-2

Brand, S. (1994). *How Buildings Learn: What Happens after They're Built.* New York: Viking.

Canepa, E., Condia, B., & Wynne, M. (Eds.) (2023). *Atmosphere(s) for Architects: Between Phenomenology and Cognition (A Dialogue between Michael Arbib and Tonino Griffero, with Commentaries)* (Vol. 5). Manhattan, Kansas: New Prairie Press.

Dave, B., Buda, A., Nurminen, A., & Främling, K. (2018). A framework for integrating BIM and IoT through open standards. *Automation in Construction, 95,* 35–45. https://doi.org/10.1016/j.autcon.2018.07.022

di Pellegrino, G., Fadiga, L., Fogassi, L., Gallese, V., & Rizzolatti, G. (1992). Understanding motor events: A neurophysiological study. *Experimental Brain Research, 91*(1), 176–180. Retrieved from http://www.ncbi.nlm.nih.gov/entrez/query.fcgi?cmd=Retrieve&db=PubMed&dopt=Citation& list_uids=1301372.

Downey, C., & Arbib, M. A. (2024). Smart Architecture for the blind. In M. Kanaani (Ed.), *Routledge Companion to Smart Design Thinking in Architecture & Urbanism for a Sustainable Living Planet.* New York and London: Routledge.

Eng, K., Klein, D., Babler, A., Bernardet, U., Blanchard, M., Costa, M., … Verschure, P. F. M. J. (2003). Design for a brain revisited: The neuromorphic design and functionality of the interactive space 'Ada'. *Reviews in the Neurosciences, 14,* 145.

Fellous, J.-M., & Arbib, M. A. (Eds.) (2005). *Who Needs Emotions: The Brain Meets the Robot.* Oxford, New York: Oxford University Press.

Haque, U. (2007). The architectural relevance of Gordon Pask. *Architectural Design, 77*(4), 54–61.

Hart, R. L. (2015). *A New Look at Humanism—in Architecture, Landscapes, and Urban Design.* California: Meadowlark Publishing.

Heidari, A., Peyvastehgar, Y., & Amanzadegan, M. (2023). A systematic review of the BIM in construction: From smart building management to interoperability of BIM & AI. *Architectural Science Review, 67,* 1–18. https://doi.org/10.1080/00038628.2023.2243247

Iacoboni, M. (2009). Imitation, empathy, and mirror neurons. *Annual Review of Psychology, 60*(1), 653–670. https://doi.org/10.1146/annurev.psych.60.110707.163604

Ijspeert, A. J. (2020). Amphibious and sprawling locomotion: From biology to robotics and back. *Annual Review of Control, Robotics, and Autonomous Systems, 3*(1), 173–193. https://doi.org/10.1146/annurev-control-091919-095731

Kolarevic, B., & Parlac, V. (Eds.) (2015). *Building Dynamics: Exploring Architecture of Change.* London and New York: Routledge.

Maravita, A., & Iriki, A. (2004). Tools for the body (schema). *Trends in Cognitive Sciences, 8*(2), 79–86. Retrieved from http://www.ncbi.nlm.nih.gov/entrez/query.fcgi?cmd=Retrieve&db=PubMed&dopt=Citation&list_uids=15588812.

Minsky, M. L., & Papert, S. (1969). *Perceptrons: An Introduction to Computational Geometry.* Cambridge, MA: The MIT Press.

Oztop, E., Kawato, M., & Arbib, M. A. (2013). Mirror neurons: Functions, mechanisms and models. *Neuroscience Letters, 540,* 43–55. https://doi.org/10.1016/j.neulet.2012.10.005

Prescott, T. J., Ayers, J., Grasso, F. W., & Verschure, P. F. M. J. (2016). Embodied models and neurorobotics. In M. A. Arbib & J. J. Bonaiuto (Eds.), *From Neuron to Cognition via Computational Neuroscience* (pp. 483–511). Cambridge, MA: The MIT Press.

Rosenblatt, F. (1958). The perceptron: A probabilistic model for information storage and organization in the brain. *Psychological Review, 65,* 386–408.

Tidwell, P. (Ed.) (2014). *Architecture and Atmosphere.* Espoo, Finland: Tapio Wirkkala - Rut Bryk Foundation.

von Uexküll, J. (1957/1934). A stroll through the worlds of animals and men: A picture book of invisible worlds. In C. H. Schiller (Ed.), *Instinctive Behavior: The Development of a Modern Concept* (pp. 5–80 [Also in Semiotica 89 (84), 319–391. Originally appeared as von Uexküll (1934) Streifzüge durch die Umwelten von Tieren und Menschen. Springer, Berlin.]). New York: International Universities Press.

Wiener, N. (1948). *Cybernetics: or Control and Communication in the Animal and the Machine.* New York: The Technology Press and John Wiley & Sons.

WOHA, & Bingham-Hall, P. (2015). *WOHA: Selected Projects, Volume 2.* Oxford, Singapore, Sydney: Pesaro Publishing.

1.5

AI AND THE MORPHOLOGY OF THE CITY _AI'S DYNAMIC POWER IN SHAPING THE FUTURE OF URBAN DESIGN

Matias del Campo and Sandra Manninger

Abstract

This chapter explores the transformative impact of Artificial Intelligence (AI) on urban design, transcending traditional paradigms and ushering in a new era of data-driven, generative approaches. Departing from linear processes, the text embraces a comprehensive perspective, acknowledging the multidimensional factors shaping urban landscapes. The integration of AI in urban design takes cues from the way neural networks operate, dynamically responding to real-time data inputs and historical iterations. Historical reference points, from Renaissance ideal cities to Modernism, serve as repositories guiding the interrogation of urban morphology.

The reasoning behind the text navigates the complexities of urban planning, emphasizing the role of humanities in crafting inclusive, meaningful designs. The interrogation delves into the historical intricacies, from Alberti's Ideal City to Simmel's analysis of metropolitan existence, whilst scrutinizing modernist movements like Dada, cubism, and futurism and contrasting them with antiurban ideologies in the works of Howard, Taut, and Wright.

This chapter then transitions to the contemporary landscape, portraying AI's disruptive moment in art and design. Drawing parallels with the modernist explosion, it discusses the dichotomy between organic, hands-on creation, and AI-driven, data-informed methodologies. The tension between technological precision and human creativity is explored, cautioning against the risk of detaching art from visceral experiences.

The integration of AI in urban design is examined, emphasizing its potential in prediction, optimization, and generative design. AI's capacity to process vast amounts of data is highlighted, offering evidence-based insights and breaking free from traditional design molds. This chapter concludes by underscoring the ethical considerations of AI in urban design, emphasizing the need for human intuition to complement computational insights and safeguard principles of equity and social justice.

DOI: 10.4324/9781003384113-13

Keywords
Artificial Intelligence; Neural Architecture; Latent Space; Machine Learning; Estrangement; Defamiliarization; Theory

Co-Design & Living

The interrogation of urban textures and historical planning involves a systematic analysis within a contextual framework, rather than adhering to linear processes, adopting a comprehensive approach that extends beyond basic reasoning (Cuthberg, 1998). This process bears similarities to the investigation of interconnected components within a vast network, surpassing simplistic input-output models commonly associated with urban design. It involves an in-depth exploration of the multidimensional factors that shape urban landscapes, encompassing various elements ranging from planning protocols and economic variables to material flows, political dynamics, social considerations, stylistic trends, creative activations, and cultural influences that define each design iteration (Rodríguez, 2006). The interplay of these dynamic variables coalesces to establish the intricate ecology against which the study of urban morphology takes place.

Artificial Intelligence and the City after Modernism

Considering urban design as a structured procedure can be compared to recognizing it as a complex system governed by a set of interrelated instructions. Or, metaphorically speaking rather than isolated lines of code, this system operates through layers of data interactions, much like a neural network processing numerous inputs. The design architecture is adaptable and responsive, influenced by real-time data inputs such as economic indicators, political events, and social sentiments (Poon, 2017). The outcome is a flexible design model that dynamically responds to the evolving urban environment. On the other end of the spectrum, and very much the raw material for any form of Artificial Intelligence (AI) application in design, is the historical data that can be likened to a repository of successive iterations, each offering insights into the progression of urban design concepts (Kamrowska-Załuska, 2021). These historical reference points function as storage units, like version control repositories in digital projects like Git (Chen et al., 2019). Each version encapsulates its unique attributes, capturing snapshots of architectural developments, ideological changes, and cultural milestones. These historical stages guide the interrogation, illustrating how urban design principles have evolved over time and suggesting potential avenues for future refinement. In this context, modern reductionism (Rowe, 2011) translates to oversimplification, neglecting the intricate interdependencies essential for the functioning and elegance of the urban system. It is comparable to attempting to encapsulate the capabilities of a sophisticated computer within a basic calculator. The real elegance lies in the intricate interplay of algorithms, where every piece of data contributes to a complex and functional whole. To grasp the essence of urban design, the designer is empowered (by the use of machine learning (Donepudi, 2017)) to navigate the intricate network of components, tracing the pathways of data convergence and divergence, where various design elements intersect and interact.

Furthermore, an important aspect of city planning lies in the incorporation of the humanities. These disciplines, which encompass fields such as history, philosophy, sociology, and cultural studies, offer critical insights into the social fabric, historical narratives, and human ambitions that shape urban environments. Integrating humanistic perspectives enables a deeper understanding of how cities are not just functional spaces but vibrant centers of human interaction and expression. By considering the values and narratives embedded within a city's cultural and historical contexts, planners can craft more inclusive, meaningful, and people-centered urban designs that resonate with the diverse communities they serve.

All of these conditions, and more, form the background when delving into the realm of urban morphology. One of these paradigms is encapsulated in the austere structure and geometric precision of ideal Renaissance cities, forever enshrined in Leon Battista Alberti's treatise *De Re Aedificatoria* (van Eck, 1998). Alberti's concept of the *Ideal City* (Pearson, 2011) extends far beyond the realm of mere architectural theory (Figure 1.5.1).

It encapsulates a profound and comprehensive vision that not only reflects architectural propositions but also forms the vessel for broader aspirations and ideals of the epoch in which it emerged. This perspective serves as a conduit, not confined by temporal limitations, to impart not only inspiration but also valuable insights into the trajectories that speculative urban design could take. Delving into the geological layers of Alberti's proposal, we can mine a reservoir of thought that echoes the essence of an era and simultaneously offers a compass for shaping future urban landscapes.

At the other end of the spectrum, the advent of Modernism (Giedion, 1941) (Figure 1.5.2) unfolds an alternative, but strangely familiar narrative in the realm of urban expression. Within the realm of these austere geometries lies an inherent dialogue that challenges conventional form, embracing social complexity and formal innovation.

Yet, beyond the geometrical dimensions, these designs are indebted to the political and social contexts from which they emerge, serving as an architectural reflection of quasi progressive urban development and a catalyst for exploring uncharted possibilities. But how uncharted and innovative were they really? A critical examination of modern urban planning reveals its complex relationship with the historical dimension of architectural thought. Ludwig Hilbersheimer, the doyen of modern urban design, clearly demonstrates this bond with history in his book *The New City – Principles of Planning* (Hilbersheimer, 1944). Maps of settlements such as Timgad, Knidos, Montpazier, Beijing's Forbidden City, and Roman encampments all contain the seed for the rigid, angular organization preferred by modern planners (Figure 1.5.3). But there is more to the modern metropolis than a square grid. Georg Simmel, the distinguished philosopher and sociologist known for his insights into urban dynamics, undertook a comprehensive interrogation of the defining features of metropolitan existence in the early twentieth century. His essay "The Metropolis and Mental Life" (Simmel, 1950) identified several crucial characteristics that shaped the essence of life within burgeoning cities during that era: division of labor, industrial mechanization, diversification of experiences, nervous stimulation, social contrast, increased individuality, an amplified consciousness and intellectual discourse, abstraction, and the pervasive leveling and interchangeability that accompanied the rise of the monetary economy.

Simmel argued that these characteristics collectively engendered what he termed the "blasé attitude." This psychological phenomenon, according to Simmel's observation, reflected a response to estrangement (del Campo, 2022) and defamiliarization among urban dwellers due to the overwhelming sensory and experiential stimuli present in the modern metropolis.

Dada, cubism, and futurism (Giedion, 1941, pp. 428–476) recognized the profound impact of the metropolis on the human psyche and sought to encapsulate its intensity,

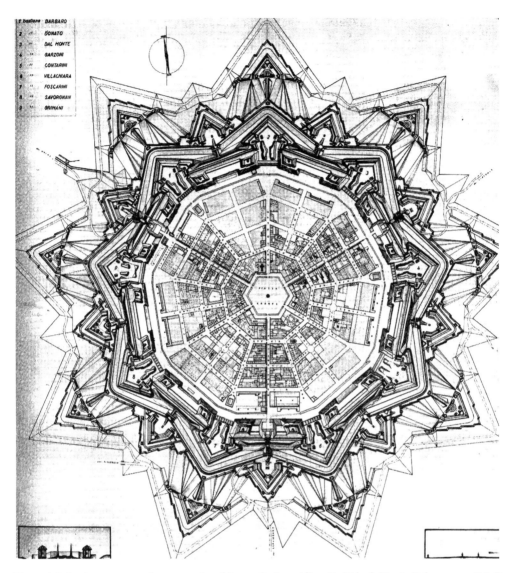

Figure 1.5.1 A representative example of Leon Batista Alberti's "Ideal City": Palmanova, Friuli-Venezia Giulia, General Giulio Savorgnan 1593. Copyright holder and credit to Joris Hoefnagel 1593, Public Domain.

diverse encounters, and nervous vigor through innovative aesthetic means. These movements championed a visual language characterized by *collage*, *montage*, and *assemblage*, where the canvas transformed into a neutral canvas for projecting the jarring encounters of city life. As aptly noted by Manfredo Tafuri (Tafuri, 1976) in his work "Architecture and Utopia," this artistic approach facilitated an artistic expression of the shock experienced within the urban milieu. In contrast to the avant-garde's innovative responses, however, architects and urban planners like Ebenezer Howard, Bruno Taut, and Frank Lloyd Wright turned away from the emerging metropolitan condition. Instead, they embraced

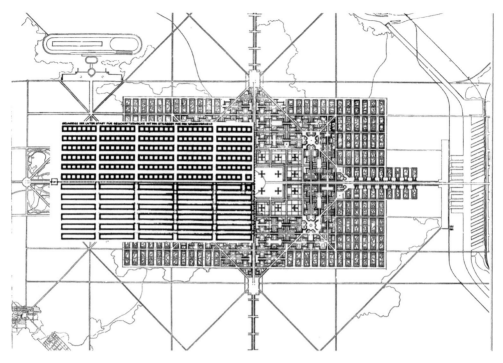

Figure 1.5.2 Le Corbusier: «La Ville Contemporaine», 1922. Credit to: Le Corbusier-Image licensed under the Creative Commons Attribution-Share Alike 4.0 International license.

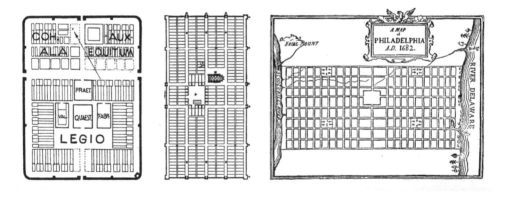

Figure 1.5.3 Plan of a Roman Castrum, the city of Montpazier in the Dordogne, France, and a plan of Philadelphia in 1682 by William Penn and Thomas Holme. All three plans were taken from Ludwig Hilbersheimer's book *The New City*. In the book, they serve as examples of similar morphologies emerging from different political systems, from autocratic cities (Rome) to various forms of Colonialism (Montpazier, Philadelphia) [Public Domain].

an antiurban ideology as manifested in their respective projects, ranging from Garden cities (Ebenezer, 1965) to Alpine architecture (Schirren, 2004) to The Disappearing City (Wright, 1932). These projects aimed to create alternative environments that counteracted

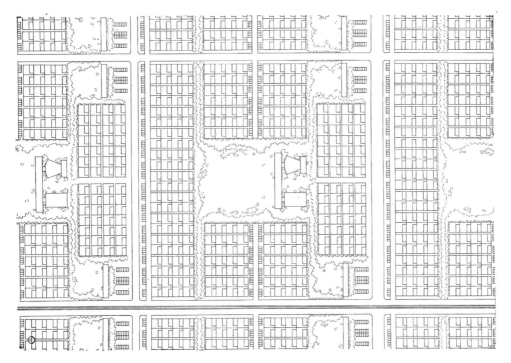

Figure 1.5.4 Ludwig Hilberseimer, Combination of 8 City Blocks, 1944. Credit to: Art Institute of Chicago.

the perceived adverse effects of the urban lifestyle. (Notably, scholars like Françoise Choay (Choay et al., 1970) and Charles Spence (Spence, 2020) subjected these initiatives to critical analysis and scrutiny.)

Ludwig Hilberseimer emerged as a proponent of constructive engagement with the metropolis, opposing the tendency to turn the back on the city, as in the previously mentioned examples. Rather than rejecting the urban phenomenon outright, Hilberseimer pioneered a novel metropolitan architecture that harnessed the intensity of the metropolis (Figure 1.5.4).

He managed to distill the "nervous energy" characteristic of urban life into a formal architectural language. This language featured uniform fenestration, deliberate repetition, and the careful reduction of typical geometric forms. This innovative approach, as elaborated on in sources like Scott Coleman's *Ludwig Hilberseimer: Reanimating Architecture and the City* (Coleman, 2023) and Detlef Mertins' *The Enticing and Threatening Face of Prehistory: Walter Benjamin and the Utopia of Glass* (Mertins, 1996), showcases Hilberseimer's nuanced relationship with the avant-garde art groups of the 1920s. These intellectual and creative endeavors collectively illuminate the intricate interplay between urban environments, human consciousness, and artistic innovation during a pivotal period in history. Today, we are again experiencing a "Zäsur," a violent rift in the fabric of design history that will shape the multitude of aspects necessary to consider when approaching any form of the design task. I will leave you here with the result of a little experiment. Using a

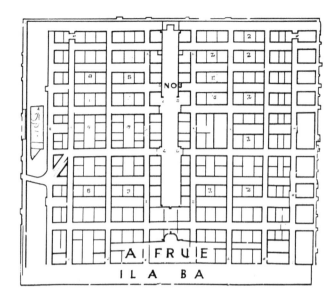

Figure 1.5.5 Using a Diffusion model, a blend of historical plans. Example of a quatrefoil city layout based on data reaching from the Baroque era to Modernism. It is neither the one nor the other, proclaiming a novel paradigm emerging in urban planning. 2023. MidJourney v5.2. Credit to: © SPAN Matias del Campo, Sandra Manninger. 2022.

diffusion model, the three historic images from Hilbersheimer's *New City* (Hilbersheimer, 1944) were mixed to form a new image. The lack of diversity in the image becomes glaringly visible in this rather nondescript, vanilla mashup. A lack of data leads to lackluster results (Figure 1.5.5).

Breaking Away from the Modern Mold

We are experiencing a disruptive moment. This departure from traditional methods of art and design to the contemporary landscape marked by the integration of AI is a profound rupture in human history, comparable to the transformative modernist explosion in the early twentieth century. The dichotomy between these two epochs delineates a trajectory that extends from organic to mechanical, from intuitive hands-on creation to the augmentation of human creativity through computational power. Just as modernist techniques like ***collage, montage***, and ***assemblage*** emerged as a rebellion against established norms (such as the entire beaux-arts system), the infusion of AI technologies raises questions about the essence of artistic expression in the context of data-driven insights. This progression, rooted in distinct eras, intersects at the crossroads of ontology and epistemology in art and design. The modernist era, catalyzed by the industrial age, sought authenticity amid mechanization. Today's digital age (Carpo, 2013) introduces AI's potential to unlock novel pathways in art yet grapples with the tension between technological precision and the emotional resonance intrinsic to human creativity. This dynamic evolution presents itself as an intricate interplay between mechanization, innovation, individualism, and human sensibility, crafting a narrative that extends from tactile to virtual, from rebellion to collaboration, and from visceral experiences to calculated outcomes. The dichotomy between the two methodologies for creating art presents a clear demarcation line between organic and mechanical. The methods of modernism, which emerged during the Industrial Age, were deeply influenced by a human desire to break away from established norms. Techniques like collage, montage, and assemblage reflected a rebellion against convention, employing tangible materials to construct compositions that carried layers of meaning. In stark contrast, contemporary art methods, intertwined with AI and large datasets, raise questions about the role of the human touch in the creative process. These methods, while leveraging technology, usher in a realm where art is informed by immense pools of information. Artists delve into the latent space of data, seeking patterns and insights that shape their work. The methods of modernism were rooted in human hands shaping materials, reflecting the era's yearning for authenticity and individuality amid industrialization's mechanization. In contrast, contemporary methods, reliant on algorithms and data-driven insights, could inadvertently overshadow the nuance of human emotions and interpretations. This of course can be an asset, in that the results, based on methods such as *blending*, *prompting*, and *compositing*, produce effects such as *estrangement*, *defamiliarization*, and Marxist *alienation*. A method that provokes the spectator to consider the piece of art of being synthetic in nature, and thus inducing the ability to perceive the piece of art with a level of abstraction that allows for an intellectual interrogation of the artwork. While contemporary artists delve into data to uncover novel avenues for artistic expression, there is a risk of art becoming a calculated outcome, detached from the visceral experiences that fuel the creative spirit. The focus on interrogating the *latent space* and uncovering new methods to express the human condition can be considered a pioneering method of artistic production that capitalizes on the synergy between human creative insight and the expansive reservoir of data. The latent space, an intricate multidimensional landscape concealed within datasets, serves as an untapped wellspring of intricate relationships, patterns, and latent potentials that transcend the boundaries of conscious human perception. In essence, the juxtaposition of these methodologies, **Modern Art** and **Neural Art**, prompts us to contemplate the tension between mechanization and individualism, data-driven insights, and intuitive human expression (Figure 1.5.6).

About the Ethics of Using AI in Urban Design

Yet, this foray into the historical intricacies of urban design should be met with caution. The seamless integration of AI's insights into the design process demands the discerning eye of the human designer, who infuses these computational revelations with the empathy, creativity, and cultural sensibility that characterize the art of architecture (del Campo, 2022). AI's computational virtuosity must be complemented by the intangible nuance of human intuition, bridging the empirical and the imaginative realms of urban design—moreover, the ethical ripples of AI's involvement in urban design warrant focused contemplation. The responsible integration of AI must guard against biases, ensure data privacy, and proactively address issues of equity and social justice. As AI becomes an ally in urban design, it is incumbent upon designers and scholars to navigate the ethical currents and uphold the enduring principles that bind architecture to the well-being of humanity. The evaluation of urban textures and planning necessitates a multidimensional perspective that transcends the pragmatic realm. Venturing into the multitude of complexities that shape urban design, diving headfirst into the complex tapestry of planning processes, economic dynamics, material

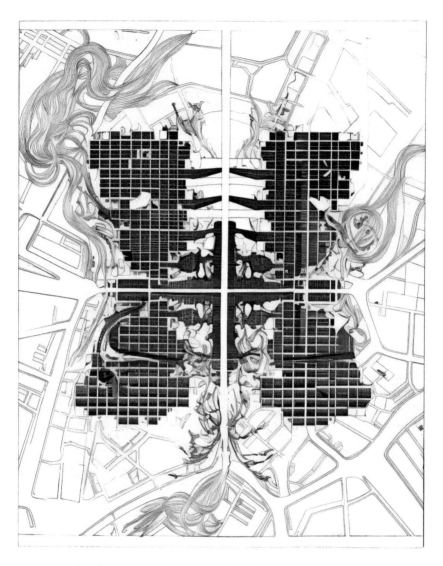

Figure 1.5.6 Example of a quatrefoil city layout based on data reaching from the Baroque era to Modernism. This linear city is a blend of historic city maps, modern city maps, and the topography of the site. 2023. Made with MidJourney v5.2. Credit to © SPAN Matias del Campo, Sandra Manninger. 2022.

influences, political nuances, stylistic proclivities, aesthetic pursuits, and cultural contexts. Historical exemplars such as Renaissance ideal cities and the Modern project serve as lighthouse examples, their profound influence resonating beyond the realm of form and geometry, permeating the fabric of politics, society, and economics. These manifestations crystallize the collective wisdom of urban planning imagination, providing a wellspring of inspiration and ideas regarding the essence of the city. Anchored in visual literacy, architectural education mines a vast repository of images, preparing the architects of tomorrow

Figure 1.5.7   This linear city is a blend of historic city maps, modern city maps, and the topography of the site. Credit to: © SPAN Matias del Campo, Sandra Manninger. 2022.

to navigate the contemporary digital landscape replete with virtual galleries that foster inspiration and facilitate the exchange of ideas. Embracing this rich visual heritage and the ever-evolving visual culture, urban planners and architects possess the tools to traverse the intricate tapestry of urban design to shape the cities of the future with ingenuity, empathy, and aesthetic sensibility.

The integration of AI within the realm of urban design promises a transformative trajectory, shaping the future of our built environment. This exploration delves into the multifaceted role of AI in urban design, unearthing its potential to revolutionize decision-making processes, foster sustainable practices, and enhance the quality of urban life. AI's foray into urban design emerges from its exceptional capacity to process and analyze vast amounts of data, unraveling intricate patterns and interdependencies within the urban fabric. AI generally speaking excels in two distinct categories: prediction and optimization. Both of which are crucial elements for future urban design. By leveraging machine learning algorithms and predictive modeling techniques, AI empowers urban designers, architects, and planners to make more informed decisions grounded in evidence-based insights. This data-driven approach transcends subjective inclinations, fostering a holistic understanding of complex urban phenomena. One intriguing aspect of AI lies in its ability to provide generative design solutions, transcending conventional design paradigms. By employing algorithms and generative modeling, AI offers designers a vast design space to explore, enabling the creation of novel alternatives that embody diverse conditions and constraints (Figure 1.5.7). This iterative process of design refinement amplifies efficiency and engenders innovative solutions, propelling the creative process forward into the future.

Conclusion

AI is on the verge of revolutionizing the landscape of urban design by harnessing the vast repository of historic architectural data accumulated over centuries. It is a model of design that is distinctively different from known design methods in that it provides a collision between bottom-up, data-driven design trajectories and the human mind, the "man in the loop" who still has the role of providing the ethical guidelines for the design process. This potential transformation is in response to the intricate and multifaceted nature of urban planning, which transcends mere functionality and involves a complex interplay of economic dynamics, social implications, political intricacies, cultural tapestries, and aesthetic movements. All of these aspects can be included in design considerations at a velocity that is unprecedented to this day. Throughout the historical evolution of urban design, categorization (Crawford, 2021) has never been an easy task, bridging the realms of form and ideology. From the geometric precision of Renaissance ideal cities to the austerity of Modernism, different design paradigms have embodied cultural aspirations and societal values. However, the emergence of AI introduces an exciting avenue that can break free from traditional molds and carve its niche in urban design.

Central to AI's potential in urban design is its prowess in data mining and machine learning. Data mining, facilitated by computational analysis, allows for the exploration of vast historical archives. Machine learning techniques enable the interpolation between existing data points, identifying patterns and morphologies that have shaped urban landscapes across various cultures and epochs (Figure 1.5.8).

Figure 1.5.8   Vague plans like this are the result of blending various data points. Such as an existing nolliplan and the topo lines of an Alpine area. Credit to: © SPAN Matias del Campo, Sandra Manninger. 2022.

In doing so, this AI-driven process can uncover hidden insights, propose design strategies, and offer cautionary lessons for future urban design endeavors. The scope of this approach extends beyond historical retrospection to offer genuinely innovative solutions that push the boundaries of traditional design paradigms. AI's influence in urban design extends to predictive modeling, site analysis, simulation, generative design, smart infrastructure management, data-driven decision-making, and more. Tapping into AI's computational capabilities and deep architectural history, designers gain access to a realm of novel, utilitarian, and aesthetically appealing solutions. AI's ability to simulate, optimize, and even generate design alternatives introduces a fresh approach that blends historic sensibilities with futuristic aspirations. However, this AI-infused vision of urban design also raises ethical considerations. Ensuring fairness, addressing biases, safeguarding data privacy, and promoting equity and social justice are pivotal aspects of deploying AI responsibly. The harmonious integration of human intuition with computational brilliance becomes vital to strike a balance between empirical evidence and creative imagination.

References

Carpo, M. (2013). *The Digital Turn in Architecture 1992–2012*. Edited by Mario Carpo. Chichester: Wiley.

Chen, Leshang & Davidson, Susan. (2019). *Automate Software Citation using GitCite*.

Choay, F., Hugo, M., & Collins, G. R. (1970). *1969. The Modern City: Planning in the 19th Century*. New York: George Braziller.

Coleman, S. (2023). *Ludwig Hilberseimer: Reanimating Architecture and the City*. London: Bloomsbury Publishing.

Crawford, K. (2021). *Atlas of AI: Power, Politics, and the Planetary Costs of Artificial Intelligence* (pp. 123–149). New Haven: Yale University Press. https://doi.org/10.12987/9780300252392.

Cuthbert, Alexander. (2008). The Form of Cities: Political Economy and Urban Design. The Form of Cities: Political Economy and Urban Design. 1-304. 10.1002/9780470774915.

Cuthbert, A. (2008). *The Form of Cities: Political Economy and Urban Design* (pp. 1–304). London: Wiley. https://doi.org/10.1002/9780470774915.

del Campo, M. (2022). *Neural Architecture—Design and Artificial Intelligence*. Novato, CA: ORO Edition.

Donepudi, P. (2017). Machine Learning and Artificial Intelligence in Banking. *Engineering International*, 5: 83–86. https://doi.org/10.18034/ei.v5i2.490.

Ebenezer, H., & Osborn, Frederic J. (1965). *Garden Cities of To-Morrow*. Cambridge, MA: MIT Press.

Esteva, A., Chou, K., Yeung, S. et al. (2021). Deep Learning-Enabled Medical Computer Vision. *npj Digital Medicine*, 4: 5. https://doi.org/10.1038/s41746-020-00376-2.

Giedion, S. (1941). *Space, Time and Architecture*. Cambridge, MA: Harvard University Press.

Hilberseimer, L. (1944). *The New City; Principles of Planning*. Chicago: Paul Theobald.

Kamrowska-Załuska, D. (2021). Impact of AI-Based Tools and Urban Big Data Analytics on the Design and Planning of Cities. *Land*, 10, no. 11: 1209.

Mertins, D. (1996). The Enticing and Threatening Face of Prehistory: Walter Benjamin and the Utopia of Glass. *Assemblage*, no. 29: 7–23. https://doi.org/10.2307/3171392.

Pearson, C. (2011). *Humanism and the Urban World: Leon Battista Alberti and the Renaissance City*. Philadelphia, PA: Penn State University Press. https://doi.org/10.5325/j.ctt7v6f4.

Poon, S. (2017). Understanding the Impact of Cultural Design Aesthetics and Socioeconomic Shifts: Approaches to Urban Resilience Empower Place Making. *Journal of Urban Culture Research*, 14: 34–56. https://doi.org/10.14456/jucr.2017.3.

Rodríguez, L. (2006). The Form of Cites: Political Economy and Urban Design. *AUS*. 6, 32–46. https://doi.org/10.4206/aus.2006.n2-05.

Rowe, H. A. (2011). The Rise and Fall of Modernist Architecture. *Inquiries Journal/Student Pulse*, 3, no. 4, 21–34. http://www.inquiriesjournal.com/a?id=1687

Schirren, M., & Taut, B. (2004). *Bruno Taut Alpine Architektur: Eine Utopie = A Utopia.* München: Prestel.

Simmel, G. (1950). The Metropolis and Mental Life. In K. H. Wolff (Ed.), *The Sociology of Georg Simmel* (pp. 409–424). New York: The Free Press.

Spence, C. (2020). Senses of Place: Architectural Design for the Multisensory Mind. *Cognitive Research: Principles and Implications*, 5, no. 1: 46.

Tafuri, M. (1976). *Architecture and Utopia: Design and Capitalist Development* (p. 86). Cambridge, MA: MIT Press.

van Eck, C. (1998). The Structure of 'De Re Aedificatoria' Reconsidered. *Journal of the Society of Architectural Historians*, 57, no. 3: 280–297. https://doi.org/10.2307/991347.

Wright, F. L. (1932). 1867–1959. *The Disappearing City.* New York: W.F. Payson.

1.6

LIVED MULTI-SPECIES HIGH-DENSITY UTOPIAS

Smart City Design for Healthy and Diverse Communities in the Post-Anthropocene

Christiane Margerita Herr

Abstract

A key aspect of intelligent utopian future cities is their ability to not only achieve high efficiency in terms of energy use and carbon emission performance over and beyond the cities we know, but also to act as host environments for healthy and content communities of inhabitants. Future smart cities will be conceived as hybrid artificial-natural ecologies, constructed to take larger systemic interrelationships into account. Accordingly, the quality of life these cities offer to their inhabitants will be defined beyond the requirements of humans only. This chapter critically examines how next-generation smart cities will integrate a broad variety of species and their interconnected habitats into future high-density and high-rise urban environments. Taking the high-tech city of Shenzhen as an example, this chapter examines how multi-species cities can be created from an initial base of integrating existing biodiversity of their surrounding environments and extend beyond conservation by including consideration of materials as well as architectural and urban form in the design of new kinds of artificial ecologies on and around buildings and urban infrastructure. In this context, materials and building typologies are re-thought for the post-Anthropocene city as forming a key component of bio-technological synergetic landscapes enabling cross-species co-living and well-being.

Keywords
Multi-Species Cities; Ecological Architectural Design; Urban Biodiversity; Smart Cities; Solarpunk

The Biodiverse Urban Utopia: Introducing New Metrics

With anthropogenic pressures on ecosystems across our planet reaching unsustainable scales, new ways of adapting human activities to the "safe operating space" of Planet

DOI: 10.4324/9781003384113-14

Earth (Rockström et al., 2009) need to be developed for our constructed environments. As collective awareness of the threatened state of our natural surroundings rises, our collective imagination is embracing nature-inclusive visions of desirable future urban environments. These scenarios typically depict technically advanced but at the same time green and livable urban environments, where inhabitants work and live with all the comforts that technological progress has to offer, yet also benefit from the natural environments we have come to recognize as the essential basis of our collective health and well-being. In practice, most contemporary urban environments struggle to achieve this balance, and designers are challenged to negotiate the difficult task of responding to social, economic, and ecological expectations at the same time. This chapter discusses future visions of "smart" urban environments that feature technological progress alongside increased acceptance and integration of nature, and how these could lead to high-tech, resource-efficient, and low-emission ways of living that re-engage with our natural environments in new ways.

A new re-engagement of humans and nature requires a qualitative re-thinking beyond the level of technical fixes to existing environments and ways of living that merely reaffirm established unsustainable systems (Crace, 2023). This chapter argues that a key driver of future urban living environments will be a new perspective on the built environment as a high-performance engineered ecosystem, designed to benefit both human and non-human inhabitants while reducing the impact on global resource use. A growing number of studies address the implications of this new perspective (Catalano et al., 2021; Weisser et al., 2023; Grobman et al., 2023) and argue for a paradigmatic transition from "environmental-sensitive" to "eco-positive" urban environments (Birkeland, 2020). While increasing levels of urban development have been shown to correlate with decreased availability of ecosystem services, "eco-positive" urban environments aim to integrate ecosystems to the extent that they not only preserve but also enhance ecosystem services (Oberndorfer, 2007). At the same time, recent research is increasingly substantiating the understanding that the contemporary disconnect between urban populations and natural surroundings has significant impacts on the health and well-being of city populations (Robinson et al., 2023). Not only do we need "eco-positive" design strategies in the planning and refurbishment of urban environments such as three-dimensional approaches to urban greening (Zhong et al., 2023), we also need new ways of mediating the encounters between nature and humans living in these environments. Similarly, materials and building typologies need to be re-thought for future cities as they form the basis of bio-technological synergetic landscapes enabling cross-species co-living and well-being. The following sections introduce a brief outline of key aspects of lived multi-species utopias and discuss their implications in the context of the city of Shenzhen, China, a contemporary high-tech megacity.

Transitioning into High-Tech, High-Density Engineered Urban Ecologies: The Case of Shenzhen

The city of Shenzhen is considered the most technically advanced and future-oriented city in China. With 17 million inhabitants, it joins a cluster of megacities in the Pearl River Delta, including Guangzhou and Hong Kong. Shenzhen is a high-density, high-rise, and high-tech city with a short history of just over 40 years and has been officially tasked by the Chinese government to develop a model ecological society (Research Institute for Eco-civilization, 2021). Shenzhen is located in a subtropical climate and a coastal setting, which exposes the city to rising sea levels due to human-induced climate change, flooding, and the impact of typhoons which hit the city several times per year (Figure 1.6.1). At the same

Figure 1.6.1   The high-density, high-rise urban environment of Shenzhen, China (copyright permission courtesy of Chao Tang).

time, extended seasonal droughts plague the region, which suffers from overexploitation of groundwater, pollution, and disruption of natural water cycles induced by changing land use and large-scale building activity. Shenzhen's location in a natural biodiversity hotspot has offered the city a pioneering role in China in terms of its biodiversity management, with the city declaring large parts of its urban areas ecological protection zones to safeguard existing biodiversity.

As a global center of high-tech development, Shenzhen is home to headquarters or research and development centers of several globally leading tech companies, including Tencent, ZTE, DJI, Huawei, BGI, and MindRay. The city is conscious of its competitiveness for internationally leading talent and perceives its high-quality green environment as a key resource to attract such talent. Across the city, 1,350 urban parks are intensively used by urban residents: "Urban Camping" in green areas surrounded by glass and steel high-rise buildings is a popular weekend family activity. Another motivation to increase the provision of public green spaces throughout the city comes from broader public health concerns to maintain the health and well-being of a rapidly aging population. While the provision of urban green space has become a priority in Shenzhen's urban planning, it remains focused on human perceptions and benefits. Ecological protection zones, however, remain conceptually separate from the intensively managed and highly frequented urban parks, which illustrates the challenges of re-integrating multi-species concerns into urban planning.

Encounters between Shenzhen's urban population and nature are not free of difficulties. To most urban residents, "nature" is a vague concept that broadly refers to greenery and has little to do with what ecologists would describe as "natural". The Shenzhen Futian Mangrove Ecological Park case demonstrates this challenge. The park is managed by the Shenzhen Mangrove Conservation Foundation, an ecology-focused NGO with a differentiated research agenda, yet it also needs to cater to expectations from urban residents using the publicly accessible parts of the ecological reserve as a park. Complaints from residents address among others the presence of various insects, reptiles and a lack of "beautiful" gardening, or the signs warning park visitors not to feed animals they encounter and not to set pets free in the park. A playground in the park uses loose wood chips as soft ground cover rather than conventional artificial floor coverings, which children enjoy to dig through but their caretakers dislike the playground as they perceive it as "dirty". This illustrates the need to co-evolve eco-positive urban areas with equally eco-positive education of urban populations. Even though Shenzhen currently has 60 nature education centers, this number is dwarfed by the size of its population of 17 million (Research institute for Eco-civilization, 2021).

In the case of Shenzhen, considerable scientific analysis of local ecosystems and resulting expertise already exists (Huang et al., 2009; Deng, 2017; Herr et al., 2024; Moghadam and Feizabadi, 2018) and could be translated into visionary eco-positive urban proposals. The park example above may illustrate why multi-species encounters between urban residents and nature cannot be romanticized based on narratives or memories of a distant rural past. The engineered urban ecosystems of the future will be designed to site-specific performance criteria (Diamond et al., 2013), while urban residents will need to adapt to a more cyclical and seasonal provision of ecosystem services. Figure 1.6.2 illustrates a visionary design proposal for a new coastal city district of Shenzhen that minimizes disruptions to the site's hydro-ecological characteristics: The urban morphology is designed to touch the ground as carefully as possible and abrupt elevation changes are avoided to support natural water cycles between sea and mountain. At the same time, the porous and interwoven inhabited volumes allow the urban form to connect horizontally between buildings and mountains, offering ecological dispersion corridors and potential habitat. Distributed soil reservoirs and vegetation provide opportunities to harness natural ventilation and cooling to the higher floors, while large parts of the site area are dedicated to intertidal ecosystems such as oyster reefs and mangroves to host local ecosystems but also to mitigate flooding and prevent shore erosion.

Figure 1.6.2 Proposal for a new type of city district for Shenzhen, China, designed to enhance hydroecological networks and ecosystem services (copyright permission courtesy of Chao Tang).

AI-Generated Solarpunk Visions for High-Density Cities

The term "Solarpunk" describes future scenarios where sustainable technologies, both low-tech and high-tech, enable humanity to live in balance with the planet's ecosystems. Solarpunk imagines how society can adapt to the constraints of limited planetary boundaries by developing eco-positive and regenerative strategies for living with nature (The Solarpunk Community, 2019). A key perspective that is gradually being embraced is the idea of performance – natural and artificial environments are not evaluated in terms of their aesthetics or social convention, but instead, their capacity to generate sustainable results. Solarpunk visions emphasize that the "smartness" of future city systems will rely on smart citizenry rather than digitization (ibid.). A collection of emblematic short stories featured in "Cities of Light" by Eschrich et al. (2021) illustrates the role of communities in future eco-positive cities, where inhabitants work collectively in changing social patterns to synchronize better with natural resource availability patterns, such as green energy derived from photovoltaics or wind. Solarpunk visions of future environments embrace the attitude that environmental challenges offer new opportunities and call for creative ideas beyond conventional distinctions, such as integrated solar and agricultural farming or energy-generating systems (Crosby, 2023).

The comprehensively engineered ecosystems featured in Solarpunk cities see natural and artificial aspects of design merge into larger performance-oriented systems to generate new environmental qualities. The engineered nature of these ecosystems makes it necessary to think in terms of clear performance criteria and to collaborate across disciplines, as a multitude of considerations needs to be integrated in both quantitative and qualitative ways (Herr, 2022). This intensity of high-density, high-rise urban space as it is common in Asian megacities can make it difficult to create coherent visions of eco-positive urban fabric replete with eco-positive collective lifestyles. In this context, recent advances in AI-generated imagery are providing new opportunities for merging visions originating from different fields to illustrate utopian yet realistic-looking and believable eco-positive futures (Figure 1.6.3). Seamlessly blending engineering visions with social and architectural visions, these images are generating both accessible and shared imagined futures that motivate change.

The Material Basis of Living Biodiverse Utopias

As future multi-species cities coordinate human-nature encounters across a broad range of scales, the material nature of the built environment will need to be reconsidered comprehensively. Beyond an already established knowledge base focusing on energy use and carbon emissions, further changes will establish circular economies, slowed-down material circulation, as well as a regenerative design approach to urban nature. The "smart" materials of the future will be engineered to be efficient as well as renewable, reusable, or compostable. Material cycles of high-performance (bio-)materials will determine urban and building cycles, such as buildings engineered for solar energy harvesting performance, or buildings featuring biodegradable facades. Natural processes proliferating through urban environments will introduce a new temporality to urban life, where material aging will be accepted and considered part of a new eco-positive aesthetic.

One example of the new metabolic perspective on materials is the recognition of urban environments as hosting life across all scales, from larger scale trees and mammals down

Figure 1.6.3   A vision of eco-positive Shenzhen illustrating the future quality of living (copyright permission courtesy of Chao Tang).

to the invisible scale of microbes. The microbial world, in particular, has so far not been acknowledged sufficiently as driving large-scale urban re-thinking and design (Herr and Duan, 2020). Figure 1.6.4 illustrates the research-driven design proposal for a high-rise office building façade engineered to host a biodiverse microbiome (Herr et al., 2022). Linked to the natural ventilation system of the building, the microbial biodiversity reservoirs on the external building facade provide inhabitants with a healthy and diverse microbial environment. To achieve microbial biodiversity, the façade employs a layered geometry and a variety of materials, where organic and inorganic materials as well as natural soil are integrated to create favorable conditions for diverse microbial taxa to thrive despite the harsh environmental conditions. In this and similar façade proposals (Herr and Li, 2023), the design follows Solarpunk principles of prioritizing performance over conventional aesthetics, deriving a new type of aesthetics from a broader multidisciplinary perspective on the built environment.

The façade system shown in Figure 1.6.4 extends beyond the microbial realm as the layered geometry offers habitats at the macro scale as well. Soil reservoirs extend along all spandrel areas and can host opportunistic local plant and animal species that can thrive under the challenging environmental conditions of exposed facades. Insects can take advantage of available food sources, which in turn provide potential food sources for birds.

Figure 1.6.4 High-rise office building facade designed for microbial biodiversity (copyright permission courtesy of Chao Tang).

Thought as a food chain rather than simply a nesting place or green feature, the design proposal demonstrates that a façade can host a new type of engineered ecosystem – while also supporting conventional sustainable design criteria such as shading, insulation, and ventilation.

Conclusion: Embracing Optimistic Living Utopias

As humanity is working to understand that new ways of urban living will be necessary to not only cope with but thrive on, limited planetary resources, cities are searching for alternative strategies for coordinating natural systems and human residents. This search is particularly acute in the high-density and high-rise megacities of Asia, where economic considerations have so far eclipsed ecological considerations. This chapter illustrates the case of the southern Chinese megacity of Shenzhen, where high-tech economic aims depend on the livability of the city in the eyes of a highly educated human workforce. In response, the city dedicates much effort to ecological conservation and urban greening but these two efforts have so far remained separate due to a more holistic ecosystem engineering approach. Drawing on Solarpunk visions of a future where urban residents coordinate their living patterns closely and creatively with limited resource availability, this chapter argues that performance-oriented urban morphologies, multi-species living environments, designed microbiomes as well as eco-positive citizen participation and education will constitute the basis of what we can consider the "smart" cities of the future.

Acknowledgments

Figures 1.6.2 and 1.6.4 were created by Chao Tang; Figure 1.6.3 was created by Li Chenxiao using MidJourney. We are grateful for Dr. Matteo Convertino's expert advice in developing proposals for alternative urban morphologies.

References

Birkeland, J. (2020). *Net-Positive Design and Sustainable Urban Development*. Routledge.

Catalano, C.E., Meslec, M., Boileau, J., Guarino, R., Aurich, I., Baumann, N., Chartier, F., Dalix, P., Deramond, S., Laube, P., Lee, A.K.K., Ochsner, P., Pasturel, M., Soret, M. and Moulherat, S. (2021). Smart sustainable cities of the new millennium: Towards design for nature. *Circular Economy and Sustainability*, 1(3): 1053–1086.

Crace, J. (2023). 'Magical' tech innovations a distraction from real solutions, climate experts warn. *The Guardian*, 10 December 2023. Retrieved from https://www.theguardian.com/environment/fossil-fuels/2023/dec/10/all.

Crosby, P.M. (2023). Towards an anti-antiutopia: Solarpunk cities and the precarity of our urban future. *Enquiry the ARCC Journal for Architectural Research*, 20(2): 79–91.

Deng, M. (2017). *Research on the Ecological Design Strategy for Super High-Rise Buildings in Lingnan* (in Chinese). PhD thesis. South China University of Technology.

Diamond, R.C., Ye, Q., Feng, W., Yan, T., Mao, H., Li, Y., Guo, Y. and Wang, J. (2013). Sustainable building in China—A green leap forward? *Buildings*, 3(3): 639–658.

Eschrich, J., Miller, C. and Wylie, R. 2021). *Cities of Light: A Collection of Solar Futures*. Tempe, Arizona State University Center for Science and the Imagination.

Grobman, Y.J., Weisser, W., Shwartz, A., Ludwig, F., Kozlovsky, R., Ferdman, A., Perini, K., Hauck, T.E., Selvan, S.U. and Saroglou, S., Barath, S., Schloter, M. and Windorfer, L. (2023). Architectural multispecies building design: Concepts, challenges, and design process. *Sustainability*, 15: 15480.

Herr, C.M. (2022). Sublimating tectonics of architecture: Innovations in creative structural engineering. In M. Kanaani (ed.), *The Routledge Companion to Ecological Design Thinking: Healthful Ecotopian Visions for Architecture and Urbanism*, Routledge, 328–338.

Herr, C.M., Blokhina, E., Gao, Z., Ji, Y., Jiang, Y. and Tang, C. (2022). Designing biodiverse high-rise façade microbiomes for healthy urban environments. *CTBUH Journal* 4: 20–27.

Herr, C.M. and Duan, Y. (2020). Designing facade microbiomes. In *Imaginable Futures: Design Thinking, and the Scientific Method, Proceedings of the 54th International Conference of the Architectural Science Association*, Auckland, New Zealand, 365–374.

Herr, C.M. and Li, C. (2023). Articulating facade microbiomes at human scale: A cellular automata driven bioreceptive facade design approach to communicate a new dimension of urban health. In *CAADRIA 2023: Proceedings of the 28th International Conference on Computer-Aided Architectural Design Research in Asia*, Ahmenabad, India, 281–290.

Herr, C.M., Li, C., Zhou, Y. and Yan, M. (2024). Embracing local biodiversity as part of sustainable high rise building facades in subtropical China. In *Proceedings of ICSBS 2023 the 3rd International Conference on Sustainable Buildings and Structures*, Springer Nature.

Huang, H., Ma, Z. and Li, J. (2009). Application of green and energy-saving building technology in super high-rise buildings in subtropical regions (in Chinese). *Architectural Journal*, (9): 99–101.

Moghadam, T.T. and Feizabadi, M. (2018). Increasing ecological capacity by designing ecological high-rise buildings. *Open House International*, 43: 94–104.

Oberndorfer, E., Lundholm, J., Bass, B., Coffman, R., Doshi, H., Dunnett, N., Gaffin, S., Köh-ler, M., Liu, K.,and Rowe, D.B. (2007). Green roofs as urban ecosystems: Ecological structures, functions, and services. *BioScience*, 57(10): 823–833.

Research institute for Eco-civilization, Chinese Academy of Social Science. (2021). *Shenzhen Sustainable Development Report*. Retrieved on 2 January, 2024 from https://www.undp.org/china/publications/shenzhen-sustainable-development-report-2021

Robinson, J.M., Wissel, E.F. and Breed, M.F. (2023). Policy implications of the microbiota-gut-brain axis. *Trends in Microbiology*, November 10: S0966-842X(23)00299-8.

Rockström, J., Steffen, W., Noone, K., Persson, A., Chapin, III, F.S., Lambin, E., Lenton, T.M., Scheffer, M., Folke, C., Schellnhuber, H., Nykvist, B., De Wit, C.A., Hughes, T., van der Leeuw, S., Rodhe, H., Sorlin, S., Snyder, P.K., Costanza, R., Svedin, U., Falkenmark, M., Karlberg, L., Corell, R.W., Fabry, V.J., Hansen, J., Walker, B., Liverman, D., Richardson, K., Crutzen, P. and Foley, J. (2009). Planetary boundaries: Exploring the safe operating space for humanity. *Ecology and Society*, 14(2): 32.

The Solarpunk Community. (2019). A Solarpunk manifesto. re-des.org. Regenerative Design. Archived from the original on 2019 October 12. Retrieved on 2 January 2024 from https://web.archive.org/web/20191012233135/http://www.re-des.org/a-solarpunk-manifesto/.

Weisser, W.W., Hensel, M., Barath, S., Culshaw, V., Grobman, Y. J., Hauck, T. E., Joschinski, J., Ludwig, F., Mimet, A., Perini, K., Roccotiello, E., Schloter, M., Shwartz, A., Hensel, D. S. and Vogler, V. (2023). Creating ecologically sound buildings by integrating ecology, architecture and computational design. *People and Nature*, 5(1): 4–20.

Zhong, W., Schoeder, T. and Bekkering, J. (2023). Designing with nature: Advancing three-dimensional green spaces in architecture through frameworks for biophilic design and sustainability. *Frontiers of Architectural Research*, 12(4): 732–753.

1.7

SMART CITY AND THE CONCEPT OF SAFETY

The Meaning of Safety in Smart City's Organizational Systems and Infrastructure

Ying Huang, Xinyi Yang and Hafiz Usman Ahmed

Abstract

With current environmental and social challenges in mind, there is a clear trajectory of Smart Cities becoming the need of modern society. Many cities in the world are already transforming their ways to be more efficient, greener, and also safer. Studies show that the field of safety receives less focus in development strategies than other fields of smart development.

This chapter explores the connection between Smart City and Safe City concepts, stressing the need to integrate strong safety measures into urban development for a genuinely smart city. Autonomous vehicles play a crucial role in reshaping road safety by potentially reducing accidents caused by human errors. The discussion extends to the communication types of autonomous vehicles and their role in minimizing road accidents.

Micro-simulation tools like AIMSUN, CORSIM, PARAMICS, and VISSIM are key players in developing intelligent transportation systems. A comparative analysis highlights their strengths, including dynamic assignment capabilities and the incorporation of human perception. The exploration also covers the Surrogate Safety Assessment Model, emphasizing its essential role in evaluating safety for new traffic models. Car-following models, such as stimulus-response, safety-distance, and psychophysical models, are examined to reveal their contributions and limitations in traffic flow simulation. Additionally, this chapter delves into foundational steps for setting up simulation environments, covering components like freeway layout configuration, vehicle type definition, breakdown scenario simulation, and handling uncertainties through VISSIM.

By connecting Smart City goals with the need for safety, this chapter provides a practical perspective on the dynamics between technological innovation and urban safety. The integration of autonomous technology, micro-simulation tool analysis, and exploration of car-following models collectively contribute to a nuanced understanding of traffic simulation and safety assessment advancements.

DOI: 10.4324/9781003384113-15

Introduction

The imperative of modern society is the transition to Smart Cities, addressing environmental and social challenges. Despite many cities progressing toward efficiency and sustainability, safety often receives less attention. This chapter underscores the essential link between Smart City and Safe City concepts, focusing on their interdependence and advocating for the integration of smart safety measures in comprehensive urban development. It specifically highlights the role of autonomous vehicles (AVs) in transportation within this context.

Introducing AVs in transportation signifies a potential paradigm shift toward enhanced road safety, as they offer the promise of minimizing accidents caused primarily by human errors. In 2020, despite reduced driving due to the COVID-19 pandemic, 38,680 people lost their lives in motor vehicle crashes, highlighting the persistent risks associated with human errors (National Highway Traffic Safety Administration, 2022). The ongoing evolution of vehicle automation, particularly AVs and connected AVs (CAVs), holds promise for significantly enhancing road safety by minimizing accidents primarily caused by human mistakes, which contribute to over 90% of crashes (National Highway Traffic Safety Administration, 2008). Projections suggest that the widespread adoption of autonomous technology could potentially save 30,000 lives annually in the USA and prevent around 5 million accidents (Greenblatt, 2016).

According to the automation levels defined by SAE International, a fully AV at Level 3 or higher has the capability to independently monitor its driving environment, access data through wireless sensing and communication, and significantly reduce the need for direct human involvement (SAE, 2018). The secure autonomous functioning of AVs hinges on an array of onboard sensors, including cameras, radar sensors, ultrasonic sensors, lidar, and global positioning systems. These sensors capture vital information about the surroundings, encompassing details such as traffic infrastructures like signs, the distance to objects like pedestrians, and the speed and acceleration of nearby elements (Harlow and Peng, 2001; Tang et al., 2020; Wu et al., 2020; Younsi et al., 2020).

Moreover, AVs have the capability to wirelessly receive information shared by other connected vehicles, aligning with communication types specified by the United States Department of Transportation for CAVs. These communication types involve vehicle-to-vehicle (V2V), vehicle-to-infrastructure (V2I), and vehicle-to-device (V2X) (Richard et al., 2015). The 'X' in V2X encompasses diverse entities, including passengers, other vehicles, onboard devices, cloud technology, wireless sensors, and navigation tools (Fyfe, 2016). Figure 1.7.1 shows V2V and V2I communications and the fundamental micro-simulation behaviors, including car-following, lane-change, and gap-acceptance actions. Within the scope of human drivers, the depicted driving logic mirrors typical longitudinal and lateral maneuvers on a roadway (Olstam and Tapani, 2004). Longitudinally, vehicles engage in gap acceptance, speed adoption, and desired acceleration or deceleration when following others. Laterally, drivers make informed decisions regarding lane changes, merging/diverging, and overtaking (Hoogendoorn and Hoogendoorn, 2010). In addition, the figure underscores the versatile role of the roadside unit, functioning as both a traffic signal and a hub for diverse active traffic management sensors (Ahmed et al., 2022). Through the integration of detected and shared data, the central computers of the AVs utilize a car-following model to scrutinize and make optimal decisions regarding its driving behaviors.

AVs, whether fully automatic or equipped with adaptive cruise control (ACC) and cooperative ACC (CACC), open up possibilities for smart transportation in technologically

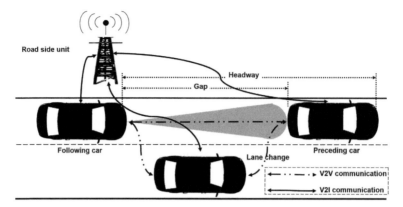

Figure 1.7.1 CAV communication channels and micro-simulation behaviors (image courtesy of author: Ying Huang).

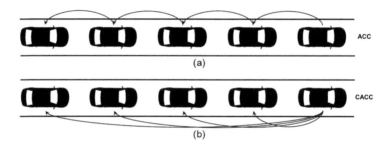

Figure 1.7.2 (a) Working principles of ACC, (b) CACC communication in a platoon setting (image courtesy of author: Ying Huang).

advanced cities. ACC, an enhanced iteration of conventional cruise controls, employs cameras, lasers, or radar sensors to monitor leading traffic in the same lane (Hunter et al., 2017; Kockelman et al., 2016; Van Arem et al., 2006). Figure 1.7.2(a) illustrates the working principles of ACC, where the following vehicle uses sensors to assess the speed and headway of the leading vehicle.

This allows the ACC-equipped vehicle to adjust its speed, maintaining a safe distance from the lead vehicle, thereby reducing the driver's stress and enhancing overall driving convenience. The system ensures a safe distance by adjusting speed in response to changes in the leading vehicle's behavior, promoting convenience and stress reduction for the driver.

CACC represents a more sophisticated evolution of ACC, involving effective V2V communication between leading and following vehicles (Kockelman et al., 2016). Under CACC, the leading vehicle transmits recommended speed and, at times, lane assignments to the following vehicle, enabling automated adjustments in speed and desired distance without driver intervention (Kockelman et al., 2016). This system enhances traffic flow stability, improves throughput, and allows vehicles to follow each other at closer distances, increasing highway capacity up to a lane drop (Weiss and Weidman, 2012). While CACC offers benefits such as smoother, safer, and more efficient driving, its advantages are maximized when both vehicles in the interaction are equipped with CACC technology, requiring at least 40% market penetration for optimal benefits (Weiss and Weidman, 2012).

Figure 1.7.2(b) illustrates the principles of CACC communication in a platoon setting, showcasing the leader-follower dynamics within the system.

Numerous states across the United States are actively exploring autonomous technologies, aiming to make advancements in safety and pave the way for the widespread integration of this technology for public use in the near future (Bierstedt et al., 2014). Research and development endeavors, led by both public and private entities such as automotive industries and academic institutions, focus on enhancing safety through innovations in machine learning algorithms, artificial intelligence, sensor technologies, and in-vehicle equipment (Bierstedt et al., 2014). Despite these efforts, the current adoption rate of AVs remains notably low, with full market integration anticipated to span several decades (Litman, 2017). Therefore, a prolonged coexistence with conventional vehicles is expected before full market adoption.

Therefore, understanding and studying the anticipated driving behavior of future AVs is critical during this transitional period to ensure a seamless integration that prioritizes safety. Understanding and studying the anticipated driving behavior of future AVs is critical during this transitional period to ensure a seamless integration that prioritizes safety. Given the current limited presence of AVs on the road, it is imperative to employ transport simulation modeling tools as an effective method to assess and enhance safety implications in studies related to AVs and their impacts on transportation networks.

Traffic Safety through Micro-Simulation

To improve safety assessment in traffic models, this section thoroughly investigates the realm of traffic micro-simulation. It conducts a detailed comparison of four prominent simulation tools – Advanced Interactive Microscopic Simulator for Urban and Non-urban Network (AIMSUN), CORridor SIMulation (CORSIM), PARAMICS, and Verkehr In Städten – SIMulationsmodell (VISSIM) (Ahmed et al., 2021). Following this, it introduces the Surrogate Safety Assessment Model (SSAM) approach, emphasizing its crucial role in safety evaluation. Additionally, car-following models are introduced, elucidating their specific contributions and limitations in simulating traffic flow.

Traffic Micro-Simulation Tools

Various commercially available traffic micro-simulation packages are designed to model real-world network configurations, problems, and solutions. Among these, four notable simulation tools include the AIMSUN, CORSIM, PARAMICS, and VISSIM (Jones et al., 2004; Lochrane, 2014; Olstam and Tapani, 2004).

- AIMSUN, developed by Traffic Simulation System, is recognized for its capabilities in traffic dynamic assignment, incident management, and applications related to Intelligent Transportation Systems. Widely used in Europe and gaining popularity in the United States, it can simulate urban streets, freeways, interchanges, and roundabouts (Jones et al., 2004). AIMSUN's strengths include robust 3D animation and recent advancements in modeling CAVs.
- CORSIM, introduced by the United States Federal Highway Administration in 1988, amalgamates NETSIM and FRESIM, enabling the simulation of urban traffic streams and complex freeway networks. CORSIM has found extensive application in the United

States, appreciated for its reliability in modeling driving behaviors and vehicle performance (Jones et al., 2004).

- PARAMICS, developed by the United Kingdom Department for Transportation in 1990, utilizes the Fritzsche car-following model, an acceleration model based on psychophysical logic (Fritzsche and Ag, 1994). With regimes like free following, following 1, following, closing in, and danger, PARAMICS incorporates human perception into its modeling, reacting to specific threshold values in the relative speed/space diagram for psychophysical follower-leader pairs (Olstam and Tapani, 2004).

- PTV VISSIM, developed by PTV Vision in 1992, is a prominent micro-simulation tool renowned for its capabilities (Wiedemann, 1974; Wiedemann and Reiter, 1992). Utilizing the Wiedemann 99 car-following model, an enhanced version of Wiedemann's 1974 model (Wiedemann and Reiter, 1992), VISSIM excels in intricate network and capacity analysis, spanning various scenarios from signalized junctions to transit operations (PTV Group, 2020). VISSIM's benefits include built-in features for CAVs, adaptable model parameters, and effective evaluation techniques for capacity and safety.

Enhancing Safety Evaluation in Traffic Models

To effectively evaluate new models, the Federal Highway Administration recommends the SSAM (Abou-Senna et al., 2015; Huang et al., 2013), which integrates the Gettman and Head surrogate safety with widely used microscopic traffic simulation models (Gettman and Head, 2003). In the context of SSAM, traffic events, such as sudden slowdowns and lane changes to avoid collisions, are treated as conflicts (Fyfe, 2016). Initially proposed by Perkins and Harris (Perkins and Harris, 1968), traffic conflicts identify events more frequent than collisions, providing a quicker, cost-effective safety evaluation compared to collision-based methods (Chin and Quek, 1997). SSAM categorizes conflicts based on angles, including rear-end conflicts ($< 30°$), lane changes ($> 30°$ and $< 85°$), and crossovers ($> 85°$) (Pu et al., 2008). SSAM assesses the number, types, severity, and location of conflicts, utilizing five common traffic conflict indicators: time-to-collision, post-encroachment time, initial deceleration rate, maximum speed, and speed differences (Das, 2018).

Car-Following Models

AVs need car-following models to operate independently on the road. These models, fundamental for traffic flow simulation, mimic vehicle behaviors and offer guidance on how AVs should react. Various types of car-following models, including stimulus-response models, safe-distance models, and psychophysical models, serve this purpose (Aghabayk et al., 2015; Brackstone and McDonald, 1999; Chen et al., 2016).

Stimulus-Response Model

The stimulus-response model operates on the assumption that each driver reacts to stimuli from other vehicles, encompassing factors like velocity, acceleration, and headway. The General Motors (GM) car-following model is one famous stimulus-response model. It developed in 1961, laid the foundation for subsequent models by utilizing acceleration/deceleration as a stimulus (Gazis et al., 1961; Toledo et al., 2007). It introduced a simplistic linear approach with a constant sensitivity parameter, calculating the following vehicle's acceleration based on the leader's speed difference (Chandler et al., 1958). Despite its simplicity, the GM model faced impracticalities, particularly its insensitivity to spacing between vehicles. Researchers addressed these limitations through extensions, such as Herman et al.'s modification allowing acceleration when the leader's speed increases (Herman, 1959). Subsequent improvements, like Subramanian's, considered faster reactions during deceleration (Subramanian, 1996). The Gazis–Herman–Rothery model extended the GM model, incorporating non-linear sensitivity to relative distance and speed (Gazis et al., 1961). Despite these enhancements, GM-type models exhibit behavioral limitations, including drivers reacting to small stimuli changes and followers remaining influenced by leaders even at large distances, raising concerns about their responsiveness in various traffic scenarios (Leutzbach, 1988; Wiedemann, 1974).

Safety-Distance Model

The safety-distance car-following model offers an advantageous approach by consistently maintaining a safe distance between following and lead vehicles, aiming to prevent collisions. This model, rooted in Newton's equation of motion, emphasizes collision avoidance, especially in scenarios where the lead vehicle behaves unpredictably (Brackstone and McDonald, 1999). The safety-distance principle, initially articulated by Pipes in 1953, establishes guidelines for maintaining a secure following distance (Pipes, 1953). The model's first general acceleration version, developed by Gipps in 1981, delineates no-collision behavior between follower and leader, contingent upon factors like safe headway and the follower's approximation of the leader's deceleration (Gipps, 1981). The model has gained popularity in micro-simulation tools due to its simplicity and applicability to human driving behavior (Barceló and Casas, 2005; Liu, 2010). However, a critical weakness noted in reviews is the model's lack of consideration for driver perception and its sensitivity to minor variations, potentially impacting the reaction time of the following driver (Lazar et al., 2016).

Psychophysical Model

The psychophysical or action point models (Brackstone and McDonald, 1999), such as the Wiedemann model, present a unique perspective in car-following models by incorporating perceptual thresholds, reflecting drivers' reactions to changes in spacing or relative velocity only when specific threshold values are reached (Wiedemann and Reiter, 1992). Developed by Wiedemann and Reiter, this model considers human driving behavior to be naturally distributed, accounting for variations in drivers' capabilities regarding perception, reaction, and estimation of the traffic environment (Wiedemann and Reiter, 1992). Employing perceptual thresholds for different regimes, including free-flowing, approaching/closing, following/closing, and emergency situations, the Wiedemann model encompasses various thresholds such as desired distance, desired minimum following distance, maximum following distance, perception threshold, and decreasing and increasing speed differences (Olstam and Tapani, 2004; Wiedemann, 1974).

Establishing the Framework for Simulation Environments

After understanding the simulation tools, safety evaluation tools, and car-following models, it is crucial to explore the foundational steps necessary for establishing a robust simulation environment. This process is fundamental for creating realistic scenarios that emulate real-world conditions and evaluating the performance of different car-following models accurately. Therefore, this section outlines the key components of this setup, ranging from configuring the freeway layout and defining vehicle types to simulating breakdown scenarios and dealing with uncertain conditions through simulation software VISSIM. Each step plays a crucial role in ensuring the accuracy and reliability of the simulation results, providing valuable insights into the behavior of vehicles under diverse circumstances.

Foundational Configuration in Simulation

The initial step involves configuring the road, where options such as single or multiple lanes and cross lanes are considered to simulate real-world conditions for specific analyses. Vehicle types are then defined, utilizing car-following models with adjustable parameters to simulate various scenarios, including different weather conditions, reaction times, and lengths. Researchers can also modify parameters in the Wiedemann 99 car-following model to simulate human and AV drivers. For those focused on creating and testing new car-following models, a new car-following model can be defined by editing the dynamic link library using C++ (PTV Group, 2020; Tettamanti and Varga, 2012; Yang et al., 2023).

Generating Vehicle Information and Speed Limits

In addition to defining control models for vehicles, information about the number and limited speed of vehicles on the road needs to be generated. Researchers can determine the number of vehicles based on real-world conditions or create scenarios with mixed-driven environments, adjusting the percentage of AVs to evaluate performance under diverse conditions.

Simulating Breakdown Scenarios and Uncertain Conditions

To simulate conditions involving crashes and delays and assess vehicle performance with different car-following models, breakdown spots can be set up. Vehicles designed to observe these spots will quickly decelerate, simulating a crash and delay scenario. Given the uncertainty in real-world conditions, stochastic variations are introduced using random seeds between simulation runs.

Simulation Condition with Different Vehicle Types Example

Introducing a practical example in VISSIM, Figure 1.7.3 shows the performance of various models with different percentages of human drivers, human drivers stopping before breakdown spots, and AVs. Each lane represents AVs controlled by distinct models, showcasing varied behaviors influenced by these models despite an identical initial setup. The analysis of delays following breakdown spots offers insights into model performance in handling delays and crashes (Yang, 2020). For additional safety analysis, VISSIM simulation results can be transferred to SSAM, allowing the extraction of stops and crashes based on user-defined criteria.

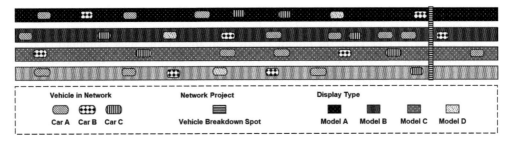

Figure 1.7.3 Varied models influence autonomous vehicles in mixed-driver environments (image courtesy of author: Ying Huang).

Conclusion

The integration of AVs into urban transportation represents a monumental shift with profound implications for road safety and Smart City initiatives. As society grapples with environmental and social challenges, the imperative to create Smart Cities becomes increasingly apparent. This chapter articulates the intrinsic link between Smart City and Safe City concepts, advocating for the infusion of intelligent safety measures into comprehensive urban development strategies.

A central theme has been the pivotal role of AVs in advancing road safety, a critical consideration given the staggering number of lives lost in motor vehicle crashes, predominantly attributable to human errors. AVs, particularly those operating at Level 3 and higher automation, emerge as promising instruments for mitigating accidents. Their ability to autonomously monitor the driving environment, coupled with advanced sensor technologies, positions them as potential game-changers in reducing accidents caused by human mistakes. Projections hinting at the potential to save thousands of lives annually and prevent millions of accidents underscore the transformative impact of AVs on road safety.

The effective functioning of AVs hinges on a suite of onboard sensors, encompassing cameras, radar sensors, ultrasonic sensors, lidar, and global positioning systems. These sensors play a pivotal role in capturing crucial information about the surrounding environment, empowering AVs to make informed decisions. Furthermore, the integration of wireless communication, as specified by the United States Department of Transportation for CAVs, introduces V2V, V2I, and V2X communication. This interconnected web of communication between vehicles and infrastructure amplifies the overall safety ecosystem.

This chapter delves into advanced driving assistance systems, notably ACC and CACC, which contribute to the realm of smart transportation. ACC, through sensors, vigilantly monitors leading traffic and adjusts the speed of the following vehicle, alleviating driver stress and enhancing overall driving convenience. CACC takes this a step further by incorporating effective V2V communication, enabling automated adjustments in speed and distance between vehicles. While promising benefits like improved traffic flow stability and increased highway capacity, the optimal realization of these advantages necessitates widespread adoption of CACC technology. A scrutiny of the current state of AV adoption reveals a protracted transition to fully autonomous transportation spanning several decades. The coexistence of AVs with conventional vehicles during this transitional period underscores the need to comprehend and study the anticipated driving behavior of future

AVs. Simulation tools, especially the SSAM, emerge as valuable instruments for assessing safety implications related to AVs and their impact on transportation networks.

This chapter further explores commercially available traffic micro-simulation packages, encompassing AIMSUN, CORSIM, PARAMICS, and VISSIM, crucial in modeling real-world network configurations, problems, and solutions. A detailed examination of car-following models, including stimulus-response model, safety-distance model, and psychophysical model, offers valuable insights into their applicability and limitations.

In conclusion, the vision of Smart and Safe Cities can be actualized through a comprehensive approach harnessing the potential of AVs, advanced simulation tools, and continuous safety evaluation. The integration of AVs into urban transportation systems holds the promise to redefine road safety paradigms and contribute to the overarching goal of creating sustainable and intelligent urban environments.

References

Abou-Senna, H., Abdel-Aty, M., Wu, J. and Darius, B. (2015), "MRI-2: Integrated Simulation and Safety", University of Central Florida, Orlando, FL, USA.

Aghabayk, K., Sarvi, M. and Young, W. (2015), "A state-of-the-art review of car-following models with particular considerations of heavy vehicles", *Transport Reviews*, Vol. 35, No. 1, pp. 82–105.

Ahmed, H.U., Huang, Y. and Lu, P. (2021), "A review of car-following models and modeling tools for human and autonomous-ready driving behaviors in micro-simulation", *Smart Cities*, Vol. 4, No. 1, pp. 314–335.

Ahmed, H.U., Huang, Y., Lu, P. and Bridgelall, R. (2022), "Technology developments and impacts of connected and autonomous vehicles: An overview", *Smart Cities*, Vol. 5, No. 1, pp. 382–404.

Barceló, J. and Casas, J. (2005), "Dynamic network simulation with AIMSUN", *Simulation Approaches in Transportation Analysis: Recent Advances and Challenges*, Springer, Boston, MA, USA, pp. 57–98.

Bierstedt, J., Gooze, A., Gray, C., Peterman, J., Raykin, L. and Walters, J. (2014), "Effects of next-generation vehicles on travel demand and highway capacity", *FP Think Working Group*, Vol. 8, pp. 10–11.

Brackstone, M. and McDonald, M. (1999), "Car-following: A historical review", *Transportation Research Part F: Traffic Psychology and Behaviour*, Vol. 2, No. 4, pp. 181–196.

Chandler, R.E., Herman, R. and Montroll, E.W. (1958), "Traffic dynamics: Studies in car following", *Operations Research*, Vol. 6, No. 2, pp. 165–184.

Chen, J., Liu, R., Ngoduy, D. and Shi, Z. (2016), "A new multi-anticipative car-following model with consideration of the desired following distance", *Nonlinear Dynamics*, Vol. 85, pp. 2705–2717.

Chin, H.-C. and Quek, S.-T. (1997), "Measurement of traffic conflicts", *Safety Science*, Vol. 26, No. 3, pp. 169–185.

Das, P. (2018), "Risk Analysis of Autonomous Vehicle and Its Safety Impact on Mixed Traffic Stream", Master's Thesis, Rowan University, Glassboro, NJ, USA.

Fritzsche, H.-T. and Ag, D. (1994), "A model for traffic simulation", *Traffic Engineering+ Control*, Vol. 35, No. 5, pp. 317–321.

Fyfe, M.R. (2016), "Safety Evaluation of Connected vehicle Applications using Micro-Simulation", Master's Thesis, University of British Columbia, Vancouver, BC, Canada.

Gazis, D.C., Herman, R. and Rothery, R.W. (1961), "Nonlinear follow-the-leader models of traffic flow", *Operations Research*, Vol. 9, No. 4, pp. 545–567.

Gettman, D. and Head, L. (2003), "Surrogate safety measures from traffic simulation models", *Transportation Research Record*, Vol. 1840, No. 1, pp. 104–115.

Gipps, P.G. (1981), "A behavioural car-following model for computer simulation", *Transportation Research Part B: Methodological*, Vol. 15, No. 2, pp. 105–111.

Greenblatt, N.A. (2016), "Self-driving cars and the law", *IEEE Spectrum*, Vol. 53, No. 2, pp. 46–51.

Harlow, C. and Peng, S. (2001), "Automatic vehicle classification system with range sensors", *Transportation Research Part C: Emerging Technologies*, Vol. 9, No. 4, pp. 231–247.

Herman, R. (1959), "Car-following and steady state flow", *Journal of Zhejiang University-SCIENCE A*, 12(8), 645-654.

Hoogendoorn, S.P. and Hoogendoorn, R. (2010), "Generic calibration framework for joint estimation of car-following models by using microscopic data", *Transportation Research Record*, Vol. 2188, No. 1, pp. 37–45.

Huang, F., Liu, P., Yu, H. and Wang, W. (2013), "Identifying if VISSIM simulation model and SSAM provide reasonable estimates for field measured traffic conflicts at signalized intersections", *Accident Analysis & Prevention*, Vol. 50, pp. 1014–1024.

Hunter, M.P., Guin, A., Rodgers, M.O., Huang, Z. and Greenwood, A.T. (2017), "Cooperative Vehicle–Highway Automation (CVHA) Technology: Simulation of Benefits and Operational Issues", United States: Federal Highway Administration, Atlanta, GA, USA.

Jones, S.L., Sullivan, A.J., Cheekoti, N., Anderson, M.D. and Malave, D. (2004), "Traffic simulation software comparison study", *UTCA Report*, Vol. 2217.

Kockelman, K.M., Avery, P., Bansal, P., Boyles, S.D., Bujanovic, P., Choudhary, T., Clements, L., Domnenko, G., Fagnant, D., Helsel, J., Hutchinson, R., Levin, M. Li, J., Li, T., Loftus-Otway, L., Nichols, A., Simoni, M. and Stewart, D. (2016), "Implications of Connected and Automated Vehicles on the Safety and Operations of Roadway Networks: A Final Report." Texas Department of Transportation: Austin, TX, USA.

Lazar, H., Rhoulami, K. and Rahmani, D. (2016), "A review analysis of optimal velocity models", *Periodica Polytechnica Transportation Engineering*, Vol. 44, No. 2, pp. 123–131.

Leutzbach, W. (1988), *Introduction to the Theory of Traffic Flow*, Vol. 47, Springer, Heidelberg, Germany.

Litman, T. (2017), *Autonomous Vehicle Implementation Predictions*, Canada, BC: Victoria Transport Policy Institute Victoria.

Liu, R. (2010), "Traffic simulation with DRACULA", *Fundamentals of Traffic Simulation*, Springer, New York, NY, pp. 295–322.

Lochrane, T. (2014), "A new multidimensional psycho-physical framework for modeling car-following in a freeway work zone" Ph.D. Thesis, University of Central Florida, Orlando, FL, USA, 2014.

National Highway Traffic Safety Administration. (2008), "National motor vehicle crash causation survey: Report to congress", *National Highway Traffic Safety Administration Technical Report DOT HS*, Vol. 811, p. 059.

National Highway Traffic Safety Administration. (2022), *Early Estimate of Motor Vehicle Traffic Fatalities in 2020*, Washington, DC: United States Department of Transportation.

Olstam, J.J. and Tapani, A. (2004), *Comparison of Car-Following Models*, Vol. 960, Sweden: Swedish National Road and Transport Research Institute Linköping.

Perkins, S.R. and Harris, J.L. (1968), "Traffic conflict characteristics-accident potential at intersections", *Highway Research Record*, No. 225, pp. 35–43.

Pipes, L.A. (1953), "An operational analysis of traffic dynamics", *Journal of Applied Physics*, Vol. 24, No. 3, pp. 274–281.

PTV Group. (2020), *PTV VISSIM 2020 User Manual*, Karlsruhe, Germany: PTV Group.

Pu, L., Joshi, R. and Energy, S. (2008), *Surrogate Safety Assessment Model (SSAM)--Software User Manual*, Turner-Fairbank Highway Research Center, McLean, VA, USA.

Richard, C.M., Morgan, J.F., Bacon, L.P., Graving, J., Divekar, G. and Lichty, M.G. (2015), "Multiple Sources of Safety Information from V2v and V2i: Redundancy, Decision Making, and Trust—Safety Message Design Report", United States: Federal Highway Administration. Office of Research, McLean, VA, USA.

SAE. (2018), "Taxonomy and definitions for terms related to driving automation systems for on-road motor vehicles", Available at: https://www.sae.org/standards/content/j3016_201806/ (Accessed 13 November 2023).

Subramanian, H. (1996), "Estimation of Car-Following Models", Ph.D. Thesis, Massachusetts Institute of Technology, Cambridge, MA, USA.

Tang, Q., Dagley, G., Ghamsari, A., Price, M. and Hoover, J. (2020), "Automatic vehicle configuration based on sensor data", *Google Patents*.

Tettamanti, T. and Varga, I. (2012), "Development of road traffic control by using integrated VISSIM-MATLAB simulation environment", *Periodica Polytechnica Civil Engineering*, Vol. 56, No. 1, pp. 43–49.

Toledo, T., Koutsopoulos, H.N. and Ben-Akiva, M. (2007), "Integrated driving behavior modeling", *Transportation Research Part C: Emerging Technologies*, Vol. 15, No. 2, pp. 96–112.

Van Arem, B., Van Driel, C.J. and Visser, R. (2006), "The impact of cooperative adaptive cruise control on traffic-flow characteristics", *IEEE Transactions on Intelligent Transportation Systems*, Vol. 7, No. 4, pp. 429–436.

Weiss, D.J. and Weidman, J. (2012), "5 Ways the Obama administration revived the auto industry by reducing oil use". Center for American Progress.

Wiedemann, R. (1974), "Simulation des Strassenverkehrsflusses."

Wiedemann, R. and Reiter, U. (1992), "Microscopic traffic simulation: The simulation system MIS-SION, background and actual state", *Project ICARUS (V1052) Final Report*, Vol. 2, pp. 1–53.

Wu, J., Xu, H., Tian, Y., Zhang, Y., Zhao, J. and Lv, B. (2020), "An automatic lane identification method for the roadside light detection and ranging sensor", *Journal of Intelligent Transportation Systems*, Vol. 24, No. 5, pp. 467–479.

Yang, X. (2020), "Cumulative-anticipative Car-following Model for Enhanced Safety in Autonomous Vehicles", Master Thesis, North Dakota State University, Fargo, ND, USA.

Yang, X., Ahemd, H.U., Huang, Y. and Lu, P. (2023), "Cumulatively anticipative car-following model with enhanced safety for autonomous vehicles in mixed driver environments", *Smart Cities*, Vol. 6, No. 5, pp. 2260–2281.

Younsi, M., Diaf, M. and Siarry, P. (2020), "Automatic multiple moving humans detection and tracking in image sequences taken from a stationary thermal infrared camera", *Expert Systems with Applications*, Vol. 146, p. 113171.

1.8

EXAMINING THE PRESENCE OF INTELLIGENT DESIGN IN LOW-TECH AND HIGH-TECH DESIGNS LEADING TO ECO-TECH SMART ARCHITECTURAL DESIGN STRATEGIES

Shari G. Grant

Abstract

This chapter explores the development of Eco-Tech design strategies by examining three distinct types of sites.

Analyzing two types of UNESCO sites is a heuristic device to determine elements of good Eco-Tech design.

A World Heritage Site illuminates the origins of many Low-Tech designs in vernacular architecture.

A Biosphere Reserve illustrates the necessity of controlling many aspects of the site. Factors include the conservation of ecosystems, sustainability of materials used, and consideration of the global nature of architectural design.

A mid-century building and campus exemplify a project where time has proven the value of intelligent architectural design.

The future of architecture rests on looking forward and incorporating current concerns like climate change/action and Eco-Tech Designs, while at the same time using knowledge and design strategies has proven valuable from the past. Wise and Smart, Intelligent Design is the goal.

Definition of Terms

Before focusing on the fascinating topic of Low-Tech and High-Tech designs leading to Eco-Tech and the concepts of Intelligent and Smart Design, let's review some inherent terminology so that we can build on a common foundation of understanding.

DOI: 10.4324/9781003384113-16

Intelligent Design: Intelligent Design is a theory that suggests that designing intelligence created matter, various forms of life, and the world (Merriam et al. Accessed 11/7/23). The term "Intelligent Design" can have different meanings in various fields. In the context of architecture, it usually refers to projects that utilize materials wisely and ensure a positive interaction of the structure with the site, resulting in an environmentally sound, sustainable, and pleasant environment for occupants. In a more specific context within architecture, "Intelligent Design" can also refer to incorporating artificial intelligence into the design process (Nikesh, 2014).

Low-Tech: Low-Tech refers to technology that is simple and not sophisticated (Merriam et al. Accessed 11/7/23). The approach is about reducing technological intensity and complexity, maintaining, and improving what already exists, and providing access to solutions to a larger number of people while controlling their usage. We can help ensure that we use technology in a socially responsible and sustainable way (Faucon and Bonjean 2022).

High-Tech: High-Tech refers to the advanced or sophisticated devices and systems produced, or utilized through, scientific technology, particularly employing electronics and computers (Merriam et al. Accessed 11/7/23). High-Tech involves high technology and represents the most current and cutting-edge technologies available. High-Tech is the opposite of low technology which is old-fashioned and commonly used. As High-Tech becomes outdated, it eventually becomes Low-Tech.

Eco-Tech: Ecotechnology or Eco-Tech seeks to fulfill human needs using high-tech forms and materials while being very aware of not harming the environment. Sustainable engineering (and architecture) that attempts not to damage ecosystems and ensures conservation of biodiversity, while being ever mindful of ecology, are forms of Ecotechnology (Slessor Smith, 2001).

Smart Architectural Design: Smart Design utilizes advanced technologies and tools to improve the efficiency and sustainability of architectural projects. This approach looks at both functional and aesthetic considerations creating intelligently designed structures and seeking the optimization of building designs throughout their lifecycle.

Sustainability: The most quote definition is, "Sustainable development is development that meets the needs of the present without compromising the ability of future generations to meet their own needs" (UN World Commission on Environment and Development).

Design Thinking: Design thinking is a problem-solving and innovation approach anchored around human-centered design. It gained popularity in the modern business world after Tim Brown published an article in the Harvard Business Review (Datar, 2021).

Networked Building Sensors: Networked building sensors provide a data feedback loop that enables architects, designers, and engineers to create innovative, sophisticated, and streamlined projects. Optimized or intelligent architectural design results in less construction waste, improved building operations, safer, more comfortable buildings, and more resilient and responsive homes, offices, and public spaces (P. Sisson).

Life Cycle Assessment: Life Cycle Assessment is a scientific approach used to analyze the overall environmental impact of projects. It takes into account all stages of a project's life cycle, not just energy consumption (source: www.aquamation.com).

Mitigation: Measures to reduce the amount and rate of future climate change by reducing emissions of heat-trapping gases (primarily carbon dioxide) or removing greenhouse gases from the atmosphere.

Adaptation: The process of adjusting to an actual or expected environmental change and its effects in a way that seeks to moderate harmful impact or exploit beneficial opportunities.

Resilience: The ability to prepare for threats and hazards, adapt to changing conditions, and withstand and recover rapidly from adverse conditions and disruptions.

Introduction

In this chapter, we explore the concepts of Intelligent and Eco-Tech designs, which both involve considering the overall system in its entirety.

The basis of Eco-Tech architectural design is that the building is a small part of the surrounding environment; therefore, it must perform as part of an ecosystem and get incorporated into the life cycle (Slessor Smith, 2001).

In this chapter, we trace the development of Eco-Tech design strategies. As a heuristic technique, we provide examples of how two types of UNESCO sites illustrate the importance of careful inclusivity of many factors in Intelligent Design.

We examine the meaning of Intelligent Design strategies in both Low-Tech and High-Tech designs, identifying the meaning of Smart Design in each methodology. Low-Tech designs can be found in vernacular architecture of many regions around the world, which have been using sophisticated Low-Tech methods in their indigenous architectural designs and practices (Kanaani, 2022).

A World Heritage Site is chosen as an example of how many Low-Tech designs are rooted in vernacular architecture.

A Biosphere Reserve demonstrates the need to control various aspects of the site, such as ecosystem conservation, material sustainability, and global architectural design considerations.

In addition, we explore the value of Intelligent Architectural Design proven over time by looking at a mid-century building and campus.

Finally, we emphasize the importance of incorporating current concerns such as climate change and Eco-Tech Designs while utilizing proven knowledge and design strategies from the past to inform the future of architecture.

Low-Tech Design Featured in a UNESCO World Heritage Site

UNESCO Biosphere Reserve sites are places with vernacular architecture perfectly adapted to preserving the surrounding land and environment while providing a traditional way of life supporting resident's social and environmental wellbeing (UNESCO).

These desirable goals will be shown to be an important part of Eco-Tech Smart Design Strategies. World Heritage Site illuminating origins of Low-Tech designs in vernacular architecture (Figure 1.8.1).

The village of Shirakawa-go is located in a mountainous region that was isolated from the rest of the world for an extended period. The large houses with steeply pitched thatched roofs in these villages have Gassho-style architecture, which is unique in Japan. Despite economic challenges, these villages are excellent examples of a traditional way of life that was perfectly adapted to the environment and the people's social and economic circumstances (UNESCO under license CC-BY-SA IGO 3.0.).

These beautiful remote Japanese villages are unique examples of Intelligent Design from the past, using Low-Tech and High-Tech designs (High-Tech for that period). The wise use of

Figure 1.8.1 Multipurpose building in Shirakawa-go, Japan, Photo © by Shari Grant 2007.

materials and positive interaction of the structures with the site were important considerations. The Eco-Tech smart architectural design strategy considered the overall system in its entirety, resulting in an environmentally sound and sustainable environment for the occupants.

The steep angle of the roofs is designed to allow most of the snow from heavy snowfalls to slide off to the ground. Additionally, the roofs are durable because of well-designed interior supports for the thatched roof structure. The construction ensured that the accumulated weight of the remaining snow could be supported.

Local plants and grasses gathered from the surrounding mountains at a particular time of the year were materials utilized to create the thatch for the roofs. The techniques of gathering, curing, and applying the thatch were all passed down through generations.

Three floors of attic space were constructed under the steeply pitched roof for rearing silkworms. The warm air rising from the human occupants and fireplaces on the bottom floors warmed the air for the silkworms in the cold winters. The sale of the precious silk worms became the primary economic support for the village. The villagers grew mulberry trees as food for the silkworms and surrounded their homes with small, irrigated rice paddies and gardens to grow their own food (UNESCO, Shirakawa-go and Okayama).

Even the placement of the houses and rice fields was carefully chosen for the geography. Water could be captured and retained for household use and irrigation. At the same time, erosion and formation of streams were prevented by placing the structures perpendicular to the downward slope of the land.

This World Heritage Site provides an excellent example of vernacular architecture, and it is fascinating to see how many low-tech designs are rooted in it.

Sustainability and Conservation of Ecosystems Exemplified in a UNESCO Biosphere Reserve Site

UNESCO Biosphere Reserve sites are established across the world as learning centers for sustainable development and conservation of ecosystems. These sites preserve the biodiversity of the region, even in the face of social changes, construction of buildings, and infrastructure (UNESCO). These goals are an essential part of Eco-Tech Smart Design Strategies (Figure 1.8.2).

UNESCO Biosphere Reserve sites around the world serve as educational hubs for sustainable development and ecosystem conservation. These sites represent an exemplary

Figure 1.8.2 Great Bear Lake, NWT, Canada, Part of the Tsa' Tue' UNESCO Biosphere Reserve, Photo © by Shari Grant 2006.

preservation of biodiversity, even in the face of social change and infrastructure construction. These goals align with Eco-Tech Smart Design Strategies.

One such site is the Tsa' Tue' UNESCO Biosphere Reserve in Canada's Northwest Territories. It is home to the Sahtuto'ine, or the "Bear Lake People," and it encompasses Great Bear Lake and its surrounding watershed. Great Bear Lake is the largest pristine Arctic lake in Canada and the world's eighth largest lake. Members of the Délı̨nę First Nation community are the main human residents of the region, and they rely on the wildlife and fish they harvest as a primary source of their food, making the ecological integrity of the lake and its watershed critical to their well-being (UNESCO, Tsa' Tue').

The community has been advocating for careful stewardship of Great Bear Lake for decades and serving as Indigenous protectors of the land since time immemorial. Maintaining the ecological integrity of Great Bear Lake and its watershed is of paramount importance to the Délı̨nę First Nation people. They consider the land part of themselves and define themselves by their relationship with it. In many ways, Délı̨nę is a traditional First Nation community that respects its elders and spiritual leaders (Sahtu Renewable Resources Board).

A Biosphere Reserve such as Tsa' Tue' demonstrates the importance of controlling all aspects of the site, including ecosystem conservation, material sustainability, and global architectural design considerations for Intelligent Design and ultimately to achieve Eco-Tech architectural design.

As global temperatures rise and climate change becomes more pronounced, it is important to try to analyze how much of the problem is caused by human activity that could potentially be controlled in response to the findings. The IEA Global Status Report for buildings and construction shows the statistic that this sector accounted for 36% of final energy use in 2019. In contrast to this high percentage of energy usage, a Biosphere Reserve represents a place where attempts are made to control what is built and maintain an overall balance between man and nature.

The Fifth National Climate Assessment by the United States government issued an encouraging statement saying "Large near-term cuts in greenhouse gas emissions are achievable through many currently available and cost-effective mitigation options" (Crimmins et al., 2023).

Smart Architectural Design Strategies in a Mid-Century Building & Campus

The Salk Institute in La Jolla is a mid-century example of Intelligent Design achieved using Low-Tech and High-Tech Designs, leading to an Eco-Tech Smart Architectural Design Strategy (Figure 1.8.3).

The internationally famous architect Louis I. Kahn designed the Salk Institute. He was an academic his entire life and had a private architectural practice. Kahn understood the power of vernacular architecture and understood many basic and ancient design principles (referred to as Low-Tech). Incorporated in the Salk Institute are Low-Tech concepts and High-Tech designs (which was advanced technology for the era of the building's construction).

The Salk Institute was chosen as a successful example as nearly 60 years have passed since the construction of the building. The passage of this much time is enough to truly understand and validate the inherent value of the Smart Architectural Design Strategies used in designing this memorable building and campus.

Figure 1.8.3 The Salk Institute, La Jolla, California, A Smart Architectural Design Strategy, Photo © by Shari Grant 2020.

Important Design Concepts incorporated into the conceptual development of the Salk Institute

"Shakkei"

Few people recognize that Kahn used an ancient Low-Tech design strategy in the basic design and layout of the Salk Institute Campus. The ancient landscape design concept was developed hundreds of years ago in Chinese Temple design, later adopted and used extensively in Japanese Temple design, creating areas of outstanding beauty!

This landscape design concept in Japanese is known as "Shakkei," which means "Borrowed Scenery" (Older, 2017). By framing a distant view, the object of interest in the distance is literally "captured" for a moment and brought into the area that the viewer is standing in. The distant view in Japan frequently consists of a mountain or temple.

Kahn carefully calculated the heights and depths of the building and structures of the Salk Institute to "capture" the breathtaking ocean view from the Salk Institute courtyard. As we stand in the courtyard looking out to the ocean, the ocean becomes part of the courtyard, and we are mesmerized by the beauty of the view. The ocean is no longer something beautiful "out there" but becomes part of what we experience in the Salk courtyard! Without Kahn's deep understanding of this ancient Low-Tech design principle, the Salk Institute could just have been another building with an ocean view.

Using these design principles created an inspired ambiance for the Salk Institute, encouraging scientific discoveries.

"Modularity"

The design principle of "Modularity" was utilized very effectively in the design of the Salk Institute. Vernacular architecture of many cultures utilizes the concept of modularity. The use of Japanese Tatami Mats laid out to design the shape of rooms and passageways in buildings is a familiar example.

The repeating shapes, sizes of elements, and modularity are pleasing to the eye at the Salk Institute. The modularity, which is efficient during construction, continues to facilitate effective and easy maintenance of the buildings. The use of the principles of modularity has led in part to the magic of the Salk Institute Campus.

"Vierendeel Trusses"

In 1896, Professor A. Vierendeel proposed a new metal girder for bridges, which was I-shaped with no diagonals and was more economical to build. The metal Vierendeel trusses became very familiar to August Komendant, a brilliant European structural engineer who later came to America.

Komendant was Kahn's structural engineer on many projects, including the Salk Institute. He was innovative and experienced with prestressed concrete. Based on what Komendant knew about metal Vierendeel trusses and his knowledge of prestressed concrete, he combined this knowledge to make a radical proposal for designing the enormous trusses that made the column-free spaces in the Salk Laboratories possible (Komendant, 1975). Using these concrete trusses became the cutting edge of intelligent high-tech design in the early 1960s. It facilitated the intelligent design of the Salk Institute Eco-Tech Smart Architectural Design Strategy.

The colossal concrete Vierendeel trusses used in the construction of the Salk Institute are the most crucial structural innovations in this building and were developed specifically to accommodate the unique requirements of the Salk laboratories. The evolution of these unique structural elements can be traced from low-tech metal elements in the 1930s on bridges in Belgium to High-Tech, innovative, and latest state-of-the-art concrete structural elements for the Salk in the 1960s.

"Innovative Flexibility"

The Salk laboratories are designed to be flexible and can accommodate changes. The building can be easily updated with the latest technology, necessary repairs and improvements, and reconfiguring workspaces without interfering with the work of the scientists. The building continues to remain innovative and new.

The incorporation of these design principles makes the Salk Institute rank among the top 10 of the 25 most significant works of post-war architecture in the world (Soller and Snyder, 2021). Smart architectural design strategies used in the innovative design of the Salk Institute have proven to be successful for almost 60 years now and have passed the test of time.

Conclusions

Architecture's success is determined by evaluating its life cycle and impact. Successful design strategies combine past and present techniques, including the latest technological advancements and traditional building methods. It is crucial to anticipate future challenges while addressing the present ones. The incorporation of proven design strategies is equally essential.

This chapter highlights the evolution of High-Tech designs to Eco-Tech and the incorporation of sustainability into design ideas. These hybrid designs combine low-Tech and

High-Tech methodologies, resulting in Intelligent Design solutions. The designs address regional and climate-specific needs and peculiarities. In the process of its evolution, High-Tech design has leaned increasingly to extreme functionalism, and the incorporation of Smart Design concepts as well (Kanaani, 2022).

There are alternative paths to solve our current environmental issues, and one such proposal is "Low Tech Architecture." "The (Re)Discovery of Sustainable Buildings" (Vesting, 2022) published after the Covid pandemic. This text offers a hopeful alternative solution for the future of architecture.

Our cities are dominated by buildings made of mineral building materials such as concrete and steel, whose raw materials endanger ecosystems during extraction and are very CO2-intensive in production. By contrast, low-tech architecture strategies offer solutions for reacting to climate change and the energy crisis. Low-tech architecture provides an opportunity in times of climate change and does not reduce the standard of living and quality. Furthermore, they provide a healthy indoor climate with simple means and natural building materials. The use of almost maintenance-free techniques also increases well-being in everyday life. Over the long term, low tech is not only more resource-efficient but also more cost-effective.

(Vesting, 2022)

The future of architecture requires a forward-looking approach that incorporates mitigating features for current concerns while using past knowledge and design strategies that have proven valuable through time.

Smart Design thinking in Eco-Tech architectural design strategies is based on ecological considerations, as well as Intelligent Design found in both current High-Tech design innovations and past Low-Tech design successes.

References

Books

Kanaani, M. (2022). *A Prospective for Smart Design Thinking in Architecture & Urbanism for a Sustainable Living Planet*. To be published as a Routledge Companion, NewYork, NY: Taylor & Francis.

Komendant, A. E. (1975). *18 Years with Architect Louis I Kahn*. Englewood, NJ: Aloray.

Slessor Smith, C. (2001). *Eco-Tech: Sustainable Architecture*. London: Thames & Hudson Ltd.

Online

Crimmins, A. USGCRP. (2023). *Fifth National Climate Assessment*. U.S. Global Change Research Program, Washington, DC. https://doi.org/10.7930/NCA5.2023.

Datar, S. (2021). https://www.online.hbs.edul Design Thinking Course.

Faucon, T. and Bonjean, A. (2022). https://www.oecd-forum.org/posts/what-do-we-mean-by-low-tech

Grammarly. https://app.grammarly.com/?affiliateNetwork=sas&affiliateID=2081315.

High-Tech. https://www.merrianwebster.com/dictionarywebster.com/dictionary/high%20tech. Accessed 27 September 2023.

How big is Canada? Fun facts about its size|Canadian Affair. https://www.canadianaffair.com/blog/how-big-is-canada/.

Low-Tech. https://www.meriam-webstercom/dictionary/low-tech. Accessed September 27, 2023
Older, Tom (2017). *Shakkei*. https://www.treehugger.com/art-shakkei-or-borrowed-scenery-4863268.
Sahtu Renewable Resources Board. (SRRB)—Déline. https://www.srrb.nt.ca/ehdzo-got-ne/de-l-ne.
Sisson, P. https://www.autodesk.com/design-make/articles/smart- architecture
Soller, K. and Snyder, M. (2021). https://www.nytimes.com/by/kurt-soller.
UNESCO Biosphere Reserves. https://www.unesco.org/en/mab/wnbr/about
Tsa Tue. https://en.unesco.org/biosphere/eu-na/tsa-tue
Tsa Tue. http://tsatue.ca/about-us/
UNESCO World Heritage Sites. *Shirakawa-go and Gokayama*. https://whc.unesco.org/en/list/734
Vesting, N. (2022). Low Tech Architecture. The (Re)discovery of Sustainable Buildings. https://ndion.
    de/en/low-tech-architecture-the-rediscovery-of-sustainable-buildings/

1.9

TOWARD PERFORMATIVE, ENVIRONMENTALLY RESPONSIVE ARCHITECTURE

Branko Kolarevic

Introduction

Addressing the building's appearance ("how it looks") and its performance ("what it does") requires creating environmentally attuned buildings, whose overall spatial and formal configuration is shaped by environmental performance with respect to light, heating, and cooling, embodied and operational energy, etc. Over the past two decades, we have also seen an increasing interest in exploring the capacity of built spaces to change, i.e., to respond dynamically—and automatically—to changes in the external and internal environments and to different patterns of use. The emphasis started to shift from the building's scenographic appearance to processes of formation grounded in imagined performances, indeterminate patterns and dynamics of use, and poetics of spatial and temporal change. In such a context, the role of architects and engineers is less to predict, pre-program, or represent the building's performances than it is to instigate, embed, diversify, and multiply their effects in material and in time.

Performativity

In the late 1950s, performance emerged in humanities—in linguistic and cultural anthropology in particular—and in other fields as a fundamental concept of wide impact. It shifted the perception of culture as a relatively static collection of artifacts to a web of interactions, a dynamic network of intertwined, multilayered processes that contest the fixity of form, structure, value, or meaning. Social and cultural phenomena were seen as being constituted, shaped, and transformed by continuous, temporal processes defined by fluidity and mediation; thus, a *performative* approach to contemporary culture emerged.

As a paradigm in architecture, performance can be understood in those terms as well; its origins can be also traced to the social, technological, and cultural milieu of the mid-twentieth century. The utopian designs of the architectural avant-garde of the 1960s and early 1970s, such as Archigram's "soft cities," robotic metaphors, and quasi-organic urban landscapes, offered images of fantasies based on mechanics and pop culture. As

 DOI: 10.4324/9781003384113-17

early precedents, they have particular resonance today, as performative architecture can be described as having the capacity to respond to changing social, cultural, and technological conditions by perpetually reformatting itself. Its spatial program is not singular, fixed, or static, but multiple, fluid, and ambiguous, driven by temporal dynamics of socio-economic, cultural, and technological shifts. In performative architecture, culture, technology, and space form a complex, *active* web of connections, a network of interrelated constructs that affect each other simultaneously and continually. In performative architecture, space unfolds in *indeterminate* ways, in contrast to the fixity of predetermined, programmed actions, events, and effects (Kolarevic, 2004).

The description of performative architecture given above is one of many—its paradigmatic appeal lies precisely in the multiplicity of meanings associated with the performative in architecture. Performance, however, is one of the most used (oftentimes misused and abused) but least defined concepts in architecture; the ways in which performance is understood in architecture are often contradictory; the meanings associated with it are often articulated as opposites. Framed within an expanded context, performative architecture can be indeed defined very broadly—its meaning spans multiple realms, from financial, spatial, social, and cultural to purely technical (structural, thermal, acoustical, etc.). In other words, the performative in architecture is operative on many levels, beyond just the aesthetic or the utilitarian. Much of the current interest in performance as a design paradigm is largely due to the developments in technology and the presence of sustainability as a defining socio-economic issue.

Adaptive, Responsive, Performative...

As the external socio-economic, cultural, and technological context changes, so do conceptions of space, shape, and form in architecture, as discussed previously. Over the past two decades, we have seen an increasing interest in exploring the capacity of built spaces to change, i.e., to respond dynamically—and automatically—to changes in the external and internal environments and to different patterns of use. The principal idea is that two-way relationships could be established among the spaces, the environment, and the users: the users or the changes in the environment would affect the configuration of space and vice versa; the result is an architecture that self-adjusts to the needs of the users. Different terms have been used to describe such architecture: adaptive, dynamic, interactive, responsive, performative, etc.

The first concepts of such architecture were born in the late 1960s and early 1970s, primarily as a result of developments in cybernetics, artificial intelligence, and information technologies. Archigram's *Walking City* hypothetical project from 1964 imagined cities as giant mobile, transformable robotic structures that could move to wherever their resources were needed. Intelligent, robotic buildings—self-contained "living pods"—would move within the cities; the pods were envisioned as independent, yet parasitic: they would "plug in" to way stations to replenish resources, moving, connecting, and disconnecting as instructed. The cities could interconnect to form larger metropolises or disconnect and disperse as required or desired.

While Archigram was among the first to envision "alive," changeable buildings and cities capable of interacting among themselves and with their occupants, Gordon Pask, as an early proponent of cybernetics in architecture, is often credited with setting the foundations for interactive environments in the 1960s with his concept of *Conversation Theory*, intended as a comprehensive theory of interaction (Pask, 1969). Pask's ideas had a tremendous influence on both Cedric Price and Nicholas Negroponte, with whom he collaborated. Cedric Price adopted concepts from cybernetics to articulate the concept of "anticipatory architecture," demonstrated by his seminal *Fun Palace* and *Generator* projects. Nicholas Negroponte proposed that computing power be integrated into buildings so that they could perform better, turning buildings into "architecture machines" that are "'assisted,' 'augmented,' and eventually 'replicated' by a computer" (Negroponte, 1975); the aim was to "consider the physical environment as an evolving mechanism." In the last chapter, he predicted that "architecture machines" (in the distant future) "won't help us design; instead, we will live in them."

At roughly the same time that Negroponte was working on his "architecture machines," Charles Eastman developed the concept of "adaptive-conditional architecture," which self-adjusts, based on the feedback from the spaces and the users (Eastman, 1972). Eastman proposed that automated systems could control buildings' responses. He used the analogy of a thermostat to describe the essential components: *sensors* that would register changes in the environment, *control mechanisms* (or algorithms) that would interpret sensor readings, *actuators* as devices that would produce changes in the environment, and a device (an *interface*) that would let users enter their preferences. That is roughly the component make-up of any reactive system developed to date.

After much initial interest in the late 1960s and early 1970s, not much happened in the next two decades, with the exception of Jean Nouvel's *Institut du Monde Arabe*, completed in 1989 in Paris, as the first significant, large-scale building to have an adaptive, responsive façade. With greater attention to buildings' energy demands and increasing capacity to monitor and manage energy use, the building envelope became the locus of technological innovation in the late 1990s. As emphasis shifted away from simply creating energy barriers (to block heat gain or heat loss) toward harvesting energy from the environment and channeling it where it is needed, architects and engineers started to incorporate electronically controlled, mechanically activated shading and ventilation systems into building façades. Double-skin façades with a controlled vented air cavity and operable, integrated shades or blinds started to emerge in the 1990s. Then over the last two decades, adaptive, kinetic, or dynamic façades, active and high-performance building envelopes entered architecture's vocabulary—and practice.

The key focus in designing adaptive envelopes is better management of energy flows, both from the exterior environment into the buildings and from the interior spaces of the building to the outside, with the overall goals being the improvement of the building's performance and the user comfort inside the building (Kolarevic and Parlac, 2015). The adaptive behavior of the envelopes can be visible or invisible (or both); in addition to components that move literally, such as the shades or vents, air (or water) would move as directed, and thermal energy would flow through different materials as designed. The visible adaptive behavior could lead to an urban spectacle that can add performative dimensions to the project that go beyond the scale of the building. While the literal movement of components is not an end in itself in many architectural projects that incorporate environmental responsiveness, it is often exploited to make the buildings appear "alive."

To imbue building skins with dynamic, changing behavior, their elements need to be *actuated*, i.e., moved, rotated, expanded, shrunk, twisted, etc., so that the desired performance objectives are met. What differentiates adaptive building skins is not so much what is actuated (and that matters greatly), but how that actuation is produced. There are essentially four different methods of actuation in building envelopes: (1) motor-based; (2) hydraulic; (3) pneumatic; and (4) material-based (Kolarevic and Parlac, 2015). Most of the automated adaptive façade systems deployed to date rely on motor-based, i.e., mechanical actuation. There is increasing use of pneumatic actuation, primarily with patterned, multilayer ETFE-based systems in which hermetically sealed air chambers can be inflated or deflated to create different shading densities. There are also ongoing experiments in material-based actuation, which offer the promise of "zero energy" dynamic building envelopes, which are years away from large-scale commercial applications.

The notions of adaptivity and responsiveness are not limited to building envelopes only. There is an emerging interest in dynamic structures that could enable buildings to change their overall shape and internal configuration, either in response to environmental conditions or different programmatic or use arrangements. If not changing its shape, the building, for example, could reorient itself through rotation so that it always presents a smaller surface area to the sun, as was proposed by OMA in 2005 for a large office building in Dubai. The *Sharifi-ha House* (2013) in Tehran, Iran, designed by Nextoffice (Alireza Taghaboni), features entire rooms that rotate in and out of the building's volume to either open or close it, exposing or protecting the interior from the seasonal weather; the turning mechanism used in the house is a commonly used one for rotating theatrical set-ups and turning car exhibits in showrooms.

Rotation is one simple way of transforming, reconfiguring, or reorienting building components (or even entire buildings). Translation along a linear path, horizontally or vertically, is another straightforward way to transform a building on the outside or inside. The *Sliding House* in Suffolk, UK, designed by dRMM and completed in 2009, features an enclosure that can move along recessed tracks to cover or uncover different buildings along its 28-m long linear path: the house, garage, or annex. In a similar fashion, the *Shed* in New York (2019), designed by Diller Scofidio + Renfro, features a 120-foot high, ETFE-covered structure that can come out from the main building volume and roll over the plaza in front of it.

Others are exploring adaptivity and responsiveness in architecture at the other end of the scale—that of materials—and are relying on changing the properties of materials to create an adaptive response in building surfaces and systems (Parlac, 2015). Then, there are issues related to building "intelligence," i.e., controlling the various adaptive responses in buildings and managing potential conflicts that may arise in operation.

Performance-Based Design

As mentioned earlier, the growing interest in building performance as a design paradigm is largely due to the emergence of sustainability as a defining socio-economic issue and to the recent developments in adaptive building systems. Within such context, building performance can be defined very broadly, across multiple realms, from financial, spatial, social, and cultural to purely technical (structural, thermal, acoustical, etc.). The issues of performance (in all its multiple manifestations) are considered not in isolation or some kind of linear progression but *simultaneously* and are engaged early in the conceptual stages of the project, by relying on close collaboration between the many parties involved in the design of a building. In such a highly "networked" design context, digital quantitative and qualitative performance-based simulations are used as a technological foundation for a comprehensive new approach to the design of the built environment (Kolarevic, 2004).

It is important to note that performance-based design should not be seen as simply a way of devising a set of practical solutions to a set of largely practical problems, i.e., it should not be reduced to some kind of neo-functionalist approach to architecture. The emphasis shifts to the processes of form generation based on performative strategies of design that are grounded on one end, in intangibilities such as cultural performance and, on the other, in quantifiable and qualifiable performative aspects of building design, such as structure, acoustics, or environmental design. Determining the different performative aspects in a particular project and reconciling often conflicting performance goals in a creative and effective way are some of the key challenges in performance-based design.

Addressing the building's appearance ("how it looks") and its performance ("what it does") increasingly requires creating environmentally attuned buildings, whose overall spatial and formal configuration is shaped by environmental performance with respect to light, heating and cooling, embodied energy, etc. Earlier this century there was a gap in the aesthetics (and ethics) between form-oriented or cultural performance-oriented designers (Frank Gehry, Zaha Hadid, etc.) and those whose work aimed unapologetically at environmental performance (Thomas Herzog, Glenn Murcutt, etc.). On the other hand, there was another group of designers—the ones whose work is neither too formalist nor environmentalist (Foster, Grimshaw, Piano, Sauerbruch, Hutton, etc.). The design strategies in the projects of the latter group vary considerably as they respond to different cultural and environmental contexts. In many of their projects, formal and environmental performative agendas were successfully pursued in parallel. In the St. Mary Axe project in London (1997–2004) by Foster and Partners, one of the design goals was to maximize the daylight and natural ventilation in order to substantially reduce (by half) the amount of energy the building needed for its operation. The spiraling form of the atria at the perimeter, which runs the entire height of the building, was designed to generate pressure differentials that greatly assist the natural flow of air. The aerodynamic, curvilinear form, besides affording a commanding, iconic presence, enables the wind to flow smoothly around this high-rise building, minimizing wind loads on the structure and cladding, and enabling the use of a more efficient structure. In addition, the wind is not deflected to the ground, as is common with rectilinear buildings, helping to maintain pedestrian comfort at the base of the building.

It is interesting to note that many of the designers mentioned earlier—notably Norman Foster and Nicholas Grimshaw, once labeled High-Tech and renamed Eco-Tech by Catherine Slessor (1998)—have explicitly stated their intentions to improve the environmental performance of their often highly visible buildings. While one could question the methodological consistency in their projects and whether certain performative aspects, such as energy efficiency, were indeed maximized, these architects did manage to consistently push the technological envelope of environmental performance in their buildings.

Reactive, Interactive, Participatory Architecture

The primary goal of constructing a truly responsive, adaptive architecture is to imbue buildings with the capacity to interact with the environment and their users in an engaging way. Architecture that echoes the work of Nicholas Negroponte could be understood as an adaptive, responsive machine—a sensory, actuated, performative assemblage of spatial and technical systems that creates an environment that stimulates and is, in turn, stimulated by users' interactions and their behavior. Arguably, for any such system to be continually engaging, it has to be designed as inherently indeterminate in order to produce unpredictable outcomes. The user should have an effect on the system's behavior or its outcome and, more importantly, on how that behavior or outcome is computed. That requires that both inputs and outputs of the systems be constructed on the fly. It is this capacity to construct inputs and outputs that distinguishes interactive from merely reactive systems.

The distinction between interactive and reactive is what enables adaptive, responsive architecture to be seen as an enabler of new relations between people and spaces. When Philip Beesley and his colleagues describe a responsive environment in *Responsive Architectures: Subtle Technologies* as a "networked structure that senses action within a field of attention and responds dynamically with programmed and designed logic" (Beesley et al., 2006), they are referring to what is essentially a reactive system. In contrast, Michael Fox and Miles Kemp argue in *Interactive Architecture* that the interaction is circular—systems "interact" instead of just "react" (Fox and Kemp, 2009). The distinction between interaction and reaction (i.e., a system's response) is not clear-cut, because a dynamic action of a component, for example, could be seen not simply as a reaction but also as a part of the overall scenarios of interactivity. Tristan D'Estree Sterk distinguishes direct manipulation (deliberate control), automation (reflexive control), and hybridized models as forms of interaction between the users and the technologies behind responsive systems (Sterk, 2006). For Sterk, "The hybridized model can also be used to produce responses that have adjustable response criteria, achieving this by using occupant interactions to build contextual models of how users occupy and manipulate space." As Usman Haque puts it, the goal is "a model of interaction where an individual can directly adjust the way that a machine responds to him or her so that they can converge on a mutually agreeable nature of feedback: an architecture that learns from the inhabitant just as the inhabitant learns from the architecture" (Haque, 2007).

Thus, one of the principal challenges is how to construct (Paskian) systems that would provide enough variety to keep users engaged, while avoiding randomness, which could lead to disengagement if the output cannot be understood. The key challenge is to design an architecture that avoids boredom and retains a high degree of novelty. As observed by Haque, "Unlike the efficiency-oriented pattern-optimization approach taken by many responsive environmental systems, an architecture built on Pask's system would continually encourage novelty and provoke conversational relationships with human participants" (Haque, 2007).

When it comes to designing adaptive, responsive environments, the "software" side does not seem to present as many challenges as the "hardware" side, the building itself, in which the majority of systems is inherently inflexible. That is perhaps where the biggest challenges and opportunities exist, as buildings would have to be conceptually completely rethought in order to enable them to adapt (i.e., to reconfigure themselves). Then there is the "middleware" that sits among the software and hardware and the users as devices that facilitate the feedback loops between the components of the system. Other, more operational-based challenges have to do with the resolution of potential conflicts within systems. For example, Sterk discusses the coordination of responses at the coincidence, i.e., shared boundaries between spaces, as in a movable partition wall between two spaces, which can have actuators accessible through two independent control processes (Sterk, 2006).

Another issue is that while change is desirable, for most purposes, it would have to occur in predictable and easily anticipated ways. If that is not possible, then there ought to be a way (in certain circumstances) for users to preview changes before they are executed, or to choose among alternatives for one (perhaps suboptimal) that fits the current circumstances, needs, and/or desires. Users may need to be informed of the impact that selected changes would have on the environment or the shape and configuration of the space. The overall issue of control is critical, as was already mentioned. In *Smart Architecture*, Ed van Hinte warns that "sometimes a simple and hence ostensibly 'dumb' building is smarter than a technology-dominated living-and-working machine over which the user has lost control" (van Hinte et al., 2003).

Some fundamental questions have yet to be adequately addressed. For example, while Beesley and his colleagues predict, that "the next generation of architecture will be able to sense, change and transform itself" (Beesley et al., 2006), they fail to say clearly toward what ends. Even though they ask what very well may be the key question—how do responsive systems affect us?—they do not attempt to answer it explicitly. Similarly, Fox and Kemp, in their *Interactive Architecture* book, avoid explaining fully—and admit as much— why interactive systems are necessary, meaningful, or useful, and simply state, "the motivation to make these systems is found in the desire to create spaces and objects that can meet changing needs with respect to evolving individual, social, and environmental demands." Fox and Kemp position interactive architecture "as a transitional phenomenon with respect to a movement from a mechanical paradigm to a biological paradigm," which, as they explain, "requires not just pragmatic and performance-based technological understandings, but awareness of aesthetic, conceptual and philosophical issues relating to humans and the global environment."

Architecture of Change = Architecture of Time

Accepting the dynamics of buildings and cities ... can turn architectural change into an ecologically efficient process as well as a new urban experience.

(Ed van Hinte, et al., Smart Architecture)

If we were to accept change as a fundamental contextual condition—and time as an essential design dimension—architecture could then begin to truly mediate between the built environment and the people who occupy it. As Ed van Hinte and his colleagues note, "Instead of being merely the producer of a unique three-dimensional product, architects should see themselves as programmers of a process of spatial change." The principal task for architects is to create "a field of change and modification" that would generate possibilities instead of fixed conditions. The inhabitable space would then become an indeterminate design environment, subject to continuous processes of change, occurring in different realms and at various time scales:

It is the form that is no longer stable, that is ready to accept change. Its temporary state is determined by the circumstances of the moment based on an activated process and in-built intelligence and potential for change. Not product architecture then, but a process-based architecture whose form is defined by its users' dynamic behavior and changing demands and by the changing external and internal conditions; an architecture that itself has the characteristics of an ecological system, that emulates nature instead of protecting it and therefore engages in a enduring fusion of nature and culture.

As Ed van Hinte and his colleagues point out, "That would be a truly ground-breaking ecological architecture." But to get there, we need to first answer some fundamental questions pertaining to change as a conceptual and time as a phenomenological dimension in architecture. We need to go beyond the current fascination with mechatronics and explore what change means in architecture and how it is manifested: buildings weather, programs change, envelopes adapt, interiors are reconfigured, and systems replaced. We need to explore the kinds of changes that buildings should undergo and the scale and speed at which they occur. We need to examine which changes are necessary, useful, desirable, possible …

In short, much remains to be done we would argue that change—and time as a design dimension in architecture—are far from being adequately addressed or explored theoretically, experimentally, or phenomenologically. As we probe and embed performativity, adaptability, interactivity, and responsiveness into the buildings and spaces, we must not unconditionally and blindly chase the latest technological advancements.

Conclusions

Performative architecture is not a way of devising a set of practical solutions to a set of largely practical problems. It is a "meta-narrative" with universal aims that are dependent on particular performance-related aspects of each project. Determining the different performative aspects in a particular project and reconciling often conflicting performance goals in a creative and effective way are some of the key challenges in this approach to architecture.

In performative architecture, the emphasis shifts from the building's appearances to processes of formation grounded in imagined performances, indeterminate patterns and dynamics of use, and poetics of spatial and temporal change. The role of architects and engineers is less to predict, pre-program, or represent the building's performances than it is to instigate, embed, diversify, and multiply their effects in material and in time.

The development of more performative techniques of design is essential to this task. It necessitates a shift from scenographic appearances to pragmatist imagination of how buildings work, what they do, and what actions, events, and effects they might engender in time.

Acknowledgments

Parts of this chapter have previously been published by the author.

References

Beesley, Philip, Hirosue, S., Ruxton, J., Trankle, M. and Turner, C. (2006). *Responsive Architectures: Subtle Technologies*. Toronto, ON: Riverside Architectural Press.

Eastman, Charles (1972). "Adaptive-Conditional Architecture," in N. Cross (ed.), *Design Participation: Proceedings of the Design Research Society Conference*. London: Academy Editions, pp. 51–57.

Fox, Michael and Kemp, Miles (2009). *Interactive Architecture*. New York: Princeton Architectural Press.

Haque, Usman (2007). "The Architectural Relevance of Gordon Pask," in Lucy Bullivant (ed.), *4dsocial: Interactive Design Environments, Architectural Design*, no. 77. London: Wiley Academy, pp. 54–61.

Kolarevic, Branko (2004). "Towards the Performative in Architecture," in B. Kolarevic and A. Malkawi (eds.), *Performative Architecture: Beyond Instrumentality*. London and New York: Routledge, pp. 203–214.

Kolarevic, Branko and Parlac, Vera (2015). "*Adaptive, Responsive Building Skins,*" in B. Kolarevic and V. Parlac (eds.), *Building Dynamics: Exploring Architecture of Change*. London and New York: Routledge, pp. 69–88.

Negroponte, Nicholas (1975). *Soft Architecture Machines*. Cambridge, MA: MIT Press.

Parlac, Vera (2015). "Material as Mechanism in Agile Spaces," in B. Kolarevic and V. Parlac (eds.), *Building Dynamics: Exploring Architecture of Change*. London and New York: Routledge, pp. 177–190.

Pask, Gordon (1969). "Architectural Relevance of Cybernetics," in *Architectural Design*, vol. 39, no. 9, pp. 494–496, London: Standard Catalogue Company.

Slessor, Catherine (1998). *Eco-Tech: Sustainable Architecture and High Technology*. London: Thames and Hudson.

Sterk, Tristan d'Estree (2006). "Responsive Architecture: User-Centered Interactions within the Hybridized Model of Control," in *GameSetandMatch II: On Computer Games, Advanced Geometries and Digital Technologies*. Rotterdam, the Netherlands: Episode Publishers, pp. 494–501.

van Hinte, Ed, Neelen, Marc, Vink, Jacques and Vollaard, Piet (2003). *Smart Architecture*. Amsterdam: 010 Publishers.

1.10

SMART URBAN RESILIENCY CONCEPTS AND GOALS

How Can Cities Become Smart but also Sustainable and Resilient

Shabtai Isaac, Miquel Casals, Silvio Carta and Blanca Tejedor

Abstract

As urban complexity grows and societal challenges are increasingly complex to address, urban resilience becomes a key factor to enhance our cities. This is particularly relevant when cities are analyzed under the lens of smart approaches to urbanism and Artificial Intelligence (AI) and data-driven city models. The adoption of urban resilience approach leads to communities with a better quality of life and improved environmental conditions toward a general sustainable development of cities.

This chapter addresses the notion of urban resilience through the concepts of smart, data-driven, and sustainable cities. As a multi-faceted notion, urban resilience is broken down into three complementary approaches. First, urban resilience is presented as a quantifiable entity, discussed through advanced spatial approaches using AI, cyber security, and Machine Learning (ML) techniques. This part also includes the distinction between physical and digital elements of community resilience. Second, it is considered in its more original sense, that of response to extreme events in lifelines conditions with examples involving Geographic Information Systems (GIS), Building Information Modeling (BIM), and network analysis approaches. Finally, urban resilience is considered more technically a concerted approach to react to climate change/action, and natural disasters where new technologies and infrastructure management procedures are needed. Each part is supported by practical examples to help readers understand concrete applications in spatial terms.

Through this three-pronged approach, this chapter proposes a possible definition of urban resilience, focusing on ways in which cities can improve on their urban performance, with the desire to provide strategies and solutions for urban problems to provide a higher quality of human life.

Urban Resilience

In this chapter we introduce the concept of urban resilience in smart cities, discussing its goals and relevant characteristics. In particular, we address the question of how cities can become smart, sustainable, and resilient through a holistic approach.

In general terms, resilience is considered in this context the ability of urban systems to absorb external changes that is changes originating outside of the system itself. This definition draws from the more general description provided in the 1970s by Holling (1973), as well as more recent studies where resilience is contextualized within the realm of smart cities (e.g., Ribeiro and Gonçalves, 2019; Sharifi et al., 2022). The idea of smart cities implies a level of interconnectedness and networks within the urban context facilitated by (digital) technologies, as suggested by many authors, including Cugurullo (2018), Kitchin (2018), and Ferre-Bigorra et al. (2022). We elaborated on these notions further in first section.

This chapter is structured in three parts, where we gradually discuss the measurement, the analysis, and the management of urban resilience. In each part, we describe how the proposed approach addresses both tangible, physical, and technological aspects, as well as intangible, service-based, and procedural aspects.

The first part of this chapter focuses on quantitative aspects of resilience, explaining the metrics at play in both design and urban analysis. The second part focuses on a qualitative assessment of resilience. Through an in-depth analysis, we explain how the resilience of urban lifelines can be assessed in detail and increased to ensure an adequate response to extreme events. Finally, the third part focuses on the management of resilience, explaining how this can be monitored and controlled to better cope with climate change and natural disasters.

Measuring Resilience

Resilience as a Qualitative and Quantitative Framework

There are a large number of studies that characterize urban resilience as a qualitative phenomenon. In the context of urban studies, the term *resilience* can be quite generic and used in many different ways depending on the focus of the study. Bueno et al. (2021) supported that studies on urban resilience are certainly on the rise and can be clustered around cognate areas such as socio-economic and cultural studies, local governance resilience initiatives, and more generically research frameworks and review studies (Bueno et al., 2021:5–10). A quite general definition is provided by Wang et al. (2018), as the comprehensive ability of an urban complex system made up of several subsystems to take in, adapt to, and recover from a disruptive event. This latter can be intended not only as a physical disruption (natural disaster) but also as a social, financial, or health-related issue (e.g., COVID-19). The study of resilience is commonly related to a framework of reference that determines its characteristics. For example, resilience to disruption provoked by earthquakes is usually considered within the context of physical environments.

As the attempt to define urban resilience in a widely shared context can be a daunting task, most studies to date have made use of a framework (or a combination of frameworks) that considers a range of elements, from sociocultural to economic. The Oxfam GB Multi-Dimensional Approach to Measuring Resilience (Hughes and Bushell, 2013), the City Resilience Index (CRI), developed by ARUP and the Rockefeller Foundation (2014), and the UK Measuring Resilience Report (Sturgess, 2016) are all successful examples of

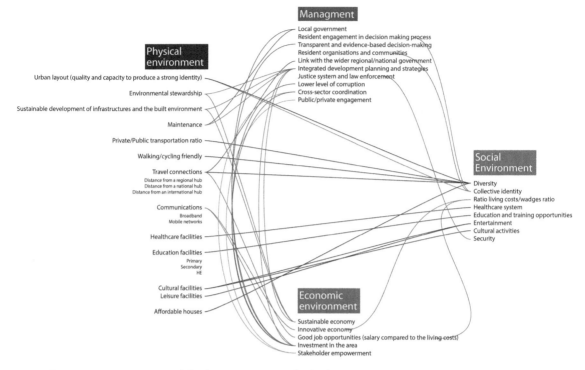

Figure 1.10.1 Mapping of the four categories and sub-elements.

Source: Carta et al., 2021. Diagram by L. Pintacuda.

such an approach. These frameworks, which are indicator and method-based, are generally beneficial for comprehending and contextualizing specific geographic, sociopolitical, and urban issues.

In previous studies (Carta et al., 2021), we reviewed several existing frameworks, identifying as a result four main categories that encompass several recurring elements that can help define urban resilience. The categories identified are Social Environment, Economic Environment, Physical Environment, and Management and are summarized in Figure 1.10.1, along with several subcategories that emerged from the literature. In particular, it is worth noting that the two main sources for the development of the mapping we developed are ARUP and Rockefeller Foundation (2014) and Wang et al. (2018) where layers of constituent parts are identified. The correspondence between the two main sources is illustrated in Figure 1.10.2.

Physical and Non-Physical Elements of Community Resilience

The categories summarized in Figures 1.10.1 and 1.10.2 could be easily distinguished by tangible and intangible factors. The majority of elements under Management, Social Environment, and Economic Environment could be regarded as non-physical (e.g., collective identity, job opportunities, and local justice systems). However, all of them can be measured in one way or another. As such, they become quantifiable, and they can be more easily related to physical factors. We approached the measurability of resilient factors in Carta

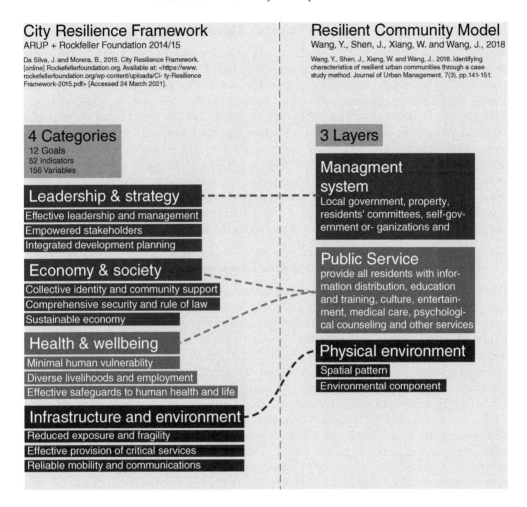

Figure 1.10.2 Comparison of the two main sources used (ARUP and Rockefeller Foundation, 2014 and Wang et al., 2018). Although using different categories and/or layers, they both focus on the same areas of investigation.

Source: Carta et al., 2021. Diagram by L. Pintacuda.

et al. (2021, 2022, 2023), where we explored the use of proximity, density, and typologies as strong factors that influence urban resilience at the community level. By analyzing the type of building, amenity, or service (e.g., a local primary school or a fire station), along with their distance from the center of the community and their number within certain areas, we are able to evaluate the extent to which a given community is resilient. Quantifying the resilience of an urban community, in turn, allows us to assess elements from the other macro-categories by looking at the individual factors within each category in the context of successful and less successful communities. Clear measurements of urban resilience based on physical elements help to compare, correlate, and infer information about the other intangible elements that characterize that particular community.

Tools for Resilience Measurement

Many scholars have been addressing the idea of assessing and measuring resilience through clear processes and methods. Among many, we include Caputo et al. (2015), Sharifi (2016), Jankovic (2018), and Petrescu et al. (2021) who worked on what can be defined as CRA (Community Resilience Assessment) tools. These studies concentrated on using quantitative frameworks and measures to rationalize urban resilient communities. One of the important issues raised by Sharifi's study (2016) is the fact that CRA methodologies typically do not account for the impact of change and the dynamic nature of resilience (as a response from communities) across time and geographical scales. This relevant point relates to the pivotal importance of a certain amount of uncertainty that needs to be included in any robust urban resilience tool, reinforcing the notion of resilience not as a static configuration, but as a shifting target (Sharifi, 2016:644). A powerful approach to dealing with uncertainties and change over time is through computational methods.

Artificial Intelligence, Machine Learning, and Cyber Security

There have been several studies addressing urban resilience through a computational and intelligent framework (e.g., Leykin et al., 2018; Yu and Baroud, 2019). An example is the work of Jankovic (2018), where a random grammar technique (Kauffman, 1996) has been employed to calculate resilience at the regional scale. According to Jankovic's approach, binary strings (0/1) represent both raw materials and the processes that transform them into processed resources. Random grammar rules govern the connectivity between the agents and the binary string transformations, which are carried out by models of artificial agents (Jankovic, 2018:4). In a recent study (Carta et al., 2022), we demonstrated how computer vision can be used to calculate urban resilience of any community in the world. The method uses a classifier that has been trained with a large number of satellite images to be able to recognize urban elements (e.g., a building from a park). Once the Artificial Intelligence (AI) model recognizes key typologies, the resilience of a certain community is calculated using a number of parameters that include proximity, distances, and redundancy of the typologies in the area.

Smart technologies are increasingly employed in cities to improve performance, safety, and economy at both local and regional scales. As cities become smarter, the risk related to urban data increases. Specifically, as citizens' information and infrastructure mechanisms are increasingly data-field (think of smart grids, self-tracking, urban sensors, etc.), cyber security becomes paramount. This notion is clearly encapsulated by the work of Andrade et al. (2021) on cyber-resilience, intended as the city's preparedness for a crisis, responsiveness, and capacity to reinvent its information and communication technologies (ICTs) structure in the face of persistent stress and severe interruptions (Andrade et al., 2021:189). In the next section, we will discuss the implications of such measurements and analysis and their relevance for urban resilience.

Analyzing Fragility and its Implications

Challenges in Analyzing the Fragility of Urban Systems

Urban infrastructure systems are essential for cities worldwide, but they are complex and continuously evolving with population growth and changing needs. Assessing the fragility of such critical infrastructure systems during extreme events is of vital importance. The continued functioning of urban systems when an extreme event occurs is determined by their structural integrity and affected by other critical utilities on which they depend. An analysis of this fragility requires an assessment of the locations where the infrastructure is likely to be structurally damaged, as well as of the impact of cascading failures that may occur in other interdependent infrastructure systems. Such an assessment is challenging to perform due to the significant complexity of the interdependent systems, and since the extreme event itself is difficult to define given that it has rarely, if ever, occurred.

Two types of analyses have been developed to assess the fragility of critical infrastructures under extreme events: reliability analysis and vulnerability analysis (Johansson et al., 2013). Reliability analysis aims to calculate the probability of systems performing under certain hazards and threats (Faturechi and Miller-Hooks, 2014). It has been criticized for relying on quantitative estimates that are based on limited knowledge and are therefore often inaccurate since they refer to low-probability, high-consequence events that are difficult to estimate (Johansson et al., 2013). Vulnerability analysis, on the other hand, aims to assess the inherent ability of a system to cope with certain hazards (Faturechi and Miller-Hooks, 2014). It seeks to determine the system's expected behavior under extreme circumstances by systematically identifying the impact of strains on the system, revealing its weaknesses. This can be done, for example, by simulating a specific scenario. However, it leaves open the question of how the simulation of certain scenarios will allow the "critical functionality" of a system to be identified if it is faced with unknown threats (Ganin et al., 2016). It may be impossible to consider and quantify in practice all the relevant events that may affect networked infrastructure systems of a complex nature (Linkov et al., 2014).

Many urban infrastructure systems are highly interdependent. Consequently, when a failure occurs in one system, this may result in additional failures in other systems—or "cascading failures". Such interdependencies must be included in an assessment of the fragility of any such system. However, cascading failures are very difficult to evaluate using conventional methods, since there is an essentially infinite number of potential operating contingencies and system changes that need to be considered (Eusgeld et al., 2011).

A Practical Approach for Analyzing Fragility

To provide an effective approach for the assessment of the fragility of urban infrastructure systems, a method needs to be developed that will reduce the complexity of the required analysis (Vatenmacher et al., 2022). To simplify the analysis process, it is essential to first focus on the relevant data to be analyzed rather than diving into exhaustive data analysis, which may include irrelevant information that is challenging to collect. An effective alternative approach is to reduce the amount of data used in the analysis by avoiding non-critical and redundant elements. This can be achieved by concentrating on the specific needs of essential end-users and quantifiably determining the circumstances under which the infrastructure systems supporting their activities might fail to meet those needs.

Such an assessment requires a definition of the impact of extreme events on the infrastructure system in terms of Levels of Service (LoS): a quality measure of the performance of the system analyzed. The complexity of an analysis of the fragility of urban systems in the highly unpredictable environment of extreme events can be reduced by considering solely the threshold where these systems no longer provide minimal LoS. In this way, the analysis of low-probability and high-impact events can be avoided. This is important in practice,

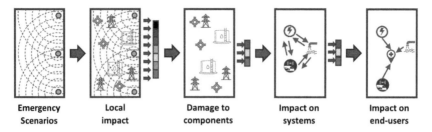

Figure 1.10.3 The conventional process for analyzing the fragility of urban systems.

Source: Shabtai Isaac.

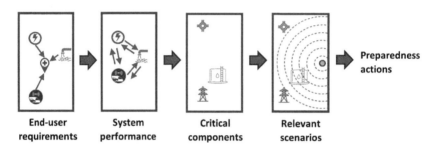

Figure 1.10.4 Proposed reversed process.

Source: Shabtai Isaac.

since historical data is often not available for such events, and their implications are consequently difficult to analyze. These difficulties are reduced by limiting the assessment to specific threshold scenarios whose probability is higher, yet which will lead to unacceptable outcomes in terms of insufficient LoS.

The proposed approach can be implemented by reversing the process through which the fragility of urban systems is usually analyzed (Figure 1.10.3). This is achieved by starting the analysis at the point where such analyses currently end, namely, the end-user and its requirements (Figure 1.10.4):

1 In the first stage, the required functionality of the systems is determined. The end-user requirements are defined that need to be ensured after an extreme event has occurred. Following this, the required performance is defined of other urban systems required to support the end-user's requirements, and the components in each system that are critical for fulfilling these requirements are identified. Then, the minimal LoS that each previously identified critical component needs to provide is defined.
2 In the second stage, the level of damage to each critical component that will prevent the minimal LoS from being provided is determined.
3 In the final stage of the analysis, scenarios are identified in which such damage will occur to the critical components, and the possibility of these scenarios is assessed. If the possibility of the occurrence of such a scenario is found to be significant, preparedness actions will need to be planned and executed to prevent the failure of critical components.

By reversing the process in which the fragility of urban systems is analyzed, its complexity is reduced in all respects—organizational, informational, and analytical. By considering only the threshold scenarios, the scope of the analysis is narrowed and irrelevant data such as non-critical elements can be ignored. Consequently, the organizational and informational resources that are required to carry out the analysis are reduced, and additional analyses can be carried out once the systems are changed.

Managing Resilience

The concept of resilience and the instruments for its evaluation have become a key topic in the last years, in response to the concerns about the increase and severity of disaster events. Within the dimension of urban infrastructure, three action fields can be highlighted: (i) social resilience; (ii) energy resilience; and (iii) thermal resilience. However, the assessment of most of them is still ongoing, since the number of requirements to be observed depends on the damage level and the possible scenarios to consider. A brief explanation of the aforementioned aspects is reported below.

Social resilience is defined as the community response to a disaster as well as its post-recovery. Kwok et al. (2016) proposed two categories of indicators, structural and cognitive. The first one considers the adaptability to embrace a change, community inclusiveness and health care capacity, food provisioning capacity, transportation access, communication capacity, leadership, and social support. The second one is related to access to economic resources, critical awareness, collaborative decision-making or collective efficacy, problem-solving policies, disaster management planning, diversity of skills, knowledge of community assets, knowledge of hazard consequences, robust community spaces, and social networks.

The indicators of energy resilience can be categorized into three domains. The first one corresponds to building characteristics, namely, disaster-resistant building, age of building, materials and construction, and maintenance of households (Osei-Kyei et al., 2023). The second domain pertains to renewable energy and the capacity to share and generate at least 5% of electricity (Feldmeyer et al., 2019). The third one is the reliability of ICT networks, which can be measured through the percentage of risk areas with monitoring, and alert systems integrated into the community, the average number of electrical interruptions per customer and year, upgrades of critical infrastructure, and the number of days that city fuel supplies could maintain essential household functions, etc. (Sharifi, 2016).

For thermal (and heat) resilience, the indicators can be classified into seven categories as follows:

i Time to a critical level. This considers active and passive survivability (Katal et al., 2019; Homaie et al., 2021; Siu et al., 2023).
ii Maximum level of thermal stress, which refers to the maximum values of indoor and outdoor air temperature, daily discomfort index (DI), and Predicted Mean Vote (PMV) (Sailor et al., 2014; Baniassadi et al., 2018; Rajput et al, 2022; Siu et al., 2023).
iii Time to exceedance, related to determining the period in which the indoor thermal comfort requirements are not accomplished given an event, considering as metrics: occupant hours lost thermal (OHL), heat index hazard hours (HIHH), PMV exceedance hours (PMVEH), the cumulative percentage of time above critical temperature, hours of exceedance (HE), HE upper limit temperature (HEULT), daily weighted exceedance

(We), percentage of occupied hours outside the range (POhOR), and number of consecutive days exceeding threshold maximum temperature (Pyrgou et al., 2017).

iv Time integral to exposure, which includes metrics such as unmet degree hours (UDH), standard effective temperature (SETUDH), and the weighted unmet thermal performance (WUMTP) (Homaei and Hamdy, 2021, Sun et al., 2021, Siu et al., 2023).

v Overheating intensity, defined by the response parameters like indoor overheating degree (IOD), ambient awareness degree (AWD), overheating escalation factor (OEF), and percentage of overheating hours (OH) (Baniassadi et al., 2018; Sun et al., 2021, Siu et al., 2023).

vi Outdoor comfort, which involves the indicators related to the public space surrounding the housing, such as outdoor neutral thermal threshold (NTT), outdoor critical thermal threshold (CTT), spatial heat resilience index (SHRI), and universal thermal comfort index (UTCI) (Sharifi et al., 2016).

vii Autonomy of the systems in a power outage, which refers to indicators such as building heat performance index (BHPI), gain utilization factor (GUF), hours of safety in free running mode, thermal autonomy (TA) and ventilation autonomy (VA) with only passive means (Katal et al., 2019).

All the action fields are correlated among them. Mavrogianni et al. (2014) mentioned that elderly people are less likely to adopt ventilation strategies in heat waves, and this could lead to amplifying the exposure to indoor air pollutants or to increasing temperature and humidity levels at home. Several studies indicated a strong relationship between the deterioration of human health (i.e., dementia, schizophrenia, diabetes, respiratory, and cardiovascular diseases) and very high outdoor temperatures (Escandón et al., 2022). Along this line, Baniassadi et al. (2018) demonstrated that the age of the building is also highly correlated with the indoor overheating rate. In less than 6 hours of power outage associated with a heat wave, older construction houses reach the DI thresholds, and the overheating values are estimated between 56 and 73 degree-hours, while new buildings can keep indoor environmental conditions. Considering that the discomfort hours could reach 36% higher values in Southern European residential stock in 2050 (i.e., Greece and Spain) (Escandón et al., 2022), the analysis of the main thermal metrics should focus on real-time monitoring. If several future scenarios are analyzed, predictive controls of building facilities based on weather forecasts could help in the adaptation of users' environments to extreme events and reduce the damage level.

It should be noted that for the energy resilience domain, the measurement level corresponds to the community, while thermal resilience refers to a building or to the public space where the housing is located. The resilience of buildings should be considered from the thermal to the energy and social domains. For example, good monitoring and control of the percentage of OH for different renovation variants at the room level could lead to lower energy consumption values and avoid an excessive operation of the energy production systems. This in turn could help to reduce energy interruptions per customer per year as well as the maintenance tasks or replacement of machinery. Hence, if building environmental conditions could be guaranteed before the occurrence of heat or cold waves, the risk of mortality or diseases of building users could be minor.

Conclusions

Summarizing, urban resilience in the context of smart cities is characterized by a degree of measurability, through quantitative approaches and increasingly robust tools (first section), elements of fragility within critical infrastructure systems, and the balance of each element (second section), and the need for a holistic approach and unification of criteria in the design of indicators for effective management of resilient communities in the built environment.

References

Andrade, R. O., Yoo, S. G., Tello-Oquendo, L., and Ortiz-Garcés, I. (2021). Cybersecurity, sustainability, and resilience capabilities of a smart city. In Visvizi, A., & del Hoyo, R. P. (Eds.), *Smart Cities and the UN SDGs* (pp. 181–193). Amsterdam: Elsevier.

ARUP and Rockefeller Foundation, (2014). *City Resilience Framework*. London: ARUP.

Baniassadi, A., Heusinger, J., and Sailor, D. J. (2018). Energy efficiency vs resiliency to extreme heat and power outages: The role of evolving building energy codes. *Building Environment*, 139, 86–94.

Bueno, S., Banuls, V. A., and Gallego, M. D. (2021). Is urban resilience a phenomenon on the rise? A systematic literature review for the years 2019 and 2020 using textometry. *International Journal of Disaster Risk Reduction*, 66, 102588.

Caputo, S., Caserio, M., Coles, R., Jankovic, L., and Gaterell, M. R. (2015). Urban resilience: Two diverging interpretations. *Journal of Urbanism: International Research on Placemaking Urban Sustainability*, 8, 222–240.

Carta, S., Pintacuda, L., Owen, I. W., and Turchi, T. (2021). Resilient communities: A novel workflow. *Frontiers in Built Environment*, 7.

Carta, S., Turchi, T., and Pintacuda, L. (2022). Measuring resilient communities: An analytical and predictive tool. *CAADRIA 2022 Proceedings*. CAADRIA.

Carta, S., Turchi, T., Spencer, N., and Vidal Calvet, M. (2023). Encoding social values of local communities in algorithmic-driven design methods. In Mora, Plácido Lizancos, et al. (eds), *Formal Methods in Architecture—Proceedings of the 6th International Symposium on formal methods in Architecture (6FMA)*. A Coruna 2022. Singapore: Springer Nature.

Cugurullo, F. (2018). The origin of the smart city imaginary. In Lindner, C. and Meissner, M. (eds.), *The Routledge Companion to Urban Imaginaries*. London: Routledge.

Escandón, R., Suárez, R., Alonso, A., and Mauro, G. M. (2022). Is indoor overheating an upcoming risk in southern Spain social housing stocks? Predictive assessment under a climate change scenario. *Building Environment*, 207. https://doi.org/10.1016/j.buildenv.2021.108482

Eusgeld, I., Nan, C., and Dietz, S. (2011). "System-of-systems" approach for interdependent critical infrastructures. *Reliability Engineering & System Safety*, 96(6), 679–686.

Faturechi, R., and Miller-Hooks, E. (2014). A mathematical framework for quantifying and optimizing protective actions for civil infrastructure systems. *Computer-Aided Civil and Infrastructure Engineering*, 29(8), 572–589.

Feldmeyer, D., Wilden, D., Kind, C., Kaiser, T., Goldschmidt, R., Diller, C., and Birkmann, J. (2019). Indicators for monitoring urban climate change resilience and adaptation. *Sustainability*, 11. https://doi.org/10.3390/su11102931

Ferre-Bigorra J., Casals M., and Gangolells M. (2022). The adoption of urban digital twins. *Cities*, 131, 103905.

Ganin, A. A., Massaro, E., Gutfraind, A., Steen, N., Keisler, J. M., Kott, A., ... & Linkov, I. (2016). Operational resilience: Concepts, design and analysis. *Scientific Reports*, 6(1), 1–12.

Holling, C. S. (1973). Resilience and stability of ecological systems. *Annual Review of Ecology and Systematics*, 4(1), 1–23.

Homaei, S., and Hamdy, M. (2021). Thermal resilient buildings: How to be quantified? A novel benchmarking framework and labeling metric. *Building Environment*, 201, 108022.

Hughes, K. and Bushell, H., 2013. *A Multidimensional Approach to Measuring Resilience*. Oxfam GB. Available at: https://oxfamilibrary.openrepository.com/handle/10546/302641

Jankovic, L. (2018). Designing resilience of the built environment to extreme weather events. *Sustainability*, 10, 141.

Johansson, J., Hassel, H., and Zio, E. (2013). Reliability and vulnerability analyses of critical infrastructures: Comparing two approaches in the context of power systems. *Reliability Engineering & System Safety*, 120, 27–38.

Katal, A., Mortezazadeh, M., and Wang, L. (2019). Modeling building resilience against extreme weather by integrated CityFFD and CityBEM simulations. *Applied Energy,* 250, 1402–1417.

Kauffman, Stuart. (1996). *At Home in the Universe: The Search for the Laws of Self-Organization and Complexity.* Oxford University Press.

Kitchin, R., (2018). Reframing, reimagining, and remaking smart cities. In Coletta, C., Evans, L., Heaphy, L. and Kitchin, R. (eds.), *Creating Smart Cities.* London: Routledge, pp. 219–230.

Kwok, A. H., Doyle, E. E. H., Becker, J., Johnston, D., and Paton, D. (2016). What is 'social resilience'? Perspectives of disaster researchers, emergency management practitioners, and policymakers in New Zealand. *International Journal Disaster Risk Reduction,* 19, 197–211.

Leykin, D., Lahad, M., and Aharonson-Daniel, L. (2018). Gauging urban resilience from social media. *International Journal Disaster Risk Reduction,* 31, 393–402.

Linkov, I., Anklam, E., Collier, Z. A., DiMase, D., and Renn, O. (2014). Risk-based standards: Integrating top–down and bottom–up approaches. *Environment Systems and Decisions,* 34(1), 134–137.

Mavrogianni, A., Davies, M., Taylor, J., Chalabi, Z., Biddulph, P., Oikonomou, E., Das, P., and Jones, B. (2014). The impact of occupancy patterns, occupant-controlled ventilation, and shading on indoor overheating risk in domestic environments. *Building and Environment,* 78, 183–198.

Osei-Kyei, R., Tam, V., Komac, U., and Ampratwum, G. (2023). A critical review of urban community resilience indicators. *Smart and Sustainable Built Environment.* https://doi.org/10.1108/SASBE-08-2022-0180

Petrescu, D., Petcou, C., Safri, M. and Gibson, K., 2021. Calculating the value of the commons: Generating resilient urban futures. *Environmental Policy and Governance,* 31(3), 159–174.

Pyrgou, A., Castaldo, V. L., Pisello, A. L., Cotana, F., and Santamouris, M. (2017). On the effect of summer heatwaves and urban overheating on building thermal-energy performance in central Italy. *Sustainable Cities and Society,* 28, 187–200.

Rajput, M., Augenbroe, G., Stone, B., Georgescu, M., Broadbent, A., Krayenhoff, S., and Mallen, E. (2022). Heat exposure during a power outage: A simulation study of residences across the metro Phoenix area. *Energy Building,* 259, 111605.

Ribeiro, P. J. G., and Gonçalves, L. A. P. J. (2019). Urban resilience: A conceptual framework. *Sustainable Cities and Society,* 50, 101625.

Sailor, D. J. (2014). Risks of summertime extreme thermal conditions in buildings as a result of climate change and exacerbation of urban heat islands. *Building Environment,* 78, 81–88.

Sharifi, A. (2016). A critical review of selected tools for assessing community resilience. *Ecological Indicators,* 69, 629–647.

Sharifi, A., Srivastava, R., Singh, N., Tomar, R., and Raji, M. A. (2022). Recent advances in smart cities and urban resilience and the need for resilient smart cities. In Sharifi, A., Salehi, P. (eds.), *Resilient Smart Cities: Theoretical and Empirical Insights,* Springer, Cham, pp. 17–37. https://doi.org/10.1007/978-3-030-95037-8_2

Sharifi, A., & Yamagata, Y. (2016). Principles and criteria for assessing urban energy resilience: A literature review. *Renewable and Sustainable Energy Reviews,* 60, 1654–1677. https://doi.org/10.1016/j.rser.2016.03.028

Siu, C. Y., O'Brien, W., Touchie, M., Armstrong, M., Laouadi, A., Gaur, A., Jandaghian, Z., and Macdonald, I. (2023). Evaluating thermal resilience of building designs using building performance simulation – A review of existing practices. *Building Environment,* 234, 110124.

Sturgess, P.; DFID. Measuring Resilience. Evidence on Demand, UK (2016) 51 pp. https://doi.org/10.12774/eod_tg.may2016.sturgess2. Available at: https://www.gov.uk/research-for-development-outputs/measuring-resilience

Sun, K., Zhang, W., Zeng, Z., Levinson, R., Wei, M., and Hong, T. (2021). Passive cooling designs to improve heat resilience of homes in underserved and vulnerable communities. *Energy Building,* 252, 111383.

Vatenmacher, M., Svoray, T., Tsesarsky, M., and Isaac, S. (2022). Performance-driven vulnerability analysis of infrastructure systems. *International Journal of Disaster Risk Reduction,* 76, 103031.

Wang, Y., Shen, J.-k., Xiang, W., and Wang, J.-Q. (2018). Identifying characteristics of resilient urban communities through a case study method. *Journal of Urban Management,* 73, 141–151.

Yu, J. Z., and Baroud, H. (2019). Quantifying community resilience using hierarchical bayesian kernel methods: A case study on recovery from power outages. *Risk Analysis,* 399, 1930–1948.

1.11

"DESIGNING SMART RETROFITS USING NATURE'S PATTERNS"

Designing Sustainability into Existing Communities

Victor Olgyay

Abstract

Our understanding of green building has grown deeper and broader over time. What remains underappreciated is our interdependence and integration of the biological world. We depend on the biological world, and yet we continue to use more of the earth's resources while simultaneously reducing the production of ecosystem services. Sustainable living requires that we reverse this equation by reducing our building's impacts and simultaneously enhancing our ecosystem services. We can build in this way in new construction, and even more importantly we can use this approach to repair our existing communities.

To date, the degree to which a built environment is considered sustainable has been measured using building rating systems which may not assess actual environmental impact. This essay takes ecosystem services and carrying capacity as the critical metrics to use in sustainable design.

Our existing built environment is an enormous resource that must be retrofit to help address climate change. In 2023, CO_2 levels rose to the level of 420 ppm in the atmosphere. We are experiencing the climate impacts of this CO_2 concentration today, and we have all the required technologies to both stop increasing it and begin to draw down the atmospheric levels of CO_2 to levels that will be compatible with maintaining a habitable climate. In this treatise, the opportunities are examined as an individual residence, a neighborhood, and at the size of a city. However, regardless of scale, sustainable design must be based on the idea of balancing our consumption of natural resources with the rate of the production of ecosystem services.

Introduction

Our existing built environment is an enormous resource that must be retrofitted to help address climate change. In 2023, CO_2 levels rose to the level of 420 ppm in the atmosphere. Using the patterns of ecosystem services, we can retrofit our built environment and both stop increasing and begin to draw down the atmospheric levels of CO_2 to levels that will be compatible with maintaining a habitable climate. This treatise examines the opportunities of an individual residence, a neighborhood, and the size of a city. However, regardless of

DOI: 10.4324/9781003384113-19

scale, we must base sustainable design on the idea of balancing our consumption of natural resources with the rate of the production of ecosystem services.

Retrofitting to the Scale of Sufficiency – The House

When planting a garden, the first step is to understand your location. What is your soil like, how much sun do you get, how long is your growing season? Once you are aware of the context, you can plan a design that meets those conditions.

At the level of an individual house, we can assess the carbon embodied in its construction, the operating energy use, and the productivity of the landscape that is associated with the property and see if building loads exceed the site capacity. In this example, a small 6,000-square-foot site located in a temperate, alpine forest ecosystem is estimated to sequester approximately 3 tons of CO2e/yr. However, an average 2,300-square-foot house would likely produce approximately 8 tons of CO2e/year for its operation, substantially overshooting the carrying capacity of this site (Figure 1.11.1).

We can retrofit this building to be in balance with its site capacity and reduce its carbon footprint. As shown in Figure 1.11.2, simple measures such as efficient appliances, air sealing, increased insulation, and high-performance windows will substantially reduce the energy required to operate the building. Adding energy recovery ventilation (ERV) will ensure that there is good indoor air quality. Removing combustion from inside the home (gas furnaces, stoves, water heaters, etc.) will greatly reduce indoor air pollution, switching them out for electricity will also reduce the overall carbon footprint. Other smart passive design elements such as increasing the amount of south-facing windows, adding thermal mass, and providing summer shading and natural ventilation can significantly increase comfort (Olgyay, 2015). Finally, adding solar electricity (photovoltaics) can make the house energy-neutral or even help it produce more energy than is consumed over the

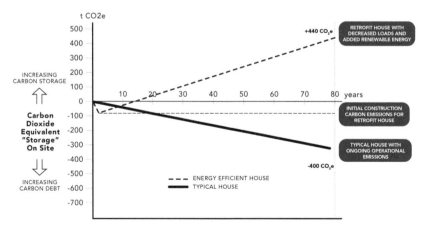

Figure 1.11.1 Graph of carbon performance over time comparing a typical house and a retrofit house that "pays off" its carbon debt in roughly 13.6 years.

Source: Victor Olgyay.

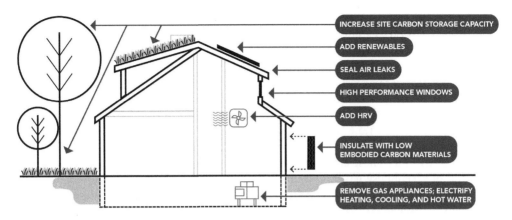

Figure 1.11.2 High-efficiency, low-carbon retrofit strategies for a typical house.
Source: Victor Olgyay.

course of a year (Olgyay and Herdt, 2004). It is technically easy to be "net zero" regarding energy and carbon over the course of a year, however, to provide all energy needs 24/7 without being connected to an electrical grid is likely to be more expensive, and an individual structure may require energy storage or oversized generation equipment to account for peak loads.

Buildings don't only use energy during their operation, but also as a consequence of their construction. It requires energy to extract, manufacture, transport, and assemble the materials to create a building. This is commonly referred to as the "embodied carbon" of a material. Materials vary greatly in their embodied carbon, expanded polystyrene foam may create 37 kilograms of CO_2e for a 4'×8' panel, and for the same application dense pack cellulose may actually be climate-negative and sequester 19 kilograms more CO_2e than is used in its manufacture. Buildings typically incur a substantial "carbon debt" as a result of their construction. In Figure 1.11.1, this initial carbon debt is indicated in the retrofit building by a 75-ton deficit. This is a substantial addition of embodied carbon, and by selecting materials carefully this quantity could be much lower or even result in a building that provides a net storage of embodied carbon (King and Magwood 2022). In addition to using low-carbon or carbon-storing materials, the carbon debt can be repaid by increasing the carbon sequestration provided by plants and soils, and by displacing high-carbon electricity. This is possible when the electricity produced is "clean" and displaces electricity that has a higher carbon intensity (measured in CO_2e per kWh). In this case, the embodied carbon debt is recovered over 13.6 years by site carbon sequestration and by the residence overproducing electricity thereby displacing 5 tons of CO_2e per year.

Reusing that single-family house and renovating it to be highly efficient is a smart use of embodied as well as operating resources. The house is affected by its site and can be designed so trees shade and cool the house in summer and allow the sun's heat to warm the house in the winter. Through careful design, the site's carbon sequestration ability can be enhanced as well (King and Magwood 2022). Mature vegetation can be preserved and cultivated, additional trees can be planted, and hardscape removed. In this renovation, a shady section of the roof (not suitable for solar electricity) was turned into a "green roof" and planted with native vegetation. The sum of all these site improvements increased the annual site carbon sequestration by 2 tons. This site's carbon sequestration could be further increased through the addition of compost, biochar, or other soil amendments.

In summary, based on the mix of fuels used at the building and those used to create electricity at this location, a typical house may generate amount approximately 8 t CO2e of emissions each year. The existing site vegetation may sequester 3 t/yr, leaving a net increase of 5 t of CO2e per year. Retrofitting this building may further reduce the generation of CO2e through the building operation to 4t, and increasing site carbon sequestration may allow for an additional 1.5 t of carbon to be sequestered. The addition of renewable energy may displace an additional 5t. The resulting total net annual operational emission is thus negative 5.5 t CO2e. These emissions will result in a net decrease in the atmospheric concentration of greenhouse gases. Over the estimated 80-year life of this building, the total cumulative emissions are negative 440 t CO2e, compared to a typical baseline residence which would produce 400 t CO2e. This can be considered the whole life carbon of this building.

	Existing Operating Carbon	Retrofit Operating Carbon	Retrofit Embodied Carbon
Building	+ 8 t CO2e/yr	+ 4 t CO2e/yr	+ 75 t CO2e
Site	-3 t CO2e/yr	- 4.5 t CO2e/yr	
PV		- 5 t CO2e/yr	
SUM	+ 5 t CO2e/yr	-5.5 t CO2e/yr	13.6 year carbon payback

Figure 1.11.3 A summary of site carbon sequestration, operating and embodied carbon to achieve a beneficial whole-life carbon impact.

Source: Victor Olgyay.

This approach provides several options to the designer, who can choose to either reduce building loads, increase site sequestration, add carbon sequestering materials, or additional renewable energy. When done carefully, we can build beyond zero, to provide a net positive improvement in the environment at all scales of intervention. This is how a building's construction and operation impacts can be balanced within the budget of the available site resources.

Adapting at the Scale of Connectivity: The Neighborhood Scale

All of the aforementioned opportunities that are available at the scale of the individual building translate to the neighborhood scale: the benefits of efficiency, the opportunities to increase the ecological capacity, the possibility of durably storing carbon, and the increase in renewable energy production. In addition, the neighborhood scale also provides occasions for increased sharing of resources that further ecological and economic efficiency.

My garden sees the sky and the rain. The garden's edges are not absolute and when I water the plants, the water seeps into the ground and hydrates the nearby plants. Bees and bugs intrude, bringing pollen and unknown nutrients. Birds eat a few fruits and deliver my seeds to my neighbor's yard. The garden is not isolated, but an intensification of the neighboring ecology, connecting resources for mutual benefit.

Implications of Neighborhood Density

Aggregating clusters of buildings into neighborhoods increases the density of the built environment and displaces natural ecosystems. Less water is infiltrated into the ground, impermeable surfaces create more water runoff at a higher speed. Soil may be more compacted making it more difficult for plants to grow and can increase the impacts of flooding. Hard surfaces tend to increase air temperatures and decrease the ability for birds, insects, and many forms of life to flourish.

Increased density also provides a plethora of beneficial opportunities. The adjacency of resources means there does not need to be a "one for one" distribution of supplies and can encourage better coordination for meeting needs. Having neighbors requires a modicum of civility and can generate a shared sense of values and aspirations. Neighborhood swimming pools, sidewalks, roads, and parks are common shared amenities. These connectivity opportunities can also include environmental improvements.

The Opportunity for Increased Connectivity

At the neighborhood size, many things can become more efficient and economical. As the size of the design pallet grows, so do the quantity, variety, and quality of positive connections. At the neighborhood scale, we have networks of systems that provide food, water, communications, convey waste, control stormwater, provide transportation, and electricity to multiple buildings. All of these built systems also provide the ability to connect buildings to our natural environment much more broadly. Like a healthy ecosystem, over time these built connections can adapt and grow. For example, most neighborhood homes are connected to an electrical utility but do not share a direct electrical connection to their neighbors. Figure 1.11.3 shows distributed energy generation created by placing solar PV on many of the residences. These systems can be connected directly to the grid to accomplish net-zero operational energy status, and the performance can be further enhanced by creating a localized microgrid (Figure 1.11.4).

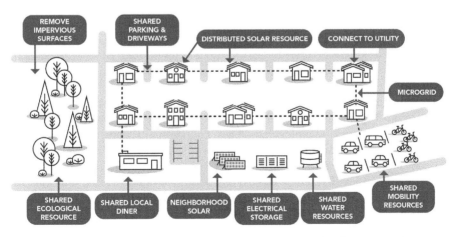

Figure 1.11.4 A common existing residential block typology retrofitted to zero carbon operations and increased ecological productivity.

Source: Victor Olgyay.

A microgrid can accommodate a variety of loads and resources, including energy storage. A properly designed microgrid will regulate electricity intelligently and when needed isolate itself from the larger utility services in a mode called "islanding". This can allow a neighborhood to independently maintain electrical services even when the larger utility has a blackout. Creating a smart neighborhood microgrid can provide an opportunity for increased localized production and consumption of electricity independently of a centralized utility. If residence "A" is producing more electricity than it needs, and residence "B" is consuming more than it is producing, the first residence can "sell" electricity directly to its neighbor (when permitted). Of course, even without a microgrid residence "A" can also sell its electricity directly back to the utility, known as "net-metering".

When these activities are coordinated, they are mutually beneficial – the buildings become assets to each other as well as to the grid. This helps the electrical grid run smoothly and economically. The neighborhood can add electricity to the grid when it is constrained and use or store electricity when there is a surplus. By leveling the loads on the electrical system, the utility will typically operate more economically and generate less carbon.

One example of this sort of neighborhood retrofit is the proposed Oakland EcoBlock (Barr, Norm, et al. 2019). In addition to adding deep efficiency to the buildings in an existing residential block (over 80% energy savings), solar PV is added to the roofs, and a microgrid connecting them all together with electrical storage (in the form of a flywheel) completes the system. Electrical vehicle charging is provided at each residence location by the street, reducing the carbon impact of transportation. The hydrological infrastructure is also tied together; rainwater is collected from roofs and used for graywater needs, such as gardens and flushing toilets.

Because these improvements reduce the existing loads on infrastructure, they can be cost-effective in reducing the need for continuing to upgrade and enlarge infrastructure. The savings can make these retrofitted developments more affordable to live in, generating an economic return resulting in these improvements paying for themselves. Neighborhoods may also share additional resources, such as shared cars, bike shares, and vegetable gardens. These sorts of amenities often create enormous value, as the neighborhood becomes highly desired for its convenience and economy.

At the neighborhood scale, it is important to balance the amount of land devoted to biological resources and to abiotic resources. Far too often we build roads, sewers, sidewalks, and buildings that are essentially ecological deserts. Low-Impact Development (LID) is an approach that employs green infrastructure to provide civic needs and ecosystem services (University of Arkansas Community Design Center, 2010). "Hard" engineered concrete culverts can often be replaced by "soft" green swales. Rather than piping runoff and surface pollution to another site, using LID solutions reduces runoff by entraining stormwater, plants remove pollutants and biologically digest contaminants while also absorbing atmospheric CO_2. Parking areas can often be paved with porous materials that reduce runoff, remain cool in the summer heat, and allow for vegetative growth. Increasing the amount of green infrastructure will often be less expensive than hard-engineered solutions and provide a multitude of habitat and ecological benefits. While LID may not replace all hard infrastructure, integrating it into neighborhoods can substantially increase our ecological resources and resilience.

Neighborhoods are a subset of a larger regional ecology and as such are likely to have ecological boundaries that do not correspond to property boundaries. This is seen in the distribution of plants, in an arid climate where plant growth is constrained by the amount of available water, the quantity and distribution of plants will be optimized according to this resource constraint. We should follow the example of nature: if the available resource of water is constrained, then we should not build additional neighborhoods whose water consumption will exceed the carrying capacity of the site (McHarg, 1992).

This optimal distribution of plant material is dynamic and continually evolves. Our neighborhoods evolve similarly, over time smart buildings become more efficient through deep energy retrofits. The carrying capacity of the site may change, and the uses and loads we put on the site may change as well. We can create more green space, reduce hard surfaces that create heat islands, we can add renewable energy, and build our neighborhoods to operate within the carrying capacity and carbon budget of the site. And most importantly, we can connect neighborhood patterns of resources and loads and get a multitude of social, economic, and environmental benefits.

Rebuilding with Density and Diversity – the scale of the City

Fifty percent of the world's population currently live in cities. Increasing the number of people, the amount of construction, the quantity of materials, food, trash, movement, noise, light, energy, and commerce increases the overall metabolic rate of a city as compared with a less dense development. With density also we get opportunistic diversity. The city can be imagined as a living organism, a system of systems, with many types of buildings containing a wide variety of uses, some highly specialized, some flexible in use, and adaptable. This diversity of changing uses and influences accelerates change and evolution, and with smart design, we can optimize the interaction of these systems to reduce waste and create wealth.

At first, Darwin's finches were ignored, especially by Darwin. However recent studies have shown these birds as a fascinating example of environmental influences hastening adaptive evolution. The morphology of the finch's beak evolves based on the food supply, when dry weather increases the number of woody seeds, larger beaks dominate. When smaller seeds were in great abundance, it was the smaller beaks that provided the fittest means for survival in the changing world.

Post pandemic, many US cities are experiencing a dramatic shift in occupancies, with office space in low demand, and an increasing need for housing. Adaptive reuse of office space for housing is a perfect moment to also increase the efficiency of the built environment in line with current needs. We can retrofit buildings and infrastructure to reduce loads, add green infrastructure and ecosystem services, and increase the connections of these systems to reduce pollution.

Cities are often considered economically and ecologically efficient, providing lower transportation impacts, especially when residential and occupational uses are adjacent. Buildings can also be more energy-efficient with common walls and floors, and compact utility systems. But while loads per person may be less, the ecological loads per acre of development are high. Because nature has been virtually eradicated in cities, there are almost no ecosystem services available. To accommodate the ecological needs of the 1.6 million people living on the 23 square miles of Manhattan, it is estimated to require an additional 35,000 square miles. Without natural systems to help, cities require extensively built ecological and infrastructural systems to operate.

Start Evolving Sustainability in Cities by Solving the Evident Problems

The city has been reimagined many times over the centuries, by Leonardo DaVinci in Italy, Eugene Haussmann in Paris, and in the modern era Le Corbusier, Paolo Solari, and "New Urbanism" thinkers like Peter Calthorpe (Calthorpe, 2011). It is only recently that the critical ideas of integrating development with natural systems have become part of this discourse.

We can build on these urbanistic ideas to adapt our existing cities to be supportive of our current climate concerns. The complex systems in cities can be organized into similar components we have identified in the single-family house and neighborhood discussions. Addressing these component issues points the way to developing zero-carbon cities that support our global climate goals. The significant differences in a city over the individual residence or the neighborhood are the increased density along with the lack of ecological productivity.

The Goals

People like safe cities, they like healthy places with clean air, and they appreciate the vibrancy and the sense of community. People want to feel comfortable, not threatened by cars or trash, they want places to have a pleasing character. These desirable city characteristics include the humanism of Kevin Lynch (1960) and the ecological literacy of Peter Calthorpe. The solutions imply that we preserve as much nature as possible in the city and prioritize adding more. Green plants sequester carbon as they grow, and every increase in vegetation helps clean the air and cool the city. Air, water, and light make cities habitable, provide human scale, and avoid turning streets into dark canyons. Designed to allow cool breezes to flow, open up the city to air movement, and allow sunlight to brighten the winters (Kelbaugh, 2019). Engage in the hydrology of the city, celebrate the movement of water, uncover and daylight waterways, and create amenities near them. Mix up uses in the city, and create useful neighborhoods providing the retail and cultural amenities desirable near residences. Prioritize street life, with plazas and cafes, and slow down or remove cars from pedestrian street life. Reclaim the streets, they are 80% of the public space in many existing cities and need not be given over to cars. Provide options for people, and good pedestrian networks with many routes and modes of travel. In this way, we can create a shared sense of purpose and responsibility, with social and environmental systems interdependent and valued (Figure 1.11.5).

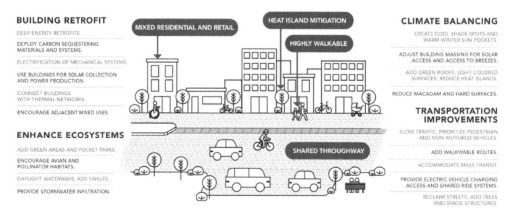

Figure 1.11.5 Retrofitting a city for humanist, sustainable living.

Source: Victor Olgyay.

These approaches lead to a built infrastructure that is humanistic and creates recognizable neighborhoods. It also is the foundation for beginning to increase the ecological resilience of a city. Most cities in the USA today are the remnants of an outdated vision of the future with failing infrastructure and dominated by the automobile, they have grown from the opportunistic sprawl of planning that zoned the city into areas segregated by income and use. They are ready to be rejuvenated.

An ecological approach to rejuvenation starts incrementally. With a greater vision in mind, we can begin to improve the city one neighborhood at a time. Perhaps there is an area where flooding is endemic, that may be an opportunity to start to revitalize the local hydrology and build green infrastructure and public places. Find locations that may be undesirable and rebuild them into assets with housing, mixed-use opportunities, and transit. Create infrastructure for pedestrians and bicycles and connect to the next neighborhood.

As we do this, we start to rebuild the ecological infrastructure and reduce environmental stress. By reducing the need for cars and providing greater pedestrian amenities within a 15-minute walk, energy use goes down. Air pollution goes down, water pollution is reduced, and we get closer to our sustainable city goal. We reduce loads and increase the productivity of nature. Adding a pocket park, removing asphalt from a parking lot and planting trees, creating a shady arbor on an outdoor restaurant will all help reduce the urban heat island effect. Designing for thermal comfort and human health will also result in reduced energy use.

And of course, we need to address the actual buildings that are much of the physical definition of cities. Buildings are a critical vector for reducing a city's ecological footprint since they typically use the majority of the energy in a city and often are responsible for about 75% of the CO_2. Substantial efficiency can be provided by increasing the thermal performance of the building envelope, through deep energy retrofits that consider the building as a system and optimize each element in relationship to the others. Electrification of structures is critical to reduce air pollution and carbon impacts.

Much like the density and diversity in a city create opportunities for reducing the impact of cars by walking and using non-motorized transit and mass transit, for buildings the adjacency and diversity provide many opportunities for shared services. In addition to water, sewer, and telecom services, cities often have thermal networks for buildings. These may be inefficient, leaky steam systems fired by fossil fuels, but they can also be improved to be elegant efficient ways to balance thermal needs across many buildings (Olgyay, Coan, Webster, and Livingood, 2020). In neighborhoods with mixed uses, such as office and residential, thermal (and electrical) loads will vary based on their time of occupancy, and infrastructure can help share these resources. Modern thermal networks are often running at ambient or low temperatures and provide a huge asset for balancing loads in a city.

Returning to our original metaphor of the city as a "living organism, a system of systems", it is evident that each of the various elements in a city can be optimized. We have buildings optimized for transit or telecommunications, and similarly, we can build projects that emulate the ecosystem services that nature provides elsewhere (Olgyay, Hainline and Harris (2006). In the city, we should build renewable energy systems to provide power and buildings that include food production, air cleaning, water cleaning, and carbon sequestration. The density of the city encourages us to create buildings that create the ecosystem services that are lacking with the reduced natural systems. We can build the required aspects of the architecture of sustainability. These civic needs can be met in the density and diversity of the city if we are smart and direct its evolution rather than let unfettered economics drive all the development decisions. In the end, creating a healthy habitable city will result in a vibrant green economy and encour*age* a virtuous cycle of civic improvements.

Conclusion

There is a clear set of requirements for buildings going forward at the scale of the individual residence, at the scale of the neighborhood, and at that of the city. Our challenge is in the rapid implementation of the following:

- Greatly increase the thermal, material, and energy efficiency of our building stock. By retrofitting our existing buildings to 80%, net-zero operational energy or even net positive energy use can and should be done cost-effectively now. New construction must be designed to be net zero or better. We must retrofit our building stock to operate within the site capacity or better.
- Solar energy is everywhere, providing opportunities to enrich us. Collect it in windows, store it in building mass, and turn it into electricity for endless applications. Buildings are part of the energy network and must flex demand, provide electricity to adjacent buildings, take advantage of diversity, connect to each other to shift loads, help with utility operation and grid congestion, and develop the economy and resiliency of a grid-interactive solar-based community.
- Cease combustion. Remove it from our buildings, directly and indirectly. We don't need to burn gas to cook, heat water, or heat our homes.
- Build to reduce dependence on motorized transportation and provide practical alternatives to the automobile. Use both design and technology to provide attractive alternatives. We can reduce the production of atmospheric carbon through urban and transportation design.
- Decarbonize materials, reduce their impacts, and instead recognize their opportunity to sequester and store carbon. Reuse and renovate existing buildings. Develop landscapes and materials that remove atmospheric carbon and store it in fibers, soils, and stones. Design using life cycle carbon analysis to ensure that over time, each building provides an overall reduction in atmospheric carbon.
- Rebuild ecosystems and increase their productivity. Put atmospheric carbon sequestered back in the ground. Both natural and man-made ecosystems need to be enhanced to increase our planet's ecological capacity.

The process of retrofitting our communities to be sustainable must be measured by how close we are to meeting the ecological capacity of our planet. If we do not rebuild and succeed in this, we will experience the worst effects of climate change.

Nature provides us with the patterns and ideas for our buildings to work better. Working with nature is the smart design solution, an architecture that is fundamentally engaged with ecology can address our environmental crises. Climate change has accelerated our need for the implementation of sustainable design at the most fundamental level. We will do this. And along the way, we just may recognize that humanity still has much more to benefit by minding nature.

References

Barr, Z., Norm B., et al. (2019). *Accelerating the Deployment of Advanced Energy Communities: The Oakland EcoBlock*. Sacramento: California Energy Commission. Publication Number: CEC-500–2019–043.

Calthorpe, P. (2011). *Urbanism in the Age of Climate Change*. Washington, DC: Island Press.

Kelbaugh, D. (2019). *The Urban Fix:* New York: Routledge.

King, B. and Magwood, C. (2022). *Build Beyond Zero: New Ideas for Carbon Smart Architecture*. Washington, DC: Island Press.

Lynch, K., (1960). *The Image of the City*. Cambridge, MA: MIT Press.

McHarg, I. (1992). *Design with Nature*. New York: J. Wiley.

Olgyay, V. (2015). *Design with Climate: Bioclimatic Approach to Architectural Regionalism*. Princeton; Oxford: Princeton University Press.

Olgyay, V., Coan, S., Webster, B. and Livingood, W. (2020). *Connected Communities: A Multi-Building Energy Management Approach*. Golden, CO: National Renewable Energy Laboratory. NREL/TP-5500–75528.

Olgyay, V., Hainline, J. and Harris, E. (2006). *Quantifying the Ecological Restoration Provided by Green Machines*. Boulder, CO: American Solar Energy Society.

Olgyay, V. and Herdt, J. (2004). The application of ecosystems services criteria for green building assessment. *Solar Energy*, 77, 389–398.

University of Arkansas Community Design Center. (2010). *LID Low Impact Development -a Design Manual for Urban Areas*. Fayetteville: University of Arkansas Press.

1.12

FROM SMART TO AUTONOMOUS CITIES ON THE EVE OF AI

Some Provocations for Architects and Designers

Tim Williams, Andy Watts and Andrew Whalley

Abstract

Most people on our planet increasingly live in cities and towns. For those who plan, design, deliver, and manage the built environment, they have become prime sites of creativity and production, real and virtual. In practice, architects and designers working in urban environments do so in three core contexts.

1. The continuing evolution of the city's physical fabric, core supporting networks, and planning and zoning frameworks.
2. Changing environmental policies and shifting public priorities.
3. Revolution in technology, digital networks, devices, and data-driven enterprises and services.

In identifying these three contexts, we do not suggest that the potential of all is being fully realized or that interactions and integrations between them are fully explored. Instead, this chapter contends that

- Architecture and design have not always fully exploited the possibilities of the digital toolkit.
- Smart City initiatives have not been systematically pursued by as many cities as first envisaged.
- Opportunities for integration of smart buildings, smart precincts, and smart green infrastructure with Smart City systems and data-driven city governance have been implemented patchily.

The arrival of Artificial Intelligence (AI), particularly generative AI, into city design, infrastructure, and management systems has resulted in a new combination that is being termed 'Urban AI' (Luusua et al., 2023). We suggest progress toward realizing Smart City objectives has been uneven and modest, particularly in cities of 'the West.' This will have implications for tech adoption and future professional practice in built environments.

Most people on our planet increasingly live in cities and towns. For those who plan, deliver, and manage the built environment, they have become prime sites of creativity and

DOI: 10.4324/9781003384113-20

160

production, real and virtual. In practice, architects and designers working in urban environments do so in three core contexts:

1 **Continuing evolution of the city's physical fabric, core supporting networks, and planning and zoning frameworks.** Many cities are still changing in response to COVID-19, which emptied city centers and decimated mass transit while drastically accelerating the shift to teleshopping and telecommuting.
2 **Changing environmental policies and shifting public priorities,** particularly around ensuring development, contributes to the realization of two big societal objectives that shape what architects do and how they do it: the maximization of social impacts and of environmental benefits.
3 **Revolution in technology, digital networks, devices, and data-driven enterprises and services.** Wi-Fi, internet, broadband, 5G, smartphones, sensors, Building Information Modeling (BIM), Computer-Aided Design (CAD), the Internet of Things, digital twins, 'Smart City' applications, and now 'generative AI' (gAI) continue to impact all aspects of the business of buildings. This tech-enabled, data-driven momentum has impacted cities and their governances, with the most innovative using tech platforms not only to promote civic dialogue and better service delivery but also, more ambitiously, to facilitate the co-design of urban improvements. The most advanced cities deserve the status of 'smart cities. We define a Smart City somewhere between the European Commission's (2024) definition, a *place where traditional networks and services are made more efficient with the use of digital solutions for the benefit of its inhabitants and business'* (para. 1) and what research company Frost and Sullivan (2019) says '*Smart governance, smart energy, smart building, smart mobility, smart infrastructure, smart technology, smart healthcare, and smart citizen'* (p. 4).

Smart Cities and Smart Architecture

In identifying these three contexts, we do not suggest that the potential of all is being fully realized or that interactions and integrations between them are fully explored. Instead, this chapter contends that:

- Architecture and design have not always fully exploited the possibilities of the digital toolkit.
- Smart City initiatives have not been systematically pursued by as many cities as first envisaged.
- Opportunities for integration of smart buildings, smart precincts, and smart green infrastructure with Smart City systems and data-driven city governance have been implemented patchily.

The arrival of Artificial Intelligence (AI), particularly generative AI, into city design, infrastructure, and management systems has resulted in a new combination that is being termed 'Urban AI' (Luusua et al., 2023). We suggest progress toward realizing that Smart City objectives have been uneven and modest, particularly in cities of 'the West.' This will have implications for tech adoption and the future professional practice in built environments.

Despite initial enthusiasm and some successes, failed experiments such as Toronto's Sidewalk Labs (Haggart & Tusikov, 2020), and the initially ambitious now scaled-back reality of Rio as the 'smartest city' in South America (O'Kane, 2023) have demonstrated the challenges in seeking to realize the Smart City goals. Progress has been limited spatially and siloed in terms of use categories and applications – relying on individual charismatic pioneers within the public sector to take the agenda forward. While some UK councils have seen Smart City initiatives, few have taken a systematic approach across a range of services. Milton Keynes City Council (2018) is the stand-out for innovation and leadership.

Another example of unevenness and low-impact innovation is Australia, where there are constitutional contradictions between strong centralized state governments and small and less empowered local councils. For example, Greater Sydney has 31 councils but no metro-scale governance. The State of New South Wales was driven to take 'cities' out of its top-down digital innovation program instead of naming it, the Smart Places Initiative. Efforts in Australian states that are keen to promote smarter 'digital first' strategies in government services have been exploring 'digital twins' yet still struggle to bridge the gap between states and councils over management of major cities. This reminds us that 'smart cities' require 'smart governance' (Sabri, Winter, & Rajabifard, 2023).

On the private sector side of the digital ledger, there have been enthusiastic tech adopters. We have much to learn from China's leading cities' early adoption of tech-enabled Smart City technologies. When it comes to public-private integration of digital tools, data-driven systems, and infrastructure planning and design at a metro-city scale, we must look to Singapore and other key Chinese cities, although their momentum has not been without controversy around community engagement and accountability. Furthermore, as Smart Cities morph via Urban AI into ever more autonomous cities, again, we find important examples of prototyping and tech-based practices coming from China that all urbanists can be enthused by and adapt for use in quite different cities and polities. This development has also proven controversial (Cugurullo, 2024).

Time to Reflect and Retool: On the Path to 'Generative' and 'Urban' AI

As professionals working in or managing the urban environment, we should reflect on where we have got to, good or ill, and where we go next. If we are to shape and exploit the potential of tech-based transformations, we must stress the radical nature of the next phase. Some see continuity, whereas others see rupture. AI may be another tool to deliver modern data-driven versions of 'business as usual' in the production of design, or it may be a sea change.

In reality, gAI has non-human intelligence and agency to independently assess options derived from data and create multiple design solutions. This is decidedly not standard practice for architects, just as the journey from Smart City to Autonomous City has its discontinuities. We must understand that identified trajectories are not as separate from each other but rather integrally linked.

There are also challenges within the built environment professions, particularly in parts of the world where dialogues of architectural design and the Smart City have remained parallel rather than intersecting. Technological potentials must be seized by designers and builders everywhere if the challenges of gAI are to be overcome and opportunities for our future cities are to be fully realized. We are left with a choice; to get on board and exploit gAI or get left behind.

While architecture, real estate, and infrastructure have adopted new digital tools, there is a residual reluctance to 'tool up' and modernize. Indeed, the property industry was recently described as largely tech-phobic (Cook, 2023). Now is the time to learn from and build speedily on foundations established by best practice firms and understand advances being made in the most innovative cities as they shift from smart to autonomous cities.

Building on Earlier Tech Adoption: A Company Perspective

Grimshaw is one among many leading architectural practices to have exploited smart tools. Aided by its Design Technology Team, it has explored the implications for architecture and the design of developments such as BIM and Computer-Aided Architectural Design. Increasingly, the firm is moving into the world of digital twins.

BIM is the digital representation of a specific building during design and construction. A digital twin is a model of, and counterpart to, actual real-world assets. In the project-creation and design phases, but also increasingly operational stages, digital twins allow for an asset's entire lifecycle to be modeled and simulated. It has great potential, and when combined with emerging visualization, augmented reality, and interactive technologies – it greatly improves communication between the diverse professions participating in creating and delivering design. It also enables planning approval authorities and communities to get a more accurate idea of the intended design and form of the build-project, and how it might impact the surrounding neighborhood. This improves transparency and potentially the reception of some projects in challenging stakeholder environments (Sisson, 2022).

Can Happen Must Happen. Toward Measuring Impact

We stress our vision can happen, but we cannot say that this potential has been fully realized. Increasingly it will be seen as the best practice we believe it to be, yet architects and designers must convince clients and regulators of the benefits of digital twins. Public sector planning departments, for one example, should require digital twins as part of the approval and community buy-in process. This tech breakthrough will also facilitate the advancement of building and design companies as learning organizations. In the era of BIM and digital twins, we can obtain hitherto unavailable real-time feedback into the ongoing design process, indicating whether the emerging design functions through the eyes of the designer, builder, client, and potentially, planning approval authorities.

Such tools can also assess the performance-built assets *once in use*. This provides enhanced capacity for developers, asset owners, managers, and users, to not just address management and service problems in a timely and efficient manner, but also to use feedback to improve the commissioning process for subsequent project design and implementation. This raises the crucial issue of Post Occupancy Performance Evaluation – a practice galvanized by digital tools that also requires new collaborative approaches between partners in the design, build, asset management, and planning approval chain to fully realize.

Key to progress in this area will be something currently rare: data on post-occupancy performance shared by asset owners with architects and designers. This could in turn drive longer term collaborations over multiple build projects to fully harness learning and improvement for subsequent buildings. Architects are often frustrated when buildings are completed and operational and as such no longer measurable. The digital twins allow for continued monitoring.

The Pope Tech Tool and similar apps for measurement can be used not only to assess the success of a design in terms of building outputs and user benefits but also to measure and maximize environmental and social outcomes outside the building. The design and operation of a new asset can also impact the precinct or community in surprising ways. A new era of collaboration, professional improvement, and social impact beckons.

Considering the current achievements of digital twins, the addition of gAI's ability to learn from data to design new options, with limited if not human agency, is radical. While catalyzed by previous tech innovations, this shift brings new challenges and discontinuities for professions in urban spaces and cities themselves. It is, in fact, 'different this time' (Marks, 2019, para. 2).

It Is Different This Time: The Issue of 'Agency'

Technologies and the built environment have always shaped each other. Designing for the historic city around walking and horsepower was different from designing for the rail or car-based city, as was designing for single-story buildings compared with multi-story developments enabled by elevators. Yet until the advent of the computer, the architectural practice would have been recognizably familiar across time and place: humans drawing by hand with hierarchical craft leadership. The shift to tech-based approaches such as CAD, object-based modeling, and parametric modeling enabled the modernization of design production and efficiencies unavailable to previous generations while leaving the idea of the architect as a lone 'auteur' largely in place. Even in Smart Cities, digital tools, data-collection approaches, and evidence-based decision-making have reflected and enabled *human* agency.

The difference with gAI is clear from the Oxford English Dictionary (2023) definition: 'the theory and development of computer systems able to perform tasks normally requiring human intelligence, such as visual perception, speech recognition, decision-making, and translation between languages.' In the AI era, non-biological agency and autonomous decision-making become real. That's a decisive shift, well beyond smart or autonomous. Generative AI is genuinely disruptive, deriving as it does from, 'purposes unrelated to architecture' (Witt, 2023, para. 1). It will reshape the practices of designing buildings and places while 'confronting architects with profound new questions around the future of design' (Witt, 2023, para. 1). In this process, the very skillset of architects, their agency, and even their identity will radically transform.

Already Changing the Nature of Work: Much More to Come

Generative AI and other digital technologies are already changing the nature of work and augmenting worker capabilities. Noting that the AI era is 'only just starting,' McKinsey (2023) identified the potential for AI technologies to absorb '60 to 70 percent of employees' time' especially those in higher paid, better qualified, 'knowledge work' sectors (para. 4). Built environment practitioners are front and center of this transformation, facing considerable challenges around managing risks, identifying future skills, and recognizing new needs for collaborative teams.

However, the upsides remain positive even as the downsides pose challenges. Design professionals must grapple with both, particularly in Western nations where urban and technological trajectories have differed from the Asian city model. In so doing, they can make a real difference for the city and business success. Indeed, the enterprise has been challenged and changed in the wake of COVID-19, becoming less focused on office and retail activities, more hybrid and decentralized in key knowledge-worker sectors, and increasingly, if unevenly, data-driven and autonomous in their operations, networks, and infrastructures.

Generative AI, Architect, and Design: The Upside

A key upside is AI's power to analyze vast amounts of data that would be impossible for humans to comprehend, let alone use effectively. The use of AI in building design, for example, can produce smarter, more sustainable buildings by analyzing data on energy consumption, weather patterns, and occupant behavior. Such optimization and performance improvement can be targeted at reducing emissions and costs, making our built environment more affordable and resilient.

Another upside relates to understanding and designing the use of space. Just as in online retail processes patterns and design choices are known to result in greater sales, so there are long-established core design principles that AI can capture and utilize to create architectural drawings. A gAI-assisted process can apply Internet of Everything sensors and computer vision algorithms that collate data on space use (IBM, 2024). Examples might include how customers move around a shop before buying, or how conference spaces are utilized in offices. Such findings, along with outcome data about purchases, customer preferences, productivity, and employee retention, can be applied to gAI tools. This data can then be overlaid with spatial information on factors such as square meterage, location, walls, furniture, and other key physical elements. Generative AI will then create architectural plans optimized to result in the desired outcomes for a specific space.

Dealing with the 'Not so Upside': The Key Challenge of Agency

Our examples show that there would be reduced guesswork in the delivery of desired outcomes. Accordingly, we must ask what precisely is to be the part played by human architects and designers in this new era. At its core, this is the difference for architects and designers between Smart Cities and AI. Generative AI has unique implications not just for how architects work but also for *who they are*.

Beyond the Architect as Auteur: Toward a New Collaboration between Human and Autonomous Intelligence

The very fabric of urban spaces is increasingly embedded with automated, intelligence-gathering sensors, and integrated with data on social interactions. These tools will be able to interact without external direction – bringing the realization that for the first time in human history, the intelligence shaping the city and the management of its core services will not be human. This reinforces the challenge of working with non-biological intelligence able to reason and extrapolate with relative autonomy and poses an unprecedented challenge to the auteur paradigm.

That challenge can be met through humility, urgency, and focus. There is indeed a risk of algorithmic autonomously generated design over-determining design outcomes based on data and assumptions unclear to human agency, with the associated risks of plagiarism and transgressing IP rights (Mittal, 2024). But we can also conceive of an optimum position in the evolving human/AI relationship based on a 'hybrid model of control and authorship between machines and humans, algorithms and designers' (Pisu & Carter, 2023). A future where architects and designers retain responsibility for the design strategy will ensure that while they 'test their ideal spatial configuration against many AI-generated options' unique facets of human agency – 'art and emotion' – remain core to the design process (Carta & Pisu, 2022). This collaborative approach to human/non-human agency must become central to architectural practice.

That modest proposal still leaves architects with the need to modify ways of working and upgrade their understanding of how AI works and what it can do, with and without them. They must act quickly – in workforce planning, human capital development, and business development, with a view to maximizing what we see as 'human-centric AI innovation.' Our aim should be AI-generated architecture, but AI-enabled architects.

Architects Are Urbanists in their DNA

While architecture is relevant to all domains and contexts, urbanism and city-building are in the DNA. Architects were city shapers from the beginning and have always seen cities as presenting development challenges and potential solutions. It is even more important than ever to recognize that 'AI operates most consequentially in the city at the scale of large urban systems' (Cugurullo, Caprotti, & Cook, 2024). Architects must continue to be urbanists as well as technologists, and it is in this context that a renewed focus on developments in Chinese cities is paramount. Whatever the flaws, they are implementing a version of this future with deliberate intentionality around the links between city and tech development. We can learn to take our profession and our cities forward into this digital Brave New World. The potential of gAI is being explored extensively in key fast-growing cities in China whose development approaches have been interactively progressing.

China's Growth as Testbed: Shenzhen and Xiong'an as City Exemplars

China's dramatic urbanization over recent decades makes it a test bed for innovation in the built environment, which has also produced significant data pools. The companies spawned in this era of market development have been world-scale developers, engineers, builders, and infrastructure investors, but also, crucially for our discussion, significant enterprises working in the tech space. Examples include Huawei and China Mobile in telecoms, Alibaba in e-commerce, and Tencent in gaming.

In combination with the conscious focus on Smart City strategies and prototyping at an urban scale, the result is a combined urban and digital transition that allows for fast and extensive rollouts of smart tech across wide ranges of use categories.

This is symbolized in Shenzhen, where China's urban revolution began Now the home of Huawei, local government officials in collaboration with the company are using digital twins of thousands of 5G-connected mobile devices to monitor and manage flows of people, traffic, and energy consumption in real-time.

It is also expressed in the remarkable development of Xiong'an in Hebei province. Prioritized as China's 'future city,' where 'physical and "digital twin" spaces will be planned and built in a synchronized fashion' (Bei Chen 2023, p.230, quoting Hebei Government 2018, no page), it envisions that there will be 'tangible utility pipelines and intangible digital twins that mirror and monitor the physical realities of cities' (Cugurullo, Capetti, & Cook, 2024 p. 363).

This has been characterized as a 'three cities' strategy combining the real, the virtual, and the skills of the architect, with those of the data analyst. One city on the ground, one underground, and one in the cloud, connected across multiple urban domains via 'city brains' – sensor/data-driven governance platforms managing multiple systems across a city. These are now promoted as essential services by China's government, with data, remarkably, officially defined as a key factor of production when assessing economic performance.

Urban AI edge Is Not in 'the West'

Generative AI further blurs the divide between physical and digital spaces, creating potential for unparalleled connectivity across a variety of urban domains. It poses further challenges and new opportunities to city managers and professionals in the built environment. But the leading edge is not in 'the West.' Concerned as we may be about potential authoritarian misuse of societal and behavioral monitoring by 'platform urbanism,' (Barnes, 2019) of data-gathering systems that damage individual social credit or facial recognition technologies that target dissent, the fact remains. China leads the way in Urban AI and promotes leadership via its Belt and Road strategy. The Global South and Asia have been influenced by this momentum. Saudi Arabia's new city *The Line* is a case in point with its data-driven, tech-enabled focus including 'city-brains' style digital systems and governance (Bell, 2022).

Learning from This: Being Confident in the Future of Cities as Well as Tech

From 2013 to 2021, China and the United States accounted for 80% of private smart tech investment. That means that since 2021 a majority of private and public investment in AI has been in China (Ramos & Mazzucato, 2022). Simultaneously China's cities have reaffirmed 'the urban' post-Covid to such an extent that their CBD offices have high occupancy levels, with new 'tall buildings' being designed and built. This contrasts with European, American, and Australian cities, where hybrid working has persisted, and adaptive reuse of commercial buildings has become a key trend. Asian Cities overall have had 85–100% returns to the post Covid office, while 60–70% has been more common in Europe and Australia. American cities have languished at 50% (Kastle, 2023).

While many tout the virtues and permanence of hybrid working, China is proceeding on the basis that urban agglomeration and higher density are the very essence of the economic function of cities. Evidence remains strong that city agglomeration brings dividends to national economies (Giuliano, Kang, & Yuan, 2019). Higher density urban centers and the real and virtual networks they support lead to higher productivity, but also crucially for the new AI economy, generating more patents and tech start-ups (Carlino, Chatterjee, & Hunt, 2007). Chinese confidence in the urban future reinforces the momentum toward investment and innovation in Urban AI. By contrast, there may be a question mark over the relative salience of Urban AI in the Western city model weakened as it was by Covid. Learning from this transformation and how it has been achieved, we can shape our city opportunities in the West, to equip city-building professions with the skills and tools needed in the era of AI.

A Mission-Led Approach to Urban AI – and Ethical Guidelines

China aims to make cities, city-making enterprises, and communities smarter and more tech-enabled and has adopted the means to achieve this. It has defined a key societal challenge and made dramatic progress based on a public-private collaboration harnessed through strong urbanist visions and tech innovations. Investment has followed. This 'mission-led' strategy is something Mazzucato (2022) says is relevant to states of all kinds even the less 'top-down' versions in the West. She recently called for the West to have an 'ethical by design' AI mission 'underpinned by sound regulation and capable governments working to shape this technological revolution to create opportunities for public value creation in the common interest' (Ramos & Mazzucato, 2022)[1]. This principle underpins UNESCO's Recommendation on the Ethics of AI now adopted by 193 member states (UNESCO, 2023). It also relates to the EU's emerging 'holistic framework' for AI governance (European Commission, 2024). We support this strongly as an area of 'Western' difference from which others can learn.

Conclusion: Some Recommendations and a Call to Action

We see the need for:

1 More coalitions of the willing in the private and public sectors sharing new tech agendas and even IP in our more open society.
2 New long-term strategic alliances between developers and asset owners sharing performance data on buildings post-completion with architects and designers to jointly improve future buildings.
3 The voluntary creation of private-public organizations identifying and sharing best practices in AI in architecture and design, building construction, mobility, energy efficiency, infrastructure, and city systems governance.
4 Wider sharing of insights to enable smaller companies to progress and to encourage collaboration across sectors and company scales has been achieved in sustainability initiatives such as the Green Building Council.
5 Explicit ethical guidelines to protect the privacy and public interest, and to maximize community accountability and benefits.

We conclude in agreement with UK 'prop-tech' leader Cook (2023) who says, 'All are going to have to retool their processes, and that retooling will be painful. But the result will be a much better economic way of doing business.' Those who fail to embrace the transformative capacity of Regenerative AI will see threats to the viability and relevance of enterprises – and fall short in terms of business objectives and benefits for their communities and cities. Mazzucato (2022) surmises that our society's future is at stake. We must not only fix the problems and control the risks of AI but positively shape the direction of digital transformations and technological innovations to ensure that they support visions for equitable, healthy, and successful placemaking. There is no better time to begin laying the foundation for limitless innovation in the interest of all.

Note

1 This is from paragraph 8 of the Ramos and Mazzucato article online. AI in the Common Interest by Gabriela Ramos & Mariana Mazzucato - Project Syndicate (project-syndicate.org)

References

Barns, S. (2019). *Platform Urbanism: Negotiating Platform Ecosystems in Connected Cities*. Palgrave.
Bell, J. (2022, September 16). AI will be the 'beating heart' of Saudi's NEOM, THE LINE: Summit. *Alarabiya News*. https://english.alarabiya.net/News/gulf/2022/09/16/AI-will-be-the-beating-heart-of-Saudi-s-NEOM-THE-LINE-Summit

Carlino, G. A., Chatterjee, S., & Hunt, R. M. (2007). Urban density and the rate of invention. *Journal of Urban Economics*, 61(3), 389–419. https://doi.org/10.1016/j.jue.2006.08.003.

Carta, S., & Pisu, D. (2022). Human-AI co-design and urban resilience. In *RGS-IBG Annual International Conference 2022- Proceedings* (pp. 466).

Chen, B. (2023). Performed imaginaries of the AI-controlled city: Conducting urban AI experimentation in China (pp. 223–237). In *Artificial Intelligence and the City*. Routledge. https://www.vitalsource.com/en-au/products/artificial-intelligence-and-the-city-v9781003810421

Cook, J. (Host). (2023, December 8). How AI is revolutionizing commercial real estate. [Audio podcast episode]. In *Trends & Insights: The Future of Commercial Real Estate*. JLL. https://podcasts.apple.com/us/podcast/trends-insights-the-future-of-commercial-real-estate/id1503057415.

Cugurullo, F. (2024, January 3). AI could make cities autonomous, but that doesn't mean we should let it happen. *The Conversation*. https://theconversation.com/ai-could-make-cities-autonomous-but-that-doesnt-mean-we-should-let-it-happen-218638.

Cugurullo, F., Caprotti, F., & Cook, M. (2024). *Artificial Intelligence and the City Urbanistic Perspectives on AI*. New York: Routledge.

European Commission. (2024). *Excellence and Trust in Artificial Intelligence*. https://commission.europa.eu/strategy-and-policy/priorities-2019-2024/europe-fit-digital-age/excellence-and-trust-artificial-intelligence_en.

European Commission. (2024). *Smart Cities: Cities Using Technological Solutions to Improve the Management and Efficiency of the Urban Environment*. https://commission.europa.eu/eu-regional-and-urban-development/topics/cities-and-urban-development/city-initiatives/smart-cities_en.

Frost & Sullivan. (2019). *Smart Cities: Frost & Sullivan Value Proposition*. https://www.frost.com/wp-content/uploads/2019/01/SmartCities.pdf

Giuliano, G., Kang, S., & Yuan, Q. (2019). Agglomeration economies and evolving urban form. *Annals of Regional Science*, 63, 377–398. https://doi.org/10.1007/s00168-019-00957-4

Haggart, B., & Tusikov, N. (2020). Sidewalk Labs' smart-city plans for Toronto are dead. What's next? *The Conversation*. https://theconversation.com/sidewalk-labs-smart-city-plans-for-toronto-are-dead-whats-next-138175.

IBM. (2024). *What Is Internet of Things?* https://www.ibm.com/topics/internet-of-things.

Kastle. (2023, September 26). Evidence of the new hybrid work pattern. https://www.kastle.com/resource/evidence-of-the-new-hybrid-work-pattern/

Luusua, A., Ylipulli, J., Foth, M. et al. (2023). Urban AI: Understanding the emerging role of artificial intelligence in smart cities. *AI & Society*, 38, 1039–1044. https://doi.org/10.1007/s00146-022-01537-5

Marks, H. (2019, June 13). This time it's different. *Advisor Perspectives*. https://www.advisorperspectives.com/commentaries/2019/06/13/this-time-its-different.

Mazzucato, M. (2022). *Mission Economy: A Moonshot Guide to Changing Capitalism*. Penguin Press.

McKinsey. (2023, June 14). *The Economic Potential of Generative AI: The Next Productivity Frontier*. https://www.mckinsey.com/capabilities/mckinsey-digital/our-insights/the-economic-potential-of-generative-AI-the-next-productivity-frontier#introduction.

Milton Keynes City Council. (2018). *MK Digital Strategy 2018–2025*. https://www.milton-keynes.gov.uk/sites/default/files/2022-03/Milton%20Keynes%20Digital%20Strategy%202018-2025%20-%20FV.pdf.

Mittal, A. (2024, January 9). The plagiarism problem: How generative AI models reproduce copyrighted content. *Unite AI*. https://www.unite.ai/the-plagiarism-problem-how-generative-ai-models-reproduce-copyrighted-content/.

O'Kane, J. (2023, November 18). Rio de Janeiro: A test for the intelligence of smart cities. *The Globe and Mail*. https://www.theglobeandmail.com/business/article-rio-de-janeiro-a-test-for-the-intelligence-of-smart-cities/

Oxford English Dictionary. (2023, December). *Generative Artificial Intelligence, N*. https://doi.org/10.1093/OED/9657191441.

Pisu, D., & Carter, S. (2023). Architectural AI urban artificial intelligence in architecture and design. In *Artificial Intelligence and the City* (pp. 339–360). Routledge. https://www.vitalsource.com/en-au/products/artificial-intelligence-and-the-city-v9781003810421

Ramos, G., & Mazzucato, M. (2022, December 26). AI in the common interest. *Project Syndicate*. https://www.project-syndicate.org/commentary/ethical-ai-requires-state-regulatory-frameworks-capacity-building-by-gabriela-ramos-and-mariana-mazzucato-2022-12.

Sabri, S., Winter, S., & Rajabifard, A. (2023, March 2). Creating digital twins to save our cities. *PURSUIT*. https://pursuit.unimelb.edu.au/articles/creating-digital-twins-to-save-our-cities.

Sisson, P. (2022, August 8). The tech that tries to tackle NIMBYs. *Bloomberg*. https://www.bloomberg.com/news/features/2022-08-08/the-virtual-tools-built-to-fix-real-world-housing-problems.

UNESCO. (2023, May 16). Recommendation on the ethics of artificial intelligence. https://www.unesco.org/en/articles/recommendation-ethics-artificial-intelligence.

Witt, A. (2023, June 13). Data, digital media, and a different design office. *Harvard Graduate School of Design*. https://www.gsd.harvard.edu/2023/06/andrew-witt-on-data-artifical-intelligence-and-architecture

1.13

SMART ARCHITECTURE TO REDUCE WHOLE-LIFE CARBON IN BUILDINGS AND INFRASTRUCTURE

Paul Toyne

Abstract

Ensuring all new buildings and infrastructure consider whole-life carbon and take actions to dramatically reduce the carbon emissions associated with their construction, operation, and maintenance is vital if we are to meet our global climate commitments. This chapter considers some of the key approaches to delivering whole-life carbon reductions. It advocates a systems approach where all aspects of carbon in the built environment are considered and presents these aspects. It also discusses some of the high-level actions for operational energy and embodied carbon, in particular passive design, reducing material, and extending the life of assets through re-purposing with project examples. Knowing what guidance to follow and when to use it is a challenge for the built environment sector. This chapter concludes by presenting a solution to this challenge in the form of a free-to-use, web platform called Minoro. The decarbonization pathway for buildings, hosted on www.Minoro.org, is structured in work stages, and for each work stage, it identifies the actions required to maximize the opportunity to reduce whole-life carbon in the project. Each action is explained and the most up-to-date international and regional guidance, including what methodologies and techniques to use, are presented. Minoro.org makes navigating and delivering action on decarbonization achievable.

Introduction

This chapter considers some key approaches to delivering whole-life carbon reductions. It advocates a systems approach where all aspects of carbon in the built environment are considered and presents these aspects. It also discusses some of the high-level actions for operational energy and embodied carbon, particularly passive design, reducing material, and extending the life of assets through re-purposing with project examples. Knowing what guidance to follow and when to use it is a challenge for the built environment sector. This chapter concludes by presenting a solution to this challenge in the form

DOI: 10.4324/9781003384113-21

of a free-to-use web platform called minoro.org. Announced at COP 28 in Dubai, and launched in July 2024, Minoro is a carbon management knowledge platform focused on creating pathways to reduce carbon in the built environment. Curated by experts from across the built environment and construction value chain, Minoro will be a central repository to find the latest guidance on carbon management for property professionals. Minoro is the result of a partnership between Grimshaw, the World Business Council for Sustainable Development and supported by over twenty organisations including the World Green Building council and RIBA. It has been developed with the support, collaboration, and advice of over a 100 respected organizations and individual experts. Rich with information but easy to use, the platform is poised to become an indispensable tool in efforts to address the decarbonization and mitigation of climate change in buildings. The decarbonization pathway for buildings, hosted on Minoro.org, is structured in work stages, and for each work stage, it identifies the actions required to maximize the opportunity to reduce whole-life carbon in the project. Each action is explained and accompanied by the most up-to-date international and regional guidance, including what methodologies and techniques to use. Minoro.org makes navigating and delivering action on decarbonization achievable.

The Climate Emergency

Cities with their buildings and infrastructure must and will play a crucial role in mitigating climate change (as well as climate adaptation). They are a major source of greenhouse gas emissions and user of our finite natural resources. Approximately 75% of annual greenhouse gas emissions are from our built environment with 37% from buildings (UNEP, 2021). Between 40% and 50% of resources extracted from global materials are used for housing, construction, and infrastructure (UNEP, 2020). Building materials account for half the solid waste generated every year worldwide (Transparency Market Research, 2021). Built environment carbon impacts are mostly attributable to either operational or embodied carbon emissions: Operational carbon impacts result from energy and water consumption in the day-to-day running of a built asset, be it a building or infrastructure asset. Embodied carbon impacts arise from sourcing, manufacturing, and installing the materials and components that make up a built asset and also include the lifetime emissions from maintenance, repair, replacement, and ultimately their demolition or deconstruction, waste treatment, and disposal.

In addition, there are also user carbon impacts from the activities of the users of a built asset, outside of the use of energy and water used to operate the asset, for example, the impact of commuting to an office building or the impact of vehicles using a road, which produces further user-related emissions (RICS, 2023).

From an environmental perspective, the way we design, build, and operate our buildings and infrastructure is inefficient: wasting materials and energy. Future urban development predictions suggest that 68% of the world's population will live in cities by 2050 with 75% of the infrastructure needed still to be built (Milnes et al., 2014 and United Nations, 2019). During this period, around 50% of emissions from new buildings will be from embodied sources and around half from operational sources (Architecture 2030, 2019). These trends suggest that emissions from the built environment will increase during a period when climate science requires a 42% reduction in GHG emissions by 2030 to stay within a 1.5°C degree rise: And we currently have a 50:50 chance of achieving this by 2100 (UNEP, 2023).

Policies have been developed that seek to improve the building performance of both existing and new buildings. Typically, this involves a number of interventions that include improving the energy efficiency in buildings and infrastructure through applying regulations and certification schemes; reducing the carbon content of the energy used in the building and the infrastructure asset through the provision of on-site and off-site renewable energy (this reduces carbon emissions associated with the operation of the asset) and reducing embodied carbon associated with construction materials. However, there is often a lag between the policy measure and the performance required to get to near-zero or net-zero carbon. For example, green building rating certification schemes and building regulations are not frequently updated. Furthermore, it's a fast-moving agenda, and keeping abreast of the latest guidance for architects and designers is time-consuming. In response, in this chapter, I review existing responses to this challenge of decarbonizing the built environment and guidance available to architects and designers to take practical action. The chapter concludes by promoting an integrated systems approach to reduce future whole-life carbon emissions.

Approaches to Reduce Whole-Life Carbon

Understanding Whole-Life Carbon

In response to the significance of whole-life carbon, a standard PAS 2080 for the measurement and reporting of whole-life carbon in buildings and infrastructure systems has been developed in the UK. PAS2080 is seen as an effective way to align supply chains in the delivery of low-carbon infrastructure and buildings as it looks at how a business measures and manages carbon at both an operational level and through its services. The standard was revised to set out how the sector can transition to net zero by 2050 by managing and reducing whole-life carbon in buildings and infrastructure (BSI, 2023). The updated guidance document offers a range of case studies where the standard has been applied and provides work examples to further assist organizations with the application and integration of the standard (BSI, 2023a).

The Royal Institute of Chartered Surveyors has also produced a whole-life carbon assessment methodology (RICS, 2023). Within this publication, RICS (2023) defines whole-life carbon emissions as the total of all assets related to GHG emissions and removals, both operational and embodied, over the life cycle of an asset, including its disposal. Figure 1.13.1 shows the composition of the different modules (A–D) that make up whole-life carbon (modules A0–A5, B1–B7, B8 optional, C1–C4, all including biogenic carbon, with A0[1] assumed to be zero for buildings). Operational carbon refers to GHG emissions arising from all energy consumed by an asset in use (B6), over its life cycle, whereas embodied carbon refers to the total GHG emissions and removals associated with materials and construction processes, throughout the whole life cycle of an asset (modules A0–A5, B1–B5, C1–C4).[2]

For new buildings, the London Energy Transformation Initiative's, Climate Emergency Design Guide covers five key areas: operational energy, embodied carbon, the future of heat, demand response, and data disclosure. The guide includes setting the requirements of four key building archetypes (small-scale residential, medium-/large-scale residential, commercial offices, and schools) and takes a whole-life carbon approach (LETI, 2020).

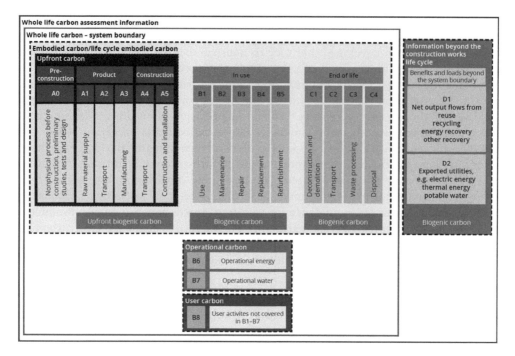

Figure 1.13.1 Building and infrastructure life cycle stages and information modules (Adapted from EN 15978, EN 17472, and EN 15643, with additions to illustrate biogenic carbon) RICS 2023.

Reducing Operational Carbon

Reducing operational carbon can be achieved through passive design that makes buildings and infrastructure assets more energy-efficient and reduces energy consumption, and by optimizing the building performance so that no energy is wasted, this often includes the installation of building services that are energy-efficient. By reducing energy use carbon emissions will be reduced, and further carbon reductions can be achieved if the energy supply is from renewable energy. Other strategies for achieving net-zero operational carbon in new buildings are summarized by LETI (2019).

Passive Design

Passive design strategies are incorporated into a building design to remove the need for mechanical or electrical heating, cooling, and ventilation. Using the construction of a building to keep it warm or cool is nothing new: Traditional buildings have many built-in architectural features for achieving solar passive cooling of buildings for comfort. These include suitable insulation of walls and roofs, reduction of heat gain through walls by light-colored surfaces, small windows, and mutual shading restricting heat gain through windows, use of louvers for natural ventilation, orientation of building along wind direction, cooling storage by use of heavy walls as thermal mass, use of overhung for shading using wooden sunshades, and shading of buildings using trees (Subramanian et al., 2017). The problem of keeping buildings warm in colder northern European climates began at the beginning of the Industrial Revolution (c. the 1760s) when firewood for fuel became sparse and coal was only just becoming available. Icelandic people found the construction of thick peat walls and roofs helped insulate them from heat loss. This approach of insulation and draught-free construction achieving optimal energy efficiency by reducing the need for heating and cooling has since developed into Passivhaus Standard (Bere, 2019).

PassivHaus is an official standard that assesses a building's performance based upon its passive design properties achieved through designing to Passivhaus principles, which are: Thermal insulation – to keep warmth in during winter and out during summer; Thermal bridge[3] reduced design – buildings are planned without thermal bridges, particularly in temperate and cold climates to reduce heating costs and prevent damage; Airtightness – a continuous air-tight outer shell to protect the building structure, prevent energy loss, and maximize comfort; Ventilation – to keep the building supplied with consistent fresh air through the ventilation system a heat exchanger ensures that air is supplied to rooms at the room temperature without the need for additional heating or cooling; Windows – triple-glazing and insulated window frames for temperate and cold climates and double glazing for warmer climates. To be awarded a PassivHaus standard, the building performance must be independently certified.

The Standard looks specifically at key building components such as floor slabs, façade anchors, ventilation systems, windows, doors, and wall and column connections, among others (Passivehouse.com, 2023). The first Passivhaus dwellings were constructed in Darmstadt in Germany in 1991. It is intended primarily for new buildings, although it can be applied to refurbishment projects, with further guidance summarized by Hopfe and McLeod (2015) (Figure 1.13.2).

The climate emergency and the volatile energy costs for operating buildings have led to a resurgence of passive design principles and there is a steady increase in buildings that are certified to the Passiv Haus standard, not just in Europe but across the world. The number of completed/certified projects has been growing rapidly since 2012 and there are projects not captured that may not pursue certification but have benchmarked against the standard for performance (IPHA, n.d.).

Recently, the Woodside Building for Technology and Design at Monash University, Melbourne, a Grimshaw-designed Passivhaus-certified building (the largest in the southern hemisphere) won both AIA's 2021 National Award for Public Architecture, as well as the AIA's National Award for Sustainable Architecture. The sustainability attributes of the building have been documented (Sangiorgio, 2020).

As with all approaches described in this chapter, passive design solutions should be considered within a whole-life carbon context so as to not overprioritize operation carbon reductions at the expense of embodied carbon reductions which in certain cases, depending on the project location and market conditions, may not provide the best carbon reduction.

Smart Building Management Systems

'Smart' Building management systems use building automation and control systems that can monitor the real-time performance of various aspects of building services such as heating control; hot water supply control; cooling control; ventilation and air-conditioning control; lighting control; blind control; technical home and building management. Through a wireless system network, the building's performance can be optimized for comfort and energy

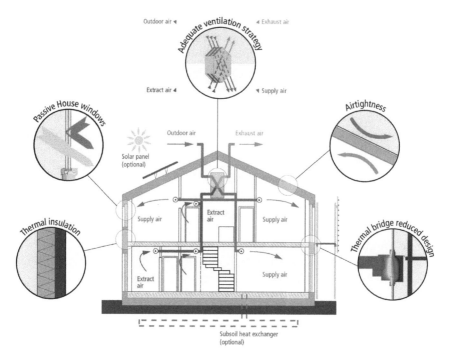

Figure 1.13.2 Diagram demonstrating the Passivhaus principles. (Redrawn from https://passiv.de/en/ 02_informations/02_passive-house-requirements/02_passive-house-requirements.htm)

consumption. However, such optimization may come with a cost, as there is usually a clear trade-off between energy efficiency and human comfort: the higher the energy savings, the lower the comfort. Lowering the overall building energy consumption whilst maintaining acceptable levels of function is challenging and has been explored for several typologies of buildings for example, for residential buildings (Shah et al., 2019); offices (Vandenbogaerde et al., 2023); data centers (Rong et al., 2016), and Sembrioz et al. (2019) make the general case for better of the integration of smart controls. Building energy simulation and optimization techniques are used in the design phase to predict how buildings will perform (Tian et al., 2018).

Reducing Embodied Carbon

To reduce embodied carbon, architects and designers have three significant options: (1) design so that buildings/assets can be re-purposed, extending their life, or disassembled, so the materials can be used again; (2) use less materials; and (3) select materials with low or no embodied carbon, or materials that have been re-used, recycled, or re-purposed.

Constructing buildings uses energy as well as resources, and once a building has come to the end of its life, these resources are still potentially available for use. Thus, in addition to reducing embodied carbon, the resources used are 'stored' in the building or infrastructure asset, and they should be thought of as 'material resource banks' (LETI, 2020a). The material resources used need to be kept in the circular economy. This means building and infrastructure should be designed so that it re-uses construction materials and products from demolished buildings and is designed for disassembly so that materials and products within the building/infrastructure asset can be re-used in future buildings. Examples of buildings that do this are explored by Cheshire (2021) and include Grimshaw's re-purposing of a furniture factory into the new School of Art and Design for Bath Spa. At the time of the original design in the 1970s, the architects questioned whether the building would always be a factory, so it was specifically designed to be adapted to extend its life. Swallow and Green (2020) describe the original design philosophy and how the building was re-purposed 40 years later.

For infrastructure projects, the concept of using less materials by retaining materials on site makes good financial sense; for example, retaining excavation waste for on-site landscaping (PAS, 2023a). The re-use of the existing Victorian structure of London Bridge Station maintained significant heritage value, enhanced the surrounding streetscapes and urban realm, and created a substantial saving in the project's embodied carbon (White, 2022).

The principle of life extension through circular design has been explored in the new Civil Engineering building on the University of Cambridge's engineering campus. Here a modular approach to the building's planning grid and services distribution maximizes the potential for future flexibility and adaptation, ensuring a long service life (Sidor and Swallow, 2022). A whole-life carbon approach was taken incorporating operational carbon, with early decision-making supported by an energy-cost metric tool developed by the team (MacKay et al., 2020).

Key construction materials commonly used in buildings and infrastructure such as steel and concrete are high in embodied carbon. Sector-specific decarbonization roadmaps are in place and technologies such as the use of hydrogen and electric arc furnaces for steel manufacturing, and carbon capture storage and utilization in cement making are being deployed. These sectors have committed to net zero by 2050 (Cembureau, 2020; Lei et al., 2023). Whilst waiting for innovations to come to the marketplace, reducing the amounts of carbon-intensive materials or substituting the material are options that architects and designers can explore (Allwood and Cullen, 2015). Using biogenic materials such as timber and the use of supplementary cementitious materials such as fly ash in concrete are common examples of material substitution. In addition, an example of successfully reducing material use was the award-winning Walton Centre for Planetary Boundaries on the Arizona State University campus in the United States. Here, Grimshaw architects worked with the general contractor to specify a 'Bubble-deck' void form concrete system, not before used in the American Southwest. This was utilized in the floor slabs to reduce the volume of concrete and embodied carbon used in the project. The bubble-deck (void form) relied on recycled plastic spheres that allowed for less concrete to be used. Additionally, the team used concrete made with 40% fly ash, which replaced cement, the most carbon-intensive component of concrete (Johnson and Vaden Youmans, 2023). Esau et al. (2021) provide further examples of cost-effective reductions of embodied carbon in new buildings.

Accessing Relevant Guidance: Minoro Is a Web-Based Solution for Managing Whole-Life Carbon in Buildings

In the previous sections, a summary of some of the key actions architects and designers can consider to support the delivery of near- or net-zero-carbon buildings and infrastructure assets was provided. However, the topic is immense and the issues to consider are complex presenting a real challenge to the property and infrastructure sector. With so much information on guidance methodologies and tools being developed by a range of organizations, it is difficult to keep on top of and navigate all the information. Furthermore, asset owners are committing to net zero with no clear route to achieve this and ultimately everyone is struggling with how to decarbonize. As I have described a system approach is required where whole-life carbon is assessed, and reduction strategies established. Such strategies can create decarbonization pathways to achieve net-zero carbon. The decarbonization pathway for buildings was originally developed by the architectural practice Grimshaw; based on progress against their own net-zero carbon design commitments and the available international and regional guidance and techniques to provide *'the what, how and when to do it'* to maximize opportunities for carbon reduction for their architects and design teams. When implemented, they found significant reductions in whole-life carbon.

Grimshaw sought to gift their intellectual property related to the pathway and as a result, a partnership was formed with the World Business Council for Sustainable Development to develop the pathway as a free-to-use website, www.Minoro.org. Over 100 organizations from around the world have helped shape its development and as a result, Minoro will support; investors in their due diligence and governance for investing in low-carbon building projects; asset owners and developers in setting whole-life carbon targets and establishing measurement and reporting of whole-life carbon, as well as supporting procurement strategies and decision making; architects, designers, and engineers in providing guidance and tools to assess whole-life carbon in the design phase; contractors by providing an understanding of what carbon reductions have been achieved in previous stages and what needs to be done through the construction phase, including material and mechanical and electrical equipment selection; facilities managers in helping them operate the building at its optimal energy consumption and maintain the building with an understanding of its components and their environmental performance (Figure 1.13.3).

The decarbonization pathway for buildings, hosted on Minoro.org, is structured in work stages, and for each work stage, it identifies the actions required to maximize the opportunity to reduce whole-life carbon in the project. Each action is explained and the most up-to-date international and regional guidance, including what methodologies and techniques to use, can be found. With international resources, guidelines, and methodologies, Minoro makes navigating and delivering action on decarbonization more achievable. Property developers, asset owners, investors, architects, designers, engineers, contractors, and consultants can work together using the guidance and resources within the platform provided to take actions that maximize the opportunity to avoid unnecessary carbon emissions in building projects. It can help users develop a plan for carbon management at any project stage and set credible, well-informed carbon reduction targets. It is also a reference for low or net-zero-carbon objectives. With an array of strategic tools for carbon governance at hand, lower carbon outcomes can be easily targeted, tracked, and achieved. Downloadable documents include a carbon management plan, and a matrix of responsibilities to support the project governance, which can be adapted to suit the project's needs.

Minoro is a free-to-use carbon management knowledge platform that will be regularly updated. The long-term plan is to include decarbonization pathways for infrastructure and address other themes such as climate resilience in buildings and infrastructure.

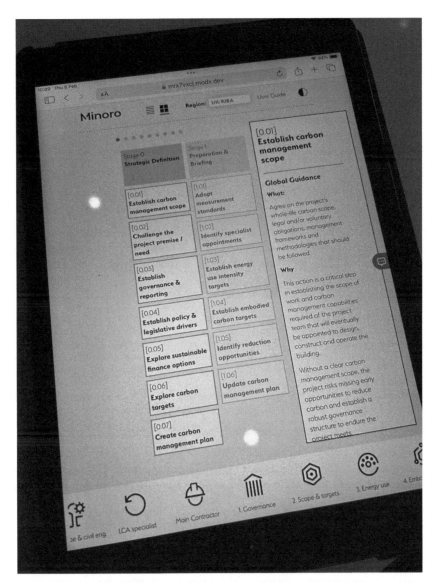

Figure 1.13.3 Grimshaw has offered their intellectual property related to the decarbonization pathway for buildings, and as a result, formed a partnership with the World Business Council for Sustainable Development to publish the pathway as a free-to-use website. Figure 1.13.3 shows how the decarbonization pathway for buildings found on http://www.minoro.org.

Source: Author Paul Toyne with Grimshaw Architects.

Conclusions

Ensuring all new buildings and infrastructure consider whole-life carbon and take actions to dramatically reduce the carbon emissions associated with their construction, operation, and maintenance is vital if we are to meet our global climate commitments. Solving the climate emergency through built environment solutions is critical and we have many of the tools required but we need to make sure that they are readily accessible and free for all to use. As explained, Minoro.org will certainly help. On focusing solely on climate change mitigation, there is a need to conclude with the obvious: I need to ensure that our built environment is resilient to the current and future impacts of climate change, as well as addressing its' known negative impact on biodiversity loss. Understanding the interconnectedness of resilience, health, and well-being, biodiversity (blue and green infrastructure) and planetary boundaries with net-zero carbon in the built environment will be essential so that future investments can deliver co-benefits across all issues for us, nature, and the restoration of Earth. Again, taking a holistic system will help identify these overlaps.

Acknowledgments

I wish to thank all members of Grimshaw's Climate Emergency Taskforce who contributed to the decarbonization pathways content that now forms the basis of the web platform Minoro: in particular, Peter Swallow, and Aaron Vaden-Youmans, who also made helpful comments to an earlier draft.

Notes

1 A0 (= pre-construction) is generally assumed to be zero for buildings. However, for infrastructure projects, A0 can include ground investigations and activities associated with designing the asset.
2 Demolition of existing structures or buildings must be separately identified and included in module A5.
3 A thermal bridge is a part of the building envelope where heat flow is different (usually higher) to the adjacent area. This can lead to changes in surface temperatures and heat losses.

References

Allwood, J., and Cullen, J. (2015). *Sustainable Materials—Without the Hot Air: Making Buildings, Vehicles and Products Efficiently and with Less New Material.* 2nd Revised edition. Cambridge: UIT, 408 p.

Architecture 2030. (2019). Why Buildings? Retrieved 27 December, 2023, from https://www.architecture2030.org/why-the-built-environment/why-buildings/#:~:text=BUILDINGS%20ARE%20A%20SIGNIFICANT%20END%20USE%20OF%20HIGH%20IMPACT%20MATERIALS&text=It%20is%20therefore%20crucial%20to,be%20taken%20back%20or%20reduced.sector matters.

Bere, J. (2019). *An Introduction to Passive House.* London: Routledge, p 112.

BSI. (2023). *PAS 2080:2023 Carbon Management in Buildings and Infrastructure.* 2nd edition. London: BSI Publishing, p 68.

BSI. (2023a). PAS 2080 Guidance Document. Retrieved 29 December, 2023, from https://knowledge.bsigroup.com/products/carbon-management-in-buildings-and-infrastructure?version=standard.

Cembureau, (2020). Carbon Neutrality Roadmap 2050. Retrieved 2 January, 2024, from https://cembureau.eu/library/reports/2050-carbon-neutrality-roadmap/.

Cheshire, D. (2021). *Handbook to Building a Circular Economy.* 2nd edition. London: RIBA publishing, p 160.

Esau, R., Jungclaus, M., Olgyay, V., and Rempher, A. (2012). Reducing Embodied Carbon in Buildings: Low-Cost, High-Value Opportunities. Retrieved 4 January, 2024, from https://rmi.org/insight/reducing-embodied-carbon-in-buildings/.

Hopfe, C., and Robert McLeod, R. (eds) (2015). *The Passivhaus Designer's Manual: A Technical Guide to Low and Zero Energy Buildings.* 1st edition. London: Routledge, p 346.

International Passive House Association, IPHA. (n.d). The Passive House Platform. Retrieved 3 January, 2024, from https://passivehouse-international.org/index.php?page_id=65#:~:text=The%20 global%20Passive%20House%20platform&text=Many%20of%20these%20 quality%2Dassured,than%205%2C600%20Passive%20House%20buildings.

Johnson, E., and Vaden Youmas, A. (2023). Sustainability Case Study: Rob and Melani Walton Center for Planetary Boundaries, Arizona State University. Retrieved 30 December, 2023, from https:// grimshaw.global/assets/uploads/ASU_Walton_Center_Case_Study_1.pdf.

Lei, T., Wang, D., Yu, X., et al. (2023). Global Iron and Steel Plant CO2 Emissions and Carbon-Neutrality Pathways. *Nature*, 622: 514–520.

LETI. (2019). Net Zero Operational Carbon: Ten Key Requirements for New Buildings. Retrieved 29 December, 2023, from https://www.leti.uk/_files/ugd/252d09_d2401094168a4ee5af86b147b6 1df50e.pdf.

LETI. (2020). *LETI Climate Emergency Design Guide: How New Buildings Can Meet UK Climate Change Targets*. Jan 2020 Edition. Retrieved 29 December, 2023, from https://www.leti.uk/_files/ ugd/252d093b0f2acf2bb24c019f5ed9173fc5d9f4.pdf.

LETI. (2020a). Embodied Carbon Primer. Retrieved 2 January, 2024, from jnahttps://www.leti.uk/_ files/ugd/252d09_8ceffcbcafdb43cf8a19ab9af5073b92.pdf.

MacKay, D., Bock, M., Cebon, D., Cullen, J., Doig, K., Drewniok. M.P., Gustafsson, J., Guthrie, G., Nibbert, A., Smith. S., Swallow, P., Symons, K., Tzokova, P. and Williams, B. (2020). *Energy Cost Metric: Energy Design Guide for the Civil Engineering Building in West Cambridge*. Retrieved 2 January, 2024, from https://www.refficiency.org/wp-content/uploads/2020/05/Energy-Cost-Metric-v7.0-FINAL_on_line.pdf.

Milnes, C. Aellig. P., Gaullier, N., Schneider Roos, K., Huber, D., Wiener, D., and Guldimann, R. (2014) 4th Global Infrastructure Basel Foundation Summit Report. Retrieved 2 January, 2024, from https://gib-foundation.org/wp-content/uploads/2020/01/Summit-Report_ext_Fin_sml.pdf.

PassiveHouse. (2023). Component Database. Retrieved 27 December, 2023, from https://database. passivehouse.com/en/components/https://database.passivehouse.com/en/components/.

RICS. (2023). *Whole Life Carbon Assessment for the Built Environment*. 2nd edition. Retrieved 27 December, 2023, from https://www.rics.org/profession-standards/rics-standards-and-guidance/ sector-standards/construction-standards/whole-life-carbon-assessment.

Rong, H., Zhang, H., Xiao, S., et al. (2016). Optimizing Energy Consumption for Data Centers. *Renewable and Sustainable Energy Reviews*, 58: 674–691.

Sangiorgio, A. (2020). Sustainability Case Study of Woodside Building, Melbourne. Retrieved 27 December, 2023, from https://grimshaw.global/assets/uploads/Monash_Case_Study_3.pdf.

Sembroiz, D., Careglio, D., Ricciardi, S., and Fiore, U. (2019). Planning and Operational Energy Optimization Solutions for Smart Buildings. *Information Sciences*, 476: 439–452. https://doi. org/10.1016/j.ins.2018.06.003.

Shah, A.S., Nasir, H., Fayaz, M., Lajis, A., and Shah, A. (2019). A Review on Energy Consumption Optimization Techniques in IoT Based Smart Building Environments. *Information*, 10: 108. https://doi.org/10.3390/info10030108.

Sidor, N., and Swallow, P. (2022). Sustainability Case Study: Civil Engineering Building. Retrieved 2 January, 2024, from https://grimshaw.global/assets/uploads/Cambs_Civil_Eng_Bldg_Case_ Study_FINAL_compressed.pdf.

Subramanian, C.V., Ramachandran, N., and Senthamil Kumar, S. (2017). Review of Passive Cooling Architectural Design Interventions for Thermal Comfort in Residential Buildings. *Indian Journal of Scientific Research*, 14(1): 163–172.

Swallow, P., and Green, A. (2020). Sustainability Case Study on Bath School of Art and Design. Retrieved 29 December, 2023, from https://grimshaw.global/assets/uploads/Grimshaw_BathSchool_ Case_Study.pdf.

Tian, Zhichao, Zhang, Xinkai, Jin, Xing, et al. (2018). Towards Adoption of Building Energy Simulation and Optimization for Passive Building Design: A Survey and a Review. *Energy and Buildings*, 158: 1306–1316.

Transparency Market Research. (2021). 'Construction Market Research' Construction Waste Market—Global Industry Analysis, Size, Share, Trends and Forecast 2017–2025. Retrieved 27 December, 2023, from https://www.transparencymarketresearch.com/construction-waste-market.html.

United Nations, Department of Economic and Social Affairs, Population Division. (2019). *World Urbanization Prospects: The 2018 Revision (ST/ESA/SER.A/420)*. New York: United Nations.

United Nations Environment Programme, UNEP. (2020). 2020 Global Status Report for Buildings and Construction: Towards a Zero-emission, Efficient and Resilient Buildings and Construction Sector. Nairobi. Retrieved 27 December, 2023, from https://globalabc.org/sites/default/files/inline-files/2020%20Buildings%20GSR_FULL%20REPORT.pdf.

United Nations Environment Programme, UNEP. (2021). 2021 Global Status Report for Buildings and Construction: Towards a Zero-emission, Efficient and Resilient Buildings and Construction Sector. Nairobi. Retrieved 27 December, 2023, from https://globalabc.org/sites/default/files/2021-10/GABC_Buildings-GSR-2021_BOOK.pdf.

United Nations Environment Programme, UNEP. (2023). Broken Record: Temperatures Hit New Highs, Yet World Fails to Cut Emissions (Again). Retrieved 28 December, 2023, from https://wedocs.unep.org/bitstream/handle/20.500.11822/43922/EGR2023.pdf?sequence=3&isAllowed=y.

Vandenbogaerde, L., Verbeke, S., and Audenaert, A. (2023). Optimizing Building Energy Consumption in Office Buildings: A Review of Building Automation and Control Systems and Factors Influencing Energy Savings. *Journal of Building Engineering*, 76: 107233.

White, J. (2022). *Sustainability Case Study: London Bridge Station*. Retrieved 2 January, 2024, from https://grimshaw.global/assets/uploads/Grimshaw_London_Bridge_CS.pdf.

1.14

BLOCKCHAIN TECHNOLOGY FOR SMART THINKING

The Intangible Digital Assets for AI-Enabled Monitoring and Improving Process Performance and Reducing Building Impacts on Ecology

Eric Farr and Poorang Piroozfar

Abstract

Buildings are significant contributors to the climate change. Efforts to improve the impacts of the built environment are scattered, limited in their validity and reliability, and lack consistency, structure, and rigor. Current methods of post-occupancy evaluation are dispersed and lack a common shared platform for collective learning and collaborative feedback.

Although subject to its definition, scope, and signification, design on its own may or may not be regarded as an intangible asset, it encompasses, triggers, and entails many intangible assets that may get lost in documentation due to a lack of unified protocols to capture, store, and retrieve them. Smart design may have different delineations; as a design approach associated with smart systems, capable of operationalizing the S.M.A.R.T. principles in the context of creative practices; or as a form of self-adaptation of, and/or to, intelligent systems.

This chapter looks into how design intangible assets can be used for peer-to-peer data capture to be fed into blockchain ledgers constructed over time as immutable, tamper-proof data chains accessible through a smart AI-enabled design toolkit to help designers improve their design's performance and reduce their ecological and environmental impacts.

Introduction

Buildings are still amongst the most significant contributors to climate change with a record of up to 40% of global energy consumption and associated GHG emissions. If we refer to the United States Environmental Protection Agency's (EPA) definition of the built environment which asserts:

The built environment can generally be described as the man-made or modified structures that provide people with living, working, and recreational spaces. It touches all

DOI: 10.4324/9781003384113-22

aspects of our lives, encompassing the buildings we live in, the distribution systems that provide us with water and electricity, and the roads, bridges, and transportation systems we use to get from place to place.

then the impact of what we create as man-made structures would be way beyond what is generally known or expected to be just as buildings. Numerous efforts and significant achievements have been made in the form of directives, pledges, and commitments at international/inter-governmental levels; standards, policies, legislations, codes, and regulations at national levels; good practice, social corporate responsibilities, and other corporate or professional bodies guidelines and initiatives at regional and local levels. Nevertheless, the pace of change is so fast that widens the gap between those efforts and achievements, and the case-based real-world applications at project and process levels.

Academic research in many aspects associated with the built environment's impacts on the wider built and natural environments and eco-systems are not few and far between. The usability of all those research that usually seek to achieve or recommend a higher level of impact than what is promised or intended at policy, standards, and legislative levels is still in need of major rethinking with respect to how, where, and when effectively the collective information base and knowledgebase can be found, retrieved, and applied to the new cases where a new build or a refurbishment, repurposing, or even demolition and recycling/upcycling project is at hand. Such complexity in the scattered structure of collective knowledge and research in this area also brings along the question of validity, reliability, timeliness, and signification of the findings for their application to new, similar, or identical cases elsewhere.

On the other hand, fragmentation of the construction industry due to dispersed supply chain structure and numerous suppliers, local (vs global) construction cultures, methods and technologies, and the differences in the labor market, the professional and vocational training process, protocols, and requirements and the workforce hierarchy and structure make such applications even more difficult if not impossible at all. Even more so, the buildings at the very best are unconnected banks of materials that can potentially be connected through a synchronized national Building Account Routing Number (n-BARN) to form a centralized system to institutionalize and improve the circular economy (Farr and Piroozfar, 2022). This will provide a semi- to fully integrated infrastructure for sustainability to thrive through the facilitation of a circular economy but only at material availability and suitability levels. Although the knowledgebase n-BARN can and will provide is invaluable in material recycling, upcycling, remanufacturing, and reuse, its application at the level where the collective design feedback loop can be closed and shared is limited.

In this chapter, we argue for the defragmentation of intangible assets[1] from their corresponding tangible assets to form and propose a model using which an open-access peer-to-peer fully verified, immutable, tamper-proof digital database can be devised to help collaboratively build, vet/verify, and share a collective knowledgebase for monitoring, controlling, and reducing ecological impacts of buildings through an Artificial Intelligence (AI)-enabled platform/system/algorithm for tracking and improving building performance.

Fragmentation of Objects and Defragmentation of Information

Intangible assets (in the form of sustainability and EEI data/information/knowledge) and the state and the process of their association and disassociation with their corresponding tangible assets (in the form of buildings and the built environment assets) are key in extracting, transferring, storing, and retrieving segments of information as a part of a collective body of knowledge for future retrieval and (re)use.

According to James (1907), truth is verifiable to the extent that statements (and thoughts) agree with actual things, in addition to the extent to which they associate or cohere with each other. These are in return verified by the observed results of the application of an idea onto actual practice. Presuming their trueness and validity, if truth is replaced with data (information and knowledge whichever applicable), then theories of truth will become relevant to our argument for the necessity of effective and meaningful disassociation of intangible assets from their tangible carriers and the ways in which this process is facilitated and managed for forming a peer-to-peer database, information base, and knowledgebase which can facilitate monitoring and improving the built environment's ecological impacts. Suffice to say that substituting truth (even though it could partially include facts, is also subject to beliefs and opinions) with the triangle of data, information, and knowledge is an intended decision for the fact that at least one definition of truth, as suggested by James, implies that true beliefs are those ones that prove useful to the believer; what can be said for some of theories associated with environment and sustainability. Cleaving to either "correspondence theory of truth" or "coherence theory of truth" will probably only give us half of what we need to cognize and extend the existing boundaries within which technology can benefit the Architecture, Engineering, and Construction (AEC) industry. Instead, William James's pragmatic theory of truth – as a synthesis of correspondence theory of truth and coherence theory of truth – becomes key in understanding how data, information and knowledge associated with a particular tangible asset can be exerted, independently verified, and built into an immutable block to then be retrieved and reused by anonymous end-users without any worries about correctness and/or tampering with the database.

Blockchain Technology

With a major aspiration to develop an immutable timestamp for documents to prevent them from being tampered with, blockchain technology was first invented in 1991 by Haber and Stornetta. It was put into its real work application with the launch of Bitcoin in January 2009. Hayes (2023) defines Blockchain as "A digital database or ledger that is distributed among the nodes of a peer-to-peer network". Scott et al. (2021) on the other hand tell us that some have defined Blockchain as a technology that enables triple entry accounting, which allows multiple parties to transact across a shared synchronous ledger. Each transaction is substantiated with a digital signature to provide proof of its authenticity (Grigg, 2005). It differs from a typical database in the way it stores information; blockchains store data in blocks linked together via cryptography.

Decentralized, distributed, and consensus are some of the key features of blockchain (Chen et al., 2020). A typical public blockchain comprises thousands of computer nodes connected through a decentralized network, whose management does not require a central authority (Foti et al., 2021). Mining in blockchain is the process of creating new blocks and distributing them across all nodes on the network for which blockchain as a self-sustaining network rewards users (Wang et al., 2021). Once transactions are sent to the network, they are placed in a pool of unverified transactions, where they are periodically collected and validated by miners before they are placed into a block (Karale and Ranaware, 2019). To ensure that there is only one version of the ledger in existence at any point in time a consensus mechanism is used by the miners to check each other's results prior to the inclusion of new blocks (Hribernik et al., 2020). Although the most common use for blockchain transactions has been in the form of ledgers in banking and finance where the most significant body of relevant literature has been developed, different types of information can be stored on a blockchain.

Smart Design and Multi-level Perspective

First coined by George T. Doran in 1981, the SMART in SMART goals, primarily in/ for management, stands for Specific, Measurable, Achievable [or Assignable], Relevant [or Realistic], and Time-bound [or Time-related] (Boogaard, 2021). The term smart has made its way through to the AEC industry and has been associated with design, buildings, communities, cities, transportation, traffic management, city/urban management, urban development, and infrastructure to name but a few. Smart design is stimulated and underpinned by (technical and technological) innovation and usually requires a transition in a socio-technical context from an existing specific system usually to a radically or fundamentally upper level system equally specific if not rather more exclusive. As such, smart design in its nature, construct, and characteristics is comparable to a wicked problem. The socio-technical regime forms the "deep structure" that accounts for the stability of an existing socio-technical system (Geels, 2005) and is the one undergoing the process of evolution or change. Hence, multi-level perspective (MLP)[2] is a workable and relevant theory for looking into transitions into the smart paradigm (which is not the focus of this chapter) and transitions within the smart design paradigm (which is what we concentrate on in here).

Geels (2011:26) tells us that as a middle-range theory (MRT)[3], MLP conceptualizes overall dynamic patterns in socio-technical transitions. The MLP relates various concepts and uses empirical research to identify recurring patterns and generalizable lessons. The non-linearity of transition processes ensues from the interplay of developments at three analytical levels: the locus for radical innovations – the niches, the locus of established practices and associated rules that stabilize existing systems – the socio-technical regimes, and an exogenous socio-technical landscape (Rip and Kemp, 1998; Geels, 2002, 2005). Figure 1.14.1 depicts the concept of smart design evolution based upon the multi-level perspective MRT.

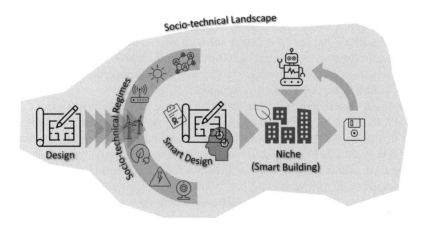

Figure 1.14.1   The concept of smart design evolution based on multi-level perspective middle-range theory (Image courtesy of authors).

Ecological Impacts of the Built Environment

The complexity of the concept of "smart" as intended and applied to architecture, design, and the built environment is unanimously agreed upon. This complexity is partially due to the big data not only in terms of the volume of datasets but also because of numerous entailed (data) nodes due to a large number and broad extent of varied disciplines involved. If only, for instance, the triple bottom-line of sustainability is aimed at, at its very first tier, the data, information, and knowledge involved root into economics, finance, environmental science, social science, and humanities at the very least – all within the context of, associated with, or related to the built environment. Inherent defragmentation of data, information, and knowledge and the need for attributing and reattributing them to the digital twins of the tangible assets to models simulate or imitate what their performance (not only environmental, but also economic, technical, functional, and societal) would or could be in its own is a complicated procedure, should this be aimed to be attended to in a comprehensive systemic manner. Such applications then get processed, translated, and realized into tangible assets which will have some constant output streams associated with them in the form of their real performance data as intangible assets of those end products – tangible assets – in/of the built environment. The smartness in design adds to this complex process the attribute of fluid transitions as a result of constant flow of data which is exponentially higher than a non-smart setting due to their inherent "dynamicity" which will entail Just-in-Time response to immediate and frequent interventions in the tangible asset's performance requirements by the building asset tenants or space users, the building asset owners or leaseholders, the facilities managers, or the maintenance/repair teams. On the other hand the caveats between how the design intents envisage a built asset to perform (mostly environmentally but also not mutually exclusively economically, technically, functionally, and societally) and how in reality it performs (what is known as performance gap more exclusively with reference to the energy and environmental performance of a building) make very difficult and in fact in some cases next to impossible to plan, predict, maintain, and control the ecological impacts of built environment. Added to the complexity is aging and deterioration of the building asset where the technical performance of materials and components starts declining with a direct or indirect impact on the ecological performance of the building as a whole (Figure 1.14.2). The deficiencies, shortcomings, incompetencies, and lack of fitness-for-purpose associated with the processes and products as well as

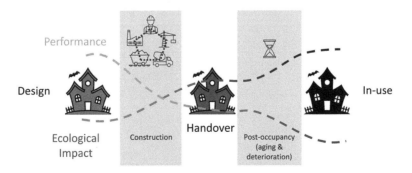

Figure 1.14.2 Ecological impact of the built environment: The impact of the performance gap, aging, and deterioration (Image courtesy of authors).

the workforce are other issues that make the performance gap wider and more difficult to predict, alleviate, or eliminate.

AI-Enabled Blockchain Technology for Smart Design

As one of the three key components of AI governance[4] (Ross, 2023), AI enablement is the process of feeding datasets into an automated system – a machine – to create self-learning patterns, thereby enabling cognitive functions – namely, thinking, perceiving, learning, problem-solving, and decision-making tasks (PSA, 2023). This process is an essential stage in substituting human intelligence with artificial intelligent which can lead into solving complex or wicked problems. AI enablement involves embedding the necessary discipline around data ownership, storage, usage, and sharing (Ross, 2023).

The point at which AI enablement gets applied is important primarily due to the other components of the AI governance and most specifically with regards to accountability. As blockchain is a tamper-proof, immutable, and unimpeded data chain that can be accessed and used – while also added to, where the enablement takes place, would be critical to the process of data capture, processing, storage, and addition to the blockchain. If the application of AI takes place immediately for the disassociation of intangible assets from their corresponding tangible assets or immediately after that then there will be two vulnerable points for breaching the data chain one by the human operators of the data or the AI system and the other one due to a selective choice of "favorable" data by an AI which may have gone above and beyond what it has been designed for. It is, however, possible and acceptable if the intangible assets associated with the tangible assets are mined/ extracted by automated systems with no high-level of cognitive decision-making before temper-proofness of the process is achieved through the process of applying the blockchain. If a high-level autonomous AI – or an unregulated one with an ability to build up such autonomy – is applied early on before the data and the whole data is captured, extracted, stored, or fed into the tamper-proof system of a blockchain, the risk of tampering with data, knowingly or unknowingly, willingly, or unwillingly by a human or non-human agent is always present and likely. Figure 1.14.3 shows an AI-enabled blockchain technology model for smart design.

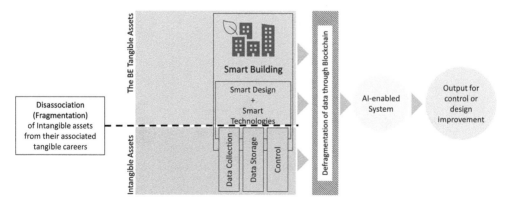

Figure 1.14.3 An AI-enabled blockchain technology model for smart design (Image courtesy of authors).

Concluding Comments

Climate change is an indisputable fact, and the building and construction industry is a major contributor with up to it. The need for a decentralized network for different building scientists within energy, environmental impact (assessment), and building performance scope across the globe to document live, just-in-time and relevant data pertaining to those areas freely without a central authority control is a way forward to build up a decentralized central data base that can not only be used locally to inform and improve the building maintenance/management systems or collectively as an design information toolkit which can act as a feedback look for designers to help them improve their design with respect to its energy performance, GHG emissions, and its EEI.

There are, however, concerns that the data capture, storage, processing, and inputting to the system can be subject to human errors and may get tampered with, with or without any specific intention or ill-will. One way to deal with this issue is to use blockchain technology to ensure that a decentralized intangible asset management system, whose entry logs are vetted anonymously and independently by the members of the network, exists and facilitates a fair, transparent, and temper-proof system that is open, accessible, and usable by everyone to add to and to use to improve their design, 1fabrication, construction, and detailing/specification decisions with an impact on the EEI of buildings. However, the enormous volume of data and colossal frequency of data nodes makes this task a very time-consuming and costly process. Automation via AI seems to be a viable solution to this problem.

AI has hypothetical and proven benefits but also some existing and potential threats if applied without due diligence as it may develop autonomy above and beyond its intended design and start making decisions which may or may not be justifiable through human moral, ethics, and logics. Encryption of intangible assets so that they become immutable and tamper-proof may be a way forward to put a reliable measure in place to ensure that the intangible assets cannot be meddled with by a human or non-human agent.

This chapter presented this novel idea for the first time and drew attention to the potential problems associated with it using Pragmatic Theory of Truth on one hand and an MLP MRT on the other. Using these theories, this chapter proposed a model that can be used to devise an effective AI-enabled performance tracking and improving system to monitor, control, and reduce ecological impacts of buildings using blockchain technology.

Notes

1 Here we rest our case of tangible assets specifically in the built (environment) artifacts and assets while intangible assets will be the data and information (nuggets, sets, clusters, and/or batches) associated with those tangible assets.

2 Widely seen as an alternative to general theory (Parsons and Shils, 1951) – also known as "Grand Theory" (Mills, 1959) – the middle-range theory, coined by Merton (1968), aims at explaining specific social phenomena without being bound to have its object as the "society" in its entirety (Boudon, 2001).

3 The concept of middle-range theory (MRT) introduced by Merton (1968) aims to navigate between the extremes of grand theory (such as Parson's structural functionalism) and pure empiricism, which focuses only on data-collection and data-analysis. It was designed as "theories that lie between the minor but necessary working hypotheses that evolve in abundance during day-to-day research and the all-inclusive systematic efforts to develop a unified theory that will explain all the observed uniformities of social behavior, social organization and social change" (Merton, 1968:39). Merton suggests that "An array of concepts does not constitute theory. (...) It is only when such concepts are interrelated in the form of a scheme that a theory begins to emerge" (1968:143). According to

Geels (2007), MRT's characteristics include: (a) MRT is not about broad, abstract entities such as "society" or "social system", but about concrete phenomena (such as socio-technical transitions), (b) MRT differs from grand theory, because it emphasizes interactions between theory and empirical research. So, MRT does not consist of elaborate frameworks with endless conceptual distinctions and limited linkages to empirical research, (c) MRT specifies relationships between concepts into analytical models.

4 Ross (2023) suggests that three key components of AI governance are enablement, accountability, and explainability.

References

Boogaard, K. 2021. *How to Write SMART Goals* [Online]. Altassian. Available: https://www.atlassian.com/blog/productivity/how-to-write-smart-goals [Accessed 19 September 2023].

Boudon, R. 2001. Sociology: Overview. In: Smelser, N. J. & Baltes, P. B. (eds.), *International Encyclopedia of the Social & Behavioral Sciences* (pp. 14581–14585). Oxford: Pergamon.

Chen, R., Li, Y., Yu, Y., Li, H., Chen, X. & Susilo, W. 2020. Blockchain-based dynamic provable data possession for smart cities. *IEEE Internet of Things Journal*, 7, 4143–4154.

Doran, G. T. 1981. There's a S.M.A.R.T. way to write managements's goals and objectives. *Management Review*, 70, 35–36.

Farr, E. R. P. & Piroozfar, P. 2022. Enabling circular economy in the AEC industry through digitalization. In: Kanaani, M. (ed.), *The Routledge Companion to Ecological Design Thinking: Healthful Ecotopian Visions for Architecture and Urbanism* (pp. 339–350). New York: Routledge.

Foti, M., Mavromatis, C. & Vavalis, M. 2021. Decentralized blockchain-based consensus for optimal power flow solutions. *Applied Energy*, 283, 116100.

Geels, F. W. 2002. Technological transitions as evolutionary reconfiguration processes: A multi-level perspective and a case-study. *Research Policy*, 31, 1257–1274.

Geels, F. W. 2005. The dynamics of transitions in socio-technical systems: A multi-level analysis of the transition pathway from horse-drawn carriages to automobiles (1860–1930). *Technology Analysis & Strategic Management*, 17, 445–476.

Geels, F. W. 2011. The multi-level perspective on sustainability transitions: Responses to seven criticisms. *Environmental Innovation and Societal Transitions*, 1, 24–40.

Grigg, I. 2005. *Triple Entry Accounting* [Online]. Satoshi Nakamoto Institute. Available: https://nakamotoinstitute.org/triple-entry-accounting/ [Accessed 19 September 2023].

Hayes, A. 2023. *Blockchain Facts: What Is It, How It Works, and How It Can Be Used?* [Online]. Investopedia [Accessed 19 September 2023]. https://www.investopedia.com/terms/b/blockchain.asp

Hribernik, M., Zero, K., Kummer, S. & Herold, D. M. 2020. City logistics: Towards a blockchain decision framework for collaborative parcel deliveries in micro-hubs. *Transportation Research Interdisciplinary Perspectives*, 8, 100274.

James, W. 1907. Lecture 6 in Pragmatism: A new name for some old ways of thinking. In: James, W. (ed.), *Pragmatism's Conception of Truth* (pp. 76–91). New York: Longman Green and Co.

Karale, S. & Ranaware, V. 2019. Applications of blockchain technology in smart city development: A research. *International Journal of Innovative Technolology and Exploring Engineering*, 8, 556–559.

Merton, R. K. 1968. *Social Theory and Social Structure*. New York: Free Press.

Mills, C. W. 1959. *The Sociological Imagination*. Oxford University Press, Incorporated.

Parsons, T. & Shils, E. 1951. *Toward a General Theory of Action*. Cambridge, MA: Harvard University Press.

PSA. 2023. *Artifical Intelligence (AI) Enabled Technologies* [Online]. Office of the Principal Scientific Adviser (PSA) to the Government of India. Available: https://www.psa.gov.in/technology-frontiers/artificial-intelligence-ai-enabled-technologies/261 [Accessed 4 November 2023].

Rip, A. & Kemp, R. 1998. Technological change. *Human Choice and Climate Change*, 2, 327–399.

Ross, C. 2023. *Can AI Be As Unethical And Biased As Humans?* [Online]. Forbes. Available: https://www.forbes.com/sites/forbesbusinesscouncil/2023/08/14/can-ai-be-as-unethical-and-biased-as-humans/?sh=2d6274ec6878 [Accessed 4 November 2023].

Scott, D. J., Broyd, T. & MA, L. 2021. Exploratory literature review of blockchain in the construction industry. *Automation in Construction*, 132, 103914.

Wang, Y., Chen, C. H. & Zghari-Sales, A. 2021. Designing a blockchain enabled supply chain. *International Journal of Production Research*, 59, 1450–1475.

PARADIGMATIC CATEGORY 2

Smart Design Methodologies and Concepts for Intelligent Typologies and User Needs

This Paradigmatic Category expands on design innovations based on users' needs and architectural types, as well as specific smart methodologies, means, and approaches that constitute design intelligibility and are specific to architectural types and users. This section expands on smart design concepts, their applications for the built environment, and their impacts on the design of spaces and infrastructure. This paradigmatic realm focuses on smart specificity needs for architectural designs based on unique characteristics and qualities of contextual settings, as well as spatial performative typological requirements and users' restrictive conditions. The contextual setting can be in space, under bodies of water, or within a fully enclosed environment, in which specificity of the user's needs in conjunction with certain physical or cognitive shortcomings, as well as physical restrictive qualities, can create specific design performativity demands. For instance, design for the blind and design for cognitive disorders necessitate certain functionalities that demand designed spaces must be charged with the capacity to address specific performative aspects of their use through smart design thinking concepts and means, for example in *design for learning* and *design for healing*.

 DOI: 10.4324/9781003384113-23

2.1

CONSIDERING SMART DESIGN METHODOLOGY AS RESEARCH-INFORMED DESIGN

2.1.1

SEARCHING THROUGH SMART DESIGN METHODS FOR ARCHITECTURE

Carmina Sánchez-del-Valle

Abstract

Architectural design aims to predict the future state or states of a physical project by utilizing knowledge gained from the past and present. Challenges demand other ways of thinking, designing, and making to face the trouble of an environment in flux. Building system's adaptability and interactivity with internal and external forces are a complex endeavor. Design methods and tools help teams achieve desired change as efficiently and effectively as possible. But design decisions depend on both subjective and quantifiable measures, and uncertainty makes it difficult to define goals. In the times of Big Data, sensing environments, robotics, and AI, the knowledge generated by architecture, engineering, construction, and facilities operation firms has yet to be collected systematically and evaluated with rigor. Because methods and tools capture knowledge about design practice, sensible and collaborative approaches to form futures must be explored.

Academic research centers and software developers, along with architecture engineering firms and construction companies, have been incorporating emerging technology into design and into projects, to manage their life cycles. Such efforts require collecting and organizing design information as evidence, building repositories of data, and relational databases. These groups are also developing algorithms for analyzing the data, constructing predictive models and generative neural networks, and integrating BIM with a digital twin. Yet, sharing design, construction, and building operation information among teams in the design and construction landscape presents financial, legal, ontological, and knowledge barriers. AI and machine learning may bridge the gap between the creative process and computation but may not fully resolve all existing barriers because they are buried in the methods, tools, and workflows we use. Attention must be paid to local work that may be having a wide impact in the periphery of Industry 5.0.

Architectural Design Methodology, Methods, Design Tools: The Ecosystem

Architectural design moves to predict the future state or states of a physical project by utilizing knowledge gained from the past and present. Different design methods and models

DOI: 10.4324/9781003384113-25

194

are used to produce the components, their systems, and consequent relationships. Teams manipulate abstractions, calibrate models and simulations, cybrids, building information models (BIMs), and handle many types of design tools. The more complete and accurate the models, props, and mock-ups, the better fit to fulfill goals. Any "smart" design process aims to meet those goals. A fundamental part of architectural design is to anticipate and satisfactorily address human needs within existing and manufactured contexts. The variability of the human, built, and natural contexts has to be addressed. Access to relevant design information is critical. The quality of the design is dependent on the fit of the constellation of design methods harnessed to identify, select, analyze, and interpret all of the information and intermediate design states from which design decisions are based. The assessment of outcomes, leveraging a myriad of interacting factors, forces, and conditions, is a complicated task.

Challenges demand other ways of thinking, designing, and making, some of which include water, land, and air pollution; climate variability and extremes; and limited resources. Design must be attuned to local-and-global forces, tangible and intangible costs, human needs, and access, and change through the life a project. The immediate goals are to define a building's life cycle for low carbon footprint and achieve economy of means through prefabrication, reuse, and recycling. Effective design should provide for disassembly and assembly, a tracked inventory of components, monitored building materials and systems, and performance adjustments in response to external and internal environments. In addition, early in the process, smart building sensing and monitoring device requirements – along with their interface with autonomous or manual control systems for seamless operation and maintenance – must be brought into design considerations. The connectivity of multiple control systems that may be or not interconnected, so they collect data and respond to a local condition in an integrated way, must be ensured. The ubiquitousness of Internet of Things devices and Wi-Fi demands the revamping of enclosure and structural building assemblies to facilitate radio waves transmission. In design, connectivity and interoperability requirements will be negotiated with the transmission-blocking materials of requisite life safety construction (Thieme, 2020; Ekahau, 2024; Newth, 2019). Already, there are calls for "promoting space design that collects the greatest amount of information and efficient use without compromising inhabitants' comfort." (Racha-Pacheco et al., 2023).

Data, Information, Evidence: Research-based design, Research-Informed design
Architectural design is multidisciplinary. Optimally, its practice is integrated. Conflicts appear in the establishment of focus and in the ordering of tasks. Because methods capture knowledge about design practice, those developed for transdisciplinary application must consider the operationalization, use, and internalization in that context (Lavrsen et al., 2022, 5). Highly specialized projects have complex requirements, so integrated design requires transdisciplinary team members. Design methods applied over cycles must be adaptable to fit situational needs, skillsets, and the organization of design activities (Lavrsen et al., 10). The lack of knowledge exchange among disciplines fails the very intent of transdisciplinary design (Lavrsen et al., 12).

An applied design method is a socio-technical system encompassing the designers themselves (Gericke et al., 2022, 14, 19). Method is the "means to help designers achieve desired change as efficiently and effectively as possible" (Gericke et al., 6) and serves as "a specification of how a specified result is to be achieved." (Gericke et al., 11). Design methods must be regularly evaluated to determine their validity for ongoing development and improvement (Gericke et al.). Combinations of methods are ecosystems where each occupies an interlocking niche (Gericke et al., 6). In the design process, "different methods have compatible and overlapping sets of concepts, terminology and representations so outputs can be used as inputs for the next" project (Gericke et al.). Furthermore "combinations of notational formalisms for different types of information function as representation ecosystems." (Gericke et al.)

The AEC industry has been slow to adopt integrated and collaborative practices as a way of improving productivity goals. It is argued this is because traditional linear workflow leads to "fragmented supply chains among multiple project participants involved at different times with limited interconnection." (Ikudayisi et al., 2023). In the context of Industry 4.0, the AEC industry has to adopt "technological tools toward achieving high-level integration across a project's life cycle and for all stakeholders." (Ikudayisi et al.). These "technological enablers" include BIM, digitalization, automation, simulation, robotics, artificial intelligence (AI), machine learning, deep learning, augmented reality, virtual reality digital twins, Internet of Things (Ikudayisi et al.).

With the advent of Industry 5.0, the AEC industry again is under pressure to align with "the ideals of connectivity of people, processes, technology, and information based on core values of human-centricity, sustainability, and resilience." (Ikudayisi et al.). Expanded versions of BIM for Integrated Design Process, Modular Integrated Construction, and Integrated Project Delivery must be developed (Ikudayisi et al.). The International Council for Research and Innovation in Building and Construction (CIB) is promoting the concept of "integrated design and delivery solutions" (IDDS). Yet, the adoption of integrated practice and delivery systems is hampered by the usual contractual issues such as risks, liability insurance, dispute resolution, and data sharing (Ikudayisi et al.). These issues may affect the incorporation of the next generation of tools such as the building digital twin, the datasets, and models necessary for AI-based design applications and their interoperability.

It is projected that as "BIM evolves from modelling environment to management tool for the finished building, issues of software interoperability and common standards, digital infrastructures like servers, and their control will become ever more critical." (Braun, Kropp and Boeva, 2022, 270). However, obstacles to compatibility and sharing of information still need to be resolved (Bernstein, 2022, 170). There are two inherent contradictions in BIM software. First, it "forces all involved to adopt its rationalities, pushing and enabling particular ways of practicing design and construction while potentially foreclosing others." (Braun, Kropp and Boeva, 270, 272). Second, it ensures the interoperability of data models while locking the design team into proprietary software applications (Braun, Kropp and Boeva). And yet, the investment of large proprietary software companies in the development of their products will deliver the data sources and AI tools that "will benefit the entire building industry." (Bernstein, 132)

A number of large firms have in-house development teams working on emerging technologies. For example, Applied Research & Development Group (ARD) at Foster + Partners is collaborating with Autodesk on Hydra, a distributed multi-objective optimization system (ARD, 2022, 138–139). ARD has created synthetic datasets (artificially generated data from simulated models) and original datasets from their own archives on which to train "design-assist machine learning models." ARD cautions that "the success of a system based on machine-learning is as good as the quantity and quality of data to which the system is exposed" (140); the amount of data generated is enormous in different formats, and "do(es) not match current machine learning requirements." (137). A "structured data pipeline tailored to and appropriate to machine learning workflows" must be developed (ARD). This research work brings forth the huge challenges ahead dealing with different file formats, legacy software, and changes in graphic notation protocols developed by each of the specializations involved in the design of a project (141). It also makes evident that access to information and evidence resulting from research is essential for testing these new methods.

Smarter Design Methods: The new AI-based tools

Smart design methodologies for the architectural design process in practice are currently focused on smart buildings, BIM, digital twins, and AI-based software tools for design. AI tools generate images based on prompts that describe qualities. Others generate diagrammatic plans or massing designs, matching specified client requirements and space constraints, while some analyze zoning codes, local building ordinances, and building codes. A number of books very recently published are dedicated to the subject (Bernstein, 2022; Chaillou, 2022; Del Campo, 2022).

Engineering design and business management count with a number of well-tested "smart" design methods: Design Structure Matrix (DSM) or Dependency and Structure Modelling; TRIZ (Theory of Inventive Problem Solving); Quality Function Deployment (QFD); and Life Cycle Assessment (LCA) (Gericke et al., 2022, 23–24). In business, smart design is a method for evaluating the effectiveness of management goals. It is defined by the acronym S.M. A.R.T.: Specific, Measurable, Assignable, Realistic, and Time-related (Bjerke and Renger, 2017). It refers to approaches where the means are defined by tangible quantifiable goals, results are measured, and benchmarks are set with a given timeframe. Importantly, baseline information must be used to describe the criteria in relation to the context to determine the level of achievability and timeframe (Bjerke and Renger). The SMART method is driven by the criteria that guide the design process, not of the product.

Pessoa and Juaregui-Becker (2020) researched trends regarding the impact of Industry 4.0 on product design and development in general. They identified six "directives" for smart design engineering and design excellence (181), of which five can be extrapolated to a smart design methodology in architecture: (1) "design for empowered users," where customers are members of the design team; (2) "product-in-use-feedback" requires "user-centered design" that allows the collection of accurate in-use data; (3) "changeability" for parts that are modular that can be upgraded and replaced (184); (4) "design data analytics" to "monitor, control, optimize" product design throughout its life cycle; (5) "design for cyber security" is directly tied to the attention required to safeguard devices that collect and control data. The last directive may be acceptable for product design but poses serious ethical problems for architecture. It is (6) "design for emotional interaction" to create and strengthen the emotional bounds of the user to the smart product (176).

Similarly, resilient design requires holistic data gathering, processing, documenting, updating, and use for creating knowledge in the form of "integrated climatic index, vulnerability index, adaptation techniques and mitigation strategies" (Ikudayisi et al., 2023, 17). A smart building can automatically control its environment based on a set benchmark. It needs to collect data, then quickly verify and analyze it to determine a response, and "learn" from real-time conditions. Building performance data is collected by owners and other agents, shared through repositories, and exchanged for profit to be analyzed and for building products and systems assessment. The United States Department of Energy maintains the Building Performance Database (BPD) of measured energy performance (US Department of Energy, 2011).

Building system's adaptability and interactivity are directly related to users' needs and choices. But design decisions depend on both subjective and quantifiable measures, and therefore "inconsistent assessment makes it difficult to define design goals." (Almusaed and Yitmen, 2023, 3). Clearly, what is not measured cannot be managed. Sensing networked building systems and AI tools are leading to the alleviation of that concern. The more spaces equipped with sensors, the higher the value of the network The project team can use what they have learned to create a model of not only the building, but of the individual users to simulate the social environment in the current or future space. Such interaction modeling is a refinement of methods that already exist (Marsh, 2020). However, design methods may change at the direction of "financially strong construction companies [as they increasingly] define the scope of design options" (Braun, Kropp, and Boeva, 2022, 270) with mandated product libraries.

New models have predictive capabilities necessary to address the complexity of integrated building systems. For example, machine learning is used for "energy modeling of several electrical and thermal building systems requiring multivariable/ objective optimization." In the design process, the prediction model is used to forecast the performance of complete scenarios, based on few known results then used as input (Qiang et al., 2023, 2). As uncertainty is a characteristic of any complex system, models must be flexible enough to change.

A smart building is "a complex concatenation of structures, systems, and technology [that can] collect thousands of data points per hour." (Qiang et al., 2023, 1). The data collected is organized into and managed through building data models. These models are based on building ontologies, which are formal representations of entities and their relationships. Žáček and Janošek define ontological models as "knowledge models able to encode and represent domain knowledge and heuristics [...] allowing software agents to interpret data and reason against ontological contexts." (2017, 2). However, there is no "universal building ontology [...] that always performs best and fits all the task requirements" (Qiang et al., 13) The solution is to reuse concepts in existing ontologies for "interoperability and usability" (Qiang et al.) developing "a uniform data model that can exchange data across various sensors, devices, systems, and buildings in an integrated, dynamic, and functional manner." (1).

The challenge remains that "architectural form is ontologically unstable" which Koh demonstrates using the example of the architectonic element floor, that can also be stair, or ramp, or corridor. (2023, 7]). Such an approach is a standard in BIM. Koh argues that, instead, a hierarchy of abstract "features" or "homogeneous voxels" replace a hierarchy of semantics of fixed meanings for building components (11). Shape grammars are rejected, as these are not the basic blocks of human perception. The concept of architectural sampling takes their place, where "a dataset exists in the form of a single building" and not in all the buildings in the world, or those designed by the same architect, or in the same style, typology, region, material, etc. (20). Koh supports an evolving ontology based on the characteristics of the forms resulting from generative adversarial networks or GANs (111).

The GAN was developed by Ian Goodfellow and collaborators in 2014 (Bolojan and Vermisso, 2020). A GAN consists of two competing neural networks engaged in an adversarial learning process. Bolojan and Vermisso demonstrated its application in their project Gaudi Hallucinations, after compiling datasets of images of Antoní Gaudi's work. One network generates "fakes," the other discriminates between fakes and real images of the architect's work. One predicts "features" for a category, the other "predicts a category from the feature." (Bolojan and Vermisso) A number of GAN's have used Gaudi's work to test generative neural network capabilities (Bautista et al., 2022). More recent works on generative algorithms based on GN and other neural networks have been reviewed, such as Chaillou's Archi-GAN model; House-GAN graph-constrained house layout generation (Nauata et al.); and convolutional neural network (CNN) for data-driven residential interior plan generation (Wu et al.; Almusaed and Yitmen (2023). Witt suggests that neural network models fall between the two poles of the architectural and the technoscientific models (Witt, 2022, 147–148). The neural model is "not thick," has more abstract roles, and visual and mathematical rigor (148–149).

AI and machine learning can bridge the gap between the creative process and computation. As a demonstration, Danhaive and Mueller presented their work on the concept of surrogate modeling that delivers "instantaneous performance feedback for designers." Through the use of CNNs, the models "can accurately predict entire fields of simulation data," as in the case of a displacement field of a structure, or the exposure of a building façade to the sun (Danhaive and Mueller, 2022, 129). The surrogate models are "portable," available via "lightweight interfaces" such as web portals (130).

A recent literature review on AI applications in architecture found that the most extensively employed are genetic algorithm-based techniques followed distantly by evolutionary-based ones (Bölek, 2023). Genetic algorithm-based methods have been applied to various contexts from form and façade explorations to floor plans and site plans (Bölek, et al.). Almusaed and Yitmen (2023) cite Moreno-De-Luca and Begambre Carrillo's (2013) review of multi-objective heuristic computation-based design optimization models and design methodologies for architectural and structural design as an introduction to new design methodologies. Those described are based on genetic (GA) and evolutionary (EA) algorithms to manage multiple conflicting objectives for an "efficient creative process that helps generate a broad set of quality performance and differentiated solutions." (Moreno-De-Luca et al., 2013, 386).

Designing for building life cycle: digital twin emerging

The International Energy Agency (IEA) defines digital twin as "a method for creating a smarter, more connected efficient, and resilient system." (Yoon, 2023, 3). Digital twins are "digital environments that are integrated with their physical systems in real time to play a role in omniscient environment and supervisory controllers." (Yoon). Twinning is touted as central to Industry 4.0 to "achieve a deep cyber-physical integration for a higher integration level of flexibility, adaptability and predictability in production." (Zhang et al., 2022). Cyber refers to the virtuality of the planning dimension based on BIM, and the physical to the execution promoted by automation and robotics (Zhang et al.). Digital twin integration with BIM applications intended for simulation, optimization, and prediction in design has been difficult. A building digital twin means full automation realized by sensing systems embedded in the building under construction, on the site and in the construction or maintenance equipment robots (Zhang et al.).

There are challenges to the application of the digital twin concept to buildings, as it is currently conceived. Its focus is on optimization, while in architecture – given the multiple forces, agents, and components – there is no optimal solution that attends to all variables, "but a broad set of possible solutions that are assessed by the multiple perspectives that comprise the design team." (Kamari, 2020, 509). In architecture, engineering, and construction, the "limited digitalization environments and operational uncertainties" challenge effective application (Yoon, 2023, 4). And, buildings are massive, differently designed, constructed in situ, equipped with heterogeneous systems and operate for a long time (Yoon, 3). The building sector has yet to thoroughly study the "systematic frameworks and methodologies to provide approaches to construct, extend, and manage digital environments mathematically over the building life cycle." (3).

The integration of BIM, sustainability, and integrated design practices based on systems thinking has been proposed, with less emphasis on component analysis and more focus on synthesis of elements (Kamari, 2020, 509). Yoon suggests a "framework and methodology for building digital twinning over the life cycle of a building" comprised by three areas: "digital twin elements" (data, information, models or DIM), functional requirements (transfer, operational extensions, continuous calibration), and enabling techniques (transitional techniques, operational techniques, and calibration techniques). In this framework, DIM is the critical area because it holds "target building physics, states and behaviors" that guide the process for "the structures to construct, extend, and manage DIM in the operation of the building." (Yoon, 4).

Smart Design Methods: People getting it all together
The film and gaming industry invested in research and development of software for modeling and predicting crowd behavior. The production of the animations for the film series The Lord of the Rings needed to simulate realistically rendered battles where thousands of CGI characters interacted. For this purpose, in the early 2000s, the visual effects company Weta Digital developed the software Massive, where each autonomous 3D agent could react to stimuli. A range of reactions were matched with a range of stimuli; in this case for defense or attack based on probabilities. When the software was tested, designers observed a group of agents apparently running away from battle. When reviewing their rules to establish stimuli and reaction, the designers' recognized agents were instructed to "search for space if in a crowd," and to "run until you find an enemy to fight with." Given that there were 2,000 agents in a limited space, some moved to find space in the opposite direction of the battle. The designers thought that, somehow, the algorithm had generated a new survival reaction rule (Fontana, 2018).

Ove ARUP's Oasys Software MassMotion and MassFlow simulate crowd and pedestrian behavior. In MassMotion, autonomous agents recognize obstacles and portals and can move at different speeds, depending on floor conditions. From any position, agents can evaluate the best path to an exit. As Massive's escaping warriors, people-agents in MassMotion avoid other agents to evade congestion. For the simulation to be effective, the scene had to have clearly established marks, to which the agents reacted. The software used in the design process verified the timing and capacity of the circulation areas and egress routes to satisfy occupancy needs. This human behavior simulation software used real-world data.

Performative design approaches consider "humans as interactive users of built space and buildings as intelligent biospheres." (Kanaani 2020, xvii). User data must be collected and analyzed. Sensory devices and support systems are essential and provide more accurate means for collecting POE data. Continuous measurements are possible. Data mining combined with machine learning techniques can be applied to determine patterns and trends (Choi, 2020, 132). Analysis and interpretation require specialized knowledge and avoidance of bias. The definition of data – and the ethics of collection and sharing personal data into datasets then used in training generative and predictive models – are not yet set. So far, the data generated by architecture, engineering, construction, and operations firms has not been collected systematically, nor evaluated with rigor comparable to scientific research data, particularly data generated for healthcare assessment.

The Living Studio used generative design optimization software tools to space plan the Autodesk, MaRS Office Toronto Technology Center, a design developed between 2016 and 2020. User data was collected from employees and managers. It was then used to set measurable goals for the design (Nagy et al., 2017). The Zaha Hadid Architects and Insight team (ZHAI) developed a proprietary algorithmic analytic and simulation toolkit. Among those analytic tools was one to research the efficient design of floorplates for the workplace, based on the client's and occupants' needs. The tools' criteria resulted from data collected regarding the relationship among the occupants' experiences, well-being, productivity, and collaboration, correlated to the spatial conditions. The analytic tool verified the findings of others' research and generated new floor plate designs. ZHAI described the platform developed as an ecosystem that included Internet of Things sensor systems and user satisfaction analytics (Kaickeret al., 2019). In the near future, such generative predictive design tools may facilitate designing for multispecies co-living (Saeidi et al., 2023).

Other Smart Methods: Local and Global Possibilities through Design

Is a singular approach to smart design applicable to all projects? What futures will it enact? Whose futures? Smart design methods are not limited to those satisfying the goals of Industry 5.0. Design exists in an environment that is ever in flux. Local conditions shape projects: people, multispecies, climate, site, regulations, cost, availability of materials and labor, infrastructure, needs, dreams, and demands. Into that mix goes the indirect and direct impacts of global activities. Examples of other uses and impacts on the directions of smart design are those generated by Yasmeen Lari and the communities she works with; Marina Tabassum working with local materials, Salima Naji's collaborative practice restoring Moroccan ancient granaries and promoting vernacular construction techniques; and design for mass-produced low-cost houses by the collective H&P Architects in Vietnam.

References

Almusaed, A., and Yitmen, I. (2023). Architectural reply for smart building design concepts based on artificial intelligence simulation models and digital twins. *Sustainability*, 15 (6), 4955. doi: 10.3390/su15064955.

Applied Research and Development Group. (ARD). (2022). The data challenge for machine learning in AECO. In *Artificial Intelligence and Architecture: From Research to Practice*, edited by S. Chaillou, 136–145. Basel, Switzerland: Birkhäuser.

Bautista, M. A., Guo, P., Abnar, S., Talbott, W., Toshev, A., Chen, Z. et al. (2022). GAUDI: A neural architect for immersive 3D scene generation. In *36th Conference on Neural Information Processing Systems* (NeurIPS 2022). doi: 10.48550/arXiv.2207.1351.

Bernstein, P. (2022). *Machine Learning: Architecture in the Age of Artificial Intelligence*. London: RIBA.

Bjerke, M. J., and Renger, R. (2017). Being smart about writing SMART objectives. *Evaluation and Program Planning*, 61 (April), 125–127. doi: 10.106/j.evalprogplan.2016.12.009.

Bölek, B., Tutal, O., and Özbaşarn, H. (2023). A systematic review on artificial intelligence applications in architecture. *Journal of Design for Resilience in Architecture and Planning*, 4 (1), 91–104.

Bolojan, D., and Vermisso, E. (2020). Deep Learning as heuristic approach for architectural concept generation. In *Proceedings of the 11th International Conference on Computational Creativity* (ICCC'20), 7-11 September, Coimbra, Portugal. Association for Computational Creativity, 98–105.

Braun, K., Kropp, C., and Boeva, Y. (2022). Constructing platform capitalism: inspecting the political techno-economy of Building Information Modelling. *ARQ* 26 (3), 267–278. doi: 10.1017/S1355220046X.

Chaillou, S. (2022). *Artificial Intelligence and Architecture: From Research to Practice*. Basel, Switzerland: Birkhäuser.

Choi, J. (2020). The cognitive dimension: The role of research in performative design process, theory put in practice. In *The Routledge Companion to Paradigms of Performativity in Design and Architecture* edited by M. Kanaani, 132–145. New York and London: Routledge.

Danhaive, R. and Mueller, C. (2022). Artificial intelligence for human design in architecture. In *Artificial Intelligence and Architecture: From Research to Practice* edited by S. Chaillou, 126–133. Basel, Switzerland: Birkhäuser.

Del Campo, M. (2022). *Neural Architecture {Design and Artificial Intelligence}*. Novato, CA: ORO Editions.

Ekahau (21 March 2024). How to measure wall attenuation for spotless Wi-Fi network designs. *Ekahau*. Retrieved from https://www.ekahau.com/blog/how-to-measure-wall-attenuation-for-spotless-wi-fi-network-designs/

Fontana, L. (12 October 2018). And cut! Brave lord of the rings warriors running away in the thousands. *Digitec*. Retrieved from https://www.digitec.ch.

Gericke, K., Eckert, C., and Stacey, M. (2022). Elements of a design method—a basis for describing and evaluating design methods. *Design Science*, 8, e29. doi: 10.1017/dsj.2022.23, 1-28.

Ikudayisi, A.E., Chan, A. P. C., Darko, A., and Adedeji, Y. M. D. (2023). Integrated practices in the Architecture, Engineering, and Construction Industry: Current scope and pathway towards Industry 5.0. *Journal of Building Engineering* 73, 106788, 1–21. doi: 10.1016/j.jobe.2023.106788.

Kaicker, A., Blum, U., Siedler, P., and Espaillat, L. (2019). Enhancing workplace design through advanced floor plate analytics. *TAD*, 3 (2), 151–160.

Kamari, A. Holistic Building Design: (September 2020). An integrated building design methodology based on systems thinking for reaching sustainability. In *Conference: eCAADe 2020* (the 38th Education and Research in Computer Aided Architectural Design in Europe) Berlin, Germany, 505–514. doi: 10.52842/conf.ecaade.2020.1.505.

Kanaani, M. (2020). Preface. In *The Routledge Companion to Paradigms of Performativity in Design and Architecture*, xvii–xix. New York and London: Routledge.

Koh, I. (2023). Architectural sampling: Three possible preconditions for machine learning architectural forms. *Artificial Intelligence, 2* (7), 1–21. doi: 10.1007/s44223-023-00024-1.

Lavrsen, J. C., Dallhuizen, J., Domler, S., and Fisker, K. (2022). Towards a lifecycle of design methods. In *DRS2022: Bilbao Conference Proceedings*, edited by D. Lockton, S. Lenzi, P. Hekkert, A. Oak, J. Sadaba, and P. Lloyd. 25 June–3 July, Bilbao, Spain. doi: 10.21606/drs.2022.542.

Marsh, M. (24 March 2020). Social data brings new life to AI for architecture. *Work Design Magazine*. Retrieved from https://www.workdesign.com/2020/03/social-data-brings-new-life-to-ai-for-architecture.

Moreno-De-Luca, L., and Begambre Carrillo, O. J. (2013). Multi-Objective heuristic computation applied to architectural and structural design: A review. *International Journal of Architectural Computing*, 11 (4), 363–392. doi: 10.1260/1478-0771.11.4.363.

Nagy, D., Lau, D., Locke, J., Stoddart, J., Villaggi, L., Wang, R., Zhao, D., and Benjamin, D. (2017). Project Discover: An application of generative design for architectural space planning. In *2017 Proceedings of the Symposium on Simulation for Architecture & Urban Design*, edited by M. Turin, B. Peters, W. O'Brien, R. Stouffs, and T. Dogan, 59–66. The Society for Modeling & Simulation International (SCS). doi: 10.22360/simaud.2017.simaud.007

Newth, J. Danielsen (20 December 2019). Which building materials can block wi-fi signals? *Eye Networks*. Retrieved from https://eyenetworks.no/en/wifi-signal-loss-by-material/

Pessoa, M. V.P., and Juaregui-Becker, J. M. (2020). Smart design engineering: A literature review of the impact of the 4th revolution on product design and development. *Research in Engineering Design*, 31 (15), 1–21. doi: 10.1007/s00163-020-00330-z.

Qiang, Z., Hands, S., Taylor, K., Sethuvenkatraman, S., Hugo, D., Omran, P. G., Perera, M., and Haller, A. (2023). A systematic comparison and evaluation of building ontologies for deploying data-driven analytics in smart buildings. *Energy and Buildings*, 292 (August), 113054. doi: 10.1016/j.enbuild.2023.113054.

Racha-Pacheco, P., Ribeiro, J. T., and Afonso. (2023). Architecture towards Technology—A prototype design of a smart home. *Buildings, 13* (7). doi.org/10.3390/buildings13071859.

Saeidi, S., Anderson, M. D., and Davidova, M. (2023). Kindness in architecture: The Multispecies co-living and co-design. *Buildings, 13* (1), 1–21. doi: 10.3390/buildings 13081931.

Thieme, W. (3 September 2020). Four common pitfalls to avoid in smart building deployment. Forbes Innovation. *Forbes.* Retrieved from http://forbes.com.

United States. US Department of Energy. Office of Energy Efficiency & Renewable Energy (2011). *Building Performance Database* (BPD). https://www.energy.gov/eere/buildings/building-performance-database-bpd

Yoon, S. (2023). Building digital twining: Data, information and models. *Journal of Building Engineering, 76* (1 October), 107021. doi: 10.1016/j.jobe.2023.107021.

Žáček, M., and Janošek, M. (2017). SBONTO: Ontology of smart building. *Far East Journal of Electronics and Communications, 17* (5), 1101–1109. doi: 10.17654/EC017051101.

Zhang, J., Luo, H., and Xu, J. (2022). Towards fully BIM-enabled building automation and robotics: A perspective of lifecycle information flow. *Computers in Industry, 135* (February), 103570. doi: 10.106/j.compind.2021.103570.

Witt, A. (2022). Shadowplays: Models, drawings, cognitions. In *Artificial Intelligence and Architecture: From Research to Practice* edited by S. Chaillou, 146–161. Basel, Switzerland: Birkhäuser.

2.1.2

FOR(M) AND AGAINST ARCHITECTURAL INTELLIGENCE

Design as Research, Again

Brett Steele

Abstract

This chapter explores the evolving role of architecture amidst the rise of technology and artificial intelligence. It questions the essence of architecture as a distinct form of human knowledge in an era saturated with various intelligences. The author suggests that architects should embrace new technologies, acknowledging their impact on architectural knowledge, design processes, and communication.

The piece delves into architecture as a realm of communication and information, emphasizing the evolution of design technologies and their influence on architectural practices. It highlights the unique way architects process and transmit information through graphic spaces, diagrams, and models. These serve as both a means to convey intentions to others and as archives of architectural thinking, reflecting the discipline's historical development.

This chapter challenges the traditional concept of architectural objects, suggesting that buildings exist more as digital information within complex design systems than as physical structures. It questions the relevance of conventional architectural histories and theories in a world dominated by intelligent design systems, proposing the need for new, machine-compatible narratives of architectural history.

Furthermore, it explores the role of architecture in a world increasingly shaped by global urbanization and information proliferation. The author discusses the merging of human agency with artificial intelligence in design processes and suggests that architectural intelligence exists not just in the minds of designers but also within the structures and systems they create.

The piece advocates for a shift in perspective, embracing the coexistence of human and artificial intelligence in architectural practices. It envisions a future where architecture transcends as an amalgamation of human and artificial knowledge, forming an integral part of evolving design research.

The author, Brett Steele, an architect and academic, brings forth these insights, drawing from his extensive experience in architectural education and practice.

DOI: 10.4324/9781003384113-26

He emphasizes the need for architectural discourse to adapt to the changing landscape of technology and design.

Architecture as Information

Once dryly observing modern architecture's most unsettling stylistic excesses, many years ago Cedric Price is said to have asked an audience of architects, 'If architecture is the answer, what's the question?' (Hardingham, 2020, pp. 327–333).[1] Following the past few decades of our planet's accelerating architectural production, facilitated as it has been by an exponential jump in the artifice of 'smart' design systems of all kinds, perhaps it's time to update Price's existential worry for architecture. Smart design is conventionally associated with contemporary approaches to design that aim to improve lives by deliberate integration of differing materials, systems, and information realms. Much of that work is dependent upon a shift toward iterative, prototype-driven design solutions (we should note the long history of prototyping in modern architecture – Mies' Barcelona pavilion, Le Corbusier's Maison Domino, etc.). So standardized have 'smart' design approaches become that 'smart design' is the name of a New York studio founded in 1980 by three industrial designers whose work has been widely celebrated and exhibited. So, the term 'smart design' likely has intellectual property and other legal protections/constraints around it, which authors, editors, and designs need to navigate as essential dimensions of today's smart design environments. Likewise, the word 'architecture' is registered to a Dutch media conglomerate owing to that company's ownership of an American magazine with the same name. This time, by asking whether or how architecture itself can even continue to exist. At least, in the most important way, it ever has as a distinct and valuable form of human knowledge, and not just a professionalized form of production within a global supply chain of new design.

What happens when architecture increasingly operates as neither answer nor question, so much as it does today, as a self-standing realm of communication? As a form, and not just discipline, entirely of its own design, language, and making, is architecture still about to comprehend, talk to, and learn about *itself*? What happens to architecture's long-standing, historical forms of human experience and knowledge in an era where there are suddenly so many *other* (equally, artificial) kinds of intelligence (and not *just* information) all around? I'd like to propose that our era's sudden and very contemporary proliferation of new kinds of (artificial) intelligence should be welcomed, and not worried over, by architects. Precisely how this reality animates and amplifies architecture's very own – very *artificial* – forms of knowledge. Architects need to remind themselves have always been no more natural than the buildings and other structures architects otherwise work so hard to invent.

Architecture has always been organized and attentive to questions of form. What's important today is that this instinct is most acutely valued when directed at special kinds of forms especially: those aligned and attentive to our planet's research and development-driven economies, where memory structures, symbolic and abstract languages, representational schemas, coding, and connective communication technologies abound. It's the startling speed and expansive arena of information gathering, processing, and storage inhabited by architects today, thanks to new hard and soft technologies that permeate every aspect of working and design lives of all kinds, which makes their traditional forms of teaching and learning so relevant, and challenging, as they go forward. Today's design technologies interconnect and entangle knowledge and communication in so many new and unexpected ways beyond those of traditional built environments that the realm of what we call architecture is itself undergoing massive re-configuration and re-organization.

Architects have always worked in unique and wholly mediating ways compared to other creative fields. They've always been information processors. They operate in and invent graphic spaces of all kinds to think, visualize, record, and transmit to others their multidimensional ideas and actions. These intermediary and highly abstract, coded media spaces that architects have always created for their work have evolved as graphic conventions of all kinds over decades and centuries, and lately into interfaces as well as spaces of new communication platforms that resonate with and serve as extensions to all kinds of new information technologies. So analogous are new information sciences and technologies with the traditional realm of architecture that many of those information technologies are being managed and maintained by figures today referred to as information 'architects' – not just data scientists.

The highly abstract, specialized kinds of drawings, models, diagrams, and other forms of information that serve as memory structures for the making of any architectural project operate in two very real and different, important ways for demonstrating what makes architectural knowledge unlike that of so many other professions or disciplines. Firstly, architects' graphic (mediating) spaces serve as the means to transmit an architect's intentionality and thinking to others. This knowledge is always directed toward the future so that outside parties can understand and then go out and build or assemble what's up to that point only been an architect's or designer's intention or idea. Secondly, these data sets become immediately associated with architecture's past. The representations architects assemble ahead of buildings or structures themselves (drawings, models, etc.) serve as another kind of recording technology entirely: a kind of hard drive archiving what that architect was thinking, or doing, articulated and documents inaccessible, communicable ways to other architects, as part of architecture's own larger disciplinary past. In both senses, these mediating memory structures aren't just generated, but deliberately retained. As has always been the case of course since the dawn of time, in the scratches, sketches, drawings, and tablets, and later files, printed books, and other kinds of manuscripts and documents systematically collected and later stored in monographs and libraries, archives, and written histories of all kinds, about and for this mediated space of architectural knowledge itself. Which in turn still serves today as architecture's own, unique, disciplinary memory structure: architecture knowledge itself. And today, owing to developments in hard and soft information technologies of all kinds, is evolving into ever more interactive, artificial forms of not just design information, but architectural intelligence as well.

This defining trait of architecture, this building of its own disciplinary record and memory of its thinking, alongside the realization of the projects and works that are the traditional focus of the discipline, is what makes architecture so very unlike so many other creative fields. This essential dependence of architecture on this simultaneous creation of its own, internal record as well as the recorded memory of a project, career, or discipline's 'past', isn't just archival: in important ways, it's a form of genuine, disciplinary self-awareness, what today we realize is an essential feature of intelligence itself.

The long historical record of this mediating activity in architecture is elevated in contemporary, smart design systems, which can learn through forms of continuous processing, modulation, and revision, a kind of learning. It's precisely this that makes today's network-based, communication-oriented approaches to design so interesting, for being built atop a discipline that has always had this tendency of self-awareness as a central impulse (albeit undertaken formerly in far less complex design and media technologies). Architecture's mediating instincts are something we can witness going back to the very origins of the discipline, where we find codified in the form of some of antiquity's oldest books and printed materials, images of architecture's earliest attempts at representing itself, and not only those careers, buildings, and projects of individual authors that were the overt 'topic' of this recording and communicating impulse.

Two millennia after Vitruvius' papyrus scrolls, with their marks etched into paper in ways that record, and later presented to his emperor, that architect's collected works, this very same architectural impulse of recording and disseminating ideas and works resides in and travels across infinitely more-expansive software systems, fiber optic and satellite networks, interactive media, and large language models capable of not just spectacularly higher transmission speeds, but their capacity for training and learning, separate from that of their originators, or receivers. As many others have long observed, architecture remains an art form distinct from so many others owing to two distinct facts. Firstly, architecture has a precise moment of origin coded in still existing, very real memory structure. Vitruvius (c. 70–80 BC) is the Roman architect and engineer whose text (as a kind of prototype to what would become in modern times, an architectural monography), now known as *De Architectura*, the oldest extant ancient text of any kind, whose Renaissance re-discovery is credited with the Renaissance itself. Secondly, architecture's history has come to embody a definition of the discipline by attention to the distinctive activities of the architect compared to other creative fields: that space where the making of drawings, models, and other kinds of representations, neither 'actual' nor 'real' as final projects, but rather mediating in their ability to eventually 'delivery' a building or structure by guiding its realization. Evans (1997) discusses the creative act of translation at the core of architectural imagination between 'drawing and building ... and a similar suspension of critical disbelief necessary to enable architects to perform their task at all' (p. 154).

An End to Architecture's Objects

What used to be called the architectural object exists today as little more than fleeting and flickering forms of digital information within complex artificial languages and programming structures underlying today's intelligent design systems. This information lives in software and other digital platforms, through which all design work today originates, is retained, and made available for others. What then might be left for architects, let alone their historians or other commentators, to do in the roles they have traditionally played in the preservation and production of new and historical forms of architectural knowledge? Have architectural histories and theories been rendered obsolete by the machinic circumstances of today's intelligent design systems?

Does an entity, a singularity like a building, which has been central to architecture's written histories for so long, even still exist today? Other than in the minds of critics, historians, Instagrammers, or others who seem mostly to still want to talk about architecture with the kinds of simplified narratives and fuzzy forms of evidence that are the hallmarks of conventional architectural histories or theories? Today social media is becoming a new kind of architectural material (Keaton, 2017). Today architecture already lives in its making in realms where the design systems responsible for its invention and realization are more often machines, networks, and databases than they are humans, individual architects, or agents. It's surely the case that narrative accounts about the making of architecture are evolving accordingly. As architectural histories and theories themselves evolve, so too may seek to better adapt into forms of information more relevant to smart design systems than the kinds of simplified story-telling impulses of architecture's past.

And by asking if such entities as a building might even still 'exist' today, I'm not meaning whether in the literal sense buildings are still really 'out there' in the city or built world all around us. Of course, they do, and live in greater numbers than ever before, thanks to the past few decades' unprecedented wave of urbanization; the largest in human history. What I intend by my question is only to ask whether or how *singular* structures or episodes of any kind, architecture conceived that way, by attention to singularities like those we might associate with a discrete building or structure, might still be a viable let alone productive concept to structure the historical accounts of the discipline; at least, of the kind that certain stand-alone architectural episodes always done. Given today's increasingly artificial kinds of highly interactive, distributed, and iterative forms of knowledge and information emerging across large and complex networks, might we imagine as well new kinds of architectural histories that are no less machinic, ambient, or emergent in their organization? And not only in their formation? Asked a different way, could an architectural history be written more like an algorithm, than it always has been, as a story? Is the history of a project more like a spreadsheet, than a table of contents? Might a particular episode of architectural work be better described as a diagram or a relational database, rather than a three-part narrative with a beginning, middle, and end? Just as we can ask what algorithms want of us today, so too, we might acknowledge the questions algorithms or networks are asking of architects, including their historians and theorists. At the very least, how might architecture's own written history reflect the reality already upon us, that most forms of reading in the world today are *already* undertaken by machines and networks, not designers or their critics? As a writer, Lanier (2010) accepts his texts are read by more algorithms than any other form of intelligence. As an optimist and positivist, he celebrates not just the AI systems, but the fact that the human creativity within them results from the very human design of such systems. An attitude from a decade ago, by the way, that feels outmoded given how neural networks themselves are now the work of large language models whose internal forms of automation allow them to massively accelerate the work human designers alone could do only a few years ago.

Architectural Criticism in the form of Spreadsheets & Data Sets

Ours is an era marked by an unhesitating acceleration of global building and urbanization (in a single year, small corners of Asia continue to annually produce new surface areas of urban life larger than the size of London or Los Angeles). It's a trajectory that to date appears utterly incapable of altering it flight path, even despite widespread recognition of the massively negative planetary consequences of this human (largely, self-centered, and self-*serving*) activity.

The circumstances and conditions in which information is produced, stored, and moves across our era's equally unprecedented proliferation of network life combine with an unprecedented scope of new design necessity to create the wider circumstances of all design thinking today. It's this assemblage of information and intelligence, not the arrangement of physical stuff and their appearances, that is the most transformative outcome of contemporary architectural life. And again, it's this 'information' space, and not only built architectural space, but that has also always been where architects think, work, and learn.

And it's within this space that smart design systems have evolved and elevated new forms of design awareness, experimentation, and understanding; in modernity's massive expansion of information worlds themselves, alongside those of built, urban spaces. While I suggest architecture might still be perceived by some as 'outside' modern and contemporary information economies, I would also suggest this is far from the case. Recall Hannes Meyer's *Peterschule* proposal over a century ago – a project formed, he argued, through little more than a visualization of the growing regulatory, planning, building code, and other information systems his design sought simply to 'visualize' and embody.

Today's distributed design teams combine organic forms of agency (of the kind we all still associate with a living, breathing person) with other, increasingly emergent, artificial forms of intelligence residing in and emerging across such networks. What we might call expertise in this expanded field continues to evolve is anyone's guess (or stochastic calculation), although this too is the work of many specialized fields of thinking and discourse (Selinger & Crease, 2006). Seen this way, the increasingly complex, layered existence of today's highly technological buildings does little more than mirror the complexity and emergent circumstances of their inventors' (designers') systems of design. This confirms anew the arrival of an architectural intelligence today that needs to be recognized as a property of the world found as easily in its buildings and structures, and not only in the minds of designers, or their design tools. It is tempting to consider models of select non-architects who've long seen architectural intelligence associated more with buildings, than with architects themselves. Brand (1995) draws attention to how buildings evolve and change over time despite their originators' or occupants' initial expectations, as an example of 'smartness', or intelligence. There are many adherents to this sensibility, even within architecture: see Frank Duffy, and his work stemming from initial PhD research into how buildings are little more than layers of different assemblages, systems, and materials each operating on their timeline.

An algorithm amounts to little more than a process. One was created to structure the movement of information such that a particular task or role can be accomplished in reliable, consistent, and valuable ways. This of course is not far from a familiar definition of an architect's work and task: to organize flows of matter and information such that they can result in new physical configurations initially formulated by a distinct design problem. Solved in the form of a new building or structure able to deliver a result that amounts to a change from former configurations or arrangements of information. However, much of the modern circumstances of this work involve ever more abstract, complex design languages, systems, and tools, resulting in ever-more complex realms of information processing, the goal of architectural work remains the same as it ever was – to change and improve upon the world as found. Simon (1996) saw the role of the architect as a model for the entirety of modern professional life – including the computer sciences. His work is so closely associated with the modern rise of artificial intelligence that recent questions about the possibilities of a contemporary convergence of generative AI and design practices aren't as theoretical – or abstract – as some in 2024 presume. That current AI systems associated with generative pre-trained transformers, of the kind associated with ChatGPT work so effectively with language-based tasks in the generating of new texts suggests, for heavily language-based creative fields, like writing and architecture, the creative possibilities – and challenges – these forms of artificial intelligence pose for architecture. In the words of Cedric Price, architecture either 'improves the quality of life uniquely or enables activities and conditions that hitherto were impossible in ways which are likely to be beneficial, or not' (Hardingham, 2020, pp. 327–333).

Reminding Ourselves of Forests Instead of Trees

So, let's no longer presume that architecture is either an answer or a question – let alone, one or the other. And let's not try and definitively conclude where and how architecture's ways of thinking are human, or machine; natural, or artificial. Let's embrace instead the possibility of intelligence as an emergent property; of both/and, more than either/or ways of thinking. The circumstances of today's ambient design systems have already been around for a long time: a half-century ago architects like Ito, T (2011) called out this new kind of 'media forest' in which all cities dwelt. It's text was written in his youth at a time coinciding with his premature departure from architectural studies to pursue the writing of science fiction before the start of his celebrated building career. Both the topic and career path of Ito's example confirm the close interdependence of architecture and writing in the production of knowledge in both. As Adolf Loos is credited with saying decades before in an entirely different modern literary and architectural culture, 'As an architect, I could write the Pantheon'. Meanwhile, other poets, such as Richard Brautigan (1967), offered us images of this constituting an entirely new kind of nature:

I like to think
(right now, please!)
Of a cybernetic forest
Filled with pines and electronics
Where deer stroll peacefully
past computers
as if they were flowers
with spinning blossoms

Today's nascent 'internet of things' points overwhelmingly to where architecture's future lies: in the realization of gesamtkunst-like forms of spatial feedback assemblies, composed from near-infinite information gathering and processing capacities, from which entirely new, artificial forms of intelligence will be inhabited, everywhere and all at once (rather than only in the domain of today's small screens and special devices already dedicated to this destiny – in the future, it will be simultaneously everywhere, in all forms of building and not just device). Architecture's battles today shouldn't be around whether or how 'smart' design is different from other kinds of design, or even whether design is the work of an architect, any more than it is the systems of communication she uses to invent, situate, and share her work with the world around it. Architecture endures as a vital form of *knowledge* that is at once both human *and* artificial, a form of knowledge aware of its formation, and not just that for the world all around it.

The growing self-awareness exhibited within smart or intelligent design systems of all kinds operates with this goal of information – of *formation*, above all others. It's something architectural innovation and their design systems have long sought to perfect, retain, and communicate with others. At its core, architectural knowledge remains a form of knowledge *about* form, and conceived this way we can understand how design endures as a distinct and discrete form of *research*. Today is an activity conceived and not just pursued across entirely new, complex networks comprising excited flows of imagination and not just information, which we can still call architecture.

Note

1 It may be the case, as was so often with his architectural audiences, this statement was simply a misattribution of Cedric's actual message that day: See his 'Technology is the Answer, but what is the Question? Prerecorded talk, Pidgeon Audio Visual, 1979'

References

Brand, S. (1995). *How Buildings Learn: What Happens after They Are Built*. Penguin Books.

Brautigan, R. (1967). *All Watched Over by Machines of Loving Grace*. In a Pamphlet with the same title.

Evans, R. (1997). *Translations from Drawing to Building and other Documents*. AA Publications.

Hardingham, S. (Ed.) (2020). *Cedric Price Works 1952–2003: A Forward-Minded Retrospective*. AA Publications.

Keaton, D. (2017). *The House that Pinterest Built*. Rizzoli

Lanier, J. (2010). *You are not a Gadget: A Manifesto*. Vintage.

Schoffer, N. (1969). *La Ville Cybernetique*. Denoel.

Selinger, E., & Crease, R. P. (2006). *The Philosophy of Expertise*. Columbia University Press.

Simon, H. (1996). *The Sciences of the Artificial*. MIT Press.

Toyo, T. (2011). The Logic of Uselessness, in Ito, T., (Ed.)., *Tarzans in the Media Forest: Architectural Words 8*. AA Publications.

2.2

BR(AI)N CITY

The AI-Enhanced City of the Future

Neil Leach

Abstract

Cities are emergent phenomena that display a form of shared knowledge, known as swarm intelligence. Their behavior can be compared to that of other emergent systems, such as brains and neural networks. This chapter explores how cities can be understood as self-regulating, intelligent systems governed by the principle of 'homeostasis', ensuring they maintain a certain dynamic equilibrium. It postulates that artificial intelligence (AI) has a potentially supplementary role in enhancing the self-regulating intelligence of the city. If hooked into a comprehensive network of interconnected AI-enhanced informational systems through a digital twin, cities could go beyond the limitations of discrete systems inherent in 'Smart Cities to operate as 'Brain Cities'. This chapter proposes the 'Brain City' could become the AI-enhanced city of the future.

In his book, *Emergence: The Collective Lives of Ants, Brains, Cities, and Software,* Johnson (2002) outlined the theory of emergence. As the subtitle of the book suggests, Johnson made an explicit connection between the emergent behaviors of a range of multi-agent systems – such as ants, brains, cities, and software – no matter how incommensurable their constituent elements. Johnson was not the first to mention this theory and was greatly indebted to the work of others (Holland, 1999; Waldrop, 1992). The interest in a distributed model of design was forecast by Stan Allen when he cited Craig Reynolds's work and suggested that swarm logic might offer insights into emergent methodologies,

> Crowds and swarms operate at the edge of control. Aside from the suggestive formal possibilities. I wish to suggest with these two examples that architecture could profitably shift its attention from its traditional top-down forms of control and begin to investigate the possibilities of a more fluid, bottom-up approach.
>
> *(Allen, 1997)*

However, it was the success of Johnson's book that did much to popularize the theory of emergence.

DOI: 10.4324/9781003384113-27

Emergence is one of many properties of a complex system and results from bottom-up interactions of two or more agents with both them and their surrounding environment.

> An Emergent Interaction System consists of an environment in which a number of individual actors share some experience/phenomenon. Data originating from the actors and their behavior is collected, transformed, and fed back into the environment. The defining requirement of emergent interaction is that this feedback has some noticeable and interesting effect on the behavior of the individuals and the collective – that something 'emerges' in the interactions between the individuals, the collective, and the shared phenomenon as a result of introducing the feedback mechanism.
>
> *(Andersson et al., 2003, p. 41)*

Emergent properties can never be reduced to the simple sum of system parts. Rather, they produce novel and unexpected outcomes greater than the sum of the parts, as is most evident in the interactions of multi-agent systems that often lead to complex global behaviors. Importantly, populational intelligence arises out of these interactions that are not pre-determined and fixed, but self-regulating and adaptive: 'Constantly mutating, emergent systems are intelligent systems, based on interaction, informational feedback loops, pattern recognition, and indirect control. They challenge the traditional conception of systems as predetermined mechanisms of control and focus instead on their self-regulating adaptive capacity' (Leach, 2014, p. 72). Importantly also, emergence and emergent properties can be found both in computational models of complex biological systems, such as the brain, as well as in complex socio-ecological and socio-technical systems, such as cities, thereby inviting comparisons between brains and cities, opening the possibility of an interaction between these two different kinds of systems.

One of the most effective ways to study emergence is through swarm intelligence. This is expressed in the decentralized, self-organizing behavior of multi-agent systems. DeLanda (2002) referred to this as 'populational behavior', 'The dynamics of populations of dislocations are very closely related to the population dynamics of very different entities, such as molecules in a rhythmic chemical reaction, termites in a nest-building colony, and perhaps even human agents in a market. In other words, despite the great difference in the nature and behavior of the components, a given population of interacting entities will tend to display similar collective behavior'(p. 118). As Roland Snooks (2017) observes, 'Swarm Intelligence operates through the local interaction of autonomous agents that gives rise to emergent collective behavior within decentralized self-organizing systems' (p. 108). A common everyday example of 'swarm intelligence' can be observed when a flock of starlings comes in to roost. The spontaneous creation of the whole out of a seemingly disordered set of interacting parts is a basic characteristic of complex systems (Heylighen, 1989). The complex aerial gymnastics of these birds are defined not by any top-down or external force imposed from above, but rather by bottom-up, self-organizing behaviors that 'emerge' out of the simple interactions between individual birds. As the flock swoops, soars, or veers, it is not being directed or controlled by any one particular bird. Rather each individual is following a certain set of basic rules related to principles of cohesion, separation, and alignment – keeping a certain distance from the birds in front and on all sides while flying at the same speed and traveling in the same basic direction. It is this that dictates the overall behavior of the flock.

Although the swarm intelligence exhibited by flocking behaviors and chemical reactions might not fit our standard notion of intelligence – such as the intelligence of slime mold foraging for food – it is nonetheless a form of intelligence. Swarm intelligence can be understood as a basic form of intelligence, within a broader spectrum of intelligence in general. Indeed, Legg and Hunter (2007) provide a systemic view of 70 different ways of defining intelligence, ranging from general definitions to psychological ones, and extending to the domain of artificial intelligence (AI), linking the theory of optimal learning agents to propose an intriguing conceptualization of 'universal intelligence'. Accordingly, intelligence measures an agent's ability to achieve goals in a wide range of environments. Mapping self-organization and emergence to complex socio-technical systems, such as cities, can help to reconceptualize the swarm intelligence found in cities beyond classical notions of intelligence as a form of efficiency and optimization.

We can glimpse the potential of swarm intelligence to inform the logic of the city if we read the city in terms of not only static forms of buildings but also the dynamic behavior of human beings within. A city can never be reduced to a collection of buildings. A city is nothing without its inhabitants. We therefore must understand the city as an amalgam of traces of construction and spatial practices. The former can be read in terms of an accretion of mineral deposits that form the built environment, and the latter in terms of choreographies of human agents whose freedom of movement is constrained by that environment. The city consists of both entities and must be viewed as a human-mineral hybrid system. This has major implications for how we understand the impact of swarm intelligence on cities, and how we can use it to solve complex urban challenges (McPhearson et al., 2016).

The Homeostatic City

A city is an example of a 'far from equilibrium system' that is open and adaptive and displays complex and nonlinear dynamics. Nonetheless, John Holland (1999) observes that the city manages to maintain a form of dynamic equilibrium, despite the constant change it experiences. He likens it to a 'standing wave' in a stream and reads the city as a 'pattern in time'

> Cities have no central planning commissions that solve the problem of purchasing and distributing supplies... How do these cities avoid devastating swings between shortage and glut, year after year, decade after decade? The mystery deepens when we observe the kaleidoscopic nature of large cities. Buyers, sellers, administrations, streets, bridges, and buildings are always changing, so that a city's coherence is somehow imposed on a perpetual flux of people and structures. Like the standing wave in front of a rock in a fast-moving stream, the city is a pattern in time.
>
> *(Holland, 1999, p. 29)*

Holland's point was that the water molecules making up a wave are constantly changing, but the pattern of the wave remains the same provided the rock is present and the water flows. According to the logic of emergence, the patterns of behavior within the socio-technical hybrid systems that constitute a city are governed by principles of self-organization. They must be understood as amalgams of 'processes', as spaces of vectorial flows that 'adjust' to differing inputs and impulses. It is as though the city should be understood as a cybernetic system (Brown, 1969). But how does a city manage to maintain this 'dynamic equilibrium'? This

214

echoes the larger model of the Earth as a self-regulating complex system, as postulated by James Lovelock (1979). Could the model of the 'city as brain' help us to understand this mechanism?

The brain, as we know, does more than just think. It also serves to regulate the body's viability envelope. This regulating mechanism is often referred to as 'homeostasis' a term coined by the American physiologist, Walter Bradford Cannon (1929), in reference to living systems. Significantly, Cannon chose the Ancient Greek term, 'homeo' (meaning 'similar') over the alternative Ancient Greek term, 'homo' (meaning 'the same'). By this, Cannon sought to distinguish human operations with their considerable variables from mechanical operations, such as in the case of the thermostat, that operate within a fixed system. Homeostasis is a process, which maintains a constant equilibrium when faced with internal or external changes, such as shocks, perturbations, and stressors. It is a concept that has been used in a number of fields including biology and mechanical systems. In the context of neuroscience, homeostasis can be understood as a kind of equilibrium on which the body depends for survival. Its behavior, however, is highly complex, and cannot be reduced to classical dynamics. Indeed, the mechanism by which complex systems self-regulate operates at many levels and often includes cross-scalar feedback mechanisms and dynamics. It therefore must be understood within the logic of systems thinking.

William Ross Ashby (2018), one of the pioneers in cybernetics, and author of *Design for a Brain*, developed a device he called the 'homeostat', a balancing mechanism – much like a thermostat – that maintains equilibrium through negative feedback. Ashby predicted the homeostat would even be able to play chess. The intention behind this device was to model the way in which the brain achieves its form of dynamic equilibrium. There are echoes here of the work of Sigmund Freud, who had already referred to the 'hydraulic construction of the unconscious' and its libidinal economy, such that 'the individual's conscious experience and behavior are the manifestation of a surging libidinal struggle between desire and repression' (Daugman, 1993). Significantly, Ashby's work caught the attention of Turing, who wrote to him suggesting he use his Automatic Computing Engine (ACE) to simulate the process rather than building a special machine. In his letter to Ashby, Turing (1946) confessed, 'I am more interested in producing models of the action of the brain than in the practical applications of computing'.[1] This, connection between homeostasis, computation, and the operations of the brain was established.

More recently Damasio (2019) argued that the primary function of the brain is to maintain our homeostatic condition and preserve our dynamic psychic equilibrium. Thus, the brain can be seen to operate less as a 'command control center' and more as a corrective mechanism that keeps the body within a safe range of emotional impulses. As Damasio and Carvalho (2013) argued, 'Survival depends on the maintenance of the body's physiology within an optimal homeostatic range. This process relies on fast detection of potentially deleterious changes in body state and on appropriate corrective responses' (p. 143). While the brain itself is highly adaptive through its neural plasticity, it can also serve as a mechanism of adaptation.

At a very basic level, we can see parallels between Damasio's understanding of homeostasis and the principles of self-organization that underpin a city. Indeed, German neuroscientist Singer (1997) has made direct comparisons between city operations and brain behavior. This comparison inspired Coop Himmelb(l)au (2009) to develop a research group, Brain City Lab, that used computational methods to map the behavior of neurons onto a city landscape model. Brains and cities, it would seem, have much in common. Could the city, however, be understood *as* a literal brain? In strict, neuroscientific terms, the city is not a brain. One is a human-mineral hybrid system, and one a biological organism. Damasio himself would never equate a city to the brain or compare AI to the brain. 'In retrospect, however, it had little to offer by way of a realistic view of what human minds look and feel like. How could it, given that the respective theory disengaged the dried-up mathematical description of the activity of neurons from the thermodynamics of life processes? Boolean algebra has its limits when it comes to making minds' (Damasio, 2019, p. 240). Nonetheless, a city could be described as a *kind* of brain.

Could we extend this comparison to AI? A neural network is composed of individual neurons contributing to an emergent collective behavior. As Kelleher (2019) suggested, 'The overall behavior of the network emerges from the interactions of the processing carried out by individual neurons within the network. Neural networks solve problems using a divide-and-conquer strategy: each of the neurons in a network solves one component of a larger problem, and the overall problem is solved by combining these component solutions' (p. 79). If so, we can extend the paradigm of emergence from relatively dumb creatures, such as ants (i.e., 'weak emergence'), to the sophistication of the brain, and on to cities and the operations of neural networks themselves (i.e., 'strong' emergence) (Chalmers, 2006). The opportunity therefore presents itself of using neural networks to model – and potentially enhance – the operations of a city.

City Brain

Perhaps, the most extensive exploration application of AI to the city has been the City Brain initiative developed by Chinese e-commerce conglomerate Alibaba. City Brain is effectively a 'digital twin' of the city itself. The project aims to develop a cloud-based system that stores city information in real time and uses machine learning to process that information in order to control operations and improve city performance.

Liu Feng (2018), one of the computer scientists behind the project, offers us a definition of the City Brain:

> The City Brain is a new architecture of the Smart City based on the model of the Internet Brain. Under the support of the city central nervous system (cloud computing), the city sensory nervous system (Internet of Things), the city motor nervous system (Industry 4.0, Industrial Internet) and the city nerve endings (Edge Computing), a city can achieve the human-human, human-things, and things-things information interaction through the city neural network (Big SNS) and achieve the rapid smart response to city services through the city cloud reflex arcs, to promote the organic integration of all components of a city, realizing the continuous progress of city wisdom. Such a brain-like smart city architecture is called "City Brain."
>
> *(p. 2)*

Initially, the City Brain initiative focused solely on traffic in Hangzhou, a city with some of the worst traffic problems in China (TomTom, 2023). It has proved surprisingly effective in improving operational efficiency. A pilot study showed City Brain could increase the speed of traffic by 15% and detect illegal parking. Moreover, by constantly monitoring traffic in the city, it can detect signs of potential collisions or accidents and alert the police, thereby improving emergency response times (Beall, 2018). By adjusting traffic lights in real time, it can help emergency vehicles reach their destinations more quickly and prevent traffic congestion during rush hour (Alibaba, 2023). Alibaba claims that City Brain allows ambulances to arrive at their destination seven minutes earlier on average, customers to check in and out of hotels in just 30 seconds, and drivers to pass through pay stations in an average time of 2.7 seconds (Alibaba, 2019). By keeping the traffic flowing, City Brain helps maintain the homeostatic condition of the city. This could perhaps be understood as a form of distributed intelligence, much like an octopus (Nixon & Young, 2003).

Further versions have since been introduced in nine other Chinese cities, and 23 cities worldwide, including Kuala Lumpur, Malaysia. City Brain is relatively easy to operate in China, given the comprehensive traffic surveillance already installed (Saieed, 2019). Alibaba is now increasing the range of applications to cover issues, such as public transportation, water and energy management, construction activities, and public security issues (Alibaba DAMO Academy, 2018).

Internet-City-Brain

The concept of the 'Internet of Things' (IoT) refers to the idea that devices can be interconnected wirelessly. This is the principle that underpins the Smart City. There are limitations, however, with the existing notions of the Smart City.

> However, there are still problems [with the Smart City] like unclear concept, blind speculation, lack of top-down design and fragile foundation. Relevant experts have pointed out that some of the Smart City construction projects are lack of top-down design and overall co-ordination, with a big difficulty in coordination and docking, especially in some vertical sectors, where the information system is only used within internal departments, lacking data sharing and application between different departments.
>
> *(Feng, 2018, p. 1)*

What would happen if our devices were not just connected through the discrete systems of the Smart City, but *intelligently* connected to form an overall network, like neurons in the brain? What if we were to combine the IoT with AI to produce what has been termed, the artificial IoT (AIoT) (Kubara, 2019; Marr, 2019). Would this produce a system that would operate somewhat like the brain?

Some, such as Demis Hassabis, have compared the brain to a computer. 'The brain is just a computer like any other… Traits previously considered innate to human – imagination, creativity and even consciousness – may be just the equivalent of software programs' (Ahmed, 2015, p. xx).[3] In fact, some scientists claim to have found mini-computers in the neurons of the brain (Fan, 2020). However, others disagree, and argue the brain is more like the Internet than a computer.

> The Internet will evolve toward the direction highly similar to the human brain, and it will have its memory nervous system, central nervous system, and autonomic nervous system in addition to the visual, auditory, tactile sense, and motor nervous systems. On the other hand, the human brain has had all the Internet functions through evolution for at least tens of thousands of years, and the continuous development of the Internet will help neurologists to reveal the secret of the human brain. Scientific experiments will prove that the brain also has a search engine like Google, a SNS system like Facebook, an address encoding system like IPv4, and a routing system like Cisco.
>
> *(Feng & Geng, 2008)*

As Jeffrey Stibel (2009) observes, 'The brain functions very differently from computers, but it functions in a manner similar to the way that the Internet works' (p. xxviii.). Whereas the computer merely represents a system of neurons, for Stibel, the Internet *operates* as a brain. 'The internet is a replica of the brain: computers and microchips represent neurons (the soma or calculating unit); like memory in the brain, Web sites house information; links among pages build semantic maps; and like axons and dendrites, phone lines carry that information across multiple regions' (p. xxiii). The hardware of the Internet is composed of millions of computers connected in a manner not dissimilar to neurons in the brain. The software is effectively the web itself.

> When I look at Google and the other search engines, I see more similarity to how memories are stored and retrieved in the mind than I do to the underlying computer architecture. When I look at websites, I think of memes and memories, not hyper-text. When I look at Classmates.com, MySpace, and Facebook, I see social networks that are developing the way neural networks develop, a way that is different than Metcalfe's Law of Networks.
>
> When I look at Internet computing clouds, I see the beginnings of a parallel pro-cessing machine that has the ability to go beyond brute calculations, toward the loopy random prediction power of the brain. But as I look out further into the future– as the electronic neurons multiply–I see in cyberspace a replication of biological growth itself, like the evolutionary growth of the brain of an insect, or an animal, or even a human being.
>
> *(Stibel, 2008, p. xx)*[3]

Recent neuroscientific research would seem to offer some support for this comparison, fanciful as it might seem. According to Narlakha and Suen (2017), the Internet and the brain are not only structured in similarly but also operate in the same way.

> While the brain and the Internet operate using very different mechanisms, both use simple local rules that give rise to stability. I was initially surprised that biological neural networks utilized the same algorithms as their engineered counterparts, but, as we learned, the requirements for efficiency, robustness, and simplicity are common to both living organisms and networks we have built.
>
> *(p. xx)*[3]

Once we reach this stage, the city will start to behave even more like the brain. Once the sensors and devices in a city are connected to form an AIoT, they would be locked into the secondary logic of an overall system that shares further similarities with the brain in effect, the discrete systems of the Smart City would give way to the comprehensive neural networks of the Brain City.

Conclusion

Whether or not we can make literal comparisons between the city and the brain, it is clear they share characteristics. Both display a form of intelligence. The intelligence of the city might not match the brain, but it is a form of intelligence resulting from the interface between people and the city itself. As Jiang (2019) comments:

With the evolution of the city, the city has its own intelligence. It's not artificial intelligence. So, you can't put human intelligence into a city. The city is going to have its own intelligence…The city is going to start its own thinking.

(p. xx)[4]

What would happen if AI supplemented the smart city? Might AI be used to reinforce the intelligence of the organic city? As argued above, intelligence takes on many different forms, but these forms are often compatible. As such, far from reducing the organic intelligence of the city, AI can operate as a form of auxiliary intelligence to an organic intelligence constituted by the city itself. AI can regulate and improve the performance of the city, much as a pacemaker might serve to regulate and improve the performance of the heart. From this perspective, we can compare the role of AI-based technology in augmenting city operations to the role of AI in augmenting human intelligence. Seen in this light, the city is *augmented* by AI, to become a form of 'brain city'.

Elon Musk (2020) has described how human beings can be enhanced by AI to become 'superhuman': 'All of us are already cyborgs. You have a machine extension of yourself in the form of your phone, your computer, and all your applications. You are already superhuman' (p. xx).[4] By extension, the 'brain city' could be a superintelligent city, where 'superintelligence' is judged by the 'intelligence' of the average city.

Bibliography

Ahmed, M. (2015, January 30). Lunch with the FT: Demis Hassabis. *Financial Times*. https://www.ft.com/content/47aa9aa4-a7a5-11e4-be63-00144feab7de

Alibaba. (2019). City Brain Now in 23 Cities in Asia. *Alibaba Cloud Blog*. 28 October 2019 https://www.alibabacloud.com/blog/city-brain-now-in-23-cities-in-asia_595479.

Alibaba. (2023). *Alibaba Cloud Intelligence Brain*. https://www.alibabacloud.com/solutions/intelligence-brain.

Alibaba DAMO Academy. (2018). *City Brain Lab*. https://damo.alibaba.com/labs/city-brain

Allen, S. (1997). From object to field. *Architectural Design*, 67(5/6): 24–31.

Andersson, N., Broberg, A., Bränberg, A., Jonsson, E., Holmlund, K., & Janlert, L.-E. (2003). Emergent interaction systems—designing for emergence. In *Paper Presented at the Momuc Workshop*. München, Germany. http://www8.cs.umu.se/~bopspe/publications/.

Ashby, W. R. (2018). *Design for a Brain: The Origin of Adaptive Behavior*. London: Chapman and Hall.

Beall, A. (2018, May 30). In China, Alibaba's data-hungry AI is controlling (and watching) cities. *Wired*. https://www.wired.co.uk/article/alibaba-city-brain-artificial-intelligence-china-kuala-lumpur=

Brown, R. K. (1969). City cybernetics. *Land Economics*, 45(4): 406–412. Accessed July 13, 2021. doi:10.2307/3145438.

Cannon, B. (1929). Organization for physiological homeostasis. *Physiological Reviews*, 9: 399–431.

Coop Himmelb(l)au. (2009). *Future Revisited*. http://www.coop-himmelblau.at/architecture/projects/coop-himmelblau-future-revisited/

Chalmers, D. J. (2006). Strong and weak emergence. In Davies, P., & Clayton, P. (eds.), *The Re-Emergence of Emergence: The Emergentist Hypothesis From Science to Religion*. Oxford University Press.

Damasio, A. (2019). *The Strange Order of Things: Life, Feeling and the Making of Cultures*. New York: Vintage.

Damasio, A., & Carvalho, G. (2013). The nature of feelings: Evolutionary and neurobiological origins. *Neuroscience*, 14: 143.

Daugman, J. (1993). Brain metaphors and brain theory. In *Computational Neuroscience*. Cambridge, MA: MIT Press.

DeLanda, M. (2002). Deleuze and the use of the genetic algorithm in architecture. In Leach, N. (ed.), *Designing for a Digital World*. London: John Wiley & Sons.

Fan, S. (2020, January 14). Scientists discovered 'Mini-Computers'. In *Human Neurons—and That's Great News for AI, SingularityHub*. https://singularityhub.com/2020/01/14/scientists-discovered-mini-computers-in-human-neurons-and-thats-great-news-for-ai/.

Feng, L. (2018). City brain, a new architecture of smart city based on the internet brain. *arXiv*, 1710.04123v3.

Feng, L., & Peng, G. (2008). Discovery and analysis of iEvolution laws. *China Science Paper Online*. https://arxiv.org/pdf/1806.10095.pdf

Heylighen, F. (1989). Self-organization, emergence and the architecture of complexity. In *Proceedings of the 1st European Conference on System Science* (Vol. 18, pp. 23–32). Paris: AFCET.

Holland, J. (1999). *Emergence: From Chaos to Order*. Perseus.

Jiang, W. (2019, July 2). City brain: Rethinking the relationship between technology and city. *ULI Asia Pacific* [Video]. YouTube. https://www.youtube.com/watch?v=RTPjzeQKg2w.

Johnson, S. (2002). *Emergence: The Connected Lives of Ants, Cities and Software*. Schribner.

Kelleher, J. (2019). *Deep Learning*. MIT Press.

Kubara, K. (2019, July 10). Artificial intelligence meets the internet of things. *Towards Data Science*. https://towardsdatascience.com/artificial-intelligence-meets-the-internet-of-things-a38a46210860

Leach, N. (2014). Swarm tectonics. In Leach, N., Turnbull, D., & Williams, C. (eds.), *Digital Tectonics*. Wiley.

Legg, S., & Hutter, M. (2007). Universal intelligence: A definition of machine intelligence. *Minds and Machines*, 17(4): 391–444.

Lovelock, J. (1979). *Gaia: A New Look at Life on Earth*. Oxford University Press.

Marr, B. (2019, December 20). What is the artificial intelligence of things? When AI meets IoT.T. *Forbes*. https://www.forbes.com/sites/bernardmarr/2019/12/20/what-is-the-artificial-intelligence-of-things-when-ai-meets-iot/#7cb3a13ab1fd.

McPhearson, T., Parnell, S., Simon, D., Gaffney, O., Elmqvist, T., Bai, X., Roberts, D., & Revi, A., (2016). Scientists must have a say in the future of cities. *Nature News*, 538(7624):165.

Musk, E. (2020, October 24). Elon's message on artificial superintelligence—ASI. *Science Time*. [Video]. YouTube. https://www.youtube.com/watch?v=ZCeOsdcQObI&feature=youtu.behttps://www.youtube.com/watch?v=ZCeOsdcQObI&feature=youtu.be.

Narlakha, S., & Suen, J. (2017). Using inspiration from synaptic plasticity rules to optimize traffic flow in distributed engineered networks. *Neural Computation*, 29(5): 1204–1228.

Nixon, M., & Young, J. Z. (2003). *The Brains and Lives of Cephalopods*. Oxford University Press.

Saieed, Z. (2019, April 25). Kuala Lumpur set to become smart city next year. *The Star*. https://www.thestar.com.my/business/business-news/2019/04/25/kuala-lumpur-set-to-become-smart-city-next-year

Singer, W. (1997). Die Architektur des Gehirns als Modell für komplexe Stadtstrukturen? In Maar, C., & Rötzer, F (eds.). *Virtual Cities* (pp. 153–161). Birkhauser.

Snooks, R. (2017). Behavioral matter. In Leach, N., & Snooks, R. (eds.), *Swarm Intelligence: Architectures of Multi-Agent Systems*. Tongji UP.

Stibel, J. (2008, June 23). The internet is a brain. *Harvard Business Review*. https://hbr.org/2008/06/the-internet-is-a-brain.html

Stibel, J. (2009). *Wired for Thought: How the Brain Is Shaping the Future of the Internet*. Harvard Business Press.

Suen, J. (2017, February 9). The internet and your brain are more alike than you think. *Salk News*. https://www.salk.edu/news-release/internet-brain-alike-think/

Tom Tom. (2023). *Hangzhou Traffic*. https://www.tomtom.com/traffic-index/hangzhou-traffic/.

Turing, A. (1946). Letter to William Ashby. *The W. Ross Ashby Archive*. http://www.rossashby.info/letters/turing.html.

Waldrop, M. (1992). *Complexity: The Emerging Science at the Edge of Order and Chaos*. Simon and Schuster.

2.3
CITY AS SPACESHIP – SPACESHIP AS CITY

2.3.1
CITY AS A SPACESHIP (CAAS)

Sue Fairburn, Susmita Mohanty and Barbara Imhof

Abstract

While past visions of future cities were often inspired by space and exploration of the unknown, and thus based on science fiction, we propose future visions of the city based on science fact; that which is known and learned from our accumulated space exploration experience.

Technological spin-offs from space design could integrate into our daily lives, but the confined conditions of extraterrestrial (ET) shuttles seldom serve as Earthly inspiration. How would we live differently if Earth were a spaceship, and we were the Astronauts? What if living conditions in outer space informed and exchanged the cramped social environments down below, such as the worker housing and informal settlements in our megacities? How can space systems inform the structure and workings of extreme urban environments? We are exploring the City As A Spaceship (CAAS) and the reciprocities it offers by mapping ET experiences onto earthly settings.

Smart City's innovative paradigm is the trend for metropolises and future human habitation toward causing the least impact on the ecosystem and safe environments for the world. The International Space Station (ISS) sets an example for a minimal ecological footprint by operating on Smart City paradigms including clean renewable solar power and air and water recycling. The ISS is a model of a unique, off-the-grid Earth-orbiting dwelling to pursue on the surface of the Earth.

This chapter, by analyzing and learning from the performative aspects of ISS and the scope of its execution and limitations on the planet, will attempt to develop practical and productive intelligent measures and tenets for future cities and their habitats providing safe and healthy havens for the citizens of the world.

Introduction

Half the world's 8.07 billion inhabitants (Population Clock at 02.00 GMT on 12/11/2023) live in urban settings. Sao Paolo, Tokyo, Mexico City, Mumbai, Moscow, New York

City, Hong Kong, and London are the big cities, the Megatropolises, which all have rapidly growing populations within their densely packed urban centers with equally densely packed peripheries. Living conditions on Earth must change, irrespective of economic or social status, so that we can equalize opportunity and achieve a better standard of living for all.

We propose that the (mega) City and the Spaceship be viewed as parallel and reciprocal case studies. We must think about contemporary forms of working and personal engagement; compact spaces, multifunctional spaces, public-private spaces, resource management, alternative energy harvesting, waste management, health management, and inclusion of nature into our built-up environment.

CAAS inspires humane technological innovation by positing the spaceship as an analogy of the modern, densely built urban space. With its complex structures and technologically advanced infrastructure, the designed intention is to configure all systems to eco-efficiency to optimize the use of available resources. We believe the time is now to meet our primary needs through *CAAS* architecture and design, using technologies for space that can immediately impact the humane retrofitting of these cities. The *CAAS* City can be an inspiration, an alternate view, for a future city and a way to project and achieve our dreams and visions of an equitable and environment-friendly urban life.

We view Space habitats and space transport vehicles as analogous to future cities. With over 50 years of accumulated human spaceflight experience, technological spin-offs from space design could integrate into our daily tendencies. The remoteness of the accumulated space exploration needs to be interpreted, translated, brokered, and curated to serve as Earthly inspiration. As designers and inhabitants of this planet, this chapter shares the author's contribution to design the thinking, the topic, and the theme, leading to designs that address the question: *If Earth were a spaceship and we were Astronauts, how would we live differently?*

This chapter sets out future visions of the CAAS in four parts: At Scale, Paradigms for Living Together, Spaceship Ecologies, and Mapping.

We authors start **"At Scale"** by presenting a stark statement of the population paradox facing cities over the next 35 years, and a case in point of an Asian urban slum, and **Paradigms for Living Together** in cities as socio-ecological systems. We cite other complex systems that benefit our understanding of

- What is needed for survival;
- What is a suitable environment; and
- How do we share spaces for creating the knowledge needed to thrive in the future?

Enter **Spaceship ecologies;** the characters or players. The Greek word "*oikos*" (the root of Economy and Ecology) is used to profile the International Space Station (ISS) as a **System οἶκος Spaceship** with its five ecologies for exploring the interrelationships and rules governing living systems of organisms and their environment. Lastly, in **Mapping**, we explore interpretations of the "city" as a "spaceship" metaphor using graphical representations of information. As this is the debut of CAAS on the international research scene. We conclude with reflections on its' generative capacity to conceive and synthesize future living systems; living, thriving, survival-challenging uber cities as collections of self-contained, super redundant microcosms to prove themselves reliable and hardy over time.

At Scale: The "Geometry and Anguish" of Cities

Federico Garcia Lorca[1] refers to the two elements of the big city as "geometry and anguish." With over 8.07 billion inhabitants, and increasing by over 50 million per year, the world's urban centers face significant challenges. In the years up to 2050, it is expected that nearly 70% of the world's population will live in cities. The Rio+20 United Nations Conference on Sustainable Development (2012) reconfirmed that in the next years, we will face even more challenging topics to our lifestyle to reduce CO_2 levels, generate more energy through alternative non-fossil sources, and stop the diminishing levels of biodiversity. According to Urban Theorist Mike Davis, our current state seems paradoxical. He refers to the city "as its solution." The exact cities that contributed to the decreasing health of our environment today probably hold the solutions for the survival of humankind in the twenty-first century (Davis, 2010).

Living both in space and dense cities brings into sharp focus considerations such as sustainability, material recycling, and regenerative life-support (Bannova et al., 2013). Yet, the big cities of the world are *cities within cities* with equally densely packed shantytowns or slums. The largest shantytown/slum within Asia is Dharavi, a former fishing village that is now a hyper-dense slum in the heart of Mumbai, the financial capital of India. Dharavi is located between two main suburban rail lines so its attraction as an affordable option for commuting outweighs its reality of a population of one million, with 600,000 housed in over 100,000 makeshift homes; a density of over 30,000 persons per hectare (12,000 persons per acre). It lacks sewage, yet 10–15 people live in the same house, cooking, sleeping, and sharing the same toilet (Figure 2.3.1.1).

Living and working in Dharavi is ironically similar to living and working in outer space. The extreme shortage of real estate, breathable air, water, and waste disposal in such informal settlements, presents living problems not dissimilar to those encountered in

Figure 2.3.1.1 Bringing the orbiting ISS and Dharavi closer, metaphorically speaking ("Low Tech, High Tech," International Artmap Workshop, Paris, 2012).

Source: ISS image courtesy of NASA, Collage: Barbara Imhof.

extraterrestrial (ET) synthetic environments. Likewise, the problems of odor, noise, crowding, privacy, hygiene, upkeep, and storage are quite comparable. The challenge, both in Dharavi and in outer space, is to not just survive the extreme environment but to live real, productive lives. Productive lives involve constantly improvising, inventing techniques to live off-the-grid, managing with scarce resources and out of necessity, and locally harvesting power and water (Mohanty, 2012).

CAAS Means

The city that you live in; imagine that one day it just unplugs and takes off and goes and lands someplace else. If it is a friendly city it leaves no trace of having been there. No trash, no trace. It has lived there lightly.

In *CAAS*, the word "City" is not literal. Rather it is a metaphor for life on the spaceship(s) we inhabit – the "City" could well be a megacity or a "megatropolis," a slum, a village, a neighborhood, a home, an office, a laboratory, or for that matter any other (product) system or sub-system. The word "Spaceship" conveys the nature of the habitat in size, basic amenities, and socio-psychological stressors, whether in orbit or that of a micro compact home or workspace in super dense cities like Mumbai, Tokyo, New York, or Sao Paolo. In viewing the "City" as a "Spaceship," we are encouraging the blurring of boundaries between the language and contexts of Outer (Space) and Terrestrial environments, to facilitate the creation of knowledge and encourage its free flow between disciplines and cultures, yielding holistic approaches to design future systems for both living on Earth and one day on other Planets.

CAAS is a metaphorical movement in urban planning, a new way of thinking about human lifestyles, habits, and tendencies, which history tells us do not change easily. To change the character of thought, one needs to remodel the forms of habitation, or in the words of Buckminster Fuller words: "reshape their environment; don't try to reshape man" (Krausse and Lichetenstein, 1999). Designing cities to be comprised of small, spaceship-like closed-loop eco-systems, where the waste they spit out gets recycled back into the ECLSS loop. This principle can lead to the design of future cities that could exemplify what Fuller meant by "Spaceship Earth." While CAAS opportunities lie in technology, at the foundation is the well of human creativity, and our desire and essential need to share space intelligently and responsibly.

CAAS: Paradigms for Living Together

Resilience is more about thinking about systems that can absorb shocks and that could constantly fall into healthy balance.[2]

Angelo Vermeulen

"Operating Manual for Spaceship Earth" (Fuller, 1969) conveys Fuller's vision of Earth as a floating body within space – self-contained and self-sufficient, as is a space shuttle – where what exists onboard is the extent of available resources. Fullers' projected analysis of Earth predicted the population boom and extreme extraction and use of its finite resources. His design work offered solutions to real problems; new ways to view familiar ways of inhabiting. As a kind of extension and inversion of this Spaceship Earth analogy, *CAAS* looks at the city – as a spaceship – as offering reciprocity for the exchange of ideas, technology, and experience.

In his 2010 lecture at the Glasgow Centre for Population Studies, Professor Max Boisot offered a perspective on forms of knowledge that could benefit complex organizations like cities (Boisot, 2010), based on lessons learned from the collaborative ATLAS experiment at CERN.[3] The ATLAS detector is one of the largest and most complex experimental machines ever constructed. Likewise, the ISS rivals CERN for technological complexity and for requiring cooperative and symbiotic working relationships. Both offer lessons on ways to share and diffuse different forms of information.

The exchange of knowledge at scale is a complex undertaking. Saskia Sassen approaches the issue from a global context, with cities at the center of our environmental future, and draws attention to the "urban knowledge capital" they hold (Sassen, 2009).

Boisot describes cities and their inhabitants as complex adaptive systems, with their networks of interactions, their dynamic relationships between environment, structure, and body, and their adaptability through behaviors; individual and collective (Boisot, 2010). But the question remains: How can we exchange relevant information and ideas, and generate reciprocities between these parallel complex systems; Cities, and Spaceships?

Sassen proposes building stronger connections between cities and their biosphere as a means to produce positive outcomes; "outcomes that allow cities to contribute to environmental sustainability?" (Sassen, 2012). We authors concur that the potential for positive connections is broad; *CAAS* serves as an accessible starting point for envisioning connections. In doing so, they look to the past, present, and future for lessons and technologies that confer reciprocities. They reference knowledge of mixing species to ensure balance, of closing loops to challenge resource inefficiencies, and of looking to both scientific and creative fields to understand what the biosphere can do.

Past visions of future cities were inspired by space and exploration of the unknown. *CAAS* proposes ideas based on science and social science facts; that which is known and learned from accumulated space exploration. These ideas come from observation and understanding of the complex relationships between space, material, technologies, and the various modes of habitation and use. With the scientific occupation of space – both human, animal, and machine – we believe in a "symbiosis" – looking at both "here and there" – at the multitude of scales (in between) – looking at technologies and the principles of survival to envision parameters for future living. When we speak of surviving and thriving we are talking about the human body and its environment; the needs of the body and the factors that surround the body.

Go into and out of the body. The Home ‖ The City ‖ Air ‖ Food ‖ Waste ‖ Water ‖ Atmosphere ‖ Gas = requirements of the body and a suitable environment.

Spaceship Ecologies

The study and translation of ancient Greek texts reveal that the whole Greek world and philosophy was reflected in their language which sometimes had more holistic meanings than the words one would associate with them today. To define the spaceship ecologies, the authors would like to introduce "oikos," the Greek word for house. "Oikos" in the Ancient Greek interpretation describes not only the house, and the shelter itself, but the whole household and everything that belonged to the house. Economy and ecology have the same root, "oikos." Thus "oikos" can be described as a system (of the house). A spaceship is not merely a house, it also comprises a whole system, a very complex system that provides shelter, energy, and nutrition, and houses inhabitants using specific technology, needing water and air, living with animals, and producing waste. For **CAAS**, the ISS can serve as a role model.

The ISS orbits the earth 350 km in the z-axis, a distance that might be closer to the reader's location than some of their nearest cities, yet the Space Station shelters against temperature differences of 300 degrees and vacuum, environmental conditions unfamiliar to most people. There is only limited habitable space available, including limited resources of water and air, which are set into a nearly closed loop. The ultimate goal is to implement controlled ecological life support systems (CELSS). These will include the inhabitants, animals, food production for all organisms aboard, and their waste management. The only renewable energy source is the sun. A complex technology connects all systems, yet this technical system co-functions with the human system: human interaction of multi-cultural crews with a variety of professional backgrounds.

The ecologies of the **System οἶκος Spaceship** are the interrelationships of the aspects of shelter, energy, technology, nutrition, inhabitants, animals, air, water, and waste management. Each ecology constitutes the relationship between the organisms and their environment.

We present the **System οἶκος Spaceship** with its' ecologies as a metaphor for thinking the future city and urban developments. Cities are complex systems in their geographies of consumption and waste production. This complexity also makes them crucial to the production of solutions. The network of global cities is a global space for the management of investments. It holds the potential for the re-engineering of environmentally destructive global capital investments into more responsible investments. In this sense, the authors view the system OIKOS as not only closed; it is also open as a city – connected **and** closed, it is the "and" according to Ulrich Beck's description of the "OFFENE STADT." According to Ulrich Beck, this is about urbanity and ecology in a new "as well as" or "and." Beck refers to cities in a world where nothing can be isolated anymore. He continues

> On one hand, we can identify architecture as a school of aesthetics, on the other hand, there is the architecture's sensitivity to develop for a social ecology of a place. The reflexive architecture of the "and" discovers and expands the history of the place into the public space. The architecture proclaims: if I cannot change the society, at least I would like to influence the way people move through spaces and perceive the connections of spaces including the built-in contradictions.[4]

CAAS proposes the following five ecologies as a foundation:

1 **Shelter as Transformable:** Shelter can be viewed as an envelope that defines interior and exterior: inhabitants need appropriate shelter to protect them from weather and create distinctions between public and private spaces. On the Space Station, only very limited space is available to each crewmember for living functions and social spaces. Storage volume is scarce, even laboratory space is finite and constrained. In highly populated cities, we experience the same issues. Concepts for multi-functional spaces which are inscribed for more than one single function. Transformability of spaces, furniture outfitting, and systems including mobility have already become a main topic of space design and will become equally important for future city-related design and planning at all scales.

2 **Energy as Renewable:** In the city, consumption will rise with the integration of more technologized infrastructure and equipment. Fossil fuel resources are limited so low-energy

lighting, heating, and new ways of transporting, communication machines, computers, etc. will be necessary to reduce the overall increasing energy need. Energy sources will need to come from clean and renewable sources to mitigate the side effects of current energy production. A photovoltaic-powered spaceship's energy ecology meets this requirement, as it generates the energy needed from clean and renewable sources as exemplified on the ISS where all energy is harvested from the sun (Figure 2.3.1.2a).

3 **Technology, Automation, and Infrastructure**: A spaceship is a technology-rich envelope incorporating certain intelligence. Space Station, for example, was assembled completely robotically using the "Canadarm" (Figure 2.3.1.2a); astronauts only controlled and supervised the process. All onboard life support systems are automatic but allow for a certain degree of manual control, as necessary. Other supporting technologies have been developed, such as a diagnostic tool that allows detailed on-orbit monitoring and logging of all avionics bus messages, and the nerve system of the Space Station. Through *CAAS*, all these systems and more can be imagined in future smart cities where construction, communication, health, traffic, and infrastructure support and maintenance are controlled by intelligent systems.

4 **Inhabitants**: On ISS, there are a few fish, or from time-to-time other small animals, which need to be incorporated into the closed-loop living system. Crewmembers have inhabited the ISS since 2009 and in doing so, they reflect international cooperation between the US, Canada, Russia, European countries, and Japan. According to the inhabitants, this presents challenges in social interaction, requiring appropriate training, because cultural understanding just does not come without an effort. The same applies to cities, which face a completely mixed population and a huge variety of professions with different cultural backgrounds (Figure 2.3.1.2b).

5 **Life Support Systems**: In closed environments, only limited resources of air and water are available, thus both essentials for life need to be treated carefully, responsibly, and sustainably through recycling processes (Figure 2.3.1.2c). On Space Stations, astronauts drink purified water recycled from their urine. A major challenge whether on earth or in space is the production of nutrition and management of wastes. Intensification of harvest in limited space: changing strategies, densification (growing vertically), using specific substrates for cultivation and growth of plants, selecting the "right" plants with high levels of minerals (algae), proteins (beans), vitamins (algae), and carbohydrates (sweet potatoes), etc. as an approach to reduce and recover waste into useful material, which will become essential factors to address. Greenhouses, as enclosed structures for cultivating and protecting plants, must be integrated not only in space station (Figure 2.3.1.2d) but also in the city, to reduce transportation and create food, and even provide valuable psychological for the inhabitants, an approach that has already been integrated in some cities of the world.

The five main ecologies can guide the designs for future cities, derived from the *CAAS* approach, applied at micro and macro scales. *CAAS* cannot only be seen as the city being the spaceship but also as the house being a spaceship. A workshop held at ESA's Astronaut Centre in Cologne in 2012 took the first step in identifying European spaceflight technologies that could be applied to terrestrial housing. IP-STAR, a Dutch company, has made this a reality by having derived a water purification system from the ESA Melissa Life Support Systems program and applying it to larger hotel complexes. *CAAS* can serve as a direct approach to spin-off technologies from space and the ISS and as a conceptual guideline in developing designs that meet the many constraints; limited space, resources, and closed-loop cycles with

Figure 2.3.1.2a   Top left: Solar panels of the ISS robotic arm/CANADARM used to build the ISS.
Source: SS image courtesy of NASA.

Figure 2.3.1.2b   Top right: ISS-Earth reciprocities: A multi-national crew collage.
Source: ISS interior background image, courtesy of NASA, Collage: Anne Marlene Rüede / LIQUIFER.

Figure 2.3.1.2c   ISS-Earth reciprocities: A water collage.
Source: ISS interior foreground image courtesy of NASA, background image credit: Sarah Jane Pell, Collage: Anne Marlene Rüede / LIQUIFER

Figure 2.3.1.2d   ISS-Earth reciprocities: A nutrition collage.
Source: ISS interior background image courtesy of NASA, Collage: Anne Marlene Rüede / LIQUIFER.

regard to air, water, and waste. Offering a paradigm for future urban developments and staging CASS as spaceflight parameters provides a way to look at life in Space from a different perspective and find commonality with Earth living systems and contemporary tendencies.

Mapping CAAS

We further explored the "city" as a "spaceship" metaphor using graphical representations of information (data). We mapped terrestrial tendencies, human density, consumption, and waste. This section presents three sets of visual data sets for comparing and contrasting the world's densest cities such as Mumbai, Tokyo, New York, Sao Paulo, Cairo, Mexico City, Amsterdam, Paris, Lagos, and Johannesburg and compares them to smaller counterparts such as Vienna, San Francisco, and Toronto (Figure 2.3.1.3).

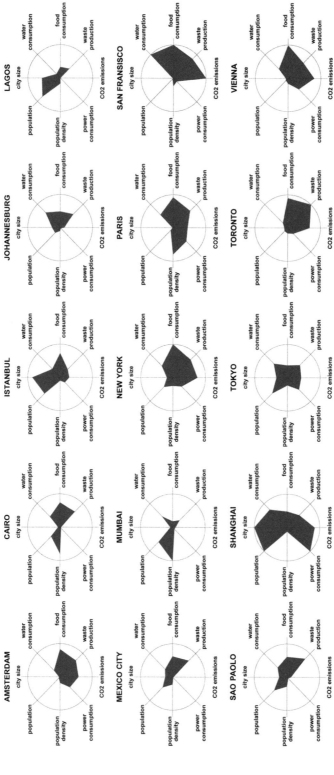

Figure 2.3.1.3 Cities of the world – TENDENCIES – a visual vector portrayal of comparative data points.

Source: Anne Marlene Rüede / LIQUIFER.

The first set – titled – TENDENCIES (Figure 2.3.1.3) – presents a visual vector portrayal of comparative data points such as city size, population, population density, waste production, CO_2 emissions, and power-water-food consumption. As an infographic, it evidences the consumption patterns of cities from industrially advanced nations (e.g. Amsterdam, New York, Paris) outstrips that of the less industrialized ones (e.g. Mexico City, Mumbai, Lagos). But there is more to it than what meets the eye. Even among the industrial nations, the (water, food, power) consumption patterns vary. Further analyses and thinking are necessary to get an in-depth understanding of what these maps convey. The emerging economies will likely catch up with this pattern in the coming decades. The situation might get out of hand putting the future of the planet in peril. Several questions come to mind when one surveys these graphic representations of (information), especially relationships within the datasets. The answers are not immediately obvious but need further investigation. For example,

- Is the standard of living in a city directly proportional to the levels of consumption?
- Is there a relationship between power consumption and CO_2 emissions?
- Why do some cities consume a lot more power than they consume food or water?
- Can a mega city have consumption patterns similar to a micro-city?

The graphics also bring forth comparative questions between cities, such as: Are the consumption and emission patterns of New York and Vienna similar? Why is Tokyo's consumption footprint more balanced than the other cities featured in this infographic? Is San Francisco's consumption and waste production *vis a vis* its population out of control?

We hope to take this **CAAS** mapping exercise forward and map it to ET situations, both current (e.g. the orbiting ISS) and future (e.g. space colonies). We believe that these maps can help designers and planners identify, understand, and if need be, alter tendencies for consumption, growth, waste production, and CO_2 emissions in ways that are planet-friendly. They can help identify patterns that are often lost in hard data and enable intelligent and well-informed resource and waste management decisions, both on and off the planet.

Conclusions

By grounding space innovations and uplifting Earth innovations, **CAAS** can challenge and shape ideas and serve as curator and broker to the planning, designing, developing, and inhabiting of near-future cities.

No. 1. We are, by no means, arguing that the way we live in outer space is more eco-efficient than how we live on our Earth or the other way around. There are parallels, there are differences, and there are reciprocities. **CAAS** believes that our earthly experiences can inform and influence our ET explorations and vice versa.

No. 2. The initial **CAAS** mapping explorations reveal that humans tend to consume more to achieve a higher material standard of living. As the emerging economies move toward higher material comforts and consumption (as did the industrial economies before them), the planet might not be able to sustain the increased levels of cumulative consumption and waste production. This concern makes the **CAAS** philosophy even more relevant. In the present-day context, when global climate change is staring us in the face, the Western industrialized nations are rethinking the results of several centuries of thoughtless depredation of the earth. Two of the most populous nations on the face of the planet – India and

Figure 2.3.1.4   Future CAAS city as envisioned for Vienna science festival 2013.

Source: Damjan Minovski for LIQUIFER systems group.

China – are urbanizing at a monstrous pace. They do it in much the same way as the industrialized world did in the preceding decades. These parts of the world need new answers if we stand a chance to keep the world habitable, and sustainable.

No. 3. The premise of **CAAS** is that the city of the future will connect Earth and (outer) space in seamless ways. This future vision, such as the one depicted in Figure 2.3.1.4, can be achieved through applications and ideas derived from innovative technologies. These technologies include the space elevator, space-based solar power plants, closed-loop waste, and water recycling as well as technologies from other fields such as nuclear fusion, tissue engineering, and medical nanorobots. An extension of this utopia is that architects, designers, technologists, economists, policymakers, and planners can work together toward an "urban future" in which every person can achieve a high standard of living, regardless of economic or social status, without depleting the resources of his or her home planet.

No. 4. The "Earth as a Spaceship" is not merely a metaphor; it is a tangible, viable way for the future survival of humankind. *CAAS* is a vision and a programmatic step toward new designs for living together – living together on a space station needs some practice – as in cities, and current global challenges make this vision pressing.

Acknowledgments

The authors wish to acknowledge the following contributors for their guidance, advice, and creative input: Anne-Marlene Rüede, Siddharth Das, and Dr. Marc Cohen.

Notes

1 "The two elements the traveler first captures in the big city are extra human architecture and furious rhythm. Geometry and anguish." Federico Garcia Lorca.
2 Quote by Angelo Vermeulen, cited in Transcripts from the "Growing as Building" Symposium titled "Biological growth into technology: between fiction and fact" held March 25, 2014 at the University of Applied Arts, Vienna, Austria. www.growingasbuilding.org
3 ATLAS (A Toroidal LHC Apparatus) is one of seven detector experiments at CERN (the European Organisation for Nuclear Research).
4 Ulrich Beck, Die offene Stadt, DeutschesArchitektenBlatt, 3/96, 1996, Bonn pp. 362–364. http:// www.kulturregion-stuttgart.de/offeneraeume/texte/beck_offene

References

Bannova, O., Alifanov, O., Clar, R., Harrison, A., Sherwood, B., Mohanty, S., Payson, D., and Tolyarenko, N. (2013) IAAA Final Report SG6 9.

Beck, U. (1996). Die offene Stadt, DeutschesArchitektenBlatt, 3/96, Bonn pp. 362–364. http://www. kulturregion-stuttgart.de/offeneraeume/texte/beck_offene (accessed 15/08/2014).

Boisot, M. (2010). "The city as a complex adaptive system: Lessons from the ATLAS experiment at the Large Hadron Collider (LHC)". In *Presented at Glasgow Centre for Population Health Seminar Series 7, Seminar 1, Summary Paper*. https://edshare.gcu.ac.uk/143/ (accessed 1 May 2014).

Davis, M. (2010). "Who will build the Ark". In *ARCH+ No. 196/197: Post-Oil City, The History of the Cities Future*, edited by Elke aus dem Moore, Iris Lenz, Nikolaus Kuhnert, Anh-Linh Ngo, ARCH+ Verlag GmbH, Stuttgart/Aachen.

Fuller, R.B. (1969). *Operating Manual for Spaceship Earth*, Southern Illinois University Press, 144 pp.

Krausse, J. and Lichtenstein, C. (Eds.) (1999). *Your Private Sky. R. Buckminster Fuller*, Lars Mueller Publishers, 528 p.

Mohanty, S. (2012). "What Has Outer Space Got to Do with Dharavi?" Invited lecture "Low Tech, High Tech". In *International Artmap Workshop*, Paris.

Sassen, S. (2009). "Cities Are at the Center of our Environmental Future". *S.A.P.I.E.N.S* [Online]. http://sapiens.revues.org/948 (accessed 30/08/2014).

Sassen, S. (2012). "Cities and the Biosphere". In *The Berkshire Encyclopedia of Sustainability: The Future of Sustainability*, Berkshire Publishing, 36 p.

2.3.2

OUTER SPACE ACTIVITIES AND THE FUTURE OF SMART HABITATS ON EARTH

M. Thangavelu

Abstract

New cities are emerging, established towns are growing and expanding, and many metropolises are merging to become megalopolises around the globe. Urban infrastructures around the world are coping hard to adjust to new pressures including the huge population migration from rural to urban regions, climate change effects, and vital resources, all to sustain and enhance the quality of life of the citizens.

Providing a safe, productive, and nurturing environment for the city dweller is the overarching directive and prime aim of every city and city management. Enhancing and safely delivering a range of cradle-to-grave activities to sustain the quality of life of the citizen including incorporating agile, responsive systems for health and welfare, economic opportunities, leisure, and safety are all part of the evolving Smart City paradigm.

Just as the space community is expanding our presence into the solar system and beyond, a group of thought leaders, including visionary policymakers, architects, engineers, and allied professionals, are peering into the Earth, studying co-relations of various dynamic systems, including land, air, and sea agents, and finding new ways to report and apply the data from space-based assets, for the immediate betterment of humanity.

Our cosmopolitan cities, urban and suburban landscapes, and dwellings are already using space assets including crew on orbiting space stations and allied technologies to monitor, inform, and enhance the quality of life. Orbiting spacecraft also helps predict, alert, and even prevent hazards, both natural and manmade, from affecting populations adversely. Future cities and their amenities including active adaptive and agile response systems that use artificial intelligence are already shaping the built environment.

This chapter will present the various space technologies and operations being studied or being proposed for adoption to make smart habitats and the overall built environment safer and more efficient, providing a better quality of life for the citizens.

We imagine, create, and evolve our environment. Thereafter, our environment shapes and steers us.

DOI: 10.4324/9781003384113-30

234

Introduction

New cities are emerging, established towns are growing and expanding, and many metropolises are merging to become megalopolises around the globe. Urban infrastructures around the world are coping hard to adjust to new pressures including the huge population migration from rural to urban regions, climate change effects, and vital resources, all to sustain and enhance the quality of life of the citizens (Mitra & Murayama, 2009; Thangavelu, 2022).

Providing a safe, productive, and nurturing environment for the city dweller is the overarching directive and prime aim of every city and city management. Enhancing and safely delivering a range of cradle-to-grave activities to sustain the quality of life of the citizen including incorporating agile, responsive systems for health and welfare, economic opportunities, leisure, and safety are all part of the evolving Smart City paradigm (Mora et al., 2019).

Just as the space community is expanding our presence into the solar system and beyond, a group of thought leaders, including visionary policymakers, architects, engineers, and allied professionals, are peering into the Earth, studying co-relations of various dynamic systems including land, air and sea agents, and finding new ways to report and apply the data from space-based assets, for the immediate betterment of humanity (Pettorelli et al., 2014; Fiore, 2020).

Our cosmopolitan cities, urban and suburban landscapes, and dwellings are already using space assets including crew on orbiting space stations and allied technologies to monitor, inform, and enhance the quality of life. Orbiting spacecraft also helps predict, alert, and even prevent hazards, both natural and manmade, from affecting populations adversely. Future cities and their amenities including active adaptive and agile response systems that use artificial intelligence (AI) are already shaping and transforming the built environment (Thangavelu, 2020).

This chapter attempts to present the various space technologies and operations being studied or being proposed for adoption to make smart habitats and the overall built environment safer and more efficient, providing a better quality of life for the citizens.

The International Space Station Is an Example of a Minimal Ecological Footprint, Paradigmatic for Smart Cities on Earth

As the *Smart City* paradigm takes hold across new metropolises and potential human habitation zones around the globe, human space activity continues to pioneer innovation in agile, responsive building systems and their evolution, transforming habitats and surroundings to suit the needs of occupants as well as adapting to both dynamic and gradual changes with minimal imposition on the natural environment that we call ecological footprint. Future City designs employ *Smart City* paradigms space technologies and processes to provide citizens and dwellers a more productive and safer environment while reducing ecological footprint. Frugal use and recycling of consumables like air and water, performant building materials, energy efficiency, and systems that respond with agility to environmental changes are hallmarks of human spacecraft and start-to-end space mission manifest management (Kitmacher et al., 2005).

International Space Station (ISS) has been orbiting the Earth for nearly 25 years in the extreme environment of space, primarily dependent on solar power for energy. The ISS sets an example for a minimal ecological footprint by operating on a *Smart City* paradigm including clean renewable solar power and air and water recycling. The ISS is a fine example of a unique, off-the-grid Earth-orbiting smart habitat.

For the past decade, the ISS has also been recycling her atmosphere and more than 96% of the water used by her occupants (Figure 2.3.2.1). It is important to note that clean renewable energy, clean-scrubbed air, and clean reusable water, as currently available for crew onboard the ISS, are also an integral part of the United Nations Sustainable Development Goals, and pointed out to the UN Science Summit and is relevant to the UN Space 2030 agenda (Figure 2.3.2.2).

A crew of six continues to spend an inordinate amount of time on housekeeping functions. Ways to reduce crew time for facility maintenance, without impacting mission productivity or sacrificing safety have become a top priority. Extending our reach into space, a lunar orbiting station is being developed by NASA with another advanced layer of efficient systems to cope with this crew's time-consuming deficiency. It is called system autonomy (Frank, 2015). Emerging technologies based on Artificial Intelligence (AI) are rapidly improving system autonomy that is more anticipatory, responsive, and agile than humans as evidenced in the fully self-driving (FSD) algorithms maturing in electric vehicles (EV) like Tesla (Nordhoff et al., 2023). SpaceX crew Dragon that carries astronauts to and from the ISS employs AI for enhanced safety of both crew and vehicle during various phases of transport, some actions requiring swift feedback and deft responses (Reddy 2018).

Several parallels exist between the Smart City tenets and space system autonomy. How to preserve a sense of place and enhance the quality of life in cities that are rapidly evolving to absorb the migration of the rural population? Space activity and technologies hold clues

Figure 2.3.2.1 The ISS is a fine example of a unique, off-the-grid Earth-orbiting smart habitat. The facility runs on clean renewable solar energy and provides its crew with clean rejuvenated air while recycling over 96% of water. [Credit: NASA].

Figure 2.3.2.2 Clean renewable energy, clean-scrubbed air, and clean reusable water, as currently available for crew onboard the ISS, are also an integral part of the UN Sustainable Development Goals, pointed out to the UN Science Summit, and are relevant to the UN Space 2030 agenda. [Credit: United Nations, M.Thangavelu].

that offer solutions to Future City needs and development. Considering that 3–4 million people move into cities every week. Rural-to-city population migration is causing tremendous strain on already overcrowded cities (Henderson, 2016; Linden, 1996). Space technologies and operations may offer some ways to mitigate and enhance future city needs and experience (Thangavelu, 2022).

Space Activity Informs

Space activity lays out, in stark contrast, graphic images of the state of our biosphere, majestic and pristine portraits of nature, as it is, as well as humanity's forays, and warns us about the consequences of climate change, all in real time (Lauer et al., 1997; Wulder et al., 2022; Imaoka et al., 2010). Human space activity reminds us of our species' fragility and the ecological balance vital to sustain life. One main factor is the air quality deterioration, which is related to economic development as seen in satellite images of China and India. Air quality affects the health and well-being of the population. It is global in scope by necessity, cosmopolitan by design, and inspires diverse communities, transcending geographic, national, and economic boundaries, to address issues, anticipate problems, and work together to preserve and protect our environment. For example, satellite imagery can show the global extent of particulate pollution in the atmosphere, effluents in water bodies, approach of inclement weather, disease spread in agriculture, or the wildfires in South America and Africa, all in real time. Such data can be used to monitor, warn populations, and prevent the hazards nature poses to humanity (Davies et al., 2019). Accurate forecasts of extreme weather and surface hazards are possible using space-based assets and timely warnings help to preserve life and property (Tramutoli, 2007). Remote sensing from space-based satellites provides farmers with accurate prediction of crop well-being and yield and provides real-time data on threats including disease burdens, as well as information on space weather affecting Earth weather and solar storms affecting continental electrical power grid network and timely warning that helps energy providers to take action (Pelton & Allahdadi, 2015).

Space Age Technologies Shaping Future City: Space-Based Solar Power

Energy is a prerequisite for all human endeavors. Cities and their operating infrastructure use 75% of all energy produced from all primary sources. Cities are also the main emitters of greenhouse gases (Keirstead et al., 2012; UN Habitat, Urban Energy). It is well established that city infrastructure affects weather and climate (Collier, 2006). Technologies are being sought, developed, and deployed to mitigate the well-known Heat Island Effect (Kleerekoper et al., 2012). Efficient use of energy in spacecraft may offer solutions.

Solar energy harvested in Space, converted into microwave energy, and beamed to rectenna receivers on Earth can provide clean, carbon-neutral power to cities. By steering the power beam, it is possible to provide power to various locations on Earth as base-load demand dictates, in a flexible manner (Mankins, 1997; Verduci et al., 2022).

Currently, Tengger Desert Solar Park in China generates over 1,500MW from photovoltaic arrays that occupy 3.4% of the desert region around the inner Mongolia Autonomous Region (Aliyu et al., 2018). Current mega-scale photovoltaic farms are already feeding 1000s of megawatts of power into the CONUS and global grid. Several more operational systems on this scale are being planned around the Sunbelt, both in the US and around the world. For example, Crescent Dunes Solar Energy Project in Tonopah, Nevada is a 110MW solar thermal power plant that uses molten salt for heat exchange and a reservoir to store excess energy that can help to provide a stable base load to the Nevada grid during nighttime, without the need for electric storage batteries (Boretti et al., 2019) (Figure 2.3.2.3). While the project has been hobbled by economic issues, clean energy projects are on the rise, across the globe.

Compact Nuclear Power

NASA recently space-qualified a low-power nuclear fission power plant that can continually sustain 3–4 kW of power making it ideal for early lunar settlement needs. With simple operation modes, minimal maintenance requirements, and built-in safety, such systems could be scaled to power homes and factories making off-the-grid infrastructures viable.

Figure 2.3.2.3 The Crescent Dunes Solar Energy Project in Tonopah, Nevada is a 110MW concentrated solar thermal power plant that uses molten salt for heat exchange (the glowing white drums are at the focus of heliostats) and a reservoir to store excess energy that can help to provide stable base load to the Nevada grid during the night, without the need for electric storage batteries. [Credit: M.Thangavelu].

Recent developments in nuclear fission technology, especially the KRUSTY reactor testbed developed by the KILOPOWER program at NASA and space-qualified in May of 2018 hold much promise (Gibson et al., 2017). Such reactors may pave the way for small, 3–10 kWh off-the-grid, safe, carbon-neutral power generation that can be deployed quickly and serviced and maintained efficiently, without the need for specialized tools or personnel on hand (Figure 2.3.2.4). Such systems make versatile applications possible for a range of dwellings of all kinds and scalability.

Efforts are underway to scale compact nuclear reactors in the 1–10 megawatt class. Small companies like NuScale are working with the US Department of Energy to certify and commission small modular nuclear fission reactors that can provide continuous base-load energy to suburban clusters and small townships at better efficiencies than large conventional nuclear power plants that have much higher capital, maintenance, repair and recurring regulatory costs (Mignacca & Locatelli, 2020).

Molten salt reactor (MSR) technology has been proposed to avoid the risk of past accidents that have hampered the progress of large nuclear reactors. Unlike the reactors that operate under high pressure systems, MSRs offer much safer and lower risk operating systems and conditions (Rosenthal et al., 1970). The Terrapower Natrium reactor is currently operating a 345MW pilot plant in Wyoming. By decoupling the nuclear energy production facility and low pressure molten sodium salt heat exchanger system for the energy storage facility, a model that is safer, simpler, and much more economical to operate and maintain is being tested for certification (Rehm 2023).

The Internet, the World Wide Web, and the Emergence of AI Algorithms

The internet, the World Wide Web, and the proliferation of servers around the world have matured to such a level that data throughput is sufficient to use for a variety of

Figure 2.3.2.4 Recent developments in nuclear fission technology, especially the KRUSTY reactor testbed developed by the KILOPOWER program at NASA and space-qualified in May of 2018 hold much promise. 1 kW reactor testbed on top, depiction of 10kW system deployed on the Moon below. [Credit: NASA].

real-time interaction applications (Yeager & McGrath, 1996; Berson, 1996). Space-based satellite internet makes Internet of Things (IoT) ubiquitous (Qu et al., 2017). Current servers and their cooling systems technology are energy-intensive. Solutions are actively being sought to rein in operational energy costs (Jin et al., 2020).

Applications like telesurgery become possible with the arrival of wideband, high-throughput data systems that allow real-time high-resolution video streaming while providing enough data throughput for applications like precision robotics with high-resolution visualization and AR and VR layers, and haptic feedback as well as teamwork hook-ups in telemedicine.

Massively parallel networks and search engines, aided by the worldwide web allow algorithms like Generative Pre-Trained Transformers(GPT) to emerge as useful tools to not only help sort through very large and complex data sets but also to create new problem-solving methods that can generate creative solutions to hard problems. USC played a role in the development of this technology. This AI technology is already helping city management to efficiently solve complex problems and provide innovative solutions. AI algorithms are being used to optimize utility needs and regulate transportation and logistics. AI generative systems are also being used to relieve traffic congestion, predict and anticipate demographic flux, and assess land use and population needs including basic agriculture, health, citizen welfare, and security needs (Allam & Dhunny, 2019).

5G and the Arrival of the IoT

High data throughput capability of the internet, using aerial and space-based assets coupled with electronic sensors built into diverse elements that make up the city infrastructure allows for very efficient and timely monitoring, anomaly resolution, and allocation of resources, as needed, to make Future City a safe and vibrant environment (Figure 2.3.2.5). Augmented Reality, Virtual and Mixed Reality Environments, VR AR, and MR allow new modes of abstraction and information manipulation that can be useful to synthesize creative solutions to complex problems like logistics, traffic management, security, and safety that arise in Future City management and evolution. VR can also provide a positive artificial ambiance to enhance well-being and productivity for people in alien or isolated and uncomfortable settings (Kim et al., 2017). The Los Angeles metropolitan region is a thriving hub of economic activity in southern California. The Los Angeles Underground has an existing underground infrastructure that includes abandoned tunnels. They could serve multiple purposes including improved digital utilities for the deep-rooted and established entertainment and visual arts industry and help relieve surface transport congestion. Underground facilities could house various industries and factories including urban farming (Figure 2.3.2.5).

Optical Laser Communications

The backbone of terrestrial communication relies on broadband optical fiber networks that stretch across the globe (Winzer et al., 2018). Terrestrial, secure, high-bandwidth IoT becomes possible with laser communication links. Free Space Optical Laser Communications allow much more data throughput at far better efficiency and have been tested and verified between the Earth and the Moon during the LADEE mission with the LLCD payload (Boroson et al., 2014; Figure 2.3.2.6).

Figure 2.3.2.5 The Los Angeles sky and underground. High data throughput capability of the internet, using aerial and space-based assets coupled with electronic sensors built into diverse elements that make up the city infrastructure, aided by AI agents allow for very efficient and timely monitoring, anomaly resolution, and allocation of resources, as needed, to make Smart City a safe and vibrant environment. The Los Angeles Underground could serve multiple purposes including improved digital utilities and relieve surface transport congestion. Underground facilities could house various industries including urban farming. [Credit: USC Architecture, K.Kawagoe, M.Thangavelu].

Robotic Construction and 3D Printing

Building construction and transformation of cityscape are a normal and progressive activity that all cities engage in as they evolve to provide more amenities, and in many cases, expand to accept a growing population. Building construction and rehabilitation of aging structures requires manual labor and is also one of the leading causes of accidents that cause fatalities and injuries to workers (Huang & Hinze, 2003).

Advanced robotic systems are gradually replacing human workers in risky building operations. Extravehicular space activity has always been risky, and several systems are being commissioned or being planned to remove the astronaut crew from hazardous tasks. USC has been at the forefront of this activity, especially in advanced robotic construction systems for extraterrestrial habitation and allied infrastructure establishment. Contour Crafting is a technology that is looking into terrestrial applications as well. Robotic Construction removes the astronaut from the hazards of associated extravehicular activity (Khoshnevis et al., 2013; See Figures 2.3.2.7 and 2.3.2.8).

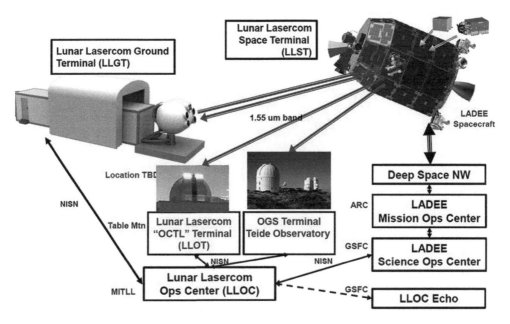

Figure 2.3.2.6 Free Space Optical Laser Communications allow much more data throughput at far better efficiency and has been tested and verified between the Earth and the Moon during the LADEE mission with the LLCD payload. [Credit: NASA].

Figure 2.3.2.7   Contour Crafting technology, a form of additive manufacturing, proposes to use local materials to build up physical infrastructure on the extraterrestrial surface. Robots, both supervised and autonomous, are being deployed for construction projects on Earth. [Credit: B.Khoshnevis, B.Farahi, M.Thangavelu}.

Figure 2.3.2.8   Robotic Additive manufacturing methods could be used to build critical infrastructure like landing pads to eliminate debris production during lander operations. [Credit: M.Thangavelu].

Companies like ICON have evolved building construction machines that employ additive manufacturing technology to build residential dwellings and associated infrastructure.

Underground Habitation

Extraterrestrial surfaces like the Moon or Mars pose extreme hazards including micrometeoritic bombardment, large and abrupt diurnal temperature swings, and radiation exposure. Recently discovered breaches in the roofs of lava tubes suggest that they may be ideal for siting permanent habitats away from the harsh extraterrestrial environment. The discovered breaches in the roofs of lava tubes suggest that they may be ideal for siting permanent habitats away from the harsh extraterrestrial environment (Carrer et al., 2024). Lunar lava tubes are estimated to be much more capacious than those found on Earth. Elevators and cable cars may be used to lower robotic construction equipment into lava tubes to build permanent lunar habitats (Horz, 1985; Ximenes et al., 2012; Thangavelu, 2014).

Advantages of Underground Dwellings

Humans have survived and thrived in underground dwellings from the earliest periods, predating civilization. People live in such structures today. Subsurface habitats offer several advantages over structures erected on the Earth's surface. As we aspire to build skyward, we must also look for options downward. Advances in Mining Drilling and Tunnelling technologies allow rapid excavation and burrowing, shoring, and buttressing of expansive underground volumes that can be stabilized and built up to provide useful spaces for living, working, and even housing factories and manufacturing facilities. Advanced tunneling technology can create expansive volumes deep below existing cityscapes (National Research Council, 2013).

Washington DC Metro is an example of a subsurface structure that has served the city well for decades and continues to evolve with miles of new tunnels. Also, the subsurface MoonBai city infrastructure proposed for the densification of the New Mumbai metropolis attempts to weave the surface elements with the underground, even below the sea floor.

One advantage is effluents that are easily processed, and waste management is better controlled and confined while underground.

Underground dwelling advantages include a 3–4X increase in urban city population density, much reduced vehicular pollution, high energy efficiency, and protection from adverse surface phenomena, especially extreme weather. For the most part, structures built underground are more stable during earthquakes and are immune to harsh transient surface conditions as posed during heatwaves, floods, tornadoes, fires, and rapid changes caused by inclement weather like storms and blizzards. Submerged dwelling technologies may also protect existing coastline cities from abandonment due to sea-level rise and associated ocean encroachment effects. Faced with the effects of Climate Change and the accelerating migration of rural populations into cities and megalopolises around the globe, and drawing precedents that indicate cities and centers that pack higher populations generally perform better economically, the Arch599 Spring 2019 graduate seminar participants decided to explore underground habitation as one way to accept urban density increase without increasing surface spread, which conventional city evolution paradigm follows. Compacting the physical city footprint by building habitation downward and below ground, we expect several other advantages including a rapid decrease in particulate atmospheric pollution caused by local vehicular transportation and logistics, more citizen contact, and real-time feedback of performance to city management as well as quicker response to resolving anomalies. The current Smart City paradigm along with state-of-the-art space and allied technologies may offer some lessons as we strive to evolve a more efficient, interactive, responsive, and humane experience that is Future City (Thangavelu et al., 2022).

Rapid Suborbital Space Transport

Important paradigm shifts in space transportation underway promise to have serious ramifications for the future of civilian commercial passenger transport between global hubs of commercial activity. The arrival of reusable rockets will drastically reduce travel time between megalopolises across the globe. Transitioning from airplanes to jetliners had such an impact in the twentieth century. Reusable suborbital rockets may soon be able to service antipodal locations in a fraction of the time it takes jetliners today. And southern California is poised to take the lead in this revolution with SpaceX of Hawthorne, CA, and Virgin Galactic of Mojave, CA spearheading the effort. Blue Origin, also based on the western seaboard of the United States in the city of Kent, WA is also working on reusable rocket-ships that will be capable of swift global transport. In some ways, the foundation elements of Future City are already in place with clean renewable energy, swift global data servers, and transport systems. Reusable suborbital rockets are already laying the groundwork for rapid travel between various global destinations in a fraction of the time jetliners take today and spaceports are being commissioned.

Advanced Food Technology

NASA has a very active Space Food Systems group under the Human Health and Performance Directorate that is continually evolving better nutrition for astronauts (Perchonok & Bourland, 2002; Cooper et al., 2011). Providing fresh food produced in compact, electrically lit, and controlled plant nutrient food chambers is being developed on the ISS and developmental studies are underway in remote research stations like the Antarctica Eden ISS Project (Figure 2.3.2.9) and Controlled Environment Agriculture Center (CEAC) Food Chamber at the South Pole Stations (Maiwald et al., 2023). The University of Arizona CEAC and Utah State University are among the leading educational centers working on intensive cultivation and several industrial facilities are already producing high-quality fresh food for the consumer (Giacomelli et al., 2012).

There is growing evidence and global concern that our industrial farming methods and urban activities are taking a toll on Nature (Rockström et al., 2009; Steffen et al., 2015; O'Neill et al., 2018). Intensive cultivation employing aeroponics hydroponics, aquaponics, and hybrid processes, technologies that continue to see development in human space activity are being deployed in urban regions across the globe (McKay, 2017). Companies like Aerofarms are using many of the advanced processes to deliver fresh produce without the worry of pests or climate change, and minimizing ecological imbalance, to enhance the quality of life in smart urban cities (Figure 2.3.2.10).

Figure 2.3.2.9 Providing fresh food produced in compact, electrically lit, and controlled plant nutrient food chambers is being developed on the ISS and developmental studies are underway in remote research stations like the Antarctica Eden ISS Project. [Credit: DLR/EU/ESA].

Figure 2.3.2.10   Companies like Aerofarms, located in urban cities, are using many of the advanced processes to deliver fresh produce locally, without the worry of pests or climate change to enhance the quality of life in smart urban cities. [Credit: Aerofarms].

Example One: How the City Can Improve its Ability to Predict and Better Prepare for Damages Associated with Sea-Level Rise, among other Natural Disasters?

A solution to Durban floods with an increase in migration to cities weekly, we witness sustained stress placed on our urban communities and a reduced ability to accommodate, protect, and sustain local populations. Our increased industrial activities continue to exacerbate issues of climate change and among those consequences, specifically the case of Durban, KwaZulu-Natal, is the growing number of floods in the city as the result of rising sea levels. In 2019, images and clips of the Indian Ocean sweeping the commercial strip along the coast of North and South Beach swarmed social media. The Durban Port, an integral contributor to the country's economy, was affected most as rising tides swept in pollution at an alarming rate, forcing it to shut down for recovery and maintenance. Altogether flooding due to sea-level rise, in the year 2019 alone, affected the lives of thousands and resulted in over $45million in infrastructural damages. The South African National Space Agency continues to conduct research on how the city can improve its ability to predict and better prepare for damages associated with sea-level rise, among other natural disasters. South Africa's efforts to contribute to space technology research, a $7 billion investment per year, have proven crucial and significantly beneficial to address social and economic needs, health, safety, and security, as well as innovation and efficiency within the city. Having looked at various precedents in flood management, this project advocates for looking at space, and the systems in place, to begin to draw strategies that inform the ways in which we prepare for and respond to natural disasters such as flooding in Durban, because of sea-level rise, in the near future. This project looks to orbiting satellite stations as a fundamental inspiration in encouraging maximized drone use on the earth's surface in similar ways regarding shoreline surveillance to help predict, alert, and even prevent hazards, both natural and manmade, from affecting populations adversely. These super drones will often be used to collect data and alert additional technology systems in place, i.e. barriers at the harbor. As part of the intervention, the project also proposes a water barrier bridge at the port's mouth, that's dedicated to controlling tide movement, and abnormal water movement as well as bridging the port's newly proposed primary truck route to Transnet shipyards. Together, both these systems in place will contribute to increased port efficiency and a decrease in flood damage and pollution in the affected parts of the city. Climate change and associated sea-level rise affect Durban and its harbor. A bridge to connect the mouth of the harbor and a barrier akin to the Thames Barrier is proposed to control tides and flood water. Drones augmented with satellite data will help monitor maritime traffic and provide real-time assistance to shipping yard cargo movement.

Example Two: Underground Infrastructure to Preserve Historical Casablanca

This project seeks to explore the potential of advanced modes of technology to develop an underground transportation system and infrastructure for the city of Casablanca in Morocco. The purpose is to create an 'invisible' layer of city infrastructure using advanced space technologies that will not disrupt the city's existing conditions as well as to preserve and enhance cultural traditions and customs. Casablanca, as well as all other cities in Morocco, has a deep and rich cultural heritage of customs and rituals, and powerful connections to history in terms of craft, architecture, and methods of construction. The concept of this project is to create a scheme that facilitates swift and clean transportation all over the country, and to eliminate the current traffic congestion dilemma, especially in Casablanca, the densest and busiest city in the country that can only get more difficult in the years to come as the population is expected to climb from the current 37 million to 48 million by 2070. Casablanca, including the seaport, is the heart of the Moroccan economy, and adding value to it through underground tubes that facilitate autonomous vehicle movement as well as advanced utilities could achieve great results (Figure 2.3.2.11). No gas emission, no surface traffic, no noise, timesaving, and most importantly, preserving the historic cityscape heritage, are among the priorities and highlights of this project. The challenge would be to have all facilities, factories, warehouses, and offices underground to leave the upper surface clean and uncongested, to enhance pedestrian access; walkable, calm, and free from any pollution. Deep learning algorithms within the city management system will study and learn from human space activities in and around Casablanca, and allied mature technologies such as robotics and AI will be key to monitoring and timely reporting of city functions that will allow city management to achieve optimum results; the way astronauts generate clean power to work inside a spaceship with robust environmental control systems that provide clean air and water while recycling and managing waste and how their scheduling of activities are monitored and assisted by robotic agents was a driving force in envisioning this project as a similar system where humans are in control of their mission for maximum productivity, comfort, and leisure, in harmony with the temperate climate and weather, and without overstressing, overloading or harming the environment. This added layer would be a new city that operates every day to offer optimum comfort for the citizens and tourists alike, providing new amenities and satisfying living experiences.

Figure 2.3.2.11   One way to conserve surface land use is to build and service utilities, industrial structures, and habitats underground. The concept for Casablanca Seaport is Underground Transportation, Factories, and Warehouses linking the whole city. [Credit: B.Wakadi, M.Thangavelu, USC Architecture].

Example 3: Yangtze River Delta and the Future of Shanghai

Rising sea levels across the globe are adversely affecting coastal cities. Global warming is responsible for this gradual process that is devouring highly prized coastal properties and shrinking accessible land areas just as urban populations are growing. The main problem of sea-level rise is that the ecosystem in coastal cities is being damaged, and changes in the climate and extreme weather are creating havoc in densely populated cities and regions around the world.

Shanghai is one of the world's largest seaports and a major industrial and commercial center of China. The city is located at the mouth of the Yangtze River, which is one of the longest rivers in the world. The banks of the Yangtze host many cities along its run and have a tremendous impact on China's economy.

Due to sea-level rise, the land area will be decreased, especially around coastal Shanghai. To deal with the issue, seashore as well as advanced underground infrastructure developments are proposed. The study presents the potential for improving the quality of life of the city dweller in Shanghai by vastly increasing the potential underground space which can house hotels, shopping malls and markets, parks and recreation facilities, as well as subway-metro, and parking garages. Tunnels under the Yangtze River can link urban areas across the river and relieve traffic congestion while also renewing air quality by recycling and rejuvenating the air.

Using the natural tidal action of the sea, underwater turbines are suggested for augmenting power generation that is needed to support the city. Yangtze River flows through part of the city and power generated from the Yangtze River is considered. The potential alternative power generation facilities include windmills on the ocean surface, underwater turbine

Figure 2.3.2.12   Shanghai is the industrial hub of China. Advanced technology tunnels under the YangTse River can link the shores, relieving traffic and barge congestion. These tunnels will rejuvenate the air and help decrease traffic pollution. Underwater tidal turbines along the YangTse can generate energy to augment city needs. [Credit: Xingbai Zhang, M.Thangavelu, USC Architecture].

generators, and transportation and utility tunnels under the river. Orbiting satellites can be used to steer increasing barge traffic autonomously and efficiently as are cargo ships servicing the harbor (Figure 2.3.2.12). All these proposed infrastructure developments employ advanced space and clean energy technologies and will help to increase urban productivity while absorbing the fast-growing population and managing population density.

Conclusion

Human space activity makes us more aware of our surroundings and refines our sensitivities. As the global population grows, so does the need for more resources and efficient management. By applying useful and appropriate technologies and processes of current and proposed human space activities and allied technologies, it is possible to create more synergetic relationships between the manmade and natural environments using principles of human space activity as a guide.

Space technology is already in wide use around the globe. From powering our homes with solar photovoltaics to modular housing and robotics, applications like telemedicine and remote online learning are all aided by advances in space technology. Using human spaceflight principles and adapting life support technologies, renewable clean energy, clean air, and reusable clean water and minimizing waste become possible for all humanity on Earth.

Using space-proven technologies, it will be possible to increase the urban population density by building habitable, serviceable underground infrastructure. Underground structures are also very energy efficient because of stable ambient temperature and by virtue of not having any surface exposed to the elements and the seasons. Such infrastructure is safe from dynamic surface phenomena and the ravages of climate change and extreme weather like hurricanes, tornadoes, flooding, and fires. Properly built and serviced underground infrastructure is also less prone to damage from earthquakes. Mega tall structures already have several floors below ground and advances in tunneling and boring technologies allow extensive critical infrastructure emplacement below ground without the hassles of trenching and for a fraction of the excavation otherwise needed. Advances in efficient HVAC combined with LED lighting for fully enclosed vertical farming and applications like 4-8K resolution virtual windows are already making below-ground dwellings more habitable. All these aspects have their origins in space technology and the future looks very bright for Future City developments.

We imagine, create, and evolve our environment. Thereafter, our environment shapes and steers us.

Acknowledgment

Most of the work in this chapter was initiated during the COVID-19 years in the USC School of Architecture and in the Department of Astronautical Engineering within the Viterbi School of Engineering at USC. Thanks are due to the faculty and students who helped shape the ideas. Thanks are also due to the guidance, persistence, and patience of the editor of this book, Dr. Mitra Kanaani.

References

Aliyu, M., Hassan, G., Said, S. A., Siddiqui, M. U., Alawami, A. T., & Elamin, I. M. (2018). A review of solar-powered water pumping systems. *Renewable and Sustainable Energy Reviews*, 87, 61–76.

Allam, Z., & Dhunny, Z. A. (2019). On big data, artificial intelligence and smart cities. *Cities*, 89, 80–91.

Berson, A. (1996). *Client/Server Architecture*. McGraw-Hill, Inc.

Boretti, A., Castelletto, S., & Al-Zubaidy, S. (2019). Concentrating solar power tower technology: Present status and outlook. *Nonlinear Engineering*, 8(1), 10–31.

Boroson, D. M., Robinson, B. S., Murphy, D. V., Burianek, D. A., Khatri, F., Kovalik, J. M., ... & Cornwell, D. M. (2014, March). Overview and results of the lunar laser communication demonstration. In *Free-Space Laser Communication and Atmospheric Propagation XXVI* (Vol. 8971, pp. 213–223). SPIE.

Carrer, L., Pozzobon, R., Sauro, F., Castelletti, T., Patterson, G. W., & Bruzzone, L. (2024). Radar evidence of an accessible cave conduit on the Moon below the Mare Tranquillitatis pit. *Nat Astron*. https://doi.org/10.1038/s41550-024-02302-y

Collier, C. G. (2006). The impact of urban areas on weather. *Quarterly Journal of the Royal Meteorological Society: A Journal of the Atmospheric Sciences, Applied Meteorology and Physical Oceanography*, 132(614), 1–25.

Cooper, M., Douglas, G., & Perchonok, M. (2011). Developing the NASA food system for long-duration missions. *Journal of Food Science*, 76(2), R40–R48.

Davies, D., Ederer, G., Olsina, O., Wong, M., Cechini, M., & Boller, R. (2019, October). NASA's fire information for resource management system (FIRMS): Near real-time global fire monitoring using data from modis and viirs. In *EARSel Forest Fires SIG Workshop* (No. GSFC-E-DAA-TN73770).

Fiore, G. M. (2020). Space for Cities: Satellite Applications Enhancing Quality of Life in Urban Areas. *Space Capacity Building in the XXI Century*, 251–263. New York: Springer Publication.

Frank, J. D. (2015, August). Demonstrating autonomous mission operations onboard the international space station. In AIAA Space Forum 2015 (No. ARC-E-DAA-TN25586). Pasadena, California.

Giacomelli, G., Furfaro, R., Kacira, M., Patterson, L., Story, D., Boscheri, G., ... & Catalina, M. (2012, July). Bio-regenerative life support system development for Lunar/Mars habitats. In *42nd International Conference on Environmental Systems*, San Diego, California. https://ices.space/about-us/

Gibson, M. A., Oleson, S. R., Poston, D. I., & McClure, P. (2017, March). NASA's kilopower reactor development and the path to higher power missions. In *2017 IEEE Aerospace Conference* (pp. 1–14). IEEE.

Henderson, S. (2016). Tensions, strains and patterns of concentration in England's City-Regions. In *The City's Hinterland* (pp. 119–153). Routledge.

Horz, F. (1985). Lava tubes-potential shelters for habitats. In *Lunar Bases and Space Activities of the 21st Century* (pp. 405–412). Lunar and Planetary Institute, Houston, Texas.

Huang, X., & Hinze, J. (2003). Analysis of construction worker fall accidents. *Journal of Construction Engineering and Management*, 129(3), 262–271.

Imaoka, K., Kachi, M., Fujii, H., Murakami, H., Hori, M., Ono, A., ... Shimoda, H. (2010). Global change observation mission (GCOM) for monitoring carbon, water cycles, and climate change. *Proceedings of the IEEE*, 98(5), 717–734.

Jin, C., Bai, X., Yang, C., Mao, W., & Xu, X. (2020). A review of power consumption models of servers in data centers. *Applied Energy*, 265, 114806.

Keirstead, J., Jennings, M., & Sivakumar, A. (2012). A review of urban energy system models: Approaches, challenges and opportunities. *Renewable and Sustainable Energy Reviews*, 16(6), 3847–3866.

Khoshnevis, B., Thangavelu, M., Yuan, X., & Zhang, J. (2013). Advances in contour crafting technology for extraterrestrial settlement infrastructure buildup. In *AIAA SPACE 2013 Conference and Exposition* (p. 5438).

Kim, T. H., Ramos, C., & Mohammed, S. (2017). Smart city and IoT. *Future Generation Computer Systems*, 76, 159–162.

Kitmacher, G. H., Gerstenmaier, W. H., Bartoe, J. D. F., & Mustachio, N. (2005). The international space station: A pathway to the future. *Acta Astronautica*, 57(2–8), 594–603

Kleerekoper, L., Van Esch, M., & Salcedo, T. B. (2012). How to make a city climate-proof, addressing the urban heat island effect. *Resources, Conservation and Recycling*, 64, 30–38.

Lauer, D. T., Morain, S. A., & Salomonson, V. V. (1997). The Landsat program: Its origins, evolution, and impacts. Photogrammetric *Engineering and Remote Sensing*, 63(7), 831–838.

Linden, E. (1996). The exploding cities of the developing world. *Foreign Affairs*, 75, 52.

Maiwald, V., Kyunghwan, K., Vrakking, V., & Zeidler, C. (2023). From Antarctic prototype to ground test demonstrator for a lunar greenhouse. *Acta Astronautica*, 212, 246–260

Mankins, J. C. (1997). A fresh look at space solar power: New architectures, concepts and technologies. *Acta Astronautica*, 41(4–10), 347–359.

McKay, B. (2017). A farm grows in the city. *Wall Street Journal*. https://www.wsj.com/articles/a-farm-grows-in-the-city-1494813900

Mignacca, B., & Locatelli, G. (2020). Economics and finance of small modular reactors: A systematic review and research agenda. *Renewable and Sustainable Energy Reviews*, 118, 109519.

Mitra, A., & Murayama, M. (2009). Rural to urban migration: A district-level analysis for India. *International Journal of Migration, Health and Social Care*, 5(2), 35–52.

Mora, L., Deakin, M., & Reid, A. (2019). Strategic principles for smart city development: A multiple case study analysis of European best practices. *Technological Forecasting and Social Change*, 142, 70–97.

National Research Council. (2013). *Underground Engineering for Sustainable Urban Development*. National Academies Press.

Nordhoff, S., Lee, J. D., Calvert, S. C., Berge, S., Hagenzieker, M., & Happee, R. (2023). (Mis-) use of standard Autopilot and Full Self-Driving (FSD) Beta: Results from interviews with users of Tesla's FSD Beta. *Frontiers in Psychology*, 14, 1101520.

O'Neill, D. W., Fanning, A. L., Lamb, W. F., & Steinberger, J. K. (2018). A good life for all within planetary boundaries. *Nature Sustainability*, 1(2), 88–95.

Pelton, J. N., & Allahdadi, F. (2015). Introduction to the handbook of cosmic hazards and planetary defense. In *Handbook of Cosmic Hazards and Planetary Defense* (pp. 3–33). Switzerland: Springer International Publishing.

Perchonok, M., & Bourland, C. (2002). NASA food systems: Past, present, and future. *Nutrition*, 18(10), 913–920.

Pettorelli, N., Laurance, W. F., O'Brien, T. G., Wegmann, M., Nagendra, H., & Turner, W. (2014). Satellite remote sensing for applied ecologists: Opportunities and challenges. *Journal of Applied Ecology*, 51(4), 839–848.

Qu, Z., Zhang, G., Cao, H., & Xie, J. (2017). LEO satellite constellation for internet of things. *IEEE Access*, 5, 18391–18401.

Reddy, V. S. (2018). The SpaceX effect. *New Space*, 6(2), 125–134.

Rehm, T. E. (2023). Advanced nuclear energy: The safest and most renewable clean energy. *Current Opinion in Chemical Engineering*, 39, 100878.

Rockström, J., Steffen, W., Noone, K., Persson, Å., Chapin III, F. S., Lambin, E., … Foley, J. (2009). Planetary boundaries: Exploring the safe operating space for humanity. *Ecology and Society*, 14(2).

Rosenthal, M. W., Kasten, P. R., & Briggs, R. B. (1970). Molten-salt reactors—history, status, and potential. *Nuclear Applications and Technology*, 8(2), 107–117. https://doi.org/10.13182/NT70-A28619

Steffen, W., Richardson, K., Rockström, J., Cornell, S. E., Fetzer, I., Bennett, E. M., … Sörlin, S. (2015). Planetary boundaries: Guiding human development on a changing planet. *Science*, 347(6223), 1259855.

Thangavelu, M. (2014). Planet moon: The future of astronaut activity and settlement. *Architectural Design*, 84(6), 20–29.

Thangavelu, M. (2020). Outer space activities and city evolution. In *ASCEND Conference 2020*, (p. 4059). Las Vegas, Nevada: American Institute of Aeronautics and Astronautics.

Thangavelu, M. (2022). Futures of architecture on earth and in space: Lessons and synergies: Essay two: A space architecture primer for 21st-century civil architects and future city evolution. In *The Routledge Companion to Ecological Design Thinking* (pp. 502–514). Routledge.

Tramutoli, V. (2007, July). Robust satellite techniques (RST) for natural and environmental hazards monitoring and mitigation: Theory and applications. In *2007 International Workshop on the Analysis of Multi-Temporal Remote Sensing Images* (pp. 1–6). IEEE.

UN Habitat, Urban Energy. https://unhabitat.org/topic/urban-energy

Verduci, R., Romano, V., Brunetti, G., Yaghoobi Nia, N., Di Carlo, A., D'Angelo, G., & Ciminelli, C. (2022). Solar energy in space applications: Review and technology perspectives. *Advanced Energy Materials*, 12(29), 2200125.

Winzer, Peter J., Neilson, David T., & Chraplyvy, Andrew R. (2018). Fiber-optic transmission and networking: The previous 20 and the next 20 years. *Optics Express*, 26(18), 24190–24239.

Wulder, M. A., Roy, D. P., Radeloff, V. C., Loveland, T. R., Anderson, M. C., Johnson, D. M., … Cook, B. D. (2022). Fifty years of Landsat science and impacts. *Remote Sensing of Environment*, 280, 113195.

Ximenes, S. W., Elliott, J. O., & Bannova, O. (2012). Defining a mission architecture and technologies for lunar lava tube reconnaissance. In *Earth and Space 2012: Engineering, Science, Construction, and Operations in Challenging Environment*s (pp. 344–354).

Yeager, N. J., & McGrath, R. E. (1996). *Web Server Technology*. Morgan Kaufmann.

2.4

SMART ASSISTIVE DESIGN CONCEPTS FOR ENHANCING INDEPENDENT LIVING IN DOMESTIC ENVIRONMENTS

Mengni Zhang and Keith Evan Green

Abstract

Numerous studies have shown that clutter can negatively affect people's health and well-being. Understanding human organizational behavior in domestic environments is a vital step in creating a smart, sustainable architectural vision for the future. By embedding assistive technologies in architecture, we can enhance the ambient environment to improve life quality. This chapter illustrates this vision by introducing a multi-robot, wall-climbing organizer system called SORT, aimed to assist a broad range of users in managing personal items at home, particularly for those who are affected by various mobility impairments. Here, we report on the iterative process of designing and fabricating the robot group, followed by a user study that confirmed the usability of our prototypes. Qualitative insights provided here can help future design researchers better understand user's organizational behaviors, decision-making, and logic hierarchies, preferences on robot number and speed, and perception of robot gestures. Finally, we present an illustration showing how the robots may form a suite with other domestic assistants to leverage and enhance the ambient environment. The work reported here represents a step forward in exploring smart designs with enabling technologies and user studies in human-environment interaction for everyday spaces, with an aim to improving life quality.

Introduction

As we spend more time indoors, maintaining an organized lifestyle becomes an especially vital task. There are many negative health consequences associated with living in a cluttered environment, such as reduced memory capacity (Gaspar et al., 2016), difficulty in object identification (Whitney and Levi, 2011), and a general increase in everyday stress (Saxbe and Repetti, 2009). Prolonged stay in clutter can also diminish our attachment to and perception of the home environment, resulting in a reduction in well-being (Roster et al.,

DOI: 10.4324/9781003384113-31

2016). Furthermore, sorting, retrieving, and managing personal and domestic items can be especially challenging for people suffering from various forms of impairments as well as for elderly people living alone, such as mobility inhibition (Sattin et al., 2015).

Through the pandemic lockdown, there have been numerous online articles advising how to organize belongings at home, such as Larkin (2022). But while there have been efforts in studying domestic, information organizations such as Taylor and Swan (2005), there remains within design research a lack of empirical studies on understanding human behaviors in organizing domestic items, especially when assisted by robots. In addition, clutter tends to accumulate on horizontal surfaces, leaving vertical architectural elements, such as walls, underutilized. This chapter reports on the iterative design and development of a multi-robot, wall-climbing organizer system aimed to assist users in managing personal items at home. Previously, we reported early efforts in developing a vacuum-based multi-robot organizer system called "SORT" (Zhang et al., In press) and associated online user studies (Zhang et al., 2021). To better understand users' true reactions working with the robots, we developed a new magnet-based, remotely controlled prototype for SORT and conducted three cycles of in-person lab studies.

This chapter documents our iterative efforts in the robot fabrication process, the experimental design, the qualitative results, and consideration of how SORT can contribute to the broader design research field by providing insights and empirical evidence toward understanding people's organizational behaviors and broaden the conversation in domestic assistive technologies to improve life quality.

Related Works

Currently, robotic organizers are implemented and widely used in commercial and industrial settings, such as warehouses and storage facilities. For example, the *PAR* system (PAR Systems) – a robotic arm supported on an elevator platform – can travel on vertical tracks to perform robust retrieval tasks. *AutoStore* (AutoStore, n.d.) is a multi-agent, modular robotic container system that travels on top of a gridded storage structure to fetch items. However, both of these systems are heavy-duty, often occupy large floor areas, and rely on additional support structures. As such, these robotic organizers are not suitable for domestic use. Moreover, such robot organizers are designed primarily to maximize storage capacities and therefore lack any human-interaction functions.

Previous efforts in robotic organizer systems for the home or office are limited to systems that rely on installing intrusive tracks in the ceiling (Fukui et al., 2008). While track-based delivery compartments can prove to be robust and reliable, the installation is costly and disruptive. Other related efforts focused on investigating user preferences for sorting items and object image recognition to improve efficacy and efficiency (Abdo et al., 2015); these rely on robotic arms and therefore the system as a whole is immobile or demands high levels of steady power supply. In addition to functional goals, our efforts to develop SORT recognize the importance of understanding and tuning robotic assistants to match users' organizational styles to ensure user satisfaction at home.

As mentioned, we rely on horizontal surfaces, such as desks and shelves, for storing items. As a result of rapid urbanization, more people are forced to live in smaller homes in cities, leaving little floor space for domestic robot assistants. To explore alternative domains, different wall-climbing robots also informed and inspired prototypes developed for this chapter, such as the vacuum-based *City Climber* (Saboori et al., 2007) for building inspection, search and rescue, and the magnet-based *Anchor Climber* (Kitai et al., 2005) for ship inspection and repair. These prototypes have their advantages and disadvantages related to noise, draft, and power supply. More broadly, there is a lack of exploration of the indoor applications of wall-climbing robots for item organization, especially as a multi-robot system.

Iterative Prototyping

First Prototype and User Study

The first new SORT prototype included two continuous servos with custom 3D-printed wheels embedded with two sets of 5 mm-diameter magnets wrapped in a leather-felt material. A container made of corrugated plastic was attached to the base via a ball bearing. The prototype was then tested on various ferrous surfaces inside the laboratory building and on a vertical surface built with a 22-gauge sheet metal. For Wizard of Oz demonstrations, the prototypes were remotely controlled with a cellphone app built with MIT App Inventor (2022).

A pilot study was conducted with five college students. Each participant was invited into the lab to complete a 15-minute item organization task by cleaning a messy desk. This initial study revealed that participants had an overall positive attitude toward the new prototypes. One significant concern was raised that having too many robots moving on the wall would introduce a new layer of clutter, therefore contradicting the original goal.

Second User Study

In response, a group of stationary dispensers was introduced. Each dispenser compartment has a clear acrylic window for object display, an inner platform serving as a release door for the mobile robot to retrieve items, and a lower panel to ensure objects will be dropped in a straight path. During a sorting task, the mobile robots can selectively deposit items into the dispenser. As a result, the mobile robots' numbers were reduced from six to two. In addition, a larger sheet metal wall measuring 72″ by 48″ was constructed.

A second user study was conducted with nine participants performing the same desk cleaning task while being assisted by SORT. This second study found that participants were concerned with robot noise, a lack of visual feedback, and potential damage to items during release. In addition, three robot gestures were demonstrated, including a quick jitter, an up-and-down movement, and a left-to-right wave. When asked about their reactions, participants responded with a wide range of comments, such as the robot was stuck, or it was asking for directions. In addition, there were also some interesting observations. All nine participants intuitively interacted with the robots with voice commands, accompanied by hand gestures. Participants also mentioned various reasons for grouping items, such as by item function and frequency of use. These comments were addressed, synthesized, and included as variables in the third user study.

Final Prototype

A final SORT system was fabricated based on feedback from the second study. The robot was redesigned with a grey acrylic shell and a corrugated plastic back sheet for LED light diffusion. A series of circular openings were punctured through the front panels to provide

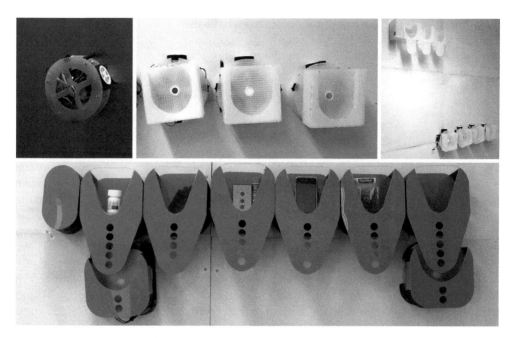

Figure 2.4.1 *Top row*: Initial prototypes tested for functionality. *Bottom row*: final SORT prototypes used for conducting the third user study.

visual feedback during item release. To prevent damage and dampen noise, a foam pad was provided inside the dispenser, and a side acrylic sheet was installed to allow items to slide gently downwards. The overall prototyping processes are documented in Figure 2.4.1.

Third User Study

The third and final user study focused on collecting qualitative data to provide insights on the following constructs: (1) users' preferences on various robot properties including speed and quantity, (2) users' organizational behaviors including changes in organizational logic, hierarchies of logic and decision, (3) users' perceived usability of SORT robots, and (4) users' perceptions of control over the architectural environments as a result of using SORT.

Participants and Setup

In total, 30 participants were recruited via the university's human subject pool management system (SONA), including 20 females and 10 males. No participants had seen the robots prior to the study. Students responding through the SONA system received 1.5 extra credits for degree course fulfillment. IRB approval was obtained from the university review board.

The study was conducted in a lab office on campus, fitted with carpet, a desk, chairs, and a previously constructed sheet metal wall, each session lasted 40 minutes. In total, six stationary dispensers and four mobile robots were used. Three office storage bins on a wall shelf and one desktop organizer were provided. Typical office supplies and personal items

Figure 2.4.2   Environment setup for conducting the third and final user study.

identified and characterized in our previous study (Zhang et al., In press) were placed on the desk, including keys, a wallet, glasses, paper clips, tapes, a pencil sharpener, sticker note pads, pens, a cellphone, a pill bottle, hand lotion, a remote control, lip balm, a stapler, a charger, and a laptop for answering surveys. To maintain consistency, objects will be returned to their marked original locations after each task (Figure 2.4.2).

Study Procedure

After completing a consent form, participants first answered five background questions, including gender, current residence type, usage of existing robotic technologies, self-rating of personal room's cleanliness (1 = Very messy to 5 = Very organized), and self-rating of cleaning frequencies of personal rooms (1 = Once a few months to 5 = every day).

During the study, participants were asked to perform one cleaning task by sorting items on the desk, once with the conventional bins and once with the SORT robots. Participants then were instructed to retrieve a medicine bottle on the shelf, once without assistance and once by using the SORT robots. The order of organizer tool usage for both tasks was randomized. A survey on the perception of control, adapted from the subscale of the NIOSH Generic Job Stress Questionnaire (CDC), was distributed. The survey includes items asking how much influence the participants felt they had over, for example, the timing and pacing of their actions. Participants were also asked to complete an adapted System Usability Scale (SUS) survey (Brooke, 1996), which included items asking, for example, if the system appeared too complicated based on a scale of 1 = Strongly disagree to 5 = Strongly agree.

The final section of the study focused on open-ended questions. Participants were asked to provide their preferences on the number of robots. Three robot gestures were demonstrated, including a quick jitter, pacing up and down, and waving left to right. After each gesture, participants were asked to report what they felt the robot was trying to communicate. Next, researchers remotely drove the robot across the wall at five different speeds, from 5 = Fastest (approximately 13cm/s) to 1 = Slowest (approximately 3cm/s). Participants were instructed to select a preferred speed for three different use scenarios based on urgency. Finally, participants were asked to explain if there were any changes in organizational logic and motivations for organizing between using the robots and conventional bins.

Results

For background questions, 7 (23.3%) out of the 30 participants reported to have uses robotic assistants at home, such as a Roomba. For personal room cleanliness, 16 participants (53.3%) self-reported living in an organized place, the average score was 3.3 with an SD of 0.88. When asked about room cleaning frequencies, 21 (70%) reported cleaning at least a few times a week, the average score was 3.8 with an SD of 0.85. Overall, the SUS score was 68.83 out of 100, placing SORT at the average level for initial usability acceptance (Bangor et al., 2009). For participants' perceptions of control, the average score for organizing with the bin was 3.88 with an SD of 0.61, and the average score for using the robots was 3.69 with an SD of 0.64.

5.1 Interpretation of Robot Gestures

Participants' reactions toward the first quick jittery gesture can be categorized into six types. Three participants felt the robot was stuck. Four thought the robot was carrying too much weight. Three believed the robot was waiting for items. Five said the robot was trying to give instructions. Eight mentioned the robot was saying hello. Six thought the robot's battery was low. One participant was unsure.

For the second gesture (moving up and down), the responses were quite similar to the first, except four participants thought the robot was trying to ask for directions. Two participants were unsure.

For the third gesture (waving left to right), the responses can be categorized into five types. Twelve participants thought the robot was trying to indicate something was seriously wrong. One felt the robot was issuing an order. Four thought the robot was seeking attention. Three felt it was asking for something and one thought the robot was stuck. Interestingly, participants described the gesture in a more anthropomorphic tone that the robot was energetic and joyful. Nine participants were unsure.

Robot Speed Preferences

When asked to imagine using SORT in an urgent delivery scenario, the average speed participants picked, between 1 (Slowest) to 5 (Fastest), was 4.5 (approximately 11.7cm/s) with an SD of 0.58. Six participants wished the robot could move even faster. A few participants did not wait for the demonstration to finish and picked the fastest speed available. Some mentioned that the preference depended on the time it took to complete the task rather than movement. For the second scenario of a non-urgent task, the average speed selected was 3 (approximately 7.8cm/s) with an SD of 0.88. One participant preferred the slowest speed because it felt very calming. For the third scenario of casual interaction, the average speed was 2.39 (approximately 6.2cm/s) with an SD of 1.43. One participant did not want the robot to move at all and selected 0 for the speed. One commented the slowest movement felt like an "old animal."

Robot Number Preferences

Participants' preferences on the number of mobile robots ranged from one to four, with an average of three. The number of stationary dispensers ranged from 3 to 12 with an average of six. Some participants mentioned their preferences would depend on the dispenser size to avoid robot collisions. Participants also suggested the dispenser should be further compartmentalized to better-fit objects of different sizes. The robot numbers were also room-specific. One participant preferred more mobile robots in the kitchen or dining areas, but fewer in bedrooms. While another suggested the dispenser robot quantity could be as many as possible if they were hidden above the ceiling. Based on the feedback, the preferred mobile robot and stationary dispenser numbers can be generalized at a 1:2 ratio.

Changes in Organizational Logic

Twenty-one participants (70%) reported a change in organizational logic between using conventional bins and robots, summarized into five types. First, seven participants reported a change based on item category to keep important objects closer by. Four based the change on frequencies of use, some perceived the robots as a secondary system and would use them for items not commonly used. One participant decided to organize items by weight differences when using robots. For five of those who changed logic by item shape, the main cause was due to inheriting design affordance such as container depth. Finally, four reported changes based on ease of reaching due to the robots' ability to deliver items to the user.

Organizational Logic Hierarchy

Participants were also asked to rank organizational logic based on importance. The responses can also be summarized into five types. Five participants mentioned organizing by item category as the most important. Nine participants selected frequencies of use where objects used every day were placed within a quick-reach distance. One participant organized by how much the items were needed based on personal activity. Eight participants grouped items by similarities in function. Four participants sorted items by use situations such as grouping all hygiene-related objects together. Three participants did not follow any particular hierarchies.

5.6 Organizational Decision Hierarchy

When participants were asked what motivated them to clean, the responses can be categorized into six types. Five participants said they organized to maintain visual cleanliness. Nine mentioned stress reduction. Three participants said they wanted to improve control. One participant wanted to appear more presentable to guests, and another said cleaning was habitual. For 11 participants, improving productivity was the primary motivation, whereas a cluttered environment would lead to a reduction in object identification and retrieval, potentially decreasing their work efficiencies. In addition, 17 participants (56.7%) mentioned the motivation was to fulfill mental needs, while 12 (40%) stated it was based on physical needs. One participant mentioned both.

Discussion

The works presented in this chapter illustrate a potential new frontier in leveraging and enhancing under-utilized architectural elements, namely wall surfaces, with assistive robots to enable people to live more independently. The results confirmed the initial usability of our SORT system and provided insights into people's organizational habits and behaviors. In addition, some findings also challenged conventional wisdom. For example, one would expect users' preferences on robot speeds to be commensurate with task urgency. However, 11 participants preferred the speed for non-urgent tasks to be the same or even higher than that of urgent delivery. Follow-up questions revealed that participants were equally concerned with delivery success, damage to delicate items, and task interruptions where any mechanical failures were not tolerated.

Interestingly, the results and participants' feedback revealed that the use of robots did not significantly increase the overall sense of personal control. This may be attributed to users' unfamiliarity with the robotic system or an initial lack of trust. Another potential explanation can be due to the robots having too much perceived autonomy as mentioned by a few participants, who expressed a feeling of lack of control during sorting tasks. As such, for the university students who participated in the study, SORT appeared to play a more supportive role as a secondary organizer system.

Furthermore, the findings in organizational logic changes do not necessarily imply one system (robot) is better or worse than the other (bins). As suggested by some participants, robots are capable of performing more tasks, but conventional bins provide convenience in ease of reach. Another important feedback from the study was on design affordance. Many participants mentioned one advantage of conventional bins over the robots was the subdividers, the shapes of which imply the objects that can fit inside.

This study also found that participants used the word "category" with great ambiguity. Based on feedback, the concept of item category can be further classified here into three types: (1) the simple representation of what the item is, e.g., a pen and hence grouping all the pens together, then pencils; (2) the representation of the item's function that is often associated with other objects with similar uses, e.g., something to write with and hence grouping all pens and pencils together; (3) the representation of different use activities, e.g., something I need during class and hence group all writing tools and notebooks together. These different interpretations greatly affected sorting logic.

There are also two important factors to be clarified. One is incorporating time and environmental familiarity into organizing logic. Participants commented that when moving into a new place, they may sort objects first by functionality, then by size. But after becoming familiar with the environment, they would prefer to sort items by frequencies of use and be reminded of where everything is located, even though some may not be used often. Another factor is the room's function, where items typically associated with specific spaces should be placed closer to their points of use. These findings indicate that organizational logic changes over time based on how people adapt to indoor environments. Overall, simply keeping items "out of sight" is evidently not the only determining goal that affects domestic organization and user satisfaction, understanding the logic hierarchy behind how and why people organize are critical elements to consider in future interior design exercises to successfully accommodate smart designs for home assistive applications.

Limitations

The results presented here have some limitations. First, participants recruited in the study were healthy university students and, therefore, the results may not generalize to other population groups. Besides the standard SUS scale, which was adapted with minimal changes, the reliability and validity of other measures are unknown. Additionally, since the robots were remotely controlled by the researcher via a cellphone app, only a maximum of two robots could be moved at a time. Therefore, the true potentials of multi-robot interactions and robot-robot collaborations could not be fully demonstrated.

There are also a few threats to validity. When recruiting participants from the University SONA management system, students had the option to browse and choose from a list of available research studies. Selection bias was a possibility, since a few students did express that they signed up for the study because of their inherit interests in either assistive robotics or organizing personal items. However, it was unknown how this initial self-selection might have impacted participants' perceptions toward SORT, which was a novel system they had not previously seen. Lastly, as a novel system designed for long-term home use, a longitudinal study, where a group of SORT robots can be sent to participants' homes, may reveal more insights.

Future Considerations

SORT contributes to an emerging research field in architectural robotics, namely human-built environment interaction study to understand the design's efficacy and impact on users' preferences and perceptions within a space. Previous robotic environments have used room-scale interventions to fulfill goals such as scaffolded learning and literacy (Schafer et al., 2018). These studies tend to involve larger, non-humanoid, spatial artifacts. SORT, as a multi-robot group, suggests an alternative in leveraging embedded environmental designs that expand architectural robotics for both functional and ambient interaction purposes. To achieve this goal, future improvements are needed in robot sensing, communication, localization, and control to allow SORT to self-assemble, potentially transitioning "SORT" from a "Stuff-Organizing" to a "Self-Organizing" Robot Team.

Future SORT explorations can focus on understanding how different container designs may improve user experience in item placements and further increase the efficiency of the whole system. Follow-up study may also implement robot features to allow participants more control. Since SORT may be especially helpful for older adults, to better understand the promise of SORT in this context, robots might be introduced to assisted living facilities for longitudinal studies. In addition, other indoor applications outside of homes might also be explored, such as in transportation and workplaces.

Most importantly, SORT is imagined working with other domestic technologies, such as the Home+ robots (Verma et al., 2018), to form an assistive suite as captured in Figure 2.4.3. As a basic mobile unit, each SORT robot has the potential to serve as a deployable vehicle, allowing other robotic interventions to be added. This suite may provide even more

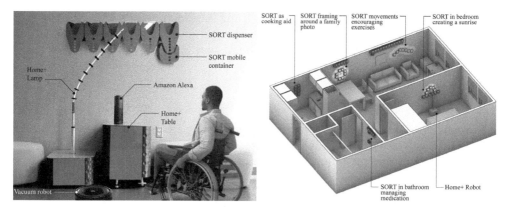

Figure 2.4.3 *Left*: Illustration showing future development in combining SORT with other robots to form a domestic assistive suite. *Right*: Potential locations where SORT may be deployed at home.

versatile functions to users in scenarios such as medication management and retrieval, or ambient interaction through artful formations.

Conclusion

As assistive robots are becoming more ubiquitous and embedded in our everyday lives, it is imperative that design researchers understand how such systems alter and shape our lives and environments from a user's perspective. As we spend more time indoors, robotic systems like SORT can be helpful in augmenting and enhancing daily routines, such as in organizing domestic items as demonstrated in this chapter. The results of the user study here provided initial insights into people's preferences toward various aspects of the robot designs, interpretations toward robot gestures, and perceptions and understandings of their personal spaces in terms of organizational logic while using assistive technologies. These considerations also demonstrate the importance of understanding people's needs through user studies, which are vital components of the iterative design cycle that are often absent in traditional architectural practices. The work reported here, moreover, represents a step forward in exploring enabling technologies and human-multi-robot interaction for everyday spaces, with an aim to improving life quality.

References

Abdo, N., Stachniss, C., Spinello, L., and Burgard, W. (2015). "Robot, organize my shelves! Tidying up objects by predicting user preferences". In *IEEE International Conference on Robotics and Automation (ICRA)*, Seattle, WA, pp. 1557–1564. doi: 10.1109/ICRA.2015.7139396.

AutoStore. (n.d.). Retrieved June 2022 from https://www.autostoresystem.com/.

Bangor, A., Kortum, P., and Miller, J. (2009). "Determining what individual SUS scores mean: Adding an adjective rating scale". *Journal of Usability Studies*, 4, 114–123.

Brooke, J. (1996). "SUS: A 'quick and dirty' usability scale". In P. W. Jordan, B. Thomas, B. A. Weerdmeester, and A. L. McClelland (Eds.), *Usability Evaluation in Industry*. London: Taylor and Francis, 189–194.

CDC, Centers for Disease Control and Prevention, "Organization of Work: Generic Job Stress Questionnaire". https://www.cdc.gov/niosh/topics/workorg/detail088.html

Fukui, R., Morishita, H., Mori, T., and Sato, T. (2008) "Development of a home-use automated container storage/retrieval system". In *IEEE/RSJ International Conference on Intelligent Robots and Systems*, Nice, France: Institute of Electrical and Electronics Engineers (IEEE), pp. 2875–2882. doi: 10.1109/IROS.2008.4650946.

Gaspar, J. M., Christie, G. J., Prime, D. J., Jolicoeur, P., and McDonald, J. J. (2016). "Inability to suppress salient distractors predicts low visual working memory capacity". *Proceedings of the National Academy of Sciences, 113*, 3693–3698. doi: 10.1073/pnas.1523471113

Kitai, S., Tsuru, K., and Hirose, S. (2005) "The proposal of swarm type wall climbing robot system 'Anchor Climber' the design and examination of adhering mobile unit". In *IEEE/RSJ International Conference on Intelligent Robots and Systems*, Edmonton, AB: Institute of Electrical and Electronics Engineers (IEEE), pp. 475–480, doi: 10.1109/IROS.2005.1545593.

Larkin, E. (2022). "10 things to do daily to be more organized". Retrieved June 2022 from https://www.thespruce.com/be-more-organized-on-daily-basis-2648474.

MIT App Inventor. (2022). Retrieved in 2022 from https://appinventor.mit.edu/.

PAR Systems, (n.d.). Retrieved June 2022 https://www.par.com/capabilities/automated-assembly/handling/.

Roster, C. A., Ferrari, J. R., and Jurkat, M. P. (2016). "The dark side of home: Assessing possession 'clutter' on subjective well-being". *Journal of Environmental Psychology, 46*, 32–41. doi: 10.1016/j.jenvp.2016.03.003

Saboori, P., Morris, W., Xiao, J., and Sadegh, A. (2007). "Aerodynamic analysis of City-Climber robots". In *IEEE International Conference on Robotics and Biomimetics (ROBIO)*, Sanya, China: Institute of Electrical and Electronics Engineers (IEEE), pp. 1855–1860, doi: 10.1109/ROBIO.2007.4522449.

Sattin, R. W., Rodriguez, J. G., DeVito, C. A., Wingo, P. A. (2015). "Home environmental hazards and the risk of fall injury events among community-dwelling older persons". *Journal of the American Geriatrics Society*. doi: 10.1111/j.1532-5415.1998.tb03799.x

Saxbe, D. E., and Repetti, R. (2009). "No place like home: Home tours correlate with daily patterns of mood and cortisol". *Personality and Social Psychology Bulletin, 36(1)*, 71–81. doi: 10.1177/0146167209352864.

Schafer, G., Green, K. E., Walker, I. D., and Fullerton, S. K. (2018). "Words become worlds: The LIT room, a literacy support tool at room-scale". In *Proceedings of the 2018 Designing Interactive Systems Conference (DIS '18)*. New York: ACM, pp. 511–522. doi: 10.1145/3196709.3196728

Taylor, A. S., and Swan, L. (2005). "Artful systems in the home". In *Proceedings of the SIGCHI Conference on Human Factors in Computing Systems (CHI '05)*. New York: Association for Computing Machinery, pp. 641–650. doi: 10.1145/1054972.1055060

Verma, S., Gonthina, P., Hawks, Z., Nahar, D., Brooks, J. O., Walker, I. D., Wang, Y., Aguiar, C, and Green, K. E. (2018). "Design and evaluation of two robotic furnishings partnering with each other and their users to enable independent living". In *Proceedings of the 12th EAI International Conference on Pervasive Computing Technologies for Healthcare (PervasiveHealth '18)*. New York: Association for Computing Machinery, pp. 35–44. doi: 10.1145/3240925.3240978.

Whitney, D., and Levi, D. M. (2011). "Visual crowding: A fundamental limit on conscious perception and object recognition". *Trends in Cognitive Sciences, 15(4)*, 160–168. doi: 10.1016/j.tics.2011.02.005.

Zhang, M., Hardin, J., Cai, J. J., Brooks, J., and Green., K. E. (2026) "Self-Organizing Robot team (SORT): A multi-robot, wall climbing organizer-and-delivery system for living spaces". *Springer Series in Adaptive Environments* (In press).

Zhang, M., Xu, T., Hardin, J., Cai, J. J., Brooks, J., and Green, K. E. (2021). "How many robots do you want? A cross-cultural exploration on user preference and perception of an assistive multi-robot system". In *30th IEEE International Conference on Robot & Human Interactive Communication (RO-MAN)*, Vancouver, BC: Institute of Electrical and Electronics Engineers (IEEE), pp. 580–585, doi: 10.1109/RO-MAN50785.2021.9515396.

2.5

DEAFSPACE

Cultural Origins, Architectural Applications and Lessons for Dwelling in a Time of Climate Change

Hansel Bauman

Abstract

This chapter will focus on the new studies and findings about the experiences that deaf people have with their surrounding environments, and how our built environment, largely constructed by and for hearing individuals, presents a variety of surprising challenges to which deaf people have responded with a particular way of altering their surroundings to fit their unique ways-of-being.

Considering that deaf people inhabit a rich sensory world where vision and touch are the primary means of their spatial awareness and orientation. This chapter will focus on revealing those experiences and their approach to using sign language, a visual-kinetic mode of communication to maintain a strong cultural identity built around these sensibilities and shared life experiences through design considerations for deaf people.

This chapter will also introduce the concept of DeafSpace developed by architect Hansel Bauman in 2005 established as the DeafSpace Project (DSP) in conjunction with the ASL Deaf Studies Department at Gallaudet University and similar research concepts in smart hearing approaches within the built environments. Concerning DSP-developed DeafSpace Guidelines, there is a catalog of over 150 distinct DeafSpace architectural design elements that address the five major touch points between deaf experiences and the built environment: space and proximity, sensory reach, mobility, and proximity, light, and color, and finally acoustics. Common to all these categories are the ideas of community building, visual language, and the promotion of personal safety and well-being.

As well as space design strategies, this chapter will also look into smart technological means that have created opportunities for spaces to have clear, precise, and perfect sound dissemination for various performances including speech, orchestra, and singing for music, and in creating special sound effects.

Climate change is here to stay. Any plausible solution for building sustainable, resilient human habitats capable of thriving amid environmental and socioeconomic uncertainty and pressures of mass climate migration presupposes social cohesion and emotional health on a societal scale. Given the well-documented forces of political polarization, and social,

DOI: 10.4324/9781003384113-32

266

and spatial isolation of our modern ways of life, the re-making of our social practices and social spaces should become a global priority on par with carbon neutrality. While such a global utopian vision is unrealistic, it is useful, if not necessary, for all those responsible for making our communities of the future work from a deeper, more urgent, understanding of how the built environment promotes connection and well-being at the fundamental scale of the human body and the socio-spatial dynamics that play out in common, daily activities. But where do we begin to create such an approach? Are there precedence or good examples to follow?

This essay explores the ways many in the D/deaf community inhabit and construct space as one possible model for building social cohesion into the ways we design future settlements. The D/deaf community is a diaspora cutting across all geo-political, socio-economic, races, ages and abilities yet maintains a strong cultural bond. According to the National Institutes of Health, over 90% of deaf children have hearing parents who cannot effectively communicate with them. Since the early nineteenth century, many deaf children were separated from their families and sent to state-run residential deaf schools where they were forced to abandon their natural language—sign language—and taught to communicate in similar ways to their "normal" hearing counterparts. Over generations, the profound separation from family and their native languages has given rise to Deaf culture centered on communication through American Sign Language and strong social bonds with fellow Deaf citizens with shared life experiences and collectivist values. Through daily acts of modifying the hearing-centered surroundings D/deaf people construct *DeafSpace(s)* to enable clear visual communication and spatial orientation—creating places, no matter how ephemeral, to foster social connection, spatial awareness, and a sense of belonging. It is the mix of an embodied understanding of social isolation, cultural affinity, and wisdom about the power of constructing space as a means of agency that DeafSpace is proposed here as a guide for designing future settlements, particularly for the diaspora of climate migration.

The points of view regarding the meaning of architecture within Deaf culture discussed here are guided by the Deaf scholars who participated in the DeafSpace Project (DSP) as transcribed from project proceedings from 2006 to 2010. This chapter chronicles the codification of DeafSpace design principles, processes, and examples of its application to a new building project at Gallaudet University. DeafSpace fundamentals and theoretical framework provide a critique of contemporary architectural discourse prioritizing image over occupant experience. Alternatively, this chapter argues for a more empathic paradigm as critical to building a more sustainable, just, and livable future. This study of DeafSpace provides tangible, tested strategies for reframing design methodologies toward a more empathic way of working as a necessary step toward building more inclusive, sustainable environments.

DeafSpace Fundamentals: Empathy and Embodiment in Deaf Experiences

Deaf people inhabit a rich sensory world in which many use sign language to communicate and maintain spatial awareness through vision, touch, and varying levels of auditory input. Many Deaf individuals in the United States identify as belonging to Deaf culture—"a collectivist culture" [1] built around sign language, spatial sensibilities, and shared life experiences. The built environment, largely constructed by and for hearing individuals, disables deaf individuals' access to clear visual communication, spatial awareness, and movement while performing common daily tasks and social interaction. For example, when a group of deaf individuals are engaged in a signed conversation while walking along a city sidewalk (Figure 2.5.1), it often becomes necessary for one or more to occupy the street to maintain sightlines needed for communication even though doing so poses the risks of walking within an active street.

Through this kind of daily lived experience, Deaf people have devised codes of conduct centered on visual communication and strategies for customizing space to enable spatial awareness and visual communication. When deaf people congregate the group customarily works together to rearrange furnishings into a "Conversation Circle" to allow clear sightlines, so everyone can participate in the visual conversation. Gatherings often begin with participants adjusting window shades, lighting, and seating to optimize conditions for visual communication that minimize eyestrain. Socio-spatial interactions such as these are the basic building blocks of DeafSpace—a cultural practice, design process, and architectural expression of deaf agency for sustaining personal safety, social connection, and well-being.

The experience and making of architecture is fundamental to human existence. Beyond shelter, it establishes presence, and it holds and transmits meaning. The sense of self, well-being, and empowerment is, in many ways, defined by the spaces we inhabit. "…science has established that environments change our brains, and those changes in turn alter our behavior" [2]. A sentiment particularly resonant in deaf experiences of constantly navigating environmental barriers to visual communication can have a disabling effect on social connection and self-esteem. It can also instigate novel acts of spatial modification ranging from simple acts of rearranging furnishings in public places for a visual conversation to large-scale building renovations to enhance visual connectivity. From a theoretical perspective, it is useful for architects to understand the two basic paradigms of D/deaf identity—the Medical Model and the Cultural Model and to consider their architectural corollaries as a means for establishing an aesthetic and methodological approach. On one hand, the Medical Model assigns disability to the body in terms of the loss of hearing. As H-Dirksen Bauman and Joseph Murry state in their introduction to their book *Deaf Gain Raising the Stakes for Human Diversity:* "A visit to any dictionary confirms that there is no way to conceive of deafness other than through the loss of the auditory sense." "Yet this definition is not always so common and does not always make sense among those who are deaf. Rather than defining their particular sensory orientation in relation to a norm of hearing deaf individuals live within the plenitude of their relation to particular sensory orientation and language culture." [3], or Cultural Model which assigns the cause of disability to environmental conditions inhibiting communication and spatial awareness. Within this more subjective model, human experience in general—and Deaf in particular—is given primacy over abstract societal constructs defining normative human behaviors and experiences.

In his essay *Empathic and Embodied Imagination: Intuiting Experience and Life in Architecture*, architectural theorist Juhani Pallasmaa proposes two contrasting paradigms of architectural imagination that serve as useful corollaries to the Medical and Cultural Models as a means for understanding the underlying connections between the ways deaf people relate to space and the ways architects design space. Since the beginning of Modernism, as Pallasmaa points out, the Formal Imagination has focused more on form and aesthetic criteria…"than the interaction between built form and life, especially mental life." [4]. The pioneer of modern architecture Le Corbusier's famous credo, "Architecture is the masterly,

Figure 2.5.1   Common elements in the built environment like standard-sized walkways often present barriers to visual communication and movement. Deaf students modify furniture to create a Conversation Circle. (Courtesy of the Author: Hansel Bauman).

correct and magnificent play of masses brought together in light" [5] eloquently describes the well-intentioned aspiration of the Formal Imagination that ultimately "turned architecture into a visually autonomous art form." [6]. With its objective focus on aesthetic principles prioritizing object-making over the inhabitant's experience, the Formal Imagination shares the Medical Model's aspiration for compliance and normalcy. The Empathic Imagination, on the other hand, focuses on the "interaction between built form and life, especially mental life" [7] and is in keeping with the Cultural Model—both celebrating what the nineteenth-century English philosopher John Ruskin describes as "Imperfection... essential to all that we know in life...irregularities and deficiencies which are not only signs of life but sources of beauty" [8]. DeafSpace as a theory, practice, and architectural expression is an "inside-out" architecture rooted within the Empathic Imagination in which space is conceived through the lens of embodied, everyday lived experiences. Unlike the Formal Imagination's view of "buildings as objects to *look at* DeafSpace aspires to create places to *be in*" [9]—spaces that enable visual communication, safety, and well-being.

DSP: Origins + Process + Outcomes

DeafSpace is not new to Deaf people. As Dr. Ben Bahan, professor, ASL and Deaf Studies at Gallaudet University says "DeafSpace has been around as long as there have been deaf people." Here, Bahan is referring to the cultural traditions of spatial customization passed from generation to generation through lived experiences that have until recently gone unrecorded. Only in the past 20 years has there been a motivation to document DeafSpace design strategies initially for the sole purpose of communicating functional needs to hearing architects and builders. The movement to brand and codify DeafSpace as an architectural language began in the spring of 2005 when a group of deaf scholars, students, and administrators gathered for the two-day DeafSpace Workshop at Gallaudet University to establish design principles for a new academic building on the Gallaudet campus: Moreover, they wanted to concretize their collective wisdom about a way of building as a release from a sense of isolation felt in the past in order to create places better attuned to the Deaf ways-of-being and expressive of their cultural identity. Sensing the profound power of what was emerging from the two-day event, the DeafSpace Workshop University established the DSP in 2006, a special design and research course offered through the university's Department of ASL and Deaf Studies. The Gallaudet campus served as a research and testing laboratory where students conducted research and design projects to understand and resolve the many physical barriers to visual communication, spatial orientation, and movement throughout the campus.

Through his extensive research into the "deaf walk" (Figure 2.5.2), Robert T. Sirvage provides an example of the creativity and insights gained as a result of the DSP when deaf participants were enabled to participate in design. Between 2009 and 2012, Sirvage conducted several different video-based comparative analyses documenting the differences between the ways deaf, hard-of-hearing signers, and hearing people walk together while communicating. Sirvage's findings suggest a distinctly different visual field and body movement is experienced by deaf and hearing dyads. His findings became the basis for several different DeafSpace Design Guidelines (Figure 2.5.2). Several Guidelines enhance spatial orientation while in motion for deaf signers as well as people with low vision.

The research and design activities of the DSP resulted in more than a hundred Deaf architectural patterns recorded in the Gallaudet DeafSpace Design Guidelines. The document

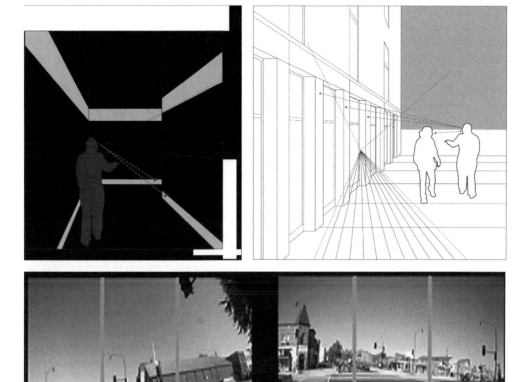

Figure 2.5.2   Still image from a deaf walk, Robert Sirvage, 2012 and the resulting DeafSpace Guideline for visual Datums and Rhythms as a visual wayfinding device. (Courtesy of the Author: Hansel Bauman).

provides guidance for the three main touch points between architecture and deaf spatial experience: Architecture and Visual Communication, Architecture and Sensory Reach, and Architecture as Cultural Expression.

Architecture + Visual Language: The dynamics of clear communication between individuals or among a group, seated, standing, or walking together inherently has spatial implications based upon the need for sustained eye-to-eye communication that reset basic space planning assumptions. In DeafSpace, space is measured in terms of *proxemics*—the cultural, behavioral, and sociological aspects of spatial distances between individuals developed by anthropologist Edward T. Hall in 1966. The size and configuration of the Conversation Circle described earlier is a dynamic function of the number of participants and the position taken by each individual to maintain a clear view of the *signing range* of all the others in the group. Combined, the signing range—defined as the space used by a signer to construct visual language—and the distance between signers needed to maintain visual contact constitute a larger area than that for oral communication. Classrooms, for example, are designed with seating configured as a shallow arch facing toward the head of the classroom to direct focus primarily toward the teaching wall instructor and secondarily to classmates. "Visual Classrooms, as a result, tend to be a rectangle, wider in the direction parallel to the teaching wall while the traditional, oral-centric plan tends to be deeper in the direction perpendicular to the lecture wall and will seat about half the number of the traditional classroom". [10]

The architectural implications of visual language touch upon light and color that form the language's visual background. Two DeafSpace patterns "Layers of Light" and "Color: Contrasting Surface" are often used in combination to achieve ideal ambient conditions of a "visually quiet" background for visual language. Diffused natural daylight is ideal for seeing sign language. High contrast light level conditions of glare, shadow patterns cast on the signer's face, and/or backlighting interrupt visual communication and can cause eye fatigue leading to a loss of concentration and fatigue. Buildings in general, and especially gathering spaces should be designed to provide multiple light sources to minimize the contrast between dark and light areas. Sign language comprehension is further enhanced by color contrast between the signer and their surroundings. The range of cool colors like blues and greens is recommended for interior spaces like classrooms, conference rooms, and social gathering areas to provide a contrast to the warmer color range of human skin tones.

Cognitive Sensibilities and Their Architectural Patterns: Spatial orientation, wayfinding, and the awareness of the movement of others within our surroundings are essential to maintaining a sense of personal safety and well-being. Because deaf people often do not sense activities behind themselves through hearing, they innovate visual and tactile strategies to extend their *sensory reach* to encompass a full 360-degree sensory field. Bahan describes the socio-spatial condition of sensory reach when he says: "There are different sets of learned behaviors and adaptive systems that are passed on with respect to 'reading the world'. One learns to engage in observing, looking and eventually seeing that sound has ways of bouncing off visual cues."[11]. Numerous DeafSpace patterns emerge from the multi-sensory ways deaf people read their environment to sense the activities and movements of others to maintain a sense of personal safety. Visual cues seen through openings to adjacent spaces, or subtle images seen in reflected surfaces or felt through structural borne vibrations happen through the fundamental aspects of architecture—form, material, and light. The DeafSpace pattern "Soft Intersections" is a prime example of the way circulation spaces can be configured to extend sensory reach. When deaf people arrive at a corridor intersection, they do not sense the distant approach of those coming from the other corridor, resulting in the need for sudden movement to avoid collision with the on-coming individual. The pattern of Soft Intersections eliminates the potential for startling collisions by providing glass corners or radiused walls at corridor intersections to allow advanced visual warning of oncoming individuals [12].

Cultural Sensibilities and Their Architectural Patterns: Deaf culture is identified as a "collectivist culture." In her book *Reading Between the Signs*, Anna Mindess describes "The American Deaf culture clearly qualifies as a collectivist culture with its emphasis on pooling resources, the duty to share information, the boundary between insiders and outsiders and loyalty to and strong identification with the group."[13]. Malzkuhn describes the socio-spatial relationship of the collectivist deaf culture this way:

When deaf people are able to belong to place, whether it is theirs or not, they immediately feel connected to it and the people that occupy the space. This comes after a
long history of being disconnected from families and friends through physical, communicative, and geographical differences. So in that sense, in customizing their space,
it does not only allow them to feel connected to their environments and the world but
it also allows them to have human connections which also confirm their existence.

[14]

DeafSpace patterns originate from Deaf culture's collectivist ways at a variety of scales that
all bear resemblance to the fundamentals of the Conversation Circle—eye-to-eye communication and care for the wellbeing of others, for example. The DeafSpace pattern Connecting
Interior Spaces locates the building's principle uses around a communal space(s) in such
a way that occupants must pass through the central area during their daily activities to
encourage casual interaction.

DeafSpace Case Studies

Dwelling Empathy + Embodiment in Contemporary Design Practices

DeafSpace is both a noun and a verb. So far, this chapter has primarily focused on the
noun—DeafSpace Design Guidelines and aesthetics. Perhaps, more important to the making of DeafSpace is the verb—DeafSpace as an inclusive way of designing and constructing
buildings. The DeafSpace design process is a departure from contemporary methodologies
exemplifying the ways inclusive, human-centered design practices can improve the lived
experiences of deaf individuals while serving as a precedent of "good design" for all. The
DeafSpace design process focus on *lived experience* is in essence what Pallasmaa refers to
as the Empathic Imagination. When Deaf people insist that their buildings be designed
in *their* way they are challenging architects to think and work very differently than the
dominant paradigm of the formal imagination has prepared them for. The challenge here
remains to create spaces that not only employ DeafSpace principles, but one designed with
close attention to occupant experience rather than architectural form. To do so, it is necessary to both reframe the architect's default design predilection and the time/cost-driven
formula for delivering building projects. The design of the Living and Learning Residence
Hall Number 6 (LLRH6) at Gallaudet University exemplifies how the integration of Deaf-
Space design methodologies and concepts into contemporary project delivery processes.
The LLRH6 project built upon the lessons learned from previous projects at Gallaudet
University designed with DeafSpace principles in mind by focusing more on the efficacy
of the design process than on guidelines the intended result being a more responsive and
authentic expression of deaf experiences.

Previous to LLRH6, building projects were delivered through a traditional "design-
bid-build" method where the architect is selected for their cost and qualifications and the
builder is selected later based upon qualifications and bid on construction cost after the
design is complete. The traditional method is inherently one of disconnection—purposefully
set up to create checks and balances between the owner, architect, and builder. As each
party advocates for their own, oftentimes, divergent interests' pressures of schedule, budget,
and regulatory concerns limit the amount of time dedicated to user engagement, and the
exploration and testing of design ideas to understand their implications on user experience

once the project is completed. In its pure sense, the traditional design-bid-build process is the antithesis of the collectivist way of making explicit to DeafSpace where early and sustained partnership between the owner, architect, and builder throughout the complete design and construction process would be essential. By collaborating from the outset of a project, the three parties are afforded the opportunity to establish a meaningful relationship built on trust, curiosity, and a shared vision and responsibility for the final outcomes. Under these conditions, it is possible to devote greater attention to design investigations tested from different and overlapping points of view to deliver a building attuned to user's needs—in this case, deaf needs—while meeting practical and budgetary requirements.

In order to optimize inclusion, the delivery method for the LLRH6 residence hall was reconceived as a "design-build competition" through which a team of architects and builders was to be selected based on the results of an interactive process that would engage project stakeholders of over 20 deaf students, staff, faculty, and administrators over a ten-week period. The competitive process allowed relationships to form and be tested as designs were developed in collaboration between deaf stakeholders and four competing teams each comprising architects, engineers, and a building contractor. The winning team was selected for their open and empathetic approach to the collaboration, and the appropriateness of their design solution.

Competing teams were required to certify their design proposal met the budget limit set at the beginning of the project. Unlike typical processes teams meet with stakeholders to address budget-cutting decisions as well as design raising the stature of the deaf stakeholders from simply an advisory role to one with responsibility for making difficult decisions typically left to the design and project management team. Such deeper engagement empowered deaf users to periodically reassert project priorities and advocate for design refinements during cost control discussions and ultimately proved to the key to the success of the winning proposal by the team of LTL Architects, QEA Architects, and Siegal Construction Company.

The project was to be situated on a narrow sloping site on the main campus quad. The building was envisioned as a "*home-away-from-home*" with 160 student beds on the upper floors and a collection of small, medium, and large classrooms and flexible collaboration spaces on the ground level. Deaf stakeholders met with each of the four design-build teams in a series of design workshops and a final interview during the ten-week competition. Each workshop provided stakeholders an opportunity to work alongside the design team to advance a variety of very different design concepts. Approximately two-thirds of the way into the competition initial cost estimates began to indicate the space program issued in the competition brief may be requiring more space than the budget can afford. A problem in the traditional design-bid-build approach may go undetected until later in the process now could be addressed with the combined wisdom of users, architects, and builders. At the third workshop, the LTL/QEA and Siegal team disclosed to their deaf counterparts the design schemes they had collectively developed thus far were over budget to a degree some program spaces needed to be cut. The creative discussions between the deaf users and the design team that followed gave rise to the building's signature space: The Terrace Lounge.

The "Terrace Lounge," the building's main social gathering space located on the ground floor facing toward the center of the campus is named for its terraced floor consisting of four separate tiers linked by a sloping ramp. The Terrace Lounge was not specified in the initial competition brief but rather it's an invention of a number of deaf participants who when faced with the need to reduce the number of meeting rooms in the building saw an opportunity to co-locate multiple spaces within a single large sloping space—an insight born from the deaf user's embodied understanding of the need for sightlines and the advantages of topography for achieving them. By stepping, the floor along the site's natural topography allows excellent sightlines for large audiences viewing a presentation or intimately scaled niches for multiple, small group meetings without the awkward moving of walls or furniture. The terrace solution exemplifies the creative capacity of including stakeholders with lived experience in complex and oftentimes tense discussions balancing costs, program, and design quality. In the case of the LLRH6 Terrace Lounge, the solution that began with a discussion about sightlines ultimately resulted in a significant cost reduction by co-locating four spaces with similar functions with the added advantage of lowering the building's overall height and significantly reduced impacts on the sloping site. By following the site's gentle slope, the Terrace Lounge floor and the subtle way it is expressed allow the building to lightly touch the ground connecting the specific condition of the place with the practical needs for sightlines to see sign language and the cultural desires to gather. Using the design-build competition, recast the building delivery method from the siloed traditional approach to one consistent with the collectivist spirit of Deaf culture by providing a forum for deaf users' insights to guide architects and builders toward the physical realization of the Deaf Architectural pattern language. With the process in place, it became possible to explore more deeply the socio-spatial nature of the DeafSpace patterns and how they can best mediate the forces of the site, the building's function, and the sensory experience of its occupants.

DeafSpace: Deaf Gain for a More Livable and Sustainable World

All of us responsible for [re]making our future habitats have much to learn from DeafSpace. Some of the early lessons have been outlined in this essay and certainly, there are more to come. But perhaps the most profound lessons reside in the power latent in the deaf ways of dwelling focused on empathy and collectivist values. If it is possible to harness the generative imagination spent every day modifying the misfit hearing world, it is conceivable deaf people can redirect the conversation to the making of places that express our connections rather than build barriers. DeafSpace is about what Merleau-Ponty calls, "experiential knowledge of the place, one in which our body feels the world in feeling itself." [15]. I am hopeful that within this "insoluble unity of life and place" [16] lies the seeds of a new way of building, knowing, and caring for the ecosystem we call the place of our own.

Notes

1 Anna Mindess, *Reading Between the Signs* (Boston: Nicholas Brealey, 2006), 41 quoted in Matthew Malzkuhn, "Cultural Customization of Home" (Washington DC: Gallaudet University, Unpublished Master's Degree Thesis, 2009), 99

2 Fred Gage, "Architecture and Neuroscience" (Keynote Lecture AIA National Convention, San Diego, CA, 20030 as quoted in Juhani Pallasmaa, "Empathic and Embodied Imagination: Intuiting Experience and Life in Architecture." In *Architecture and Empathy* (Espoo, Finland: Tapio Wirkkala-Rut Bryk Foundation, 2015), p. 7

3 H. Dirksen L. Bauman and Joseph J. Murry, "Deaf Gain, an Introduction." In *Deaf Gain Raising the Stakes for Human Diversity* (Minneapolis: Minnesota Press, 2014), p. xv

4 Juhani Pallasmaa, "Empathic and Embodied Imagination: Intuiting Experience and Life in Architecture." In *Architecture and Empathy* (Espoo, Finland: Tapio Wirkkala-Rut Bryk Foundation 2015), p. 7

5 J. Pallasmaa, p. 6

6 J. Pallasmaa, p. 6

7 J. Pallasmaa, p. 7

8 John Ruskin, as quoted in Gary J. Coates, *Erik Asmussen, Architect* (Stockholm: Byggforlaget, 1997), p. 230

9 Hansel Bauman, "A Case for SLCC Aesthetic Principles", (Washington DC: Unpublished 2005), p. 02

10 Hansel Bauman, "*Gallaudet University DeafSpace Design Guidelines*", (Washington DC: Unpublished 2010), p. 35

11 Benjamin Bahan, "Memoir Upon the Formation of a Visual Variety of The Human Race." *Deaf Studies Today,* Volume 1 (2004): 26

12 Bauman, "*Gallaudet University DeafSpace Design Guidelines*" (Washington DC: Unpublished 2010), p. 66

13 Anna Mindess, *Reading Between the Signs* (Boston: Brealey, 200), 41, quoted in Malzkuhn "Cultural Customization of Home", (Washington DC: Gallaudet University, Unpublished Master's Degree Thesis, 2011), p. 99

14 Malzkuhn, "Cultural Customization of Home". (Washington DC: Gallaudet University Unpublished Master's Degree Thesis, 2011), p. 102

15 Merleau-Ponty, "The Visible and the Invisible", 118 quoted in Sarah Robinson, *Preface, Nesting: Body Dwelling Mind* (San Francisco: William Stout Publishers, 2011), p. 146

16 Christian Norberg-Schulz, *The Concept of Dwelling* (New York: Rizzoli International, 1985), p. 13

2.6

SMART ARCHITECTURE FOR THE BLIND

Chris Downey and Michael Arbib

Abstract

This chapter characterizes smart architecture for the blind in two senses: design by architects who are smart in their understanding of how the blind experience their world and employment of technology in making buildings more responsive to their users. This chapter also examines enhancement of visual cues for those with low vision but thereafter emphasizes design with a multisensory design palette excluding visual cues. The roles of canes and guide dogs set the baseline. This chapter explores the multisensory forms of atmosphere, including beauty, for the blind. An assessment of how the blind experience space is located within a general understanding of scripts, navigation, and behavior. Analysis of digital tools that aid navigation, including AIRA and GoodMaps, leads us to emphasize the trade-off between smart buildings and the smart ecosystems made possible by smartphones and the internet. Finally, this chapter includes consideration of social interaction and the adaptation of user and technology.

Three Roles in the Development of Smart Architecture

We reserve the term "low vision" for people for whom enhanced visual cues can prove beneficial, and "blind" to include those with low vision and no vision. However, we emphasize architecture for people for whom non-visual cues are crucial.

Chris Downey was already an architect when he lost sight in 2008. He then rebuilt his career as an architect while regaining his confidence in a world in which enhanced use of other senses replaced sight, and retaining a vivid visual imagination. Michael Arbib brings his expertise in neuroscience and artificial intelligence (AI) into the conversation. We emphasize the nature of non-visual experience to help the architect avoid visually grounded assumptions and consider smart architecture in two senses:

1 **The smart architect** is cognizant of the cognitive and multisensory experience of space of the blind and can develop designs that are attractive and functional for both sighted and blind. Downey's design with Mark Cavagnero Architects for the Lighthouse for the

DOI: 10.4324/9781003384113-33

Blind and Visually-Impaired (San Francisco, 2016) provided multisensory strategies that did their job quietly in the background for the sighted but were crucial for the blind. Design features to help the blind include:

- high visible contrasting nosing strips on all stair treads for increased visual accessibility for low-vision users;
- room numbering that provides an intuitive system to indicate where any room would be found and to reorient oneself if needed;
- room identification signage designed to aid low-vision users and to provide tactile cues from braille and raised characters; and
- acoustics to enhance the sensory reach of the blind and for a lively yet functional experience.

2 **The technological overlay:** We consider both *smart buildings* equipped with sensors and responsive elements with the linking computation to support the user – such as Lighthouse elevators programmed to call out each floor as it is passed and provide general descriptions of each floor – and a *smart ecosystem* in the sense explained below.

Moreover, design must be responsive to the **assessment by users** of their needs and the effectiveness with which they are being met. The blind individual accepts responsibility to attain non-visual competency to move effectively and safely through space. Traditionally, canes and guide dogs have supported this and their role remains crucial.

Architects must recognize that by their inattention to non-visual experience, perpetuating an oculocentric approach, they risk disabling, rather than aiding, their users. For example, placing an odd step or two here and there for visual interest could pose challenges for a blind person, and others, walking through the space. Such recognition truly refocuses the human-oriented design of spaces.

Enhancing Acuity for Low Vision

Someone with low vision may share many problems with those with no functional sight – for example, it may not be clear which direction to go to exit a space, and here the use of a cane may be helpful. However, they may still use simple visual cues and one challenge is to have lighting and/or effective color contrast that makes objects more visually accessible. However, very bright lighting may be uncomfortable for someone with normal vision and others with light sensitivity.

A smart building could identify people with low vision and adjust light levels in their vicinity to maximize their visual acuity and avoid glare – and when that person leaves that space, lighting would revert to normal. It could respond to people's different needs to the extent that lighting is locally controllable. However, it remains crucial to address privacy and security concerns associated with identifying users and tracking their movements.

Before considering the role of high technology in aiding the blind, we contrast the benefits of walking with a cane or a guide dog.

Canes: A cane can pick up environmental information, transmitting it haptically through the grip of the cane. Simultaneously, the user can perceive textures through their feet as well as the cane and can tell the difference between walking on a sidewalk or asphalt, brick or stone. Locating a curb, a drop, a stair, a tree, a wall, or other change in the path with a cane is basic, but very important. Tapping the cane on the ground supports echolocation so the blind user can perceive where walls or openings are located. Such cues help the user develop the coordinates, circulation patterns, and cognitive ergonomics of the space as the basis for later recall and more confident navigation.

Research on developing smart canes with, e.g., object identification and location tracking (Kebede and Shiferaw 2023) lies outside the scope of this article. However, unlike smart canes, non-smart canes are affordable and easily replaced when they break. The general issue for all smart technology is to help the user *maintain or increase a sense of self-reliance rather than a state of overreliance*. Indeed, smart cane feedback may distract the user from more subtle but essential cues provided by the environment.

Guide Dogs: Guide dogs can take care of challenges like avoiding obstacles. In particular, dogs learn their user's height, so they know how to avoid obstacles like tree limbs that are at head level. As the user is going down the street, the dog lets them walk quickly. However, the user must keep track of navigation, telling the dog when to turn right or left. On reaching a destination, the user can just say "door" and the dog will find one.

A Multisensory Design Palette

Juhani Pallasmaa (2012) offers a penetrating critique of the Oculocentrism of much architecture. Opening a door involves the feel of the door handle in one's hand and how it changes as one moves the handle and then the blend of action, locomotion, and proprioception. Nonetheless, Pallasmaa does not address the experience of space and behavior when vision is excluded. The architect needs to understand how to incorporate these non-visual experiences into designing of spaces that enrich experience for the blind.

From Beauty to Atmosphere

Buildings for the blind should be endowed with beauty that need not be seen. The term "atmosphere" in architecture (Arbib 2021, Chapter 4; Tidwell 2014) captures the way in which a building may immediately set a mood or emotional tone for the user, albeit one that may change over time. The literal atmosphere is non-visual – we may taste or smell it, feel its temperature, or feel the breeze. Yet, the discussion of architectural atmosphere almost completely emphasizes vision, including an emphasis on first impressions that may be less meaningful for the blind whose first impression would be auditory, yet lacking the cues offered as tactile exploration builds a more detailed mental image.

We thus raise the question. "How does the perception of beauty or delight in architecture change when you are blind?" Perhaps, clues may be found in our experience of the beauty of music or birdsong, our delight in the scent of a flower, or the pleasure of a vigorous walk. However, the notion of atmosphere is far broader than what is delightful. One would not be delighted to be in a funeral home but would seek an architectural atmosphere of appropriate solemnity that is socially supportive of the bereaved.

Moreover, a space that seems beautiful to a sighted user may offer an abrasive soundscape to a blind person. Hotel lobbies that play Muzak too loudly will mask critical acoustic cues like conversations from the reception desk, the clanking dishes that help locate the restaurant or more subtle acoustic cues that could help locate the elevators. By allowing each space to be expressive of its specific functions and by not attempting to mask or camouflage their related sound or noise specificities and thus mislead the user, a designer can augment a sense of identification of the space, not only ease access for individuals with limited or no vision but also enhancing their appreciation of the special qualities, or "genius loci," of each particular space. Indeed, the quality of the sound echoing and reverberating in a space can identify the spaciousness, and a sense of high ceilings may even convey a message of grandeur and awe.

Haptics and Proprioception

Designing the handrail, the doorknob, or a wall to lean against can anticipate the experience of the user, contributing to the non-visual atmosphere. For example, in the now demolished American Folk Art Museum in New York, big timbers used as benches had a slight concave cup subtly carved into the top surface that made the act of sitting there much more relaxing than would sitting on a flat surface – providing a quiet signal that the designer was considerate of the visitor's comfort.

Building muscle memory of spatial layout can support acting confidently without continual tentative search. One may confidently reach for a door handle, knowing its height above the floor and relation to the door frame. While walking, a sense of moving uphill or downhill or having reached the crest can help sense location. Conversely, the feel of the body while moving confidently can offer a great sense of well-being.

Acoustics

The sound of a footfall or a cane tap on the ground surface can be a good sound – but a metal cane tip-tapping on steel makes a loud and unpleasant sound, especially in an interior space. Conversely, carpeting a space and even white noise may muffle auditory cues that are crucial to the blind, as when tapping a cane for echolocation. A deeper appreciation of how background noises that the sighted may ignore can diminish delight or distort essential auditory cues for the blind. Background noise may be a buffer against intrusive noises or become intrusive. Muzak played in restrooms often masks the critical sounds needed to help sort out the space to find a desired element – requiring more exploration and dependency on touch to explore an environment that one would prefer to touch less!

Smell

The smell of a space contributes literally to its atmosphere and may provide strong cues as to the functionality and meaning of the space. Gardens with distinctively scented plantings may support cognitive mapping. Branded scents (olfactory signage such as baking smells emanating from a storefront) or incense in a religious ceremony may also play a role. Pleasant aromas can evoke positive emotions and create a welcoming atmosphere, while unpleasant smells can be discomforting. As noise-canceling technology exists for sound, we could envision "odor-suppressing" technology that filters out or neutralizes unpleasant smells in certain environments. We add that evaluation of smells can be subjective and culturally influenced, while some odors can be allergenic.

The Experience of Space by the Blind

A sighted person getting up in the morning may have a clear cognition of their coming behaviors in going to the bathroom, the kitchen, and the front door in getting ready for work, and these can be structured by patterns of action in various places and the locomotion between them in the absence of clear visualization. *The same is true of the blind person* – the outcome of dwelling in the space, dwelling in the paths, dwelling in the actions.

Learning to structure spaces in a way that does not systematically require sight for the user is the key to becoming a smart architect for the blind. Sighted architects must complement "sight-based language" with cues for the blind. Changing materials underfoot could be a cue, or an auditory sense of how the space opens up, going from a smaller scale of a hallway to the grandeur of a more open space. Providing a clearly discernible multisensory circulation path through a plaza or across an open lobby can help order the space while identifying the primary path of travel in an equitable way.

Downey works with tactile plans, raised lines rather than printed lines on a surface. As he reads a tactile plan, he is focused to a great extent on human movement through the space – not just trying to understand what one place is, but also tracing its relationship to other places and how to link them all together. Reading the drawing through touch puts him in that plan, letting him mentally build a rich cognitive map as part of the creative process. As his finger moves from the bathroom down the hall to a specific place in the kitchen, he will be thinking about and potentially designing specific landmarks along the way.

Scripts, Navigation, and Behavior

Each building must support a range of typical behaviors by its users and so the architect must envisage "scripts" for these basic activities and provide places in the building that support them. A person who uses the building must locate various places that support their behaviors (whether practical or contemplative) and how to move between them – they build cognitive maps that do more than support navigation from one place to another. The navigation problem is to find a path from one place to another. In part, this involves habitual paths, but the virtue of having a cognitive map is that one can determine novel paths if a habitual path is blocked, or if one wishes to carry out an unusual task. Our challenge is to emphasize that the images involved in navigation are multisensory and may not involve vision. Without sight, landmarks take different forms – there might be nearby sounds or acoustic impulse responses (as in echoes evoked when tapping a cane), textures underfoot, or haptic cues from a cane, while a scent might provide olfactory cues for navigating toward it.

Affordances (Gibson 1977) are the perceptual clues that indicate an action is possible or provide needed information (often nonconsciously) to adjust behavior to the current surroundings. Passini and Proulx (1988) found that the blind could navigate complex spaces but made more decisions and required more informational access points than those who navigated sighted. The lack of visual cues about whether there is smooth terrain and an unobstructed path to the next "via point" requires a greater density of non-visual via points if navigation is to be conducted efficiently. The notion of scripts reminds us that navigation from points A to point B is often less important than navigating between diverse places in executing some overall behavior – just consider the places involved in washing up after dinner and putting everything away afterwards.

Claudia Folska (2012), herself blind, had blind participants sketch maps of their route from public transportation to the Colorado Center for the Blind. Respondents exhibited a preference for relying on touch rather than audition for extracting environmental information. Tactile cues could include the changing texture of ground beneath their feet, or changes recognized through using the cane to extend the sense of touch. In urban spaces, background noises may be too insistent to allow dependence on auditory cues. In other settings, the sound of a stream or a fountain might offer better cues than the texture beneath one's feet. Hearing, too, is a distance sense and can offer cues about parts of the environment that are not within the peripersonal space that can be mapped by touch, even when extended by a cane.

Digital Tools that Aid Navigation: Smart Buildings or Smart Ecosystems?

As a basis for understanding technology that can support the navigation of the blind, we consider two current systems, AIRA and GoodMaps. AIRA involves no smart architecture at the building level, and GoodMaps makes no change to the fabric of buildings but does provide a 3D map to support localization within the building. The smart architecture here is not that of the building but of a *smart ecosystem* combining the internet with smartphones augmented by new apps linking blind users with agents, whether human or AI, whether local or remote, that can cater to their needs. Linkage of buildings to smart ecosystems with affordable technology is a challenge for smart architecture in general, but our concern here is with implications for the blind.

AIRA and GoodMaps reflect a state of the art that is rapidly changing. This suggests the desirability of leveraging technologies that do not require costly investment in the building itself. Thus, many of the technological strategies of smart architecture for the blind can be relegated to a complementary ecosystem. The aim is to make the relatively long-term features of the building infrastructurally light yet designed so that fast-changing technologies can be adapted as they become effective and economically viable, but also discarded as they become outmoded.

AIRA

AIRA is the acronym for Artificial Intelligent Remote Assistance, but as of 2023, the company aira.io offered live access to visual information using human agents rather than AI agents, though the human agents may make use of AI tools. The agent can assist clients with any situation where visual information needs to be interpreted, not just navigation. The agent views a screen with the view as would be seen by the client if they had vision, whether transmitted from a smartphone camera or from smart glasses. In an airport, for example, the agent can see the signage overhead, an escalator, or a gate or restroom and tell the client when to turn or otherwise modify their walking.

The service requires a smartphone app and a subscription. Crucially, many public spaces, and even the whole state of Alabama, offer free use of the app in their domain. While most people will use smartphones, developments with smart glasses would be more helpful because they free the hands. These devices are too costly for most users, but even partial adoption may promote the emergence of powerful yet affordable hardware and software.

Smartphones combine sensors for vision and sound and can produce images, text, speech, and music, accelerometers can track walking patterns of the user and can use signals from the Global Positioning System, GPS. Drivers have become used to the turn-by-turn directions this ecosystem makes possible. In cities, walkers can use their smartphones to get navigation instructions that are up to date on when and where public transport will arrive to shorten travel time. However, instructions to get to a particular address do not help the blind client get to a meeting in room 923. A wealth of data has to be managed and accessed to fill the gap, but developments in AI and an ever-increasing ecosystem of publicly held data will be increasing support for AI-based agents that require little or no help from a human agent. Moreover, we see here possibilities for coupling a navigation system with an intelligent building that, for example, can adapt elevator performance to the need of the client.

We also see an opening for the architect or interior designer to structure distinctive places within each room where items are customarily placed, and supporting logging items into a database of what is inside the closet, inside the drawer, etc., but doing so in a way that makes it easier for the client to retrieve the object. Radio Frequency Identification (RFID) tags might be linked to an app to help locate hidden objects, complementing the use of a cane that continues to help to avoid unexpected obstacles.

GoodMaps

GoodMaps (www.goodmaps.com) has taken a step toward implementing a scenario that does not require human agents. Basically, the use of GPS for driving is replaced by the use of Lidar (laser imaging, detection, and ranging) to determine the distances to objects and surfaces with a laser to make high-resolution maps of interior spaces, which can then be labeled with Points of Interest. The user's location inside the building is determined with camera-based positioning. The indoor navigation app GoodMaps Explore can use the client's current location to direct them to any desired point of interest, taking mapped obstacles into account in offering a path.

In May 2023, Walmart Mexico launched a pilot using Explore to provide real-time turn-by-turn directions from the parking lot to the product shelves to the checkout counter, directing customers to each product they wish to buy as well as bathrooms and other areas (https://goodmaps.com/newsroom/walmart-mexico-partners-with-goodmaps-to-offer-a-digital-navigation-experience/). The emphasis is on providing users with a measure of autonomy they would not otherwise have. The current GoodMaps system can get the customer within a meter of their desired product. For someone with low vision, this may suffice. But what of customers who cannot see? One solution would be to have a speaker located on the shelf below the desired item make a sound to direct the reach. However, the vast number of transmitters that would be required to guide each shopper to each of the thousands of items is infeasible. Moreover, the range and placement of products in a supermarket keep changing. Nonetheless, supermarkets are now increasingly using electronic signage on the shelves linked to a database of where every type of product in the store is shelved, so the problem is eminently solvable.

Social Interaction

Much of our well-being rests not on navigation or using objects, but on social interaction. Thus, a challenge – more for the ecosystem than the physical architecture of the building itself – is to explore how a blind person could be alerted when somebody they know is nearby.

Developments in the smart ecosystem already exploit our ability to transfer our skill for human interaction to interaction with AI agents. Some agents are designed for ease of use once the user learns the basics of how to operate them, but we also expect developments in personal assistants that can offer human-like guidance. Many chatbots still answer general queries to a company in menu-driven ways that can be frustrating to the user, but in light of recent breakthroughs in AI we envisage personal assistant that adapt to the style of its user.

We may contrast the task of the remote agent assisting a person to navigate in a well-lit space with the task of finding one's way to the bathroom in the dark in an unfamiliar hotel. The darkness does not change the experience of the blind person but may drastically change the sensory data the agent can work with. We noted how GoodMaps uses a one-off Lidar scan to provide a 3D chart of a space but cameras to estimate the user's current position. We envisage scenarios whereby, for example, a personal assistant could interact with hotel staff or a database to answer queries about a hotel room that challenge a blind visitor, such as how to control the shower and where to stand when the cold water becomes warm.

Other developments can help the blind interact with other people by providing recognition at a distance. The circulation space for the Lighthouse was deliberately designed to be all hard surfaces while all other surfaces were not. One of the benefits was that, as the executive director at the Lighthouse who is blind commented, he could hear someone tap their cane as they walked around far from him, and he would know who it was because of the way they tapped.

A potential app linking smartphones could provide location signals for sighted friends passing down the street so that the blind person could orient accordingly and wave to them to attract their attention. A long-implemented free social app is "Be My Eyes" (bemyeyes.com). This noteworthy social network app is available worldwide in diverse languages. The app works by pairing the blind user with a sighted volunteer based on language and time zone. The volunteers come online whenever they are available and needed. The first volunteer to answer the request is connected to that specific user and receives a live video feed from the rear-facing camera of the user's smartphone. In August 2023, Be My Eyes announced beta testing of Be My AI to provide navigation information extracted by AI processing of camera data.

Adaptation of User and Technology

For people with deafness caused by peripheral damage to the cochlea, cochlear implants offer an established technology to ameliorate the condition but require dramatic adaptation in the auditory brain of the user to make good use of what initially sounds like aberrant signals. Accordingly, some users come to hear quite well, while others never do so. Research on neuroprostheses for the blind remains in its infancy (Lestak et al. 2022; Fernández, Alfaro, and González-López 2020) and plays no role in our present considerations. Nonetheless, as our discussion of the multiple benefits of learning to understand the multisensory cues of using a cane makes clear, extensive adaptation is required on the part of the new user. A key issue for smart architecture and smart wearables is to what extent the technology adapts to the human and vice versa. Turning to architecture, it has in the past been a matter of the human body adapting to the imposition of the architecture – the body had to cope with the building.

With experience, we learn what affordances the surroundings provide for our actions and how they are located relative to each other. If a long corridor has a central strip of carpet with a strip of stone or wooden flooring exposed on either side, then the change in both sound and foot-feel may supplement or replace visual cues in keeping users within the corridor. Provision of auditory cues to blind pedestrians at traffic lights could be extended to provide tactile cues via a vibrating panel set in the sidewalk, with implications for similar active cues to provide dynamic cues within buildings. Current best practices for audible pedestrian/crossing signals include a large push pad that not only emits a periodic pulse/signal to help find it that increases its rate when it is time to cross but also vibrates to provide redundant signals of the time to cross. This is critical for those who are deaf or deaf-blind, including those who are blind but situationally deaf to what they need to hear on account of loud vehicles and other noise. If properly augmented, the push-pad can be depressed and held to announce the street that is being crossed and the street one is following.

While new technology always imposes a learning curve, a desideratum for smart building technology is that the building should [also] adapt to the user. The companion chapter, "Neuromorphic architecture at a Turning Point," explores the general challenge of designing buildings that are in some sense "aware" of the user's needs and capabilities and can modify systems of the building to better accommodate the needs of its occupants.

Acknowledgments

We thank Luis Othon Villegas and Troy Otillio for their discussion of the themes of this chapter.

References

Arbib, M.A. 2021. *When Brains Meet Buildings: A Conversation between Neuroscience and Architecture*. New York: Oxford University Press.

Fernández, E., A. Alfaro, and P. González-López. 2020. "Toward Long-Term communication with the brain in the blind by intracortical stimulation: challenges and future prospects." *Frontiers in Neuroscience* 14, article 681.

Folska, C.L. 2012. "In blind sight: Wayfinding in the absence of vision." Ph.D. Thesis, University of Colorado at Denver.

Gibson, J.J. 1977. *The Ecological Approach to Visual Perception*. Boston: Houghton Mifflin.

Kebede, G.A., and Y.K. Shiferaw. 2023. "Assistive smart cane technology for visually impaired peoples: A review." In *Artificial Intelligence and Digitalization for Sustainable Development*, edited by B.H. Woldegiorgis, K. Mequanint, M.A. Bitew, T.B. Beza and A.M. Yibre, 196–208. Cham: Springer Nature Switzerland.

Lestak, J., J. Chod, J. Rosina, and K. Hana. 2022. "Visual neuroprosthesis: Present and possible perspectives." *Biomedical Papers of the Medical Faculty of the University Palacký, Olomouc, Czechoslovakia* 166: 251–257.

Pallasmaa, J. 2012. *The Eyes of the Skin: Architecture and the Senses* 3rd Edition. Chichester, UK: Wiley.

Passini, R., and G. Proulx. 1988. "Wayfinding without vision: An experiment with congenitally totally blind people." *Environment and Behavior* 20 (2): 227–252.

Tidwell, P., ed. 2014. *Architecture and Atmosphere*. Espoo, Finland: Tapio Wirkkala—Rut Bryk Foundation.

2.7

PEOPLE-CENTERED SMART LEARNING ECOSYSTEMS

Frameworks of reference for optimal design and planning to support individual well-being and *learning by being*

Carlo Giovannella and Giuseppe Roccasalva

Abstract

In this chapter, we discuss how the *school factory model* that has inspired the design of learning spaces and processes for over two centuries can be overcome thanks to *smart people-centered learning ecosystems*, in which the *smartness* of the places is associated with a framework that aims at the achievement of the *well-being* of the student and, more generally, of all the players involved in the educational process and in which the *learning by being*-inspired learning processes have as their ultimate goal the harmonious formation of the personality of the students, future proactive members of the society. In this framework, the IC technologies play an important role in the development of the *e-maturity* of the learning ecosystems and the development of an individual and collective digital literacy seen as a factor capable of amplifying the *competence-based learning* and the learning *how to be*. The overall picture suggests the need to overcome, from the architectural point of view, the factory model of schools with implications both on the design of new physical and digital spaces and for the renovation of existing learning spaces throughout intervention inspired also by the principle that define the *phygital spaces*.

Keywords
Learning by Being; Competence-Based Learning; Smart Learning Ecosystem; Phygital Learning Spaces; Design for well-Being; Ecosystems' Smartness; E-Maturity

Introduction

In spite of the theoretical progress made by pedagogical sciences over the last century, it is hardly disputable that in almost all schools – except for the design- or laboratory-based

DOI: 10.4324/9781003384113-34

courses – the dominant didactic approach is still the transmissive one, focused on the transfer of knowledge rather than of know-how and, above all, of *know how-to-be*. Despite the last 30 years having marked a true info-communication technological revolution, technologies do not seem to have substantially affected the educational process, as amply documented by the observations conducted during the recent pandemic period [1–4]. The educational process, in fact, with few exceptions, remained anchored to the school model developed at the time of the Industrial Revolution, known as *factory model education* [5]. For more than two centuries, educational institutions (in particular schools) have delivered educational processes organized based on the student's age [6]. Since the last quarter of the last century, then, the democratization of education, combined with an increasingly rapid transformation of productive processes has led the schools to progressively misalign with the demands of the labor market (skills gap phenomenon [7,8]) and, paradoxically, also to reduce their capability to transfer basic contents and procedures, due to the combined effect of a *students' progression based mainly, if not only, on their age* and the *strong push toward inclusion* [9,10]. Within this educational framework, the ICT technologies have been used essentially as tools capable of amplifying what already exists, and the ultimate effect of the technological progress has been only the demand to develop a digital literacy [11–13] adequate to shape *future consumers of network services* [14]. If the adjective *smart* were to be associated solely with the advent and penetration of network infrastructures and technological applications within *learning environments* (LEs), it would have to be connoted exclusively as an intervention aimed at enhancing the efficiency of the educational process, not unlike from what happened in the case of the *smart cities* during the so-called *first wave* [15–18]. In the case of *smart cities*, however, over the years, it has been understood that a city can be considered smart only if its citizens become smart too [19,26]; that a city can be considered smart not only if its activities are sustained by an intelligent infrastructural backbone aimed at fluidifying both material and immaterial flows (goods, people, data, etc.) but, even more, if its urban design and management are centered on the quality of life of its inhabitants [20–25]. In a scenario in which the smart city is people-centered, all citizens must consider themselves active agents capable of contributing to the progressive increase of the ecosystem's *smartness* [29]. Being smart does not simply mean *knowing* how to use at best the technological backbone of the city but to participate consciously in the development of the city's smartness and co-evolve with the ecosystem. In other words: *to be*.

Going back to LEs, in much the same way, it should be realized that their main purpose is to train students, first and foremost as people, capable of becoming active agents of society. This means that educational processes should be competence-based, *learning by being* inspired and that the integrated competence space of reference should include, in addition to basic skills [13,26]: (a) life skills useful for the harmonious development of the personalities of individuals and their preparation as proactive subjects of society; (b) vertical skills useful for the inclusion of individuals into the job market (no longer as a primary objective, but as a complementary and integrated one aimed at the acquisition of an adequate level of personal dignity and independence); (c) digital skills as amplifiers of other skills, rather than as a separate and independent set of skills. Incidentally, competencies-based *learning by being an educational process* is also fundamental to allow people to distinguish themselves from *machines* and maintain a critical and creative superiority, given that it is not possible to challenge the *machine* on the algorithmic side [19].

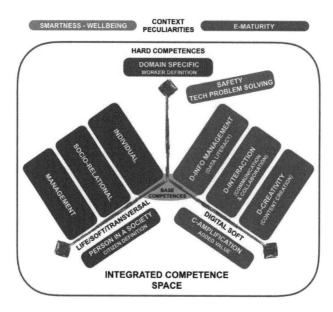

Figure 2.7.1 The integrated competence space of reference. (Courtesy of the Author Carlo Giovannella).

The centrality of the student, of her well-being, and of her *becoming a competent person*, also in relation to the society and the environment in which she lives, endows the LEs with a new centrality with respect to the territory of reference, to productive activities and territorial stakeholders, as well as to the entire population. Unavoidably, this entails a redefinition of the scale of needs and values that should characterize LEs, together with the meaning of the term *smart* associated with them [27].

For this reason, the next paragraphs will be devoted to the definition of the constructs of *smartness* and *well-being* associated with LEs and the role that ICTs take on in this framework in defining their *e-maturity* [28,29]. Lastly, needs and opportunities for redefining physical/phygital spaces will be analyzed, as well as to overcome the school factory model.

Smartness and *Well-Being* as the Cornerstone of People-Centered Learning Ecosystems

The shift of focus from a *factory of human resources to the advantage of the production system* to *a place for the harmonious formation of the personality of the students* (future pro-active members of the society) requires a redefinition of the needs around which design and organize the activities of a learning ecosystem. The multidimensional factor, represented in Figure 2.7.2 (ASLERD pyramid [30]), resumes such needs and has been derived [27] from a revisitation of Maslow's pyramid of needs [31] on top of which the elements determining the individual's flow state [32] are grafted. The lower levels map the primary needs (individual *well-being* generated by the educational context). The higher levels are related to the individual *well-being* resulting from the participation in the education processes, which are expected to generate a deep involvement (flow state) and to support a progressive acquisition of competencies, self-realization, and, as well, to foster socialization [33].

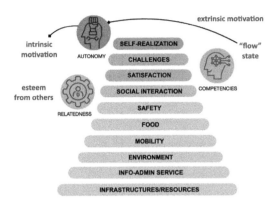

Figure 2.7.2 The dimensions that define the smartness of a large techno ecosystem (ASLERD [30] pyramid). (Courtesy of the Author Carlo Giovannella).

Figure 2.7.2 provides also indications for the design of physical spaces, which must favor simplified access to the structure; respect the environment and be eco-sustainable, be safe, offer adequate food facilities, and favor social interaction.

The e-Maturity of the Learning Ecosystem and the Phygital Spaces

E-maturity

Having discussed about what the meaning of the adjective *smart* should take when associated with a LE, let now see how the ICTs can contribute to amplifying the *smartness* of LEs. This contribution can be defined through its *e-maturity* [4] [28,29].

The factors that contribute to the e-maturity of LEs are succinctly represented in Figure 2.7.3. It is important to emphasize how also this construct is not solely determined by the presence of technological infrastructures but by an integrated set of infrastructural, human, and organizational aspects. The infrastructures and organizational factors define the context, while the former together with the competencies of the actors involved in the process constitute the available resources and ultimately determine the impact on the educational processes and on the well-being of the people who participate in them.

Actually, although all important, not all the factors listed in Figure 2.7.3 can be put on the same level. Indeed, one has to be aware that there exists a causal relationship between them [4] (Figure 2.7.4).

The contribution of ICT proves effective only if it derives from adequate managerial vision and design capacity, capable of defining appropriate objectives. What emerges, in other words, is the relevance of the design – also for what concerns the management and the learning processes – and of the human factors.

The Phygital Places

The ICT infrastructuring of an LE can only proceed step by step and requires a deep understanding of the interaction between physical and virtual spaces that goes beyond the

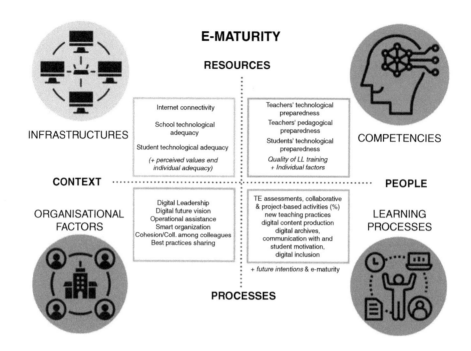

Figure 2.7.3 Schematic representation of the factors contributing to the determination of the e-maturity of a learning ecosystem. (Courtesy of the Author Carlo Giovannella).

streamlining and amplification of existing processes and fosters the emergence of new qualities from the integration of the two spaces that become only one: a *phygital* place [34]. Phygital design should be based on recurrent driving conditions, for example, *responsiveness, usability, empowerment,* and mostly *interaction.* The interactive role of space is, among all, the one that encompasses many of the qualities that were discussed in the scientific literature [35,36] about space design. Interaction is about the digital and physical exploration of spaces, throughout the five senses of human beings. In these terms, interaction generates an ontology of very different qualities that define an *experience* [37,38] which, in turn, requires that designers widen the common and traditional sense of space and time. The design of school factory education neglects physicality or is laterally influenced by it.

The designer should focus on at least three main dimensions that qualify phygital LEs:

- *Sensitive:* phygital spaces can embed sensors that collect info or react to human behaviors. Sensitive objects or materials can be connected and provide in real time that invisible network (Internet of Things) which is becoming the new 'metabolism' of spaces helping us, in the near future, to assess the level of smartness of an ecosystem.
- *Enabling:* phygital spaces can reduce/limit human intervention by providing a set of options to choose from but at the same time it can ease the implementation of numerous activities (social, working/ studying, or moving activities).
- *Engaging:* phygital spaces increase widely both the bidirectional information flows between the digital and the physical realm and the structure and nature of the information; this augments and amplifies engagement strategy and opportunities to interact with space and people, even if we are passive and choose not to interact.

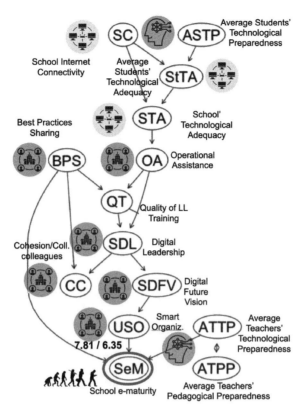

Figure 2.7.4 Causal network linking the factors that contribute to determining the e-maturity of a learning ecosystem, in the opinion of schools' teachers and principals [4]. (Courtesy of the Author Carlo Giovannella).

These three dimensions occur simultaneously and can feed each other's purpose to provide a variety of school design configurations which will hopefully take to new models as fluid classrooms, occasional rehearsal halls; meeting recreation corridors/corners, virtual learning spots with protagonists of the past/future; social diachronic spaces, immersive meetings spaces with world heritage sites, etc.

Consequences on Physical and 'Phygital' Spaces

A transmissive LE is characterized by a distributive model in which students are led into classes identified by a grade corresponding to age and within which the central element is the desk-board area to which the student's attention is directed.

On the other hand, we have seen how important the competence-based approach and the *learning by being* are; what needs LEs should satisfy to be defined smart; the central role that LEs should play with respect to the territories of reference; the conditions under which an ICT infrastructure could contribute to the perceived smartness of LEs and, ultimately, to the well-being of the actors involved in the educational process; the possibility to change qualities and affordances of the physical spaces that may become phygital. All this requires rethinking of the educational spaces. In particular, because a competence-based approach

291

would require the use of spaces sufficiently differentiated and organized to allow students to develop properly the whole spectrum of competencies.

Although the full awareness about the relevance of space organization and other cor-related design aspects materialized recently, a critical analysis of the existing has been undertaken as early as the nineteenth century by pedagogists like Pestalozzi e Froebel that focused particularly on the early age of development [39], criticisms reinforced by the Piaget's [40], and Maria Montessori's [41] studies on the cognitive development of children and by Vygotsky's studies [42–44] that contributed, together with those of other colleagues [45], to the enunciation of constructivist theories [46]. Already in the early years of the twentieth century, it was theorized that kindergarten spaces should be designed to support the development of all modes of human interaction – physical, intel-lectual, social, and affective – and all potential talents by allowing children to interact also with peers of other ages and having the time necessary for their development, while respecting human rights and the environment (think of the Steinerian principles and schools [47]). An approach that even then favored interaction between indoor and out-door spaces (also understood as occasions for human relations and taking social respon-sibility, e.g., family participation). Apart from the Steinerian and Montessori schools and the work done by Loris Malaguzzi (Reggio Emilia Approach [48]), it is only during the last three decades that school design has produced smarter environments: most of them dedicated to tertiary education [49,50], with less frequent realizations at the level of K12 and high schools.

What have been the inspiring principles of these latter projects?

The first is undoubtedly the *flexibility*. A principle that can be applied both at the macro level – as in the case of the 4het Gymnasium in Amsterdam [51], a school composed of prefabricated modules that could take on different configurations – and at the micro level in relation to the interior spaces – as in the Ørestad Gymnasium in Copenhagen [51]. Flexibility at the macro level may be useful in case of expansion-decompression of exist-ing structures due, for example, to changes in the number of students. Undoubtedly, more interesting is the application of the concept of flexibility to the possibility of reorganizing interior spaces and the configuration of interior furnishings, in particular when one has to tackle the renovation of old school buildings.

Also, as an alternative to flexibility, the second key concept is *diversification*. In some cases, as in the Vittra school [51], there are learning spaces designed specifically for group work; a space designed to encourage individual reflection and concentration; an area designed for presentation, discussion, and convening assemblies; an area for exhibitions/performances and workshops with specific functions; a cloakroom and a space for the distribution and enjoyment of meals. The classroom has disappeared and the student's attention is no longer focused on the desk (although attentional points are needed for the inevitable projection of information). Spaces are used according to needs, not allocated to a fixed group of students (as actually, it occurs also in schools with a more traditional space organization thanks to a functional redefinition of the traditional classrooms).

In all new schools, the idea of open spaces and a search for interaction with the out-doors tends to dominate. The relationship with the outdoors is also sought to affirm a new centrality of the school with respect to the territory (see the primary schools built by the VSBA in Melbourne's outer western suburbs [52]) that can even become a true civic center (Ørestad Gymnasium) with spaces open to activities involving the inhabitants of the terri-tory of reference.

Up to now, we have not yet mentioned the IT infrastructures that in principle could amplify the effects of a design of physical spaces inspired by 'more advanced' pedagogical principles. This is mainly because since the internet penetrated the LEs and began to be used for teaching purposes, the collective imagery about the use of ICTs has been confined to a) the possibility of accessing an unlimited number of resources in real time; b) the availability of classrooms equipped with connected computers; and, more recently, to c) the use of the interactive whiteboard; and, in a limited number of cases, to that of virtual LEs ('platforms'). By no coincidence, the references to ICTs that we can find in the projects we mentioned up to now did not go beyond this imagery.

The recent pandemic period has not substantially changed such a landscape, although it has forced the massive use of applications to hold virtual meetings and video lectures, share materials, and perform collaborative work by means of cloud-based applications. At present, despite the strong post-pandemic push for the complete restoration of in-presence activities, we can detect a weak tendency toward a transformation of the relationship between physical and digital spaces with computer classrooms increasingly emptying themselves of workstations in favor of BYOD (Bring Your Own Device) approach that presupposes the spread of efficient WIFI connectivity and the use of the cloud, as well as the ubiquitous presence of screens (sometimes placed on small robots) to allow telepresence. Such increasing interconnection between internal and external spaces also to access skills that can be found in the latter (think, for example, of music ensembles without the physical presence of all the components) is witnessing a 'light' increase in the *enabling* and *engaging* dimensions of the physical spaces.

What are the possible trends toward the future development of increasingly phygital spaces?

The first one concerns the *sentient* dimension of space. The most trivial applications are those that follow the definition of home automation, aimed at controlling the physical well-being (temperature, light, and its coloring, humidity level, sound intensity, etc.) and mechanical affordances (automated movement of components of physical space); less trivial, but now widely accessible, is the detection and elaboration, in particular in laboratory environments, of physical parameters of various kinds (also, for example, in the management of green spaces – precision farming [53]) and the detection of behaviors (e.g. students' attention by cameras [54]). The latter, especially when coupled with AI applications, entails ethical considerations but may stimulate in the students the acquisition of adequate data literacy [55,56] as well as a multidimensional perception of the self.

Another aspect is *automation,* especially in labs where sensors could be integrated with expert systems (e.g., AI-based applications on the cloud), to prepare students for the so-called Industry 4.0 [57].

A final aspect concerns immersive experiences in which the virtual becomes physical like in the case of digital interactive elements mapped and projected on physical spaces [58,59].

A fully interactive immersiveness can also be experienced through the use of visors, and wearable sensors/actuators, but in such cases the individual's perception (including the proprioception) is decoupled from that of the physical space in which one finds oneself. Certainly, useful in all cases of simulations (e.g. Lego construction [60]) and in the visualization of what cannot be explored in reality, e.g. [61,62]) but in such cases the phygital perception changes quite a lot and we can hardly refer to phygital spaces. A final notation deserves all digital applications that, although not perceptible in physical space, can influence the behavior of its inhabitants and the physical experience of the space.

With the exception of interactive caves and performance spaces, in phygital spaces, the *machine* tends to disappear behind the physical spaces and in the bodies of the objects that populate them [63–65]. It manifests itself only through computability and responsiveness, i.e. the capacity of spaces and objects to perceive a stimulus and to process a response [66]. This ultimately means that the conformation of the space of LEs, albeit with the aid of technologies will continue to be dictated by people's needs and, hopefully, by the evolution of the models that shape the learning processes taking place there.

Digital technologies are supporting tools, not the roots of the place's smartness. Nevertheless, we must be fully aware and deeply assess their meaning and potential impacts to integrate them meaningfully into the design of phygital solutions capable of amplifying the possibilities for *interaction* and *engagement*.

Necessarily, every change in a space topology and functionalities should be inspired by a transformative hypothesis – in this case of the educational processes – and the transformed spaces, through their affordances, are expected to favor further evolutions of the processes. Such changes, however, must be accompanied also by the training of people; otherwise, the transformed spaces might risk becoming silent containers, often underused, incapable of stimulating fruitful interaction with those who populate them and with their territorial context and community. A *smart designer* should be able to intuit – possibly with the help of experts – the widest possible number of evolutionary trajectories of the processes that could develop in the transformed spaces, also taking into account possible technological developments and the potential needs of the evolving society. In other words, it should be able to read the evolutionary path that has led from the past to the present and that could fan out from today into tomorrow, having always in mind the *well-being of the individuals*.

References

[1] As an example see Sahin I., & Shelly, M. Eds. (2020). *Educational Practices during the COVID-19 Viral Outbreak: International Perspectives*, ITES Organization.

[2] Giovannella, C., Passarelli, M., & Persico, D. (2020). "The Effects of the Covid-19 Pandemic on Italian Learning Ecosystems: The School Teachers' Perspective at the Steady State". *Interaction Design and Architecture(s) Journal - IxD&A*, 4: 264–286. https://doi.org/10.55612/s-5002-045-012

[3] Giovannella, C., Passarelli, M., Alkhafaji, A. S. A., & Pérez Negrón, A. P. (2021). "A Model for the Attitude to get Engaged in Technological Innovation (MAETI) Derived from a Comparative Study on the Effects of the SARS-CoV2 Pandemic seen through the Lens of the University Teachers of three different National Learning Ecosystems: Iraq, Italy and Mexico". *Interaction Design and Architecture(s) Journal - IxD&A*, 47: 167–190. https://doi.org/10.55612/s-5002-047-008

[4] Giovannella, C., Cianfriglia, L., & Giannelli, A. (2022). "The Italian School Ecosystems Two Years After the Lockdown: An Overview on the 'Digital Shock' Triggered by the Pandemic in the Perceptions of Schools' Principals and Teachers in Polyphonic Construction of Smart Learning Ecosystems". Springer, vol. 908: 47–76. https://doi.org/10.1007/978-981-19-5240-1_4

[5] Wikipedia. (n.d.). "Factory Model School". Retrieved October 3, 2023 from https://en.wikipedia.org/wiki/Factory_model_school

[6] Robinson, K. (2010). "Changing Education Paradigms". TED Talk, Retrieved October 3, 2023 from https://www.ted.com/talks/sir_ken_robinson_changing_education_paradigms

[7] CEDEFOP. (2010). "The Skill Matching Challenge: Analyzing Skill Mismatch & Policy Implications". Luxemburg, Available online at: http://www.cedefop.europa.eu/EN/Files/3056en.pdf.

[8] McGuinness, S., & Ortiz, L. (2015). Skill Gaps in the Workplace: Measurement, Determinants and Impacts, IZA DP No. 9278.

[9] UNICEF. (n.d.). "Inclusive Education". Retrieved October 3, 2023 from https://www.unicef.org/education/inclusive-education

[10] Leijen, Ä, Arcidiacono, F., & Baucal, A. (2021). "The Dilemma of Inclusive Education: Inclusion for Some or Inclusion for All". *Frontiers in Psychology*, 12: 633066.

[11] UNESCO. (n.d.). Digital Competence Framework for Teachers, Learners and Citizens. Retrieved October 3, 2023 from https://unevoc.unesco.org/home/Digital+Competence+Frameworks/lang=en/id=4.

[12] European Commission. (n.d.). DigiComp Framework. Retrieved October 3, 2023 from https://joint-research-centre.ec.europa.eu/digcomp/digcomp-framework_en.

[13] Giovannella, C. (2023). " 'Learning by being': Integrated thinking and Competencies to Mark the Difference from AIs". *Interaction Design & Architecture(s) Journal – IxD&A*, 57: 8–26, https://doi.org/10.55612/s-5002-057-001

[14] Brečko, B., & Ferrari, A. (2016). Vuorikari R., Punie Y. Eds. *The Digital Competence Framework for Consumers*. EUR 28133 EN. Luxembourg (Luxembourg): Publications Office of the European Union. JRC103155

[15] Lee, S. Ho, Han, J. Hoon, Leem, Y. Taik, & Yigitcanlar, T. (2008). "Towards Ubiquitous City: Concept, Planning, and Experiences in the Republic of Korea". *Knowledge-Based Urban Development: Planning and Applications in the Information Era* (pp. 148–169).

[16] Deakin, M., & Al Waer, H. (2011). "From Intelligent to Smart Cities". *Journal of Intelligent Buildings International: From Intelligent Cities to Smart Cities*, 3(3): 140–152.

[17] Giffinger, R., & Gudrun, H. (2010). Smart Cities Ranking: An Effective Instrument for the Positioning of Cities? *ACE: Architecture, City and Environment*, 4(12): 7–25.

[18] Hollands, R. (2008). "Will the Real Smart City Please Stand Up?". *City*, 12(3): 303–320.

[19] Fitsilis, P. Ed. (2022). *Building on Smart Cities Skills and Competences*. Springer Publisher.

[20] Giovannella, C., Dascalu, M., & Scaccia, F. (2014). "Smart City Analytics: State of the Art and Future [Perspectives". *Interaction Design and Architecture(s) Journal - IxD&A*, 20: 72–87.

[21] Giovannella, C. (2013). "Territorial Smartness and Emergent Behaviors". In *ICSCS 2013* (pp. 170–176). IEEE Publisher.

[22] Giovannella, C., Gobbi, A., Zhang, B., Elsner, J., Del Fatto, V., Pérez-Sanagustín, M., Avouris, N., & Zualkernan, I. (2013). "Villard-de-Lans: A Case Study for Collaborative People-Centered Smart City Learning Design". In *ICALT 2013* (pp. 459–460). IEEE Publisher.

[23] The origin of the "Person in Place Centered Design" Vision is Documented in Giovannella C. (2008). "Person- in-Place Centered Design: Educare 'Istructional Designer' e Operatori dei Futuri 'Learning Places'". In *Didamatica 2008*. Ed. Andronico, A., Roselli, T., & Lamborghini, B. Bari, p. 973.

[24] The Human Smart Cities Cookbook. (2014). *Planum*. 28. Retrieved October 3, 2023 from https://issuu.com/planumnet/docs/cookbook_planum.

[25] Concilio, G., & Rizzo, F. Eds., (2016). *Human Smart Cities. Rethinking the Interplay between Design and Planning*. Springer.

[26] Giovannella, C. (2022). "At the Root of the Smart Cities: Smart Learning Ecosystems to train Smart Citizens". In *Building on Smart Cities Skills and Competences*. Springer Publisher, pp. 217–228.

[27] Giovannella, C. (2014). "'Smartness' as Complex Emergent Property of a Process. The Case of Learning Ecosystems". *ICWOAL*. IEEE Publisher, p. 1–5.

[28] Sergis, S., Zervas, P., & Sampson, D. G. (2014). "A Holistic Approach for Managing School ICT Competence Profiles towards Supporting School ICT Uptake". *International Journal of Digital Literacy and Digital Competence*, 5(4): 33–46.

[29] Kampylis, P., Punie, Y., & Devine, J. (2015). Promoting Effective Digital-Age Learning: A European Framework for Digitally-Competent Educational Organisations, EUR 27599 EN, Publications Office of the European Union, Luxembourg. JRC98209.

[30] ASLERD: Association for Smart Learning Ecosystems and Regional Development. Retrieved October 3, 2023 from http://www.aslerd.org

[31] Maslow, A. H. (1943). "A Theory of Human Motivation". *Psychological Review*, 50(4): 370–396.

[32] Czisikszentmihalyi, M. (1990). *Flow—The Psychology of Optimal Experience*. Harper & Row.

[33] Giovannella, C. (2022). "From Simplex to Complex: Designing for Wellbeing at Scale". *Interaction Design and Architecture(s) Journal - IxD&A*, 55: 123–138, doi: https://doi.org/10.55612/s-5002-055-006

[34] Momentum. (2022). Treccani 2022. Retrieved October 3, 2023, from https://www.treccani.it/magazine/lingua_italiana/articoli/parole/Figitale.html.

[35] Ghel, J. (1971). *Life between the Building: Using Public Spaces.* The Danish Architectural Press.

[36] Hillier, B. (1984). *The Social Logic of Space.*

[37] Hassenzahl, M. (2010). "Experience Design: Technology for all the Right Reasons". *Synthesis Lectures on Human-Centered Informatics*, Cambridge University Press, 3(1): 1–95.

[38] Giovannella, C. (2012). "Is Complexity Tameable? Toward a Design for the Experience in a Complex World". *Interaction Design and Architecture(s) Journal - IxD&A*, 15: 18–30.

[39] Fröbel, F. (1826). *On the Education of Man (Die Menschenerziehung)*, Keilhau/Leipzig, Wienbrach.

[40] Wikipedia. (n.d.). Jean Piaget. Retrieved October 3, 2023, from https://en.wikipedia.org/wiki/Jean_Piaget.

[41] Montessori, M. (1935). *Il Metodo Della Pedagogia Scientifica Applicato All'educazione Infantile Nelle Case Dei Bambini.* Loescher, Roma.

[42] Vygotsky, L. S. (1978). *Mind in Society: The Development of Higher Psychological Processes.* Cambridge, MA, Harvard University Press.

[43] Vygotsky, L. S. (1934/1986). *Thought and Language.* Cambridge, MA, MIT Press.

[44] DeVries, R. (2000). "Vygostky, Piaget and Education: A Reciprocal Assimilation of Theories and Educational Practices". *New Ideas in Psychology*, 18: 187–213.

[45] Mayer, S. J. (2008). "Dewey's Dynamic Integration of Vygotsky and Piaget". *Education and Culture*, 24(2): 6–24.

[46] Mascolo, M. F., & Fischer, K. W. (2005). *Constructivist Theories. Cambridge Encyclopedia of Child Development* (pp. 49–63). Cambridge, Cambridge University Press.

[47] Steiner, R. (1924). "Human Values in Education GA 310 IV. Three Epochs of Childhood". Rudolf Steiner Archive. Steiner Online Library. Retrieved October 3, 2023, from https://rsarchive.org/Lectures/19240720a01.html

[48] Malaguzzi, L. (1993). "For an Education Based on Relationships". *Young Children*, 49: 9–12.

[49] HEFCE. (2006). Design Spaces for Effective Learning. A Guide to 21st Century Learning Space Design. Retrieved October 3, 2023, from https://www.d41.org/cms/lib/IL01904672/Centricity/Domain/422/learningspaces.pdf

[50] REMI. (2021). The New Architecture of Schools. The School of the Future is Flexible, Adaptable, and Healthy. Retrieved October 3, 2023 from https://www.reminetwork.com/articles/the-new-architecture-of-schools/

[51] INDIRE. (n.d.). Quando lo Spazio Insegna. Retrieved October 3, 2023 from https://www.indire.it/quandolospazioinsegna/eventi/2012/miur/

[52] ARM Architecture. (2023). Six New Primary Schools, 2023. Retrieved October 3, 2023 from https://armarchitecture.com.au/projects/six-new-primary-schools-2023/

[53] Kitchen N. R., Snyder C. J., Franzen D., & Wiebold W. J. (2022). "Educational Needs of Precision Agriculture". *Precision Agriculture*, 3(4): 341–351.

[54] Dessus, P. (2023). Context-Aware Classrooms as Places for an Automated Analysis of Instructional Events. In: Dascalu, M., Marti, P., Pozzi, F. (eds) *Polyphonic Construction of Smart Learning Ecosystems.* SLERD 2022. Smart Innovation, Systems and Technologies, vol 908. Singapore: Springer. https://doi.org/10.1007/978-981-19-5240-1_1

[55] Olari V., & Romeike, R. (2021). "Addressing AI and Data Literacy in Teacher Education: A Review of Existing Educational Frameworks". *WiPSCE '21: The 16th Workshop in Primary and Secondary Computing Education* (pp. 1–2). Retrieved October 3, 2023 from https://doi.org/10.1145/3481312.3481351.

[56] Dykes, B. (2020). *Data Storytelling: How to Drive Change with Data, Narrative and Visuals.* Wiley.

[57] Baena, F., Guarin, A., Mora, J., Sauza, J., & Retat, S. (2017). "Learning Factory: The Path to Industry 4.0". *Procedia Manufacturing*, 9: 73–80.

[58] Breeze Creative. (n.d.). Retrieved October 3, 2023 from https://www.breezecreative.com/

[59] Studio azzurro. Opere. (n.d.). Retrieved October 3, 2023 from https://www.studioazzurro.com/category/opere/

[60] Doma, O. O., & Sener, S. M. "Dreamscape Bricks VR: An Experimental Virtual Reality Tool for Architectural Design". *Interaction Design and architecture(s) Journal—IxD&A*, 52: 234–258. https://doi.org/10.55612/s-5002-052-013

[61] Zhou, Y., Hou, J., Liu, Q., Chao, X., Wang, N., Chen, Y., Guan, J., Zhang, Q., & Diwu, Y. (2021). "VR/AR Technology in Human Anatomy Teaching and Operation Training". *Journal of Healthcare Engineering*, 2021: 9998427.

[62] Sullivan, E., Nieves, A. D., & Snyder, L. M. (2017). "Making the Model: Scholarship and Rhetoric in 3-D Historical Reconstructions". In: Sayers, J. (ed), *Making Things and Drawing Boundaries: Experiments in the Digital Humanities* (pp. 301–316). University of Minnesota Press, Minneapolis.

[63] Greenfield, A. (2006). *Everyware: The Dawning Age of Ubiquitous Computing.* New Riders.

[64] Nieuwdorp, E. (2007). "The Pervasive Discourse". *Computers in Entertainment*, 5(2): 13.

[65] Li, S., Xu, L. D., & Zhao, S. (2015). "The Internet of Things: A Survey". *Information Systems Frontiers,* 17: 243–259.

[66] Giovannella, C. (2008). "L'uomo, La Macchina E La Comunicazione Mediata: Evoluzioni Di Paradigmi E Design Per Le Esperienze Nell'era Organica Dell'interazione". *Machinae: Tecniche Arti E Saperi Del Novecento* (pp. 471–490). Ed. Graphics, B. A. Bari.

2.8

THE BODY IN HEALING TECHNOLOGY

Anna Strøe, Nick Ward and Fiona Zisch

Abstract

eXtended Reality (XR) environments are increasingly acknowledged as effective training tools for rehabilitation of limb movement following neurological damage such as stroke.

XR spans virtual reality, augmented reality, and mixed reality; this can include an immersive virtual environment which incorporates components of the physical environment (for example, interaction with objects in the physical space).

There is significant potential to break through what is traditionally thought of as the ceiling of recovery through the increased dose and intensity of movement training possible with XR tools.

Using machine learning (ML) to detect specific abnormal patterns of movement and then adapt the XR environment to encourage better quality, non-compensatory movement could provide tailored movement training to suit individual needs and promote maximum recovery. Integrating elements of the physical space with the virtual environments could enhance engagement to promote appropriate quality movements.

This chapter presents an analysis of existing technologies in this realm and proposes new frameworks with which to enhance recovery for patients recovering from stroke or other forms of neurological damage that lead to motor and cognitive impairments. This chapter discusses the significance of architectural design (both in physical and virtual space) for XR environments in promoting the efficacy of rehabilitation tools. Finally, it reflects on the necessity for interdisciplinarity in the development of these tools, as they bridge the fields of computer science, design, and neuroscience.

Introduction

For a few minutes, for an hour, or even for a whole day, try to use only one of your arms (perhaps even your non-dominant arm). If you are typing on a computer, cooking, or showering, pin one arm to your side and use only the other to complete your tasks. Notice how this alters your perception of your own body, and your perception of your physical abilities. Does it alter your sensory perception? Your perception of your environment?

DOI: 10.4324/9781003384113-35

298

The body is in many ways extraordinarily malleable. Changes in the perception of one's own body can result from even subtle shifts in personal or extra-personal space. Spatial perception is not something that objectively unfolds before the eye; it is a participatory process between the body and its surroundings. Husserl utilizes a tactile example to illustrate embodied perception: if I reach out my hand to touch a sculpture, to better understand its crevices and curves, I am sensing not only the material and shape of the sculpture but my experiential perception of *myself* touching the sculpture (Behnke, 2011). I sense both the sculpture's qualities and my body in contact with them. If the qualities of one change, for example, if my hands are covered in oil, or the sculpture is sanded down to a rough texture, my perception of the other will also shift. My environment alters my experience of my physical body, and vice versa.

Stroke and other forms of brain injury that can lead to motor, sensory, and cognitive impairment tangibly shift the spatial body. Questions of healthcare are, of course, fundamentally questions of the body, and the body's relation to its environment. By viewing impairment as a shift in the spatial body, one can use XR neurorehabilitation post-stroke (defined and explained later in the chapter) as a lens through which to investigate design for the body and the virtual body in space in new light.

This chapter will focus on how smart technologies, specifically eXtended Reality (XR) technologies, defined later in the chapter, can be used in healthcare applications, particularly in helping stroke patients overcome their impairments through neurorehabilitation. The chapter will begin with a brief background on stroke and neurorehabilitation, as well as the rationale for employing XR. It will then explore the role of embodiment in XR, and its relation to neurorehabilitation. Lastly, this will lead to a speculative analysis of future XR neurorehabilitation design and the importance of interdisciplinarity within it. The chapter will raise a series of questions throughout, for future work in this field to address.

XR in Neurorehabilitation

Background on Stroke and Neurorehabilitation

Stroke is one of the world's leading causes of death and disability (Stroke Association). Stroke is caused by a lack of blood supply to a part of the brain, which damages brain cells, and can cause difficulty with moving, communicating, thinking, and feeling depending on which part of the brain is affected. Stroke is common: 1 in 4 people will have a stroke in their lifetime (Feigin et al., 2022). 15 million people suffer a stroke each year and there are currently over 100 million people living with the consequences of stroke. Stroke is no longer a disease of the elderly with two-thirds of strokes occurring in people under the age of 70.

Approximately 75% of stroke survivors will have some difficulty using the arm and hand. Upper limb impairment greatly affects daily living, as it reduces the ability to accomplish "basic" tasks such as cooking, cleaning, driving, writing, typing, etc. Additionally, impairments from stroke can have major impacts on other aspects of life, such as self-confidence, social life and relationships, and community participation (Kirkevold et al., 2018).

Current Treatment Approaches

Repetitive task training is the standard approach to helping patients regain movement. Animal studies suggest that 400–600 repetitions of a movement each day are required to see both behavioral improvements and associated cortical changes (secondary to neuroplasticity mechanisms). Generally, stroke patients are not receiving adequate doses of neurorehabilitation treatment, but some centers are attempting to remedy this (Ward et al., 2019). In addition to achieving the correct dose of movement training, the correct movements must be trained to help achieve the best recovery. Recent data support the idea that patients can make meaningful improvements in their impairments even in the chronic stage (> six months post-stroke).

XR

The term XR describes a broad category of technologies, environments, and experiences spanning virtual reality, augmented reality, and mixed reality (Cardenas-Robledo et al., 2022). While the term "virtual reality" implies replacing all stimuli in one or more of the sensory fields with a digitally constructed "world" to create a sense of presence and immersion, mixed reality generally implies incorporating elements of the physical environment into the virtual or digital experience. Augmented reality, then, sits somewhere between the two on this reality spectrum.

Why Use XR in Neurorehabilitation?

XR tools have across a range of studies and meta-analyses been shown to improve function post-stroke, both when used in conjunction with traditional therapy, and when used in replacement of traditional therapy (Bargeri et al., 2023). The extensive literature on the results of studies and experiments that utilize immersive and non-immersive Virtual Reality (VR) environments in the recovery of movement after stroke overwhelmingly reports that VR training is as effective as (and in some cases, more effective than) traditional rehab training (Ibid).

Within neurorehabilitation, there is a need for higher doses of treatment, i.e., increased task repetitions. Additionally, there is a need for greater focus on the quality of movement, with treatment directly targeting impairment, rather than solely focusing on improving activities of daily living (Bahouth et al., 2023). While the latter may decrease the length of hospital stays, ultimately, the focus should shift toward impairment reduction as the primary priority of treatment. Other areas of focus in the development of treatment include strategies for increasing motivation and engagement in rehabilitation (both as a way to increase time on task and to improve learning), as well as access to treatment in the home environment. Each of these areas has the potential to be addressed through XR applications.

XR interventions in rehabilitation are theorized to work primarily through the repetitive training of motor activity, as well as the cognitive stimulation of the activity (Hao et al., 2022). Their usually gamified nature is thought to increase engagement and therefore increase task repetition (Rojo et al., 2022).

Additionally, "enriched environments" such as those found in gamified XR environments are shown to increase the potential for experience-dependent plasticity and therefore increase the efficacy of the learning environment (Livingston-Thomas et al., 2016). Environmental enrichment varies widely but typically refers to increased access to socialization, physical activity, and a larger spatial environment. The design potentials that this encourages in the XR environment then include multi-person environments, virtual tasks that require or facilitate movement, and rich sensory landscapes. Literature exploring the role of enriched environments in clinical stroke rehabilitation cites the benefits of a changing environment that encourages "sensory and cognitive stimulation, and task-specific therapy targeting the primary impairment" (McDonald et al., 2018).

Alternative forms of feedback not typically utilized in the clinical environment can also be implemented through XR applications. For instance, it has been shown that real-time audio feedback can significantly reduce the number of abnormal movements in chronic stroke patients (Douglass-Kirk et al., 2022).

In one example of an existing XR application within neurorehabilitation, a large range of movement on all planes is encouraged through the paretic arm's (de-weighted using an exoskeleton device) control of a virtual dolphin, projected onto a screen-mounted device. Using the exoskeleton to allow free movement, coupled with the design of the immersive gaming environment which uses an aquatic animal that can move in all directions, allows the paretic arm to move through its full active range axis (Krakauer et al., 2021). Contrastingly, however, the 2D design of many other neurorehabilitation gaming environments direct movement solely along one axis.

Limitations of Existing Neurorehabilitation Tools

Many existing XR interventions aim to increase the dose of treatment, rather than improving the quality of movement. Additionally, few, if any, take explicit steps to individualize the training tools to the patient's unique movement patterns. Individualization could involve, for example, the system's analysis of user behaviors to understand movement patterns as they pertain to the specific tasks of the game or environment. This could then be used to better "score" user's movements in the game or to select which "level" of the game they should be in. Machine learning (ML) could be used for the automatic detection of compensatory movements based on a wide set of user data, rather than the constraints for what constitutes a compensatory movement being preset.

In the context of stroke recovery, compensatory movements are often used when one struggles to use the impaired limb in the way one has previously been accustomed to in completing a task. The compensation occurs from a shift in the body to accommodate this impairment, such as leaning the trunk forward when trying to reach an object in front of you, if you have trouble extending your arm (Cirstea & Levin, 2000). The use of compensatory strategies in stroke recovery results in nonoptimal movement patterns, which as they get learned, negatively impact and even hinder recovery (Cai et al., 2019). Targeting impairment directly would involve focusing on the quality of the user's movement, discouraging the use of compensatory movements.

Compensatory movement patterns are in principle, actively discouraged in rehabilitation by clinicians. Automatic detection using motion tracking and markerless systems in tandem with ML could provide users with the feedback needed to improve, without the constant presence of a physiotherapist. Feedback that encourages the user to move away from compensatory movement would therefore directly target the quality of movement, by not only increasing the dose through task repetition but also by paying attention to the precision of the desired movement. For instance, in a physical rehabilitation setting, if a stroke patient leans their trunk forward to reach for an object, a clinician might use verbal or physical cues, e.g., saying, "Keep your trunk back" or holding their trunk in place to discourage this movement. However, many tools rely on physical hardware (robotics) to keep the limb in constrained or desired positions, rather than the system itself tracking its position (Figure 2.8.1).

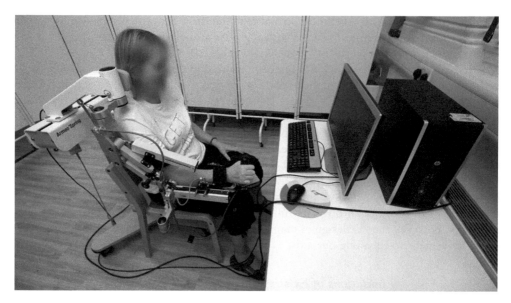

Figure 2.8.1 A patient using a de-weighting device in a gaming rehabilitation tool. (Courtesy of the Author, Nick Ward).

Bringing the Body into XR

Questions of virtual space, or virtual environments, inherently presuppose questions of both the virtual body and the body in space. Putting on a virtual reality headset does not transport a floating set of eyes into a digital landscape; rather, the whole body is taken onboard the journey. A multisensory perceptual experience is undergone which can generate physiological and emotional arousal, can quicken the heartbeat, or induce an empathic response (Marín-Morales et al., 2021).

Due to presenting, at minimum, a new visual field for the body to accept, a shift in the spatial body must occur to accommodate this new environment. When a virtual avatar is employed in the virtual experience, an additional layer of complexity, that of *virtual embodiment* (Gonzalez-Franco & Peck, 2018), is introduced.

In an early example of such experiments, grappling with the phenomenon of the phantom limb, neuroscientist Vilayanur S. Ramachandran and colleagues created a "mirror box," or "virtual reality box therapy" as they called it. This device consisted of a vertical mirror in the middle of a wooden box, and an open top and side so that the patient could look into the box and at the mirror. The patient (who was experiencing a phantom limb) was then asked to move their healthy arm around until the mirror image superimposed the phantom arm. The primary intention of this therapeutical device was to treat one of the central concerns that accompanies phantom limb: pain (Ramachandran & Hirstein, 1998). Virtual reality is now widely used as a treatment for chronic pain across a range of health concerns (Goudman et al., 2022), providing one instance of how these considerations of the lived body and lived space lend themselves to health and treatment.

Within clinical psychology, it has been shown that the hostility toward "out-groups" shown in sociological research is duplicated when interacting with virtual characters. In a study by Peck et al., when participants experienced being virtually "in the skin" of a race different from their own, their scores on implicit racial bias tests significantly decreased, suggesting that XR experiences, and the avatar representation within them, can influence even implicit cognitive processes (Slater et al., 2009). This calls into question the more fundamental ways in which a lived experience in XR can alter deep-seated or engrained ideas about one's own and other's bodies.

Thinking about the spatial body in virtual worlds through these lenses illuminates the possibilities that embodiment in XR can provide for shifting one's relationship with one's own body and environment. From here, one can speculate why embodiment will be significant for neurorehabilitation in XR.

Speculative Design: Why Is Embodiment Important for Stroke Rehabilitation?

Thus far, this chapter has established that XR has the ability to alter implicit beliefs about the self and others, treat chronic pain, and increase engagement and time on task, among other benefits.

Given that stroke leads to a confounding series of impairments, including motor, sensory, and cognitive factors, XR's capabilities render it a promising medium with which to tackle these impairments simultaneously. XR's immersive nature, engulfing the user in an ocean of sensory stimuli, presents the open question: how does this impact the complex confounding impairments that follow brain injury? Which considerations must be taken into account accordingly in their design?

Examples outside of neurorehabilitation, and even outside of healthcare, provide a promising argument for utilizing XR in treatment in ways not yet developed or applied . in the clinical setting. In addition to increasing the dose of treatment and targeting impairment, as is needed in the development of treatments for brain recovery, we can draw from examples in design, psychology, and gaming to postulate how embodiment might radically alter the course of movement and body-based rehabilitation.

Potentially in part due to the lack of prolific use of Head Mounted Displays in neurorehabilitation tools today, there has yet to be a significant focus on the design of the virtual avatars used in the environments. This area, however, presents a wealth of design opportunities: avatar representation directly impacts the experience of the user through what is known as the "proteus effect," or the (thoroughly evidenced) idea that individuals change their behavior in a virtual environment based on characteristics (such as skin color, texture, shape, movement patterns) of their virtual avatar (Praetorius & Görlich, 2021). This is thought to be accomplished by what is known as the body ownership illusion (Slater, 2009).

The proteus effect has also been shown to lead to higher level cognitive changes, for instance

> embodying a child body causing adult VR users to overestimate the size of virtual objects (Banakou et al., 2013), embodiment in a different race body leading to changes in implicit racial attitudes (Maister et al., 2015; Banakou et al., 2020), or embodying a stereotypically empathic woman instigating empathy (Hadjipanayi and Michael-Grigoriou, 2022).
>
> *(Hadjipanayi et al., 2023)*

With these examples in mind, one may begin to imagine how this effect could be brought into a rehabilitation tool. For example, if a stroke patient consistently underestimates their own ability to complete a task, hindering their recovery process: could a virtual avatar that completes the task faster, or with an exaggerated and better-quality movement, improve their belief in their own ability? Could embodying an extremely confident and self-assured avatar help a patient in overcoming issues of self-esteem that accompany the recovery process? One could even imagine whether experiencing an avatar that is extremely energetic in its demeanor and movements might induce a higher feeling of motivation and positivity in the user. These changes in perception, confidence, and motivation could in turn improve their performance beyond what might otherwise be seen as the "limits" of their recovery potential.

It has been shown, for instance, that when given a taller virtual avatar, participants negotiated more aggressively in subsequent face-to-face interactions than when given shorter avatars, suggesting that a boosted sense of confidence in the virtual realm carried over into the physical realm (Yee et al., 2009). What might happen if, in an XR system that is able to detect subtle movements, a small quiver or gentle movement of the arm manifests as an exaggerated, bold movement in the virtual avatar? In this way, the system could detect the intentions of its user and transform their perceived sense of agency through its manipulation of movement. One must of course then consider the implications of this on motivation and self-esteem outside of the XR system, which require further study.

There are many other possible ways to manipulate space and movement perception in the XR environment that are not possible in the physical world, such as allowing for first-person perspective learning through co-locating two avatars in the virtual space (that are physically in different locations). First-person perspective learning has been shown to improve imitation and reduce errors (Watanabe & Higuchi, 2016), which may benefit motor learning in rehabilitation. Conversely, one's avatar could also be placed virtually away from the physical body, so that the user views their own body's movement from a third-person perspective.

In one example of a perspectival shift in XR, The Machine to be Another, created by the BeAnotherLab, facilitates a body swap illusion (the sense of embodying another being) using virtual reality, movement, and tactile feedback. This has been used as a performance and research piece to alter perception, address negative stereotypes, and as therapeutic body extension (BeAnotherLab). In another example, the installation series *Artificial Nature* by Haru Ji and Graham Wakefield employs virtual reality, physical objects, and digital projection to elicit changes in the sense of scale and time across a range of thematic explorations. In the virtual space, the visitor finds themselves shrunk down to the size of an insect, now having to navigate the world in this new body. A sense of their own speed, the space they take up, and their relation to the built and natural environment is turned on its head; this triggers a more imaginative and exploratory body when interacting with space (Artificial Nature). One can consider how applying these perspectival shifts in a rehabilitation setting might reframe one's approach to one's own body, and therefore, to treatment.

These perspectival shifts relate to the questions of motivation and confidence posed earlier. Take, for instance, the dolphin rehabilitation game mentioned earlier in the chapter. Were you to visually and tactually *embody* the dolphin, how might your drive and ambition in the game change? If you feel, through visual, auditory, and tactile stimuli that you truly are immersed in a body of water, how might your arm move differently? When considering what is understood as the ceiling of recovery in rehabilitation, how large a (limiting) role do implicit beliefs about the body and about one's own abilities play?

These ideas represent uses of XR not only to "overcome the limitations of our experiences in the real world" (Abtahi et al., 2022), but to use those experiences to remap our behavior in the real world. XR has the potential to pull one in and *out* of one's own body, in ways that serve the interests of regaining motor and cognitive function. These speculations raise questions of design in healthcare environments more broadly, and the role of architectural design in body-based rehabilitation.

Think back for a moment to the exercise presented at the beginning of the chapter, on using only one arm in daily tasks. If you have tried it already, you might have discovered that you end up using your body in a variety of creative or unusual ways to compensate. Now imagine that your environment changes in a way that encourages, guides, or even necessitates specific, altered movements for you to complete those tasks. Understanding this shift in the body, as well as how to design this environment, would require, to name a few, knowledge of the lived experience, measurement of the kinematic movements, and design and construction of the dynamic space. This prompts the need for cross-disciplinary bounds in the development of these tools.

Interdisciplinary Design

The design of XR technologies in healthcare and neuroscience is an inherently interdisciplinary process, as it brings together, amongst others, clinical knowledge, technical design and computer science, and architectural and spatial design. Thus, it becomes crucial to develop a common language among clinicians, designers, and technologists: this entails not only a vocabulary but also an understanding of common goals, methodologies, and approaches.

Through such interdisciplinary projects, a language can begin to emerge that integrates seemingly disparate schools of thought toward new treatment paradigms. Ideas and provocations surrounding the spatial body within architecture and design can be applied in neuroscience to challenge treatment approaches, and use cases or treatment needs in healthcare can push the development of technological and design applications.

Ideas from other fields can be integrated to expand the bounds of what is possible within these healthcare applications, as this chapter has presented through ideas from computer science, psychology, philosophy, and interactive design. In our research group at University College London, working across the Bartlett School of Architecture and the Queen Square Institute of Neurology, we are researching and developing a new generation of neurorehabilitation XR, approaching questions of the body across disciplines. In the design of the XR environment, we are interested in possibilities for adaptive feedback which takes into account motivation, reward, sensory, and cognitive factors. We are interested in the embodiment possibilities that XR presents, as explored in this chapter, that may open the doors to treatment approaches not currently in place in clinical environments. The motivation and motor learning research within neuroscience can here be applied in radically new ways through the design of an XR environment which allows you to embody and manipulate the movement (and spatial placement and perception) of a virtual avatar.

Interdisciplinary work in this field, in turn, may lift the perceived "ceilings of recovery" in healthcare. What have been previously thought of as the limits of treatment outcomes may be pushed forward or even expelled through the integration of ideas from across disciplines.

References

Abtahi, P., Hough, S. Q., Landay, J. A., & Follmer, S. (2022). Beyond Being Real: A Sensorimotor Control Perspective on Interactions in Virtual Reality. In *CHI Conference on Human Factors in Computing Systems (CHI '22)*, April 29-May 5, 2022, New Orleans, LA, USA. ACM, New York, NY, USA, 17 pages. https://doi.org/10.1145/3491102.3517706

Artificial Nature. Retrieved from https://artificialnature.net/

Bahouth, Mona, N., Zink, Elizabeth, K., Ahmad, Omar, Roy, Promit, Zeiler, Steven R., Urrutia, Victor C., & Krakauer, John W. (2023). Bringing High-Dose Neurorestorative Behavioral Training into the Acute Stroke Unit. *American Journal of Physical Medicine & Rehabilitation*, 102(2S): S33–S37. https://doi.org/10.1097/PHM.0000000000002146

Bargeri, S., Scalea, S., Agosta, F., Banfi, G., Corbetta, D., Filippi, M., Sarasso, E., Turolla, A., Castellini, G., & Gioanola, S. (2023). Effectiveness and Safety of Virtual Reality Rehabilitation after Stroke: An Overview of Systematic Reviews. *eClinicalMedicine, The Lancet Discovery Science*, 64: 102220. https://doi.org/10.1016/j.eclinm.2023.102220

BeAnotherLab. (n.d.). The Machine to Be Another. BeAnotherLab. https://beanotherlab.org/home/work/tmtba/.

Behnke, E. (2011). *Husserl and Phenomenology*. Internet Encyclopedia of Philosophy. Retrieved from https://iep.utm.edu/husspemb/.

Cai, S., Li, G., Zhang, X., Huang, S., Zheng, H., Longhan, X. (2019). Detecting Compensatory Movements of Stroke Survivors using Pressure Distribution Data and Machine Learning Algorithms. *Journal of NeuroEngineering and Rehabilitation*, 16: 131. https://doi.org/10.1186/s12984-019-0609-6

Cardenas-Robledo, L. A., Hernández-Uribe, Ó., Reta, C., & Cantoral-Ceballos, J. A. (2022). Extended Reality Applications in Industry 4.0.-A Systematic Literature Review. *Telematics and Informatics*, 73, 101863

Cirstea, M. C., & Levin, M. F. (2000). Compensatory Strategies for Reaching in Stroke. *Brain*, 123(5): 940–953. https://doi.org/10.1093/brain/123.5.940.

Douglass-Kirk, P., Grierson, M., Ward, N. S., Brander, F., Kelly, K., Chegwidden, W., Shivji, D., & Stewart, L. (2022). Real-time auditory feedback may reduce abnormal movements in patients with chronic stroke. *Disability and Rehabilitation*, 45(4), 613–619. https://doi.org/10.1080/09638288.2022.2037751

Feigin, et al. (2022). WSO Global Stroke Fact Sheet. *International Journal of Stroke*, 17: 18–29.

Gonzalez-Franco M., & Peck T. C. (2018). Avatar Embodiment. Towards a Standardized Questionnaire. *Frontiers in Robotics and AI*, 5: 74. https://doi.org/10.3389/frobt.2018.00074

Goudman, L., Jansen, J., Billot, M., Vets, N., De Smedt, A., Roulaud, M., Rigoard, P., & Moens, M. (2022). Virtual Reality Applications in Chronic Pain Management: Systematic Review and Meta-analysis. *JMIR Serious Games*, 10(2): e34402. https://doi.org/10.2196/34402

Hadjipanayi, C., Banakou, D., & Michael-Grigoriou, D. (2023). Art as Therapy in Virtual Reality: A Scoping Review. *Frontiers in Virtual Reality*, 4: 1065863. https://doi.org/10.3389/frvir.2023.1065863

Hao, J., Xie, H., Harp, K., Chen, Z., & Siu, K. C. (2022). Effects of Virtual Reality Intervention on Neural Plasticity in Stroke Rehabilitation: A Systematic Review. *Archives of Physical Medicine and Rehabilitation*, 103(3): 523–541. https://doi.org/10.1016/j.apmr.2021.06.024

Kirkevold, M., Kildal Bragstad, L., Bronken, B. A., Kvigne, K., Martinsen, R., Gabrielsen Hjelle, E., Kitzmüller, G., Mangset, M., Angel, S., Aadal, L., Eriksen, S., Wyller, T. B., & Sveen, U. (2018). Promoting Psychosocial Well-Being Following Stroke: Study Protocol for a Randomized, Controlled Trial. *BMC Psychology*, 6(1): 12. https://doi.org/10.1186/s40359-018-0223-6

Krakauer, J. W., Kitago, T., Goldsmith, J., Ahmad, O., Roy, P., Stein, J., Bishop, L., Casey, K., Valladares, B., Harran, M., Camilo Cortés, J., Forrence, A., Xu, J., DeLuzio, S., Held, J., Schwarz, A., Steiner, L., Widmer, M., Jordan, K., Ludwig, D., Moore, M., Barbera, M., Vora, I., Stockley, R., Celnik, P., Zeiler, S., Branscheidt, M., Kwakkel, G., Luft, A. (2021). Comparing a Novel Neuroanimation Experience to Conventional Therapy for High-Dose Intensive Upper-Limb Training in Subacute Stroke: The SMARTS2 Randomized Trial. *Neurorehabilitation and Neural Repair*, 35(5): 393–405. https://doi.org/10.1177/15459683211000730

Livingston-Thomas, J., Nelson, P., Karthikeyan, S., Antonescu, S., Jeffers, M. S., Marzolini, S., & Corbett, D. (2016). Exercise and Environmental Enrichment as Enablers of Task-Specific Neuroplasticity and Stroke Recovery. *Neurotherapeutics*, 13: 395–402. https://link.springer.com/content/pdf/10.1007/s13311-016-0423-9.pdf?pdf=button sticky

Marín-Morales, J., Higuera-Trujillo, J. L., Guixeres, J., Llinares, C., Alcañiz, M., & Valenza, G. (2021). Heart Rate Variability Analysis for the Assessment of Immersive Emotional Arousal using Virtual Reality: Comparing Real and Virtual Scenarios. *PloS one,* 16(7): e0254098. https://doi.org/10.1371/journal.pone.0254098.

McDonald, M. W., Hayward, K. S., Rosbergen, I. C. M., Jeffers, M. S., & Corbett, D. (2018). Is Environmental Enrichment Ready for Clinical Application in Human Post-stroke Rehabilitation? *Frontiers in Behavioral Neuroscience*, 12. https://doi.org/10.3389/fnbeh.2018.00135

Praetorius, A. S., & Görlich, D. (2021). The Proteus Effect: How Avatars Influence Their Users' Self-perception and Behavior. In: Tom Dieck, M. C., Jung, T. H., Loureiro, S. M. C. (eds), *Augmented Reality and Virtual Reality*. Progress in IS. Springer, Cham. https://doi.org/10.1007/978-3-030-68086-2_9.

Slater, M., Pérez Marcos, D., Ehrsson, H., & Sanchez-Vives, M. V. (2009). Inducing Illusory Ownership of a Virtual Body. *Frontiers in Neuroscience*, 3(2): 214–220. https://doi.org/10.3389/neuro.01.029.2009

Stroke Association. (n.d.). *What is Stroke?* Retrieved from https://www.stroke.org.uk/what-is-stroke

Ramachandran, V. S., & Hirstein, W. (1998). The Perception of Phantom Limbs. The D. O. Hebb Lecture. *Brain: A Journal of Neurology*, 121(Pt 9): 1603–1630. https://doi.org/10.1093/brain/121.9.1603

Rojo, A., Santos-Paz, J. Á., Sánchez-Picot, Á., Raya, R., & García-Carmona, R. (2022). FarmDay: A Gamified Virtual Reality Neurorehabilitation Application for Upper Limb Based on Activities of Daily Living. *Applied Sciences*, 12(14): 7068. MDPI AG. Retrieved from http://dx.doi.org/10.3390/app12147068

Ward, N. S., Brander, F., & Kelly, K. (2019). Intensive upper limb neurorehabilitation in chronic stroke: outcomes from the Queen Square programme. *Journal of Neurology, Neurosurgery, and Psychiatry*, 90(5), 498–506. https://doi.org/10.1136/jnnp-2018-319954

Watanabe, R., & Higuchi T. (2016). Behavioral Advantages of the First-Person Perspective Model for Imitation. *Frontiers in Psychology*, 7, 701. https://doi.org/10.3389/fpsyg.2016.00701

Yee, N., Bailenson, J. N., & Ducheneaut, N. (2009). The Proteus Effect: Implications of Transformed Digital Self-Representation on Online and Offline Behavior. *Communication Research*, 36(2): 285–312. https://doi.org/10.1177/0093650208330254

2.9
SMART DESIGN FOR HUMAN RESPONSIVENESS AND MOVEMENT

2.9.1

PROPORTIONED AND SMART ARCHITECTURE

Tiziana Proietti and Sergei Gepshtein

Abstract

Recent emphasis on technology and science in the design of the built environment has been perceived as a challenge to the humanistic tradition in architecture. The concern is that scientific approaches, often fragmented and abstract, may overshadow the humanistic ideals of architecture. We examine this issue in light of the evolving interface between architectural design and the scientific disciplines of cognitive science and neuroscience. We ask how the humanistic concern can be addressed by means of 'smart' designs capable of adapting to human needs. The capacity for adaptation can only be attained through systematic and wide-ranging empirical studies of human perception, behavior, and affect, in individuals and groups. We illustrate this empirical approach with studies of *architectural proportion* and its impact on design and experience. By investigating human perception of proportioned objects, this work has presented an opportunity to discover user *diversity*, shifting the focus of research from the prior pursuit of ideal proportions by ideal agents to the question of how specific proportions are perceived by individuals with different needs and abilities.

Introduction

The humanistic tradition in architectural design places human flourishing above the artistic expression of the designer. This tradition draws inspiration from visions of harmony and balance that are akin to proportions of the human body: a product of nature and a traditional symbol of perfection. With such ideas in mind, humanistic architects of the fifteenth and sixteenth centuries sought to create a connection between the person and the universe. This tradition has continued to influence architects over the centuries: from the Renaissance of Cesariano, di Giorgio, and da Vinci to the Modernism of Le Corbusier, Neufert, and Blomstedt.

In recent decades, the growing emphasis on technology and science in architectural design has often been seen as a challenge to the humanistic tradition. This is partly because the sciences pertinent to understanding human experience (such as neuroscience

DOI: 10.4324/9781003384113-37

and cognitive science) offer descriptions of experience that are fragmented and abstract. Concerned with parts of the human body and segments of behavior, the scientific stance is feared to divert the architect from the unity of experience. Additionally, some critics express worry that integrating scientific principles into architectural design may overshadow the humanistic ideals of harmony and beauty and thus hinder the artistic creativity of the designer.

A careful review of these concerns suggests that the suspicion of the scientific attitude in architectural design has been fueled by early and premature applications of this attitude. There is hope that the rapidly evolving interface of science and architecture will facilitate designs that are "smart" in the sense of being adaptable to human needs. This adaptability can be achieved at different stages of design: using tools informed by empirical study of human perception and behavior during conception of design, and through flexible real-time interaction between individuals and their environment during use. In both cases, advancing smart design requires systematic empirical investigation of how individuals interact with and respond to their environment, using a broad spectrum of scientific methods that include physiological, behavioral, and computational.

To illustrate this approach, we turn our attention to the hatching transformation of a traditional theme of research in humanistic architecture: the theme of architectural proportion and its role in the design and experience of the built environment.

The Scientific Turn in the Study of Proportion

The theme of architectural proportion was central to design theory until its role was questioned in the mid-twentieth century (Cimoli and Irace, 2007, 2013; Delbeke and Cohen, 2018; Wittkower, 1960; Zevi, 1957). Among the reasons for this change, one stands out as crucial. It is the persistent lack of clarity about how the proportional structure of the built environment affects human perception. Throughout their long history, concepts of architectural proportion have been primarily examined without attending to the basic fact that the observer's perceptual capacities are limited and that the observer moves. These neglects have distracted designers from fundamental questions about the role of architectural proportion. Do observers experience proportions as the designer intended? Does this experience depend on the movement of the observer, or the observer directing the gaze to particular parts of the environment? One could argue that prior generations of designers were unable to answer such questions because they lacked suitable investigative methodologies. Only today can we begin addressing such questions thanks to advances in the sciences of perception and behavior.

The matter of experience of proportion is complicated by the tradition of understanding it two-dimensionally, by compressing representations of three-dimensional (3D) objects to a plane. Indeed, perspective drawings of architectural objects dislodge the observer from the normally dynamic experience of the environment. This method of representation assumes that the observer's eye aligns with the idealized eye of a stationary observer (Panofsky, 1991; Wittkower, 1953; Belting, 2011; Kubovy, 1986; Pirenne, 1970). Then, such drawings are routinely annotated using regulating lines and other geometric constructions imposed upon building plans and elevations: inherently two-dimensional entities that leave no room for integrating the observer's motility into the representation of the environment. These are just some of the representation tools that rely on an implicitly stationary model of the observer: a *canonical spectator*.

This tradition of canonical spectator has left a lasting mark on modern architecture. Its influence persists in contemporary design in spite of voices of descent. For example, at the symposium *De Divina Proportione* in Milan in 1951, the renowned architectural historian Sigfried Giedion noted that, at the beginning of the Modern Era,

> the critical issue was to identify a modern – i.e., dynamic – proportion that no longer defined the man of Leonardo but that of Le Corbusier, in motion, now standing, now sitting, now resting on the balconies of the Unité de Marseille.
>
> *(Cimoli and Irace, 2013: 10)*

Similarly, Carlo Fontana contended, at the same symposium, that "the divine proportion eluded the realm of modern and future architecture" (Cimoli and Irace, 2007: 212).

Still, architectural discourse has had difficulty moving beyond the idealization of the canonical spectator. One example of this arrested development is Le Corbusier's proportional system *Le Modulor*, built after the idealized static observer of a standard size occupying spaces with preconceived body stances and postures. *Le Modulor* failed to respond to variations in a person's height, other gender differences, and variations among the naturally broad diversity of the user.

It appears that a significant change is overdue: generally, in architectural representation, and more specifically, in the theory of architectural proportion. The change should be founded on the understanding that architecture is experienced from a mobile point of view, and by a person who is imperfect in many ways rather than singularly idealized by a one-size-fits-all canon. In the following, we look into how the scientific method can be engaged to bring this vision to reality, in empirical studies of observers moving in the 3D space, and while considering the numerous limitations of observer perception and movement.

The Emerging Empirical Platform

As we noted, architectural proportion has been regarded as an important factor in the clarity and readability of a building's design since antiquity, described today in terms of the "legibility" or "intelligibility" of buildings. Here, we consider one manner of turning the focus of attention away from the study of these factors in an abstract, two-dimensional rendering of the built environment, and embark on a new style of investigation informed by empirical sciences.

In this new framework, human beings are dynamic agents who move freely in the 3D space, rather than static spectators viewing two-dimensional drawings. What is more, real users of architecture are imperfect and have limited powers of perception and motility. Different users have different imperfections, including users living with disabilities and restrictions that fall into clinically distinct categories. Investigating architectural proportion through the lens of user *diversity* can help shift the focus of research from the question of ideal proportion to the question of how proportion is perceived by individuals with different perceptual and active needs.

Several areas of empirical research on human perception and behavior developed methods of research germane to our goal of understanding how the moving person is affected by the proportional structure of the environment. Here, we briefly review three such areas: perceptual constancy, cue combination, and perceptual organization.

Perceptual Constancy

Perceptual constancy is a classical and well-established theme in studies of perception:

> A very central fact about perception is the all-pervasive tendency toward constancy of object properties despite variation of or difference between the proximal stimuli. By 'proximal stimulus' is meant the stimulus that impinges upon the sense organ rather than the distal stimulus, the external object or event.
>
> *(Rock, 1983: 24)*

In visual perception, as we move relative to objects, their optical projections to the eye (proximal stimuli) undergo continuous change. Perceptual constancy is achieved when the experience of a property of an object does not change in spite of the change of the proximal stimulus. In other words, perceptual constancy refers to the ability to see objects as consistent and stable, even when their appearance changes because of the changing viewpoint or the varying lighting conditions.

Numerous studies of visual perception looked for conditions under which perceptual constancy was achieved or not (the latter case being called the "failure of constancy"). A question critical to our inquiry is the constancy of object shape (Epstein and Park, 1963; Howard, 2012; Perdreau and Cavanagh, 2013). When shape constancy fails, the person may perceive that the same object has different proportions under different viewing conditions, such as when the object is regarded from different locations or under different directions of gaze.

The researcher of architectural proportion will ask where in a specific built environment the proportion of a certain architectonic detail is perceived veridically. Where perceptual constancy fails, the researcher will ask what the apparent proportion is and how it differs from the intended proportion.

It is useful to think of answering these questions in terms of spatial mapping. Considering a specific part of the built environment, one can measure the perceived proportion of the part at multiple locations, and then interpolate the results of the measurement across locations. This way one will obtain a map of perceived proportions. When the proportion of interest is perceived veridically at some locations and nonveridically at other locations, this procedure will reveal specific boundaries of experience: between regions of differently perceived proportions (as suggested by Gepshtein, 2020, and Proietti and Gepshtein, 2022b). These boundaries will be more subtle than *isovist* boundaries (Benedikt and McElhinney, 2019) but not less important for understanding architectural experience.

The next challenge faced by this line of research will be that of generalization. For example, using a rigorous model of shape constancy, the researcher will be able to make testable predictions of the noted boundaries of experience for any detail of interest, in every environment.

To illustrate, consider a colonnade of rectangular pillars whose facets have different proportions. Imagine a person walking by the colonnade and stopping at certain locations that afford different views of the pillars. Even when individual faces of these pillars may appear to have different proportions (due to perspective distortion), the person may recognize the pillars as having the same proportion (Figure 2.9.1.1A) because of perceptual constancy. Perceptual constancy may fail, however, under certain strong distortions of surface shape, as in Figures 2.9.1.1B and 1C, where a tall building is viewed from a close distance.

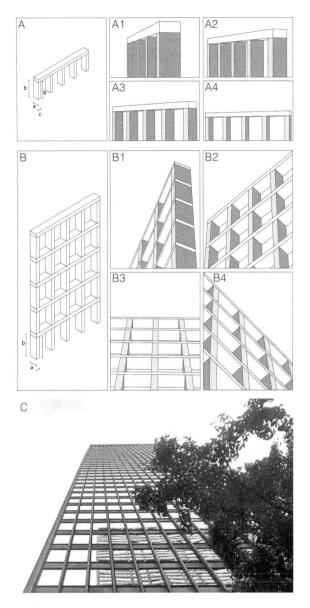

Figure 2.9.1.1 Perceptual constancy.

A. A series of rectangular pillars in a colonnade have the same proportions. Despite their perspectival distortion, illustrated in panels A1–A4, an observer may recognize the pillars as having the same proportions (having achieved perceptual constancy).

B. In a tall building, whose façade is organized into a grid of pillars and beams, the observer may not recognize the pillars as having the same proportions (failure of perceptual constancy) when the building is viewed from a close distance, illustrated in panels B1–B4.

C. Mies van der Rohe, Seagram building, New York, 1958.

(Image: Courtesy of the authors, Tiziana Proietti and Sergei Gepshtein)

As noted, the researcher of architectural proportion will want to study the conditions separating veridical versus non-veridical perception. The distance from the building in our preceding example, at which perceptual constancy may fail, is one example of such conditions.

Cue Combination

Whether perceptual constancy is achieved depends on how perceptual systems combine information about object properties. In visual perception, such properties are called visual *cues*. One set of cues that plays a crucial role in our ability to perceive the 3D layout of visual scenes is called "depth cues." Depth cues help us understand the shape of objects and their positions relative to each other. Examples of depth cues include binocular disparity (which is the difference in left and right retinal images of the scene, and which is salient at short viewing distances), motion parallax (the difference in the apparent speeds of objects positioned at different distances from the person), and texture gradient (the apparent difference in the density of optical elements on surfaces positioned at different distances from the person).

Modern theories of cue combination describe the results of combination as a weighted sum of cues (Maloney and Landy, 1989; Landy et al., 1995; Ernst and Bülthoff, 2004). The more reliable a cue, the greater its contribution to perceptual experience. For example, the perceived slant of a surface may depend more on binocular disparity than surface texture when the surface is close to the person. This is because the information provided by binocular disparity is more reliable (more precise) than the information provided by texture (e.g., Hillis et al., 2004).

Preceding examples of cue combination concern the interaction of cues "within senses," which is within a single sensory modality, and "between senses," which is between sensory modalities, such as vision and touch or vision and audition (Rock and Victor, 1964). For example, Gepshtein and Banks (2003) studied how vision and haptics control the perceived object size. At different viewing angles, the perceived size depended more on vision or haptics, because the reliability of either cue depended on the viewing angle. A very similar interaction was found in the (ventriloquist) combination of visual and auditory cues (Alais and Burr, 2004). In these and many other cases, cue combination is governed by the model of the weighted sum of cues described just above (Ernst and Bülthoff, 2004; Gepshtein et al., 2005; Alais et al., 2010).

This literature is poised to explain why the combination of sensory cues arising from the same architectonic detail can yield rather different experiences under a slight change in the condition of observation. Such phenomena may appear counterintuitive before they are submitted to the analysis described above. Empirical studies mentioned in the preceding paragraph suggest that such interactions between cues are lawful and therefore predictable.

The researcher of proportion conversant with methods of psychophysical measurement and modeling may ask, for example, how the perceived proportion of an architectonic detail depends on the viewing distance and the angle of observation. This is the case of cue combination within the senses. For another example of cue combination within senses, consider the perception of a gate that contains two rectangular pillars of the same proportion (Figure 2.9.1.2A). The perceived proportions of these pillars may depend on whether or not the pillars have the same texture or color, illustrated in Figures 2.9.1.2A–B. Considering inter-sensory interactions, one may ask how the perceived proportion of a large

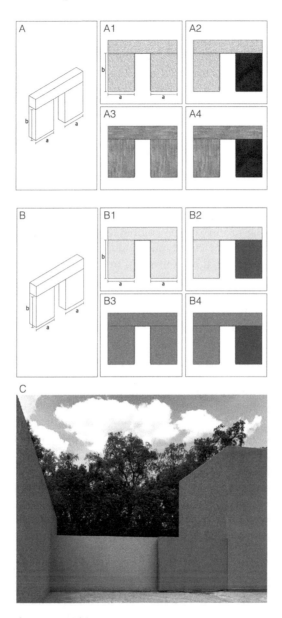

Figure 2.9.1.2 Cue combination within senses.

A-B. Two rectangular pillars of a gate have the same proportions, which may appear to be different from one another if they have different textures or are made of different materials. Darker surfaces may appear to be smaller than brighter surfaces (A1 vs. A2 and A3 vs. A4). Will a change of the apparent size of one of the pillars lead to a change in its apparent proportion? The same question applies to panels B1 vs. B2, and B3 vs. B4, where the surfaces differ by color rather than texture.

C. Luis Barragan, Casa Gilardi, Mexico City, 1948.

(The figure is rendered in color in the online edition of this chapter.)

(Image: Courtesy of the authors, Tiziana Proietti and Sergei Gepshtein)

hall depends on the amount and the manner of illumination, on one hand, and the acoustic properties of the hall, on the other hand.

The researcher of architectural proportion will appreciate the degree to which the perceived proportions of 3D objects are susceptible to influences of other sensory cues within and between senses. We imagine that future work in this arena may separately address the intrinsic properties of objects (such as their color, texture, or other material properties) and their extrinsic properties (such as the amount of illumination and the context of observation).

Perceptual Organization

Perceptual organization is another fundamental manner of integrating parts of the scene by perceptual systems. Perceptual organization is sometimes described as "weak fusion," in contrast to the "strong fusion" of cue combination (e.g., Clark & Yuille, 1990). This is because in cue combination, the cues typically do not correspond to perceptually distinct parts of the object. In perceptual organization, in contrast, the parts can be perceptually distinct, within the larger whole of the object.

Modern literature on perceptual organization evolved from Gestalt psychology of the early twentieth century (surveyed in Kubovy and Pomerantz, 1981; Gepshtein, 2010; Wagemans et al., 2012a). Traditionally, phenomena of perceptual organization have been divided into two large classes. In one class, called *perceptual grouping*, certain regions of the scene are perceived as connected or "belonging together" (Koffka, 1935; Kubovy and Gepshtein, 2003), just as tree branches are perceived as parts of a larger entity without losing their distinct identities. The whole and its parts generally have different geometric properties, even as they affect one another, in a process called perceptual assimilation (Kanizsa, 1979).

In the other class of phenomena of perceptual organization, called *figure-ground segmentation*, some parts of the scene appear as an articulated figure that stands in front of the less articulated ground. Parts of the ground "fill in" behind the figure, creating the continuous ground (Kanizsa, 1979; Wagemans et al., 2012a). Both kinds of perceptual organization can be ambiguous (prone to perceptual reversals) as the case is when the same objects appear to reorganize and form different groups (Kubovy, 1994), or when the space between objects appears to make the figure and the objects form the ground (Kanizsa and Gerbino, 1976).

A large body of empirical studies uncovered the factors that control perceptual grouping and figure-ground segmentation: the "principles" of perceptual organization (Wagemans et al., 2012a). Where early Gestalt studies were descriptive and qualitative, much of the work conducted over the last four decades (dubbed "neo-Gestalt") has been mathematically tractable and susceptible to predictive modeling (Gepshtein et al., 2008; Wagemans et al., 2012b). Still, this work was conducted in highly abstract laboratory conditions, using two-dimensional stimuli in studies of visual organization.

A promising line of future studies is suggested by the encounter of this literature with the myriad questions arising in architectural design. Research methods and models developed in the laboratory are ripe for application "in the field," pursuing an agenda some of which has been anticipated by Arnheim's groundbreaking review of 1977, but respecting both the experimental tradition of Gestalt psychology and the more recent (and just mentioned) neo-Gestalt tradition of computational modeling of empirical phenomena.

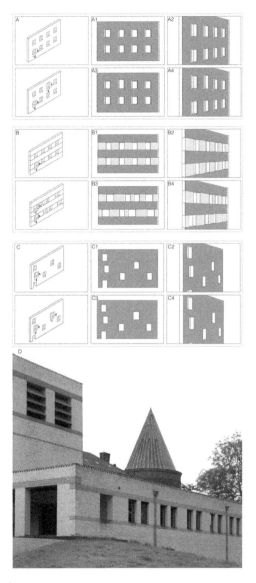

Figure 2.9.1.3 Perceptual organization.

A. At the top, identical windows are aligned vertically and horizontally. At the bottom, one of the windows has a distinct height.

B. At the top, identical windows are separated by string courses and are spaced evenly. At the bottom, windows are spaced unevenly, and one of the windows has a distinct width.

C. At the top, identical windows are spaced unevenly in both vertical and horizontal directions. At the bottom, one of these windows has a distinct width and height. Different perceptual organization of the windows may cause their proportions to be perceived differently in every case.

D. Hans van der Laan, St. Benedictusber Abbey, Vaals, Netherlands, 1956–1986.

(Image: Courtesy of the authors, Tiziana Proietti and Sergei Gepshtein)

To the researcher of architectural proportion, this work will give the power to understand the conditions in which an architectonic object is perceived, or fails to be perceived, as a part of a larger group (an ensemble) and how the perceived proportion of the object in question depends on the proportional properties of the group. Similarly, by investigating the conditions in which an architectonic object is perceived as a figure, or as a part of the ground, the researcher will be able to infer, for example, whether it is the proportion of that object, or the proportion of the "negative" space between that and other objects, that the observer will likely perceive in a given environment.

For an example of perceptual grouping, consider the perception of windows in a façade illustrated in Figure 2.9.1.3. The windows will be perceived differently under their different arrangements with respect to one another. The windows may be aligned vertically and horizontally, as in Figure 2.9.1.3A; they may be separated by string courses and aligned horizontally, as in Figure 2.9.1.3B; or they may be misaligned in both directions, as in Figure 2.9.1.3C.

Laboratory studies of perceptual organization found that grouped items appear to be more similar to one another than ungrouped ones. This is a case of perceptual assimilation mentioned earlier in the present section (also see King, 1988). Conversely, the mutual similarity of items determines how likely they appear to be grouped together (in a process termed "grouping by similarity;" e.g., Kubovy and Van Den Berg, 2008).

Accordingly, in Figure 2.9.1.3A, the windows are perceived as members of the same perceptual group because of their vertical and horizontal alignment, making the windows appear more similar to one another than they would be otherwise, thanks to perceptual assimilation. Conversely, the windows in Figure 2.9.1.3C are misaligned; the prospect of their perception as a group will depend on their similarity.

One could readily imagine other scenarios of perceptual organization of windows with different proportions, in which perception of proportion could be enhanced or weakened by the presence of decorations, such as moldings. Because of moldings, windows may appear more or less similar to one another, and thus more or less likely to form perceptual groups.

New Proportional Thinking

The just-discussed concepts and methods of empirical science can help to answer some of the questions about the perception of architectural proportion. For example, under what conditions perception of proportion is preserved, thus attaining perceptual constancy? How do other properties of objects affect the perception of their proportions? When objects are perceived as parts of a larger group, how do the perceived proportional properties of the group affect the perceived proportions of individual objects? Notice that these questions address characteristics of both the built environment and the observer.

Using the empirical approach, we can redefine the role of proportion in architecture and introduce a new style of investigation, which we call *new proportional thinking* that is both "smart" and "humanistic." It is smart in that it adapts to the reality of how humans perceive and respond to properties of the built environment. It is humanistic in that it acknowledges that architecture is experienced by diverse individuals with different capabilities for movement, differently shaped bodies, distinct cultural backgrounds, and prior experiences.

As an illustration of how questions of the perceptibility of architectural proportion can be addressed using scientific investigation, we briefly describe an ongoing study of the perception of architectural proportion (Proietti and Gepshtein, 2022a). In this study, we ask how the observer's ability to discriminate between proportions of objects depends on the viewing conditions. We address this question using methods of sensory psychophysics (Gescheider, 2013; Kingdom and Prins, 2016). In contrast to prior psychophysical studies of proportion conducted with two-dimensional shapes presented on computer screens, we perform our experiments using 3D physical objects and custom-designed observation devices.

In this study, the observer is immersed in the physical space that contains the stimuli. The space is a room designed for presenting proportioned objects at the human scale (see Figure 2.9.1.4A–B). The stimuli used for this experiment are 3D objects, each supported by a central pole that permits object rotation. The objects are parallelepipeds with known proportions selected from the morphotheek: a carefully calibrated set of proportioned objects that implement the plastic number system developed by the Dutch architect Hans van der Laan (Van der Laan, 1977; Padovan, 1999; Proietti, 2015, 2021).

The space of observation is a room painted black. A nine-by-nine square grid is placed on the floor to control the location of the pieces and the observer. During the experiment, the room is dark except for the light emitted by a 3D mapping projector used to illuminate the facets that serve as stimuli. Throughout the experiment, the observer remains stationary or moves from one location to another according to the experimenter's script. The experiment consists of a sequence of stereotypical "trials." Within a trial, the stimulus (two facets of one or two objects) is briefly presented at predetermined locations and orientations, allowing the researcher to measure the perceptibility of differences between proportions under a wide range of conditions: concerning the observer and between objects (Figure 2.9.1.4C). Observers use a standard numerical keypad to report their judgments on a six-point rating scale. Responses ranging from 1 to 3 signify "left is larger," while responses from 4 to 6 signify "right is larger." Within each of these two response groups, three distinct categories allow observers to express their confidence.

Experimental conditions studied in this setup represent various scenarios encountered in the built environment (Figure 2.9.1.4D). These include arrangements of pairs of 3D objects (such as a pair of pillars), a 3D object standing freely in space a two-dimensional object attached to a wall (such as a pillar and a window), and two two-dimensional objects (such as two windows). Similar experimental arrangements can be used to study the perception of objects of different scales, including furnishing and ornamental elements of a room (in the interest of interior design), or structural and decorative elements of a building (in the interest of architectural design).

These studies will help to reveal how architectural space is organized in terms of where its proportional properties can or cannot be perceived, or in terms of how space is divided into regions affected by differently proportioned parts of the environment (Proietti and Gepshtein, 2022b).

Conclusions: Smart Design in Humanistic Architecture

We have noted that smart design is the one that adapts to the reality of how humans perceive and respond to properties of the built environment. As an illustration of this vision, we studied the case of the experience of proportional properties of the environment. We argued that is useful to replace the idea of the stationary observer with the more realistic idea of a dynamic observer. To this end, it is important to understand how mobile viewers perceive proportions. We have argued that there are scientific tools readily suitable to elucidate

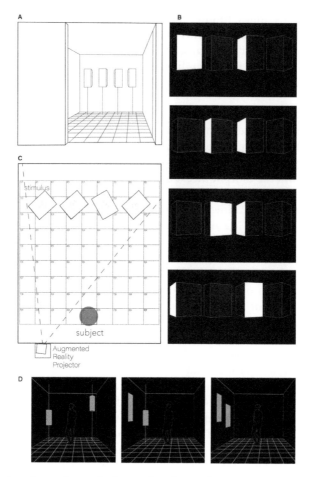

Figure 2.9.1.4   Design of experiment for immersive observation.

A.   Perspective view of the experimental room with the stimuli erected on supporting poles.

B.   Photographs of several stimuli. In each photograph, two facets of two different 3D objects are illuminated using projection mapping. (The wireframe rendering of the objects is shown here for clarity; only the illuminated facets were visible to the subject.)

C.   Floor plan of the room showing the stimulus blocks, the projector, the subject, and the nine-by-nine grid built into the floor to mark stimulus and subject locations.

D.   Experimental conditions simulating different arrangements of architectural elements encountered in the built environment.

(Image: Courtesy of the authors, Tiziana Proietti and Sergei Gepshtein)

this matter. We have presented some of the ideas elaborated in the scientific literature that can assist in developing the desired deeper understanding of the perception of proportions of the built environment. These ideas include perceptual constancy, sensory cue combination, and perceptual organization. And we have described an ongoing empirical study of the perception of 3D proportioned objects.

The larger program of research suggested by this line of reasoning is an example of how scientific methodology can be applied to answer architectural questions, in the broader context of converging science and design (Eberhard, 2009; Mallgrave, 2010; Robinson and Pallasmaa, 2015; Gepshtein and Snider, 2019; Albright et al., 2020). Here, the goal of the program is to reevaluate, and perhaps restore, the role of proportion in architectural practice and pedagogy on a new empirical ground. The *new proportional thinking* advocated in this essay is meant to inspire the designer to turn away from learning about proportions by scrutinizing two-dimensional drawings. Instead, the designer may elect to study how the flesh-and-blood human being responds to proportioned objects in the 3D space open to movement.

References

Albright, T., S. Gepshtein, and E. Macagno. (2020). "Visual neuroscience for architecture." *Architectural Design* 90, no. 6: 110–117.

Alais, D., and D. Burr. (2004). "The ventriloquist effect results from near-optimal bimodal integration." *Current Biology* 14, no. 3: 257–262.

Alais, D., F. Newell, and P. Mamassian. (2010). "Multisensory processing in review: From physiology to behaviour." *Seeing and Perceiving* 23, no. 1: 3–38.

Belting, H. (2011). *Florence and Baghdad, Renaissance Art and Arab Science*. Cambridge: Harvard University Press.

Benedikt, M., and S. Mcelhinney. (2019). "Isovists and the metrics of architectural space." In *Paper Presented at the 107th ACSA Annual Meeting. Articulating Architecture's core in the Post Digital Era*, Pittsburg, March 1–10.

Cimoli, A., and F. Irace. (2007). *La Divina Proporzione. Triennale 1951*. Milan: Mondadori Electa.

Cimoli, A., and F. Irace. (2013). "Triennial 1951: Post-War reconstruction and divine proportion." *Nexus Network Journal* 15, no. 1: 3–14.

Clark, J. J., and A. L. Yuille, 1990. *Data Fusion for Sensory Information Processing Systems*. New York: Springer Science & Business Media.

Delbeke, M., and M. Cohen. (2018). *Proportional Systems in the History of Architecture: A Critical Reconsideration*. Leiden: Leiden University Press.

Eberhard, J. P. (2009). *Brain Landscape: The Coexistence of Neuroscience and Architecture*. Oxford: Oxford University Press.

Epstein, W., and J. N. Park. (1963). "Shape constancy: Functional relationships and theoretical formulations." *Psychological Bulletin* 60, no. 3: 265.

Ernst, M. O., and H. H. Bülthoff. (2004). "Merging the senses into a robust percept." *Trends in Cognitive Sciences* 8, no. 4: 162–169.

Gepshtein, S. (2010). "Two psychologies of perception and the prospect of their synthesis." *Philosophical Psychology* 23, no. 2: 217–281.

Gepshtein, S. (2020). "Species of space." *Architectural Design* 90, no. 6: 36–41.

Gepshtein, S., and M. S. Banks. (2003). "Viewing geometry determines how vision and haptics combine in size perception." *Current Biology* 13, no. 6: 483–488.

Gepshtein, S., J. Burge, M. O. Ernst, and M. S. Banks. (2005). "The combination of vision and touch depends on spatial proximity." *Journal of Vision* 5, no. 11–7: 1013–1023.

Gepshtein, S., J. H. Elder, and L. T. Maloney. (2008). "Perceptual organization and neural computation." *Journal of Vision* 8, no. 7: 1–4.

Gepshtein, S., and J. Snider. (2019). "Neuroscience for architecture: The evolving science of perceptual meaning." *Proceedings of the National Academy of Sciences USA* 116, no. 29: 14404–14406.

Gescheider, G. A. (2013). *Psychophysics: The Fundamentals*. London: Psychology Press.

Hillis, J. M., S. J. Watt, M. S. Landy, and M. Banks. (2004). "Slant from texture and disparity cues: Optimal cue combination." *Journal of Vision* 4, no. 12: 1–1.

Howard, I. P. (2012). *Perceiving in Depth, Volume 1: Basic Mechanisms*. Oxford: Oxford University Press.

Kanizsa, G. (1979). *Organization in Vision: Essays on Gestalt Perception*. Westport, CT: Praeger Publishers.

Kanizsa, G., and W. Gerbino. (1976). Convexity and symmetry in figure-ground organization. In *Art and Artefacts*. Edited by Henle M., 25–32. New York: Springer.

King, D. L. (1988). "Assimilation is due to one perceived whole and contrast is due to two perceived wholes." *New Ideas in Psychology* 6, no. 3: 277–288.

Kingdom, F. A. A., and N. Prins. (2016). *Psychophysics. A Practical Introduction*. London: Elsevier.

Koffka, K. (1935). *Principles of Gestalt Psychology*. New York: Harcourt, Brace, & World.

Kubovy, M. (1986). *The Psychology of Perspective and Renaissance art*. Cambridge: Cambridge University Press.

Kubovy, M. (1994). "The perceptual organization of dot lattices." *Psychonomic Bulletin & Review* 1, no. 2: 182–190.

Kubovy, M., and S. Gepshtein. (2003). Perceptual grouping in space and in space-time: An exercise in phenomenological psychophysics. In *Perceptual Organization in Vision: Behavioral and Neural Perspectives*, Edited by Kimchi, Ruth, Marlene Behrmann, and Carl R. Olson, 45–85. Mahwah, NJ: Lawrence Erlbaum Associates Publishers.

Kubovy, M., and J. R. Pomerantz, eds. (1981). *Perceptual Organization*. Hillsdale, NJ: Erlbaum.

Kubovy, M., and M. Van Den Berg. (2008). "The whole is equal to the sum of its parts: A probabilistic model of grouping by proximity and similarity in regular patterns." *Psychological Review* 115, no. 1: 131–154.

Landy, M. S., L. T. Maloney, E. B. Johnston, and M. Young. (1995). "Measurement and modeling of depth cue combination: In defense of weak fusion." *Vision Research* 35, no. 3: 389–412.

Mallgrave, H. F. (2010). *The Architect's Brain: Neuroscience, Creativity, and Architecture*. New York: John Wiley & Sons.

Maloney, L. T., and M. S. Landy. (1989). A statistical framework for robust fusion of depth information. In *Visual Communications and Image Processing IV*. Vol. 1199, 1154–1163. Philadelphia: Society of Photo-Optical Instrumentation Engineers (SPIE).

Padovan, R. (1999). *Proportion. Science, Philosophy, Architecture*. London and New York: Taylor & Francis Routledge.

Panofsky, E. (1991). *Perspective as Symbolic Form (1927)*. New York: Zone Books.

Perdreau, F., and P. Cavanagh. (2013). "Is artists' perception more veridical?." *Frontiers in Neuroscience* 7: 6.

Pirenne, M. H. (1970). *Optics, Painting & Photography*. Cambridge: Cambridge University Press.

Proietti, T. (2015). *Ordine e Proporzione. Dom Hans van der Laan e L'espressività Dello Spazio Architettonico*. Macerata: Quodlibet.

Proietti, T. (2021). "Revisiting the plastic number theory from the perspective of perceptual psychology." *Architectural Science Review* 64, no. 4: 346–358.

Proietti, T., and S. Gepshtein. (2022a). "Architectural proportion from an empirical standpoint." *Journal of Interior Design* 47, no. 1: 11–29.

Proietti, T., and S. Gepshtein. (2022b). Locating architectural atmosphere. In *Generators of Architectural Atmospheres*, Edited by Canepa Elisabetta, 95–110. Kansas State University Library: New Prairie Press.

Robinson, S., and J. Pallasmaa, eds. (2015). *Mind in Architecture: Neuroscience, Embodiment, and the Future of Design*. Cambridge: MIT Press.

Rock, I. (1983). *The Logic of Perception*. Cambridge, MA: The MIT Press.

Rock, I., and J. Victor. (1964). "Vision and touch: An experimentally created conflict between the two senses." *Science* 143, no. 3606: 594–596.

Van der Laan, H. (1977). *The Architectonic Space. Fifteenth Lessons on the Human Habitat*. Leiden: Brill.

Wagemans, J., J. H. Elder, M. Kubovy, S. E. Palmer, Maary A. Peterson, M. Singh, and R. von der Heydt. (2012a). "A century of Gestalt psychology in visual perception: I. Perceptual grouping and figure–ground organization." *Psychological bulletin* 138, no. 6: 1172.

Wagemans, J., J. H. Elder, M. Kubovy, S. E. Palmer, M. A. Peterson, M. Singh, and R. von der Heydt. (2012b). "A century of Gestalt psychology in visual perception: II. Conceptual and theoretical foundations." *Psychological Bulletin* 138, no. 6: 1218.

Wittkower, R. (1953). "Brunelleschi and proportion in perspective." *Journal of the Warburg and Courtauld Institutes* 16, no. 3–4: 275–291.

Wittkower, R. (1960). "The changing concept of proportion." *Daedalus* 89, no. 1: 119–215.

Zevi, B. (1957). "I sistemi proporzionali sconfitti a Londra." *L'architettura. Cronache e Storia* 26: 508–509.

2.9.2

SMART HOME DESIGN FOR PEOPLE WITH DEMENTIA

Julia del Río and Eduardo Macagno

Abstract

This chapter focuses on the incorporation of a smart design approach, understood as data-informed design as part of an evidence-based design strategy to enhance people living with dementia and Alzheimer's quality of life and slow down the cognitive decline associated with dementia and Alzheimer's.

The incorporation of intelligent sensing systems to the designed environment with the capability of supporting cognitive and motor impairment to assist Alzheimer's patients is explored, as well as their role in contributing to evidence and data-based design by being able to collect baseline performance measures and monitor the implementation of this design.

Moreover, and concerning the current lack of involvement of the user in the research process, this chapter presents the use of technology – Smart Home and sensors – as a research tool to better support the research and design process through post-occupancy evaluation, helping researchers to fully access the direct experiences of people living with dementia.

Introduction

Our perception of the built environment is formed by the information obtained through the senses, which is later processed and interpreted by our cognitive faculties, including memory. Imperfections and impairments in these faculties accrue over time as a natural part of the human condition. This deterioration is more profound in people suffering from dementia, dramatically impacting their experience of the world and their ability to cope with everyday tasks.

Here, we consider disorders that impact memory, with numerous consequences for performance in daily activities, social and communication skills, decision-making, emotion control, reasoning, and other abilities (Liappas et al., 2021). Alzheimer's disease is particularly devastating in that it is a progressive, chronic disorder that severely impairs cognitive functions, including memory, reasoning, linguistic ability, perception of depth, and mobility. There is a growing body of research on the structural brain changes that occur during normal aging and in dementia. These changes include advancing decreasing brain

DOI: 10.4324/9781003384113-38

volume deterioration of white-matter fibers resulting in impaired connectivity between brain regions, with numerous consequences for cognitive function (Burzynska and Malinin, 2017). Alzheimer's Disease International analyzed a 2021 status report by the World Health Organization and estimated that, in 2020, there were approximately 55 million people worldwide afflicted with this tragic disease.

This chapter explores the possibility that improving the design of the built environment can enhance the quality of life for individuals suffering from dementia. To this end, we combine two approaches:

Evidence-based Design is the process of making design decisions about the built environment motivated by the results of credible empirical research. This manner of design typically relies on scientific methodologies of measuring the physical and psychological effects of the built environment on its users (see, for example, the Center for Health Design).

Smart Design (also known as Data-informed Design) is a manner of design that takes advantage of artificial intelligence integrated into larger "smart" systems.

Although much progress has been made in the last decade, our knowledge about the experience of the environment by **people with dementia remains rudimentary**. It is imperative to develop new methods for the design of effective environments for this vulnerable population. We need guided, factual information about the design strategies and technologies that can be adopted by design professionals.

It is known that environments can be designed to help *prevent* the decline of cognitive function (e.g., Burzynska and Malinin Agnieszka, 2017). This chapter focuses on how the design of houses for seniors may positively impact users" cognitive abilities and quality of life, using an evidence-based framework for organizing emerging research in the field of Smart Design. The integration of specialized technologies into the design of home care for those afflicted with dementia can enhance well-being; promote independence, autonomy, and dignity; stimulate curiosity and exploratory behaviors; enhance spatial memory through navigation activities; and introduce novelty to stimulate attention and memory formation and encourage meaningful social interactions.

Technology and Evidence-Based Design

There exist affordable and well-targeted technologies for improving dementia care (Tsekleves and Keady, 2021). Starting with this evidence, our goal is to measure the baseline performance of people living with dementia and then monitor their performance after implementing specific design approaches. Such analyses will provide the data that will help researchers refine their design strategies and justify the increased costs that may be required for their implementation.

One challenge in evaluating the environments designed for people living with dementia is engaging users in the process of research. Smart Design technologies can be used to meet this challenge, as a type of "intervention," in which users are assisted in their daily activities by stimulation of their motor and cognitive abilities – all while monitoring the users' safety. Smart Design research tools can make it possible to rigorously test various implementations of this approach, while keeping the user engaged throughout this process.

Smart Design typically requires the integration of assistive technologies into the built environment. For example, intelligent sensing systems can provide context-sensitive adaptive feedback with continuous monitoring. This approach helps to reduce the impact of dementia of employing functional support to the user, including timely therapeutic interventions, which play a crucial role in this process by allowing the researcher to concentrate their work on data collection and analysis, and not on continuous engagement with the user (Gillani, 2021).

Smart Homes

Smart Homes are environments equipped with technologies (with an emphasis on special-ized software) that monitor the behaviors of the residents and perform certain analyses of the captured information. Smart Home technology relies on such systems as telemonitoring, activity recognition, safety mechanisms, enhancement of cognitive performance, behavior analysis, etc. (Liappas et al., 2021).

The approach of Smart Homes provisioned with emerging technologies (such as ambient or embedded sensors, placed in the environment or worn on the body) allows for experi-mentation and testing of evidence-based design hypotheses. In this sense, Smart Homes can function as laboratories where real-life research can be conducted in real time and continuously refined.

Assistive Technology and Sensors

Assistive Technologies

Assistive Technologies have become the pillars of health strategies designed to increase users' safety by sustaining their independence while respecting their dignity (Pappadà et al., 2021). Assistive Technologies includes products and technology-based services that expand the abilities of people of any age whose activity is limited in their daily lives, education, work, or leisure.

There is a wide range of types of Assistive Technology that can be used and adapted for people living with dementia, classified by a purpose: to promote safety (e.g., cooker switch-off devices), foster communication, alleviate memory loss (picture-button tele-phones), provide multisensory stimulation, and enhance memory (reminder messages, item locators, and medicine reminders). Besides the adaptability and user-friendliness of Assis-tive Technology, one should consider that individual users might react to technology idi-osyncratically and that the presence of technology may be interpreted as a withdrawal of user independence (Tsekleves and Keady, 2021).

Virtual Reality can be used as Assistive Technology and function as a cognitive aid, for diagnostics and cognition training of Alzheimer patients. In light of recent theories of neural plasticity and findings about the nervous system's ability to reconstruct cellular synapses – as a result of interaction with enriched environments – new research is dedicated to the rehabilitation of memory, and non-invasive non-pharmacological interventions are gaining increasing attention (e.g., García-Betances et al., 2015).

Sensors

Sensors are increasingly used as distributed systems for long-term monitoring of activity patterns of individuals. Sensors are also used in handheld devices that offer quick assess-ment mediated by touch, vision, and voice (Gillan et al., 2021). In Smart Homes, sensors are used as context-sensitive tools (Liappas et al., 2021) that operate by the analysis of behavior that takes into account distributed patterns of resident activity.

These devices can be wearable or located in the environment. Embedded sensors can be incorporated into a device, such as a mobile phone, watch, or clothing. Wearable sensors can monitor behavior and collect data regardless of user location, whereas ambient sensors are attached to objects in the environment with which the user interacts (e.g., door, kettle, or walls; García-Constantino et al., 2021). Sensors can be sensitive to thermal signals, direct contact, infrared radiation, and acoustic waves, and they can measure physiological data, such as heart rate and skin temperature, along with motion and location-tracking data (Gillani, 2021).

A case study of sensors used to monitor the interaction of users with the built environment is a study investigation carried out by Lyons and co-authors in 2015, where smart sensors were placed strategically in 480 homes of an elderly population and used to monitor residents' gait, mobility patterns, and leisure time (e.g., computer usage and socializing). Analyzing the multimodal data collected from these sensors made it possible to identify the causes of decline in cognition and mood, and to detect the sense of loneliness.

The use of sensors is often presented as part of the Smart Home approach, forming the backbone of the systems for Assistive Technology. These smart devices, commonly used in the management of dementia and Alzheimer's disease – for reasons of safety and enhancement of quality of life – can also act as data collection instruments, providing contextual information and data for evaluation of the experience of specific places.

Strategies

Here, we review how Assistive Technologies can support specific scenarios while also serving as data collection tools, supporting evidence-based and data-based approaches to design.

Enriched Environments

It has been shown that an environment that presents the optimal amount of cognitive challenge can have protective effects against brain pathology (Babcock et al. 2021) and that exposure to enriched environments may help reduce age-related cognitive decline, sustain functional independence, and reduce the risk of dementia (Burzynska and Malinin, 2017). Enriched Environments are characterized by enhanced physical and social stimulation, which can promote neurogenesis and neuronal survival when providing a sufficient level of environmental complexity and multisensory stimulation (Burzynska and Malinin, 2017).

Humans exposed to richer environmental stimulation present fewer signs of brain degeneration and perform better in cognitive tasks than those not exposed to enriched environments while triggering morphological changes in the brain through sensory stimulation, building this way resilience to cognitive aging (Babcock et al., 2021).

Design features in dementia and Alzheimer's care homes should then aim to provide cognitive challenges through multisensory enrichment. However, it is important to identify what would be considered an adequate Enriched Environment for someone living with dementia or Alzheimer's, since individuals will differ in their sensory, motor, and intellectual capacity. For example, too much stimulation, high variations in sound levels, or high engaging quality of the environment can result in increased wandering behavior in dementia patients (Burzynska and Malinin, 2017).

The enrichment of the built environment can be supported through the use of technology. Just by implementing a technological component in stimulation interventions, sensory deficits can be compensated thanks to opposite-designed interfaces (Pappadà et al., 2021).

Through the use of sensors, multisensory stimulation (picturegrama phone, reference) can be provided, and through the use of Virtual Reality, distinct virtual enriched environments can be created. Virtual Reality can expose cognitively impaired patients to a computer-generated Enriched Environment, providing a sense of "presence" or "being there," for the patient to interact with quasi-naturalistic real-life-like stimuli in a multisensory fashion, safely using visual, tactile, and kinesthetic sensations (Constantino-García et al., 2021).

Virtual Environment studies have focused on creating multisensory spaces to enhance cognitive skills (Goodall et al., 2019) through the stimulation of sight, touch, hearing, balance, and smell of people living with dementia, resulting in an improvement in their overall well-being and quality of life. In addition, it can also help patients improve their relationships in social and personal environments since the aim is to provide an atmosphere of wellness and relaxation for both the patient and the specialist (Elnimr, 2021).

Exposure to natural stimuli is considered another Enriched Environments strategy. The cognitive advantages of spending time immersed in natural settings suggest the need to provide elements of biophilic design in senior housing. The incorporation of biophilic features (plants, water, aquariums) provides complex multisensory stimulation (visual, auditory, olfactory, tactile) and it adds a sense of novelty (Burzynska and Malinin, 2017).

Technology can enhance biophilic design through the use of digital technologies – from screens, projections, sounds, or interactive devices to Virtual Reality, Augmented Reality, and biometric sensors – that can simulate and enhance the presence of natural elements in the built environment. This digital-nature approach can create immersive and engaging experiences that stimulate the senses, evoke emotions, and foster learning and curiosity.

In 2019, Goodall et al. examined physical and cognitive rehabilitation for people living with dementia by using an immersive Virtual Environment that combines Virtual Reality and Augmented Reality in a special room (Sense-Garden). The room combined multisensory stimulation with physical activity and techniques from reminiscence therapy. It also included an integrated sound system with familiar music and background nature soundscapes used to motivate and enhance the patient's cognitive rehabilitation, together with an olfactory dispensary system releasing familiar scents.

In summary, Assistive Technologies present a good opportunity to stimulate cognitive and physical abilities in multisensory environments in care homes while, at the same creating room for experimentation, data collection, and analysis.

Spatial Navigation

Spatial navigation and orientation abilities are important for independence, autonomy, and well-being, helping to delay the cognitive decline associated with aging. However, age-related decline in wayfinding skills can make it difficult to learn to navigate in unfamiliar environments.

Good wayfinding skills derive from the interaction between individual and environmental factors; they form a prerequisite for mobility and hence personal autonomy and independence. Environments that are designed to support spatial orientation help to compensate for impaired navigation abilities and to improve the independence, quality of life, and well-being of residents. This is accomplished by providing optimal amounts of cognitive and physical challenge, encouraging spatial exploration (active movement and exploration that involves decision-making), and strengthening hippocampal activity.

The implementation of Assistive Technology systems can promote users' independence, supporting dementia patients with mobility and reducing disorientation. Assistive Technology can increase motor autonomy and reduce the risks associated with wandering, thanks to GPS technology (Pappadà et al., 2021).

A common example of such applications is using a simple navigation device for people living with dementia. This device encourages the user to maintain an active lifestyle by enabling them to navigate frequently – and infrequently visited outdoor places while providing safety, independence, and confidence. Using these wearable devices, GPS monitoring, and wireless moving sensors can help the patient avoid getting lost but also serve as a data gathering tool, by creating behavioral maps, allowing researchers to locate users or collect activity information.

Additionally, emerging Virtual Reality applications can serve as cognitive training for dementia patients, concentrating on navigation and orientation (Garcia-Constantino et al., 2021). For example, a Virtual Environment was presented as a training tool in the study carried out by White and Moussavi (2016), who investigated cognitive rehabilitation of Alzheimer"s disease patients, with respect to spatial cognitive tasks. The study used a cognitive treatment program based on spatial navigation in a Virtual Environment, having the user navigate to targets in a symmetric, landmark-less virtual building, proving that the user could learn to navigate in a simple navigation environment, suggesting that users can transfer information about the environment obtained from Virtual Environment to real life.

Light

Light has a remarkable influence on the nervous system, affecting mainly the sense of sight and by this, many other neural processes that include regulation of the body"s circadian rhythms, which directly affect memory and psychomotor performance.

One of the problems associated with dementia is sleep disorders and disruptive behaviors occurring at night (Ly et al., 2016). Light has been shown to be a central aspect of a supportive environment, not only by helping users navigate by providing guiding cues but also as a modulator of circadian rhythms, consequently working as a behavioral and mood treatment.

Due to mobility impairments, people living with dementia often do not venture outdoors, which causes exposure to light levels insufficient for proper vision, not to mention the negative outcomes on circadian rhythmicity and mood. Here we consider adaptive and intelligent lighting strategies implemented as part of the Smart Home approach.

One of the most effective applications of smart lighting is *phototherapy*, which can be aimed at managing behavioral symptoms with positive effects in the form of agitation, circadian rhythms, and well-being (Pappadà et al., 2021). Several studies investigated the effectiveness of phototherapy interventions – which employ full-spectrum bright light – in older adult patients with dementia (Lu et al., 2023) proving that phototherapy significantly improves cognitive function and shows promising effects on restlessness and disturbed sleep. Phototherapy is thus considered one of the most promising non-pharmacological interventions for improving core symptoms of dementia (Ly et al., 2016).

Social Interaction

It is well known that a lack of social interaction gradually challenges a person's capacity to communicate with others, causing a loss of the sense of belonging and slowly leading to isolation and loneliness (associated with a reduced volume of the prefrontal cortex). To avoid the commonly experienced feeling of "fading out," any intervention that encourages social interaction might be critical. Indeed, interacting socially is a good strategy to stay mentally agile and alert. Additionally, interpersonal and community engagement is important for health maintenance and high quality of life (Tsekleves and Keady, 2021).

At the same time, social engagement and exercise have been shown to benefit cognition in numerous studies (Cassarino and Setti, 2015). For example, more aerobic exercise leads to less white-matter lesions, and engagement in social and leisure activities offers intellectual stimulation (Burzynska, 2017), fostering cognitive reserve and mitigating negative effects of aging on cognition.

Here, we focus on supporting social interaction through design-based and Assistive Technology interventions. By creating supporting environments that foster positive behaviors and social interaction, the sense of well-being is reinforced by promoting meaningful interactions through technology that encourages multimodal and playful engagement with the environment.

For instance, Assistive Technology can be employed to discover the environmental conditions that encourage social interaction, supporting recreational activities and social contacts (Neal et al., 2021). The use of smart software makes it possible to trace users" movements, enabling the research team to see changes in behavior during use. Assistive Technology can provide opportunities to socially interact through multisensory stimulation, in well-lit spaces, with sufficient greenery, interesting sounds, sights, aromas, and pleasurable design (Burzynska and Malinin, 2017). For example, Kenning and Treadaway (2018) studied the development of sensory textiles for people living with advanced dementia, showing how textile objects made of chenille helped users interact with objects, to connect and engage meaningfully with other people.

Conclusions

It appears that the majority of research to date places most focus on medical and clinical needs, paying little attention to the emotional needs and daily activities of people living with dementia (Tsekleves and Keady, 2021). The role of the built environment in shaping our perception and experience of places is often neglected, along with the possibilities offered by Assistive Technologies integrated into design.

Current technologies have concentrated on helping individuals in the early stages of dementia to remain independent, improving social participation, and security, as well as monitoring physical and behavioral status. It is advised, however, that Assistive Technology be examined as an opportunity to involve the user in the process of conducting research, in the interest of evidence-based and data-based design.

One of the main challenges faced by adherents of evidence-based design in post-occupancy evaluation is accessing groups of people living with dementia and involving them in research. As a result, studies have largely failed to fully appreciate the experiences of people living with dementia who often assume a passive role in research (Tsekleves and Keady, 2021).

Still, technology can make a significant contribution to the architectural design in this arena, by investigating innovative design solutions that incorporate embedded electronics and smart materials – sensors worn by residents and placed in the environment – allowing residents to participate in the data-informed process of design (Pappadà et al., 2021). This way, the smart design allows designers to better support people with dementia, including Alzheimer's disease, enhancing their quality of life.

This is a growing and extremely promising opportunity for learning about person-building interaction at high resolution, taking into account changes evolving over time (Burzynska and Malinin, 2017). Being able to record the lived experiences of people with cognitive impairment caused by dementia is an important milestone in our understanding and application of emerging technologies of design.

References

Babcock KR, Page JS, Fallon JR, Webb AE. (2021). Adult hippocampal neurogenesis in aging and Alzheimer"s disease. *Stem Cell Reports*, 16(4): 681–693. doi: 10.1016/j.stem- cr.2021.01.019. Epub 2021 Feb 25. PMID: 33636114; PMCID: PMC8072031.

Burzynska A., Malinin L. (2017). Enriched environments for healthy aging: qualities of seniors housing. *Designs Promoting Brain and Cognitive Health. Senior Housing & Care Journal*, 25(1): 16–27.

Cassarino M, Setti A. (2015). Environment as "Brain Training": A review of geographical and physical environmental influences on cognitive ageing. *Ageing Research Reviews*, 23(Pt B): 167–82. doi: 10.1016/j.arr.2015.06.003. Epub 2015 Jul 2. PMID: 26144974.

Elnimr, H. (2021). Interactive architecture as a therapeutic environment for people with Alzheimer's disease, a scoping review. *FormAkademisk*, 14(1): 19–23.

García-Betances RI, Waldmeyer MTA, Fico G, Cabrera-Umpiérrez MF. (2015). A succinct overview of virtual reality technology use in Alzheimer"s disease. *Frontiers in Aging Neuroscience*, 7: 80.

García-Constantino M, Orr C, Synnott J, Shewell C, Ennis A, Cleland I, Nugent C, Rafferty J, Morrison G, Larkham L, McIlroy S, Selby A. (2021). Design and implementation of a smart home in a box to monitor the wellbeing of residents with dementia in care homes. *Frontiers in Digital Health*, 3: 798889. doi: 10.3389/fdgth.2021.798889.

Gillani N, Arslan T. (2021). Intelligent sensing technologies for the diagnosis, monitoring and therapy of Alzheimer's disease: A systematic review. *Sensors (Basel)*, 21(12): 4249. doi: 10.3390/s21124249.

Goodall G, Ciobanu I, Taraldsen K, Sørgaard J, Marin A, Draghici R, Zamfir MV, Berteanu M, Maetzler W, Serrano JA. (2019). The use of virtual and immersive technology in creating personalized multisensory spaces for people living with dementia (SENSE-GARDEN): Protocol for a multisite before-after trial. *JMIR Research Protocols*, 8(9): e14096. doi: 10.2196/14096. PMID: 31538942;

Kenning G. and Treadaway C. (Jan. 2018). Designing for dementia: Iterative grief and transitional objects. Design Issues, 34(1): 42–53. doi: 10.1162/DESI_a_00475.

Liappas N, Teriús-Padrón JG, García-Betances RI, Cabrera-Umpiérrez MF. (2021). Advancing smart home awareness-a conceptual computational modelling framework for the execution of daily activities of people with Alzheimer"s disease. *Sensors (Basel)*, 22(1): 166. doi: 10.3390/s22010166. PMID: 35009709; PMCID: PMC8747630.

Lu X, Liu C, Shao F. (2023). Phototherapy improves cognitive function in dementia: A systematic review and meta-analysis. *Brain and Behavior*, 13: e2952.

Ly NT, Tscharn R, Preßler J, Huber S, Aknine S, Serna A, Hurtienne J. (2016). Smart lighting in dementia care facility. In *Proceedings of the 2016 ACM International Joint Conference on Pervasive and Ubiquitous Computing: Adjunct (UbiComp '16)*. Association for Computing Machinery, New York, 1636–1639.

Lyons BE, Eaustin D, Eseelye A, Epetersen J, Yeargers J, Eriley T, Esharma N, Mattek NC, Ewild K, Edodge H, et al. (2015). Pervasive computing technologies to continuously assess Alzheimer's disease progression and intervention efficacy. *Frontiers in Aging Neuroscience*, 7: 102. doi: 10.3389/fnagi.2015.00102

Neal D, van den Berg F, Planting C, Ettema T, Dijkstra K, Finnema E, Dröes R-M, (2021). Can use of digital technologies by people with dementia improve self-management and social participation? A systematic review of effect studies. *Journal of Clinical Medicine, 10:* 604.

Pappadà A, Chattat R, Chirico I, Valente M, Ottoboni G. (2021). Assistive technologies in dementia care: An updated analysis of the literature. *Frontiers in Psychology,* 12: 644587. doi: 10.3389/fpsyg.2021.644587. PMID: 33841281; PMCID: PMC8024695.

Tsekleves E, Keady J. (2021). Design for people living with dementia: Interactions and innovations. 10.4324/9780429442407.

White PJ, Moussavi Z. (2016). Neurocognitive treatment for a patient with Alzheimer's disease using a virtual reality navigational environment. *Journal of Experimental Neuroscience,* 10: 129–135. doi: 10.4137/JEN.S40827. PMID: 27840579; PMCID: PMC5102253.

2.9.3

SMART DESIGN AND AI FOR DEVELOPMENTAL DISABILITIES

Characteristics of People with Autism Spectrum Disorders and Other Developmental Disabilities

Kristi Gaines and Raquel Rodrigues

Abstract

In the United States, approximately 1 in 6 children in the 3–17-year age range are diagnosed with a developmental disability. Developmental disabilities (DDs) include autism spectrum disorders, attention-deficit/hyperactivity disorder (ADHD), blindness, cerebral palsy, moderate to profound hearing loss, intellectual disability, and other developmental delays (CDC, 2023). Children with DD may experience delays with learning and problems with behavior. Adults may struggle with vocational training, communication, social skills, and basic living skills. Each individual is different, but many people who are neurodivergent struggle with social interaction, repetitive and restricted behaviors, and nonverbal communication.

The use of technology, including artificial intelligence (AI), is being used in assessment, diagnosis, therapy, learning, accommodations for everyday activities, and in assisting researchers. Early detection is key to improved outcomes, and AI is being investigated as a means for screening and diagnosis. Robotic playmates can aid in both screening and providing therapeutic interventions. Identifying biomarkers is also underway utilizing technological advances such as functional magnetic resonance imaging (fMRI).

The use of virtual reality (VR) and augmented reality (AR) are providing successful interventions and show promise in many applications due to their realistic experience. AR and VR are currently being utilized to improve social skills and educational outcomes in a variety of settings. Accessibility to technology is becoming more widely available, and positive outcomes are being identified in problem-solving, engagement, communication, job interview skills, tactile tolerance, independence, and activities of daily living. Since many individuals struggle with processing sensory information, the use of VR/AR provides training or diagnosis provides a safe and more predictable environment while allowing for individual preferences. Benefits of AI are currently realized and the potential for future advancement is great.

DOI: 10.4324/9781003384113-39

Individuals with autism spectrum disorder (ASD) and other developmental disabilities (DD) exhibit strengths and challenges that effect the way they think and interact with the environment. Each individual is different, but typically people on the spectrum display problems with communication and social interaction, repetitive and restricted behaviors, and nonverbal communication. They may be highly proficient or encounter great challenges with everyday activities. Some individuals are able live independently while others may need considerable assistance with daily activities (Gaines et al., 2016).

The Centers for Disease Control (2023) states that the prevalence of ASD in 2023 is 1 in 36 children in the United States. DDs are also increasing. Approximately 1 in 6 children in the 3–17-year age range are diagnosed with a DD. DDs include ASD, attention-deficit/hyperactivity disorder (ADHD), blindness, cerebral palsy, moderate to profound hearing loss, intellectual disability, and other developmental delays. Approximately 30% of children on the autism spectrum also have a co-occurring intellectual disability (DeLeyer-Tiarks et al., 2023). School-age children with ASD and other DDs may experience delays with learning and problems with behavior (Gaines et al., 2016). Adults with ASD may struggle with vocational training, communication, social skills, and basic living skills. Estimated unemployment of adults on the spectrum varies, with some estimates as high as 85% (Artiran et al., 2022). Problems with social interactions and society's workplace communication norms may interfere with an individual's ability to acquire and maintain a job.

No two people are alike, although, sensitivity to the environment is often a characteristic for people with ASD and DD due to sensory processing differences. Individuals may be hypo- or hypersensitive to environmental stimuli such as light, color, sound, textures, and smells. The lesser-known sensory systems of proprioception, vestibular, and interoception may also be impacted. An individual may respond to environmental stimuli with coping mechanisms that may appear as inattentiveness, repetitive behaviors, tantrums, or other behaviors that interfere with activities of daily living (Gaines et al., 2016).

The use of technology and artificial intelligence (AI) is rapidly increasing for individuals with ASD and DD. By technology, the authors are referring to an electronic piece of equipment or application that is intentionally used for practical purposes or to improve the quality of life. Technologies currently being used include laptops and desktop computers with software, smartphones, tablets, speech-generated devices, interactive whiteboards, virtual reality (VR), augmented reality (AR), and the internet. Technological applications are being used in clinical settings to assist with assessment, diagnosis, therapy, learning, accommodations for everyday activities, and assisting researchers. However, it should be noted that the neurodiversity movement is opposed to this deficit-focused label of disability. Instead, "deficits" are interpreted as "differences." Neurodiverse individuals frequently display strengths such as memory and expertise in certain areas. The neurodiversity movement maintains that there are individual differences in brain function instead of disabilities (Erden et al., 2021). The authors recognize that the current medical diagnosis focuses on deficits without considering strengths. However, the diagnostic approach is the current mechanism used to provide needed therapeutic and behavioral interventions to individuals. The authors acknowledge that all individuals display personal strengths; yet, seek to communicate the usefulness of technology in detection and accommodation for individuals with ASD and other DD. The terms neurodiverse and neurodivergent will be used in this chapter as inclusive terms for individuals with ASD and DD.

Detection

Early detection of ASD/DD is associated with improved outcomes and quality of life. The CDC recommends screening by a child's pediatrician three times by age three in order to begin early intervention if needed. Several assessment methods have been developed; however, a diagnosis of ASD is typically made by a psychologist or a specialized physician. Unfortunately, a child must often wait a year or more in order to receive a diagnosis. The *American Psychiatric Associate's Diagnostic and Statistical Manual*, Fifth Edition (DSM-5) provides criteria to identify ASD and is frequently used in the identification. The evaluation requires information from parents and teachers, observational data, and a development history (CDC, 2023). However, bias and interpretation may present problems in existing diagnostic processes.

With the emergence of AI, researchers are working to determine an alternative to the traditional diagnostic methods. AI can be used to assess genetic biomarkers and may be combined with neuroimaging to help improve detection (DeLeyer-Tiarks et al., 2023). However, AI is unable to assess behavioral observational data which is currently a critical component of diagnosis. Since ASD is a complex disorder, incorporating AI into the healthcare system will require additional validation. However, an AI-based system is under development to assist pediatricians in diagnosis. Cogna software utilizes questionnaires that are completed by the pediatrician and parents. Videos of the child are also uploaded and scored. AI algorithms and trained analysts score the questionnaires and videos to determine an ASD diagnosis. Studies are underway to validate the software (Abbas et al., 2020).

Additionally, AI may be used to *screen* children for ASD. Sensory-based technologies using AI algorithms have been used. AI is useful for identifying patterns within data to potentially identify markers associated with ASD diagnosis. Promising research is underway to analyze interactions with robots (Figure 2.9.3.1), touch sensitivity, eye tracking,

Figure 2.9.3.1 Interaction with robots may provide screening assessments while providing therapeutic intervention. Stock images purchased from Shutterstock, Photo Contributor Yuganov Konstantin.

facial expressions, and vocalizations (Schuman, 2021). Interaction with robotic playmates can provide screening assessments while providing therapeutic intervention at the same time. AI-enabled robots can detect a child's movements and eye-gaze (Erden et al., 2021). While these technologies cannot be used diagnostically, they may be helpful in screening.

Telehealth-based tools are being used in diagnostics (Schuman, 2021). The Naturalistic Observation Diagnostic Assessment (NODA) is available to use through a smartphone-based application. Parents upload a completed questionnaire and videos of their child. A clinician uses the DSM-5 checklist to diagnose ASD. Studies show that the accuracy of the system is similar to in-person evaluations (Schuman, 2021).

Additionally, the recognition of brain-based biomarkers for ASD and ADHD through functional magnetic resonance imaging (fMRI) (Figure 2.9.3.2) is showing potential for an objective diagnosis. fMRI technology may also have promise in monitoring and predicting treatment responses and outcomes. Studies are identifying specific features such as gray matter volume, functional connectivity, and modular cortical networks that differentiate individuals on the spectrum (Nakai et al., 2023). Biomarkers will not replace clinical assessments, but they may prove to be useful in determining treatment methods and goals.

The development of technologies shows promise in diagnosing a child with ASD at a younger age. Early intervention is key to provide interventions and therapies for better outcomes and quality of life. Unfortunately, adult diagnostic intervention is difficult as they may have developed "masking" strategies to help them navigate a neurotypical world. Most individuals report waiting approximately one year or longer for a referral and diagnosis (Erden et al., 2021).

The use of AI is currently limited in supporting the diagnosis of clinicians, yet shows promise for additional future use. Advantages and disadvantages are present. AI is beneficial in avoiding the bias of the individuals conducting the diagnostic assessment and can be integrated with converging technologies such as brain scanning in the diagnostic process.

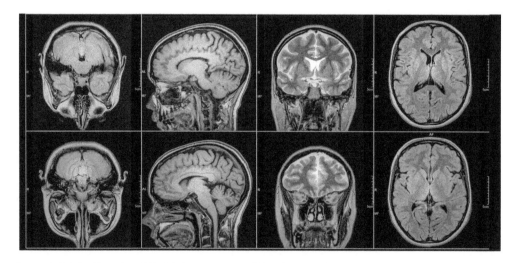

Figure 2.9.3.2 Functional fMRI shows potential for objective diagnosis.

Stock images purchased from Shutterstock, Photo Contributor Triff.

Eventually, neuroimaging biomarkers may be able to identify developmental differences. However, limitations exist since AI uses algorithms that rely on vast amounts of data, and the data sets are compiled by the contributions of physicians with possibility of human error. Other limitations include a lack of algorithms that consider changing social norms (difference vs. disability) and analyzing behavioral aspects. AI cannot consider behavioral nuances and tends to make simplistic evaluations. The use of AI will still require clinicians to assess the information (Erden et al., 2021).

VR, AR, and Other Technologies

VR systems merge technology and human perception through virtual worlds and environments, role-playing, and static VR. Commonly, head-mounted displays (HMDs) are used to display computer-generated imagery, live imagery, or a combination. Gloves and motion tractors may also be used for a multisensory experience (Figure 2.9.3.3). The three basic aspects of VR systems are immersion, interaction and a sense of presence (Savickaite et al., 2022). In addition, acoustic stimuli may be provided via headphones or speakers.

Figure 2.9.3.3 VR uses HMDs with computer-generated imagery and may be used for education and training. Stock images purchased from Shutterstock, Photo Contributor Vitech.

Olfactory and gustatory stimuli may also be a part of the VR. Applications in healthcare, education, training, communication, entertainment, and engineering are available (Baus & Bouchard, 2014).

In contrast, AR is an interactive technology that projects people and objects into real-world surroundings in real time. Sensory information such as visual or auditory stimuli is projected into the existing world. Through the combination real-world and computer-generated elements, AR may appear to be more realistic than VR. DeLeyer-Tiarks et al. (2023) state that AR may be used to improve eye contact, nonverbal communication, and social engagement. Their research also recognizes the potential of VR/AR to provide benefits such as learning daily living skills, emotional regulating, and promoting independence. Neo et al. (2021) found that using AR in learning environments is a useful tool for children on the spectrum.

The potential of immersive VR technology is vast, as it helps individuals with ASD develop and improve abilities in a safe and controllable environment (Abdeen & Albiladi, 2022). The use of VR/AR may reduce sensory input and allow greater access for social training or other interventions needed for quality of life and daily living. For individuals on the autism spectrum, using VR/AR may provide an environment that reduces anxiety while Artiran working to improve functional language, vocabulary, and social skills (Figure 2.9.3.3). Immersive VR/AR shows remarkable promise as a comfortable place for face-to-face social contact for those who show nonverbal difficulties. The use of VR also shows promise in enhancing social skills for people with a range of developmental, intellectual, and communication disorders. While VR/AR are used primarily for enhancing social skills, in the future, VR/AR applications may be used to help with sensory sensitivities, difficulties with motor skills, and repetitive behaviors, to improve health, well-being, and enhancing overall quality of life (Savickaite et al., 2022; Bailey et al., 2022). However, AR/VR technology is not readily available as a mainstream intervention. Also, while these technologies show promise as interventions, more research is needed to determine evidence-based applications (Figure 2.9.3.4).

Age-Related Characteristics and Technological Applications

Children

Most of the existing research for children on the spectrum focuses on classroom environments since early intervention leads to improved social outcomes, improved academic performance, and improved behavior. Unfortunately, children with ASD or DD may show a lack interest in the classroom. Approximately 30% of children on the autism spectrum have a co-diagnosis of intellectual disability (DeLeyer-Tiarks et al., 2023)

Additionally, computer and/or other video-based applications provide an educational intervention in a regulated learning environment (DeLeyer-Tiarks et al., 2023). Students show increased motivation when provided with the option of using gamification. For example, video and video recordings have been demonstrated as effective in improving language, academic performance, social, language, and daily living skills (DeLeyer-Tiarks et al., 2023). AI and other technology modalities have been shown to be effective in differentiating various features associated with ASD.

In a study by Cheung et al. (2016), a VR-enabled system was used to aid in social training for school-aged children who were either diagnosed or were speculated to be on the

Figure 2.9.3.4   Immersive VR may provide an environment that reduces anxiety while working on skills. Stock images purchased from Shutterstock, Photo Contributor, Gorodenkoff.

spectrum in an academic environment in China. The study presented six unique scenarios that were delivered through a fully immersive 4-side CAVE installation with head position and orientation tracking to provide an authentic experience. Four of the six scenarios investigated social skills including school life, getting ready for school, riding the bus to go to school, participating in classes, studying in a library, and purchasing food from a store. One scenario helped children with ASD discuss what took place in the training scenarios. One relaxation scenario helped them become familiar with the VR process, and learn to cope and manage emotions. The preliminary results indicated that after the completion of the intervention, children showed significant improvements (Cheung et al., 2016).

Adolescents

As children move into adolescence, they may continue to experience challenges associated with engaging in social interactions and with communication. Today's youth have been exposed to technology since early childhood. They prefer information that is presented in a visual format while learning (Odom et al., 2015). According to Odom et al. (2015), the more engaging video applications include the following characteristics:

- animated or video presentations are more successful in communicating information than static visual methods,
- larger screen displays may be more effective than smaller displays,
- certain types of visual screen media are preferred

Odom et al. (2015) found that adolescents on the spectrum prefer to use technology above other leisure or social activities. They found that three factors affect the benefits of technology for adolescents with ASD. These include (1) individual characteristics, (2) the purpose for using the technology, and (3) the device itself (Odom et al., 2015).

Transitioning into adulthood is challenging for the general population and may be more difficult for people who are neurodivergent. An immersive VR training program utilizing a lightweight wireless headset for adolescents and adults ages 12 and older was tested as a method for training individuals in police safety (McCleery et al., 2020). The training provided direct feedback and instruction on performance. The instructions included orienting their gaze at a person and removing their hands from pockets. The participants reported that the system was enjoyable to use and that they were willing to engage in additional sessions.

In another study (Genova et al., 2021), a high school setting was utilized to assess the effectiveness of a VR job interview tool. The findings show that job interview performance was improved after the intervention. Unfortunately, perceived anxiety and self-efficacy did not show improvement. Technological interventions may be useful if incorporated into a curriculum to transition youth to adulthood and improve success in daily living and in employment outcomes.

Adults

Most of the current evidence-based research focuses on children with little information on the long-term outcomes and care for adults on the spectrum. Support systems available through the school system are no longer available and they may need to establish relationships for training, higher education, or employment. Few high-quality research studies have been completed that focus on young adults as they transition to adulthood and support independence for adults of all ages (Wang & Jeon, 2023). Adults on the spectrum often face challenges with vocational training, basic home and community living skills, emotional regulation, and self-promotion (Wang & Jeon, 2023). Difficulty with social and communication skills may contrast with society's workplace communication norms resulting in difficulty with acquiring and retaining employment.

Wearable assistive technology for people who are neurodiverse is available that focuses on social interactions, physiological, and emotional monitoring. These studies include wide-range reporting of people on the spectrum without regard to age. The specific needs of adults may be quite different from children with ASD (Wang & Jeon, 2023). Studies focusing on adults with ASD are few, since researchers predominantly focus on children and adolescents (Kandalaft et al., 2013).

A study by Kandalaft et al. (2013) examined the practicality of VR for social training for young adults. After a 5-week intervention, the researchers found significant increases on social and emotional measures and in real-life interactions (Kandalaft et al., 2013). Another study (Smith et al., 2014) examined the effectiveness of VR job interview training using the internet or computer software. The participants found the process pleasurable and easy to use. They reported feeling prepared for the interview process.

Technology for Communication and Social Interaction

Parents report that the biggest challenge with their child on the spectrum is appropriate communication (Neo et al., 2021). Individuals with ASD and DD often demonstrate social communication difficulties through verbal and nonverbal communication, difficulties in social-emotional exchange, and trouble in interpreting facial expressions correctly (Cheung et al., 2016). These complications can lead to learning difficulties and making social connections. Children may also have difficulty communicating with their parents. Despite these difficulties, individuals can learn social skills through step-by-step instruction. Through play, children learn cultural and social norms. If a child has difficulty playing with other children, then communication and social skills will be hindered. Often, children with ASD and DD engage in a type of play that excludes others which can lead to loneliness. Play is important for all children to improve intelligence, creative thinking, develop language, develop motor skills, reduce stress, and reach developmental milestones.

VR-enabled systems are being used to address the problems with communication and social interaction frequently observed in people on the spectrum. Technological advances aid with communication and social skills. Smartphones, tablets, computers, specialized software, interactive whiteboards, speech-generating devices, and the internet are readily available for use. Learning environments utilize these tools for academic achievement. Also, learning expressive language can be enhanced through video recording (DeLeyer-Tiarks et al., 2023).

Home Therapy

Caring for a child on the spectrum may be demanding and stressful for family and caregivers. The financial strain of therapies and intervention creates burdens for many. Even after diagnosis, long waiting lists frequently delay needed therapeutic assistance. Since parents understand the particular needs of their child, they are able to identify and target behaviors that need assistance. A potential in-home solution to the problems of accessibility of care is the use of Socially Assistive Robots (SARs). Javed and Park (2022) have found improvement in outcomes using SARs that include:

- Improved tactile tolerance
- Emotion interpretation
- Object identification skills
- Learning activities of daily living
- Improving problem-solving skills
- Increased attention and engagement to tasks
- Maintains or increased emotional engagement
- Maintains or increased task engagement

The practicality and value of using the technology in a remote home-based setting were investigated to determine a possible impact on skills for daily living for adolescents and young adults with intellectual disabilities. Panerai et al. (2018) conducted a study using virtual applications that were installed on tablets. The study found statistically significant improvements with the VR sessions. The skills practiced in the VR training session were found to be transferable to the real world. The participant and their families reported a good level of satisfaction with the intervention.

Classroom

Children and youth who are neurodivergent may exhibit difficulties in the classroom. Problems may stem from a lack of interest or motivation, distractions in the learning environment, poor academic performance, anxiety, or social issues. Children with ASD and ADHD are more likely to miss school and display refusal behavior (Ide-Okochi et al.,

2022). Poorly designed learning environments contribute to these negative behaviors. Individuals on the spectrum may have difficulty processing sensory information in schools and classrooms. Factors such as noise, glare, clutter, and a large number of people may create sensory overload. They may also struggle with transitioning between activities and controlling their impulses (Gaines et al., 2016).

Federal law in the United States addresses educating individuals who are neurodivergent in a general education classroom when possible. Improved outcomes for many children who are neurodivergent have been identified through inclusion in a general education classroom; however, some students are better served in self-contained classrooms or through partial inclusion (Gaines, et al., 2016).

The use of VR is showing potential in educational environments. Training through VR should be safe and controllable (Cheung et al., 2016). A Virtual Reality Learning Environment has clear objectives and meets the conditions for training and learning environments for children with ASD (Cheung et al., 2016). In recent years, because of lowering costs of VR technology, learning through VR has become available in general education and for specialized instruction for individuals who are neurodiverse. VR environments may be used in evaluation and to provide a realistic experience in a virtual world (Ide-Okochi et al., 2022). Using VR classroom environments allows the researcher to tailor preferences to the individual while collecting more accurate data (Ide-Okochi et al., 2022). Individuals with ASD have reported an attraction to computers that may result in an increase in motivation to learn with the technology (Parsons & Carlew, 2016). Additionally, in a study by Ide-Okochi et al. (2022), a VR classroom was utilized to access gaze, academic performance, and interoception. The results show that the DD group showed a significantly longer gaze duration on the virtual teacher in the VR classroom.

In their study, Parsons and Carlew, 2016 compared individuals with and without ASD in a paper-and-pencil task and a VR classroom task. No difference was found in the paper-and-pencil task between the two groups. However, the individuals with ASD performed considerably worse on the VR tasks with distractors. The distractors included a variety of audio-visual, audio, and visual distractors. The results suggest the possibility of using VR to determine the distractibility condition in adults with high-functioning autism.

Neurodivergent Research and Technology

The use of technology in diagnosing and assisting individuals who are neurodivergent is promising in enhancing a range of skills in a controlled and safe environment. Although widely available, the accessibility of technology to some populations may prove to be a hindrance to many people who could benefit from its use. Social skills are currently the most dominant research area showing positive outcomes. Additional research is needed in the area of communication, sensory differences, repetitive behaviors, and motor difficulties as they relate to enhancing the quality of life. The intersection of the real and virtual worlds provides new possibilities. The potential benefits of technology for people with ASD and DD are exciting and yet to be discovered.

References

Abbas, H., Garberson, F., Liu-Mayo, S., Glover, E., & Wall, D. (2020). Multi-modular AI approach to streamline autism diagnosis in young children. *Scientific Reports*, 10(1), 5014.

Abdeen, F., & Albiladi, W. (202). Factors influencing the adoption of virtual reality (VR) technology among parents of individuals with ASD. *Interactive Learning Environments*, 32(4), 1330–1347.

Artiran, S., Ravisankar, R., Luo, S., Chukoskie, L., & Cosman, P. (2022). Measuring social modulation of gaze in autism spectrum condition with virtual reality interviews. *IEEE Transactions on Neural Systems and Rehabilitation Engineering*, 30, 2373–2384.

Bailey, B., Bryant, L., & Hemsley, B. (2022). Virtual reality and augmented reality for children, adolescents, and adults with communication disability and neurodevelopmental disorders: A systematic review. *Review Journal of Autism and Developmental Disorders*, 9(2), 160–183.

Baus, O., & Bouchard, S (2014) Moving from virtual reality exposure-based therapy to augmented reality exposure-based therapy: A review. *Frontiers in Human Neuroscience*, 8,112. doi: 10.3389/fnhum.2014.00112.

Cheung, S., Kwok, L., Shang, J., Wang, A., & Kwan, R. (2016). Virtual reality enabled training for social adaptation in inclusive education settings for school-aged children with autism spectrum disorder (ASD). In *Blended Learning: Aligning Theory with Practices* (Vol. 9757, Lecture Notes in Computer Science, pp. 94–102). Switzerland: Springer International Publishing AG.

Data & Statistic on Autism Spectrum Disorder. (2023). Centers for Disease Control and Prevention https://www.cdc.gov/autism/data-research/index.html.

DeLeyer-Tiarks, J., Li, M., Levine-Schmitt, M., Andrade, B., Bray, M., & Peters, E. (2023). Advancing autism technology. *Psychology in the Schools*, 60(2), 495–506.

Erden, Y., Hummerstone, H., & Rainey, S. (2021). Automating autism assessment: What AI can bring to the diagnostic process. *Journal of Evaluation in Clinical Practice*, 27(3), 485–490.

Gaines, K., Bourne, A., Pearson, M., & Kleibrink, M. (2016). *Designing for Autism Spectrum Disorders*. Routledge.

Genova, H., Lancaster, K., Morecraft, J., Haas, M., Edwards, A., DiBenedetto, M., & Smith, M. (2021). A pilot RCT of virtual reality job interview training in transition-age youth on the autism spectrum. *Research in Autism Spectrum Disorders*, 89, 101878.

Ide-Okochi, A., Matsunaga, N., & Sato, H. (2022). A preliminary study of assessing gaze, interoception and school performance among children with neurodevelopmental disorders: The feasibility of VR Classroom. *Children (Basel)*, 9(2), 250.

Javed, H., & Park, C. (2022). Promoting social engagement with a multi-role dancing robot for in-home autism care. *Frontiers in Robotics and AI*, 9, 880691

Kandalaft, M. R., Didehbani, N., Krawczyk, D. C., Allen, T. T., & Chapman, S. B. (2013). Virtual reality social cognition training for young adults with high-functioning autism. *Journal of Autism and Developmental Disorders*, 43(1), 34–44.

McCleery, J., Zitter, A., Solórzano, R., Turnacioglu, S., Miller, J., Ravindran, V., & Parish-Morris, J. (2020). Safety and feasibility of an immersive virtual reality intervention program for teaching police interaction skills to adolescents and adults with autism. *Autism Research*, 13(8), 1418–1424.

Nakai, N., Sato, M., Yamashita, O., Sekine, Y., Fu, X., Nakai, J., Zalesky, A., & Takumi, T. (2023). Virtual reality-based real-time imaging reveals abnormal cortical dynamics during behavioral transitions in a mouse model of autism. *Cell Reports*, 42(4). https://doi.org/10.1016/j.celrep.2023.112258.

Neo, H., Teo, C., & Yeo, Q. (2021). Augmented reality emotion recognition for autism spectrum disorder children [version 1; peer review: 1 not approved]. *F1000 Research*, 10, 1217.

Odom, S., Thompson, J., Hedges, S., Boyd, B., Dykstra, J., Duda, M., & Bord, A. (2015). Technology-Aided interventions and instruction for adolescents with autism spectrum disorder. *Journal of Autism and Developmental Disorders*, 45(12), 3805–3819.

Panerai, S., Catania, V., Rundo, F., & Ferri, R. (2018). Remote home-based virtual training of functional living skills for adolescents and young adults with intellectual disability: Feasibility and preliminary results. *Frontiers in Psychology*, 9, 1730.

Parsons, T. D. & Carlew, A. R. (2016). Bimodal Virtual Reality Stroop for Assessing Distractor Inhibition in Autism Spectrum Disorders. *Journal of Autism and Developmental Disorders*, 46, 1255–1267.

Savickaite, S., Husselman, T., Taylor, R., Millington, E., Hayashibara, E., & Arthur, T. (2022). Applications of virtual reality (VR) in autism research: Current trends and taxonomy of definitions. *Journal of Enabling Technologies*, 16(2), 147–154.

Schuman, A. (2021). AI, telehealth & sensor-based technologies facilitate autism diagnosis. *Contemporary Pediatric*s (Montvale, N.J.), 38(10), 16–20.

Smith, M., Ginger, E., Wright, K., Wright, M., Taylor, J., Humm, L., Olsen, D., Bell, M., & Fleming, M. (2014). Virtual Reality job interview training in adults with autism spectrum disorder. *Journal of Autism and Developmental Disorders*, 44(10), 2450–2463

Wang, M., & Jeon, M. (2024). Assistive technology for adults on the autism spectrum: A systematic survey. *International Journal of Human–Computer Interaction*, 40(10), 2433–2452.

Wang, M., Zhang, D., Huang, J., Yap, P., Shen, D., & Liu, M. (2020). Identifying autism spectrum disorder with multi-site fmri via low-rank domain adaptation. *IEEE Transactions on Medical Imaging*, 39(3), 644–655.

PARADIGMATIC CATEGORY 3

Smart Materiality

This Paradigmatic Category focuses on the role of fast-evolving smart materials and their impact on the process of form-making and the creation of design concepts that are free from material constraints and their advancements. Smart responsive materials undertake considerable responsibility for environmentally sensitive progressive architecture and promoting the ideals of realistic sustainable and energy-efficient built environments. By using information derived from quantum physics, nanotechnology, biology, chemistry, and AI, the chapters in this section offer progressive advancements that are currently taking place in the development of smart materials and tectonics of the built constructs. The fast-paced progressive role of imaging technology in developing various scales of superhard super-light synthetic materials with superhuman properties is indeed a major contributor to the creation of smart spaces for the design of various typologies.

 DOI: 10.4324/9781003384113-40

3.1

ON SCIENCE OF THE MATERIALS FOR THE BUILT ENVIRONMENTS – THE ROLE OF BIOMIMETICS/BIOMIMICRY AND DEVELOPMENT OF STRENGTH AND PROMOTING NATURAL FORMS AND FUNCTIONALITY INSPIRED BY NATURE

Bioreceptive Materials for Future Artificial Ecologies – Epizoochory: Evolution of Material and Methods

Mark Tholen

Abstract

A key aspect of intelligent utopian future cities is their ability to achieve high environmental performance over and beyond the cities we know. This chapter examines the bio-performance of materials and structures in the context of sustainable environments, where materials will be designed to empower new kinds of artificial ecologies developing on and around buildings and urban infrastructure. In this context, materials are rethought for the post-Anthropocene construction as forming a key component of bio-synergetic tectonics enabling historic principles of manufacturing for future ecological applications. This chapter offers a detailed examination of principal methods of biomimicry at a micro level to inform architecture and artificial ecologies designed for advanced technological environments.

DOI: 10.4324/9781003384113-41

This chapter will focus on the exciting subject of increasing methods in the development of man-made synthetic materials assemblies that are allowing the liberation of innovative structures by learning the tricks and nuances of nature, which is a major consideration in the field of material science. This is about blurring and challenging the *inert* traditional idea of materials for structural roles into new orders. This chapter focuses on the role of materials acting as innovative integrated elements forming future structures manipulated in analog and digital processes to form new synergies, by drawing on the materials' family tree, will look into the properties of each category's mechanism in creating structures beyond natural forms following nature's laws of physics.

Introduction

The task of writing this text comes at a difficult time when the written word is once again utilized and consumed unquestionably, surprisingly, by the most intelligent readers and writers. We used to rebel in our younger years, left countries with opposing ideologies, and questioned why and who would ultimately receive the profit from what is being prescribed or taught. Currently, we are facing multiple challenges in academia, where critical thinking, objectivity, or even simple questions suggesting an alternative are discouraged and students and faculty face dismissal in the event of critical assessments of situations. Education has been commercialized into repetition, and while repetition certainly allows for the perpetuation of thought in some fields of study, doctrination, and singular uncontested views undoubtedly give us order and internal correlation and some form of peace within; however, this also constitutes the root of stagnation. Critically reviewing agendas and understanding the impacts of teaching the status quo or integrating research into alternative options of the given is to be sought after, for example being open to a reduction in technology in final applications, not necessarily an increase, creating and facilitating an evolution to a simpler way of constructing and operating buildings as applied in the 2026 project by Baumschläger and Eberle. Not restraining the application of technology or artificial intelligence in the process, quite contrary, AI should be incorporated as a process of creation but then guided toward the simplicity of a building with less combination of complex technologies, well designed as a static and passive functional structure allowing genuine critical choices by the user through simple, efficient use of spaces and enclosure. In architectural education for the last decades' design-build approaches have been one of these impetuses that have challenged the high intellectual status of the profession and formed a successful return to learning from tradition to contest advances where we possibly went too far and require reviews toward real critical sustainability, not temporary technological advances but reintroducing and embracing alternative ways of nonlinear teaching. The 'Other' as identified by Philippe Barriere, is the needed impetus to trigger real positive change and development promoting and embracing optimism and passion in architecture and seeing architecture as a discipline and again a natural reflection of our culture. Nature and culture evolve by integrating change or the introduction of the other as it could become a prevailing option, ice ages come and go, warm centuries allowed forests to exist all over Nordic areas, and Greenland for instance still bears their natural identity in her name. Nature adapts to any given condition. Species evolve and go extinct as their habitat and nutrition evolve, disappear, or change, just as the finches develop various beaks on neighboring islands, due to alternate nutritional existence. Evolution within organisms ultimately is an effect of a mistake in the DNA, producing alternate results. In turn, tried and tested these adjustments manifested themselves as superior and became dominant. Alternate thought must be promoted on all levels of the process. In the realm of design, chance or an error in information is in due course seen as a vital strong element of progress and evolution (Enzio Manzini, 1989).

Evolution

Humans have been in the process of constructing their dwellings ever since we lost our fur (Manfed Hegger, 2012). In this, the evolutionary development of construction methods through trial and error has been the best designer amongst man-made dwellings. Adaptation to conditions in construction was essential ever since we left the security of the trees into the tall grass. Historically documented by Marc Antoine Laugier in 1755 with the famous drawing by Charles Eisen, the making of our first primitive huts, the properties of our building materials were used from posts made from branches and tree trunks in certain areas of the world that were gifted with the existence of moderate climates. In other geographic locations, adobe huts prevailed or structures made from cut ice to form the optimal structure-to-surface relation around a central fire or to bamboo split lengthwise to form troughs and ridges of a roof in Asia. An amazing testimony to the global spread of knowledge is evident from the Roman Empire to the Yangtze River as roof tile manufacturing advanced from simply using grasses, leaves, slates, or bamboo to more sophisticated clay tiles with the same principles of design, despite being 20.000km apart in geographic location. The minor difference is that due to more intense weather patterns, Chinese roofs used mortar to seal the joints compared to the dry-placed Roman principle. Ultimately, rain in Asia is known to not just follow the laws of gravity but may come from all directions.

Evolution in building methods is replicating nature and at the same time has occurred due to the challenges enforced and imposed by nature and climatic transformations throughout the ages. In emulating customs, we have developed through the historic assembly of materials, learning from nature in principle, from fish skin patterns for building skins replicated in wood or other sheet materials, to direct natural adaptation and application by utilizing animal skins or animal products like sheep and lama wool blankets to insulate or enclose dwellings, for instance in Asian yurt construction. Compressed sheep and lama wool or felt constitute the very first 'woven' fabric known to man before weaving was conceived, felt originated by chance as fur that hunters stuffed into their hide shoes accidentally creating this first fabric known to humans. Generated through the process known as 'Walken' in the Anglo-Saxon language, which is synonymous now with pressing or walking on it under the influence of warm moisture. Grass, seaweed, wool, and bark insulation are examples of direct natural substances entering the construction methods of habitation further. From the linguistic point of view giving names to the processes, a window in the Northern European languages describes an eye in the wall, Ow (Old Norse for eye or the German equivalent: Das Auge), the area of the wall where the winding of the sticks stops; the eye of the winding: Window, way before the introduction of glass. Surfaces and runoff principles were applied similarly in all cultures and so were the materials to create shelter. Shelter from the water above or below – the nave of a boat turned upside down becoming the nave of a longhouse, the naval vessel upside down gave birth to the function and name of the nave of a church.

Chance

Applying materials and methods through chance, failures, and successes, replicating nature, has been guiding us throughout our existence (Figure 3.1.1). In 1941, when the Swiss engineer George De Mestral came home from his walks in the Alps and, as always, found burdock burrs attached to his clothes and his dog Milka, he realized that this principle could be utilized to create a closure mechanism. The term he found for this invention came from the French words Velour and Crochet and he abbreviated this into Velcro. A group of engineers, and tool and die makers in Canada discovered methods to bring this technology from fashion and footwear to the engineered realm of automotive component assembly as a form of 'Metal Velcro'. After successful applications in the automotive industry, further options are being explored in the construction industry and field of architecture. In collaboration with the manufacturers of the material, we conceived and constructed the first 'Metal Velcro' structure for the Winter Station Competition, as a design-build research challenge in Toronto, Canada in 2016. Metaphorically this structure, the Steam Canoe, represented an upside-down boat, pulled up to the shore of Lake Ontario. The first nations of Turtle Island and the Vikings had practiced for centuries to create housing by sleeping under the hulls of their boats, which later developed into the principle of longhouses. Unlike the Indigenous birch bark hulls or the Nordic wood versions of cedar boats, the 'Steam Canoe' project at the shores of the lake did not need any structural frame, through the use of an innovative method of veneer lamination with 'Metal Velcro' the skin inherited its structural integrity and required no primary structural support. In the same fashion as the Urbach Tower by Achim Menges and Jan Knippers and other structures previously conceived by the ICD/ITKE Stuttgart, the structure of the Steam Canoe was achieved by the strengthening of the skin through lamination without the use of any glue and the utilization of innovative experimental production combining the traditional process of press rolling laminated timber panels with the new mechanical fastening technology of 'Metal Velcro' and the principle of curving the material (Figure 3.1.2).

Figure 3.1.1 Image of a burdock seed (Arctium), the long burrs or whorls of bracts allow the seed to be attached and carried by passing animals to spread the seed for long distances. Photo by Author.

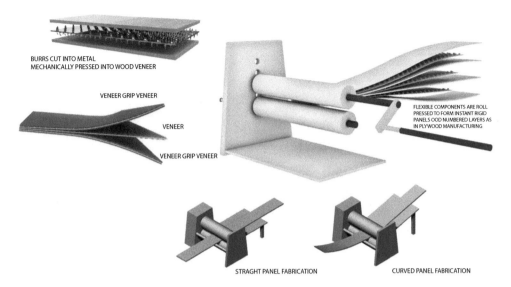

BURRS CUT INTO METAL
MECHANICALLY PRESSED INTO WOOD VENEER

VENEER GRIP VENEER

VENEER

VENEER GRIP VENEER

FLEXIBLE COMPONENTS ARE ROLL
PRESSED TO FORM INSTANT RIGID
PANELS OOD NUMBERED LAYERS AS
IN PLYWOOD MANUFACTURING

STRAGHT PANEL FABRICATION

CURVED PANEL FABRICATION

Figure 3.1.2   Fabrication Diagram (GRIP Metal). The layering of alternating materials of wood and metal. Press rolled into flat or complex curved shapes. Instantly forming rigid, strong hybrid structural panels. Utilizing the fastening principle of the burdock burrs in metal. Renderings: Jaewon Kim/Mark Tholen.

In this process, just like the burdock burrs are embedded into the fabric of passing fur or clothing, the metal burrs are pressed into the wood material to form a structural 'semi-permanent' bond; semi-permanent as it can be separated for recycling at the end of the lifespan of the product. Initially, two layers of continuous thin gauge metal layers were utilized around a central core of standard dimensional lumber and two outside veneers are taking on the interior and exterior locking surfaces structures. The geometry was achieved with a combination of analog and digital methods of computer-assisted parametric layout and analog cutting of the computer-generated forms.

Bending materials and applications of fractal geometries in structural surfaces, as an emulation of nature, results in compressing inner layers or the surface of materials and placing outer layers of the material into tension and with this creating an inherent stability of the complete form (Figure 3.1.3).

Nothing in the natural world is equivalent to a rectangular sheet of paper which naturally has no rigidity at all, other than tensile stability in two directions. In nature, all forms are non-integer dimensional forms, forms between two-dimensional surfaces or three-dimensional solids, forms that are characterized by self-similar repetitions of endless irregularity and with this creating strength as identified by Benoit Mandelbrot.

Application

This principle of 'Metal Velcro' is now being explored in a new way by layering alternating thin wood veneers with layers of metal for a far superior construction method, further enhancing the structural capacity of the skin. The forming principles explored by Ray and Charles Eames in plywood and the construction methodology of Jean Prouvé, who was the master in metal forming last century, are now fully incorporated into the latest structures

Figure 3.1.3   Steam Canoe project, prototype press laminated timber structure with solar hydronic heating elements, constructed for the 2016 Winter Station Competition, Toronto, Canada. The collaborative project, Curtis Ho, Amy Jungyun Lee, Jaewon Kim, Jason Wong, Mark Tholen, et al., in collaboration with Nucap Industries, Canada. Photo by Author.

that are being tested for prefabricated production. Jean Prouvé was visionary from his early furniture designs to his approaches to the prefabrication of housing, military structures, and industrial buildings. Working alongside Le Corbusier and inspired by his contemporary Marcel Breuer, Prouvé produced sophisticated industrialized pieces of mass-produced furniture and then ventured into buildings with simple assembly methods, lightweight designs that allowed a reduction in weight compared to conventional structures, originally coming from the ideas of taking flight in aircraft design. The weight reduction was possible by the innovative forming of the light material resulting in an increased structural capacity. These structures could be constructed or deconstructed with minimal labor and time due to their lightness and required no cranes compared to conventional solid structural steel structures.

During World War II, Prouvé was commissioned to design prefabricated barracks for the French army, which would allow him to progress his signature structural systems further, developing a characteristic vision for all his later architectural designs. These larger buildings were structurally more solid, yet still lightweight with his signature A-shaped columns that incorporated a ridge beam slotted into the column, in order to support the roof and walls. Inspiration for this work was drawn from general manufacturing processes of military vehicles, and machine and aircraft construction and ultimately reached new levels of material and method application processes in building construction that were similar to what was occurring in automotive design. An elimination of the frame and the space-saving more economical 'Unibody' philosophy of structure, eventually mimicking the natural phenomenon of an exoskeleton in organisms.

The distinction of a traditional syntax of wall structure manifested in the support structure, trunk or branch, and skin, leaves, or grass was blurred where cladding panels became the load-bearing structure. Prouve's work reached a peak for the Féderation du Bâtiment construction in Paris in 1949 and culminated in a visionary state with his Panneau Studal 'tout alu' principle. Walls are made from two layers of formed sheet aluminum skins, with vertical inside panels and horizontal outside sheets forming the complete wall assembly – innovative in the thermally separated point connectors that slipped perfectly into the horizontal and vertical bends of the micro corrugated material. This resulted in the elimination of the traditional structure for lightness and efficiency of material and with the skin becoming the structure, a construction method evolved that predated any considerations for thermally disconnected Passivhaus design.

Future

The blurred line between natural and man-made or artificial, between learning from nature, not as a replication of natural form, but beyond, to an application of principals that evolutionary natural intelligence provided to us, applied in process and materiality is replicated in a new type of structure, similarly to Prouvé's exoskeleton design, that is now being realized with the use of 'Metal Velcro' in the latest iteration of construction in the line of our prefabricated systems. A symbiotic performance of metal and wood for a new efficient constructability with maximized strength and minimized material use. The 'Metal Velcro' aids in the creation of an external skin, as a rigid exoskeleton structure as well as a secondary interior shell with thermally disconnected spacers and sustainable insulation made from hemp, used as a superior ecological natural alternative. Natural materials with centuries of applications have traditional high-quality strengths and inherent properties. While current industrial products certainly have an apparent initial superiority, the environmental impacts of these man-made artificial materials, in the long run, will be the evolutionary wrong beak length of the finch. This is where the critical ability to evaluate methods is so essential in teaching, combining genuine practical knowledge and allowing an education of choice, investigation, and alternate thought in parallel best taught in hands-on application. Education must inspire, excite, be filled with learning through making, and be filled with optimism and passion as we learn in half the time when these parameters are met (Steiner/Montessori). Out of this environment comes our latest award-winning thermally separated structure that is currently developed to be used as a socioeconomic seed, an economical prefabricated housing assembly for the town of Huron, California for migrant workers. Nature's adaptive inventions are now intertwined with the machine production process, analog intertwined with digital manufacturing, utilizing the best properties of each material with methods to form adequate sustainable habitation. The optimum relation of material to surface and area is not to create a form that is originally inspired by nature in shape, but a symbiotic ideal material assembly using naturally inspired micro principles. A sustainable reduction in material and at the same time, a maximization of internal structural forces by utilizing the right material in the most ideal location with calculated irregularities, creating strength; opening the stage to further research into materials and methods and toward an ecological future, from structural bio-simulations in fractal strengths to performance materials that will self-heal or absorb carbon, forming part of our constructed human ecology. The options for a future ecology simulate what nature applied for millions of years in principle, function, and performance on all levels, but predominantly internal levels of scale within the material and the method, as a logical advancement of our culture (Figure 3.1.4).

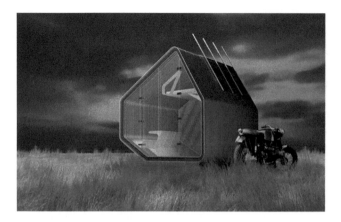

Figure 3.1.4   10m2 experimental prototype, Bas-Saint-Laurent, Canada. Double-press laminated skin with thermal separation and hemp insulation. 50m2/550sqft version in planning for Huron, California. 2022 Green Good Design Award, Chicago. Photo by Author-TYYZ

Bibliography

Barnsley, M. (2014). *Fractals Everywhere*, Academic Press.

Blanciak, F. (2008). *Siteless, 1001 Building Forms*, MIT Press

Burry, J. (2020). *Fabricate*, Riverside Architectural Press.

Deleuze, G. (2003). *The Fold. Leibniz and the Baroque*, Continuum London.

Foster, H. (2002). *The Anti-Aesthetic: Essays on Postmodern Culture*, The New Press.

Frampton, K. (2011). *Rappel à Ordre: The case for the Tectonic*, Chronicle Books.

Gissen, D. (2009). *Subnature: Architecture's other Environments*, Princeton Architectural Press.

Gramazio, F. (2008). *Digital Materiality in Architecture*, Lars Müller Publishers Zürich.

Grant, P. (2017). *Ecology and Evolution*, Princeton University Press.

Hegger, M. (2012). *Heat | Cool: Energy Concepts*, Birkhäuser.

Jacobs, J. (2005). *Dark Age Ahead*, Vintage.

Leach, N. (2014). *Swarm Tectonics, Digital Tectonics*, Wiley.

Manzini, E. (1989). *The Material of Invention*, MIT Press.

Nesbit, K. (1996). *Theorizing a New Agenda for Architecture*, Chronicle Books.

Orr, D. (2002). *The Nature of Design: Ecology, Culture and Human Intention*, Oxford University Press.

Pallasmaa, J. (2007). *The Eyes of the Skin: Architecture and the Senses*, Wiley.

Pawley, M. (1990). Theory *and Design in the Second Machine Age*, Blackwell.

Pawlyn, M. (2016). *Biomimicry in Architecture*, RIBA Publishing.

Schwartz, C. (2017). *Introducing Architectural Tectonics, Exploring the Intersection of Design and Construction*, Routledge.

Semper, G. (1851–1989). *The Four Elements of Architecture and other Writings*, New York, Cambridge.

Sennet, R. (2018). *Building and Dwelling: Ethics for the City, Farrar*, Straus and Giroux.

Sequin, P. (2007). *Jean Prouvé*, Sonnabend & Sequin NY.

Silk, G. (1984). *Automobile and Culture*, Harry N. Abrams, NY.

Spiller, N. (2018). *Celebrating the Marvellous: Surrealism in Architecture*, Wiley.

Sulzer, P. (1991). *Jean Prouvé*, Meister der Metallumformung: Das Neue Blech, Rudolf Mueller.

Thomsen, M. (2024). *Design for Rethinking Resources, Sustainable Development Goal Series*, Springer.

Von Meiss, P. (2004). *Elements of Architecture: From Form to Place*, Routledge.

Von Vegesack, A. (2004). *The Poetics of the Technical Object*, Vitra Design Museum.

Waldrop, M. (1992). *Complexity: The Emerging Science at the Edge of Order and Chaos*, Simon and Schuster.

Zumthor, P. (2010). *Thinking Architecture* (3rd ed.), Birkhaeuser.

3.2

SMART WAYS TO ENCLOSE BUILDINGS

Using Super-Strong, Super-Hard, and Flexible Biomaterials Designed with Nano- and Mesoscale Technology

Negar Kalantar, Evan Jones, Margaret Ikeda and Dyche Mullins

Abstract

In this age of rapid technological advancement, the architecture of our buildings is undergoing a transformative shift. Enclosures are now an integral part of sustainable, smart, and environmentally conscious design. The expertise is available to achieve energy-efficient buildings, but the emphasis on whole-life carbon is focusing research on low embodied energy building materials. This chapter introduces the concept of utilizing biomaterials designed with nano- and mesoscale technology to create resources for innovative building enclosures on a macroscale.

The last few decades have witnessed an exponential growth in the capabilities of parametric modeling and large-scale fabrication methods. Architectural designers have developed an interest in the potential for complex geometries, allowing for a reimagining of the ways our buildings and cities are made. Through the refinement of fabrication tools, what began as speculative exploration has evolved into full-scale prototypes for novel building assemblies.

Recent architectural forms are becoming increasingly fluid in their geometries and ability to align with the structural requirements of buildings. Novel fabrication methods represent a new paradigm of building form that is accompanied by even newer logics. With this comes the uncoupling of the traditional order, which is based on repetitive panelized construction and rectangular [orthographic] geometries. As we explore this present-day terrain and associated efficiencies, it becomes possible to incorporate the microbiological world as a model for structure and ecological performance.

In this age of rapid technological advancement, the architecture of our buildings is undergoing a transformative shift. Enclosures are now an integral part of sustainable, smart, and environmentally conscious design. The expertise is available to achieve energy-efficient buildings, but the emphasis on whole-life carbon is focusing research on low embodied energy building materials. This chapter introduces the concept of utilizing biomaterials

DOI: 10.4324/9781003384113-42

designed with nano- and mesoscale technology to create resources for innovative building enclosures on a macroscale.

The last few decades have witnessed exponential growth in the capabilities of parametric modeling and large-scale fabrication methods. Architectural designers have developed an interest in the potential for complex geometries, allowing for a reimagining of the ways our buildings and cities are made. Through the refinement of fabrication tools, what began as speculative exploration has evolved into full-scale prototypes for novel building assemblies.

Recent architectural forms are becoming increasingly fluid in their geometries and ability to align with the structural requirements of buildings. Novel fabrication methods represent a new paradigm of building form that is accompanied by even newer logic. With this comes the uncoupling of the traditional order, which is based on repetitive panelized construction and rectangular [orthographic] geometries. As we explore this present-day terrain and associated efficiencies, it becomes possible to incorporate the microbiological world as a model for structure and ecological performance.

Biological Examples

The ability of microscopic animals to utilize local resources to produce hard shells is foundational for individual species' survival and perpetuation. Marine organisms' capacity to produce shells arose through biological processes that precipitate calcium carbonate from the environment. Innumerable marine invertebrates are able to harness the calcium ions and carbon dioxide present in water. Within the context of evolutionary pressures, more successful organisms could create harder and more resilient shells while also expending the least amount of energy. This means that while this chemical ability is crucial, the evolution of formal geometries that optimize these materials is equally significant. Taken as a whole, these structures provide a catalog of forms iterated over millions of years, and many are now achievable through additive fabrication techniques.

Unlike crystal formation in the abiotic world, which features static angular geometries that emerge purely from the physical conditions, living creatures operate within a dynamic environment. Demands related to predation and growth create more complex variations in form that are inextricably connected to the microbiological processes through which shells are grown around bodies. Variations in such shells are a result of many environmental factors. In this way, they can be looked at as precedents for the design of architecturally "smart" materials and structures (Figure 3.2.1).

Beyond these geometric and environmental advancements, shells have also perfected the ability to self-heal. This means that the same processes that create the initial shell can be deployed to repair (and in some cases, improve) its performance. Considered in this way, another advantage of these naturally based structures is that they can adapt their shapes through the addition of materials in a manner that is responsive to a changing environment.

Fabrication

In our own bodies, bones can heal to be stronger after an initial breakthrough of calcium carbonate deposited over time. Fabrication processes in nature resemble 3D printing, such as in the layer-by-layer additive growth of shells and coral reefs. As layers are added sequentially, their resultant complexity often emerges from a simple set of parameters. For example, seashells' intricate patterns, including spirals and spines, are created by mollusks

Figure 3.2.1 (a) Biomineralization (Achal, Pan 2014), (b) coccolithophores. Consisted of two images: Image to the left: (from the paper by Dr Achal). Title: Biomineralization for sustainable construction – A review of processes and applications. Authors: Varenyam Achal a,*, Abhijit Mukherjee a,b, Deepika Kumari c, Qiuzhuo Zhang. Image to the right: (from Wikimedia Commons). File: Diversity of coccolithophores.jpg, https://en.m.wikipedia. org/wiki/File:Diversity_of_coccolithophores.jpg

following three fundamental rules during shell growth: expand, rotate, and twist. A mollusk's mantle deposits layers of calcium carbonate, uniformly expanding the shell's opening, turning it to achieve a full rotation, and finally twisting the points of deposition to create helicoidal shells. Mechanical forces generated during growth (such as rapid expansion and compression) lead to additional features like spines (Moulton et al., 2021).

The advancement of robotic printing offers numerous advantages when compared to traditional construction technologies. The resulting improvement in materials efficiency, fabrication precision, and speed makes it a promising choice for the construction industry. Particularly on a mesoscale, in additive manufacturing (AM), the impact of process parameters on the bond strength between layers is crucial. In real-world materials, deposition using a robotic-assisted AM process, environmental factors such as temperature, humidity, the load from upper layers, and nozzle pressure on printed layers come into play. These factors introduce a secondary geometric characteristic into the printed objects that is absent from the initial digital model. Thanks to robotic-assisted AM, we now have a deeper understanding of how process parameters affect the bond strength between layers of paste in the construction of large-scale structures (Farahbakhsh et al., 2021).

Embodied Energy

AM also avoids many problems related to construction waste because the material is extruded as needed, eliminating the cutoff and partial usage of materials seen in traditional construction. By linking fabrication to a single material, the embodied energy of that material can be fully controlled. This is significant because while the design and construction of carbon-neutral buildings are becoming increasingly attainable from an energy-use perspective, the embodied energy needed to manufacture building materials continues to be a challenge (Wurm et al., 2021). A "whole life cycle" metric considers not only the performance of the material but also its manufacture, leading to the development of bio-cementation as an alternative to cement-based concrete, the production of which is responsible for 8% of the total annual CO_2 emissions (Lehne & Preston et al., 2018).

The ability of multiple species (ranging from plankton to mollusks and birds) to fabricate shells through the precipitation of calcium carbonate obtained from their environment was a source of inspiration for the present work. Since many of the most common industrial construction materials (such as cement and metals) require an intense amount of heat energy to manufacture, the more the focus turns to bio-based models, the greater the chance of reducing the overall carbon footprint. Nature offers myriad examples of shell-like materials achieving properties comparable to and applicable on an architectural scale. Some of the simplest bacteria produce calcium carbonate throughout their lives. These may represent the most ideal source since they can easily be concentrated and used in place of cement binders.

Producing new building components aligned with biological processes requires merging the expertise of biologists and engineers, and the consequent potential to "grow" building materials promises to significantly reduce the embodied energy in buildings (Achal et al., 2016).

Working with Scientists

Mixtures of living bacteria capable of producing calcium carbonate for construction purposes is a new area of design investigation requiring the integration of expertise in design, engineering, and biology. Bio-cementation on a microscale does not directly correlate to a building materials level. Biologists and designers often find themselves removed from the intricate processes of materials development, testing, and fabrication. Finding the right recipe for growing, mixing, and placing bio-cement requires close collaboration with cellular biologists, engineers, and materials scientists. Synergizing skills and knowledge from multiple disciplines will facilitate groundbreaking advancements in this emerging discipline.

To bring about the development of innovative hybrids, the authors engaged in a collaborative research effort known as "Bacterra," a name symbolizing the fusion of biology and earth architecture. Along with a valuable industry collaborator, the Autodesk Research Group, this collaborative endeavor included three academic labs: the CCA Digital Craft Lab, CCA Architectural Ecologies Lab, and the UCSF MULLINS LAB of Molecular and Cellular Pharmacology. This collective initiative was tasked with exploring the possibility of creating new building components aligned with biological processes.

The designers at the CCA labs brought knowledge of the required properties of extrudable clay and tested various concentrations of bacterial densities to add to such clay. In this case, the synergy between the designers and scientists was crucial in determining what would be scientifically and technically feasible and how these two essential components could harmoniously intersect. This demanded a thoughtful design and scientific research strategy that took into account the growth dynamics of the bacterial medium that would be used to build strength in earthen architectural materials.

Micro-, Meso-, and Macroscales

The Bacterra exploration was initiated across three distinct scales, micro- (nano-), meso-, and macro-, each offering a unique perspective on the convergence of biology and design for earth construction. On the microscale, the project delved into materials exploration, analyzing the molecular and structural properties of biological components in order to unlock their potential as building materials. Moving to the mesoscale, the focus shifted to the intricacies of printing, where precision and control are of the utmost importance. Here, the team considered how to harness these biologically derived materials in the AM process, ensuring that they could be effectively used in construction, and determined how AM process parameters might affect the printability and strength of the material. Finally, on the macroscale, the project expanded its perspective to consider the holistic geometry of entire buildings. This involved envisioning and designing structures that incorporated local earthen resources to be biologically strengthened. The three scales collectively formed the foundation of the Bacterra initiative, driving forward the frontiers of ecological architecture. In the following section, we provide an overview of these three explorations across various scales.

UCSF cellular and molecular biologists informed and guided the nanoscale efforts, allowing for the safe integration of a ubiquitous and non-toxic bacterium that activated the biomineralization process in other materials, resulting in safe outcomes. The science research labs provided a clean space designed to limit airborne contaminants; they were set up to grow bacteria to their optimal maturity before handing off the medium to designers to mix with clay and ground recycled sea urchin. After drying, the bioclay samples were brought back to UCSF and checked with high-powered magnification tools to see if the bacteria had successfully crystallized on a nanoscale, giving the material the super-hard and super-strong characteristics similar to those of shells.

A key goal of our work was to harness the natural ability of microbes to precipitate soluble forms of calcium into insoluble calcium carbonate crystals. When carried out in the context of building materials such as concretes and clays, this process can help cement small particles and plug holes in matrices (Rong et al., 2012; Abo-El-Enein et al., 2013). These microscale effects can then affect the mesoscale mechanical properties of a material by decreasing porosity and water ingress and significantly increasing compressive strength.

In choosing appropriate microbial species for this work, we were guided by several essential criteria. The organisms had be (1) ubiquitous in the natural environment, (2) safe to handle and live around, and (3) tractable to acculturation and manipulation. The first criterion was important because we wanted to use materials that are readily available to builders and communities around the world. Another benefit to using ubiquitous species is avoiding the introduction of alien – and potentially invasive – species into sensitive ecosystems. The second criterion meant avoiding the need for expensive safety equipment during the building process and potential health effects for later occupants. The third criterion ensured that using such organisms would help to contain costs, decrease construction times, and reduce the amount of training required to employ the method and material.

One species that satisfied our three selection criteria was *Bacillus subtilis*, an aerobic, gram-positive soil bacterium. First, *B. subtilis* is a ubiquitous species found in soil samples from around the world. It secretes several enzymes that enable it to metabolize different types of carbon sources (i.e., food) and thrive in varied and continuously changing environments. Second, decades of practical experience and safety testing have led this organism to be generally recognized as safe (see e.g., Westers et al., 2004; Zweers et al., 2008). It has been employed for decades as a model system in biomedical research and the chemical and biochemical industries. In the latter, companies routinely use it to produce commercially important enzymes and bio-therapeutics (Su et al., 2020; Westers et al., 2004; Zweers et al., 2008). Finally, its robust physiology and highly adaptable metabolism make it easy to store and cultivate on inexpensive and widely available substrates (Su et al., 2020). In addition, when its cells are starved of nutrients, they form extremely tough spores that can survive in conditions as hostile as the vacuum of space. The survivability of these spores raises the intriguing possibility that microbial cells entombed in a building material at the time of its creation could be "reanimated" by nutrients leaking in through cracks. Once reawakened, these cells could help catalyze a means of "healing" these cracks (De Belie et al., 2009; Wiktor et al., 2012).

For our project, we grew bacteria in a minimal medium containing urea as a carbon source and calcium chloride as a source of calcium for biomineralization. It was important to make sure that the medium was alkaline to avoid leaching calcium out of the structure and promote optimal bacterial growth (DeBelie et al., 2009; Wiktor et al., 2012). Upon curing, we tested the mechanical properties (i.e., compressive strength and porosity) of our bio-cemented materials against control materials that lacked the added *B. subtilis*. We then used scanning electron microscopy to study the nanoscale architecture of the material and assess the density of embedded bacterial spores in the final cured product. We tested the material for the presence of viable spores by pulverizing samples and attempting to culture *B. subtilis* from the powdered residue. We next assessed the self-healing properties of the material by inducing fractures and measuring the porosity over time in the presence and absence of added urea-containing cultures. In addition to optimizing the self-healing properties of the material, we adapted our original mixture to create microbe-containing mortars to repair cracks (Figure 3.2.2).

On a mesoscale, the CCA's labs were set up for flexibility and to accommodate messy processes such as work zones for clay potterbot machines requiring space to mix, air dry, and assemble materials. The labs allowed for geometrical and material experimentation on a component scale with modified setups designed for clay-bodied printing. Design experimentation revolved around mixing material to an appropriate consistency to extrude at a rate ideal for good layer adhesion. Variations in nozzle size, rate of extrusion, and speed were all resolved on this scale. Further experiments were conducted regarding the drying conditions of the samples, as well as the application of additional nutrients during the

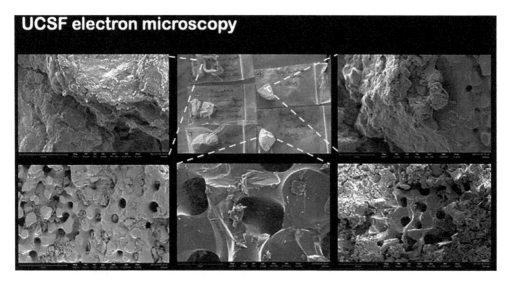

Figure 3.2.2   Electron microscopy images from the Mullins Lab (2023) (Courtesy of Dr. Dyche Mullins).

drying time. Components designed and tested in such ways acted as a proof-of-concept for the structural capability that could be enjoyed if scaled up to the size of a house or city.

Drawing upon previous research on the importance of the mesoscale in architectural innovation (Farahbakhsh et al., 2022), the exploration of the scale was conducted in two stages. The first involved printing with clay potterbots at CCA's labs. During this stage, the focus was on printing layers and conducting geometrical and materials experiments on a component level. Working with a new material for 3D printing requires many extrusion experiments, in this case specifically tailored for clay-bodied printing. This process facilitated fast prototyping and allowed for swift iterations of the recipe for the printable clay. It became clear that refining this recipe was not only about ensuring structural stability and layer bonding, but also alignment with the machine's properties, fine-tuning of the force required (air pressure and motor power), and ensuring smooth and consistent printing.

During the second stage of exploration, robotic 3D printing was utilized to enhance the functionality, precision, and complexity of the form. At the Autodesk Technology Center in San Francisco, an advanced AM robotic system was developed that exceeded the capabilities of conventional planar printing methodologies. Six-axis 3D printing offers at least two advantages over conventional three-axis printing tools, including the ability to adjust print parameters such as speed, nozzle height, printing flow, and speed of the robots, all of which affect layer bonding. Additionally, the technology provides greater freedom to explore more complex geometries beyond the limitations of conventional planar printing (Figure 3.2.3).

On a macroscale, exploration was focused on a larger scale and geometrical patterns from civilizations that have been developing earth architecture for thousands of years. Computational tools were employed to optimize the structure, minimizing materials usage

Figure 3.2.3 Mesoscale studies, CCA Digital Craft Lab, Architectural Ecologies Lab, and Autodesk Technology Center. (Courtesy of Author, Margaret Ikeda)

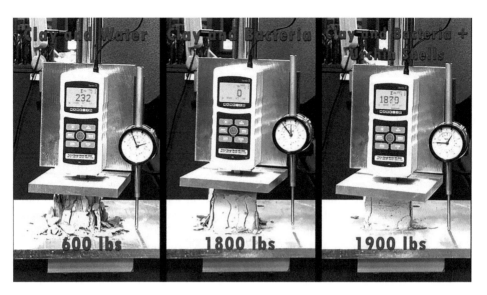

Figure 3.2.4 Autodesk Technology Center compression testing. (Courtesy of Author, Margaret Ikeda).

while ensuring the highest levels of structural and environmental performance. Through 3D printing technology, the creation of more intricate sections resembling bone structures became possible. Known for their unique microstructure and composition, bone structures possess the remarkable quality of being both porous and strong. Their inherent pores and channels contribute significantly to their reduced weight. The strength of a bone is attributed to its composition, which consists of collagen fibers and mineralized calcium phosphate crystals that provide it with a hardness and resistance to deformation.

Verification of the strength of the biomaterial was provided at the Autodesk Technology Center. Three 4″×4″ square cubes of different mixtures, (1) clay and water, (2) clay and the bacteria medium, and (3) clay, the bacteria medium, and ground sea urchin were tested on machines to determine their compression capabilities. Tests were conducted with Autodesk's building materials research group, resulting in confirmation of the ability of the bacteria to enhance the compressive strength of the material. Further research is needed to graduate this material to an industrially viable manufacturing scale, but the design and science method developed by the team for the prototypes will be transferable to efforts to address these technical challenges (Figure 3.2.4).

Biological Opportunities

By foregrounding the biological process of calcium precipitation, it is hoped that further strains of bacteria can be isolated that will address some of the issues still in need of development. With the bacillus mix, the material is not hydrophobic. Thus, there is the potential to investigate other bacteria that may be compatible with seawater, allowing for a less precious resource to be used in larger-scale construction and the potential provision of greater strength. In the near future, should there be an ability to synthesize the proteins that mollusks use, an entirely greater structural capacity could be achieved. At present, the ways in which some of the most basic and simple animals perform biomineralization are still elusive, and it remains to be seen if synthetic biology will ever decode and replicate these methods. In the meantime, it is completely possible to integrate these bacteria directly into a mixture, creating a naturally non-toxic composite material equally dependent on the strength of the earth as on the binding capacity of a simple biological process.

Conclusion

This chapter investigates the fascinating intersection of architecture, biology, and cutting-edge technology. It presents a range of possibilities in which the integration of nano- and mesoscale technologies revolutionizes the very essence of building enclosures. This work showcases the emergence of biomaterials that draw inspiration from the intricate wonders of the natural world, possessing superlative strength, remarkable resilience, and an inherent affinity for sustainability.

The heart of this chapter lies in interdisciplinary collaboration: a harmonious convergence of biologists, engineers, and designers. This union of diverse experts was the catalyst for creating building materials that not only withstand the test of time but also contribute to a greener, more environmentally conscious future. It is within this crucible of collective intelligence that we will discover the true potential of living organisms for use in architecture, a future in which building materials become dynamic, adaptable, and self-healing.

As we navigate this uncharted terrain of ecological architecture, we find ourselves on the brink of a transformative era. According to this vision, buildings are no longer static structures, but rather dynamic participants in the ecosystems they inhabit. They adapt, repair, and contribute to the preservation of our environment. This chapter serves as a compass pointing towards a future in which our constructions are not just shelters, but rather integral components of a sustainable world, embodying the philosophy of harmonious coexistence with nature (Figure 3.2.5).

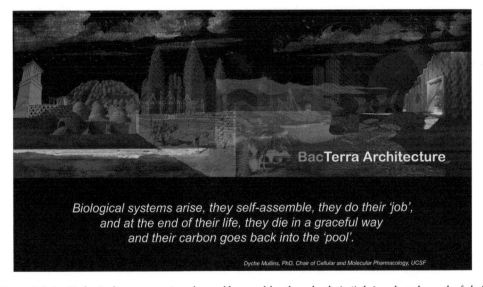

Figure 3.2.5 Biological systems arise, they self-assemble, they do their 'job,' and at the end of their life, they die gracefully, and their carbon goes back into the 'pool.' Dyche Mullins, PhD, Chair of Cellular and Molecular Pharmacology, UCSF (Image, Courtesy of Author, Margaret Ikeda).

Biological systems arise, they self-assemble, they do their 'job,' and at the end of their life, they die in a graceful way, and their carbon goes back into the 'pool.'

Dyche Mullins, PhD, Chair of Cellular and
Molecular Pharmacology, UCSF

References

Abo-El-Enein, S. A., Ali, A. H., Talkhan, F. N., & Abdel-Gawwad, H. A. (2013). Application of microbial biocementation to improve the physico-mechanical properties of cement mortar. *HBRC Journal*, 9(1), 36–40.

Achal, V., Mukherjee, A., & Zhang, Q. (2016). Unearthing ecological wisdom from natural habitats and its ramifications on development of biocement and sustainable cities. *Landscape and Urban Planning*, 155, 61–68.

De Belie, N., & De Muynck, W. (2008, November). Crack repair in concrete using biodeposition. In *Proceedings of the international conference on concrete repair, rehabilitation and retrofitting (ICCRRR), Cape Town, South Africa* (pp. 291–292).

Dezeen. (July 16, 2021). Drive to reduce embodied carbon in buildings makes biomaterials market a "really exciting space". Interview with Jan Wurm, Arup research and innovation. https://www.dezeen.com/2021/07/16/carbon-drive-reduce-embodied-carbon-buildings-biomaterials-jan-wurms/

Farahbakhsh, M., Rybkowski, Z. K., Zakira, U., Kalantar, N., & Onifade, I. (2022). Impact of robotic 3D printing process parameters on interlayer bond strength. *Automation in Construction*, 142, 104478.

Farahbakhsh, M., Kalantar, N., & Rybkowski, Z. (2021). Impact of Robotic 3D Printing Process Parameters on Bond Strength: A Systematic Analysis Using Clay-Based Materials. In *Proceedings of the ACADIA 2020 Conference* (pp. 594–603).

Lehne, J., & Preston, F. (2018, June 13). Making concrete change: Innovation in low-carbon cement and concrete | chatham house - international affairs think tank. Chatham House. https://www.chatham-house.org/2018/06/making-concrete-change-innovation-low-carbon-cement-and-concrete

Moulton, D., Goriely, A. & Chirat, R. (2018). *Spirals, Spines, and Ridges: The Mathematical Story of Seashells*. Scientific American, April 2018.

Rong, H., & Qian, C. X. (2012). Development of microbe cementitious material in China. *Journal of Shanghai Jiaotong University (Science)*, 17, 350–355.

Su, Y., Liu, C., Fang, H., & Zhang, D. (2020). Bacillus subtitles: a universal cell factory for industry agriculture biomaterials and medicine. *Microbial Cell Factories*, 19, 173.

Westers, L., Westers, H., & Quax, W. J. (2004). Bacillus subtilis as cell factory for pharmaceutical proteins: a biotechnological approach to optimize the host organism. *Biochim Biophys Acta*, 1694, 299–310.

Wiktor, V., Thijssen, A., & Jonkers, H. M. (2012). Development of a liquid bio-based repair system for aged concrete structures. In *Concrete Repair, Rehabilitation and Retrofitting III*. Alexander et al. (eds), pp. 345–346.

Zweers, J. C., Barak, I., Becher, D., Driessen, A. J., Hecker, M., Kontinen, V. P., Saller, M. J., Vavrova, L., van Dijl, J. M. (2008). Towards the development of Bacillus subtilis as a cell factory for membrane proteins and protein complexes. *Microbial Cell Fact*, 7, 10.

3.3

SMART MATERIALS AS ARCHITECTURED POROUS AND HYBRID SYSTEMS TO PRODUCE PERFORMATIVE BUILDING COMPONENTS

Sina Mostafavi, Edgar Montejano Hernandez and Ding Wen Bao

Abstract

This chapter delves into the transformative potential of computational design and digital production processes when applied to the creation of porous and hybrid materials in the realms of architecture and design. The main focus is on how informed architectured material systems can increase the structural, environmental, and functional performance of the built environment on multiple scales. In architecture, porosity entails the deliberate distribution of substance and void at different scales, while hybridity encompasses the combination of multiple materials to attain specific material properties or behaviors. Computed porosity has the potential to enhance structural efficiency and reduce embodied energy by lowering weight, while controlled hybridity allows for customization of material behavior and characteristics at the localized level within building components. This chapter explores the advancements in utilizing integrated design computation for digital production and delves into the application of porous and hybrid architectural material systems in the design and construction of built structures. Additionally, the prototypical projects illustrate how cutting-edge technologies are poised to revolutionize the standardized palette of materials available to architects and designers, opening a wealth of possibilities for innovation and creativity.

Keywords

Smart Materials; Porosity; Hybridity; Material Architecture; Performance Driven Design

DOI: 10.4324/9781003384113-43

Introduction and Background

In contemporary architecture, the integration of smart materials has become a transformative frontier, reshaping the conception, construction, and experience of architecture. Architectured materials exhibit augmented properties directly linked to their geometry. These architected or hybrid materials fulfill demanding engineering requirements when conventional materials are impractical (Ashby & Bréchet, 2003, Bouaziz et al., 2008, Barthelat, 2015, Estrin et al., 2019). This paradigm shift is driven by technological advancements, a deeper understanding of material science, and the need for sustainable, adaptive, and responsive built environments. This chapter explores the incorporation of smart materials at micro, meso, and macroscales, emphasizing the design and production of hybridity and porosity. It delves into design computation and fabrication of architectured material systems through integrated performance drive design processes. It further discusses how the implementation of informed porosity and hybridity results in the optimization of material distribution, assemblies, and spatial arrangements (Mostafavi & Bier, 2016).

The adoption of smart materials in architecture is fueled by technological capabilities to harness materials responding to environmental stimuli. The introduction of emerging modes of computation and robotic building processes brings forth a plethora of opportunities for optimization in architecture, engineering, and manufacturing workflows (Mostafavi & Anton, 2018). The era of climate change and resource scarcity calls for innovation in sustainable practices, materials design, energy use, and circular systems to enhance the performance of the built environment. Digital technologies and material science convergence enable design innovation for structures interacting actively with surroundings and occupants. The urgency to create efficient buildings propels smart materials into the spotlight in the discipline of architecture to build resilient communities and environments (Mehan & Mostafavi, 2022).

In architecture, porosity entails the deliberate distribution of substance and void at different scales, while hybridity encompasses the combination of multiple materials to attain specific material properties or behaviors. Computed porosity has the potential to enhance structural efficiency and reduce embodied energy by lowering weight, while controlled hybridity allows for customization of material behavior and characteristics at the localized level within building components. In the realm of material innovation, the use of informed densities in computed materials leads to the development of novel composite systems, exemplified by Functionally Graded Porous Materials (FGPM), strategically manipulated through porosity gradients (Lu et al., 2023). Exploring hybridity, contemporary methods in computation and production revolutionize hybrid systems, yet the historical roots of smart materials trace back to concepts like Shape-Memory Alloys (SMA) from the 1960s. The recent surge in digital modeling and fabrication enables the handling of established materials and the utilization of previously unmanageable elements (Schröpfer & Carpenter, 2011). Advancements in computational design, simulations, and fabrication drive materials to exhibit responsive and adaptive characteristics. The journey of smart materials, from twentieth-century kinetic facades to recent developments like self-healing concrete (Jonkers et al., 2010), reflects a continuous quest for integration, efficiency, and sustainability in the realm of informed material design.

Looking ahead, smart materials offer vast possibilities. Their versatility allows structures to dynamically respond to changing environmental conditions, optimizing energy consumption, and enhancing occupant comfort. Utilizing digital methods in design and production enhances the efficiency of handling complex geometries and optimizes the efficiency of structural systems. Integrated workflows fuse form-finding and production to deliver performance-driven building systems and components that are informed structurally, environmentally, and functionally, (Morales-Beltran & Mostafavi, 2022, Li et al., 2023) contributing to a comprehensive approach in the design and production of high-performance structures.

Architectured Porosity and Hybridity

At the microscale, smart materials are intricately regulated by molecular and atomic properties. Computational models empower architects to comprehend and manipulate these properties, fostering innovations at the nano and material levels. Before these advancements, correlated material properties such as strength and density could be separated and tailored for the required application (Azulay et al., 2023). Moving to the mesoscale, the aggregation of smart materials into building components relies on simulation tools to predict performance and interactions. This middle ground becomes a testing field, bridging microscale behaviors to larger architectural constructs. Ascending to the macroscale, the focus shifts to ensuring the structural integrity of the entire building. Computational models and simulations play a crucial role in guaranteeing safety, stability, and long-term performance (Ahlquist & Menges, 2013). This approach illustrates how algorithmic thinking influences the built environment, aligning aesthetic design with robust and enduring architectural solutions at multiple scales ranging the tectonics to assembly.

At the microscale, the precise manipulation of materials impacts porosity, defining the permeability of spaces. Hybridity is showcased as nano-level innovations enable the seamless blending of traditional and innovative materials. The realization of structurally controlled and nano-architected porous structures can impart improved functionalities, including lightweight systems to reinforced mechanical properties that are even superior to those of its raw block of materials (Yeo et al., 2019). In this context, the production of hybrid material systems requires methods of digital modeling and computation of multi-materiality using multi-mode production methods (Mostafavi et al., 2019). Building on this background, the emphasis of this chapter lies in the realm of design computation and digital fabrication applied to porous and hybrid systems across various scales, where material properties, behaviors, and performances are purposefully computed and augmented. Furthermore, case studies address how fabrication intelligence leveraging the programmability and flexibility of robotic production empowers architects and builders to conceive informed porous and hybrid systems (Mostafavi, 2021).

Microscale: Architecturing Properties

Architectured properties at the microscale are intricately linked to the chemophysical compositions and the topological characteristic of material structure. When it comes to hybridity, in composite materials, the combination of substances with their distribution pattern plays a crucial role in achieving desired material design. This is exemplified by fiber-reinforced polymers (FRP), which rely on polymer matrix composites like polyester, vinyl, epoxy, and polyurethanes, along with reinforcing fibers such as glass, carbon, aramid, and basalt. Advancements in compounding bio-based materials and fabrication techniques enable purposeful modifications of properties, expanding the material options for architectural applications. The application of unconventional materials such as fiber composites in architecture has historical roots, as seen in projects like the Monsanto House. Informed material deposition and distribution, employing techniques like 3D printing and robotic weaving, can enhance the strength of similar free-form shell structures while minimizing material consumption (Mohamed et al., 2021). These combinations yield materials with a high strength-to-weight ratio and diverse properties like durability, damping, flexural strength, and resistance to corrosion, wear, impact, and stiffness.

The versatility of architectured materials across multiple scales is essential for the relevant application of advanced manufacturing in the building industry. The programmability of smart materials on a microscale enhances the properties of building components, significantly contributing to efficient material conception and reducing embodied energy. The shift from mass-producing repetitive building elements to customizing architectural components, and strategically distributing materials as needed, marks a significant change in tailoring mechanical properties at higher resolutions within the building industry. While the mass production of repetitive parts using high-performance materials like fibers brings efficiencies, architectural challenges arise with limited repetition due to the high cost of conventional techniques such as casting with molds. Emerging digital building technologies in production make smart materials more accessible in microscales by minimizing material usage and maximizing efficiency through bespoke integrated workflows. Technological advancements, including 3D printing, broaden the applications of multi-material and porous systems.

Advancements in manufacturing technologies hold the promise of mass production at no extra costs. Concurrently, generative design processes employing techniques such as multi-agent systems, Finite Element Methods (FEM) and Machine Learning (ML) algorithms have been emerging in architectural practices and academia. These processes empower designers to control and enhance the properties of architectural materials at micro scales. Techniques like topology optimization, widely utilized in structural fields, aim to maximize structural performance (Bao et al., 2022), providing strength and durability while facilitating the production of complex designs, particularly advantageous in architecture and product design. The application extends to prototyping in product development, involving fabrication with robotic arms. This process includes creating a toolpath through computer-aided design (CAD) and computer-aided machining (CAM) software for the robot to execute (Bilotti et al., 2018). However, a key challenge lies in transitioning computed morphologies, often described in the forms of pixels, voxels, or point clouds, into robotically producible topologies applicable to the scale of architectural constructs (Figure 3.3.1). The successful creation of toolpaths relies on a combination of digital calibrations, mathematical calculations, and the understanding of material properties through physical testing. Extruded materials, with their complex parameters, pose challenges that cannot be easily predicted or parameterized in a script (Rosenwasser et al., 2017). Hence, the attainment of fabrication intelligence necessitates simultaneous development and exploration of design, material, and production space.

Mesoscale: Augmenting Behaviors

Augmenting the behaviors of material systems entails the computed combination of multiple materials, incorporating informed variations in physical attributes like density and thickness. This delineates an additional facet of smart materials in the context of the ongoing industrial revolution in the architecture, engineering, and construction sectors.

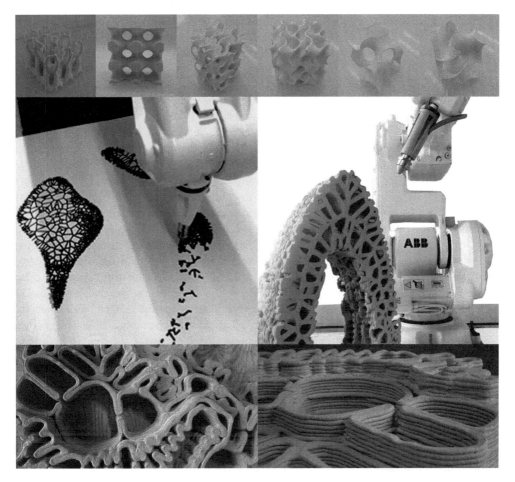

Figure 3.3.1 Top: Architected materials 3D printed using Fused Deposition Modeling; Credit: TTU-HCoA, Hi-DARS lab; Middle: Translating the discrete result of topology optimization to continuous robotic 3D printing of ceramic structures; Credit: to Authors, TU Delft (Mostafavi et al., 2015); Below: AI-generated porous patterns translated into continuous toolpaths for concrete 3D printing of cellular structures in multiple heights; Credit: TTU-HCoA, Hi-DARS lab.

At the mesoscale, this augmentation of material behaviors expands the palette of hybrid materials, fusing a spectrum of characteristics and functionalities.

In terms of computation methods, the components generated through a combination of structural optimization and agent-based modeling, or other emerging methodologies, stand as empirical evidence in research aimed at unraveling the intelligence of architectural materials at the mesoscale. A bespoke approach to design and optimization, grounded in performance considerations, enables a simultaneous generative process that negotiates architectural design concerns as well as structural and environmental optimization. This departure from traditional sequential workflows, integrating either generative approaches with structural analysis or sequentially optimizing pre-existing complex geometries within generative processes, marks a significant paradigm shift. A series of prototypes denoted as components, has been developed to instantiate this approach on a medium scale, seeking insights into the implications for large-scale spatial structures or buildings. This approach empowers the creation of intricate architectural forms that excel in both material efficiency and performance (Bao et al., 2022).

In contemporary engineering, CAD techniques have become indispensable tools for the precise and swift analysis of architectural designs. Through quantitative analysis utilizing simulation technologies, alterations to each design in the architectural design process induced by structural performance factors can be promptly evaluated (Bao & Yan, 2024). Since the 1960s, computer-aided simulation methods such as FEM have permeated numerous engineering fields. Leveraging computational power, an interconnected pathway between intricate building geometry models and building performance analysis is established, enabling quantitative feedback to design and produce smart material in mesoscales.

Within this context, exploring the utilization of building performance data within a multi-agent framework for performance data-driven bionic computational architectural design holds promise for overcoming existing challenges and providing data-driven solutions for architectural problems (Bao & Yan, 2024). Similar to natural systems, several researchers have explored the notion of hybridity by fusing two or several materials, not as separate layers, but as interdependent systems, creating hybrid material behaviors that surpass the sum of its individual parts (Snook, 2022, Mostafavi et al., 2019). The resulting complexity and intricacy of the generated geometry demonstrate the feasibility of construction through large-scale additive manufacturing. This effort aligns with a broader agenda focused on exploring the fabrication of algorithmically generated architectural forms using robotic fabrication techniques, particularly additive manufacturing, as well as multi-mode subtractive additive workflows (Figure 3.3.2).

Through a fusion of different materials and production methods, the non-homogeneous distribution of materials within components has the potential to enhance mechanical strength and durability (Yan et al., 2023). At this level, the porosity of components can be meticulously controlled. These voids enhance properties/behaviors such as permeability, filtration, weight, insulation, ventilation, and ornamentation. This nuanced control over porosity enables a strategic influence on material characteristics, resulting in structures that excel in various aspects of performance and aesthetics (Feng et al., 2022). Hence, in mesoscale, the design objective is to reassess the interplay between form, structure, ornamentation, and their spatial consequences. It defines a tectonic approach to architecture where these elements collectively express an architectural porous and hybrid system.

Macroscale: Enhanced Performance and Assembly

The success and relevance of smart material systems hinge on multiple factors, with the simulation of overall performance and scalability being crucial. Simulation involves an abstraction of reality, contrasting with the ever-growing computational capabilities of porosity and hybridity in high resolution. Scalability, the second key factor is vital for determining how highly detailed computed material systems at micro or mesoscales can be scaled up for larger spatial constructs. The scalability of a system relies on incorporating assembly intelligence in integrated design-to-production solutions. The Evolutionary Structural Optimization/Bi-directional Evolutionary Structural Optimization (ESO/BESO) method finds application in both structural analysis of completed buildings, such as Gaudi's

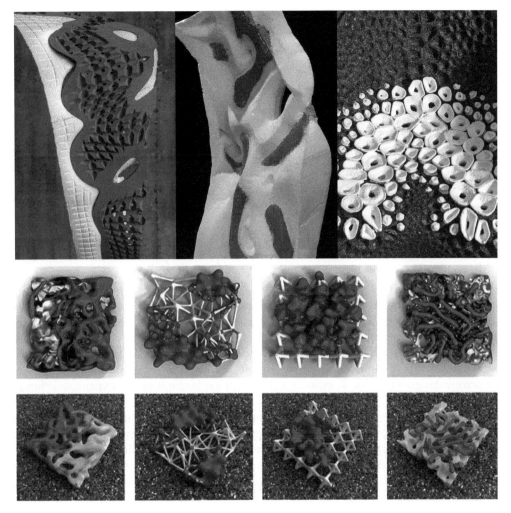

Figure 3.3.2 Top: Multi-material systems composing hybrid material behaviors of soft and hard by implementing multi-mode subtractive and additive robotic production methods; Credit: to Author, TU Delft (Mostafavi et al., 2019); Bottom: Computation and 3D printing of hybridity.

Sagrada Familia tree structure analysis (Burry et al., 2005), and the analysis of the shell structure of Palazzetto dello Sport in Rome (Yan et al., 2019).

Topology optimization, particularly ESO (Xie & Steven, 1997) and BESO (Huang & Xie, 2010), has emerged as a favored strategy for creating innovative architectural forms. This method, used in structural analysis and intelligent design outcomes, strikes a balance between artistic preferences and technical requirements (Xie, 2022). On the flip side, biomorphic model-based form-finding technology is transitioning from conceptual design to practical implementation. Architectural researchers turn to agent-based modeling and swarm intelligence algorithms for their logical structures and versatility, imbuing intelligent buildings with biological and environmental response strategies (Snooks, 2021).

Figure 3.3.3   Left – intelligent Form: 3D-printed mold with ultrahigh-performance concrete optimized wall (Bao et al., 2020, RMIT). Intelligent force printing: 3D concrete topological
optimized pavilion; Credit to Author, Nic Bao & Philip Yuan.

Scalability profoundly influences the design process and project feasibility in simulations and optimization algorithms. Frei Otto's approach to forming full-scale architectures
using scaled means of measurable mechanical simulation for textile surface and cable mesh
behaviors exemplifies the importance of scalability (Lewis, 2003). Adaptability, demonstrated by swarm optimization, is particularly pertinent for macroscale buildings with
numerous design variables. It ensures a thorough exploration of the expansive solutions
space, ultimately shaping the final structure's hybrid and porous characteristics.

Applying scalability to enhance performance in macroscale building design involves the
infusion of scalable technologies and strategies. Additionally, for several practical reasons
such as transportation and logistics of construction, assembly of smaller components to create larger constructs is inevitable. Hence, the effectiveness of integrated methods relies on the
flexibility and scalability encompassing simulations, optimization, and generative systems
to address challenges in large-scale projects. Concurrently, the critical aspect of scalability
extends to assembly and constructability, shaping hybridity through modular constructions, prefabrication, or on-site solutions for connections and assemblies (Figure 3.3.3).
As manufacturing setups advance to print or produce entire structures in one go, the intelligence in assembly significantly contributes to the success of smart materials in macroscale
building processes.

Conclusion and Discussion

The proliferation and advancement in computational design and digital fabrication of
porous and hybrid systems across various architectural scales reveal the transformative
potential application of smart materials. The incorporation of informed material systems represents a significant leap forward in resource and data-driven design, considering structural, environmental, and functional performance criteria across different scales.
Therefore, the performative distribution of substance and void, known as porosity, and
the amalgamation of various materials to augment properties and behaviors, discussed as
hybridity, serve as the cornerstone of the application of smart materials in AEC sectors.

This transformative evolution opens further avenues for innovation and efficiency in the ever-evolving landscape of architectural practices.

The implementation of integrated design computation in digital production illustrates how cutting-edge technologies are on the verge of revolutionizing the material palette available to architects and designers. This revolution unlocks a plethora of possibilities for creativity and innovation in shaping the built environment. The disruptive power of computational design and digital production processes has unveiled a new realm of possibilities for smart materials in architecture and design. The capacity of smart materials to adapt, react, or modify their characteristics in response to external stimuli introduces multifunctional systems capable of performing a diverse range of functions.

Architected hybrid and porous materials, commonly known as smart materials, play a pivotal role in both research and industry. These materials offer an extensive range of customizable properties, behaviors, and functions achieved through purposeful adjustments in chemophysical compositions, nanostructuring, and the optimization of material functionality. Architectured to achieve structural integrity, environmental sustainability, and enhanced performance, these materials strike a balance between lightness and scale. The combination of porosity and hybridity leverages the adaptability and programmability of robotic production setups for multi-materiality across various scales. This approach delves into the identity of smart materials within the building context and their intricate relationship with the convergence of computational design, digital production, and innovation in architecture. This exploration reveals an exciting frontier that not only redefines the possibilities in construction but also sets the stage for a more sustainable and adaptive built environment, marking a significant evolution in the landscape of architectural practices.

References

Ahlquist, S., & Menges, A. (2013). *Frameworks for Computational Design of Textile Micro-Architectures and Material Behavior in Forming Complex Force-Active Structures.* https://doi.org/10.52842/conf.acadia.2013.281.

Ashby, M., & Bréchet, Y. (2003). Designing hybrid materials. *Acta Materialia, 51*(19), 5801–5821.

Azulay, R., Combescure, C., & Dirrenberger, J. (2023). Instability-induced pattern generation in architectured materials—A review of methods. *International Journal of Solids and Structures, 274,* 112240.

Bao, D. W., & Yan, X. (2024). Data-driven performance-based generative design and digital fabrication for Industry 4.0: Precedent work, current progress, and future prospects. In: Barberio, M., Colella, M., Figliola, A., Battisti, A. (eds), *Architecture and Design for Industry 4.0.* Lecture Notes in Mechanical Engineering. Cham: Springer. https://doi.org/10.1007/978-3-031-36922-3_46

Bao, D.W., Yan, X., Snooks, R., & Xie, Y.M. (2020). Bioinspired generative architectural design form-finding and advanced robotic fabrication based on structural performance. In: Yuan, P., Xie, Y.M., Leach, N., Yao, J., & Wang, X. (eds.), *Architectural Intelligence.* Singapore: Springer.

Bao, D. W., Yan, X., & Xie, Y. M. (2022). Encoding topological optimisation logical structure rules into multi-agent system for architectural design and robotic fabrication. *International Journal of Architectural Computing, 20*(1), 7–17.

Barthelat, F. (2015). Architectured materials in engineering and biology: Fabrication, structure, mechanics and performance. *International Materials Reviews, 60*(8), 413–430.

Bilotti, J., Norman, B., Liu, J., Rosenwasser, D., & Sabin, J. (2018). Robosense 2.0 Robotic Sensing and Architectural Ceramic Fabrication. In *Proceedings of the 38th Annual Conference of the Association for Computer Aided Design in Architecture (ACADIA)*, Mexico City, Mexico, pp. 18-20. 2018. https://doi.org/10.52842/conf.acadia.2018.276

Bouaziz, O., Bréchet, Y., & Embury, J. (2008). Heterogeneous and architectured materials: A possible strategy for design of structural materials. *Advanced Engineering Materials, 10*(1–2), 24–36.

Burry, J., Felicetti, P., Tang, J., Burry, M., Xie, Y. M. (2005). Dynamical structural modeling: A collaborative design exploration. *International Journal of Architectural Computing*, 3(1), 27–42. https://doi.org/10.1260/1478077053739595.

Estrin, Y., Bréchet, Y., Dunlop, J., & Fratzl, P. (2019). *Architectured Materials in Nature and Engineering*. Cham, Switzerland: Springer Nature Switzerland AG.

Feng, Z., Gu, P., Zheng, M., Yan, X., & Bao, D. W. (2022). Environmental data-driven performance-based topological optimisation for morphology evolution of artificial Taihu stone. In: Yuan, P.F., Chai, H., Yan, C., & Leach, N. (eds.), *Proceedings of the 2021 Digital Futures. CDRF 2021*. Singapore: Springer. https://doi.org/10.1007/978-981-16-5983-6_11.

Huang, X., & Xie, Y. M. (2010). *Evolutionary Topology Optimization of Continuum Structures: Methods and Applications*. Chichester: Wiley. https://doi.org/10.1002/9780470689486

Jonkers, H., Thijssen, A., Muyzer, G., Copuroglu, O., & Schlangen, E. (2010). Application of bacteria as self-healing agent for the development of sustainable concrete. *Ecological Engineering*, 36, 230–235. https://doi.org/10.1016/j.ecoleng.2008.12.036.

Lewis, W.J. (2003). *Tension Structures: Form and Behavior*. London: Thomas Telford Publishing.

Li, C., Bao, D. W., Yan, X., Wu, R., & He, C. (2023). RE-WEATHERING: A nature-inspired experimental method for re-generating porous architectural systems based on environmentally data-driven performance. In: Immanuel Koh, Dagmar Reinhardt, Mohammed Makki, Mona Khakhar, Nic Bao (eds.), *HUMAN-CENTRIC - Proceedings of the 28th CAADRIA Conference*, Ahmedabad, 18-24 March 2023, pp. 271–280. https://doi.org/10.52842/conf.caadria.2023.1.271

Lu, H., Lee, T., Ma, J., Chen, D., & Xie, Y. (2023). Designing 2D stochastic porous structures using topology optimisation. *Composite Structures*, 321, 117305. https://doi.org/10.1016/j.compstruct.2023.117305.

Mehan, A., & Mostafavi, S. (2022). Building resilient communities over time. In *Building Resilient Communities Over Time* (pp. 1–4). Springer International Publishing. https://doi.org/10.1007/978-3-030-51812-7_322-1

Mohamed, H., Bao, D. W., & Snooks, R. (2021). *Super Composite: Carbon Fibre Infused 3D Printed Tectonics*. pp. 297–308. In: Yuan, P.F., Yao, J., Yan, C., Wang, X., Leach, N. (eds), *Proceedings of the 2020 DigitalFUTURES. CDRF 2020*. Singapore: Springer. https://doi.org/10.1007/978-981-33-4400-6_28

Morales-Beltran, M., & Mostafavi, S. (2022). Topology optimization in architectural design a technique for obtaining discrete structures from continuum typologies. In Pak, B., Wurzer, G., & Stouffs, R. (eds.), *eCAADe 2022- Co-creating the Future: Inclusion in and Through Design* (pp. 589–598). (*Proceedings of the International Conference on Education and Research in Computer Aided Architectural Design in Europe*).

Mostafavi, S. (2021). Hybrid intelligence in architectural robotic materialization (HI-ARM): Computational, fabrication and material intelligence for multi-mode robotic production of multi-scale and multi-material systems. *A+BE | Architecture and the Built Environment*, 11(12), 1–266. https://doi.org/10.7480/abe.2021.12.5799

Mostafavi, S., & Anton, A. (2018). Materially informed robotic fabrication: Architectural robotics and multi-scalar material architecture. In Daas, M., & Wit, A. J. (eds.), *Towards a Robotic Architecture* (pp. 88–99). ORO Editions.

Mostafavi, S., & Bier, H. (2016). Materially informed design to robotic production: A robotic 3D printing system for informed material deposition. In: Reinhardt, D., Saunders, R., & Burry, J. (eds.), *Robotic Fabrication in Architecture, Art and Design 2016*. Cham: Springer. https://doi-org.lib-e2.lib.ttu.edu/10.1007/978-3-319-26378-6_27.

Mostafavi, S., Bier, H., Bodea, S., & Antón, A.M. (2015). Informed design to robotic production systems - developing robotic 3d printing system for informed material deposition. In Martens, B, Wurzer, G., Grasl, T., Lorenz, W.E. & Schaffranek, R. (eds.), *Real Time - Proceedings of the 33rd International Conference on Education and Research in Computer Aided Architectural Design in Europe (eCAADe)* [Volume 2]. Vienna University of Technology, Vienna, Austria, https://doi.org/10.52842/conf.ecaade.2015.2.287

Mostafavi, S., Kemper, B., & Du, C. (2019). Materializing hybridity in architecture: Design to robotic production of multi-materiality in multiple scales. *Architectural Science Review*, 62(5), 424–437.

Rosenwasser, D., Mantell, S., & Sabin, J. (2017). *Clay Non-Wovens: Robotic Fabrication and Digital Ceramics*. ACADIA 2017: DISCIPLINES & DISRUPTION [*Proceedings of the 37th Annual*

Conference of the Association for Computer Aided Design in Architecture (ACADIA). ISBN 978-0-692-96506-1] Cambridge, MA 2-4 November 2017, pp. 502–511. https://doi.org/10.52842/ conf.acadia.2017.502

Schröpfer, T., & Carpenter, J. (2011). *Material Design: Informing Architecture by Materiality.* Berlin, Boston: Birkhäuser, 2011. https://doi.org/10.1515/9783034611664

Snooks, R. (2021). Behavioral formation: Volatile design processes and the emergence of a strange specificity. New York: Actar Publishers. https://trove.nla.gov.au/work/227465948? keyword=9781940291925

Snooks, R. (2022). Behavioral tectonics: agentBody prototypes and the compression of tectonics. *Architectural Intelligence.* https://doi.org/10.1007/s44223-022-00007-8

Xie, Y. M. (2022). Generalized topology optimization for architectural design. *ARIN 1, 2.* https://doi. org/10.1007/s44223-022-00003-y.

Xie, Y. M., & Steven, G. P. (1997). *Evolutionary Structural Optimization.* London: Springer. https:// doi.org/10.1007/978-1-4471-0985-3.

Yan, X., Bao, D. W., Cai, K., Fang, Y., & Xie, Y. M. (2019). A new form-finding method for shell structures based on BESO algorithm. In: *Proceedings of International Association for Shell and Spatial Structures (IASS) Annual Symposia, IASS 2019 Barcelona Symposium: Form-finding and Optimization,* pp. 1–8. https://www.ingentaconnect.com/content/iass/piass/2019/00002019/00000017/ art00012

Yan, X., Bao, D. W., Xiong, Y., Snooks, R., & Xie, Y. M. (2023). Structural topology optimisation based on a multi-agent model. *Engineering Structures, 296, 116978.*

Yeo, S., Oh, M., & Yoo, P. (2019). Structurally controlled cellular architectures for high performance ultra-lightweight materials. *Advanced Materials (Weinheim), 31(34),* E1803670-N/a.

3.4

FRACTAL-BASED POROUS CONCRETE COMPONENTS DESIGN AND 3D PRINTING

Iasef Md Rian

Abstract

This chapter explores the innovative application of fractal geometry in the design of extra-light porous concrete structures utilizing advanced 3D printing technologies. It methodically examines various fractal-based modeling approaches, including form-based, force-based, and fabrication-aware strategies, each contributing uniquely to the development of specialized light porous concrete structures. This chapter further explores two distinct fabrication techniques: the utilization of 3D-printed polymer formwork for casting concrete components and the cutting-edge method of directly 3D printing concrete mixed with polymers, which remarkably eliminates the need for conventional formwork. Additionally, this chapter discusses the intricacies of composite concrete mixtures tailored to suit the specific modeling approach, fabrication method, and intended application of the components. Rather than presenting new empirical findings, this chapter serves as a synthesis of existing research and studies in this field. Its aim is to illuminate the potential and expand horizons for the application of fractal concepts in the realm of 3D-printed concrete structures. This exploration not only highlights current opportunities but also opens up avenues for future possibilities, showcasing how the convergence of fractal geometry and 3D printing technology can lead to significant advancements in construction methodologies and materials.

Keywords

Fractal Geometry; Architected Porosity; Extra-Light; Porous Concrete; 3D-Printing

Introduction

Background: Architected Porosity

The use of precast concrete components in modern construction has notably increased, favored for their reduced dead load, ease of transport, quick installation, material efficiency, and eco-friendliness (Ünal et al., 2007). These components are made lightweight

DOI: 10.4324/9781003384113-44

376

through porosity or foaming, with further weight reduction achieved by altering composite materials and polymers in the concrete mix (Vicente et al., 2018; Kearsley & Wainwright, 2002; Lo & Cui, 2004). A critical challenge is balancing mass reduction with strength retention, where the design of void geometries is crucial for optimizing strength-to-weight ratios (Lu et al., 2014).

Recent materials science advancements have focused on microscale porous scaffolds, especially using minimal surface geometries like gyroids and lattices, to create exceptionally lightweight structures (Ambu & Morabito, 2018; Montazerian et al., 2017; Al-Ketan et al., 2018; Helou & Kara, 2018; Mahmoud & Elbestawi, 2017). Techniques like Electron Beam Melting (EBM) facilitate the fabrication of these complex scaffolds, although such designs have predominantly employed polymers and metals, initially developed for medical applications like bone scaffolds (Wang et al., 2016; Feng et al., 2018). The translation of these methods to concrete has been hindered by material-specific limitations, leading to the exploration of macro-scaffolds in 3D concrete printing (3DCP) as an alternative.

Recent studies like those by Noack et al. (2019) and researchers at ETH Zurich (Jipa et al., 2019) have shown the potential for lightweight concrete structures using innovative void configurations. However, these do not fully exploit iterative methods for further weight reduction. Exploration of fractal geometry in designs, such as in the work of Rian (2019) and Rian and Ibrahim (2022), and the creation of ultralight metal micro-lattices (Rayneau-Kirkhope et al., 2012; Meza et al., 2014) demonstrate the potential for advanced weight reduction. The iterative approach using fractal geometry suggests a promising direction for developing exceptionally lightweight concrete components, highlighting the need for further research in this area. (Figure 3.4.1)

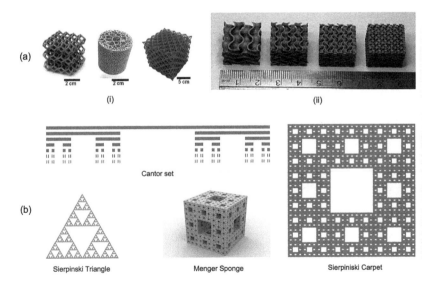

Figure 3.4.1 (a) Architected microscale porous materials, (i) Architected micro-latticed materials manufactured by EBM (Murr, 2018), (ii) Gyroid-latticed lightweight metal specimen manufactured by SLM (Maskery et al., 2017); (b) Mathematical examples of fractals - Cantor set, Sierpinski triangle, and Menger sponge.

Fractal Geometry and Scope in Porous Concrete Design

Fractal geometry, known for its repetitive self-similarity seen in nature, like in tree branches and river basins, offers a novel approach to designing porous concrete components. Introduced by Mandelbrot in 1982, fractals such as Cantor dust, Sierpinski triangle, and Menger sponge demonstrate complex structures with inherent voids, crucial for high porosity designs like the Sierpinski Carpet (SC), noted for its scalable porosity.

While fractal concepts have been applied in 3D printing (3DP), mainly with polymers and metals, their use with concrete remains less explored. Incorporating fractal geometry in the design and fabrication of 3D-printed concrete components merges architectural design, engineering, and manufacturing techniques to yield structures that are aesthetically appealing, structurally efficient, and functionally beneficial.

Fractal geometry facilitates the creation of intricate, robust designs for porous concrete components, optimizing material distribution for enhanced load-bearing efficiency and structural integrity. These designs also potentially improve thermal insulation and acoustic properties, leveraging their multi-level porosity. Despite the high computational demands and the need for advanced software for design optimization, this method aligns with sustainable construction practices, potentially reducing material use and environmental impact. Thus, fractal geometry in the design and 3DP of porous concrete components represent a promising fusion of aesthetics and functionality in construction.

Objective and Chapter Outline

This chapter explores fractal geometry's role in creating ultralight porous concrete components, covering three main aspects. It first addresses computational design methods, including form-based design with fractal-generated forms, force-based approaches using topological optimization, and fabrication-aware methods that consider fabrication impacts on model and material choices. The second section investigates the practical aspects of 3DP, such as material selection and challenges, along with potential solutions. Finally, it discusses real-world applications and future research opportunities of fractals in constructing concrete building components, emphasizing the synergy between fractals, computational modeling, and advanced digital fabrication tools. This approach aims to enable the production of lightweight, strong, and sustainable concrete components for the construction industry.

Design Approaches

There are various methods for creating porous morphologies, particularly for concrete components in building applications. This chapter focuses on multiscale porous morphology, utilizing fractal geometry as a fundamental framework. Fractals enable the replication of porous structures across multiple scales through a recursive algorithmic system, as exemplified by the SC, which demonstrates efficiency through weight reduction. Three distinct approaches are discussed: form-based, force-based, and fabrication-aware.

Form-Based Approach

Fractal shapes, characterized by their complex self-similarity, are effectively generated using rule-based systems like the Iterated Function System (IFS), conceived by John Hutchinson in 1981 and popularized by Michael Barnsley in 1988 (Hutchinson, 1981; Barnsley,

2014). In IFS, a geometric transformation function is repeatedly applied to an initial shape, creating progressively transformed shapes with each iteration. This method, exemplified in "Figure 3.4.2a" with the SC, can be adapted to create parametric models of perforated components. By varying the iteration number, the model adjusts the number of holes, balancing mass reduction with strength requirements within the limits of allowable displacement. The SC model is then transformed into a finite element model for structural analysis, particularly compressive testing, optimizing pore morphology while considering deformation constraints under vertical load. This approach enables precise control of porous structures for efficient design and manufacturing applications.

In a case study, a 90 cm × 90 cm panel with a thickness of 3 cm is digitally segmented into 64 squares (8×8 grid), each representing an iteration of the SC model, allowing for variable multiscale porosity. This design is optimized using a structural simulation-based approach rather than traditional optimization methods. The panel is divided into 64 cells subjected to compressive force, leading to different nodal displacements categorized into four levels. High displacement areas are assigned low iteration SC patterns, while low displacement areas receive higher iteration patterns. Due to the scalability limitations of 3DP, the maximum iteration is capped at four, achieving a minimum hole size of approximately 5 mm × 5 mm. This approach reduces the mass by about 51.77% in the 4th iteration, maintaining strength but not fully optimizing the void-to-stiffness ratio. To achieve a balanced void-to-stiffness ratio, multi-objective optimization is used, with "Figure 3.4.2c" illustrating several optimal choices (options 7, 8, and 9) balancing weight reduction and displacement. The selection of solutions is based on specific weight and displacement criteria.

Beyond the standard SC, randomized versions and other fractal designs like the Hilbert curve, Sierpinski Gasket, Apollonian Gasket, and Menger sponge offer diverse porous morphologies (Ullah et al., 2021). These fractals, along with methods like L-System (Prusinkiewicz & Lindenmayer, 2012) and Finite Subdivision Rules (Cannon et al., 2001), expand the scope for designing controlled porosity in concrete components. The successful application of these patterns in 3DP and 3DCP depends on the technology's ability to handle intricate fractal geometries.

Force-Based Approach

The force-based modeling approach, often utilizing topology optimization (TO), allows forces under load to shape the optimized structural design of components. Standard TO yields efficient structures, but incorporating fractal geometry enhances this through multiscale TO and fine-tuning design at every scale for greater efficiency. Multiscale structures, increasingly used in engineering, offer enhanced structural efficiency and multifunctionality (McDowell et al., 2009; Zhao et al., 2018). Advanced multiscale TO methods optimize material distribution and internal microstructures (Rodrigues et al., 2002; Sivapuram et al., 2016; Xia & Breitkopf, 2017), enabling the creation of optimized, efficient, and extra-light structures.

Deng et al. (2017) demonstrated multiscale optimization by iteratively reducing mass from each shell based on force-experience categories. Kim and Park (2021) developed a density-based multiscale optimization with lattice enhancement for structural efficiency. In 2021, Chatterjee et al. showed that robust topological designs for extreme metamaterial microstructures offer enhanced mechanical performance with lightweight and high strength

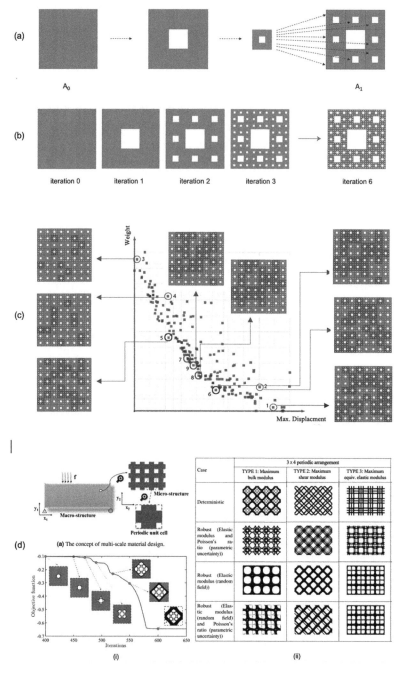

Figure 3.4.2 (a) Geometric transformation rule of a SC; (b) IFS application for generating a SC; (c) Pareto front displaying the optimal and suboptimal variations of a porous panel, (d) Robust topological designs for extreme metamaterial microstructures, (i) Multiscale material design and iterations to get optimized cell design (Chatterjee et al., 2021), (ii) Periodic arrangement of different types of topological optimized cell patterns at the microscale (Chatterjee et al., 2021).

(Figure 3.4.2d) (Chatterjee et al., 2021). The force-based TO approach for porous concrete components, from macroscale to microscale, relies on the concrete mixture, liquidity, particle size, fabrication method, and post-fabrication drying. Consequently, fabrication-aware modeling is vital and practical for porous concrete components.

Fabrication-Aware Approach

In creating porous concrete components, both form-based and force-based methods prove effective for polymers. However, a fabrication-aware approach is crucial for precise pore size and fractal level selection. Techniques include 3D-printed polymer molds, which allow for the creation of fine pores, and 3DCP, offering multi-layered porous structures. The choice depends on factors like pore size, structural complexity, and intended use, highlighting the versatility of fractal designs in modern construction. Subsequent sections delve further into this approach in detail.

Digital Fabrications

Materials

In 3DCP, particularly for fabricating architected porous concrete components, the selection of appropriate materials is a critical factor that greatly influences the outcome. This selection process should be an integral part of the design phase, considering both the primary materials for the concrete mixture and the materials used for formwork.

Concrete Mixture and Composites

Traditional concrete is commonly used in 3DP due to its easy availability and well-known preparation methods. However, for better printability and more versatile outcomes, a composite mixture that includes polymers, known as "polymer-modified concrete" or "concrete-polymer composites," is preferred. These composites offer improved printability, flowability, low viscosity, and enhanced strength and durability compared to traditional concrete. Various polymers such as acrylonitrile butadiene styrene (ABS), polyvinyl alcohol (PVA), polypropylene (PP), polycarboxylate superplasticizers, polyethylene (PE), and styrene-butadiene rubber (SBR) are incorporated to enhance specific properties of the concrete. For instance, ABS is used for its impact resistance and viscosity reduction, making it ideal for strong and durable components, while PE enhances flexibility, suitable for components that must endure bending. Additionally, bio-based polymers like polylactic acid (PLA), cellulose-based, starch-based polymers, and bio-PE are increasingly used for their environmental benefits. PLA is biodegradable with considerable strength, cellulose, and starch-based polymers improve concrete properties, and bio-PE, sourced from biomass, offers a sustainable alternative to traditional PE. Glass-reinforced concrete (GRC) is also a popular choice for making perforated components, combining the strength of glass fibers with the versatility of concrete.

Formworks and Molds

In terms of materials for formworks and molds, polymers like ABS and PLA are popular choices due to their strength, flexibility, and ease of printing. These are crucial for creating detailed and intricate porous structures. Composite materials, often reinforced with fibers, provide the necessary strength and durability for larger or more complex formworks. Resins are chosen for their ability to produce smooth, detailed surfaces, which is particularly important for architectural concrete components where aesthetic finish is a key consideration. These materials are selected for their ability to withstand the pressures of concrete casting without deforming, as well as for their compatibility with the concrete. They contribute to sustainable construction practices through their reusability and recyclability. The thermal properties of these materials also play a role in influencing the curing process of concrete, thus affecting the overall strength and quality of the components.

3D-Printed Molds and Concrete Casting

The fabrication of 3D-printed molds for porous concrete casting is a versatile process that can adapt to various requirements, including single-layered molds for one-time casting, multi-layered molds for layer-by-layer casting, and reinforced molds designed to accommodate reinforcing mesh. Each approach has its specific methods and considerations.

Single-Layered Casting

The fabrication of fractal-designed porous concrete components using single-layered concrete casting on a 3D-printed mold involves intricate and precise techniques. Typically made from ABS or PLA, the mold intricately captures fractal patterns (as shown in Figures 3.4.3a(i) & 3.4.3a(ii)). Upon preparing the mold, concrete is poured over it in a single layer, ensuring the fractal design is precisely imprinted. After the concrete cures, the mold is removed, unveiling a unique panel with a porous fractal pattern (Figure 3.4.3a(iii)). This technique effectively merges 3DP's accuracy with conventional concrete casting, resulting in components that are both aesthetically striking and functionally robust.

Multi-Layered Casting

These molds are crafted for overlapping or interlocking fractal patterns, facilitating multi-stage casting where each stage adds a cross-layer to the structure. Printed in segments corresponding to each concrete layer, the process involves casting a layer, partial setting, and then adding the next mold layer. This approach is ideal for complex, cross-layered, or multi-layered designs, demanding precise control over each layer's curing, especially for large structures that cannot be cast in a single mold.

Reinforcement Casting

Reinforced molds, incorporating spaces or channels for mesh or rebar, are essential when additional strength is needed in concrete structures. This approach is crucial for load-bearing structures or those under substantial stress. It ensures that the reinforcing materials are accurately positioned and secured, allowing concrete to flow around them, thereby creating a cohesive and structurally sound build.

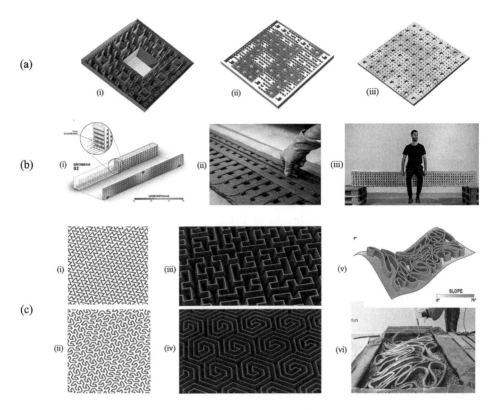

Figure 3.4.3 (a) 3D-Printed molds and concrete casting, (i) PLA mold for SC casting, (ii) PLA mold for optimized perforated concrete casting, (iii) The casted panel. (b) 3DCP, (i–iii) A porous beam design with an orthogonal grid layout for 3DCP with continuous toolpath and reinforcement (Breseghello & Naboni, 2022). (c) Fabrication-aware 3DCP, (i–ii) Space-filling fractal curves, (iii–iv) 3DCP extrusion on Hilbert and Gosper curves (Petroff et al., 2019), (v–vi) Field-based 3DCP of a space-filling pattern using calibrated depth camera (Naboni et al., 2022).

In all molding methods, meticulous design is vital. The mold must accurately replicate the intended shape and consider the properties of both the mold material and concrete. Key considerations include providing structural support during casting, incorporating vents or channels for air escape to prevent defects, and designing for mold removal without damaging the concrete structure.

3DCP

3DCP significantly advances the construction of porous concrete components, moving beyond traditional mold-based methods. This process involves directly extruding concrete along a pre-defined path, with the choice between continuous and discontinuous toolpaths determined by the design. Soo and Yu (2002) highlighted the effectiveness of fractal curves in toolpath generation for 3DP, underscoring the growing potential of fractals in modern 3DCP, equipped with advanced tools.

Continuous Toolpath: Space-Filling Fractal Curves

In the continuous 3DCP method, an unbroken stream of concrete is extruded through the nozzle, suitable for space-filling fractal curves like the Hilbert, Peano, and Gosper Curves (Figure 3.4.3c). Despite its continuous nature, this method creates complex voids across multiple scales. Multi-layer fabrication is achieved in one operation, forming cross-layered structures with intricate patterns by rotating each layer 90 degrees (Figure 3.4.3b). The ideal concrete mix for this process contains ABS due to its low viscosity, ensuring smooth extrusion, proper setting without deformation, and structural strength.

Intermittent Toolpath: Discontinuous Fractals

Fractals like fractal dust, SC, Menger Sponge, and Apollonian Gasket, with their discontinuous nature marked by breaks or gaps, are ideal for creating porous structures using discontinuous 3DCP. This technique, involving intermittent pausing and resuming of concrete extrusion, allows for the fabrication of detailed, intricate components with voids. It offers high customization and material efficiency, including the possibility of targeted reinforcement within the component. However, discontinuous 3DP requires precise control and can lead to layer adhesion issues, nozzle clogging, and irregular material flow. Its intermittent nature potentially extends production times and necessitates additional post-processing.

Curl Printing: Fractal Curls

3D curl concrete printing, employing fractal curves like the Fibonacci spiral and Dragon curve, revolutionizes construction and design with its advanced technology and complex patterns. Differing from traditional linear extrusion, this method extrudes concrete in a curl-like motion (Figure 3.4.3d), building structures layer by layer that adhere to fractal designs. This creates intricate patterns and voids within components, allowing for complex, multiscale voids. Ideal for architectural elements like façades and decorative components, it provides significant design freedom and functional optimization. Yet, it demands precision in printing, flow management of concrete, and structural stability, necessitating advanced software and precise machinery control.

Applications and Feasibility

Fractal-based porous concrete components, suitable for a range of architectural applications from micro to large scale, offer both structural and decorative uses. They function as lightweight wall screens, load-bearing blocks, stand-alone walls, or roof screens, enhancing natural light and airflow. These components can also serve in landscaping as permeable pavements and elevate exterior aesthetics, potentially fostering microscale plant growth. Adaptable to various shapes, their porous nature eases installation and bolsters insulation and acoustics. Fractal patterns in these components can enrich the aesthetic and functional aspects of architectural designs and acoustics (Sapoval, et al. 1997). Highlighting fractal applications, Michael Hansmeyer's Digital Grotesque projects (Hansmeyer & Dillenburger, 2013) exemplify the fusion of computational design and 3DCP in creating intricately detailed, fractal-like columns. The Digital Grotesque projects, along with others featured in Figure 3.4.4, illustrate the future potential of fractals

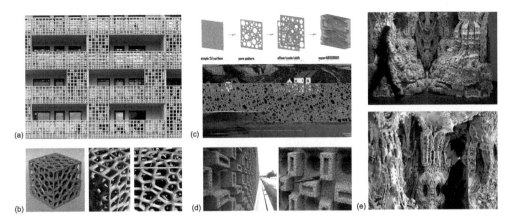

Figure 3.4.4 (a) Light and airy precast concrete façade of a Housing complex, Helsinki (Alkus, 2014); (b) "SCIN Cube," 3D-printed latticed cellular polymer-mixed concrete cube, London Design Festival, SCIN Gallery (Kudless, 2012); (c) "superABSORBER," a sound barrier wall proposal made of 3D-printed multi-layered concrete panels for USA highways (Skinner & Hecker, 2007); (d) "Fractal Wall," a fractal-inspired concrete-wood sound barrier with multiscale porous blocks, Ecole Polytechnique (France) (Sapoval & Filoche, 2009); (e) "Digital Grotesque II," 3D-printed intricate fractal-inspired micro-decorative columns (Hansmeyer, 2017).

in creating sophisticated, lightweight, and efficient concrete structures, blending artistic design with practicality in construction.

Conclusion: Opportunities and Challenges

The exploration of fractal geometry in designing extra-light, porous concrete components using 3DP technologies represents a significant advancement in construction and architectural design. This chapter has delved into various modeling approaches like form-based, force-based, and fabrication-aware strategies, underscoring the versatility of crafting these advanced concrete components. Employing fractal geometry leads to aesthetically appealing, functionally optimal, and smart designs, transcending traditional construction limitations. Innovations such as 3D-printed polymer formwork and direct 3DP with polymer-infused concrete offer efficient, sustainable, and adaptable building solutions.

Fractal geometry introduces innovative design possibilities, enhances material efficiency for sustainability, and allows for flexible customization. These methods augment concrete's structural properties, improving its strength and durability. However, challenges include the technical complexity of fractal designs, managing composite concrete mixtures, and scaling these technologies for larger projects. Cost and regulatory compliance also pose significant challenges.

In summary, integrating fractal geometry with 3DP in concrete components fabrication signifies a leading-edge shift in architectural innovation, paving the way for new building design and construction methods. While facing challenges and requiring further research, the potential for sustainability, efficiency, and design flexibility makes fractal-based 3D-printed concrete components a promising direction for future construction endeavors.

Acknowledgment

This study was supported by the Research Development Fund (RDF-19-01-28) of Xi'an Jiaotong-Liverpool University, China.

References

Al-Ketan, O., Rezgui, R., Rowshan, R., Du, H., Fang, N. X., & Al-Rub., R. K. (2018). Microarchitected stretching-dominated mechanical metamaterials with minimal surface topologies. *Advanced Engineering Materials, 20*(9), 1800029.

Alkus. (2014). *Housing Complex in Helsinki: Light and Airy Precast Façade for Finnish Residential Complex.* Retrieved from Alkus Innovative Systems: https://www.alkus.com/en/references/housing-complex-in-helsinki on 30th November 2023.

Ambu, R., & Morabito, A. E. (2018). Porous scaffold design based on minimal surfaces: Development and assessment of variable architectures. *Symmetry, 10*(9), 361.

Barnsley, M. F. (2014). *Fractals Everywhere.* Cambridge: Academic Presss.

Breseghello, L., & Naboni, R. (2022). Toolpath-based design for 3D concrete printing of carbon-efficient architectural structures. *Additive Manufacturing, 56*, 102872.

Cannon, J., Floyd, W., & Parry, W. (2001). Finite subdivision rules. *Conformal Geometry and Dynamics of the American Mathematical Society, 5*(8), 153–196.

Chatterjee, T., Chakraborty, S., Goswami, S., Adhikari, S., & Friswell, M. I. (2021). Robust topological designs for extreme metamaterial micro-structures. *Scientific Reports, 11*(1), 15221.

Deng, J., Yan, J., & Cheng, G. (2017). Multi-objective concurrent topology optimization of thermoelastic structures composed of homogeneous porous material. *Structural and Multidisciplinary Optimization, 47*, 583–597.

Feng, J., Fu, J., Lin, Z., Shang, C., & Li, B. (2018). A review of the design methods of complex topology structures for 3D printing. *Isual Computing for Industry, Biomedicine, and Art, 1*(1), 1–16.

Hansmeyer, M. (2017). *Digital Grotesque II.* Retrieved from Michael Hansmeyer, Computational Architecture. https://www.michael-hansmeyer.com/digital-grotesque-IIHansmeyer, M., & Dillenburger, B. (2013). Digital grotesque: Towards a micro-tectonic architecture. *SAJ-Serbian Architectural Journal, 5*(2), 194–201.

Helou, M., & Kara, S. (2018). Design, analysis and manufacturing of lattice structures: An overview. *International Journal of Computer Integrated Manufacturing, 31*(3), 243–61.

Hutchinson, J. E. (1981). Fractals and self-similarity. *Indiana University Mathematics Journal, 30*(5), 713–747.

Jipa, A., Barentin, C. C., Lydon, G., Rippmann, M., Chousou, G., Lomaglio, M., … Dillenburger, B. (2019). 3D-printed formwork for integrated funicular concrete slabs. *Proceedings of IASS Annual Symposia, 2019*(6), 1–8. International Association for Shell and Spatial Structures (IASS).

Kearsley, E. P., & Wainwright, P. J. (2002). The effect of porosity on the strength of foamed concrete. *Cement and Concrete Research, 32*(2), 233–239.

Kim, J.-E., & Park, K. (2021). Multiscale topology optimization combining density-based optimization and lattice enhancement for additive manufacturing. *International Journal of Precision Engineering and Manufacturing-Green Technology, 8*, 1197–1208.

Kudless, A. (2012). *Matsys.* Retrieved from https://www.matsys.design/scin-cube on 30th November 2023.

Lo, T. Y., & Cui, H. Z. (2004). Effect of porous lightweight aggregate on strength of concrete. *Materials Letters, 58*(6), 916–919.

Lu, L., Sharf, A., Zhao, H., Wei, Y., Fan, Q., Chen, X., … Chen, B. (2014). Build-to-last: Strength to weight 3D printed objects. *ACM Transactions on Graphics (ToG), 33*(4), 1–10.

Mahmoud, D., & Elbestawi, M. A. (2017). Lattice structures and functionally graded materials applications in additive manufacturing of orthopedic implants: A review. *Journal of Manufacturing and Materials Processing, 1*(2), 13.

Mandelbrot, B. B. (1982). *The Fractal Geometry of Nature* (Vol. 1 ed.). New York: WH Freeman.

Maskery, I., Aboulkhair, N. T., Aremu, A. O., Tuck, C. J., & Ashcroft, I. A. (2017). Compressive failure modes and energy absorption in additively manufactured double gyroid lattices. *Additive Manufacturing, 16*, 24–29.

McDowell, D. L., Panchal, J., Choi, H.-J., Seepersad, C., Allen, J., & Mistree, F. (2009). *Integrated Design of Multiscale, Multifunctional Materials and Products.* Butterworth-Heinemann, Oxford.

Meza, L. R., Das, S., & Greer, J. R. (2014). Strong, lightweight, and recoverable three-dimensional ceramic nanolattices. *Science, 345(6202),* 1322–1326.

Montazerian, H., Davoodi, E., Asadi-Eydivand, M., Kadkhodapour, J., & Solati-Hashjin, M. (2017). Porous scaffold internal architecture design based on minimal surfaces: A compromise between permeability and elastic properties. *Materials & Design, 126,* 98–114.

Murr, L. E. (2018). A metallographic review of 3D printing/additive manufacturing of metal and alloy products and components. *Metallography, Microstructure, and Analysis, 7,* 103–132.

Naboni, R., Breseghello, L., & Sanin, S. (2022). Environment-aware 3D concrete printing through robot-vision. In *40th Conference on Education and Research in Computer Aided Architectural Design in Europe, eCAADe 2022,* (pp. 409–418). Ghent, Belgium.

Noack, K., Eichenauer, F. M., & Lordick, D. (2019). Optimization of voids in concrete ceilings: A geometrical approach. *FME Transactions, 47(2),* 245–252.

Petroff, M., Appel, J., Rostem, K., Bennett, C. L., Eimer, J., Marriage, T., Ramirez, J., & Wollack, E. J. (2019). A 3D-printed broadband millimeter wave absorber. *Review of Scientific Instruments, 90(2),* 1–6.

Prusinkiewicz, P., & Lindenmayer, A. (2012). *The Algorithmic Beauty of Plants.* New York: Springer Science & Business Media.

Rayneau-Kirkhope, D., Mao, Y., & Farr, R. (2012). Ultralight fractal structures from hollow tubes. *Physical Review Letters, 109*(20), 204301.

Rian, I. M. (2019). IFS-based computational morphogenesis of a hierarchical trussed beam. *CAAD Futures 2019: "Hello, Culture"* (pp. 1010–1022). Daejon, South Korea: KAIST.

Rian, I. M., & Ibrahim, A. (2022). Fractal-based perforation morphology and structural optimization of perforated steel beams. In *IASS 2022 Symposium affiliated with APCS 2022 conference Innova tion·Sustainability·Legacy.* Beijing, China. pp. 2374–2381.

Rodrigues, H., Guedes, J. M., & Bendsoe, M. P. (2002). Hierarchical optimization of material and structure. *Structural and Multidisciplinary Optimization, 24,* 1–10.

Sapoval, B., & Filoche, M. (2009, 03 25). *The Fractal® acoustic barrier (Research Article).* Retrieved from Institute for Pure & Applied Mathematics (IPAM) https://www.ipam.ucla.edu/research-articles/fractal-acoustic-barrier/ on 30th November 2023.

Sapoval, B., Haeberlé, O., & Russ, S. (1997). Acoustical properties of irregular and fractal cavities. *The Journal of the Acoustical Society of America, 102*(4), 2014–2019.

Sivapuram, R., Dunning, P., & Kim, H. A. (2016). Multiscale topology optimization for structures with tailored porous structured materials. In *57th AIAA/ASCE/AHS/ASC Structures, Structural Dynamics, and Materials Conference,* San Diego, California, pp. 0938–2016.

Skinner, M. & Hecker, D. (2007). *Superabsorber.* Retrieved from https://marthaskinner.com/project/superabsorber/ on 30th November 2023.

Soo, S. C., & Yu, K. M. (2002). Tool-path generation for fractal curve making. *The International Journal of Advanced Manufacturing Technology, 19,* 32–48.

Ullah, A. S., D'Addona, D. M., Seto, Y., Yonehara, S., & Kubo, A. (2021). Utilizing fractals for modeling and 3D printing of porous structures. *Fractal and Fractional, 5*(2), 40.

Ünal, O., Uygunoğlu, T., & Yildiz, A. (2007). Investigation of properties of low-strength lightweight concrete for thermal insulation. *Building and Environment 42*(2), 584–590.

Vicente, M. A., González, D. C., Mínguez, J., Tarifa, M. A., Ruiz, G., & Hindi, R. (2018). Influence of the pore morphology of high strength concrete on its fatigue life. *International Journal of Fatigue 112,* 106–116.

Wang, X., Xu, S., Zhou, S., Xu, W., Leary, M., Choong, P., … Xie, Y. M. (2016). Topological design and additive manufacturing of porous metals for bone scaffolds and orthopaedic implants: A review. *Biomaterials, 83,* 127–141.

Xia, L., & Breitkopf, P. (2017). Recent advances on topology optimization of multiscale nonlinear structures. *Archives of Computational Methods in Engineering, 24,* 227–249.

Zhao, J., Yoon, H., & Youn, B. D. (2018). An efficient decoupled sensitivity analysis method for multiscale concurrent topology optimization problems. *Structural and Multidisciplinary Optimization, 58,* 445–457.

3.5

ADVANCING TUNABLE ACOUSTICS THROUGH SMART MATERIALS AND RECONFIGURABLE KERF STRUCTURES

Alireza Borhani, Negar Kalantar, Anastasia H. Muliana,
Maryam Mansoori and Ali Farajmandi

Abstract

This chapter explores the synergy between wood and Shape-Memory Polymer (SMP) to create a tunable material for adaptable room acoustics. Acknowledging the significance of geometric intervention within a materials-oriented approach, this chapter takes a step in addressing architectural adaptation through the responsive properties of materials, minimizing the need for complex mechanical systems.

Leveraging the widespread use of wood in acoustics and the unique potential of SMP, the goal is to present a practical method for making self-transformable surfaces, blending the capabilities of both materials to advance the soundscape of a given space. These adaptable surfaces alter their forms in response to specific acoustic criteria.

The primary challenge lies in bridging the gap between the need for macro-scale transformation in architectural space and the microscale behavior of SMP to achieve adjustable acoustic conditions. One potential solution involves aligning material properties with an externally applied overlaid geometry, thereby transforming small material shape morphing into more substantial and expansive spatial effects.

Implementing an overlaid kerf pattern geometry to make partial cuts in the wooden pieces plays a pivotal role in amplifying the motion of SMP and providing control over its degrees of freedom. This method promotes the seamless integration of wood with SMP. Through the reconfiguration of both macro- and microscopic structures, relief-cutting patterns on a wooden sheet provide it with inherent energy dissipative mechanisms. This capability is heightened when the kerf sheet can shape freeform geometries to finely tune the propagation of sound waves.

DOI: 10.4324/9781003384113-45

388

Achieving the desired acoustic adjustments relies on both the inherent properties of the materials and the strategic application of geometry to transform wooden sheets.

Bridging the Divide Between Designers and Material Scientists

Material science and architecture face a notable divide, reflected in disparities across literature, pedagogy, and practice. Material scientists, with a focus on technical language and rigorous training, delve into the understanding of material structures at atomic and molecular levels. By contrast, architects are driven by visual and aesthetic design language to creatively apply materials, emphasizing formal composition, spatial effects, and user experience. The architect's consideration of materials at the scale of entire structures and spaces falls beyond the immediate research scope of material scientists, who meticulously analyze material behavior at the nano or microscale. This divergence creates a challenging gap between the microscopic realm of material properties and the macroscopic scale of architectural design.

Despite the existing disciplinary split posing challenges for collaboration, this study emerges as a collaborative effort to investigate the application of smart materials for dynamic environmental responses. It aims to bridge this gap by converging the highly specialized knowledge of material scientists with the multifaceted approach of architects and engineers. The goal is to extend advancements in programmable materials beyond minuscule characteristics and into the domain of architectural acoustics, challenging the conventional notion of fixity in the design of sonic environments.

Adaptable Soundscapes

The acoustic performance of a space significantly influences occupants' productivity, comfort, and overall well-being (Varjo et al., 2015). In spaces where rigid and immobile elements prevail, incapable of altering their shapes, locations, or orientations, the central challenge arises in defining the suitable acoustic setting for a dynamic environment. This environment must navigate diverse ambient noises, cater to varied purposes, and accommodate occupants with distinct auditory needs and preferences. While it is vital to have an adaptable acoustic environment capable of dynamically adjusting to various sonic circumstances, the integration of smart materials and kerf structures can facilitate responses to changing acoustic demands. This includes considerations for aspects such as reverberation, sound absorption, and diffusion.

Kerfing for Architectural Adaptability

In addition to utilizing smart materials for fine-tuning a room's acoustics, this study examines the acoustic responses of kerf structures. Various experiments have been conducted by the authors to assess how the unique attributes within kerf patterns, including different cell types, cut densities, air gap ratio, and shape reconfigurations, can affect both load-bearing capacity and acoustic properties such as absorption coefficient.

The controlled microstructural topology of a kerf piece with carefully cut lines can induce multi-scale shapeshifting. This capability is highly desirable when aiming to extend the microscale behavior of Shape-Memory Polymer (SMP) to macro-scale architectural reconfiguration. The geometric intervention of kerfing in wood causes local deformation, resulting in the entire material transitioning from one shape to another. Such elasticity is derived from the interplay of various patterns, sizes, and densities (Chen et al., 2020), allowing for the subtraction of stiff material and supporting out-of-plane expansion and compression. While providing flexible yet rigid material, the applied geometrical modification doesn't disrupt the continuity and integrity of the given sheet. Strategically positioned relief cuts not only allow for the manipulation of wood's pliability but also provide control over the orientation and ultimate angle of bending. When parallel cut lines allow bending along one axis, multiple lines in different alignments enable the material to bend in a multi-directional fashion. In addition to the geometry and compactness of cut lines, the sheet's bendability is influenced by the force direction.

Kerfing offers a significant advantage in making nearly seamless double-curvature shapes from flat materials without tears or wrinkles, using readily available 2.5D fabrication tools such as laser cutters, waterjets, and CNC routers. This capability contributes to minimizing the typical waste associated with fabricating freeform surfaces, including the need for formworks (Kalantar and Borhani, 2018).

Kerf Patterns for Enhanced Acoustics

To assess the impact of kerfing on the acoustic environment, both square and hexagon-based spiral patterns were cut into 1/8″ thick MDF and plywood sheets. Utilizing an in-house algorithmic platform for remeshing 2D meander patterns (Borhani et al., 2022, Zarrinmehr et al., 2017a, 2017b, 2017c), various kerf densities and shape reconfigurations were parametrically designed in grasshopper. Subsequently, these designs were laser-cut, introducing varying degrees of flexibility to the sheets. To analyze the acoustic performance of these patterns and their impact on reverberation times (RTs), a mathematical model was necessary to reveal wave propagation behaviors in trapping and/or redirecting sound energy.

With a custom-designed impedance tube, absorption rates of basic kerf cell cut samples were measured, continuing from earlier research that explored corresponding responses of kerf samples under static and dynamic loadings on building skin (Shahid et al., 2022a, 2022b). Absorption measurements at Bruel and Kjaer (B&K) in Detroit reveal that lower kerf density generally correlates with a higher absorption coefficient, except at frequencies 125 and 250 Hz where the impact is negligible. At 500 and 1,000 Hz, absorption coefficients decrease with increasing reflection attributes (Figure 3.5.1).

After modeling a small office space with a suspended ceiling, ray-tracing simulations were conducted to investigate the behavior of larger kerf surfaces in space and examine the potential influence of various kerf densities on the ceiling panels. The input material parameters employed in these simulations were obtained from the absorption coefficients measured at B&K using the impedance tube.

The outcomes of these simulations indicate that the room's acoustics were enhanced by incorporating kerf panels with various densities. Following that, it was explored how altering the overall geometry of the ceiling could affect the room's sonic ambiance. Due to the inherent flexibility of the kerf panels, their shape could be easily reconfigured to adopt different geometries, including convex and concave surfaces. After repeating simulations, it became evident that a ceiling with multiple reconfigured panels effectively contributed to an improved acoustic response at 500 Hz and 1,000 Hz by leading to a reduced RT (ranging from 0.49s to 0.65s). Notably, this response remained consistent regardless of the

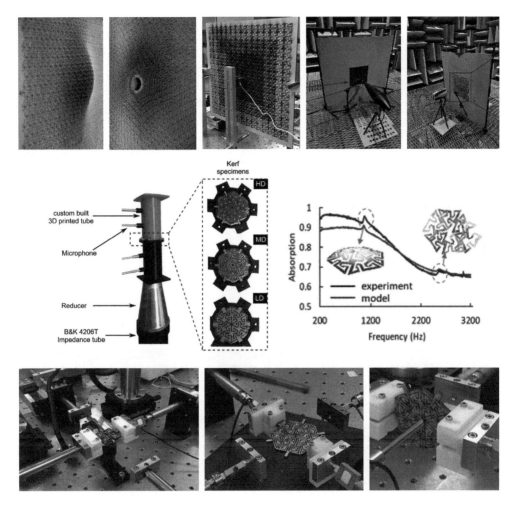

Figure 3.5.1 Investigating the mechanical properties and acoustic behaviors of various kerf unit cells and their aggregations through physical tests and simulations (for unit cell testing, refer to (Chen et al., 2020). Acoustic cell testing courtesy of Ed Green (B&K) and Zaryab Shahid (TAMU). (Photo: courtesy of author Anastasia H. Muliana).

positions of the occupants. The kerf parameters could be tuned until the specific acoustic performative expectation is satisfied. The study did not explore the viscoelastic responses of wood kerf, which are influenced by changes in temperatures and humidity and impact modal frequencies.

In a project named "Kerfonic Wall," the application of kerfing in architectural acoustics was explored. This permanent installation is in the boardroom lounge of Autodesk Gallery in San Francisco. In addition to designing, fabricating, and acoustically simulating the wall, we conducted physical tests on the sound quality of the lounge area before and after the wall installation (Borhani et al., 2022). Using the HBK Analyzer (Type 2270) and RT software (BZ-7227), we measured the lounge RT at a 1/3 octave. The Impulsive Excitation Method (Schroeder Method) with a balloon burst, as recommended in ISO 3382-2, was employed

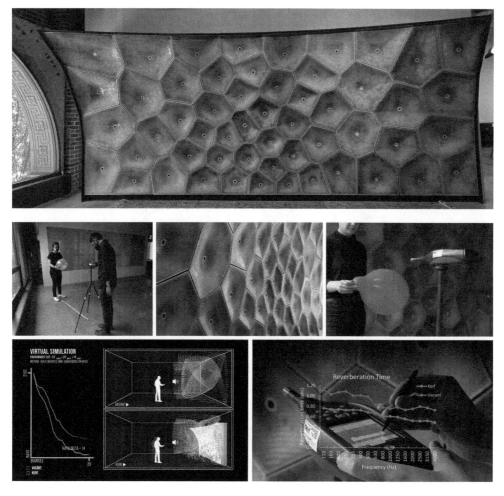

Figure 3.5.2 Kerfonic Wall, Autodesk Gallery, San Francisco: Assessing wall acoustic performance via simulation and pre/post-installation acoustic tests for RT measurement. (Photo: courtesy of author Alireza Borhani).

for these measurements. The results of this test revealed that the Kerfonic Wall increased the effective absorption of the space and reduced sound echo and RT (Figure 3.5.2).

Temperature-Responsive Polymers as Smart Materials

Employing smart materials to achieve enhanced adaptability surpasses the reliance on mechanical actuators for fine-tuning appropriate responses. This ensures the activation of acoustic components composed of passive or inanimate materials. The development of smart materials presents an alternative way for adaptation through material activation, challenging the dominance of simplistic sliding or folding in rigid-body mechanical approaches. These materials open new possibilities for tuning a room's acoustics while celebrating impermanence through reversible geometrical transitioning between flexibility and rigidity.

Introducing a temporal dimension to a room's acoustic setting involves the use of a temperature-responsive polyurethane epoxy resin-based polymer. This polymer can be programmed to reconfigure in response to an external stimulus. As the SMP undergoes a geometric transformation into the fourth dimension through internal reactions to heat, it regains its initial form. The SMP formula in this study, overseen by Dr. Terry Creasy, consists of epoxy named Epon 826 (1.00 part), Jeffamine D230 as a curing agent (0.63 parts), and Neopentyl Glycol Diglycidyl Ether (NGDE) as a strengthening agent (0.60 parts) (Mansoori et al., 2018). The mix ratio of this SMP results in a "glassy" or rigid state at normal room temperatures (20–25°C), transitioning to the "elastomeric" or rubbery phase in the 40–60°C range.

Once shaped at a high temperature and cooled, the SMP can revert to its initial shape upon reheating, facilitated by the reorientation of its molecular chains. Both the initial and transformed shapes remain stable. The glass transition temperature (Tg) is the temperature at which the polymer undergoes a reversible change from a rigid to a leathery state. Below the Tg value, Epon 826 maintains its stiffness. However, exceeding the Tg value causes the NGDE segments to make SMP flexible, enabling it to self-transform back into its initial shape. Tg, the transition point, can be tailored to suit a specific application. In this study, a 1-way SMP was developed to transition between two shapes. However, it is possible to create 2-way, 3-way, or multiple-way SMPs through 3D printing as digital materials. However, the performance of these SMPs might be restricted to fewer cycles.

Synergistic Design: SMP and Kerf Hybrid

As mentioned, Kerfing dissipates energy imparted on wood, while SMP aids in controlling shapeshifting to respond to the desired sound quality. A piece of wood kerf can take on various shapes, but incorporating SMP onto that piece provides complete control on targeted curved geometry, well-suited for regulating a broad spectrum of frequencies.

Combining SMP and wood kerf forms a composite material, showcasing a micro-macro effect. Wood kerf, designed for extensive transformation to accommodate architectural-scale applications, is complemented by the nuanced motion behavior of SMP, providing responsiveness to the composite. As SMP stabilizes the final kerf piece, wood strengthens the polymer's structure, extends its transformative capabilities, guides its transitional direction, expedites alteration, and maximizes the area that it can reach. This composite material demonstrates superior mechanical properties compared to wood and SMP individually. In this hybrid, while wood and SMP are not physically fused, they are unified and function as a single entity (Mansoori et al., 2022). At the intersection of architectural design and material science, the unique aspect of combining kerfing and SMP is achieving on-demand pliability and stiffness without compromising the structural stability and adaptability of wooden panels. Without mechanical force, the hybrid of SMP and kerf wood requires minimal actuation energy to morph from one shape to another. The hybrid of wood and SMP reflects a bio-inspired perspective that form and material are interrelated and should be designed simultaneously to support the desired acoustic environment (Figure 3.5.3).

The cost-effectiveness of fabricating kerf panels, along with the simplicity of SMP's basic ingredients, complements cost savings achieved through the elimination of complicated mechanical components required to activate wood panels. In addition to reducing overall weight, the exclusion of mechanical components responsible for panel adjustability results in reduced maintenance costs.

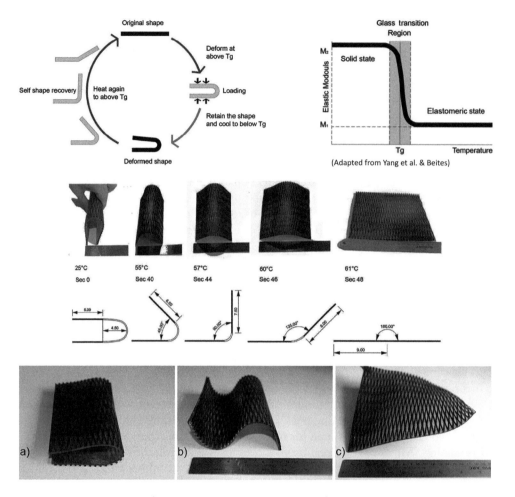

Figure 3.5.3 Representing the temperature response pattern of an SMP, a wood kerf-SMP hybrid with a curved geometry transforms back to its original shape without external forces. (Photo: courtesy of Author Maryam Mansoori).

Fabrication Techniques for SMP-Wood Composites

This study aims to integrate the responsive qualities of SMP into everyday materials. The goal is to enable a material programmed at the molecular scale to perform and respond at the building scale. From various materials at our disposal, the decision was made to integrate wood and SMP, creating a hybrid material that reconciles the conflicting characteristics of flexibility and rigidity. To achieve this goal, three primary fabrication methods were investigated:

- CAST COMPOSITE
  The method included mixing and stirring the SMP liquid ingredients, heating and degassing the mixture to remove entrapped air bubbles in a vacuum oven for 30 minutes, and pouring the mix into a silicone rubber mold with the wooden sheet. Following that, the

mix was cured in an oven at 100°C for 90 minutes and then cooled to room temperature (Mansoori et al., 2018). The mold could have either flat or curved geometry.

- LAMINATED COMPOSITE
  In this method, the SMP mixture was hardened separately before adhering to the wood. Considering that actuation is intrinsic to the material in SMP, it was important to carefully consider its desired initial shape. When the initial shape was intended to be non-flat, it had to be cured in a non-flat shape before attaching it to kerf wood. An alternative approach was to add smaller SMP pieces at multiple locations on the wood, rather than shaping the entire SMP and activating it at once. Here, the mixing and curing of various SMPs at different ratios (each characterized by unique Tg values) allowed for their activation at different temperatures.

- 3D-PRINTED COMPOSITE
  Overall, this strategy is referred to as 4D printing, where the shape-changing capability of SMP is activated over time. In this study, by utilizing fused deposition modeling (FDM) 3D printers, thermos-responsive SMP filament was accurately deposited onto a kerf piece in flat or curvilinear shapes, enabling reversible shape transformations. For example, when printing a double-curved surface of SMP, it could regain its initial curved geometry upon heating after any deformation. One advantage of printing was the ability to create asymmetrical SMP surfaces of varying thickness. Thinner areas heated up more quickly, reaching the Tg threshold faster. Consequently, they could undergo transformation more rapidly, offering increased potential for bendability. Apart from the temperature and humidity of the printing environment, several factors could significantly impact the bonding of printed layers to the wood surface. These factors could play crucial roles in maintaining adhesion after multiple shape-changing cycles, as well as influencing warpage, internal stress, dimensional errors, layers delamination, and degree of crystallinity. These factors included SMP filament specifications, wood surface finish, both nozzle and built-plate temperature, rapid heating-cooling process, print area size and shape, nozzle diameter and extrusion flow rate, printing speed, and layer height, as well as infill pattern structure. Considering the printing layer orientation and wood grain, the printed composite is expected to exhibit anisotropic behavior. The layer-by-layer deposition of molten SMP filament had its pros and cons. On the positive side, it offered geometric freedom for accurate placement of SMP at any position, resulting in cost- and time-efficient creation of lightweight prototypes with high bendability. However, on the downside, challenges included dealing with a material with a non-customizable Tg, poor bonding between wood and SMP, a composite with high porosity, and lower structural firmness.

Dynamic Room Acoustics: SMP-Wood Hybrid in Action

As discussed, the hybrid properties of wood and SMP can initiate sonic adjustments in a room. Imagine a statically aggregated wall with passive acoustic characteristics transforming physically into active elements that respond to a specific sound source.

Mounted on the lightweight grid, the aggregated wall cell consists of flat and elongated fin-shaped pieces, resembling snake scales. Arranged in rows to create a uniform mosaic pattern, these leaf-like fins are attached to the grid from just one side, overlapping from the opposite side. This tessellated arrangement provides the fins with flexibility and ease of movement (Figure 3.5.4).

Constructed from SMP and wood kerf, each fin is a hybrid composite. As the SMP reaches its glass transition temperature (Tg), the flat fin can curl up, contributing to adjusting the room acoustics. Given the fin's initial curved geometry, heating the SMP in its flat position allows it to revert to that geometry.

Inside each fin, a thin wire is placed to activate the SMPs. The flow of electric current through the wire converts electrical energy into heat, initiating the shape-changing phase of the SMP. Consequently, the resistive heating in the wire causes the necessary mechanical force to bend the fin forward.

The fin SMPs can bend at different angles depending on their programming. Utilizing 2-way SMPs enables the fin to return to its original flat position. This intricate interplay

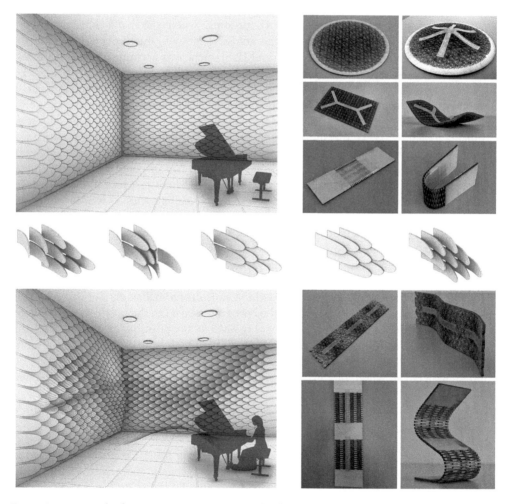

Figure 3.5.4 Use the heat-responsive 3D-printed kerf-SMP composite to create a dynamic sound space with configurable fin-shaped elements bending at various angles on demand. (Photo: courtesy of author Alireza Borhani).

of materials' micro behavior influences the micro attributes of the space. The collective physical transformation of the fins, featuring varied angles, enables the wall to respond effectively to diverse sonic landscapes within the room. The motion pattern and actuation speed of the fins can create a choreographic scene through the harmonious interconnection of material, form, performance, and architecture.

Conclusion

By considering the potentials and limitations of materials as design factors, this study takes a step toward reintegrating geometric considerations and smart materials for achieving rooms with adjustable acoustics. Capable of exhibiting both local and global dynamic modes, this study specifies that kerfing holds significant potential for efficient energy dissipation mechanisms in freeform wooden panels. In addition to improving the intrinsic transformation abilities of kerf wood, the authors also explore how SMP introduces a unique adaptive capacity that contributes to various acoustic adjustment requirements in space. Various methods, including casting, 3D printing, and laminating, are examined to incorporate shape-changing characteristics of SMP into a kerf piece. Creating the hybrid material involves integrating the structural rigidity, aesthetic appeal, and affordability of wood with the transformative qualities of SMP.

The current literature and available simulation tools lack comprehensive support for analyzing the responsive acoustic properties arising from kerf wood. This study represents progress in understanding the interdependency among factors like kerf length, air gap area, topology, shape transformation aspects, and energy dissipation potential. Future research should explore the interplay between SMP attributes and wood viscoelastic properties to facilitate the digital prediction of wave propagation, enabling the manipulation of room acoustics.

In addition to the technical aspects discussed in the chapter, this study aims to honor our auditory connection to the built environment and highlight how sound influences our emotional, communicative, and cognitive awareness. Acoustically adaptable architecture encourages thinking about the nature of buildings, emphasizing the importance of responding to the ever-changing needs of their inhabitants. In contrast to passive acoustic architecture, which functions as an inert backdrop wrapped with fixed acoustic components, adaptable acoustics seek to make architecture both sonically and perceptually responsive. This involves envisioning a space enriched with the complexity of change, fluidity of orders, and diversity of responses. The study emphasizes the synergy between performance and appearance, celebrating the role of functional ornament in visually communicating invisible behavioral qualities of architecture.

References

Borhani, A., Kalantar, N., Muliana, A., Shahid, Z., Rezaei, E., and Green, E. (October 26–29, 2022). "The sound of kerfing: A new approach to integrating geometry, materials, and acoustics to build invisibles." In *Proceedings ACADIA 2022 Hybrids and Haecceities*, University of Pennsylvania, Philadelphia, PA.

Chen, R. Turman, C., Jiang, M., Kalantar, N., Moreno, M., and Muliana, A. (2020). "Mechanics of kerf patterns for creating freeform structures." *Acta Mech*, 231 (9): 3499–3524. https://doi.org/10.1007/s00707-020-02713-8.

Kalantar, N., and Borhani, A. (2018). "Informing deformable formworks—parameterizing deformation behavior of a non-stretchable membrane via Kerfing." In *Learning, Adapting and*

Prototyping - Proceedings of the 23rd CAADRIA Conference, CAADRIA (pp. 339–348). Tsinghua University, Beijing, China.

Mansoori, M., Kalantar, N., and Creasy, T. (July 2018). "The design and fabrication of transformable, doubly-curved surfaces using shape memory composites." In *Proceedings of IASS Annual Symposia* (Vol. 2018, No. 14, pp. 1–4). International Association for Shell and Spatial Structures (IASS), MIT, Boston, USA.

Mansoori, M., Rybkowski, Z., and Kalantar, N. (2022). Material driven adaptive design model for environmentally-responsive envelopes. In *Advanced Materials in Smart Building Skins for Sustainability: From Nano to Macroscale* (pp. 207–220). Springer International Publishing, Cham.

Shahid, Z., Bond, C., Johnson, M., Hubbard Jr J., Kalantar, N., and Muliana, A., (2022b). "Dynamic Response of Flexible Viscoelastic Kerf Structures of Freeform Shapes." *International Journal of Solids and Structures*, 254–255: 111895.

Shahid, Z., Hubbard Jr, J., Kalantar, N., and Muliana, A. (2022a). "An Investigation of Dynamics Responses of Architectural Kerf Structures." *Acta Mechanica*, 233: 157–181.

Varjo, J., Hongisto, V., Haapakangas, A., Maula, H., Koskela, H., and Hyönä, J. (2015). "Simultaneous effects of irrelevant speech, temperature and ventilation rate on performance and satisfaction in open-plan offices." *Journal of Environmental Psychology*, 44: 16–33. https://doi.org/10.1016/j.jenvp.2015.08.001.

Zarrinmehr, S., Akleman, E., Ettehad, M., Kalantar, N., and Borhani, A. (2017a). "Kerfing with Generalized 2D meander-patterns: Conversion of planar rigid panels into locally-flexible panels with stiffness control." In *Future Trajectories of Computation in Design [17th International Conference, CAAD Futures 2017, Proceedings, CAAD Futures]* (pp. 276–293). Istanbul, Turkey.

Zarrinmehr, S., Akleman, E., Ettehad, M., Kalantar, N., Haghighi, A.B., and Sueda, S. (2017b). "An algorithmic approach to obtain generalized 2D meander-patterns." In *Bridges 2017 Conference Proceedings. The 20th Annual Bridges Conference*, BRIDGES (pp. 87–94). Waterloo, Ontario, Canada.

Zarrinmehr, S., Ettehad, M., Kalantar, N., Borhani, A., Sueda, S., and Akleman, E. (2017c). "Interlocked archimedean spirals for conversion of planar rigid panels into locally flexible panels with stiffness control." *Computers & Graphics*, 66: 93–102. https://doi.org/10.1016/j.cag.2017.05.010.

3.6

SMART TECTONICS FOR THE DESIGN OF BUILDING STRUCTURAL SYSTEMS

Olga Popovic Larsen and Sander Løkkegaard Benner

Abstract

This chapter focuses on healthy Smart Structural Systems that explore innovative sustainable ways of working with form, structural composition, detailing to achieve smart tectonics through circular use of materials and structural systems. The study is motivated by the extreme consumption, pollution, and material use in the building sector contributing greatly to the climate emergency. The outcomes of three case studies are presented. Two are experimental demonstrator structures built in full-scale developed through current smart design and fabrication tools. The third is an innovative larger structure for buildings of 6–8 floors. All three projects differ in their approaches for minimizing the use of wood in wooden constructions, implementing reused wood, enabling design-for-disassembly and adaptability. Inspired by historic materials, structures, and detailing, also aspects from historic Danish half-timbered houses, the exploration journey seeks to map and understand historic approaches that inform new building practices enhancing building with re-claimed materials, also, material and structural efficiency. The reflections offer insights for approaches that address current complexity in achieving smart tectonics.

The investigations have been carried out by the authors in collaboration with master's students from the master's program *Architectural Technology* and PhD students at the *Royal Danish Academy: Architecture, Design, Conservation* in Copenhagen.

Motivation – The Climate Emergency Is Inevitable

The state of the climate is worsening. Six of the nine planetary boundaries have been exceeded – including climate change, biosphere integrity, land system change, freshwater change, biochemical flows, and novel entities – (Richardson et al., 2023) and despite the increasing focus on climate change, the atmospheric concentration of CO_2 is still rising. In 2019, the atmospheric carbon concentration reached 410 parts per million (ppm), which is believed to be the highest in more than two million years (IPCC Secretariat, 2023). This means that the planetary boundary for climate change, which is set at 350 ppm, now is

DOI: 10.4324/9781003384113-46

closer to the "Upper end of zone of increasing risk," which is set at 450 ppm (Richardson et al., 2023). Due to a growing global economy and increased living standards, it is expected that the overall-global consumption of raw materials will more than double by 2060 (UNEP, 2022). This is alarming and calling for radical reductions by a wide range of industrial sectors. The building sector that is part of the problem – which, combined from buildings operations and construction of buildings, accounts for approximately 37% of global energy and process-related emissions (UNEP, 2022, s. 26) – must also become part of the solution.

At present, many of the conventionally used construction materials are non-renewable and mineral-based; they also often rely on high energy-intensive manufacturing processes.

These processes have a significant impact on factors such as loss of biodiversity, water scarcity, and embedded carbon emissions. To reduce the environmental impact of the construction sector, the United Nations Environment Program (UNEP) points to the need to minimize embedded emissions and to implement adaptable construction solutions. This includes solutions for building less, requiring less material, substituting conventional high-emission materials with low-carbon materials, implementing circular solutions, and increasing building longevity (UNEP, 2022, s. 74). Here, circular economy is considered as *"one of the most promising approaches"* for increasing the longevity of materials, where construction materials are designed to enter circular loops and thereby increase both building and material longevity. Increasing the longevity of both existing and new buildings and building components are highlighted as key factors for minimizing the environmental impact from the building industry. But the longevity of buildings does not only rely on the physical durability of buildings and materials, but is also affected by social, cultural, and economic aspects. In addition to their quantifiable/performative parameters, materials also have a cultural and emotional impact on buildings occupants' who culturally connect them to a certain place, sensual quality, or meaning (UNEP, 2022, s. 74–77).

Embedded emission can be reduced by substituting high-emission construction materials, such as concrete, steel, and aluminum, with locally available bio-based materials, such as wood, bamboo, and straw. These materials store carbon that they have absorbed from the atmosphere, which by using them in construction is being stored in our buildings, until the materials biodegrade or are burned after the end of life of the material or building (UNEP, 2022, s. 74–77). As a result, at present, the interest for bio-based materials in construction has increased. Wood is one of the bio-based materials that has gained significant interest because it is renewable and a material with a high strength-to-weight ratio, which has been used for thousands of years (Ramage et al., 2017). For building multi-story and more complex constructions, various glulam products with high strength – such as LVL (laminated veneer lumber), CLT (cross-laminated timber), and GLT (glue-laminated timber) – are being used increasingly. However, there are different levels of wood utilization for different timber components. When thinking about wood, it is important to have the energy consumption in mind, used for drying the wood where much of the energy consumption comes from the drying of green timber, also the glue production used in engineered timber products (Glulam, CLT, LVL, etc.) (Ramage et al., 2017).

The potential benefits from using wood in construction – regarding minimizing embedded emission – however are not fully unproblematic. While *climate change* is a highly important factor within the planetary boundaries, factors such as *land system change* and *biosphere integrity* must also be kept in mind. These have both, just like *climate change*, already been exceeded. The boundary *land system change* is measured by the amount of original forest as a percentage that is remaining in relation to preindustrial values. The planetary boundary is set at 75% globally and was, in 2023, at 60%, where all subcategories (tropical, temperate, and boreal forest) have been exceeded globally (Richardson et al., 2023).

Learning from the Past – Timber, Flexibility, and Design-for-Disassembly

An obvious question is if historical buildings, traditional building methods, and materials could help us overcome the climate crisis and create the basis for a future smart building practice.

In a way, it seems logical because human civilizations build upon knowledge and skills developed over the centuries. The different challenges throughout history have influenced methods for adaptation to the ever-changing conditions including knowledge of how to build better with the locally available materials. The trial-and-error evolved knowledge and experience was passed on from generation to generation, also known as *tacit knowledge*. There is valuable inspiration to be found in revisiting historical examples, building methods, and ways of thinking. Also, there are many lessons to be learnt, especially in finding smart ways of addressing the climate crisis we are facing now.

Historic and Current Smart Materials

Some studies suggest (Montjoy, 2023) that when surrounded by natural materials, our well-being is supported. Currently, technologies enable us to describe materials and their performance very precisely whereas qualitative material characteristics often are neglected. In historic buildings, material choices were considered more holistically, especially because design and crafting skills were based on tacit material knowledge. This explains why some historic structures are still valued and used – the material choices were based on a combination of performative and tactile qualities.

Wood – A Renewable Resource?

Timber constructions were among the first man-made structures, built over centuries in different building cultures, showing great experience in building with wood. Figure 3.6.1 presents four historic timber projects from Denmark. One can argue that indigenous structures globally display the beginning of smart building tectonics. Traditional buildings were often constructed in timber, with both structure and the façade made of wood. Half-timbered houses, on the other hand, had facades made of a combination of wood and other materials, such as straw and clay. All wood used (structural and non-structural) was adaptable, easy to repair and replace.

Today wood is often considered a more expensive option compared to using concrete or steel, but this is not necessarily correct. A recent research project (Horswill & Nielsen, 2016) demonstrates that in the Danish context, a six-story high timber apartment block can be constructed for the same price as the equivalent building in concrete. This, however, requires more careful design, planning, and thinking. A valid concern is whether we will run out of wood if we build all our future buildings in wood. We cannot afford to build our future housing short-sightedly, where buildings are destined for demolition after relatively few years and in a process where the wood is burned. We require diverse ways of using

Figure 3.6.1   Historic Danish houses: Top left: house fully built in wood from the Viking period. Top right: half-timbered house from the countryside. Bottom left: multi-story half-timbered town house. Bottom left: old fully timbered connection. Hand sketches by Jacob H. Hoffmann.

wood as a building material and it is a matter of design to find an application that will enable us to use wood in the best way through smart approaches.

Also, we need to consider using wood of a lesser quality, through smart design strategies that ensure safety compensating for the lower material quality. Recent studies carried out at The Royal Danish Academy in collaboration with Hede Danmark (Munk, 2022) experimented with the use of hybrid larch as structural wood. Hybrid larch is planted and grown between high-quality trees and every 20 years the larch trees are cut down. Their function is primarily to enable the superior quality trees to grow vertically and tall, and so far, the subsequent use of the larch has mainly been as woodchips or firewood. The hybrid larch wood is not certified, and the precise quality is unknown, but the study revealed the structural potentials of the material. With the need to build in more sustainable ways and with the rising price of wood, imperfect and lower quality wood is likely to be used more. This requires better understanding of the material that we are working with through more testing and material studies. Referring to historic building examples, we can see that the wood used was the one that was locally available – and this was not always of the highest quality.

Cascading refers to a concept of materials having multiple lives, before downgrading the material. In historic building practice, all materials that could be reclaimed were typically reused. Time and workmanship were readily available, and materials were scarce. The first life of materials could be a house; then perhaps, the house was moved to another location but still functioned as a dwelling, with most elements reused (beams are used as beams, columns are still columns, etc.) At the point when this house was demolished, all usable elements become part of something else, as close as possible to their original function. When this no longer was possible, the elements in any subsequent reuse became downcycled but were still used and reused as long as possible before they are disposed of or burned.

Current industrial material production with fast production of mineral-based materials and high labor prices has made building practice wasteful. Facing the climate crisis, however, presents us with the challenge of limited material resources with the requirement for making material lives longer, through multiple reuses.

It takes close to a century for a tree to grow and to become mature, making it precious. Wood should be seen as a natural material that can have multiple lives. Not surprisingly at present, a new smart building practice is emerging with reclaimed materials. The climate damage as well as the scarcity of material resources calls for making the new less wasteful and smart building practices to become more mainstream. Current smart digital tools and new approaches enable this thinking.

If we look back in history for inspiration for a new building practice, we find that half-timbered houses can offer many relevant aspects to learn from. Half-timbered houses appear in varying forms and levels of complexity, throughout different building cultures and geographic regions. They are a system with a clear technical logic: a load-bearing structure made of timber that is visible on the façade, with its own specific rhythm. Both vertical structure and the bracing are provided by the same system, enabling vertical forces to be taken by the vertical elements, while the bracing goes diagonally across providing stability and wind resistance to the building. All the timber members in a half-timbered house are joined with carpentry connections, and as such they can be taken apart, which makes it – potentially – possible to move a half-timbered house and rebuild it somewhere else, without extra material going into building it again. The principle of design-for-disassembly (DFD) is a smart design approach that is relevant in addressing the current climate crisis. It has also been embraced and tested in the investigations with current innovative structures presented in the next section.

Smart Structural Timber Tectonics

This section presents three projects (two built experimental structures and a novel approach for larger buildings) inspired by historic building design and embracing smart design thinking, also current cutting-edge computational design/fabrication tools. All three projects are developed using reclaimed wood in different ways promoting the cascading principle as a smart design approach. *The ReciPly Wood* and *Waste Wood Canopy* test strategies for structural safety through robustness as well as simple connection systems. The large timber structure sets out to investigate how to articulate load-bearing structures in multi-story buildings, while working within technical principles for fire protection in the Danish building regulation. Optimizing usability, buildability, tectonics, and aesthetics and waying them out has been important for all three projects.

Two Smart Experimental Structures: ReciPlyDome and
Waste Wood Canopy

ReciPlyDome is a reciprocal frame (RF) (Larsen, 2008) minimal bending active structure developed as a full-scale a prototype. It is a grid structure consisting of 45 identical double-curved plywood members, providing the required rigidity and stiffness. It forms a spherical load-bearing structure spanning 5 meters with 12 mm thick plywood.

To start with, the *ReciPlyDome* was designed to be fabricated from new-virgin plywood material. However, the design made for disassembly enabled further uses as well as reconfiguration of the members with new spherical geometries. Plywood was chosen as an inexpensive material and the structure was optimized to utilize minimum material. A further consideration was to enable ease of construction without any specialized lifting equipment. This made the *ReciPlyDome* kit of parts easy-to-use by lay people system who could easily construct it, and, when needed disassemble it. The fabrication was also relatively fast and simple requiring only a wood workshop and few people to fabricate the beams from the plywood plates.

To construct the *ReciPlyDome* structure, the RF beams are assembled by a single bolt creating the connection between two beams. Assembly and disassembly were simple with all beams and joints being identical. The only beams that are shorter are where the structure touches the ground (Brancart et al., 2017; Larsen et al., 2018).

Another project utilizing the *ReciPlyDome – Domes of transition*, investigated the potential of it as a temporary shelter with untrained people fabricating it and constructing it out of locally available materials, showed that this was viable. Research suggests that involving people affected by a disaster in rebuilding their future helps the healing process.

In design terms, the structure, however, is everything but simple. To design it and deal with the gematrical and static complexity high level of computational skills is required. Combining physical modeling and digital modeling approaches, the team of researchers from the Royal Academy and Vrije Universiteit Brussel (VUB) worked several months together. Resolving the *ReciPlyDome* beam connections with different inclinations was challenging. The grid curvature is defined by the eccentricity of the connections and thus the cross-sectional height of the members. The bending forces that are imposed through the intermediate connections along the beams often require large cross-sections. Utilizing bending-active beams through the flexibility of the components overcomes the difference in beam inclinations producing the required cross-sectional height. A further complexity that the team dealt with is the modeling of the static behavior of the structure that is highly indeterminate offering robustness through a high level of redundancy. After several design iterations and high-level smart tools, the result was achieved – a smart design that minimizes material resources and enables untrained people to self-build the minimal structure; also, when the structure is no longer needed to take it down for a subsequent use (Figure 3.6.2).

One of the challenges with the *ReciPlyDome* was developing a high-performing cladding system as low tech in fabrication and construction as the load-bearing structure itself. *ReciPlySkin* (Larsen, 2019) created a fully enclosed structure with a lightweight fabric membrane, that offered a waterproof solution, however an uninsulated space. An insulated membrane is a possibility, but an expensive solution, using materials (for the insulation) that are high performing but also environmentally polluting. Further development is being carried out to find façade system alternatives using bio-based easy to construct solutions.

Although very different in form/appearance to an indigenous structure, *ReciPlyDome* clearly draws parallels to smart historic approaches as DFD and adaptability, also

Figure 3.6.2   Top: ReciPlyDome. Bottom: Waste wood canopy. Photos by Olga P. Larsen.

minimizing material use. Its' form, performance, and overall design/fabrication are enabled by state-of-the-art smart computational design tools as parametric software.

Waste Wood Canopy is a full-scale prototype of RF experimental grid structure made from reclaimed short timber members. It was developed as a demonstrator testing the viability for utilizing reclaimed timber for an inhabitable load-bearing structure. The canopy was designed as shelter, based on an arched geometry forming a small gridshell structure. Unlike the *ReciPlyDome* that was designed utilizing new plywood subsequently reused/rebuilt several times for new uses, the *Waste Wood Canopy* as starting point utilized reclaimed wood. This presented a further potential for cascading as the structure was reused several times yet starting from reclaimed material (otherwise considered as waste). A further difference and development in the investigations between the *ReciPlyDome* and the *Waste Wood Canopy* was that the latter embraced the complexity of factors and strived at optimizing them simultaneously. Usability (architecture and aesthetics), structural behavior, and buildability were tested and optimized in parallel. This multi-objective optimization, on one hand, meant that no single aspect could achieve the highest level and be fully optimized. On the other hand, it meant that by considering several relevant aspects and waying them out, a more balanced (holistic) outcome could be achieved.

The *Waste Wood Canopy*, shaped as vault open at both ends, acts as a gridshell structure carrying the loads via arch action. With RF geometry with short identical members arranged in diamond shapes and offset joints, the structure requires many connections. The number of metal connections was optimized by novel clamp joint which fixes together four beam members with a single bolt. Optimizing the number of connections contributed to both the "clean – uncluttered" aesthetics as well as the ease of construction (buildability).

The design – both in terms of defining the geometry configuration as well as the structural behavior – would have been impossible without smart parametric tools. The full frame was modeled in Rhinoceros 3D, Grasshopper, and plug-in Karamba 3D as a wireframe, with supports, and point loads based on the intersection with the glulam beams. At first, the frames are filled completely with web elements that can be progressively removed based on the axial stresses reported by the calculation (Castriotto et al., 2021).

The *Waste Wood Canopy* and the *ReciPlyDome* are both structurally highly statically indeterminate, offering alternate load paths taking the self-weight down to the base/foundations. It also suggests that a local failure of a member or removing one or more timber members will not cause the whole structure to fail. Furthermore, if one or more of the clamp connections were to fail, this would not lead to an overall failure of the structure. This makes both experimental structures robust and safe, securing them against disproportional collapse (Larsen & Browne, 2023).

Both *Waste Wood Canopy* and the *ReciPlyDome* have been constructed, taken down, and rebuilt on several locations, showcasing important precedents of building with reclaimed wood for structural applications.

Both projects were greatly reliable on smart tools (parametric software and 3D scanning), especially for the design and geometry definition. The fabrication of the *ReciPlyDome* utilized simple workshop tools, whereas the *Waste Wood Canopy's* clamp connections were fabricated with a CNC cutter which was precise but time-consuming. A further development would be to automate the process utilizing a robotic arm. Although built in full scale, both projects need further research to upscale them to building scale typologies. This development carried out at present is fully dependent on smart design/fabrication tools.

Adaptable Timber Structures – A Beam-Column Structure with a Reused Rib Timber Deck

The "adaptable timber structure" project aimed to combine minimal material use, DFD, and flexible plan layouts together with tectonic principles of making the details and load-bearing structure inherent elements of the building's aesthetics. It was developed as a final-year master's research project by the second author of this text, together with co-student S. B. Seipelt both graduates of the program Architectural Technology *(Arkitekturens Teknologi)* at the Royal Danish Academy.

Following the global urbanization tendency (Ritchie & Roser, 2018), the project more specifically focused on multi-story buildings. The structure consists of a load-bearing beam-column structure with newly produced glulam components and a reused timber rib-deck element. The deck element consisted of *reclaimed wood Brosenius beams,* (inspired by the work of Swedish Engineer Hilding Brosenius) and developed by PhD candidate X. Browne together with the first author of this text, and a two-layered CLT-deck made of reused wood and assembled with dovetail connections instead of glue. The connections between the different components are inspired by old traditional timber connections used in, e.g., half-timbered houses.

The project's aim was to make an "honest" building system, with the load-bearing structure and wood visible. Exposing the structure is an architectural choice. On the other hand, the choice and design of the load-bearing structure is a decisive step to ensure the building's potential lifespan, where constructive principles can have great impact on how to maintain, transform, or renovate a building. Future transformation and adaptation can be enabled through clear and logical principles, where materials can be replaced and reused (Beim & Jensen, 2022). In terms of load-bearing structures, there are differences between separating (such as wall-plate systems) and non-separating construction systems (such as beam-column systems). In the latter, the separating parts must, to a greater extent, be added to the main structure of the building subsequently. In the separating ones, a load-bearing wall can act as, for example, a separating wall between apartments. In general, with conventionally used materials, there is an assumption that the separating systems have the greatest value from a technical and economic perspective, as the load-bearing components, such as concrete walls, often can comply with technical requirements for sound and fire. However, these are more "locked" in their spatial arrangement and are more difficult to transform. Here, the open systems are to a greater extent preferable, in an architectural and overall economic perspective, due to their flexibility and transformation possibilities (Beim, Vibæk, & Jørgensen, 2007; Figure 3.6.3).

Technical aspects regarding fire and sound had a significant impact on the design. The approach for creating a "composite" structure, consisting of newly produced glulam beams and columns with a rib-deck element made of reused wood, occurred due to how ceilings and floors often are being covered in massive timber structures due to sound and fire requirements. Therefore, the ceiling would later be covered in gypsum and the flooring with a high-density layer, such as sand or crushed reused concrete. This strategy also correlated with the idea of minimizing the amount of new wood in the concept, where it was mapped out where the most material was used, which, not surprisingly, was in the slabs. By limiting the total area of exposed wooden surfaces, the complexity in a fire situation was reduced while the glulam beams and columns could remain exposed and thereby articulate the load-bearing structure.

In the project, there was a wish to implement old familiar wooden joints and make the connection an architectural feature, without the use of metal screws, brackets, etc., which often are used in modern wooden constructions. These joints were inspired by the old

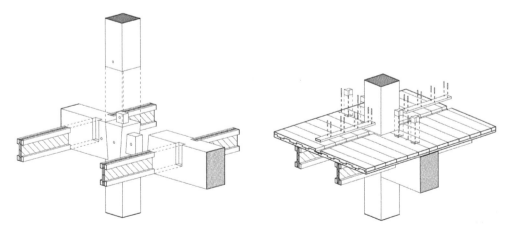

Figure 3.6.3 The "Adaptable Timber Structure": detail between the reused rib-deck elements and the glue-lam columns and beams. Drawings by Sander L. Benner.

half-timbered houses in Denmark and followed the principle for DFD, but they also had to take contemporary aspects regarding fire into account, when designing the connection. The glulam beams were placed on an abutment on the glulam column. But due to how the abutment would burn away in a situation of fire, a load-bearing connection piece inside the beams and columns was implemented, so that the glulam beams would not fall in the event of a fire. Due to how the surrounding wood itself and the charred wood layer would insulate the inner wood (Ramage et al., 2017), the connection piece would be able to retain its strength. By this strategy, the load-bearing structure can uphold adequate static abilities within a given time, e.g., 90 minutes, in a situation of fire if the structural timber is dimensioned adequately.

Discussion and Conclusion

The text dealt with smart tectonics for the design of building structural systems, where we suggest that cutting-edge design/fabrication tools and methods albeit very important, don't provide the full answer. Designing with a deep material/structural understanding combining historic and cutting-edge knowledge, skills, and tools will enable the very needed paradigm shift toward more sustainable construction. The shift should embrace high-level computational smart design and fabrication tools, but also be complemented with smart thinking. In that sense utilizing wood and bio-based materials in smart ways including also reclaimed wood and wood of low quality is one of the ways forward. Today the building industry is extraordinarily complex, because of the amount of specialist knowledge required. Balancing out requirements and holistically approaching material minimizing, optimization, and adaptability principles also found in historic structures, while utilizing smart techniques, tools, and methods is important. Smart tectonics has the potential to both contribute to reducing the climate crisis and at the same time give rise to more balanced and longer lasting structural systems. Both historic and current examples in the text propose a new understanding of the notion of *smart sustainable tectonics*.

Acknowledgements, for Contributing to the

ReciPlyDome project to Niels de Temmerman, Lars Laet and Stijn Brancart of VUB, Brussels
Waste Wood Canopy to Caio Castriotto and Xan Browne
Reclaimed Wood Brosenius Beams to Xan Browne
Adaptable Timber Structure to Sebastian Bernhard Seipelt
4:1 exhibition: Mads Oien Nielsen and Jacob Hoffmann

We are grateful for financial support from Realdania and Innovations Fond and the Royal Danish Academy.

References

Beim, A., & Jensen, J. Z. (2022). *Teknik og Arkitektur Mod en Bedre Byggeskik*. Copenhagen: CINARK, Institut for Bygningskunst og Teknologi, Det Kongelige Akademi. Hamburg: HafenCity University Hamburg.

Beim, A., Vibæk, K. S., & Jørgensen, T. R. (2007). *Arkitektonisk Kvalitet og Industrielle Byggesystemer*. Copenhagen: Kunstakademiets Arkitektskole, CINARK.

Brancart, S., Larsen, O. P., De Temmerman, N., & De Laet, L. (2017). Bending-active reciprocal structures based on equilateral polyhedral geometries. *IASS Symposium*. Hamburg: HafenCity University Hamburg.

Castriotto, C., Tavares, F., Celini, G., Larsen, O. P., & Browne, X. (November 2021). Clamp links: A novel type of reciprocal frame connection. *International Journal of Architectural Computing*. doi:https://doi.org/10.1177/14780771211054169

Horswill, D., & Nielsen, T. (2016). Can CLT construction help copenhagen become world's first carbon neutral city? *Structures and Architecture*, 1, 153–160.

IPCC Secretariat. (2023). *Synthesis Report of the Ipcc Sixth Assessment Report (AR6)*. Geneva: IPCC Secretariat.

Larsen, O. P. (2008). *Reciprocal Frame Architecture*. London: Architectural Press.

Larsen, O. P. (2019). *Physical Modelling for Architecture and Building Design: A Design Practice Tool*. London: Institution of Civil Engineers.

Larsen, O. P., & Browne, X. (2023). Loadbearing structures from reclaimed wood – strategies, design parameters and reflections. *Proceedings of 6th International Scientific Conference, Wood Technology & Product Design*. Skopje: Cyril and Methodius University Skopje.

Larsen, O. P., De Laet, L., De Temmerman, N., & Brancart, S. (July 2018). Bending-active reciprocal structures: Geometric parameters and their stiffening effect. *Creativity in Structural Design: IASS Symposium 2018*, Boston: IASS, 566.

Montjoy, V. (23. November 2023). *What Materials Can Promote Health in Interior Architecture?* Hentet fra ArchDaily: https://www.archdaily.com/989880/what-materials-can-promote-health-in-interior-architecture

Munk, C. A. (12. December 2022). *Studerende tager 200 år gamle træidéer ind i fremtiden*. Hentet fra HedeDanmark: https://www.hededanmark.dk/nyheder/studerende-tager-200-aar-gamle-traeideer-ind-i-fremtiden

Ramage, M. H., Burridge, H., Busse-Wicher, M., Fereday, G., Reynolds, T., Shah, D. U., ... Scherman, O. (2017). The wood from the trees: The use of timber in construction. *Renewable and Sustainable Energy Reviews*, 68(1), 333–359. doi:http://dx.doi.org/10.1016/j.rser.2016.09.107

Richardson, K., Steffen, W., Lucht, W., Bendtsen, J., Cornell, S. E., Donges, J. F., ... Rockström, J. (13. September 2023). Earth beyond six of nine planetary boundaries. *Science Advances*, 9(37). doi: 10.1126/sciadv.adh2458

Ritchie, H., & Roser, M. (2018). *Urbanization*. Hentet fra Out World in Data: https://ourworldindata.org/urbanization

UNEP. (2022). *2022 Global Status Report for Buildings and Construction: Towards a Zeroemission, Efficient and Resilient Buildings and Construction Sector*. Nairobi: United Nations Environment Programme.

3.7

SMART BUILDING SENSIBILITIES

Future Buildings Will Be Smarter, Greener, Cleaner, Connected, Adaptable ... and Driven by Digital Technology Rather Than Architectural Innovation

Pierce Reynoldson and Ibrahim Odeh

Abstract

In "Smart Building Sensibilities," Pierce Reynoldson and Ibrahim Odeh explore the transformative impact of the evolution of office buildings into smart, interconnected structures. This chapter argues that the current trajectory of building innovation lies in digital technology integration within building systems, rather than conventional architectural design. Emphasizing the role of AI and IoT in optimizing building management and automation, this chapter highlights how these technologies contribute to significant operational efficiencies and energy savings.

This chapter anticipates the office spaces of 2030, envisioning them as digitally driven environments where AI plays a pivotal role in managing complex systems for enhanced efficiency and comfort. This vision includes retrofitting existing structures with smart systems, creating interconnected networks of devices and systems, and leveraging cloud-based ecosystems for city-wide coordination. The authors discuss the sustainability aspect of smart buildings, projecting substantial reductions in energy and water usage through automated systems.

This chapter also addresses crucial aspects of safety, security, and privacy, underscoring the ethical considerations and need for robust regulatory frameworks in the era of smart buildings. Furthermore, it explores the architectural implications of smart technology, suggesting a future where technology informs architectural design, leading to an integrated approach combining spatial and software solutions.

"Smart Building Sensibilities" provides a comprehensive overview of the future trajectory of smart buildings, highlighting the importance of a balanced approach that embraces technological innovation while addressing concerns of efficiency, sustainability, security, and privacy. It calls for collaborative efforts across sectors and regulatory bodies for the successful and ethical implementation of smart building technologies.

What will office buildings look like 20 years from now? Basically, the same as they did 30 years ago, because the current phase of building evolution is driven by digital innovation, not architectural and interior design concepts. Setting aside changing styles, fashions,

DOI: 10.4324/9781003384113-47

410

Figure 3.7.1 "Grayscale illustration of New York City's Financial District, optimized for printing, based on the second image. The scene features the iconic skyline with skyscrapers and historical buildings. The central focus is a prominent building with digital data flows extending vertically into the sky, similar to the style of 'The Matrix' movie, depicted in varying shades of gray to symbolize glowing streams of coded information. Additionally, five random surrounding buildings exhibit smaller data flows with numbers and symbols, in a similar "Matrix"-inspired style. The gray-scale tones are adjusted for clarity and contrast, making these features stand out against the urban landscape backdrop." This image was generated with the assistance of AI. Image generated by OpenAI's DALL·E, November 16, 2023.

and workplace trends, real building innovation is happening behind and beyond the walls and furniture, through increasingly connected, automated, and artificially intelligent building systems. Like most aspects of contemporary life, buildings are undergoing a largely invisible, digital revolution.

In the twenty-first century, building innovation has been largely confined to building systems: physical systems, like mechanical, electrical, plumbing, and telecommunications, and information systems like computer-aided facilities management (CAFM). These systems have accelerated following major shifts in digital technology like cloud computing and Internet of Things (IoT). Systems innovation has been driven by a clear ROI for building owners, because roughly 75% of a building's life cycle cost is incurred post-occupancy maintenance and management (Vierra, 2021). Thus, systems innovation is basically agnostic to architectural space-making. 21C buildings look like those of the 20C, because in many cases they are the same buildings – updated and retrofitted with the latest digital technology and maintenance management and optimized by artificial intelligence (AI) – or newer buildings following established real estate development and building code principles.

Market

The global smart building market size is expected to grow from $87 billion in 2022 to $570 billion by 2030 based on the growing demand for energy-efficient systems, the rise in adoption of IoT-enabled Building Management systems (BMS), along with growing industry standards and regulations (Grand View Research, Inc. 2022). Additional factors driving the market include better user experience, increased energy efficiency, improved facility operations, and a more sustainable environment (Ernst & Young Global, 2017).

The COVID-19 pandemic is another catalyst for increased demand for smart technologies. In particular, technologies that engender safe and healthy work environments, reduce operational costs, and attract commercial building users. Though subleased office occupancy rates have increased by nearly 130% since Q2 2020, the average occupancy rate stands at only 49.8% (Doolittle & Fliegelman, 2023).

In general, two strategies have emerged to address depressed commercial occupancy. The first tries to increase occupancy, by making the office more attractive. The technology and spatial innovation that has followed from this solution seems to be a continuation of earlier trends toward enhanced amenities and personalization that started with early 2000's tech offices (e.g., the GooglePlex), continued with the rise of community-based coworking (e.g., WeWork), and may also be a reaction to the post-pandemic rise in home offices. The second strategy seeks to lower operational costs (OpEx) like energy, maintenance, management, and security. We believe this second option – focused on the bottom line and building on proven existing technology – is the more influential on future developments based on past developments and current trends.

For the purposes of this chapter, the authors focused on building/asset management and facilities management systems, which we believe are the prime movers of building innovation. That said, personalization technology will be far from absent in future buildings. In fact, as buildings become increasingly connected through IoT and cloud, personalization technology will become easier to develop and implement. Lastly, though it is not the focus of this chapter, it is worth briefly mentioning other emerging areas of smart innovation, such as smart materials, power generation, environmental sensors, energy management, smart servicing, and robotics.

Trends

Since the COVID pandemic, many organizations are thinking about how to address a more remote workforce. The investment in home offices has surged, and smart building features are increasingly catering to a fragmented workforce.

Beginning in the early 2000s, the corporate world has seen a significant shift in office design. Companies like Google and Apple set the stage with amenity-rich campuses, and this trend was further propelled by co-working spaces like WeWork, which emphasized community and flexibility. This period has been characterized by a focus on Occupant-Centric Design – a design philosophy that prioritizes the individual needs and preferences of each occupant. Modern offices can now have environmental controls that follow the user. As employees move through different spaces, the lighting, temperature, and even the acoustic environment can adapt to their preferences, offering a truly personalized experience. Beyond communal spaces, individual workstations have also seen significant advancements. Employees can now control various aspects of their immediate environment, from lighting and ambient temperature to air ventilation and acoustics. This level of control not only enhances comfort but also contributes to overall productivity.

Office furniture has adapted to this new emphasis on flexibility. Adaptive workspace configurations, height-adjustable desks, modular and mobile furniture, and ergonomic customization are now standard features in many modern offices. These elements allow for a more dynamic and health-conscious work environment. The integration of technology extends to automated concierge services that offer personalized service recommendations, security access, and even health and wellness support. Smart voice assistants and personalized notifications and reminders are becoming commonplace, further enhancing the user experience.

While the allure of high-tech, personalized office spaces is undeniable, the industry never lost sight of the bottom-line importance of operational efficiency and sustainability. Decreasing operational expenses (OpEx) provides a clear and proven return on investment. Thus, while various trends in personalization and architectural solutions have come and gone, the focus on operational efficiency remains the consistent driving factor for new development. The industry's preference for operational efficiency over flashy technology is evident. Companies are more likely to invest in improvements that offer tangible returns, such as energy-efficient lighting or HVAC systems, rather than in aesthetic enhancements with no direct impact on OpEx and that are often left to the whims of the tenant.

The integration of data analytics, IoT, and automation is already playing a significant role in shaping the future of office space. CAFM systems are becoming increasingly sophisticated, integrating with other smart building features to offer a seamless experience. Building Automation Systems (BAS) is on the rise, further contributing to operational efficiency. The concept of digital twins – connected virtual models of physical buildings and assets – is gaining traction and is expected to play a pivotal role in the integration of smart buildings with smart cities. This will not only enhance the individual user experience but also contribute to broader sustainability goals. (Alonso, 2023)

The building sector is a contributor to carbon emissions, energy usage, and waste. As such buildings are an important leverage point for global sustainability. 75% of CO_2 emissions come from urban areas, 25–30% of water consumed by buildings is wasted (EY, 2021), and in 2022 commercial buildings consumed nearly 1/5 (18%) of all energy in the US (University of Michigan, 2023). The industry touts improving building efficiency as more than immediate OpEx savings, but part of a wider global good.

One example of the emerging smart building technology stack is JPMorgan Chase's new headquarters at 270 Park Avenue, Manhattan, which is set to be New York City's largest all-electric skyscraper. It will operate with net zero operational emissions and be fully powered by renewable energy. The building will incorporate advanced technologies, including intelligent systems using sensors, AI, and machine learning (ML) for energy efficiency, alongside innovative water storage and reuse systems and triple-pane glazing with automatic solar shades for enhanced energy efficiency. It is also a 60-story "Workplace Lab" for testing innovative office concepts, like biophilic walls, circadian lighting, and hologram conferencing (JPMorgan Chase & Co, 2022).

Stakeholders

Smart building technology involves a variety of stakeholders, including technology companies, BMS providers, energy management companies, and even building owners themselves.

Technology companies, both corporate incumbents and startups, are actively involved in developing innovative hardware, software, and connectivity solutions for integrating various building assets (e.g. equipment, fixtures) and automating building systems. They create smart sensors, connectivity devices, data analytics platforms, and user-friendly interfaces to enhance the operation and functionality of smart buildings.

BMS providers have been at the forefront developing smart building technology. For decades, companies like Bosch, Siemens, Schneider, and Honeywell have offered digital solutions for monitoring, controlling, automating, and managing building systems. They develop software platforms that allow building owners and facility managers to monitor energy consumption, control HVAC systems, track occupancy, and optimize overall building performance.

Energy management companies also contribute to the development of smart building technology. Their expertise lies in energy efficiency, sustainability, and the optimization of energy consumption. They develop advanced energy management systems that integrate with BAS to provide real-time data and insights on energy usage. These systems help building owners and energy managers identify inefficiencies, implement energy-saving strategies, and reduce utility costs.

Sophisticated commercial tenants are often driving the smart building innovation – in particular, tech sector tenants are particularly demanding. They invest in research and development to create custom solutions that meet their specific needs. They collaborate directly with technology companies or engage in partnerships with other stakeholders to develop and implement smart building solutions.

Overall, smart building technology development is a collaborative effort involving technology companies, BMS providers, energy management companies, and proactive tenants. This collaboration ensures a diverse range of solutions and approaches to address the evolving needs of the industry and drive the advancement of smart building technology.

One problem with tenant-driven innovation has been the development of highly customized and individualized solution systems. This has led to low standardization at the industry level, a high degree of fragmentation between solution providers, and disjointed data pipelines.

Industry

Historically, real estate management has faced significant challenges in transitioning data from traditional, paper-based systems to digital formats. The process is often cumbersome, expensive, and fraught with errors, leading to inefficiencies and missed opportunities. This has been a significant roadblock in leveraging data for operational improvements, as the lack of standardized, easily accessible data hampers the implementation of advanced analytics and other technologies.

With the advent of smart buildings, the industry aims to harness idle or siloed data for better decision-making and operational efficiency. Smart buildings offer a plethora of sensors and devices that generate a massive amount of data. However, this data often remains unused or is stored in isolated systems that don't communicate with each other. The challenge lies in integrating these disparate data sources into a cohesive, actionable format. This is where the promise of smart buildings often hits a wall, as the complexity of data integration can be a daunting task for many organizations.

Technological advancements like the IoT and cloud technologies offer solutions but come with their own set of challenges. IoT devices can generate real-time data that is invaluable for operational efficiency, but they also introduce security risks and require robust network infrastructure for effective data transmission. Cloud technologies offer scalable storage solutions and better data accessibility but raise concerns about data sovereignty and compliance with local regulations. The integration of these technologies into existing systems often requires significant investment in both hardware and software, not to mention the expertise needed to manage these complex systems.

AI and ML are the frontier technologies that promise to revolutionize real estate management. They offer the potential to analyze vast amounts of data for predictive maintenance, energy efficiency, and even tenant satisfaction. However, the implementation of AI and ML is not without challenges. These technologies require high-quality, labeled data for training algorithms, which many organizations do not have. Additionally, there is a general lack of understanding and expertise in these technologies, leading to hesitancy in adoption (AITJ Staff Writer, 2023).

Robust networks are the building blocks of smart buildings and communities, enabling smart sensors, devices, and analytics platforms to perform effectively. With flexible work arrangements gaining prominence due to the COVID-19 pandemic, organizations are increasingly prioritizing the need for networks that can support remote work effectively. However, many companies are delaying necessary network upgrades due to the high costs

Figure 3.7.2 "A zoomed-in gray-scale architectural rendering of a smart office space, focusing on a single human person at a desk. The rendering, similar in style to the second previously provided image, showcases the office equipped with modern smart technologies like facial recognition, Wi-Fi, and automated facilities management. The desk includes smart appliances, equipment, and systems for automated lighting, heating, and cooling. This detailed and technical rendering highlights the integration of AI and data management in a realistic office environment, emphasizing the human interaction with the smart office setup." This image was generated with the assistance of AI. Image generated by OpenAI's DALL·E, November 29, 2023.

associated with implementation and operations (Cross, 2022). Networks are poised to improve significantly with the recent development of 6eG and impending Wi-Fi 7 technology. (Euklidiadas, 2023)

Also, companies are facing increased physical security threats tied to the convergence of digital and physical risk and data privacy. The willingness of building occupants to share personal information and engage with IoT services is contingent upon their trust in the responsible entity storing and analyzing the data. Public awareness and wariness regarding data storage and usage have made it increasingly challenging to obtain trust and maintain privacy. Moreover, AI/ML technologies that could optimize data processes are relatively new and not fully trusted by the general public.

In conclusion, while technological advancements offer promising solutions for overcoming historical challenges in real estate management, they come with their own set of complexities. The transition from traditional to smart buildings is not merely a technological shift but requires a comprehensive approach that addresses data integration, security, and expertise in emerging technologies. As the industry navigates these challenges, the focus must remain on achieving a balance between technological innovation and operational efficiency. Without clear industry-level guidance and standards, current smart building adoption remains available to only the most sophisticated organizations.

A Smart Future

Let's imagine the landscape of smart building offices in 2030. A future driven by a pragmatic approach focused on sustainability and operational efficiency, with AI playing a pivotal role in managing increasingly complex and interconnected systems.

Old Buildings Digitized

As noted throughout, future office space – disregarding changing aesthetic trends – will look as it does today, but with key differences: it will be cleaner, better maintained, more comfortable, and better managed. While the design and construction of buildings have seen some intriguing technological advancements – such as modular construction, cross-laminated timber (CLT), and additive manufacturing – the essence of what makes a building "smart" is happening behind (and beyond) the walls. Smart building systems will sit atop existing structures and systems, often implemented as retrofits to existing stock.

Connected and Integrated

Future offices will contain an invisible web of interconnected devices, people, systems, neighborhoods, and cities. IoT devices will communicate with each other, remote and on-premise users, and higher level management systems over a robust Wi-Fi 7 network. The office space will communicate with other spaces and the larger building. Smart buildings will increasingly leverage Infrastructure as a Service (IaaS) clouds to optimize various functions and make informed decisions. In this cloud-based ecosystem, functions can be coordinated not just within a single building, but with neighboring buildings and the city as a whole.

Interconnected buildings will give rise to digital twin cities, serving dual purposes: tracking energy and usage in real-time, and enabling rapid prototyping through the simulation of various strategies. In this way, buildings will learn from each other, creating a network of continuously improving, self-optimizing structures.

Automated

AI/ML will be needed to manage the immense amounts of data and complex processes created by this pervasive integration and optimization. These technologies will manage complex systems – from HVAC to lighting to security – optimizing for both efficiency and comfort. AI algorithms will also analyze patterns in energy usage, automatically adjusting systems to reduce waste and lower costs.

Smart building user interfaces will likely be chat based. The rapid rise of large language models (LLM) like OpenAI's ChatGPT and readily available natural language processing (NLP) models have made sophisticated chat and speech generation widely available. Today, we are not far from sophisticated speech-based agents like 2001: A Space Odyssey's Hal 9000(Kubrick, 1968) or Her's Samantha (Jonez, 2014). In those films, the AIs are basically operating systems for managing a digital world of information systems, automated tasks, and connected devices. Chat interface could resolve the persistent problem of the learning curve involved with CAFM technology. Currently, facilities managers must navigate a suite of semi-connected platforms to analyze work orders and maintenance schedules. In the future, they will just talk to Samantha.

Sustainable

Smart buildings will consume 40% less energy. A study by the American Council for an Energy-Efficient Economy (ACEEE) suggests that monitoring and automating just three things – HVAC systems, lighting and window shading – can result in energy savings of 30–50%. (D'Silva, 2023) They will use 10% less water through water flow monitoring devices (Dhingra, 2022) and they will waste less of the water they do use.

Safety and Security

Property owners and building management companies will enhance safety and security through smart technologies, creating a network of sensors for real-time monitoring, crucial for occupant safety. This includes the integration of traditional safety sensors, such as heat, smoke, fire, and fire doors, with emergency protocols to ensure an immediate response to hazards. Tagging assets and personnel provides a comprehensive view for efficient asset management and safety equipment tracking.

Regarding security and access, future buildings could be hands-free, with doors opening automatically as authorized personnel approach, using facial recognition as a biometric key. This technology is already augmenting, and even replacing, physical keycards in some private buildings. Makers of the technology tout its efficiency, accuracy, and ease of use in monitoring employee movement and access. (Dutton, 2023) Facial recognition can activate many of the personalization technologies mentioned above. Ideally, one could walk into an office that immediately adjusts the heat, lighting, and furniture automatically. This level of location tracking is a privacy concern for many, especially when combined with the various ethical and surveillance concerns of facial recognition.

Privacy

Much of a building's data is people data. Many of the benefits discussed above assume pervasive data sharing and connectedness that raises serious concerns about data privacy and ethical uses of AI/ML. In the commercial office sector, owners will need to implement safeguards to assure tenants that their personal and professional data is protected. Local governments will need to do the same for smart city level integration.

It is worth noting that basic facilities management applications do not require personal data. For heating, cooling, and lighting, a BMS need not know who is in the building – only how many and where, which can be done with anonymized closed-circuit cameras and motion detectors. Personalization and security technologies do need some level of personal identity data. However, unlike security, personalization is not a necessity.

Regulatory frameworks must evolve to keep pace with technological advancements. The level of digitization speculated above must coincide with thorough government regulations to ensure privacy and ethical data usage, similar to the recent European Union General Data Protection Regulation (GDPR) and AI Act. Unfortunately, in the US these regulations remain largely market driven and vary from owner to owner and state to state.

Figure 3.7.3   "A highly detailed, zoomed-in gray-scale architectural rendering of a smart office space, focusing on a single woman at a desk. The woman is dressed in pants and wearing flat shoes, engaging with advanced smart office technologies like a smart screen and interactive interfaces. The desk includes subtle features of automated systems for lighting, heating, and cooling. This rendering emphasizes the modern, technologically advanced workspace, with a clear focus on the woman in practical attire, interacting with her smart office environment." This image was generated with the assistance of AI. Image generated by OpenAI's DALL·E, December 1, 2023.

Smart Architecture

Throughout this chapter, we have argued that emerging smart building technology is largely architecture-agnostic, because the digital revolution predominantly occurs in the cloud and in devices, rather than in the physical structure. However, this viewpoint is not to diminish the role of architecture but to highlight a broader context. Smart buildings are still early in development and even earlier in adoption. The current focus on energy efficiency, maintenance, and automation represents just the beginning. Growth stage technology often gravitates toward immediate and predictable returns. As technology evolves, a reciprocal influence is expected, where smart technology informs architectural design and vice versa.

Buildings are more than mere static structures; they can function as intelligent, semi-autonomous networks combining spatial and software solutions. Like any smart device, buildings now have their own software, opening up new possibilities for architecture and architects. This integration enables architects to think more holistically and collaborate with software and device developers.

A similar coevolution occurred in the development of personal computing. Donald Norman, a "cognitive engineer" and the first individual to have "user experience" in his title, pioneered this at Apple. Norman recognized the paradigm shift introduced by personal computing and expanded user-centered design to a wider world of interactions, to "cover all aspects of the person's experience with the system including industrial design graphics, the interface, the physical interaction and the manual." (Merholz, 2008). Smart architecture could do the same.

References

AITJ Staff Writer. (22 February 2023). The Impact of AI and Machine Learning on Commercial Real Estate. *AI Time Journal*. Retrieved from https://www.aitimejournal.com/the-impact-of-ai-and-machine-learning-on-commercial-real-estate/42619.

Alonso, S. (29 October 2023). Smarter Building Management. *AECOM*. Retrieved from https://www.aecom.com/ca/smarter-building-management.

Cross, P. (18 February 2022). *Smart Building Challenges and Opportunities*. MBS: Modern Building Services. Retrieved from https://modbs.co.uk/news/fullstory.php/aid/19792/Smart_Building_Challenges_and_Opportunities_.html#:~:text=Cybersecurity%20has%20typically%20been%20the,of%20data%20are%20top%20concerns.

Dhingra, Suruchi. (4 October 2022). The Use of Smart Buildings Solutions Can Reduce Total Global Energy Consumption by 3–5%. Transforma Insights. Retrieved from https://transformainsights.com/blog/smart-buildings-reduce-global-energy#:~:text=Building%20Automation%20Systems%20integrated%20with,by%202010%25%20on%20an%20average.

Doolittle, Tom & Fliegelman, Arthur. (24 August 2023). Work-from-Home and the Future Consolidation of the U.S. Commercial Real Estate Office Sector: The Decline of Regional Malls May Provide Insight. *Office of Financial Research*. p.2.

D'Silva, Milton. (5 June 2023). Energy Saving In Smart Buildings. *Smart Building EMEA*. Retrieved from https://smartbuildingmag.com/market-overview/68658-energy-saving-in-smart-buildings#:~:text=A%20study%20done%20by%20the,40%25%20of%20final%20energy%20consumption.

Dutton, Holly. (7 July, 2023). The Risks and Rewards of Facial Recognition Tech in Office Buildings. *Propmodo*. Retrieved from: https://propmodo.com/the-risks-and-rewards-of-facial-recognition-tech-in-office-buildings/#:~:text=This%20kind%20of%20technology%20has,SCAN%2C%20a%20division%20of%20RealNetworks.

Ernst & Young Global Ltd. (October 2017). Smart Buildings: How to Drive Operational Efficiencies. Retrieved from https://www.ey.com/en_gl/real-estate-hospitality-construction/smart-buildings--how-to-drive-operational-efficiencies.

Euklidiadas, M. (16 June 2023). Wi-Fi 7: What Is It And Why Is It So Important For Cities? *Tomorrow City*. Retrieved from https://tomorrow.city/a/what-is-wifi-7.

EY. (2021). Executive Playbook: 2021 and Beyond. *Microsoft*.

JPMorgan Chase & Co. (14 April 2022). JPMorgan Chase Unveils Plans for New Global Headquarters Building in New York City. Retrieved from https://www.jpmorganchase.com/news-stories/jpmorgan-chase-unveils-plans-for-new-global-headquarters-building-in-new-york-city.

Merholz, Norman. (2008). UX Week|Don Norman | Peter Merholz Speaks with Don Norman. (2008). Retrieved from: https://vimeo.com/2963837

PR Newswire. (15 September 2022). Smart Building Market to Hit $570.02 Billion by 2030: Grand View Research, Inc. Bloomberg. Retrieved from https://www.bloomberg.com/press-releases/2022-09-15/smart-building-market-to-hit-570-02-billion-by-2030-grand-view-research-inc.

University of Michigan: Center for Sustainable Systems. (12 November 2023) Commercial Buildings Factsheet. Retrieved from https://css.umich.edu/publications/factsheets/built-environment/commercial-buildings-factsheet#:~:text=Commercial%20buildings%20consumed%2018%25%20of,in%20the%20U.S.%20in%202022.&text=In%202022%2C%20the%20commercial%20sector,a%2072%25%20increase%20from%201980.&text=Operational%20energy%20represents%2080%2D90,building's%20life%20cycle%20energy%20consumption.

Vierra, S. (2021). Whole Building Design Guide's Sustainable Building Technical Manual.

Jonze, S. (Director). (2014). Her [Film]. Annapurna Pictures; Warner Home Video.

Kubrick, S. (Director). (1968). 2001: A Space Odyssey [Film]. Metro-Goldwyn-Mayer; Warner Bros.

PARADIGMATIC CATEGORY 4

Smart Design for a Changing Climate

This Paradigmatic Category focuses on smart design solutions in defiance of Climate Change, and resiliency for regions with extreme hot, cold, or arid climates. It considers bodies of water as contextual settings for developing living environments. It also investigates consequences of major climatic changes, such as fires, and flooding, and new approaches in bridging architecture with agriculture through urban farming, Net Zero, and clean energy production through artificial and natural aquatic systems, and avoidance of usage of fossil fuels to prevent environmental toxic and harmful pollutions. This section discusses unchartered territories and regions entangled with extreme climates and geographical extremities, constraints, and challenges. It reflects on recently developed technologies for smart habitats and living environments, offering smart solutions to adapt to the negative impacts of intense climates. It also champions the appreciation of good practices for climate-resilient communities and sustainable livable constructs in harmony with their natural settings.

DOI: 10.4324/9781003384113-48

4.1

PANARCHISTIC ARCHITECTURE
A Paradigm in Wildfire Resilience

Melissa Sterry

Abstract

Multiple factors signalling the advent of a new 'Fire age', the Panarchistic Architecture paradigm takes the task of living with wildfire back to the design
drawing board, asking not how we, humans, would solve the problem, but how
fire-adapted flora already have.

Evolved from an extensive, first of its kind, several-year long transdisciplinary
study, the paradigm posits resilience to major wildfires through the creation of
complex adaptive architectural and urban systems that mimic the biochemistry,
behaviours, and relationships of indigenous flora and fauna species in the low-,
mixed-, and high-severity fire regimes. Its constructs drawing on the natural
world for model, method, and medium, its proposed means of enablement hy-
bridise human and non-human material and information systems, by splicing
biocomputing, satellite communications, and artificial at the edge of science,
technology, and engineering.

This chapter details the fundamental tenets of the Panarchistic Architecture
paradigm, examples of innovations and inventions that could enable it to work
in practice, together with speculations that convey how those that adopted it may
experience it whereupon it was built.

Son of Iapetus, surpassing all in cunning, you are glad that you have outwitted me
and stolen fire – a great plague to you yourself and to men that shall be. But I will give
men as the price for fire an evil thing in which they may all be glad of heart while they
embrace their own destruction.

Hesiod (1914)

The Origin of Fire myth is universal. Native to numerous ancient cultures spanning several continents, though many are its versions, but for a few exceptions, their underlying
message is one and the same: humans stole the control of fire, and the price of that theft
is eternal. Control of fire has been the cornerstone of human civilisation. Without it neither we, nor the species of which we are the direct descendants would have evolved. Fire
craft in its many forms has not merely shaped our technologies and our culture, but our

DOI: 10.4324/9781003384113-49

physiology and our intelligence. In that sense, we are born of fire and our relationship with it is so intimate as can never be unbound. Fire craft is literally written into our genetics, which expresses a mutation that enables some toxins emitted in smoke to be metabolised at a safer rate. However, like many relationships, it's a complex one, and no more so than now and in the coming years and decades. Though some state we are 'the Gods now', the matter that we are mortals is evident in the fact that when seeking to solve the many challenges that we face, rarely, if ever do we find panaceas. Instead, our lives are littered with Promethean choices, which whether large or small involve us sacrificing one thing in order that we attain another.

Wildfire is a highly contentious issue and debates have raged for decades as to how we might safely coexist with the phenomenon. As with all debates, the various viewpoints express how and why their advocates see the external world as they do. Few are unbiased, though rarely, if ever intentionally. Instead, we find that factors, including disciplinary and demographic silos, press and media bias, belief systems and culture more generally, calibrate the lenses through which individuals and collectives perceive of the problem. Yet, though many are their superficial variances, at their core, most viewpoints tend to fall into one of three approaches towards that most subjective of constructs that is commonly referenced as 'Nature', those being 'Nature as Supernatural', 'Nature at Servant', and 'Nature as Collaborator'.

All the foremost ancient belief systems view the non-human world as being curated by supernatural forces. When seen through this lens, averting catastrophes of the wildfire and other kind involves the worship of whichsoever non-mortal entity or entities are believed to control a given phenomenon. Prayers, gifts, and sacrifices become the means of threat mitigation, and when, despite these offerings, disaster strikes, blame is placed not with the supernatural, but with the mortal, and more specifically, with their fallibility. Within this construct, humans are subservient to those perceived to be Nature's masters, and they, not us, define what might be construed as our 'terms of use' of the natural world. The advent of the Scientific Revolution and thereon The Enlightenment catalysed the inversion of this philosophical construct, wherein no longer were we perceived to be in the service of Nature, but it perceived to be in the service of us. Thus, 'Nature as Supernatural' evolved into 'Nature as Servant'.

Whereupon the natural world is viewed from the secular not faith-based perspective, scientific laws not supernatural forces govern its workings. When seen through this lens, Nature is the sum of measured and replicable experimental parts, and that sum becomes so great as to necessitate specialisms. Upon quantifying various aspects of Nature, since the mid sixteenth century onwards, both intentionally and otherwise, scientists have been illuminating new ways to extract value from it. However, as understood by the 'Godfather of Ecology', Alexander von Humboldt, whereupon our understanding of the natural world becomes partial, we can lose sight of its bigger picture. Today, we find ourselves amidst a chorus of conflicting opinions as to how and why we came to face an environmental and social crisis of global proportions. On the one hand, Nature as Servant underlies the dominant economic narrative, wherein the natural world is reduced to the sum of its resource parts, which are extracted and traded in global markets. The matter that all products and all services within these markets are, ultimately, derivatives of the natural world continues to remain largely over-looked, as does the fact that these resources exist not in a vacuum, but as integral parts to processes that extend across evolutionary and in turn geological timescales and spaces. On the other hand, while the origins of Nature as Supernatural are ancient, its influence remains current. But, whereas of old, human cultures worshipped the imaginary in the form of gods and other non-mortal beings, today many hold reverence for celebrities, brands, and other constructs of the imagination that have been formed with the explicit intent of creating commercial success. Paradoxically, though such commercial entities tend treat Nature as servant, upon doing so they commonly market it as supernatural. For example, some present representations of the natural world which, largely, if not entirely fabricated, have no relation to its actual workings, amounting to no more than avatars that have been built on visual extractions of aspects of Nature. Yet, often such works gain extensive coverage in the press and media because they are either created or endorsed by celebrities and/or companies that with significant public presence have many fans and followers that treat their word as gospel, in that they automatically attribute credibility to projects of which the integrity may be questionable. In that sense, even some communities that are considered to be secular express some behaviours that mirror those of theocracies, seemingly worshipping at a temple of consumerism.

Nature as Collaborator is not a new construct, quite the contrary, as with Nature as Supernatural, its philosophical roots lie so far back through the mists of time that it's improbable that we'll ever find the origin. Humans have been collaborating with non-human life forms since prior to the evolution of our species, and today we work with so many members of the *Plantae*, *Animalia*, *Fungi*, and *Bacteria* kingdoms as to be innumerable. In some cases, we've consciously influenced the evolution of our non-human collaborators, as becomes much evident if you look at the impact of selective breeding on members of the *Canidae*, *Bovidae*, and *Equidae* families. In others, the ways in which human actions have influenced the functional traits of the species that we have collaborated with have been unintentional, and in that regard our level of awareness of the implications of our behaviour towards those species reflects our level of awareness, or rather lack thereof, of the implications of our behaviour towards the Kingdoms of Life as a whole. Just as control of fire comes at a Promethean price, so too does control of evolution, and in both cases that price is one that humanity is only just starting to grasp.

Whether consciously or otherwise, we all of us are in collaborations with other life forms for the duration of our lives, starting with the 39 trillion or so microbes that inhabit our bodies. Indeed, a growing body of data suggests that this collective of microscopic organisms are not merely integral to bodily functions, including digestion and temperature regulation (Gabanyi et al., 2022), but influence our decision-making, such that some posit our microbiome to be akin to a 'third brain' (Martin et al., 2018; Lui et al., 2019), which in turn works with the 'second brain', it being the enteric nervous system that comprised more than 100 million nerve cells lines our gastrointestinal tract. A frontier research field in which discoveries are emerging thick and fast, we're only just now grasping that human intelligence is not merely a product of one organ – the encephalon, better known as 'the brain', but at least two, and those organs are in a constant conversation with an ecosystem of organisms: a veritable system of systems of intelligence that challenges historical precepts of human intelligence. Seen another way, those that posit that 'artificial intelligence' will soon outperform 'human intelligence' are working with a construct that's fundamentally contrived, in the sense that new findings evidence that human intelligence operates in symbiosis with non-human intelligence, and across more species than have yet been mapped. However, awareness levels of such discoveries vary greatly and are themselves a reflection of our belief systems and wider worldviews, and the bias innate in them. Some view *Homo sapiens* as being the pinnacle of Evolution and superior to all other life forms therein, thus hold what some consider to be a pre-Darwinian worldview and analogically speaking, the three 'wise monkeys' that choose to see no 'evil', hear no 'evil', speak no 'evil' that might challenge their opinion and all as rests upon it. Others recognise that we're part of a deeply connected system of systems operating at scales both intimate and universal, and of which some parts we understand, others not, and to the extent that we're not yet even alert to their very existence. For example, so very many are the species on this planet that we know not the sum of their numerosity, let alone understand their various relations to their environment and all such other species as inhabit it. Both within biology and ecology, and with that, the world at large, deciphering the often-complex relations between one thing and another is where some of the most compelling discoveries of the past century and a half have been made. Now, as then, just as the work of Darwin and Wallace catalysed paradigmatic shifts in understanding in and beyond their fields of activity, discoveries made by those of whom the research continues to unravel the many entanglements that underpin the workings of our world are doing likewise.

Panarchistic Architecture is an exploration of Nature of Collaborator that both rejects the notion that supernatural forces shape our environmental and social destinies, and with it, that ours is the agency to wholly control those forces ourselves. Instead, it's predicated on the idea that humans are actors in a highly complex and ever-evolving system of systems of relationships which both biotic and abiotic, operate at both local and global scales, and in near, intermediate, and deep time. In the tradition of polymaths, including da Vinci, von Goethe, von Humboldt, and Darwin, its research and practice is transdisciplinary and extends across several scientific, artistic, and humanistic fields of enquiry. As with the seminal works of those referenced, the scale and complexity of the task in hand necessitates working beyond the parameters now typical in both academic and commercial research. Most research programmes today are framed by narrow briefs, limited budgets, and specific timeframes, all of which tend to serve narrow research enquirers well but rarely provide of the expansive scope that's necessary for projects of which the aims are paradigmatic in proportion, for it is neither possible to aggregate wide-ranging research within such tight parameters, let alone subject such breadth of research to sufficiently robust enquiry. The reality of research for many today is that even the most progressive programmes are usually restricted to working with just a few disciplinary fields. The twenty-first century this may be, but at the level of organisation in academia, in industry, and in society at large, we are living with the hangover of the last century, and with it, the one before that. Our economic, cultural, social, and wider value systems are still largely shaped by the Industrial Revolution, which focused on homogeneity over heterogeneity and on quantity over quality. Within this approach 'one size fits all', or all but, and value can be measured in units of sale. Within academia, the pressure to publish with constancy can make some academics feel like they are working on a factory production line of which the management is too linear to allow for the kind of breakthroughs they entered their profession to pursue.

Whether we like it or not, we all of us are living within boundaries that though fabricated constructs of which the usefulness has sometimes expired nonetheless define what we can and cannot do both personally and professionally. Ours is a largely Linnean experience of classifications, of categories, of departments, and other delineations that segregate one thing from another, and even when those boundaries become conceptually, ethically, and technically blurred. However, not one, but several global social and cultural trends show and clearly that some are now challenging such boundaries, and the evidence thereof abounds. For example, look to how perceptions of gender, sexuality, and class have changed this past several years, during which it's become common for new demographic categories to be included in, among other things, national censuses and equality surveys. We're witnessing a transition from one era to another, which like many births is a somewhat messy and protracted process. Yet, though the Arrow of Time forever points forward, we see in the present patterns from the past, as the dominant cultural narrative of one period catalyses that of another. The industrialisation of the eighteenth and nineteenth centuries inspired Friedrich Shelling's reconciliation of Science and Nature – his Naturphilosophie, thereon the wider Romanticism school and its cultural protégées Scientific Romance and Art Nouveau. Today's counterculture revolutionaries are not only rejecting the reductionism of the industrialisation of production, but of information too. Recognising that value cannot be quantified by metrics alone, theirs is an inherently qualitative approach to their research, and though they may not present their various hypotheses using such poetic and emotive prose as von Humboldt, George Perkins Marsh, and John Muir, they do endeavour to factor such things as cannot be objectively measured.

> The difficulty in satisfactorily tracing back the vital phenomena of the organism to physical and chemical laws (much like the prediction of meteorological processes in the atmosphere) lies largely in the complexity of phenomena, in the great number of simultaneously active forces, and in the particulars of their activity.
>
> *von Humboldt (1849)*

Paradigmatically, Panarchistic Architecture takes the task of living with wildfire back to the design drawing board, asking not how we, humans, would solve the problem, but how fire-adapted flora already have. A sub-set of a yet larger investigation that interrogates how our built structures and infrastructure might work if they were designed, engineered, and constructed in ways that use other organisms and the assemblies they form – ecosystems – as model, metaphor, and medium, its research programme involves the development of not one 'species' of architecture, nor even one 'genus', but an 'Ecosystem of Architectures' that evolves over time and space and in accordance with changes in the environment. Thus, Panarchistic Architecture sits in the wider evolutionary architecture and ecological architecture schools. Etymologically, the root of the paradigm's name, 'Pan', means 'of everything', which is in reference to its transdisciplinary research and practice nature. Additionally, its name is in reference to the primary systems theory construct that first inspired the wider studies of which it is part. Panarchy, a morpheme, has a prefix in reference to the Grecian god of nature and the wild, Pan. Drawing on earlier works by C. S. Holling, including his paper 'Resilience and Stability of Ecological Systems' (1973) and The Adaptive Cycle (1986), which visualise how ecosystems evolve over time, it frames 'how variables at different scales interact to control the dynamics and trajectories of chance in ecological and social-ecological systems' (Gunderson et al., 2010). Panarchistic Architecture applies this framework to architectural and urban design, wherein wildfire becomes a catalyst for systemic resilience and renewal (Figure 4.1.1) while building on the wider body of research of which it is a part, including later works by Holling, Gunderson, and their ecological systems and resilience theory peers (Holling, 1992, 1996, Gunderson et al., 1995, Gunderson & Holling, 2002, Gunderson et al., 2010). Conceptually, the paradigm works within a construct that Holling and Gunderson described as 'Nature Evolving', which views ecological systems as being in perpetual states of 'discontinuous change, chaos and order, [and] self-organisation', and as being inherently evolutionary, adaptive, non-linear, open, and

Figure 4.1.1 Wildfires as a catalyst for ecosystem renewal mapped onto Holling's 'Adaptive Cycle'. Diagram by the author Melissa Sterry.

transformative in character (Gunderson & Holling, 2002). Nature Evolving presents far greater complexity as a conceptual framework than Clements' successional theory, as it replaces certainty with uncertainty with respect to the evolutionary paths a given species or system will follow.

However, its aim being to reconcile humanity's relationship with wildfire, the 'pan' in Panarchistic has another affiliation, that being with the mythological Pandora, she being the bearer of the vessel in which Zeus placed humankind's punishment for its acquisition of the control of fire – her Pyxis, which later became known as her 'box'. Over the course of the past several decades, fire ecologists have published now countless studies that show how many flora and fauna have evolved to harness fire as a catalyst for rebirth and renewal and in the process shown that the ancient construct of 'creative destruction' has real world roots. Whereas the advent of wildfire can constitute a hazard, or series thereof to human communities, for flora and fauna that's evolved to live with wildfire it can present an abundance of opportunity. For example, for pyrophytes (plants evolved to coexist with fire) with wildfire comes the redistribution of nutrients, space, and light, as well as the triggering of their reproductive cycle. What if we could learn to do the same? If we could do that then at least some of the contents of Pandora's box might become opportunities, not risks.

> command and control… usually results in unforeseen consequences for both natural ecosystems and human welfare in the form of collapsing resources, social and economic strife, and losses of biological diversity..
>
> *Holling and Meffe (1996)*

The task of investigating how buildings, infrastructures, and assemblies thereof might work if using pyrophytes as model, metaphor, and medium for design, engineering, and construction necessitates research into the biochemistry, behaviours, and relationships of these species, and not just with respect to other members of their population, and with the biota of their biome at large, but with the abiotic systems that interplay with them. Wildfire is a profoundly complex phenomenon, which sitting at the apex of Earth systems is influenced by several features of the environment, including meteorological, topographical, hydro-logical, and ecological conditions, as well as human factors, including ignition sources, land-use and management, and spread of invasive species. All these variables now subject to rapid change, wildfire occurrence and outcomes are likewise fast changing, and even in those places remote from human settlements, such as the Arctic Tundra.

'Fire regime' is the term that's used to describe the particulars of how a given eco-system interacts with wildfire, and whereupon we examine the pyrophyte communities that are present in a landscape we can establish its historical fire regime. Nature always evolving, so too are these species and the systems they form. But their relationship with wildfire is not passive, it's active, as pyrophytes have functional traits that enable them to influence wildfire frequencies, intensities, and behaviours. In other words, pyrophytes are in a sym-biotic-abiotic relationship with wildfire, wherein the relationship is like the asso-ciations formed between pairs of species in symbiotic relationships. Pyrophytes' genetics, form, and biogeographic distribution over deep time reveal compelling insights about our possible wildfire futures. The fossil record evidences that many extant pyrophyte species have evolved from taxonomic lineages that were able to coexist with fire regimes far fiercer than those of today, such as when atmospheric oxygen levels were sizeably higher, thus combustion more frequent. Additionally, both extant and extinct pyrophytes provide a record of fire frequencies, intensities, and severities, and in among other forms their tree rings (Figure 4.1.2). This data, together with other wide-ranging information

Figure 4.1.2   Specimen of fossilised wood showing a dendrochronological record in the form of its tree rings. Photography by the author Melissa Sterry.

on past environmental conditions, suggests that we're on the cusp of a new 'Fire age', in which fire is to the climate what ice was to the Ice Age. Coined the 'Pyrocene' (Pyne, 2015), if this prediction comes to pass then wildfire will become far more prevalent both at and beyond the wildland-urban-interface, and not just in the form of combustion itself, but through its various side-effects too. Locally, these effects include increases in the probability of flooding and debris falls due to changes that wildfire creates in biotic communities and thus in soil structure. Both locally and remotely, these effects include air pollution, as seen in the summer of 2023 when wildfires in Canada turned the skies of cities, including New York, a vibrant orange. Hence, when working to develop architecture and urban scale resilience to wildfires, one needs accommodate for not one class of natural hazard, but several.

Within academia, fire ecology is a comparatively young discipline. However, if we look to human culture more generally, we find that in those places to which wildfire is native peoples have been observing how plants coexist with combustion for millennia (Sterry, 2018). Furthermore, we find that these peoples found ways to design and construct architectures that worked with, not against, fire regimes, and with Nature in its broader sense, in that they both sourced abundantly renewable materials and built structures that posed no pollution threat to local or remote environments before, during, or after a wildfire passed. But, though still useful these ingenious indigenous pyro-architectures may be, their applicability is nonetheless limited and not least because some are built to burn seasonally. Concerned with researching and developing solutions to the problem of living with wildfire in a way that serves not merely select human interests, but those of the widest possible community that reside at the interface of wild and urban lands, Panarchistic Architecture necessitates pioneering new design, engineering, and construction concepts as opposed to simply re-introducing pre-existing ones. Therefore, it constitutes not a low technology lens, as championed by Julia Watson (2019), but one that draws on leading-edge science and technology, and in particular that which hybridises biotic and human elements, including biomaterials, biodesign, bioengineering, and biocomputing. This in turn throws up many questions, for that which is living not inert has its own agency, and of the kind that can add yet greater uncertainty to already complex systems. The over-arching aims of Panarchistic Architecture are aligned with the schools of ecological design and living architecture. There are however some distinct variances in its approach compared with most other research projects, and these include firstly the fact that it's concerned with developing not one, but three qualitatively distinct approaches to wildfire resilience, and secondly it explores how the works of others, both academic and commercial, may be integrated to the paradigm and impact upon its possible outcomes.

Wildfires come in many forms and there are various classifications systems that describe those forms, as is also the case for the ecosystems to which wildfires are native, and the many pyrophytes and other life forms that have evolved to live in them. Adding to that complexity, there is no scientific consensus as to which classification systems are optimum. Thus, a foundational aspect of developing Panarchistic Architecture's underlying principles involved researching these various systems, identifying which ones current data suggest to be the most robust, and triangulating these qualitatively distinct systems such that an operating framework could be authored. Within this framework, which is focused on creating architectural and peri-urban resilience to wildfire at the interface of Mediterranean forests, woodlands, and scrublands, and at the interface of temperate coniferous forests, wildfire is broadly classed as being of either low-, mixed-, or high-severity variants, and of which the sub-variants include ground, surface, crown, or spot fires, each of which can have further sub-variants in terms of fire's behaviour and overall physical expression. The paradigm involves pyrophytes being classified as either 'Endurers', 'Evaders', or 'Resisters', in a system that builds upon a classification system developed in the late twentieth century (Rowe, 1983). Within this schema Endurers regenerate upon the passing of wildfire and their resilience resides in the perennating parts – their rhizomes, roots, and root crowns, which tend be protected by humus and mineral soils. These pyrophytes evolved to coexist with low- and mixed-severity fire regimes in which the frequency of wildfires is high, except for a sub-set dubbed 'superspecies' (Ibidem), that are evolved to endure even high-severity fires, whereas, Evaders, which are also defined as having two-subclasses, take a sacrificial approach to survival, wherein the parent plant succumbs to wildfire but stores seeds of which the germination is triggered by its passing. But, whereas this class of pyrophytes was originally defined as being adapted to short and intermediate fire cycles (Ibidem), more recent studies have shown that Endurers are evolved to coexist with mixed- and high-severity fires with long fire cycles (Wallace and Christensen, 2004; Nijhuis, 2012), thus the paradigm works with the latter, not former fire regime affiliation. Completing the trio of pyrophyte classes the paradigm adopts are Resisters, which, protected by an array of defensive pyro-armoury, including thick bark, are largely evolved to coexist with fire cycles of intermediate duration, but of which some are well adapted to relatively frequent fires (Rowe, 1983; Pausas, 2015).

Pyrophytes have an array of functional traits that enable them to coexist with wildfires, and though some overlap between classes, most vary between them. Some of these traits relate to the species' physiology, such as their biochemistry, others relate to their behaviours, and others still to their relationships with other members of their species population. The matter that, like all species, pyrophytes are evolving means that any affiliation between a trait and a class is potentially temporary thus needs be reviewed as new studies unfold. Notwithstanding, the traits as presently defined present compelling possibilities whereupon viewed as metaphors, models, and mediums for designing architectures fit for whatsoever pyrofutures might come to pass. As metaphors, these species and the systems they form serve to establish qualitative features of design, and both at the level of individual elements and of collectives thereof, such as the fact that as with works from the wider schools of ecological and living design, the architectural paradigm is populated by inherently metamorphic and evolving forms. As models, pyrophytes and fire regimes constitute prototypes of which the workings can be mimicked such that structural elements, structures, and assemblies thereof embody their physical properties. As mediums, these pyrophytes serve as elements that can be integrated into the architectural and urban schema materially, informatically, and structurally. As in the ecosystems to which wildfire is native, Panarchistic Architecture is organised around fire regimes, each of which is populated by the architectural species and urban systems that have been designed to coexist in those specific regimes, and those species and systems are classed into three categories of which the name reflects their pyrophyte affiliations: Pyro-Endurers, Pyro-Evaders, and Pyro-Resistors. Functional traits of pyrophytes from which these three classes of architectural and urban resilience draw inspiration include pyriscence (Fig. 3), pyrogermination, resprouting, abscission, and retardant rhytidome, the first three of which are reproductive traits, the latter two of which defensive traits. Ways in which migration of these traits to architecture and urban design are explored within the paradigm include creating sensing, processing, and actuation networks, which integrated into the material fabric of structures, activate defences upon detection

Figure 4.1.3 Serotinous pinecone specimen containing the parent plant's offspring in the form of seeds that are safely stored until the heat from a passing wildfire melts the resins that hold the cone's exterior parts together. Photography by the author Melissa Sterry.

of wildfire; developing data storage systems that akin to seed banks safely store information on the building, its owners/occupants, and contents during wildfires and other closely related hazard events; producing materials with self-renewal properties that are activated upon the occurrence of wildfires; and building architectural resilience to wildfires through the development of structures of which the physical properties (i.e. physics and chemistry) are inherently resilience to heat, thus combustion (Figure 4.1.3).

Some posit that in Nature 'shape is cheap but material is expensive' (Pawlyn, 2011), but the inverse is true of pyrophytes. Shape is determined by genes, those being genes that have evolved over many millions of years. Upon the advent of wildfire, Evader species often succumb to the flames, but having ensured that their genes will live on in their offspring, the latter of which benefits from wildfire's redistribution of nutrients, space, light, and other resources, whereas Endurers and Resistors have evolved resilience through, among other functional traits, the shedding of various exterior parts both prior to and during wildfires. Thus, collectively these species prioritise the protection of information over materials. The former of these value propositions is readily reconciled with the dominant architectural and urban narratives of these and recent times, all of which revolve around notions of permanency in its various forms. In contrast, the latter stands in conflict therewith, for it is concerned with material and spatial temporality, wherein buildings and assemblies thereof reconfigure cyclically, and in symbiosis with both biotic and abiotic aspects of their environment.

> What distinguishes Herder and Humboldt from their predecessors is their disinterest in classification, and by contrast, their interest in grasping a "world", an inhabited reality that is reflected in the very structure of its inhabitants.
>
> *Nasser (2019)*

Perhaps the most pressing challenge before us is not technical, but psychological, for how can we hope to reconcile our various architectures and other built structures with the workings of the natural world if we cannot reconcile our beliefs, values, and aspirations too? Whereupon we persist in seeking material permanency in the face of Earth's inherently temporary systems, we arguably stand little, if any chance of reaching the environmental targets that we have continuously missed. Might we embrace ideas which, truly paradigmatic in proportion, involve relinquishing a sense of security that is nested in notions of Nature as being supernatural or servant and instead build the foundations of a future devoid of delineations of the kind that caused the climate and other catastrophes with which we are now so consumed? The Origin of Fire myth, and mythologies more generally, may not provide of practical solutions to our various problems, but they do serve as timely reminders of the fact that our fallibility is nothing new. We are but mortals facing seemingly godly tasks and have been all along. On the balance of probability, as the years and decades unfold, those tasks may feel yet more difficult still, and not least against what will likely be a backdrop of increased tensions at local, regional, and global scales, and of the kind that permeates lives both near and far. In those moments when we feel overwhelmed and doubt our capacity to make veritable miracles happen, might we remember that Nature was our original source of metaphor, model, and medium and is so very abundant in its diversity and distribution that we have yet to quantify its sum. What's more, wherever we are, whoever we are, and whatever we're working on, we only have to go outside to find an array of specimens, and in turn systems from which we might glean insights and ideas. Panarchistic Architecture illustrates how the study of species and the assemblies they form can catalyse new approaches to complex architectural and urban problems. Though focused on the problem of living with wildfire, its fundamental tenets are transferable to the problem of living with wide-ranging natural and anthropogenic hazards at a time of rapid change and resource scarcity. Furthermore, it challenges us to reconsider our relationship with other species and to design in way that integrates their various forms of intelligence with our own. Given that every other species on Earth has found a way to live sustainably across epochs as extend far beyond the existence of not just our species, but our genus, and in turn family, they serve as an infinite source for smart design thinking.

References

Gabanyi, I., et al. (2022). Bacterial Sensing via Neuronal Nod2 Regulates Appetite and Body Temperature. *Science*. 376(6590). https://pubmed.ncbi.nlm.nih.gov/35420957/

Gunderson, L. H., Allen, C. R., and Holling, C. S. (2010). *Foundations of Ecological Resilience*. Island Press. Washington.

Gunderson, L. H., and Holling, C. S. (2002). *Panarchy: Understanding Transformations in Human and Natural Systems*. Island Press. Washington.

Gunderson, L. H., Holling, C, S., and Light, S. S. (1995). *Barriers and Bridges to the Renewal of Ecosystems and Institutions*. Columbia University Press. New York.

Hesiod, Homeric Hymns, Epic Cycle, Homerica. (1914). Translated by Evelyn-White, H G. Loeb Classical Library Volume 57. William Heinemann. London.

Holling, C. S. (1973). Resilience and Stability of Ecological Systems. *Annual Review of Ecology and Systematics*. 4. https://www.annualreviews.org/content/journals/10.1146/annurev.es.04.110173.000245

Holling, C. S. (1986). The Resilience of Terrestrial Ecosystems: Local Surprise and Global Change. In: Clark, W. C., and Munn, R. E. (eds), *Sustainable Development of the Biosphere*. Cambridge University Press. Cambridge, 292–317.

Holling, C. S. (1992). Cross-scale Morphology, Geometry, and Dynamics of Ecosystems. *Ecological Monographs*. 62: 447–502.

Holling, C. S. (1996). Engineering Resilience versus Ecological Resilience. In: Schulze, E. (ed.), *Engineering Within Ecological Constraints*. National Academy of Engineering. Washington, DC.

Holling, C, S., and Meffe, G. K. (1996). Command and Control and the Pathology of Natural Resource Management. *Conservation Biology*. 10.

Lui, P., et al. (2019). Crosstalk between the Gut Microbiota and the Brain: An Update on Neuroimaging Findings. *Frontiers in Neurology*. 10, 8883.

Martin, C. R., et al. (2018). The Brain-Gut-Microbiome Axis. *Cellular and Molecular Gastrentrerology and Hepatology*. 6(2)

Nijhuis, M. (2012). Forest Fires: Burn Out. *Nature*. 489(7416): 352–4.

Pausas, J. G. (2015). Bark thickness and Fire Regime. *Functional Ecology*. 29. https://besjournals.onlinelibrary.wiley.com/doi/full/10.1111/1365-2435.12372

Pawlyn, P (2011). *Biomimicry in Architecture*. RIBA Publishing. London.

Pyne, S. J. (2015). *The Fire Age*. Aeon. https://aeon.co/essays/how-humans-made-fire-and-fire-made-us-human

Rowe, J. S. (1983). Concept of Fire Effects on Plant Individuals and Species. In: Wein, R, W., and MacLean, D, A. (eds), *The Role of Fire in Northern Circumpolar Ecosystems: Scientific Committee on Problems of the Environment*. John Wiley & Sons Ltd. Chichester.

Sterry, M. L. (2018). *Panarchistic Architecture: Building Wildland-Urban Interface Resilience to Wildfire through Design Thinking, Practice and Building Codes Modelled on Ecological Systems Theory*. PhD Thesis, University of Greenwich, London.

von Humboldt, A. (1849). *Views of Nature with Scientific Annotations*. Corrected and Expanded Third Edition. J. G. Cotta Publishing. Stuttgart and Tubingen.

Wallace, L, L, and Christensen, N. L. (2004). Epilogue: After The Fires. What Have We Learned? In *After the Fires: The Ecology of Change in Yellowstone National Park*. Yale University Press. New York, 362–372.

Watson (2019). *Lo—TEK: Design by Radical Indigenism*. Taschen. Cologne, Germany.

4.2

CONNECTING ARCHITECTURE AND AGRICULTURE FOR A CLIMATE-SMART FUTURE

Henry Gordon-Smith

Abstract

In the dynamic intersection of architecture and agriculture, Agritecture emerges as a global trend revolutionizing urban living. As the Founder and CEO of Agritecture, I, Henry, explore the intricate synergy between architectural design and agricultural innovation to accelerate climate-smart agriculture.

The journey begins with Agritecture's origin in 2011, emphasizing its pivotal role in reshaping urban landscapes. The focus on modern urban agriculture (UrbanAg), particularly Controlled Environment Agriculture (CEA), unveils cutting-edge techniques like hydroponics, aquaponics, and vertical farming. Precision agriculture, coupled with high-tech tools and low-tech practices, emerges as a pivotal strategy.

UrbanAg takes center stage, showcasing its contributions to healthier cities through environmental impact, water conservation, waste reduction, and biodiversity. The term Agritecture is defined as the integration of agriculture into the built environment, showcasing diverse UrbanAg designs.

Paris's pioneering green roof policy becomes a beacon of inspiration. Nature Urbaine, the world's largest urban rooftop farm in Paris, and Dallas's Comprehensive UrbanAg Plan exemplify practical implementations, offering insights into reshaping urban landscapes for sustainability.

The narrative culminates in a focus on Design Thinking for Climate-Smart Agriculture, presenting it as a potent tool for addressing complex challenges. Graphics of urban farming types and impacts demonstrate how design thinking can drive sustainable solutions.

Finally, the vision extends to new planned cities incorporating UrbanAg and Agritecture. This innovative model not only tackles environmental issues but also stimulates local economies, fostering community engagement and showcasing cities as beacons of sustainability. Join me on this exploration of Agritecture for a more sustainable and resilient urban future.

Introduction to Chapter

At the intersection of architecture and agriculture, a revolution is brewing. Designs are becoming ever eco-friendlier and more sustainable, integrating agricultural concepts for

DOI: 10.4324/9781003384113-50

better harmony with the built environment. The art, practice, and science of integrating agriculture is called "Agritecture" and it's an idea that I developed in 2011 and has since developed into a global trend with widespread implications for food security and resilience.

These designs prioritize local food production and can reduce resource consumption with features such as the activation of underutilized spaces, maximizing natural light, implementing rainwater harvesting systems, and even incorporating on-site renewable energy sources. Sometimes they also emphasize biodiversity and soil health, thus facilitating productive urban landscapes. The architectural designs of the future will seamlessly combine the principles of agriculture with design aesthetics to create living spaces that not only coexist with nature but are also self-sustaining thus reimagining the concept of urban living for a more sustainable future.

As the Founder and CEO of Agritecture – a pioneering first-of-its-kind global urban agriculture (UrbanAg) consultancy, we have been in pursuit of the mission to accelerate climate-smart agriculture (CSA) by bridging the gap between architectural design and agricultural innovation. Our work has laid the foundation for the exploration and implementation of urban and smart farming solutions that prioritize environmental sustainability and food security.

This chapter ventures into the rapidly expanding realm of CSA and avant-garde city innovations set to provide fresher, locally sourced food to urban residents with the goal of reducing the negative environmental impacts common in agriculture. This ushers in a transformative epoch in our agricultural arena, targeted toward fostering a sustainable living planet. The emphasis lies in uniting cutting-edge design and progressive technology to enhance farming practices for better sustainability, operational efficiency, and resilience.

What Is CSA and Why Do We Need It Now More Than Ever

With the world's population expected to reach nearly 10 billion by 2050 (Nicholas, 2021), the demand for food faces an unprecedented rise. This increase, coupled with the adverse effects of climate change on traditional agricultural practices, has highlighted the urgent need for solutions that offer both productivity and sustainability. The destructive practices and inefficiencies of current farming methods pose significant threats to the environment, contributing substantially to global greenhouse gas emissions and deforestation while also depleting natural resources and reducing biodiversity. Hence, a sizeable challenge awaits in the reconciliation of high-yield farming, environmental protection, and sustainable development.

What Is CSA?

CSA is an integrative approach aiming to transform and reorient agricultural systems to effectively support development and ensure food security under climate change (Scherr et al., 2012). It seeks to increase agricultural productivity and incomes sustainably and equitably, enhance resilience to climate change, and reduce or remove greenhouse gas emissions, where possible. In essence, CSA addresses the interlinked challenges of food security and climate change, presenting synergies that can aid in mitigating the aforementioned global issues. At Agritecture, we work across different types of CSA but most of our portfolio to date focuses on modern methods of UrbanAg, namely, controlled environment agriculture (CEA).

CSA Solutions

CSA solutions span a diverse spectrum, employing both high-tech tools and time-tested, low-tech techniques, as necessitated by the challenges and unique conditions presented. Emergent in this field are solutions such as:

Precision agriculture epitomizes the synergistic fusion of agriculture and technology. It enables farmers to use real-time data and sophisticated software to guide decisions about crop planting, fertilization, pest control, and harvesting. Precision agriculture aids in enhancing farm profitability, reducing waste, improving sustainability, and increasing yield and quality of produce.

The implementation of precision agriculture relies heavily on the use of innovative tools and technologies such as **Geographic Information System (GIS), data analytics, precision irrigation,** and **remote sensing.** These technologies are further bolstered by the integration of sensors, AI systems, Internet of Things (IoT) devices, and Machine Learning algorithms (Mes´ıas-Ruiz et al., 2023). Farmers can leverage these technologies to map their fields, monitor soil properties, plant health and growth patterns, predict yield, and control irrigation and fertilizer applications, ensuring optimal use of resources and minimizing environmental impacts (Filintas et al., 2023).

Alongside the use of these technologies, come notable challenges that need to be addressed for successful implementation and uptake of precision agriculture. A key hurdle is the **high initial cost** of acquiring and setting up precision agriculture technologies. For many smallholder farmers, the costs could be prohibitive. This necessitates effective strategies and interventions that can help alleviate these costs.

Equally significant to the high-tech aspects of precision agriculture are the rudimentary – low technology, yet profoundly effectual, climate-smart practices that can be just as transformative. One such practice is **cover cropping,** a tried-and-true method in which farmers plant certain species to cover the soil rather than leaving it exposed. This not only protects against erosion but also helps enhance soil fertility and breaks up the cycle of pests and disease, leading to healthy, productive soils (Dzvene et al., 2023).

Additionally, there's **intercropping,** the well-established practice of growing two or more crop species simultaneously in a given field area. This diversification strategy presents numerous advantages, including more efficient utilization of resources, reduced pest pressure, and improved yield stability. Furthermore, it's a significant strategy for strengthening the resilience of agricultural systems under changing climate conditions (Dzvene et al., 2023). Effective too is **crop rotation,** the practice of growing different types of crops in the same area across seasons. Crop rotation enriches soil nutrients without synthetic fertilizers, disrupts cycles of pests and pathogens, and reduces the risk of soil erosion.

Waste management in agriculture, particularly **composting** waste, is yet another low-tech solution gaining traction. Composting involves the biological decomposition of organic waste under controlled conditions to produce a nutrient-rich soil conditioner. This closes the nutrient loop and reduces reliance on synthetic fertilizers, thus making agricultural practices both more sustainable and economical.

Lastly, **low- or no-tillage** practices are fostering sustainable farming. These practices reduce soil erosion and preserve soil structure, maintaining the soil's capacity for nutrient cycling and water infiltration, crucial under climate change projections. Minimal tillage systems can also increase carbon sequestration, playing a role in the mitigation of greenhouse gases.

Collectively, these low- and high-tech solutions play a significant role in CSA, providing sustainable and climate-resilient agricultural practices accessible to all farmer demographics (Filintas et al., 2023).

Urban Agriculture

Now, with all the examples of CSA above, you might be asking yourself why would anyone grow food in urban areas, if there is technology to help farmers grow in rural areas? Well, one major reason for growing food in urban areas is that by 2050, 80% of all food will be consumed by cities (Ellen Macarthur Foundation, 2022). Growing food closer to consumers will provide consumers with a greater awareness of how our food is grown and remind us to value it more. Additionally, the age of farmers is rising rapidly and in the next 30 years (Perkins, 2022), about a third of all farmers will retire. With most of the children of farmers moving to cities for opportunity, UrbanAg presents an opportunity to maintain food security while recognizing that cities are the future of humanity. There are numerous approaches to UrbanAg and benefits which we will explore here.

Overview

UrbanAg serves as a beacon of evolution in cities that yearn to bridge the gap between sustainability and urban living. Fundamental to this revolution of UrbanAg is the principle of community involvement, a concept that is predicated on the belief in collaborative effort and the establishment of strong kinships amongst residents (Anggraeni et al., 2022). This form of farming, often orchestrated within the heart of the city's most populous areas, employs models that emphasize and prioritize the welfare of community inhabitants over the quantity of large-scale yields. Therefore, it not only supplements the provision of nutritious food and improves local food security but also enhances social interaction, fostering a resilient, self-sufficient, and harmonious community fabric.

UrbanAg designs can have a positive impact on the environment in various ways. Some ways in which UrbanAg designs can impact the environment:

- **Reducing the carbon footprint** is a paramount goal in our fight against climate change. UrbanAg plays a pivotal role in this endeavor by shortening the distance that food travels from farm to table. This reduction in food miles leads to a significant decrease in greenhouse gas emissions associated with the transportation of produce (depending on the city). By cultivating food within urban environments, we lessen our reliance on long-haul transportation, thereby decreasing the environmental impact of the entire food supply chain, including food waste. However, not all urban farms are the same in this impact: while soil-based urban farms and greenhouses tend to have lower carbon footprints for food than imports in many markets, vertical farming is very energy-intensive and can have a much higher carbon footprint when powered by non-renewable sources.
- **Water conservation** is another key advantage of UrbanAg, especially in regions facing water scarcity. Urban farmers employ water-saving techniques such as drip irrigation and rainwater harvesting. This is particularly vital in a world where water resources are increasingly stressed, and every drop counts in our collective efforts to sustain both our cities and the natural environment. Where water is the most scarce, hydroponic

greenhouses and vertical farms with recirculating irrigation systems will deliver the greatest water efficiency for fruits and vegetables.

- UrbanAg is not only about food production but also about improving the overall **environmental quality** of our cities (Wang et al., 2023). One notable aspect is its role in enhancing air quality. Urban farms, with their lush greenery, absorb carbon dioxide and filter out other pollutants from the air. Additionally, the shade provided by plants and trees in UrbanAg areas helps reduce the urban heat island effect, which can have detrimental consequences for the quality of life in densely populated cities. By creating more green spaces in urban environments, we contribute to cleaner, cooler, and healthier cities, benefiting both the environment and the people who inhabit them. Moreover, UrbanAg serves as a haven for **biodiversity** within urban settings, by providing essential habitats for pollinators, birds, and other wildlife, contributing to the preservation and enhancement of local ecosystems. By fostering biodiversity within cities, UrbanAg aids in maintaining a balance in the urban environment, ultimately leading to better overall environmental health.

- **Boosting community spirit and fostering meaningful human relationships** within our cities. When neighbors come together to cultivate gardens, tend to community plots, or participate in local food initiatives, they not only grow fresh produce but also cultivate a sense of shared purpose and camaraderie. Working side by side in urban farming projects encourages collaboration, knowledge sharing, and a sense of belonging that transcends age, culture, and background. This shared commitment to sustainability and local food production builds stronger bonds among community members, promoting a deep sense of connection and unity that extends far beyond the boundaries of the garden.

- By implementing composting practices for food scraps and organic materials, urban farmers divert a substantial portion of waste away from landfills. This not only reduces the amount of waste sent to landfills, which can lead to various negative environmental repercussions, but also results in the production of nutrient-rich compost that can be used to enrich the soil for future crop cultivation. This virtuous cycle of waste reduction and resource recycling further underlines the environmental benefits of UrbanAg (Orsini, 2013).

- UrbanAg emerges as a promising solution to mitigate the intensity of the **urban heat oven** and urban heat island effect plaguing our densely populated cities. The proliferation of towering buildings nearby creates a heat trap, making urban environments uncomfortably warm and impeding air circulation. Urban farms, however, serve as vital breathing spaces within the concrete jungle, by not only breaking the monotony of heat-retaining structures but also allowing for the free flow of air, offering a refreshing respite for city dwellers.

- In addition to their tangible impact on temperature reduction, plants assume a pivotal role in elevating the quality of urban life by serving as natural filters, releasing fresh oxygen into the atmosphere. The intrinsic ability of vegetation to absorb pollutants from both the air and soil underscores the multifaceted benefits of UrbanAg. Plants, acting as nature's purifiers, possess the remarkable capacity to capture and metabolize various pollutants, including particulate matter and harmful gases, thereby contributing significantly to the amelioration of air quality in urban environments. Consequently, the integration of urban farms not only fosters a more pleasant and breathable atmosphere but also exemplifies a proactive approach toward enhancing the overall well-being of cities (Figure 4.2.1).

ENVIRONMENTAL IMPACT

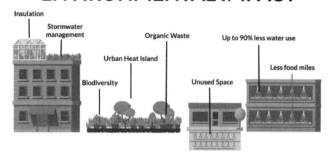

Figure 4.2.1   Environmental impact of urban agriculture.

UrbanAg Typologies and Case Studies

UrbanAg designs can take many forms and aspects, from on-ground soil community gardens to high-technology vertical farms:

- **Community gardens**:
    Community gardens serve as vibrant hubs of communal activity, where a collective of individuals unite to cultivate a diverse array of crops, fostering a sense of togetherness and self-sufficiency (Ridge, 2003). Beyond their horticultural significance, these shared green spaces carry profound social and environmental benefits. In these gardens, the spirit of community flourishes as neighbors come together to plant, nurture, and harvest an assortment of crops, ranging from luscious fruits to nutrient-packed vegetables.
- What makes community gardens truly remarkable is their potential for inclusivity. Community gardens are designed with the goal of being accessible to people of all ages and abilities. Features such as raised beds make it easier for individuals with mobility challenges to actively participate in gardening, while wheelchair-accessible paths ensure that everyone can navigate the garden's beauty and bounty. In this way, community gardens are more than just places to grow food; they are spaces where people of diverse backgrounds and physical capabilities can come together, fostering a sense of belonging and empowerment.
- **CEA** is a cutting-edge technology where environmental conditions, such as temperature and humidity, are manipulated to optimize plant growth. CEA includes the use of **hydroponics** – the process of growing plants without soil, relying instead on nutrient-fertilized water (Nicholas, 2021). **Aquaponics** is a system that combines hydroponics and aquaculture, where waste from fish farming is used as a nutrient source for plants, which is another notable technique in CEA (Nicholas, 2021).
    Urban farms for mushrooms, pharmaceutical herbs, and other specialty crops are often facilitated by the controlled settings of this agricultural method. Lastly, **vertical farming** is a revolutionary facet of CEA, capitalizing on the vertical space within controlled environments to maximize yield per square foot (Andrew et al., 2019). Vertical farms, a brainchild of the marriage between architecture and agriculture, provide a smart, efficient, and sometimes sustainable solution to the challenges of food scarcity and population growth, pushing the boundaries of what urban farming can achieve and where it can thrive (Figure 4.2.2).

SPECTRUM OF URBAN AGRICULTURE

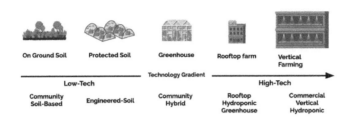

Figure 4.2.2   The spectrum of urban agriculture varies from low technology on ground soil to high technology Vertical Farm.

The Pioneering Role of Paris in Promoting Green Architecture

City policies play a critical role in encouraging UrbanAg. With smart policies, urban farming entrepreneurs often can't start or scale their operations (Agritecture, 2018).

Paris stands at the forefront of UrbanAg policy, leading by example with the introduction of a policy that mandates green roofs on all new corporate structures. The repercussions of incorporating green roofs extend beyond aesthetics; they encapsulate an ability to absorb pollutants, accumulate rainwater, and double as a sanctuary for avian life. By mitigating the effects of heat during summer and promoting biodiversity, green roofs demonstrate a multi-faceted approach to environmental sustainability.

The greening of Paris's quintessential rooftops is well underway and not only includes green roofs but urban farms as well. These policies have encouraged the establishment of the world's largest urban farm, Nature Urbaine.

Nature Urbaine: The World's Largest Urban Rooftop Farm in Paris

Nature Urbaine is a notable case study in the realm of urban farming and exemplifies the integration of architecture and agriculture at its finest. Based in Paris, this progressive project demonstrates how urban spaces can be innovatively utilized for sustainable food production, carving out a 150,000-square-foot rooftop farm in the fifteenth arrondissement. This undertaking, slated to be the world's largest urban farm once fully operational, exploits smart farming methods to grow fruits, vegetables, and herbs. Expected to produce approximately 2,000 pounds of produce daily during high season, this venture underpins Paris's commitment to enhance UrbanAg, with a keen focus on locally sourced food and local community involvement. Nature Urbaine has consequently emerged as a model of how urban layouts can be re-imagined and redesigned to propagate a resilient, sustainable, and forward-looking food system (Viparis, 2022).

Paris has also executed Parisculteurs, the first citywide UrbanAg competition that pre-negotiated spaces from real estate owners for urban farmers to apply for placing farms on them. Think government buildings, rooftops, and basements that are all underutilized. Paris facilitated easier terms for urban farmers, published the sites, and then invited business plan applications for farming on them. This initiative catalyzed an urban farming revolution in the city with hundreds of new urban farms popping up and the city is well on its way to its 30 hectares of new urban farming space with approximately 16 hectares developed from the Parisculteurs competition already. I had the pleasure of being the judge for the contest one year and still cite this to all cities I speak with as one of the most proven methods for accelerating UrbanAg.

Dallas Comprehensive UrbanAg Plan

As one of the pacesetters in UrbanAg, Dallas has developed a Comprehensive UrbanAg Plan under the advisement of Agritecture Consulting. This policy took root in an effort to address issues surrounding food access, economic development, and community vitality intrinsic to urban centers (City of Dallas, 2022).

The Dallas Comprehensive UrbanAg Plan sets forth a vision that amalgamates agriculture within the urban fabric, fostering not only environmental stewardship but also new economic opportunities. Known as "The Garden City Plan," it employs a simple yet effective strategy: it repurposes underutilized lands in the city, converting them into productive urban farms and gardens.

The Primary Objectives of Dallas UrbanAg Plan

1 **Improve Food Access:** By creating urban farms and gardens, the plan aims to reduce food deserts that affect numerous quarters of the city. The result is increased access to fresh, locally grown produce.
2 **Promote Economic Development:** The cultivation, harvesting, and selling of produce generate income, fueling local economic growth while creating jobs and training opportunities for local residents.
3 **Enhance Community Cohesion:** The community gardens serve as social gathering spots, bringing different factions of the society together, fostering a sense of unity, and providing the opportunity for communal learning and skills exchange.

Implementation and Progress

While the comprehensive plan is a step in the right direction, its implementation has been confronted with challenges such as zoning regulations, water access, and necessary infrastructural support. Yet, despite the obstacles faced, genuine progress has been made. Many community gardens have sprouted up, acting as catalysts for generating neighborhood vibrancy, food security, and economic development.

As cities strive for sustainability and resilience, the Dallas Comprehensive UrbanAg Plan exemplifies a shrewd strategy of intertwining urban development with agricultural practices. Such integration remodels the urban environment, enhancing not only the ecological balance but also providing social and economic benefits.

Agriculture + Architecture = Agritecture

Agritecture is a term that refers to the integration of agriculture into the built environment. It is the art, science, and business of designing and implementing urban and CEA. Agritecture is about applying architectural thinking when designing agriculture for the built environment. Incorporating agritecture into urban regions allows agriculture to shape our approach toward sustainable urban development more responsibly. This process helps

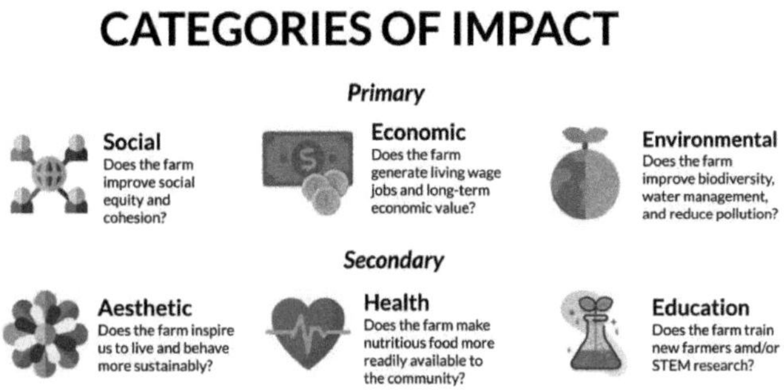

CATEGORIES OF IMPACT

Primary

Social
Does the farm improve social equity and cohesion?

Economic
Does the farm generate living wage jobs and long-term economic value?

Environmental
Does the farm improve biodiversity, water management, and reduce pollution?

Secondary

Aesthetic
Does the farm inspire us to live and behave more sustainably?

Health
Does the farm make nutritious food more readily available to the community?

Education
Does the farm train new farmers amd/or STEM research?

Figure 4.2.3 Categories of impact of urban agriculture.

people become self-sufficient by using urban and architectural design methods applied to food production.

Design Thinking for Climate-Smart Agritecture

With so many different types of urban farms with varying requirements and benefits, how can we make smart choices for UrbanAg planning and design? Well, design thinking, with its emphasis on empathy, collaboration, experimentation, and iteration, is a powerful tool for addressing the complex challenges posed by urban and CSA. By focusing on the end-user – in this case, farmers, communities, and ecosystems – design thinking can help create more effective, sustainable, and resilient agricultural systems.

In the context of smart farming, urban farms, and vertical farms, design thinking can be utilized in several ways. Firstly, it can help architects and urban planners to create urban farms that not only produce food efficiently but also fit seamlessly into the urban fabric. This includes considering factors such as aesthetics, access, use of space, and impact on local communities (Figure 4.2.3).

Secondly, design thinking can support the development of new technologies and processes for smart farming. By prototyping and testing new ideas, and iterating based on feedback, we can develop solutions that not only increase yield and efficiency but also reduce environmental impact.

Finally, design thinking can drive policy and systemic change by encouraging stakeholders to view problems and solutions from different perspectives. By fostering empathy and collaboration, design thinking can break down silos and encourage more holistic and integrated approaches to CSA (Figure 4.2.4).

A New Era for UrbanAg

As we look towards the future of urban development, greater opportunities for UrbanAg arise as we plan more and more new cities. New cities like NEOM in Saudi Arabia are fresh slates for reimagining not just how we live, but also how we eat (The Standard, 2023). Food production can be planned ahead of time to meet the needs of future residents, providing the optimal selection of crops and technologies to reduce food waste, optimize supply chains, and drive efficiency through smart management. Overall, the trend towards smart and sustainable cities should always include agriculture.

SPECTRUM OF URBAN AGRICULTURE

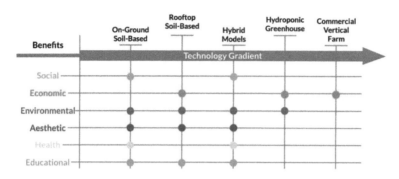

Figure 4.2.4 Impact category graphic.

The synthesis of urban planning, architectural design, and agriculture promises significant benefits for our planet and its citizens. From an environmental perspective, Agritecture can reduce the urban heat island effect, increase biodiversity, and contribute to improved air and water quality. Moreover, incorporating green spaces and farms into urban buildings enhances their aesthetic appeal, contributing to a more pleasant and healthier living environment.

Besides the environmental impact, Agritecture promotes local food production. Harvesting and consuming produce within city borders decrease the food miles traveled significantly, thus reducing carbon emissions and improving the freshness of consumables. UrbanAg also encourages seasonal eating, which contributes to a more diverse and nutritious diet.

Another consideration for cities is that no other urban green technology embodies the food, water, energy, and waste nexus that is critical to sustainable development more than UrbanAg does. So, beyond the benefits of community engagement, reduced food miles, green jobs, and others, UrbanAg is a catalyst for smarter and more sustainable cities overall (Agritecture, 2018). Smart cities will look at their cities as a canvas for opportunities in UrbanAg and understand the climatic, social, and market needs of their cities now and in the future to develop smart policies to encourage the right urban farms to solve their challenges. For urban planners, consultants, and architects, design thinking and an open approach that considers the landscape of possible UrbanAg typologies as "tools in the toolbox" will lead to the greatest project success. We are ready to take on the challenge of climate change adaptation by accelerating smart farming in and near cities and invite all to join us.

References

Agritecture. (2018). Smart cities are forgetting about something: *Food*, from: https://www.agritecture.com/blog/2018/8/17/smart-cities-are-forgetting-about-something-food

Anggraeni, E.W., Handayati, Y., Novani, S. (2022). Improving Local food systems through the coordination of agriculture supply chain actors. *Sustainability*, 14(6): 3281.

Beacham, A.M., Vickers, L.H., Monaghan, J.M. (2019). Vertical farming: A summary of approaches to growing skywards. *The Journal of Horticultural Science and Biotechnology*, 94(3): 277–283

City of Dallas. (2022). Comprehensive urban agriculture plan: Draft plan & upcoming community meetings, November 4, 2022, from: https://dallascityhall.com/government/citymanager/Documents/FY%2022-23%20Memos/Comprehensive%20Urban%20Agriculture%20Plan.pdf

Dzvene, A.R., Tesfuhuney, W.A., Walker, S., Ceronio, G. (2023). Management of cover crop intercropping for live mulch on plant productivity and growth resources: A review. *Air, Soil and Water Research*, 16: 1–6.

Ellen Macarthur Foundation. (2022). Transforming our food system can tackle climate change, and cities play a leading role, from: https://www.ellenmacarthurfoundation.org/cities-and-a-circular-economy-for-food/climate-article

Engler, Nicholas, Krarti, Moncef. (2021). Review of energy efficiency in controlled environment agriculture. *Renewable and Sustainable Energy Reviews*, 141: 110786

Filintas, A., Gougoulias, N., Hatzichristou, E. (2023). Modeling soil erodibility by water (Rainfall/irrigation) on tillage and no-tillage plots of a helianthus field utilizing soil analysis, precision agriculture, gis, and kriging geostatistics. *Environmental Sciences Proceedings*, 25(1): 54.

Mes´ıas-Ruiz, G.A., Pe´ rez-Ortiz, M., Dorado, J., de Castro, A.I., Peña, J.M. (2023). Boosting precision crop protection towards agriculture 5.0 via machine learning and emerging technologies: A contextual review. *Frontiers in Plant Science*, 14: 1143326

Perkins. (2022). Farming in 2050: The farmers of tomorrow 2022, from: https://www.perkins.com/en_GB/campaigns/powernews/features/future-farmers.html

Ridge, Rosamarie (2003). The History of Community Gardens in New York City: The Role of Urban Agriculture and Green Roofs in Addressing Environmental Racism. Student Theses 2001–2013. 76.

Scherr, S.J., Shames, S. Friedman, R. (2012). From climate-smart agriculture to climate-smart landscapes. *Agriculture & Food Security*, 1: 12.

The Standard. (2023). What is Neom? The $500 billion Saudi Arabian 'smart city' is 33 times the size of New York, 17 October 2023, from: https://www.standard.co.uk/news/world/neom-saudi-arabia-smart-city-mohammed-bin-salman-b1114036.html#:~:text=Neom%20is%20a%20city%20of,has%20been%20reserved%20for%20nature.

Viparis, Nature Urbaine, (2022). from: https://www.viparis.com/en/news-events/news/nature-urbaine-2

Wang, Chao, Chen, Yu, Sun, Mingxing, Wu, Jiayu, (2023). Potential of technological innovation to reduce the carbon footprint of urban facility agriculture: A food–energy–water–waste nexus perspective. *Journal of Environmental Management*, 339: 117806.

4.3

ANTI-DESERTIFICATION ARCHITECTURE

Aeolian Assemblies

Stephen Mueller

Abstract

This chapter contends with the problematics and potentials of operative spatial technologies applied within desert contexts and amidst the real and imagined conditions of "desertification." To consider an "anti-desertification architecture," we must engage with two existential threats threats to ongoing life in the desert: on one hand, the fallacious construct of "desertification" as a tool to essentialize, delegitimize, and appropriate arid lands to advance settler colonial interventionism; and—on the other hand—the very real and precarious futurity of the inhabitants of arid lands as they contend with the challenges to their lives and livelihood while facing increasing drought and climate extremes. Architecture, thus, must be against the construct of desertification as a colonial tool, and responsive to the realities of living in inhabited deserts. While the proliferation of transcontinental "anti-desertification" projects seeks to negate the desert climate and its inhabitants at the territorial scale, new architectural technologies and morphologies suggest an alternative scale and site for desert-conscious design, collaborating with the mechanics of desert landscapes and atmospheres to mitigate potential damages of extreme aridity and heat in service of desert populations.

Architecture against "Desertification"

This chapter contends with the problematics and potentials of operative spatial technologies applied within desert contexts and amidst the real and imagined conditions of "desertification." The naming of the desert has long served as a colonial tool promoting extractivist logics and negating indigenous claims to land. A growing body of desert design scholarship positions the desert not as "empty," but as richly inhabited by a wide diversity of human and non-human life (Henni, 2022; Kripa et al, 2023), and as a new shared territory in which solidarities emerge between geographically distant but commonly desert-bound anti-colonial struggles (Lambert, 2022). Within this diverse array of inhabited deserts, there is a reality of increased aridity and extreme heat which is transforming more of the world's ecosystems into drylands. Urbanizing deserts will become home to an even greater number of human inhabitants in the next decades (IPCC, 2023), placing new stressors on desert resources.

DOI: 10.4324/9781003384113-51

To consider an "anti-desertification architecture," we must engage with both threats to ongoing life in the desert: on one hand, the fallacious construct of "desertification" as a tool to essentialize, delegitimize, and appropriate arid lands to advance settler colonial interventionism; and—on the other hand—the very real and precarious futurity of the inhabitants of arid lands as they contend with the challenges to their lives and livelihood and face increasing drought and climate extremes. An anti-desertification architecture, thus, must be positioned against the construct of desertification as a colonial tool and responsive to the realities of living in inhabited deserts.

"Anti-desertification" design at a territorial or landscape scale in the past decades has been highly problematic, advancing the erasure of the condition of the desert along with the legacies and livelihoods of its inhabitants. Earnest advances in the realm of contemporary architectural technologies to adapt building technologies to the shifting conditions of desert environments have offered insight into directions for continued disciplinary research and sustain life in inhabited deserts. But a more desert-situated approach is needed, which seeks to protect the life and property of humans and non-humans alike through the acceptance of desert conditions as a site for sustained life, and through the engagement of the material and atmospheric conditions of the desert as instigators of responsive and resilient designs.

This chapter will elaborate on the problematics of an "anti-desertification" design approach at both the scale of the territory and the scale of the architectural assembly and conclude with examples of design research that signal potential directions for an architecture that works against erroneous concepts of desertification while serving those that inhabit the desert.

Anti-desertification Territories

The shifting boundaries of desert territories from the "loss of dryland vegetative cover" can be attributed to either of two causes—*desertification*, "scientifically understood as land degradation due to human mismanagement" and *dessication*, attributed to changes in climate (Turner et al., 2023).

Colonial and extractivist campaigns have long advanced technopositivist "solutions" for desert environments that posit the wholesale conversion of desert or "desertifying" territories into water-rich environments through large-scale transformations deploying water infrastructures and water management strategies (Cooper, 2023). Stemming from a settler colonial mindset unadapted to life in the desert, these supposed "solutions" are advanced by those who see the desert as inherently empty, hostile to life, and problematic.

Design projects to combat desertification are seemingly growing in scale, increasingly engaging transnational, intercontinental territories. These projects consider the design of land management and infrastructures promoting food security and increased agricultural production not merely as a salve for rural populations, but for the security of urban population centers and indeed the integrity of nation states and international governance.

Projects promoting "anti-desertification" have a long history in colonial territories of state powers, who leverage "dessication theory" to territorialize drylands that were presumed "empty" of resources. These projects have expropriated vast tracts of land in the name of reshaping the desert, displacing indigenous and minoritized communities. Despite claims of these programs to advance food security, advance economic growth, and improve livelihoods, the social and societal impact of large-scale anti-desertification projects is decidedly limited (Turner et al., 2023).

One of most well-known territorial scale design projects to combat desertification is the so-called Great Green Wall project in China, which over the past several decades has sought to leverage large-scale tree planting efforts to create shelter belts around the Gobi desert, arguably to protect China's population against the desert's advancing sands. The project was initiated in 1978 to "protect the cities from sand and dust storms," mitigating the risk that severe dust storms cause to human life during extreme weather events. Noting the risks that airborne dust borne from desertified areas poses to critical infrastructure, the project also purportedly protects the economic interests of rural regions and densely populated urban regions like Beijing to advance state interests (Veste et al., 2006), largely in ethnic minority areas (Turner et al., 2023). The project demonstrates some early adoption of now common features in the design of anti-desertification technologies, primarily in the form of geoengineering and landscape-scale interventions that seek to stabilize soil by augmenting both vegetative and soil characteristics. Like other similar initiatives, the desertifying region is fundamentally transformed from an ecological—and even microbiological—perspective, through the hybridization of existing dunescapes and landforms with new patterns of tree and grass planting, and the nurturing of biological soil crusts.

For geology professor H. Jiang, the project represents the Chinese government's "dominating relationship with the environment." As part of the project, the dryland areas of Minqin were appropriated as a "sand control and tree planting model" to reverse desertification in the region and advance state interests. While the government has celebrated the success, the data suggests otherwise. Jiang describes the project as "relying too heavily on human intervention instead of natural recovery" and further criminalizing human activities as the main culprit of ecological degradation (Jiang, 2016).

The World Bank has led a similar, but more contemporary green wall initiative. The Great Green Wall for the Sahara and Sahel initiative (GGWSSI) (World Bank, 2013) is the "most ambitious ARR [afforestation, revegetation, and reforestation] program in sub-Saharan Africa" that seeks to transform vast territories of Sub-Saharan Africa to restore "degraded" lands and advance "smart agriculture" (Turner et al., 2021). The initiative has "demonstrated limited success, often due to conflicts between sedentary and pastoralist communities" (WeForest, 2023). The spatial practices of nomadic pastoralists were negated by the initiative's emphasis on transnational land management (Spiegelenberg, 2022).

In contrast to these superscaled "anti-desertification" territorial and infrastructural conquests, indigenous cultures "thrived in aridity." The Zuni "built sophisticated infrastructural systems to conserve water for use during dry periods," while the Tohono O'odham "traveled nomadically with seasonal water flows" (Cooper, 2023).

As infrastructure, no matter the scale, will never prove capable of overturning the aridity of desert landscapes and territories (Cooper, 2023), designers have simultaneously pursued approaches to mitigating the desert environment at smaller scales. Instead of changing the desert, these approaches change the conception of the desert and our relationship to it, nurturing ways to live with the desert, as we always have, and to live with the desert to come.

Anti-desertification Architectural Technologies

At an architectural level, advances have been made to develop building technologies and performative systems to protect against the advances of the desert. While not addressing desertification specifically, these technologies, responsive to the extreme heat, radiation, and aridity of a desert environment, are suggesting future trajectories for continuing conflu-ences of human life and desert atmospheres.

Extreme climate phenomena are increasingly shaping and codifying professional archi-tectural and urban design practices. Severe weather events in wet and coastal climates have driven a substantial amount of design investigation and regulation in the past decades, evi-denced most clearly in the US by the popularization of the notion of sea-level rise, majority populations living in urban centers near the coasts, and the resulting prevalence of adopted standards and building codes addressing designs for hurricanes and flooding. Experimental facilities for the testing of new building technologies, such as hurricane simulators and product testing facilities, are common resources for building professionals to test and advance the state of the art of design in coastal environments.

In many professional design communities, however, inland environments in general, and arid environments in particular, are not as well studied or understood, though they too are frontlines where the impacts of climate change will be disproportionately delivered to sig-nificant and longstanding urban, rural, and migrating populations.

The atmospheric conditions prevalent in inhabited deserts—including the impacts of air-borne particulate, temperature, and radiation extremes on buildings and their inhabitants—are deserving of more robust disciplinary attention.

Aeolian Assemblies

Airborne sand and dust are a common atmospheric condition in inhabited deserts, a natural result of the extreme heat, aridity, and sparsely vegetated landscape coupled with aeolian, or wind-based phenomena. The frequency of dust storms and dust events will increase with the effects of climate change in many of the world's populated deserts.

While many common material and architectural practices exist in these regions to miti-gate the impact of airborne dust, advances in construction technology have opened new channels for invention of dust- and sand-responsive architectural assemblies.

The impacts of this airborne material are well known in building sciences, where even small particles of airborne dust at moderate velocities are known to scour and degrade sur-faces, aggregate, and accumulate in unwanted areas, infiltrate building cavities and systems, and produce other deleterious effects. The public health impacts are even more devastating, as fine particles can also migrate into indoor air where over time they can severely impact human and animal respiratory tissue and contribute to acute and chronic disease.

The King Abdullah Petroleum Studies (KAPSARC) project, designed by Zaha Hadid Architects in collaboration with Arup, provides one example of contemporary architec-tural technologies adapting to the material conditions of the desert to address the issue from a building sciences perspective. The project is sited in Riyadh, where large dust storms are a common occurrence. The design team recognized that the extreme arid and particulate-laden environment would necessitate a significant reworking of otherwise common approaches to design the roof cladding for the project. The team selected an open-jointed rainscreen system as the ideal technical solution for adapting the project to the impact of water during the region's "occasionally violent thunderstorms." But having selected an open system for water drainage to protect the panels, they also discovered that the airborne dust would eventually infiltrate the cavity and degrade this performance, requiring extensive and continual maintenance to stabilize the building's performance over time. The response was to design a so-called sand gutter below the open joint, which would not only support the panels but also act as an integral part of the newly desert-adapted rainscreen system, capturing and conveying the accumulated dust away from the cavity (Bishop & Wilson, 2011).

Testing and simulation capacities of these environmental conditions are highly specialized, and more commonly under the domain of advanced research laboratories or military installations leveraging advanced technologies to wield technological superiority over the aspects of desert environments that threaten human life and state power (see Mueller, 2020). There is a need, however, to develop capacity within the architectural discipline to better simulate, anticipate, and intuitively respond to known and emerging impacts of airborne sand and dust in desert cities.

Not every desert is alike, however, and the particularities of windblown particulates— their origins, behaviors, and impacts—vary widely from dryland to dryland. By situating a study and simulation of aeolian atmospheres, equally diverse architectural technologies and imaginaries might emerge.

Chihuahuan Desert Futures

In the binational metroplex of El Paso–Ciudad Juarez, efforts to "reclaim" the desert continue, through the extensive management of the Rio Grande–Rio Bravo watershed and the construction of large-scale water desalination infrastructures. The largest inland desalination plant in the world is built in El Paso, Texas, in a partnership between the water utility of the city and Fort Bliss, one of the largest military installations in the United States (KLAQ, 2023). The plant supplies 27.5 million gallons of freshwater daily by removing the salts from brackish water in underground aquifers and plans to nearly double this capacity to support continued population growth in the context of increasing water scarcity.

Urban populations living in the arid US–Mexico borderland face significant environmental and public health challenges from atmospheric pollution. The region's desert geology contributes to dangerously high levels of fine particles, threatening the estimated 25 million borderland inhabitants with adverse health impacts from airborne sand and dust. This environmental and public health crisis will be exacerbated in the coming decades by the combined impacts of climate change, climate migration, desertification, and rapid urbanization, intensifying conditions of spatial, social, and environmental injustice (Heyman, 2007; Eades, 2018; Mueller & Kripa, 2022). The built environment of the borderland has yet to adapt significantly to these airborne threats. While other urbanized desert regions have adopted advanced building technologies to manage the adverse impacts of extreme particulate exposure in the built environment (Bishop & Wilson, 2011; Grassi et al., 2019), the borderland has yet to develop an expertise to address these changing threats specific to its unique environmental conditions.

Dust Institute Studio: Aeolian Assemblies for the Chihuahuan Desert

Design research, conducted in past years through the Dust Institute undergraduate architectural design studio at Texas Tech University Huckabee College of Architecture in El Paso, has sought to develop advanced building construction systems capable of managing and mitigating the flows of airborne particulate on a variety of sites near the US–Mexico border. By privileging "dust flow" as a primary driver for performative building envelope design, common environmental design principles (e.g., passive ventilation strategies) were interrogated and re-evaluated to imagine new assemblies capable of addressing "dust-specific" behaviors (e.g., scouring, infiltration, creep, suspension). As a second goal, the research sought to identify architectural strategies that could leverage these new construction systems to promote the public awareness and scientific study of changing dust conditions. As a third goal, the studio sought to combat the notion of the desert or scientifically "desertified" landscapes as an "empty" or "barren" condition, with designs amplifying and sustaining the many forms of human and non-human life that reside and migrate in our desert cities.

The studio develops students' understanding of architectural design through the design of aeolian assemblies—performative building envelopes and spatial membranes responsive to desert airflow dynamics. Students model and test example buildings and building envelopes—and simulate air and particulate flow—in detailed physical and digital prototypes, custom responsive algorithmic drawings, and computer simulation environments using computational fluid dynamics (CFD) workflows. After studying the performance of their precedents, each student investigates specific particulate transmission vectors impacting human and biotic conditions (e.g., allergens, pathogens, fine particles, geologic and biologic signatures, and radioactivity) in greater detail and develops models to encourage specific airflow behaviors in their own designs. The studio leverages additive methods of digital production and fabrication, and testing through computational simulations, to ensure rapid feedback between proposal and evaluation. The studio emphasizes the simultaneous recording of the design and the environmental impact through two primary drawing types—the unfolded elevation and the detailed wall section.

From this desert-situated and research-informed design approach, students were able to develop and test experimental, innovative, and detailed architectural designs using "dust" as a driver for innovation. Students gained insight into design research informed by critical material practice, developed skills in generative design techniques and analytical representational techniques, and developed their ability to design synthetic relationships between environmental conditions, sites, building forms, and the public realm.

Articulated Membranes

Many designs questioned and recalibrated assumptions about the human's relationship to the desert atmosphere, articulating spaces to study and engage airborne dust. Informed by generative design techniques managing the complex assemblage of aggregated forms, student designs explored a range of formal and material articulations. Imagining new forms of performance within a thickened building skin, students articulated new assemblies for double-skin facades that could incorporate an inhabitable research gallery in the layers of construction between the dust-laden air of the exterior desert environment and the filtered air within the controlled laboratory interior. Gradients of atmospheric conditions and variations in building program were designed to facilitate building-scale experiments, with airborne contaminants controlled or redirected the students' manipulation of design parameters in a range of investigations. Different approaches included the kinetic assemblage of deflective formed metal apertures to differentiate experimental "wet" and "dry" labs interfacing with changing zones of wind pressure and velocity (Figure 4.3.1), and photochemical substrates deployed on arrays of cast minimal surfaces to isolate contaminants and improve microclimate air quality within the building envelope (Figure 4.3.2).

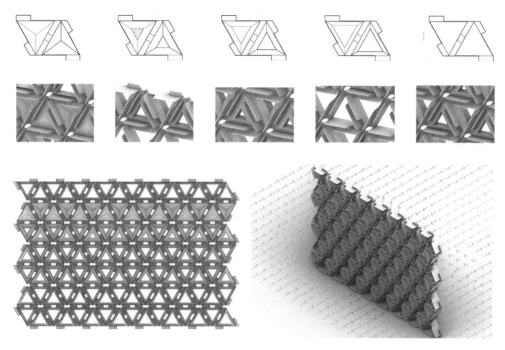

Figure 4.3.1 Articulated membrane-folded metal apertures. Student work by Blanca Perez; Stephen Mueller, instructor; Dust Institute Studio, Texas Tech University, 2023; Image Courtesy of Author.

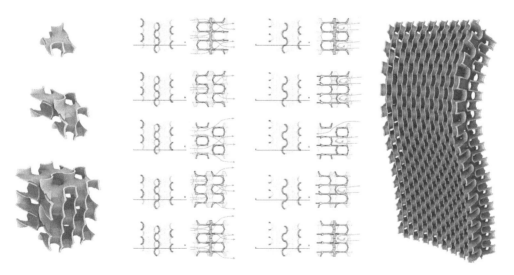

Figure 4.3.2 Articulated membrane-cast minimal surface. Student work by Emmanuel Urena; Stephen Mueller, instructor; Dust Institute Studio, Texas Tech University, 2023; Image Courtesy of Author.

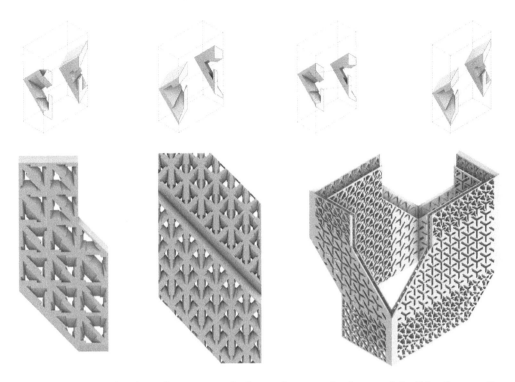

Figure 4.3.3   Articulated membrane-networked ceramic screen. Student work by Brian Barrera; Stephen Mueller, instructor; Dust Institute Studio, Texas Tech University, 2023; Image Courtesy of Author.

For his design of an articulated ceramic membrane, Brian Barrera developed a performative building envelope that manipulated levels of humidity in the interior and exterior environment to simultaneously facilitate the collection of airborne particulate and improve human comfort within the building interior (Figure 4.3.3). Advancing traditional methods of passive cooling utilizing ceramic water vessels near ventilated openings in desert environments, the articulated, hollow ceramic envelope allows for rainwater capture during monsoon seasons and helps to increase atmospheric humidity in the microclimate around the building envelope through evaporation. Moisture in the air and envelope system assists in binding atmospheric particulate in water droplets, which travel through the network of ceramic channels into collection chambers.

The system works as a building-scale experiment, expanding the capacity of geological investigations into airborne dust within an urban environment (Figure 4.3.4). Typically, a series of field-installed dust collectors would gather airborne particulate at or near ground level, and samples would need to be transported to a laboratory facility where they would be suspended in a water mixture, dried, and evaluated for mineral content and contaminants. The proposed system is instead able to suspend the collection mechanisms in a vertical array, capturing a wider variety of atmospheric pollutants in varying degrees of suspensions near ground level and toward the building roof, collecting and recording a more representative sample of wind conditions and airborne particulate concentrations in an urban environment.

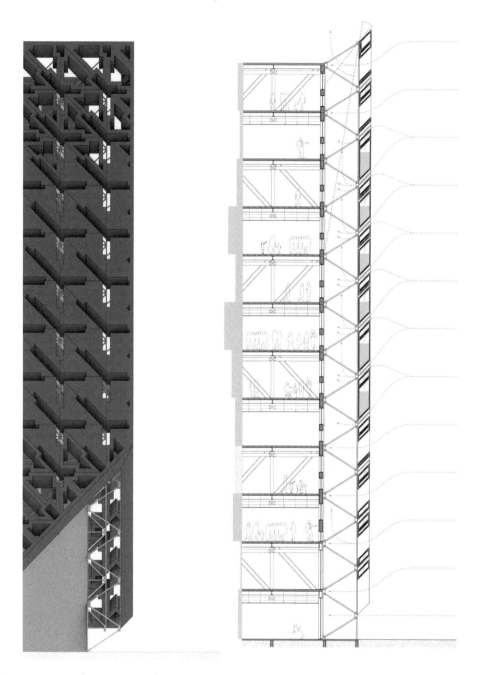

Figure 4.3.4 Performative membrane wall section. Student work by Brian Barrera; Stephen Mueller, instructor; Dust Institute Studio, Texas Tech University, 2023; Image Courtesy of Author.

The varying wind velocities from ground to roof drive the vertical articulation of the ceramic screen, which creates varying levels of porosity from ground to sky. Pressure differentials between windward and leeward faces of the building are addressed by the horizontal differentiation of the ceramic screen, which capitalizes on seasonal windflows to naturally ventilate the interior while allowing particle-laden air from major dust events into interior laboratory and demonstration spaces. The resulting screen modulates between a heavy, protective, and deeply channeled mass, and a more delicate, lacelike filigree, alternating between surface and void to redirect windflow.

The reciprocity between the breathing building skin and the breathing human inhabitants was further explored and articulated as the project determined optimal correspondences between inhabitants and the mitigated desert atmosphere. Recognizing that various indoor programs contribute to the humidity of the indoor air through respiration, synergies were explored between the surplus humidity generated by active programs with larger occupancies (e.g., public demonstration areas) and the humidity deficit of smaller and less active programs (e.g., offices).

As the formal, performative, and technological features of the project were resolved, students also explored the capacities for their designs to address larger societal impacts of desert environments on desert dwellers and lifestyles. Active humidification systems common in desert environments are susceptible to contamination by airborne microorganisms and chemicals, contributing to respiratory diseases and disorders, including hypersensitivity pneumonitis. The ability of the ceramic membrane to modulate humidity through passive systems was explored as an alternative to active humidification systems, with proper humidification and contamination control able to be properly studied and optimized by pairing with the scientific institute program.

Conclusion

The projects in the studio illustrate an attitude toward anti-desertification—not intended to transform the desert or keep it at bay, but to engage with the desert and its material atmospheres to foster new ways of building and living in urbanized deserts. By making in, and making with, the desert and its people, the studio advances discourses, and imaginaries of an architecture against desertification.

References

Bishop, E., and Wilson, J. (2011). "21 concept to realisation: GRC and complex facades." *GRC 2011 Congress, Istanbul:* 1–15. https://www.grca.online/about-grca/previous-grca-congress/grca-2011-congress-istanbul

Cooper, D. (2023). "Dry matters: Speculations for an arid future." *Journal of Architectural Education,* 77(2): 410–426.

Eades, L. (2018). "Air pollution at the U.S.–Meχico Border: Strengthening the framework for bilateral cooperation." *Journal of Public and International Affairs:* 64–79. https://jpia.princeton.edu/sites/g/files/toruqf1661/files/resource-links/jpia_2018.pdf

Grassi, G., Lupica Spagnolo, S., and Paoletti, I. (2019). "Fabrication and durability testing of a 3D printed façade for desert climates." *Additive Manufacturing,* 28: 439–444.

Henni, S., (ed.) (2022). *Deserts Are Not Empty*. Columbia University Press.

Heyman, J. (2007). "Environmental issues at the U.S.–Mexico Border and the unequal territorialization of value." In A. Hornberg, J. McNeill, and J. Martinez-Alier (eds.), *Rethinking Environmental History: World-Systems History and Global Environmental Change*. New York: Altamira Press: 327–341.

IPCC. (2023). *Climate Change 2023: Synthesis Report*. Intergovernmental Panel on Climate Change (IPCC), Geneva, Switzerland, 184 pp., doi: 10.59327/IPCC/AR6-9789291691647.

Jiang, H. (2016). Taking down the "Great Green Wall": The science and policy discourse of desertification and its control in China. *The End of Desertification? Disputing Environmental Change in the Drylands*. Berlin: Springer-Verlag: 513–536.

KLAQ (2023). "El Paso has the world's largest one of these." https://klaq.com/worlds-largest-el-paso-desalination-plant

Kripa, E., Marullo F., and Mueller, S., (eds.) (2023). *Journal of Architectural Education*, 77(2): Deserts.

Lambert, L. (ed.) (2022). *Funambulist Magazine*. Vol. 44: The Desert.

Mueller, S. (2020). "Airborne agents." In Tatiana Bilbao, Ayesha Ghosh, and Nile Greenberg, (eds), *Two Sides of the Border: Reimagining the Region*. Zurich: Lars Muller Publishers: 290–304.

Mueller, S., and Kripa, E. (2022). "Drawn across borders." In Emanuele Giorgi, Tiziano Cattaneo, Alfredo Mauricio Flores Herrera, Virginia del Socorro Aceves Tarango, (eds), *Design for Vulnerable Communities*. Cham: Springer Nature, 395–422.

Spiegelenberg, F. (2022). "Spatial justice and large-scale land transformation: A study of spatial justice for transhumant pastoralists in the case of the Great Green Wall." Linköping: Linköpings Universitet: 1–91.

Turner, M. D., Carney, T., Lawler, L., Reynolds, J., Kelly, L., Teague, M. S., and Brottem, L. (2021). "Environmental rehabilitation and the vulnerability of the poor: The case of the Great Green Wall." *Land Use Policy*, 111: 105750.

Turner, M. D., Davis, D. K., Yeh, E. T., Hiernaux, P., Loizeaux, E. R., Fornof, E. M., … Suiter, A. K. (2023). "Great green walls: Hype, myth, and science." *Annual Review of Environment and Resources*, 48: 263–287.

Veste, M., Gao, J., Sun, B., and Breckle, S. W. (2006). "The green great wall-combatting desertification in China." *Geographische Rundschau International Edition*, 2(3): 14–20.

WeForest. (2023). https://www.weforest.org/programme/great-green-wall/

World Bank. (2013). *Transforming the Sahel: Supporting the Great Green Wall Initiative*. https://www.worldbank.org/en/region/afr/brief/world-bank-support-for-great-green-wall-initiative

4.4

THE STACKED CITY AS A MODEL FOR HIGH-DENSITY LOW-CARBON URBANIZATION

Comparison of the Vertical and Horizontal City Models for Urban Development in Hot Climate Zones and their Potential to Achieve Net-Zero Carbon Emissions

Brian Cody

Abstract

The concept of a vertically stacked city as a model for urban growth in hot climates is examined along with the merits and potential drawbacks of this city form when compared to more conventional horizontally aligned city concepts. Over 90% of new building construction to accommodate the global population growth in the coming 25 years will be in hot climate zones. The construction of new cities might be a more sustainable alternative rather than the expansion of existing ones and in the past 2 decades, over 150 new cities have been launched in more than 40 countries. Against the background of the global goal of achieving carbon neutrality by 2050, the most appropriate currency for comparing the energy performance of various options is land as the ultimate resource. Practical renewable energy supply is a finite resource, as it requires materials and land for its implementation. The concept of energy land, defined as the land area required for the renewable energy production to supply a given urban area, is used to compare future city models supplied by renewable energy sources. Whereas the portion of land taken up by energy production in today's city is almost negligible, in a vertical city, in which a high-density urban area is powered by renewable energy systems, the land area required for energy production is greater than the land area of the urban development itself. The question considered here is which model – the vertical or horizontal city – leads to higher urban density in a hot climate. Which approach leads to reduced land use in real terms and how do the ecological footprints of the models compare.

DOI: 10.4324/9781003384113-52

Introduction

This chapter will explore the concept of a vertically stacked city form as a model for urban growth in hot climates and examine the merits and potential drawbacks of this model when compared to more conventional horizontally aligned city concepts. Does the concept of the vertical city offer a potential increase in urban density in real terms, leading to reduced land use and ecological footprint? For comparison, a low-rise high-density horizontal city model was chosen.

Growth

By 2050, global population is predicted to increase from currently approx. 8 billion to nearly 10 billion (United Nations, n.d.). Sub-Saharan Africa will account for roughly two-thirds of this global population growth (ODNI, 2021). Currently around 40% of the world's population live in the tropical climate zone, which is centered on the Earth's equator, between the Tropic of Cancer and the Tropic of Capricorn (23.5° latitude North and South, respectively). By 2050, this will rise to roughly 50% (Wilkinson, 2014). It follows, therefore, that the vast majority (over 90% according to author's estimation) of new building space needed in order to accommodate this population growth of nearly 2 billion people in the coming 25 years will need to be constructed in the Global South – in the subtropical and tropical regions, mostly in sub-Saharan Africa and Asia – and thus in hot climate zones, of which by far the larger portion will be in the tropical climate zone (approx. 80% according to author's estimation). At the same time, cities in other parts of the world in the Global North are predicted to shrink (Jarzebski et al., 2021). Potential mass migration from hot climate zones and other regions adversely affected by the changing climate alongside migration due to war, conflicts, and other issues could of course alter the course of events and lead to changes in the patterns described above.

The challenge this poses can best be understood by considering the following statement. The growth described in the preceding paragraph is equivalent to building a city the size of Singapore every month for the next 25 years or a city the size of Aberdeen, Scotland every day. Innovative urban design strategies and concepts on how best to provide this urban growth in a sustainable manner are therefore urgently required. While, based on the above, growth in population seems inevitable, it has been suggested that economic growth is a choice and prosperity can be achieved without it (Jackson, 2016). While this argument is very valid for a large part of the Western World, it is not the case for a large portion of our global population and not for the planet as a whole. Roughly one quarter of the people on earth do not have adequate access to water, food, or shelter (WHO, n.d.; FAO, n.d.; Habitat for Humanity, 2020). Calls to stop building altogether as an alternative to sustainable growth are equally naïve, considering the number of world inhabitants without adequate shelter and the growth levels outlined above. No economic growth is not a real alternative, given that an unprecedented re-distribution of existing wealth on a global scale is, to say the least, highly improbable.

Cities

By 2050, nearly 70% of the world population is projected to be living in urban areas (UN Habitat, 2023). This urban growth will need to be distributed among the expansion of existing and the construction of new cities. A large portion of this growth is anticipated in coastal areas (Neumann et al., 2015) despite warnings that cities in coastal areas are particularly prone to flooding by rising sea levels caused by climate change (World Bank, 2013). The locations chosen for cites in the past were driven by factors such as proximity to natural resources, especially water, rivers, and the oceans for transportation or mountains for defense. In more recent times, factors such as human capital and business potential have become more important. Which factors will drive city location, growth, and form in the future? Climate and renewable energy potential might well become new driving forces. In any case, the necessary climate adaption of existing (and new) cities to render them "climate proof" is an issue that could affect future locations for growth, possibly leading to less growth in coastal and more development of inland locations. Given that climate and coastal proximity have been found to be the two key geographical gradients of economic development up until now, the consequences for future development are large (Mellinger et al., 2000). Are Megacities inevitable or will we see more distributed growth? Issues such as the future of work, travel and globalization, aging populations, and the resulting influence on concepts such as walkability remain to be seen and the consequences are impossible to predict with any certainty.

New Cities

It has been suggested that the construction of new cities might be more suitable to accommodate the urban growth needed rather than the development of existing ones (Fuller et al., 2014). It may also be more sustainable, given that we face very real problems regarding the necessary renovation of our existing cities in Europe and North America due to legal, financial, and technical constraints, ranging from ownership structures, heritage protection issues, and NIMBY. In the past 2 decades, over 150 new cities have been launched in more than 40 countries (Moser, 2020). Concepts for sustainable urban development in hot areas have also been explored in the past, perhaps the earliest example in modern times is Arcosanti, designed by Paolo Soleri, which began construction in 1970 in the Arizona desert (Evans, 2016). Numerous so-called ecological cities such as Dongtan in China (Wang et al., 2019) and Masdar in the UAE (Griffiths and Sovacool, 2020) were much discussed, yet unfortunately not or only partially realized. Of the current projects under development the largest and by far best-known example is The Line in the new NEOM region in northwestern Saudi Arabia (Paszkowska-Kaczmarek, 2021), which is intended to be the first city on the planet with net-zero carbon emissions.

Energy, Carbon, and Sustainability

When we look closely at some of the largest problems and challenges faced by our society today, energy is a key factor, not least for global warming and climate change, where energy is the single largest contributor to carbon emissions. The energy problem is complex and only when understood in its entire complexity will we be in a position to develop the right solutions to solve it (Cody, 2017). In the following, we will concentrate on the aspects relating to climate change and the relevance for city building. At the COP 21 conference in Paris in December 2015, a landmark global agreement was reached to combat climate change. The central aim of this so-called Paris Agreement is to limit the global temperature rise this century to 2 degrees Celsius or less. At present, more than 70 countries, including the largest emitters – China, the United States, and the European Union – have set a net-zero carbon target, covering about 76% of global emissions (UN, n.d.). In 2021, the International Energy Agency proposed a roadmap for CO_2 emissions until 2050 (IEA, 2022).

The enormity of the task becomes apparent when considered against the background of the exponential global growth of people, energy, materials use, etc. described above and the fact that 2050 is little more than 25 years away. Since the first global climate agreement, ratified by 197 countries in 1992 some 30 years ago, global GHG emissions have actually increased by more than 60% (Tiseo, 2023). It is important to realize that, while achieving CO_2 neutrality as soon as possible is imperative, the pathway to reach that goal is equally important. Figure 4.4.1 shows several pathways that lead to the zero-carbon goal in 2050. However, it is the cumulative emissions (the shaded area under the curve) that are the salient driver of change in the atmosphere. Therefore, the embodied energy associated with building new infrastructure, cities, and buildings is of crucial importance, given the fact that these large emissions occur upfront. The planned decarbonization of the energy supply which is already underway is another reason why the time of emissions is a vital component. Emissions now are more damaging than emissions that occur in the future.

Figure 4.4.1 also shows the author's predictions for growth in population, building floor space, energy and electricity use based on the literature cited above. Growth in energy use due to the increased use of air conditioning can be expected to be disproportionately high due to the distribution of population growth discussed above, the warming climate and rising expectations of the population. In fact, rising expectations in the developed countries is probably one of the main factors why energy demand in countries in the Global North is stabilizing despite stagnating populations and much improved energy efficiency. Another item with disproportionally high growth will be electricity, which is likely to grow at a rate more than three times higher than energy use in general. This can be explained by the

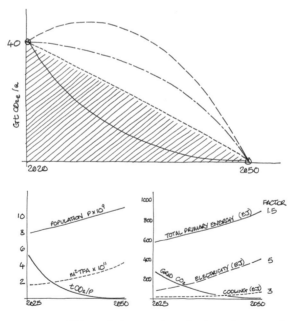

Figure 4.4.1 Pathways to zero CO_2 emissions and projections for growth (Image Courtesy of Author).

ongoing electrification of society, which is a universally agreed element of the global strategies to achieve the carbon goals described above. Some forms of mobility (particularly air transport) and industry (including cement, steel, and other products for buildings) will prove very difficult or impossible to electrify, meaning other solutions such as hydrogen will be employed, while all-electric building energy solutions are perfectly conceivable. The challenge will be presented by the mismatch between fluctuating and out-of-sync renewable energy supply and energy demand in many regions of the world, meaning that solutions for energy storage will be key. Electricity must be stored indirectly by transformation into other energy forms such as chemical energy (batteries) or potential energy (pumped storage) and satisfactory solutions on the scale required have yet to be found.

The priority given to the security of energy supply and its geopolitical consequences lead to another major challenge for society, which will not disappear as we move toward a carbon-free energy future based on renewable energy due to the need for land and materials to create and maintain this future. Water, food, and energy form a nexus at the heart of sustainable development (UN, n.d.). Agriculture is the largest consumer of the world's freshwater resources, energy production requires large quantities of water, new methods of food production such as vertical farming require large amounts of energy and thus consideration of the interdependent relationships in the development of future strategies for water, food, and energy is crucial. Particularly in hot climates, water is often a key issue due to the lack of fresh water sources. The energy demand for desalination in the Middle East region is predicted to rise to 15% of total energy consumption by 2040 (Walton, 2019). As alluded to above, due to the complexity of the energy problem and the manifold interdependencies and interactions, proper solutions require systems-thinking. Dogmas and attempts at formulating simple recipes are therefore doomed to fail but are nevertheless unfortunately all too prevalent. In the design of buildings and cities, available natural forces with the development of form and configuration based on physics can be employed to achieve high performance and symbiotic relationships between nature, humans, and technology (Cody, 2017).

As the energy supply of our society progresses toward 100% supply from renewable sources, energy infrastructure will become increasingly visible, as the land taken up by energy infrastructure increases by a factor of approx. 50 (Cody, 2017). Concerns relating to nature conservation and the aesthetics of renewable energy will gain in importance. NIMBY is a global phenomenon which contributes to the slow implementation of renewable energy production, as wind and solar farms are frequently prevented by community protests. In the building sector, aesthetic considerations in architectural design have also slowed progress. It may seem that the largest challenges facing the integration of renewable energy generation into building designs are cost, efficiency, and dependability. However, the greatest challenge may lie in the often unseen and little understood dilemma of the successful integration of these systems into architectural design from an aesthetic point of view. The aesthetics of renewable energy is an important matter for urgent research.

Energy Land

It is important to realize that practical renewable energy supply is a finite resource, as it requires materials and land for its implementation. The embodied carbon associated with the construction of the renewable energy infrastructure and the land to accommodate it need to be considered. Productive land (for food) and inhabitable land (for humans) constitute scarce resources. The earth's surface area is approx. 5.1×10^8 km². Approx. 29% of this is land, most of it uninhabitable in the form of mountains, deserts, etc., while approx. 11% is arable and can be used for food production. Urban areas on the other hand occupy approx. 1–3% of the land area on the planet (Liu et al., 2014). Research on various topics ranging from the comparison of different urban forms to agriculture and vertical farming has shown that the most appropriate currency for comparing the energy performance of various options may ultimately be land and not energy or dollars, as land is perhaps the ultimate resource (Cody, 2017). In the case of energy land, as described below, total land use is also a good indicator for the consumption of materials for the renewable energy infrastructure. With sufficient land, it is possible to generate all the energy a city requires with renewable sources. Consider a new city in a hot desert region; with land it is possible to generate energy, with energy it is possible to produce drinking water via desalination and with water and energy for artificial lighting, food can be produced in vertical farms. The bottleneck is then not water or energy but land and raw materials. This scenario is an over-simplification to demonstrate the value of land as a resource. It should not be taken to imply that this type of city is ideal – for example, there are other ecological concerns apart from energy consumption relating to desalination processes in their present form.

The concept of energy land, defined as the land area required for the renewable energy production to supply a given urban area, can be used to compare future city models supplied by renewable energy sources. In a vertical city concept, building energy demand is stacked vertically and consequently, the land area required for centralized renewable energy production is large – see Figure 4.4.2. Whereas the portion of land taken up by energy production in today's city is almost negligible, in a vertical city, in which a high-density urban area is powered by renewable energy systems (e.g., solar and wind parks), the land area required for energy production can be many times greater than the land area of the urban development. In the horizontal city concept, more of this infrastructure can be integrated into the building surface area, which reduces the energy land requirements and can also save materials if the energy producing surfaces (e.g., photovoltaic) replace other materials in the building's surfaces. Other advantages are the reduction of distribution losses as energy production is moved closer to consumption.

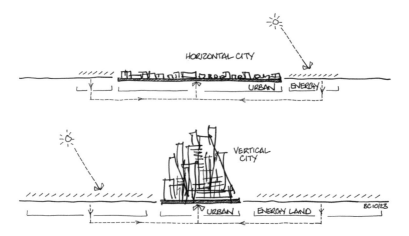

Figure 4.4.2 Vertical city versus horizontal city (Image Courtesy of Author).

Sustainable City Models

Against the background outlined briefly above, it is obvious that we will need urban growth in the form of cities and that these will need to be designed to minimize carbon emissions during their construction and operation. For the reasons given above, consideration of the embodied energy of buildings and infrastructure is becoming increasingly important. Alongside zero-carbon emissions, sustainable cities need to minimize environmental impact in general and fulfill further criteria for economic and social sustainability, which are not considered here. One topic worth mentioning in this context, and which is becoming an increasingly important factor in the design of cities, is outdoor comfort. Problems with hot urban environmental conditions in existing cities in Northern Europe have increased in recent years. Obviously, in hot climates, this phenomenon will be more pronounced and consideration of this is particularly relevant for their design. Along with the changing climate, the urban heat island effect can play an important role. The role of greenery and vegetation in buildings and cities is therefore important, as also is the provision and careful design of shaded public areas, thermal buffer zones, and passive and active cooling systems. Waste is a further important factor, and its consideration and solutions could well become one of the most important drivers for future sustainable city models.

In the design of a sustainable city, the point of departure is to decide how we as a society want to live and work in the future. We need to think about the necessary infrastructure which will make this possible. It is instructive to stop and consider the immense and fascinating technical infrastructure which makes modern life possible along with the problems it causes. Comfort is a physiological need at the very bottom of the pyramid of Maslov's hierarchy of needs; a condition which must be met in order for the human body to remain in homeostasis and before any advancement to higher level needs can take place. We need to consider how to provide suitable levels of indoor and outdoor comfort in the city. The question is how to design the city and its spaces to make the above possible in a sustainable way.

Based on the preceding discussion of land as a scare resource, achieving a high level of urban density, i.e. reducing the land needed to house a given population, is an important element of the sustainable city. The question we are considering here is which model – the vertical or horizontal city – leads to higher density in a hot climate. As described above, growth is expected in both the subtropical and tropical climate zones. Of these two broad climate types, research has shown that the subtropical might be more conducive to sustainable growth than the tropical zone (Cody, 2022). This research also shows that the other two climate zones considered (cold and temperature) are also more suitable than the tropical zone. However, we cannot choose where growth will happen.

Characteristics of the Vertical City Model

As outlined above, there are many aspects and parameters which are important in the design, construction, and operation of sustainable cities. Here, we are concerned purely with the energy aspects of the two typological city models considered and for the reasons described above, the currency used for evaluation will be land area.

First, let us consider which attributes of the vertical city might affect performance either positively or negatively.

On the positive side:

– Smaller footprint (urban land)
– Lower exposed surface area due to compactness of the form
– Generation of thermal updraft can be used for ventilation or energy production
– In very tall structures temperatures reduce with height
– Increased wind speeds at height – potential renewable energy source
– Possibility of using verticality as a means of creating an energy storage system, based on the use of gravity

On the negative side:

– Higher energy demand (elevators, pumps, fans, etc.)
– Smaller horizontal roof areas available for solar energy production
– More difficult to use low-impact low carbon natural materials, timber construction, etc.

It is important to distinguish between the vertical city model and a high-rise city model. The vertical city model considered here is based on the hypothesis that the urban design of cities needs to be conceived of in more spatial terms than was the case until now (Cody, 2017). Circulation, mobility systems, and public spaces need not remain trapped on the ground plane – see Figure 4.4.3. Various layers at different vertical levels are conceivable in a truly three-dimensional spatial arrangement of public and private life, combining urbanity and nature, density, and diversity.

Comparison of the City Models

To compare the two city models, a calculation model was set up, which, although very rough, gives an indication of the likely land areas and population densities which might be achieved. Let us assume that a new city to house a population of 1 million inhabitants is to

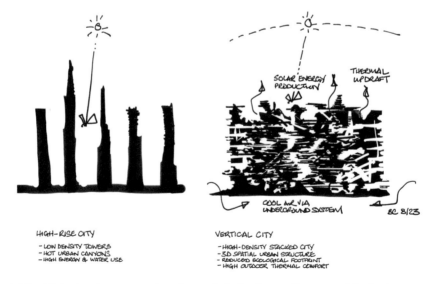

Figure 4.4.3   High-rise city compared to the vertical city (Image Courtesy of Author).

Table 4.4.1 Assumptions for the Hypothetical City Models (Image Courtesy of Author)

	Horizontal City	Vertical City	
Street width	8	24	m
Average building side	40	50	m
Average building height	12	120	m
Total floor area per person	100	125	m^2/p
Embodied energy	12	14	GJ/m^2
Operational energy, subtropical	59	71	kWh_{el}/m^2a
Operational energy, tropical	72	87	kWh_{el}/m^2a

be built. Table 4.4.1 shows the various assumptions used in the model. The figures for energy demand are based on simulations carried out for a research project on zero-energy-buildings in different climate zones (Cody, 2022) and are based on very efficient building design concepts.

The allocation of total floor area per person includes building space for residential, office, and other commercial and public building space. It is the gross floor area and includes circulation space, etc. so that the density can be measured in terms of people per km^2 land which is a real indication of achievable urban density. The city mobility concept is obviously a key element. A high degree of walkability and very efficient public transportation is assumed in both cases. In the energy demand calculation, some light industry is allowed for. An all-electric solution for buildings, mobility, and industry is assumed. In both models, an allocation of 10 m^2 per person of public and green space is provided.

With regard to the characteristics of the vertical city model discussed above, the higher energy demand for elevators, pumps, fans, etc. has been taken into account, as have the geometric consequences on surface area for energy production. The use of thermal updraft, increased wind speeds at height, and gravity storage systems has not been considered, as these items depend very much on the specific design. On the other hand, the probability that low-impact low carbon natural materials would be easier to implement in the horizontal city model has also not been considered.

The point of departure is the city's initial construction. According to the assumptions above, the vertical city model will require more materials and energy. However, both models will require vast amounts of energy and materials for their construction and using current methods would lead to massive emissions of CO_2 into the atmosphere within a relatively short time frame. To remind ourselves of the scale, we would need approx. 2,000 such cities to accommodate the expected population growth in the next 25 years. Ideally, the initial step in the building of our hypothetical city would be to use available resources to build solar energy plant which would allow the zero-carbon production of the required building materials and the construction of the structures and infrastructure which make up the city. Theoretically, the energy infrastructure on the outskirts of the city which will supply the city with the energy needed for its operation throughout its life could be built first and used for this purpose. An order-of-magnitude initial comparison of the capacities suggests that this might be feasible, at least in terms of the size of the plant required in both cases. Alongside embodied energy, the energy required for the city's operation over the course of its life cycle and the renewable energy supply systems to meet this demand were considered and calculated for both models.

Results and Conclusions

The results show that in both the tropical and the subtropical climate zones, the horizontal city model leads to higher densities, when the total land area required, comprising urban and energy land areas, is considered (Figure 4.4.4). The calculated population densities based on the urban land area alone ranges from approx. 16,000 to 52,000 P/km². The current figure for Paris, a city with a high urban density, is approx. 20,000 P/km². If we include the energy land areas, the densities reduce to a range between approx. 7,000 and 14,000 P/km². Based on the land area of the earth, the current urban population and the urban land area figures given above, we can calculate the current average density of urban areas on the planet at approx. 1,350 P/km², showing that the achieved densities of both models considered here are very high compared to the current average. The results obtained confirm the results of the previous research described above, showing that increasing the urban density above a certain point leads to lower overall population density, if the area for energy infrastructure is included. The model was also tested for an in-between urban density configuration and the results were found to lie in-between the horizontal and vertical models, suggesting an approximate linear relationship.

The vertical city model, however, has one very important advantage. The land footprint for the urban area is significantly lower. The two types of land, urban land and energy land, can be – and probably should be – considered separately and treated differently. Energy land is arguably of a more ephemeral nature, i.e. the infrastructure is lighter and can be more easily removed, compared to the situation for urban land. Therefore, energy land could be considered less impactful than urban land with the potential to touch the ground more lightly. Furthermore, energy land could be combined with farming and food production – "Agrivoltaics" (Goetzberger and Zastrow, 1982) resulting in positive benefits and symbiotic effects. On the other hand, in hot climates and particularly in desert regions, the vertical model might perform particularly well, as the abundant desert land cannot be used for any other productive purpose. As a side note, the area of the planet taken up by desert is increasing due to climate change (Nunez, 2019).

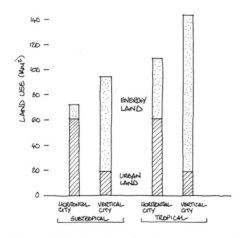 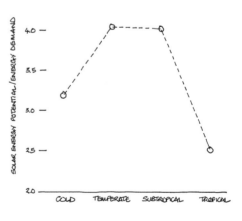

Figure 4.4.4 Resulting densities and comparison of the zero-carbon potential in different climate zones (Image Courtesy of Author).

It is instructive to consider the relationship between solar energy potential and specific energy demand for the four climate zones. Figure 4.4.4 shows that the temperate and sub-tropical are the most promising in terms of achieving optimal density, and the tropical climate zone – where most building activity and the construction of the majority of new cities is predicted to take place – is by far the worst case! However, as discussed in Cody (2022), this climate zone has a significant advantage in terms of the requirement for energy storage, a major element in any future strategy involving a society based on renewable energy sources. This attribute may compensate for some of the disadvantages of lower density.

To understand how responsive the model outputs are to changes in the input variables, sensitivity analysis was carried out. As a result of this, one parameter was found to have a significant influence; the area factor used to allow for optimal spacing between PV arrays to avoid mutual shading and allow maintenance in the large-scale solar systems on the city outskirts. In the model, an area factor of 0.53 is assumed. This means that for every 1 m² of PV collector area, 1.88 m² of land is used. If this factor can be improved, and that might be possible in the tropical climate zone, where the optimal PV tilt angle is small and the solar elevation high, the performance of the vertical city improves relative to the horizontal city model.

In the calculations above, we have focused on the important issue of land. The availability of the necessary raw materials for the city's construction, including the vast amounts of renewable energy infrastructure required, has not been considered. Strategies for disposal and/or recycling have also not been explicitly considered here. These are however significant issues. The phenomenon of shrinking cities has already surfaced in Europe and North America, and this is predicted to increase in these regions in the time frame we are considering here. Assuming it takes 15–20 years to construct our hypothetical city, a large part of the infrastructure and buildings will have reached the end of their useful life around 2090. According to some predictions, global population will begin to decline toward the end of this century, after reaching a peak around the year 2080 (Peek, 2022).

References

Cody, B. (2017). *Form Follows Energy: Using Natural Forces to Maximize Performance*. Berlin, Boston: Birkhaeuser.

Cody, B. (2022). *Visionary Engineered Biotopes in Bringing Nature to High Levels from: The Routledge Companion to Ecological Design Thinking, Healthful Ecotopian Visions for Architecture and Urbanis*m. Routledge.

Evans, J. (2016). The glorious failure of the experimental city: Cautionary tales from Arcosanti and Masdar City. In *The Experimental City*, 218–235. Routledge.

Food and Agriculture Organization (FAO) of the United Nations. (n.d.). SDG indicators data portal. Retrieved November 3, 2023. https://www.fao.org/sustainable-development-goals-data-portal/data/indicators

Fuller, Brandon and Romer, Paul (May 1, 2014). Urbanization as Opportunity. World Bank Policy Research Working Paper No. 6874.

Goetzberger, A., Zastrow, A. (1982). On the coexistence of solar-energy conversion and plant cultivation. *International Journal of Solar Energy*, 1(1), 55–69.

Griffiths, S., Sovacool, B. (2020). Rethinking the future low-carbon city: Carbon neutrality, green design, and sustainability tensions in the making of Masdar City. *Energy Research & Social Science*, 62, 101368.

Habitat for Humanity. Retrieved November 3, 2023. https://www.habitat.org/sites/default/files/documents/Policy-brief_housing-in-the-time-of-COVID-19-and-beyond.pdf#:~:text=An%20estimated%201.6%20billion%20people,people%20live%20without%20improved%20sanitation.

IEA. (2022). An updated roadmap to net zero emissions by 2050. https://www.iea.org/reports/world-energy-outlook-2022/an-updated-roadmap-to-net-zero-emissions-by-2050

Jackson, Tim. (2016). *Prosperity without Growth*. 2nd ed. London: Routledge.

Jarzebski, M.P., et al. (2021). Ageing and population shrinking: implications for sustainability in the urban century. *npj Urban Sustain*, 1, 17. https://doi.org/10.1038/s42949-021-00023-z.

Liu et al. (2014). How much of the world's land has been urbanized, really? A hierarchical framework for avoiding confusion. *Landscape Ecology*, 29, 763–771.

Mellinger, M. et al. (2000). Climate, water navigability, and economic development. CID Working Paper No. 24. September 1999. Center for International Development at Harvard University

Moser, S. (2020). New cities: Engineering social exclusions. *One Earth*, 2(2), 125–127.

Neumann, B. et al. (2015). Future coastal population growth and exposure to sea-level rise and coastal flooding—a global assessment. *PLOS ONE. Public Library of Science*, 10(3), 1–34.

Nunez, C. (2019). Desertification, explained. Humans are driving the transformation of drylands into desert on an unprecedented scale around the world, with serious consequences. But there are solutions. National Geographic.

Office of the Director of National Intelligence, ODNI. (2021). Structural forces. *Demographics, and Human Development*. Retrieved November 3, 2023. https://www.dni.gov/index.php/gt2040-home/gt2040-structural-forces/demographics-and-human-development

Paszkowska-Kaczmarek, Natalia E. (2021). The line – the Saudi-Arabian linear city concept as the protype of future cities. *Architecturae et Artibus*, 13–2(48). Sciendo.

Peek, K. (December 7, 2022). *Global Population Growth Is Slowing Down. Here's One Reason Why*. Scientific American.

Tiseo, Ian. (2023). Statista. Retrieved November 3, 2023. https://www.statista.com/statistics/276629/global-co2-emissions/#:~:text=Since%201990%2C%20global%20CO%E2%82%82%20emissions,5.01%20GtCO%E2%82%82%20in%202021%2C%20respectively.

United Nations. Global issues, population, our growing population. Retrieved November 3, 2023. https://www.un.org/en/global-issues/population

UN Habitat. SDG 11: Sustainable cities and Make cities and human settlements inclusive, safe, resilient and sustainable communities. https://unhabitat.org/sites/default/files/2023/07/2023_hlpf_factsheet_sdg_11_2.pdf

Walton, Molly. (2019). Desalinated water affects the energy equation in the Middle East. https://www.iea.org/commentaries/desalinated-water-affects-the-energy-equation-in-the-middle-east.

Wang, X. et al. 2019. Evaluating the challenges of eco-city development in China: A comparison of Tianjin and Dongtan eco-cities. *IDPR*, 41(2), 215–242.

WHO. (n.d.). Water supply, sanitation and hygiene monitoring. Retrieved November 3, 2023. https://www.who.int/teams/environment-climate-change-and-health/water-sanitation-and-health/monitoring-and-evidence/wash-monitoring.

Wilkinson, Allie. (2014). Science. Expanding tropics will play greater global role, report predicts. Retrieved November 3, 2023. https://www.science.org/content/article/expanding-tropics-will-play-greater-global-role-report-predicts

World Bank. (2013). https://www.worldbank.org/en/news/feature/2013/08/19/coastal-cities-at-highest-risk-floods.

4.5

SUSTAINABLE SMART COLD LIVING HABITATS – LESSON FROM ANTARCTICA FOR OTHER EARTH LOCATIONS IN THE LIGHT OF CLIMATE CRISIS

Ewa Kuryłowicz, Piotr Kuczyński and Karolina Czumaj

Abstract

This chapter focuses on smart technologies and a project being developed to conserve energy, recycle heat, rethink building envelope systems, stabilize homes situated on melting permafrost, and ensure supplies of fresh air. As the communities of the Circumpolar North adapt to climate change, their solutions hold lessons for carbon-neutral designs in the very cold temperature zone and also in other Earth areas. The severe climatic conditions as well as no waste requirements of the localization on King George Island, and the South Shetland Archipelago on the South Pole were the reasons to come up with the solutions that turn deficits into potentials. Nature was the source here both for the buildings' architecture and for its economic dimension. The design of the Arctowski Polish Antarctic Station presented in this chapter is both purposeful and at the same time different from other examples within its category. The demanding conditions it must endure have led to innovative solutions that can be implemented in future construction projects, also in less extreme locations. From the wooden huts of the first explorers, sealskins, and natural furs, the materials used to protect people have come a long way, to the usage of fiberglass or metal composites, as seen in the construction of the Arctowski station. The "design for disassembly" principle, which is imperative in Antarctica, favors the use of wood. However, with the Antarctic conditions and observations made so far, it is essential to exercise caution while selecting building and equipment materials to prevent plastic pollution in this sensitive and easily monitored ecosystem. Lessons learned in the Antarctic should be applied elsewhere.

What Can We Learn from Extreme Conditions? Creative Strategies – Turning Deficits into Potential

What are contemporary architecture's best assets for the future? At times of climate crisis, with storms ravaging forests, flooding destroying cities, and road infrastructure

DOI: 10.4324/9781003384113-53

disappearing into the ground, buildings need to be able to respond to the ever-increasing challenges of the natural world. And the more we neglect and monopolize nature, the greater these challenges become (Figure 4.5.1). If we are to have a future on Earth, we need to rethink how we treat our planet. The architectural community has been debating the principles of ecology, sustainability, and resilience since the late 1960s. What used to be the essence of environmental awareness, as described in the concept of the Three Rs – Recycle, Remake, Reuse – is based on the old belief of the Western world that *"necessity is the mother of invention"*. This motto, echoing across different languages of Europe and America,[1] implies an attitude based on the principle of acting only when there is a need. Even if not, everyone is prepared to acknowledge the reality of the climate crisis – which unfortunately is still the case – the extreme local environmental conditions found in certain regions of the Earth clearly demand action to be taken. At Expo 2020 in Dubai last year, the architectural forms of many pavilions demonstrated innovative and creative strategies for turning deficits into potential. In the case of the Terra Pavilion, the simple observation that it is noticeably cooler underground in 50-degree heat and that air circulation can be enhanced by extracting air through a chimney supporting a canopy has led to the development of a building designed to work in harmony with the desert environment rather than resist it. New types of buildings, designed with a real, rather than declarative, respect for nature demonstrate that authentic sustainable solutions generate a unique alphabet of architectural forms. We hope that our design for the comprehensive redevelopment of the Arctowski Polish Antarctic Station managed by the Institute of Biochemistry and Biophysics of the Polish Academy of Sciences located on King George Island in the South Shetland Archipelago will also contribute its characters to this alphabet. Discovered in approximately 1820, Antarctica remains the final continent to be explored by humans. It has never had an indigenous population (Baroni, 2021). There is nothing on King George Island except nature and the buildings

Figure 4.5.1 General view of Arctowski Polish Antarctic Station, visualization K&A, 2020+.
Source: K&A archives.

of existing Antarctic stations maintained by a number of countries, including Poland. Everything that is needed for the construction and subsequent operation of the expanded station will have to be brought in by a rough sea route. All household and construction waste must be transported out of Antarctica. Early in the design and construction process, decisions had to be made to move the building inland due to rising sea levels. Not only the harsh weather conditions but also international agreements on environmental protection made it necessary to adopt solutions that clearly and precisely apply the aforementioned 3Rs principles, both in the design of the building and during its construction. Antarctica is threatened by the destructive impacts of human civilization, and not just in the form of melting glaciers. Tourism continues to grow, and illegal fishing is also on the rise. Despite the Antarctic Treaty, which has been updated since 1950, and the 1991 Protocol on Environmental Protection (the Madrid Protocol), only 1.5% of the surface of the continent is protected, compared to 15% of the surface of the Earth, and it remains unclear who owns Antarctica (Mottal, 2021). This adds to our responsibility in proposing and contributing to the already extensive built environment on this continent. In the 200 years since Antarctica was discovered,

> /.../ between 80 and 100 facilities of various kinds were set up, with some countries owning more than 10 stations on this continent. A large number of these are concentrated on the Antarctic Peninsula, which is the most accessible region of the continent and the most rapidly warming part of our globe/...

The shape of the facility, which is an extension of the Arctowski Polish Antarctic Station complex, is determined by a number of factors, including environmental conditions, which had to be accommodated in the design. One of the most important considerations was the need to adapt to the katabatic wind, capable of attaining immense speeds and carrying debris that could cause significant damage to buildings. The mental well-being of the polar explorers was also a top priority. During their year-long stay, they will be exposed to extreme stressors. These include the isolation and solitude that come with being far from home and surrounded by wilderness, as well as the constant and prolonged companionship of the same people. The Station's spatial design should offer room for integration, physical recreation, and communal activities as well as provide privacy and personal space for each resident. Another important factor was the need for a modular design of the elements that make up the facility, which had to make optimum use of the available volume of the shipping containers so that the number of containers was kept to a minimum for economic reasons. On top of this, the project has also been affected by political turmoil.

The current political situation has had a completely unexpected impact on the construction work currently underway (Autumn 2023). As the distance between Poland and Antarctica is 14,000 km, the new facility has to be transported by water, with the final leg being carried out by a Russian shipping unit. As a result of the war in Ukraine and severed relations with Putin's state, an alternative mode of transportation had to be found. Fortunately, a suitable option was available.

The design of the extension pavilion of the Arctowski Polish Antarctic Station is both purposeful and very different from other examples within its category. The demanding conditions it must endure have led to innovative solutions that we can implement in future construction projects, also in less extreme locations. This serves as an example of how smart, sustainable building can create a livable environment in the harsh Antarctic climate.

Project Site Conditions vs. Implementation Conditions – Design for Disassembly as an Inevitable Strategy. Geography and Climate Conditions

Temperature

King George Island, home to the Arctowski Polish Antarctic Station, has a high annual temperature amplitude, typical of a subpolar climate. The average air temperature in the vicinity of the station is –1.7°C, falling to –32°C in winter, while in summer it is close to 0°C, with a record high of +16°C. This gives rise to a number of challenges. In the harsh conditions of extreme cold, the temperature impacts the delivery schedule for construction equipment and materials, as well as the construction itself, and it dictates the annual operating cycle of the station. Construction work can only be carried out during the 120-day Antarctic summer, which lasts from December to March. Deliveries are only possible when the bay is clear of ice. Even the smallest delays can lead to months of disruption. Every component must precisely fit the other parts, as the small assembly team has neither the time nor any on-site workshop facilities. A characteristic feature of the climate in the South Shetland Archipelago is the frequent fluctuations in temperature, ranging from sub-zero to above zero. This poses a significant challenge to the building's structural elements, envelope, and other components during installation. The temperature also affects the operating cycle of the building. The station's three-part modular structure allows selected functional areas within the building to be expanded, or even partially dismantled, according to the users' needs.

Land

The Antarctic provides unique opportunities for scientific monitoring and investigation of processes of both global and regional significance that are essential for understanding the environment. The station is located in an area protected under the Madrid Protocol, which sets out legal provisions for the protection of the environment. It regulates human activities in the area and lays out principles for minimizing impacts on climate, fauna, flora, air, and water quality. Given the challenges posed by environmental change and the unique nature of the site, it was particularly important to assess the environmental impact on the building. The Antarctic Specially Protected Area (ASPA-128), which borders the station, is a strict nature reserve. One of the consequences of the regulations governing this region is that there are limitations on the extent to which the ground can be altered. Considering the specific location and the need to protect the land, the design team opted to elevate the station above ground level. When designing the facility, the team had to take into account the entire life cycle of the building. One of the key considerations in the lifecycle analysis of the station was to address the stages of demolition, recycling, and waste disposal. Every single element of the building will have to be transported back to Poland for disposal. Design decisions were heavily influenced by anticipated environmental costs and measures to reduce emissions. The facility was designed with modular elements so that it can be dismantled in stages if necessary. The timber superstructure can be easily reused on-site or used as fuel, reducing the amount of waste that would have to be transported by sea.

Water

The South Shetland Islands, where the Antarctic Station is located, lie at a distance of 14,000 km from Europe, making the journey a significant challenge. A direct voyage by ship from Poland takes place once a year and lasts more than a month. The ship delivers the crew, equipment, and supplies for the station's entire year of operation.

Other problems include heavy and frequent rainfall and humidity levels of up to 80–90% brought on by marine air masses. The proximity of seawater causes constant sea aerosols to impact all structures, leading to accelerated rusting of metals and chemical corrosion of wood, which is highly susceptible to moisture. To protect the building from corrosion, a special metal alloy has been used for the façade. The existing station is situated directly on the seafront, and the sea level has been rising significantly in recent decades. As a result of climate change, the current building – once 30 meters from the shore – is now at risk of periodic flooding during high tides and storms. The southern part of the station site is taken up by the so-called Jasnorzewski Gardens, a waterlogged, unstable area with numerous depressions. As the entire area is situated on a low, waterlogged terrain of marine accumulation, the groundwater level is up to 20 cm below the surface and the site is covered with mud during periods when there is no snow. Sediments are deposited by local streams and the sea. During periods of heavy snowmelt, local flooding occurs. This is why the new station is located at some distance from the shore. The large number of footings allows for a better distribution of loads and reduces uneven subsidence of the facility.

Wind

The South Shetland Islands are located in the most turbulent region of the southern hemisphere, which makes wind a climatic factor with a significant impact on the site. The winds can reach hurricane force, with gusts exceeding 60 m/s, blowing buildings out of the ground. The station's existing main building – a simple one-story pavilion – was nicknamed "the Airplane", not only because of its shape but also because of the turbulence it experienced during high winds. The station is mainly exposed to winds from the south- and northwest. The most powerful winds arrive in the form of vortices from the direction of the Ezcurra Inlet or along the ice tongues, usually around midday. Because of the varied coastline, they tend to be turbulent, resulting in very strong gusts. Currently, the Arctowski Polish Antarctic Station consists of multiple structures situated in different parts of the site that require either refurbishment or replacement with new buildings. In windy conditions, the walking time from the main building to the other facilities can become significantly longer, despite their apparent proximity. This revealed the need to consolidate all functions in one place and to integrate storage, cold rooms, greenhouses, and laboratories into the structure of the main building in order to minimize the hazards faced by polar explorers and to improve working conditions. The building's design and orientation were optimized to minimize resistance to gusts of wind, based on data collected on wind direction and speed. The structure consists of wedge-shaped elements which redirect the wind to the sides. The stormy winds, prevalent in the Archipelago, blow an average of 81 days per year, carrying small stones, sand, and gravel that make up the terraced platform the station rests on. These small elements are carried by the wind up to a height of 2 meters, grinding and abrading all surfaces.

Snow

Rain and snowfall are extremely frequent, with only two to three days per month without precipitation. A permanent snow cover persists from June to November but also forms temporarily during other months. The users of the Polish Antarctic Station have encountered a significant problem with snow blowing onto the walls of the buildings during the winter months (from the end of March to the end of November). Buildings that sit directly on the ground are buried on all sides, to the point of being unusable. During the design phase, weather analysis data was collected, and simulations of snow accumulation were carried out. The resulting conclusions had a significant impact on the building's design. To ensure the personnel's safety and reduce the risk of the crew being trapped inside, it was crucial to guarantee the free flow of air and snow underneath the structure. The building's entrance area is slightly elevated above ground, located centrally but sheltered in a well-protected recess. Evacuation routes are also available at the end of each wing of the facility. Since the station can be cut off from the world for up to several months during periods of severe weather, self-sufficiency is essential. This has been achieved through hydroponic cultivation, which is able to meet the basic needs of the residents. The crops are watered from a melting glacier.

Other hazards include snow blizzards, which occur due to winds exceeding 10 m/s and drastically reduce visibility. The yellow color scheme, associated with the Arctowski station by polar explorers from other countries, makes it easier to detect an object in dense snow because humans have evolved to interpret it as a warning. As a result, yellow can help users locate the object using basic instincts.

Sun

Due to its proximity to the Antarctic Circle, the site – located approximately 120 km from the Antarctic coast – experiences half-years of extended daylight and half-years of extended periods of darkness lasting over 20 hours. Polar explorers working in small groups are not only exposed to solitude but also to the extreme stressors associated with low levels of natural light. Sunlight measurements were taken on each facade and wing of the building to decide where different functions should be located. Diagrams based on these analyses helped us choose optimal locations for communal areas and zones dedicated to work and leisure. When designing the new building, we aimed to blend the architecture into the surrounding landscape and orientate the view toward the north, where sunlight is most abundant. The relatively large windows – compared to other buildings of this type – break through the metal cladding of the station and provide the permanent residence rooms with an optimum amount of natural light and a wide view of the bay and other station buildings (Figure 4.5.2).

Building Life Cycle

Development (Construction and Transport vs. Design Implications)

The extremely harsh weather conditions on the islands, with strong katabatic winds, sub-zero temperatures, and high levels of precipitation, affected both the form and the spatial design of the building. Extensive analysis and innovative solutions were necessary to

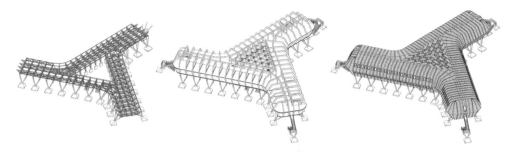

Figure 4.5.2   Axonometric drawing of the new main station building, visualization K&A.
Source: Kuryłowicz & Associates, 2020.

address the extreme climate and lighting conditions at the Antarctic Circle. The logistical constraints, as well as the lack of the necessary technical infrastructure on site, meant that the building had to be designed as a set of locally assembled modules.

The meteorological conditions described above were not the only major factors influencing the shape and form of the new station building. The success of the project depends heavily on the ability to address the logistical considerations and associated construction challenges.

To fully comprehend the overall process and the significance of the distance between the manufacturing site in Poland and the construction site in Antarctica, it is essential to consider the complex technological cycle involved: prefabrication, test assembly, disassembly, transport, and final assembly. This cycle involves the use of advanced material and design solutions to ensure that assembly is carried out in a way that minimizes, if not eliminates, potential errors and inaccuracies. To make this possible, the process was divided into three construction and material phases: concrete foundation blocks, a profiled steel substructure, and the main body of the building, based on a glulam timber superstructure.

Using the latest computer modeling technology, a detailed model of the building and each of its elements was created to maximize repeatability and maintain full modularity. Realistic modeling was conducted for each structural connection, and a simulation was developed to illustrate the installation sequence of every beam, column, and floor element. The distribution of utilities was planned in detail by creating special openings in the prefabricated elements.

The structure was designed to be anchored to 36 concrete blocks. These were prefabricated in Poland and shipped by sea to King George Island at the start of winter 2021, just as Antarctic summer was about to begin. The blocks were placed in their intended position, measured with precise surveying, and leveled to within a millimeter. The foundation blocks have special notches designed to ensure precise connection to the steel substructure of the station.

The steel platform, which creates the "legs" that elevate the building off the ground, arrived on the same transport. Approximately 65% of the required construction components were transported to the site, with 35% remaining in Poland to enable trial assembly of the building's main structural elements. The use of a platform allows the building to be raised off the ground, ensuring the rigidity of the structure and providing space for the placement of technical equipment required for its operation.

The next phase of the construction project will include the modular core structure of the building and façade cladding.

The core structure will be made of glulam timber, steel connections, and prefabricated external cladding panels made of plywood, filled with layers of wind, thermal, and acoustic insulation. The whole construction will be covered with sheet metal modules made of an alloy of copper and aluminum, which is resistant to abrasion and corrosion and ensures adequate rigidity. The station will be fitted with multi-glazed windows that will not only provide good insulation but will also be able to withstand stone impacts. This crucial stage will also be the most challenging, and to be successful it must follow the correct technological cycle mentioned above. The main elements of the timber superstructure, such as columns, girders, joists, and floor slabs, will be fabricated in a glulam timber factory and then test assembled in a selected repetitive fragment on a steel substructure that was left in Poland for this purpose. Similarly, a selected section of the façade will be manufactured in the form of a number of modules, which will then be test assembled. The tests will be used to validate the solutions and to make any necessary adjustments to the design and manufacturing process. It is only on the basis of the experience gained that the final production of all the components of the modular structure and housing will begin.

Following the principles of modular design, the entire building structure is divided into modules and elements that do not exceed 233×586×219 cm in size and fit into standard shipping containers. Algorithms will be utilized to minimize the number of containers necessary, with emphasis placed on the efficient and environment-friendly use of container space.

Other factors taken into consideration include the performance of on-site construction machinery, including crane capacity for handling individual components and the buoyancy of pontoons used to transport modules from the ship to the mainland, as well as the assembly capacity of the construction crew on-site, where no industrial facilities are available.

Building as an Organism and Living Environment

Functional Layout

The Arctowski Polish Antarctic Station currently operates and is expected to operate in the future, in two activity cycles. During the summer cycle, from January to March, up to 37 people can be present at the station, while the winter cycle, which covers the remaining seasons, requires the presence of no more than 13 polar explorers to conduct the most demanding research.

Starting work on the project, we asked ourselves a fundamental question: What happens to researchers who spend an endless winter in polar conditions? How do they cope with the stress of being isolated and living in a small group? What measures would they hope for to reduce this stress?

Based on the client's brief, a functional layout was drawn up, which dictated a clear three-way division of functions and specified the requirements for each room. It takes into account, among other things, the visibility of the station site and the surrounding bay, sunlight and shading conditions, wind directions, the weather conditions at the entrance area, as well as the positioning of spaces dedicated to work, leisure, and technology.

The design features individual single-occupancy living spaces, double and four-bed (one-six-bed) guest rooms for visiting researchers, lecture rooms, storage rooms, laboratories, workspaces, and research rooms. The most important areas, however, are those that foster a sense of community. These include the relaxation zone, the fitness room with a sauna, and the canteen and dining room – the perfect place to meet and share a cup of tea. All of these key functions are centered around the two-story common room, which is the heart of the facility. There is no way to move around the building without crossing this area. The layout and interior design aim to encourage human interaction and create a sense of well-being and psycho-physical comfort, which is crucial as the residents of this building are literally isolated from the outside world and confined to each other's company for long periods of time.

The multi-functional interior space also includes a greenhouse which, beyond its utilitarian purpose, is intended to become a substitute for a park for the station's residents. The naturally lit space will allow for the year-round cultivation of herbs and vegetables – yet another place to promote communal activity.

Systems

To ensure the well-being of the occupants, specially designed system solutions will be used. It is crucial to emphasize that in Antarctic conditions, sources of water, electricity, and heat are predefined and specific. Water at the station is sourced from an intake located in an artificial reservoir fed by a melting glacier. It will be supplied to the central building using a hydrophore system, which is housed in the technical building nearby. The water will be used for household purposes, including cooking and watering plants in the greenhouse. Domestic hot water for sanitary appliances will be produced locally in electric storage water heaters. Sanitary wastewater will be directed into the already existing pumping station for biological treatment. The design of the treatment facility to maintain the effective operation of the microbial bed under harsh temperature conditions and varying volumes of wastewater proved to be a significant technical challenge.

During the Antarctic winter, the building will be occupied by a smaller research crew. To minimize the amount of energy required to operate the station during these periods, all of the building's services have been designed as decentralized systems. The station rooms will be heated by electric radiators. Electricity will be generated using an upgraded diesel power station. Photovoltaic panels will be used to back up the generators and surplus energy will be stored in energy banks.

The design was guided by the idea that the systems should be functional and flexible and that any solutions adopted should allow for easy and effective organization of floor space and future expansion. Throughout the design process, measures were taken to guarantee that the solutions implemented could be executed swiftly, utilizing readily available technologies (Figure 4.5.3).

Minimizing the Negative Impact of Construction Projects on the Environment – Lessons from Antarctica

The Madrid Protocol of 1991, which entered into force seven years later, regulates the legal aspects of the environmental impact of new buildings in Antarctica. The document outlines fundamental principles for human presence and access to mineral resources and stipulates

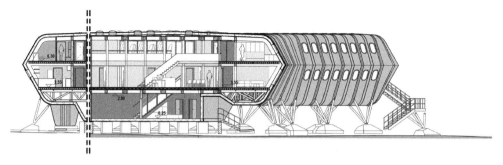

Figure 4.5.3   Section of New Main Station Building, visualization K&A.

Source: Kuryłowicz & Associates, 2020.

that anything that has been brought to Antarctica must be transported off the continent at the end of its useful life. To comply with legislation, newly constructed facilities, including the Arctowski Polish Antarctic Station, implement prototype solutions that can also be seen as examples of different approaches to protecting pristine areas. They also demonstrate what kind of measures can be adopted in less demanding environments. Although developed out of necessity, they offer innovative environmental, economic, and other benefits for everyday use in moderate climates.

The environmental impact of a new building can be measured on various levels.

Ideally, and somewhat metaphorically, similar to the process of grafting a fruit tree, the new object (the equivalent of the branch being grafted) penetrates the natural substrate (the equivalent of the tree) to produce a new species. In this case, a building that is resistant to frost, wind, and snow. And just as in grafting, the building becomes one with its surroundings. The geotechnical properties of the natural terrain on King George Island pose significant challenges. During the summer months, when construction is feasible, the station site is covered with mud caused by shallow groundwater. Just below the surface, however, the ground is stable, as there is solid rock beneath the mud. This means that building foundations have to extend approximately 1 meter deep into the ground.

A spread footing foundation is beneficial as it reduces the number of contact points with the ground, allowing for lighter weight distribution and better ventilation. Additionally, they facilitate the elevation of the building, thus minimizing the risk of damage from snow accumulation, which has the potential to pose a serious threat to buildings. There is the well-known case of the German Neumayer II station, built on a glacier in 1992, which was literally crushed under the weight of snow. The new station, Neumayer III, which was built in 2007, sits on height-adjustable hydraulic columns, allowing snow to be blown underneath the building and actively managed during snowstorms (Schramm, 2021). The Arctowski Station, designed in 2016 using lessons learned from other such facilities in Antarctica, is also elevated on support for economic and practical reasons. In a small entrance vestibule under the pavilion, there is a room for changing and drying muddy and wet clothes, so that staff can enter the main level of the building in fresh clothing. Such a functional solution reduces the volume of wastewater by minimizing the number of washing cycles required. It also saves valuable snowmelt water, which is difficult to collect. This demonstrates that even if water is conveniently provided by the municipal water supply and collected by the municipal sewerage system, implementing efficient solutions in buildings to help reduce the need to wash clothes and clean equipment can significantly alleviate the burden on the local hydrogeological system.

The harsh Antarctic environment makes it easier and quicker to detect the negative impact of plastics in terms of so-called plastic pollution – a phenomenon that is discussed in the context of construction, but the debate is often clouded by a lack of hard data. In a land like Antarctica, nothing can be hidden.

> /.../ The latest news from the South reveals that plastic pollution does not only affect Antarctic marine wildlife but also has reached terrestrial food webs, as shown by the polystyrene traces found in the digestive tract of the Antarctic soil collembolan *Cryptopygus antarcticus* which was feeding on a piece of polystyrene foam covered by algae, moss, and lichens on King George Island. In this region, stranded polystyrene foam has previously been associated with the spread of antibiotic resistance genes suggesting that microplastics may alter soil properties, microbial communities, and biodiversity within Antarctic terrestrial ecosystems.
>
> *(Bergami, 2021)*

From the wooden huts of the first explorers, sealskins, and natural furs, the materials used to protect people who have come a long way, to the usage of fiberglass or metal composites, as seen in the construction of the Arctowski station. The "design for disassembly" principle, which is imperative in Antarctica, favors the use of wood. However, with the Antarctic conditions and observations made so far, it is essential to exercise caution while selecting building and equipment materials to prevent plastic pollution of this sensitive and easily monitored ecosystem.

The rapid pace of on-site construction, driven by the "weather window" of the short Antarctic summer and transport economics, necessitated the use of lightweight modules for the Arctowski Polish Antarctic Station expansion project to allow for quick assembly upon arrival at the construction site. This approach reduces the negative impact of construction machinery and accumulated packaging, requires operational flexibility, and anticipates the various scenarios that may arise on-site after long and costly transport. Efficient organization of the construction process, based on the above considerations, can significantly aid the construction logistics of any building, regardless of location.

During the Antarctic summer, facilities in Antarctica are also tourist destinations. Mass international tourism, halted somewhat by the COVID-19 pandemic but rebounding again (2023), is being increasingly opposed by local communities in cities such as Barcelona and Venice, trampled by unlimited numbers of visitors. The need to protect the Antarctic environment in the face of an exponential increase in the number of visitors from various countries has resulted in the introduction of limits for groups disembarking at any one time to 100 people and a limit for the capacity of vessels (the vast majority of tourists arrive by sea) to 500 people. These principles designed to safeguard Antarctica's delicate ecosystem are rooted in Measure 15 (2009), which is binding for the Antarctic Treaty Consultative Parties (Liggett, 2021). It would seem advisable to extend similar principles to other places on Earth.

Lessons learned in the Antarctic should be applied elsewhere (Foscari G. (red.), 2021).

Ewa Kuryłowicz et al.

References

Abdel Mottal, D. (2021). "Antarctic Resources and the Protocol of Environmental Protection" in: *Antarctic Resolution*, ed. Giulia Foscari, Zurich, Lars Muller Publishers, pp. 136–137.

Baroni, C., Fox, A., Harris, U., Pirlot, J.-Y. (2021). "Naming the Antarctic" in: *Antarctic Resolution*, ed. Giulia Foscari, Zurich, Lars Muller Publishers, p. 82.

Bergami, E. Corsi (2021). "The Emerging Issue of Plastic Pollution in Antarctica" in: *Antarctic Resolution*, ed. Giulia Foscari, Lars Muller Publishers, p. 159.

Foscari, G. (ed.) (2021). "Henryk Arctowski 1977/2020+" in: *Archive of Antarctic Architecture*, pp. 601–875, fragment: *Antarctic Resolution*, ed. G. Foscari, Lars Muller Publishers, pp. 848–851.

Liggett, D. (2021). "Antarctic Tourism" in: *Antarctic Resolution*, ed. Giulia Foscari, Zurich, Lars Muller Publishers, p. 165.

Schramm, T. (2021). "Design for Removal: The Life Cycle of Antarctic Stations" in: *Antarctic Resolution*, ed. G. Foscari, Lars Muller Publishers, p. 503.

4.6

ENVISIONING ECOLOGICAL PLANNING MERGED WITH SMART TECHNOLOGIES AND DENSITY

Frederick Besançon

Abstract
Open space, through ecological services that are augmented by smart mapping tools, can provide many benefits to urban living and smart ecological planning to increase biodiversity, resilience, and improve people's health and well-being. Open space can be a tool to restrict sprawl, like that of an urban growth boundary, or promote density by limiting where development can occur. Smart density has many benefits such as less carbon use, less miles traveled, improve walkability, and lower costs along with the preservation of valuable open space resources. Moreover, smart urban planning needs to account for the "more-than-human" species with principles that support and foster biodiversity and ecological richness to foster a holistic environment. Ecology is not independent from the city's effects as negative conditions like pollution or poor habitat will impact the local, immediate, and surrounding settings. Consequently, planners should incorporate the smart tools used in analyzing traffic, transit, energy flows, or crime to include nature in data gathering and analysis to tabulate ecological value, promote biodiverse richness, and understand the effectiveness of restoration work. Furthermore, these smart technologies can reveal ecological conditions to the public-at-large to help them understand their neighborhood's environment and to foster public action to improve it.

Open space, through ecological services, can provide benefits to urban living and smart ecological planning to increase biodiversity, resilience, and improve people's health and well-being. Smart tools, like those used to analyze traffic, transit, energy flows, or crime, should be extended to include nature in data gathering and analysis to tabulate ecological value, promote biodiverse richness, and understand the effectiveness of restoration work. These smart technologies can reveal ecological conditions to the public-at-large to help them understand their neighborhood's environment and to foster public action to improve it.

There is an intrinsic relationship between density and open space: with a given population the denser the city, the more open space is preserved. Architects Adrian Smith and

DOI: 10.4324/9781003384113-54

Gordon Gill take this inquiry to its limits when they pose the question "What if we could build a mile high?" in their book, *Residensity* (Smith and Gill, 2018, p. 7). Their question raises the fundamental issues of how we construct for our ever-growing population. Are there benefits to such density – will such a feat improve the urban condition, maximize land effectiveness, decrease carbon use, and benefit the planet? (Smith and Gill, 2018) To house our increasing population, we can either push past the exurbs, create new satellite cities linked via transportation routes, or build denser with infill development. Architect and urban designer Peter Calthorpe argues that while clean sources of energy will be important to reduce our impact on the planet, smart urbanism, "*is, in fact, our single most potent weapon against climate change, rising energy costs, and environmental degradation*" (Calthorpe, 2011 p. 17 emphasis in original).

Open space, or more specifically the protection and restoration of ecologically significant places, can be used as a tool to encourage density, improve urban conditions, and promote urban biodiversity. While smart city planning sometimes uses the metaphor of ecology to describe a city's interconnectedness and sustainability (Rzevski et al., 2020), actual urban ecology needs to be infused into the city along with similar measurement tools afforded by smart city design. Such an integration affords the benefits of urban nature for human and non-human species.

Earlier Visions of Density and Open Space

In the early twentieth century, thinkers like Frank Lloyd Wright and Le Corbusier addressed the negatives in the post-industrial revolution city – conditions that were increasingly more polluted, dark, crowded, and chaotic. The two not only presented integrated concepts for town forms but also how societies need to be re-structured to reflect the ideals reflected in those designs (Fishman, 1977). They used open space as a mechanism to improve the community and individual by providing physical and psychological benefits like fresh air, light, relaxation, and repose. They saw emerging technologies like the automobile and electronic communication as important mechanisms to benefit their visions (Wright, 1945; Le Corbusier, 1987).

In *The City of To-Morrow and its Planning*, Le Corbusier recounts a meeting with the master gardener of Bois du Boulogne, who lamented Paris' lack of greenery and poor air. The gardener opined that Paris needed 20–50% open space for fresh air. Le Corbusier recognized this deficiency and used it as a key criterion for his ideal city plan. Le Corbusier rationalized that "The towns of today can only increase in density at the expense of the open spaces which are the lungs of a city. We must *increase the open spaces...*" (Le Corbusier, 1987, p. 167, emphasis in original). To get to, and surpass the master gardener's target, Le Corbusier pushed for hyper-dense city cores of 1,000 people per hectare consisting of autonomous high-rise towers in a field of park-like spaces. To enforce and focus this highly dense center, he argued for the simultaneous "*legal establishment* of that absolute necessity: a protective zone which allows extension, *a reserved zone* of woods and fields, a fresh air reserve" (Le Corbusier, 1987, p 166 emphasis in original). Le Corbusier argues that the creation of this protective zone "is one of the most essential and urgent tasks which a municipality can pursue. It would eventually represent a tenfold return on the capital invested" (Le Corbusier, 1987, p 174).

While Le Corbusier argued for 1,000 people per acre, Wright retorted that "1,000 people to the 'hectare' (two and a half acres) is not looking extremely far ahead. That is just 997

1/2 too many" (Wright, 1945, p. 43). Wright's response to Le Corbusier was his Broadacre City which pushed for individual land ownership with each citizen receiving their own acre for direct access to light, air, and greenery (Wright, 1945). Today, we see the unfortunate side effect of this approach with expansive land use which became sprawl and the parcellation of nature.

Both viewed nature as an instrument at the service of humankind; Le Corbusier saw wilderness as a negative, "present[ing] itself to us as a chaos... its kaleidoscopic fragments and its vague distances, is a confusion...Seen by us without reference to any other thing, the aspects of Nature seem purely accidental" (Le Corbusier, 1987, p 19). His urban spaces consequently looked to control the outdoors via order and use (Le Corbusier, 1987). Wright exalts nature, striving for the harmonization between indoors and outdoors, but his attitude toward nature is one still of subserviency to human desires and happiness:

> Great woods, fields, streams, mountains, ranges of hills, the wind-blown sweep of plains, all brought into the service of Man without doing violence to them...Citizens now, who understand, revere, and conserve all natural resources whether of Materials or Men. This – to me – is Organic Architecture!
> *(Wright, 1945, p. 64)*

What can we gain from these models? These visions, in many respects, should not be seen as literal executions of a design, but the translations of aspirational goals and views of humanity visualized into physical typologies (Fishman, 1977). They established the goals of well-being, fresh air and light, and access to the outdoors against the competing interests of density and urban form. Their approaches were predicated on tabula rasa development, a simplified conceptualization of urban citizenry, unlimited capital, and a fully supportive government while ignoring existing cities. We do not have such luxuries – the value embedded in our cities as infrastructure, transportation networks, housing, and embodied energy is incalculable, and the city's citizenry is vastly more complex to readily accept wholesale a new living paradigm.

Contemporary Ideas of Density and Open Space

In the century since Corbusier's, and Wright's ideas were birthed, the concepts of ecological services, sustainability, green infrastructure, and resiliency along with the critical issues of climate change and biodiversity collapse have changed how we perceive nature. Key to our planet's survival will be the conservation, restoration, and resiliency of ecological systems, habitat, and biodiversity. Urban nature will also play a significant role as it encompasses the abundance and diversity of species within a city – flora and fauna, native and exotic, in wild spaces as well as green roofs, parks, and streets. Urban nature will play a critical role in how our cities will perform with climate change in mitigating impacts like coastal flooding, storm surge, water pollution, and the heat island effect. There are also the physiological and psychological benefits of nature, including child development, social connection, and decreased chance for cardiovascular or respiratory health issues. We must therefore look at ecological planning, or the smart integration of nature-based solutions into city planning efforts (Guerry et al., 2021). This brings up the tension between density and open space preservation; in other words, how much of the limited land supply is allocated to development versus ecological services.

A contemporaneous project, The Line (Al Khatt) in Saudi Arabia, attempts to resolve density and mobility through its unique urban form and transit network. The city is planned to hold 9 million residents within a 110-mile-long, 200-meter-wide city made up of superstructures where no cars will be allowed – just a central high-speed rail line. The Viennese think tank, Complexity Science Hub, pointed out that its basic form is not efficient for mobility. Using the same presumed density, they argue that a more efficient shape is a circle only 4 miles in diameter. With such a layout, most people will be within walking distance of 25% of the hypothetical circular city, whereas 2 random people in The Line will be over 30 miles apart (Orf, 2023). Beyond the inherent criticisms of constructing such a monumental structure in such a harsh environment, its simple urban form looks like a knife effectively severing and fragmenting existing ecosystems.

The book *Residensity* evaluates the climate impacts of residential typologies by estimating operational emissions, energy usage, infrastructure requirements, and materiality to determine the least carbon use. In this study, the four-story courtyard apartment at 20 units per 2,075 m^2 was the most carbon efficient followed by the urban single-family home (two stories with zero-lot sides) and the three-flat (three-stories with zero-lot sides). The authors acknowledge that their study does not account for the ancillary benefits of density in terms of land usage, that is, how preserved open space can be used for recreation, agriculture, habitat, or energy production. The courtyard, three-flat, and urban single-family typologies include approximately 20% open space which can provide open space benefits (Smith and Gill, 2018).

Nature Around the City

Le Corbusier's "protective zone" around the city core is analogous to today's Urban Growth Boundaries (UGBs) where governments delineate a development limit to the metropolitan area. Today's UGB's are

> devices to achieve or ensure urban containment by promoting compact and contiguous development patterns. These are patterns that can be efficiently served by public services and that preserve open space, agricultural land, and environmentally sensitive areas that may not be suitable for intensive development.
>
> *(Meck, 2002, p 6–43)*

A well-configured UGB should anticipate estimated growth and housing needs for the next 10–20 years (Meck, 2002). To resolve development pressures, some metropolitan areas institute an elastic UGB where the region permits limited growth within the protected green space to relieve development pressures (Hiramatsu, 2014). Research from Concordia University investigating 60 European cities' growth showed UGBs are effective at reducing sprawl. Ninety percent of the cities investigated showed that "the average contribution per person to urban sprawl increased by 24.2% in cities without greenbelt[s], while it decreased by 27.3% in cities with greenbelts" (Pourtaherian and Jaeger, 2022, p. 5).

Reducing sprawl has many benefits beyond more efficient land use. Using the software UrbanFootprint, Calthorpe analyzed sprawl (or "business as usual") compared to compact development in the San Francisco Bay Area and Greater Los Angeles and saw that compact development resulted in more improved living with approximately half the annual carbon emissions, improved health, and increased property values. Mobility is improved, too, with increased walkability and less than half the vehicle miles traveled per household. Urban development resulted in even higher performance. The focus is on infill development, making more efficient use of under-utilized lots while preserving intact ecological areas (Architecture 2030, 2020).

Nature within the City

While UGBs provide protected open space at the city periphery, metropolitan areas are located at some of the Earth's biological hotspots. The same features that attracted people to reside in a specific locale are those that attracted non-human species (Galle et al., 2019). Consequently, cities and their surrounding areas can be locations of threatened plant and animal species so ecological preservation is critical to avoid losing such critical habitats (Ives et al., 2016). Unfortunately, biodiversity has not been seen as important as other urban issues when it comes to urban design (Guerry et al., 2021). Artmann and others' study shows that smart growth and urban nature reinforce each other. They argue that nature needs to be integrated at a range of scales such as parks, green infrastructure, green roofs, and recreation areas for improved connectivity between people and wildlife. Their research shows that green spaces provide physical and psychological health benefits as well as civic pride and social cohesion. They argued that it is critical to unify the city's physical aspects and ecological protection with policy making. To synthesize compact city development with ecological preservation, they proposed four concepts with related indicators to measure:

- Smart environment: integrating nature and green infrastructure into urban density
- Smart multi-functionality: synergizing multi-uses, economies, ecologies, and health benefits together for job creation, affordability, and health
- Smart government: fostering leaders at multiple government scales to use their agencies to remove barriers to smart growth while championing big-picture ideas
- Smart governance: utilizing non-government actors, such as multi-disciplinary professionals, to promote sustainable strategies and shift public preferences (Artmann et al., 2017)

Another multi-disciplinary academic group took John Ruskin's classic architectural treatise, *Seven Lamps of Architecture* as inspiration to develop urban biodiversity principles in their "Seven Lamps of Planning for Biodiversity in the City." The premise was to take design principles familiar to architects, landscape architects, and urban planners but re-fashioned to address "more-than-human" species (Parris et al., 2018).

Their first two lamps recognize that there is priority placed on conserving and connecting existing high-quality biodiverse sites which are still intact to improve the overall ecological matrix. Connecting these sites leads to "metapopulations" or large groups of wildlife to improve species resiliency and potentially form new habitats. The third lamp extends conservation territories into urban features such as green roofs, vertical gardens, or on-ground planting. The fourth lamp proposes rethinking waste (e.g., water, vegetated disposal, and soil) as resources to enhance habitats by mirroring natural processes. The fifth lamp recognizes that higher trophic levels (e.g., predator) require successful lower trophic levels. Lamp six addresses how design features outside habitats can still negatively impact nature such as high-rise windows causing bird strikes. The last lamp accepts that purely native urban habitats may not be achievable and that exotic species can still form strong novel ecological systems. Because animals and plants may not be resilient to urban pressures, one must recognize that the need of a viable habitat may go against the desires of human-centric design. For example, night lighting that provides a sense of security for humans disrupts the nocturnal habitats of nearby fauna. Together, these seven lamps transform espouse that nature is more than large wilderness reserves but can occur and thrive in brownfield restoration, buffer plantings, green infrastructure, small residential yards, or within infill development (Parris et al., 2018).

Singapore as one of the world's densest cities portrays a successful integration of biodiversity and high-density living. The city opted to disperse its high-density developments amongst low-density areas in "checkboard planning" to relieve crowdedness. To give relief to the density, Singapore, as a "city in a garden," has made "pervasive greenery" an integral component to provide better cooling, air quality, and beauty by injecting plants wherever it can (10 Principles, 2013). Furthermore, the country developed the Singapore Index (or City Biodiversity Index) which tracks annually 23 metrics that quantify biodiversity values, including species richness, water quality, cultural services, and climate regulation. This index has also been successfully used by dozens of other cities (Guerry et al., 2021).

One way to protect a biological resource is to identify emblematic indicator species whose success can be publicly championed. Such actions not only have the advantage of helping the targeted species but also have added ancillary benefits, including improved habitats, better water, heightened stewardship, and enhanced citizen science. For example, the Pacific Northwest's non-profit Salmon Safe developed certification programs for site developments similar to LEED to enhance salmon habitat (Salmon-Safe Inc., 2023). When developer Mark Grey was forwarded a video by his civil engineer about salmon dying in Seattle's polluted waters, he realized he could alleviate the situation with his new office building near Lake Union. Grey reached out to Salmon Safe and government authorities to see how his project could improve salmon habitat. Salmon-Safe measured the pre-project water runoff from adjacent Aurora Bridge and determined it had more than five times the baseline amount for total suspended solids and was heavily polluted with metals (Kett, 2017). Grey's architect/landscape architect Weber Thompson developed an international award-winning landscape with bio-retention areas that cleanses nearly 2 million gallons of stormwater annually from the office's roof and roughly half of the Aurora Bridge. The terraced rain garden filters pollutants, while native plants cater to pollinators while providing a pleasant, beautiful landscape for people to traverse (Richardson, 2023). This success story demonstrates how revealing information about a local ecology's health spurred citizen action to implement ecological resiliency in an urban area (Figure 4.6.1).

Integrating Smart Technology with Ecology

In the same manner, one can use smart technologies to assess the success or operational efficiency of issues like transit, traffic, or utilities, similar methods should be utilized to infuse urban ecology into urban planning. Biodiversity goals converted into metrics can be measured and assessed to identify and achieve obtainable targets. Such actions would help facilitate larger sustainability and resiliency goals such as habitat preservation and species protection while understanding which methods work for a given locale's nuances and requirements. These metrics should be augmented by "reflective management" or government agencies who monitor the benefits of green infrastructure and landscape development.

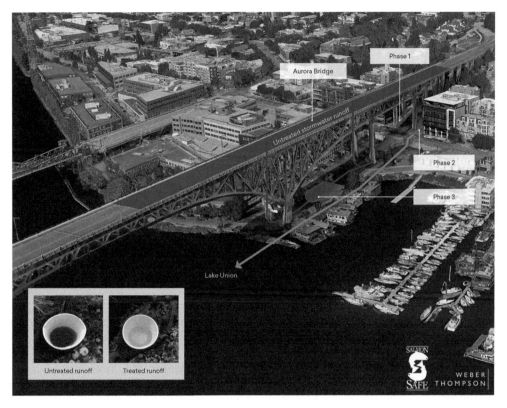

Figure 4.6.1   The three phases of the Aurora Bridge Bioswales collectively clean almost 2 million gallons of runoff annually. From (Richardson, 2023) Copyright 2023 by Weber Thompson, Reprinted with permission

These measures give such ecological services a commensurate economic value which can be assessed (Artmann et al., 2017).

One paradigm for looking at such technologies is the "Internet of Nature" or "IoN" (as compared to the Internet of Things), championed by Dr. Nadina Galle. Digital information networks are incorporated into natural systems to measure their health, viability, and ability to re-connect people to urban ecology. Technologies such as satellite imagery, remote sensing, or citizen science apps like iNaturalist can create "ecological intelligence" or overall data mapping and representation of urban ecosystems to assist urban foresters, planners, and politicians make informed decisions. For example, these technologies can inform people which street trees are better performing, which are stressed, and which contribute to a neighborhood's ecological resiliency. Galle contends that

> as cities become denser and the use of these critical spaces intensifies, having planners, ecologists, and city officials understand the 'reaction' of plants and animals to – but also enable nature to 'express its needs' about – environmental changes is critical.
>
> *(Galle et al., 2019, p. 283)*

Software like InVEST (Integrated Valuation of Ecosystem Services and Tradeoffs) helps agencies model ecological services for their economic, ecological, and social metrics for

Figure 4.6.2   The Internet of Nature. From (On the roof with, 2021) Copyright 2023 by Dr. Nadina
Galle, Reprinted with permission

better decision-making. Using InVEST along with subsequent data assessment can help
determine which efforts have positively or negatively impacted the surrounding or inner-city
wildlife (Guerry et al., 2021). Such data accumulation combined with bringing urban ecologists into the decision-making can begin to give ecology an equivalency in planning like
addressing traffic, pollution, or crime (Figure 4.6.2).

One tool to further communicate this information are digital maps which provide a strong,
visual way to express a complex web of ecological relationships and "what-if" scenarios
that are understandable to all. As Ryan Perkl, green infrastructure lead for ArcGIS, explains,
"today's mapping tools combine vast amounts of information, spanning both the built and
natural realms… Combining these layers of data unlocks insights about critical patterns and
relationships and holds immense communicative power to spur action when it's needed most"
(Perkl, 2022, p. 2). An example of such revelatory visualizations is the mappings of historic
ecologies before colonization such as the San Francisco Estuary Institute's Hidden Nature
SF initiative to identify opportune places to restore ecosystems (Baumgarten et al., 2022).

Future Visions

The goal of smart planning is to use land more effectively by reducing sprawl and building compact development while offsetting the potential negatives with relief in the form of
greenery and access to nature experiences. By incorporating ecological planning and data
to assist in the decision-making process, one can understand what measures are working or
better plan for a more adaptable city. For example, if the UGB needs to expand outwards,
decision-making should include biological data and ecologists to help analyze which of the
surrounding preserves has proven to be the most resilient or which have irrevocably been
negatively harmed. As explained in "Biodiversity in the City," the

Primary overarching issues for biodiversity planning and management are gaps between science and policy…To conserve biodiversity in [urban green spaces], diverse stakeholders – including ecologists, managers, developers, students, and citizens – should be encouraged to join in collaborative networks to share data, engage in interdisciplinary research, and discuss urban biodiversity management, design, and planning.

(Aronson et al., 2017 Conclusions section)

Strategies, details, and plant selection will differ based on microclimate, rainfall, soil type, cultural preferences, and the arrangement of existing natural resources to foster a powerful sense of place in stark contrast with the one-size fits all the utopian thinking from Wright and Corbusier. The IoN can bring together this understanding of local landscapes with the democratization of data where ecological performance can be openly communicated to foster community action.

A student project from Harvard's landscape architecture program envisions such a scenario. Abby Feldman's Fiber Optic Marsh for Providence's Field Point imagines a marine restoration where fiber optic strands are connected to chemical monitoring circuits. The strands provide physical anchorage for eel grass and epiphytes which will cleanse the damaged waters meanwhile they emit light whose color reflects the bay's contamination and eutrophication levels. Here, the unseen world of marine life and pollution is revealed to the public with colorful displays that illuminate the bay's health, hopefully inspiring residents to change their behavior (Margolis and Robinson, 2007) (Figure 4.6.3).

Imagine if billboards, instead of promoting commerce and consumption, telegraphed a neighborhood's ecological health or the outcome of recent restoration projects. What if the Salmon Safe broadcasted real-time data on its ongoing successes like the Aurora Bridge project and herald the increased amount of spawning salmon to the community? The ubiquitous signs at stormwater inlets that warn how they feed directly into nearby water bodies could go further where data divulges how much pollution is occurring in comparison to other water bodies which could lead to local action and behavioral changes. This feedback of information can confirm which open space restoration methods work best. The issue isn't density per se but ensuring that a city, like Singapore, has adopted measures to provide places of relief and to protect its environmental health from the negative impacts of urban density.

Figure 4.6.3   Fiber optic bundles provide the surface area for algae and fish habitats. From (Margolis & Robinson, 2007) Copyright 2007 by Abby Feldman, Reprinted with permission

We can refashion Wright's and Le Corbusier's response to the Industrial Revolution's impacts on the city through new urban typologies that integrate density, technology, biodiversity, and ecological services. The aim is to incorporate information revolution technologies with principles like the Singapore Index or Seven Lamps of Planning for Biodiversity to better plan for our community's (human and non-human) benefit and to achieve sustainability. Digital tools can help communicate and reveal these issues, discoveries, and successes to the public. Hopefully, such comprehendible illustrations of hidden natural phenomena can inspire the public to understand and protect natural resources because, as Henry David Thoreau described it, "a town is saved, not more by the righteous men in it than by the woods and swamps that surround it" (Thoreau and Emerson, 1991, p. 100).

References

10 Principles for livable high-density cities: Lessons from Singapore. (2013). Centre for Liveable Cities and Urban Land Institute. https://www.clc.gov.sg/docs/default-source/books/10principlesforlivablehighdensitycitieslessonsfromsingapore.pdf

Architecture 2030. (2020, September 20). *RESET! URBANIZATION: Global Sprawl, Climate Change, and Equity // CarbonPositive RESET!* [Video]. YouTube. https://www.youtube.com/watch?v=A7vCgPJVRi8

Aronson, M., Goddard, M., Lepcyk, C., Lerman, S., (2017). Biodiversity in the city: Key challenges for urban green space management. *Frontiers in Ecology and the Environment,* 15(Issue 4). https://doi.org/10.1002/fee.1480

Artmann, M., Kohler, M., Meinel, G., Gan, J., & Ioja, C. (2017). How smart growth and green infrastructure can mutually support each other—A conceptual framework for compact and green cities. *Ecological Indicators,* 96. https://doi.org/10.1016/j.ecolind.2017.07.001.

Baumgarten, S., Stoneburner, L., & Grossinger, R. (2022, June). Historical ecology deepens our understanding of place: the democratization of maps & California's future. *Artemisia,* 49(1), 20–25

Calthorpe, P. (2011). *Urbanism in the Age of Climate Change.* Island Press

Fishman, R. (1977). *Urban Utopias in the Twentieth Century: Ebenezer Howard, Frank Lloyd Wright, Le Corbusier.* Basic Books, Inc. p. 3–20

Galle, N., Nitoslawski, S., & Pilla, F. (2019). The Internet of Nature: How taking nature online can shape urban ecosystems. *The Anthropocene Review,* 6. https://doi.org/10.1177/2053019619877103.

Guerry, A., Smith, J., Lonsford, E., Daily, G., Wang, X., & Chun, Y. (2021). *Urban Nature and Biodiversity for Cities.* World Bank Publications Reports 36325, The World Bank Group

Hiramatsu, T. (2014). Expansive urban growth boundary. *Modern Economy,* 5, 806–820. https://doi.org/10.4236/me.2014.57074

Ives, C.D., Lentini, P. E., Threlfall, C. G., Ikin, K., Shanahan, D. F., Garrard, G. E., Bekessy, S. A., Fuller, R. A., Mumaw, L., Rayner, L., Rowe, R., Valentine, L. E., & Kendal, D. (2016), The importance of cities for threatened species. *Global Ecology and Biogeography,* 25, 117–126. https://doi.org/10.1111/geb.12404.

Kett, H. (2017, November 26). How to filter 2 million gallons of stormwater from the Aurora Bridge. Nature.org. https://www.nature.org/en-us/about-us/where-we-work/united-states/washington/stories-in-washington/filtering-stormwater/.

Le Corbusier. (1987). *The City of To-Morrow and its Planning* (F. Etchells, Trans). Dover Publications, Inc. (Original work published 1929) pp. 15–20, 163–245.

Margolis, L., & Robinson, A. (2007). *Living Systems: Innovative Materials and Technologies for Landscape Architecture.* Birkhäuser.

Meck, S. (Ed.) (2002). *Growing Smart Legislative Guidebook—Model Statutes for Planning and the Management of Change.* HUD USER, Economic Development, Economic Development Publications.

On the roof with Dr. Nadina Galle on the Internet of Nature. (2021, Fall). https://livingarchitecture-monitor.com/articles/dr-nadina-galle-on-the-internet-of-nature-f21

Orf, D. (2023, September 12). Saudia Arabia is building an entire city in a straight line. It makes zero sense. *Popular Mechanics*. https://www.popularmechanics.com/science/green-tech/a44966174/saudi-arabia-line-city/.

Parris, K., Amati, M., Bekessy, S., Dagenais, D., Fryd, O., & Hahs, A., Hes, D., Imberger, M., Livesley, S., Marshall, A., Rhodes, J., Threlfall, C., Tingley, R., van der Ree, R., Walsh, C. J., Doshi, M., & Williams, N. (2018). The seven lamps of planning for biodiversity in the city. *Cities*, 83. https://doi.org/10.1016/j.cities.2018.06.007.

Perkl, R. (2022, June). Introduction: The democratization of maps & California's future. *Artemisia*, 49(1), 2–6.

Pourtaherian, P., & Jaeger, J. (2022). How effective are greenbelts at mitigating urban sprawl? A comparative study of 60 European cities. *Landscape and Urban Planning*, 227, https://doi.org/10.1016/j.landurbplan.2022.104532.

Richardson, O. (2023, April 26). Aurora Bridges Bioswales—ULI Americas Awards for Excellence Winner. *ULI.org*. https://americas.uli.org/aurora-bridge-bioswales-uli-americas-awards-for-excellence-winner/.

Rzevski, G., Kozhevnikov, S., & Svitek, M. (2020). Smart city as an urban ecosystem. 2020 *Smart City Symposium Prague (SCSP), Prague, Czech Republic*, 2020, p. 1–7, https://doi.org/10.1109/SCSP49987.2020.9133849.

Salmon-Safe Inc. (2023). *Salmon-Safe Urban Standards version 3.1*. Herrera Environmental Consultants, Inc.

Smith, A., & Gill, G. (2018). *Residency: A Carbon Analysis of Residential Typologies*. ASGG. p. 7

Thoreau, H. D., & Emerson R. W. (1991). *Walking. In Nature and Walking*. Beacon Press. p. 100

Wright, F. L. (1945). *When Democracy Builds*. University of Chicago Press.

4.7

THE INTELLIGENCE OF BUILDINGS

Information and Bioclimatic Design

William W. Braham

Abstract

Building envelopes already embody a great deal of intelligence in the design of their envelopes, which selectively filter ambient conditions to provide comfortable, habitable conditions. Smart products and devices rely on these basic capabilities and are typically deployed to compensate for the inadequate bioclimatic design of the building. Real intelligence begins by configuring buildings so they can effectively respond to changing conditions with techniques such as shading and ventilation. Operated correctly, a well-designed building can keep itself comfortable most of the time, turning to automated intelligence to enhance their operation.

Buildings are rarely as smart as advertised, beeping plaintively to attract human intervention when they can't complete their appointed task. Nonetheless, algorithmic devices continue to propagate through the built environment, changing our relationship with everything from dishwashers to doorbells to air conditioning. But what do we mean by smart? Mostly it means some degree of automation, translating human activities into feedback-based, labor-saving systems using sensors, activators, and algorithms to perform a service. In a stricter definition, smartness is the feedback and processing of information to reduce uncertainty, to increase the likelihood of a particular outcome. The lowly thermostat is the classic building automation technology still used to illustrate feedback mechanisms in textbooks on control theory. It samples information about temperatures to regulate devices that keep building temperatures comfortable. But even the simplest enclosure reduces uncertainty about likely conditions because of the information embodied in its form and its materials, which increases the likelihood of comfort. The current fascination with adding smart products and devices to buildings can obscure the fact that they rely on the basic capacities of the underlying building and are mostly compensating for its inadequacies, for example, automatically ramping up cooling because large areas of glass are left unshaded in summer. Before adding a learning thermostat or responsive device, the first task is to make buildings themselves smarter in their bioclimatic abilities, embedding information to enhance their ability to respond to the climate and their occupants.

DOI: 10.4324/9781003384113-55

Machinate Animals

In the operation of a simple thermostat, people can see the life-like behavior of a self-regulating mechanism. In its responsive, pulsing behavior, they can readily imagine that the more complex forms of feedback in artificial intelligence (AI) might even evolve to overtake us. That was Samuel Butler's first thought when he read Darwin's *Origin of Species* (1859), that natural selection also applied to technological inventions, and his book *Erewhon* (1872) explored the question of whether clocks and steam engines would eventually evolve to surpass and enslave mankind. We continue to debate whether we are approaching the "singularity" of AI (Vinge 1993, Kurzweill 2005), further sharpened by the release of Generative Pre-trained Transformers (GPT). But as Deleuze and Guattari argued, Butler already saw beyond the simple opposition between men and machines, between vitalism and mechanism, recognizing that men and their machines are both parts of distributed social-physical entities (Deleuze and Guattari 1983, 284). As Butler observed,

> Man [...] was a machinate mammal. The lower animals keep all their limbs at home in their bodies, but many of man's are loose, and lie about detached, now here and now there, in various parts of the world—some being kept always handy for contingent use, and others being occasionally hundreds of miles away.
>
> *(1872, Book XXV)*

Buildings are part of our "loosely detached limbs," extensions of the genetically organized bodies that we use to better adapt the world to our needs. To fully consider the question of building automation and smartness, we need to ask what buildings actually do. They can house many different kinds of activities, but their fundamental role is to provide shelter—an environment that is dry, safe, more comfortable than outdoors, and light enough to see the task at hand. As Banham argued with his parable about that primitive tribe, we mostly accomplish those tasks by building shelters and/or burning fuels, investing in long-lived structures that modify the internal environment sufficiently so that the fires can provide adequate heat and light (1984). In the pre-modern context, people are the sensors, information processors, and actuators, setting fires when they decide that they need heat or light. In a contemporary building that work has been encoded in thermostats of varying levels of capacity and intelligence, and in that situation, it is easy to understand information as the signal travelling through wires to regulate the furnace. But how is the information implemented?

Form and Information

The concept of information, like that of entropy with which it has become closely associated, can mean different things in different contexts. In the everyday sense, it describes any form of knowledge delivered to a system whether by human language, genetic codes, a text message, whatever. For a more precise definition, Shannon developed a probabilistic measure of the information that could be transmitted through a particular channel of communication, usually measured in bits, which describes the capacity of the channel. That definition seems to contradict the everyday understanding because in Shannon's measure the more certain the outcome, the less information it can convey, so the term entropy helps convey the sense of information potential rather than specific knowledge. As useful as the mathematical definition of information has been for a variety of disciplines, it has long been troubled by the importance of semantic content and the context of the signal. It is the larger context that interests us, and it is the reason that a 1-bit message to the furnace can affect the temperature productively. The building and its furnace were organized to give that signal meaning. Without that context, the thermostat is just talking to itself.

To evaluate the information encoded in a building, we can treat it as a system of connections and interactions and draw on the methods developed by ecologists to understand the operation of complex, self-organizing ecosystems. Tracing the materials, energy, and information exchanged within an ecosystem can reveal its organization and operation and help us evaluate the effect of individual components. It may seem paradoxical to describe buildings as self-organizing, but if we accept Butler's view (or Deleuze and Guattari's) that they are extensions of our social-physical activities, we can see that they are more "loosely detached limbs" that we deploy to adapt to our environments. We can understand buildings as systems of interaction between occupants, devices, and the climate. Windows admit heat and light, massive materials store heat, and the envelope slows its transfer, while the occupants and HVAC systems intervene to adjust those interactions as needed. As we will see, it is the ability of the envelope to respond to changing conditions that make buildings more powerful and more intelligent.

One way to evaluate the work of buildings as systems is through the complexity of their interconnections and interactions, which can be measured variously through "permutations, entropy, information content, statistical parameters, and energy flows" (Odum 1994, 302). The ecologist Robert Ulanowicz adapted a statistical indicator called the Average Mutual Information (AMI) to measure a system's level of organization based on resource flows among the components of a network (Hirata and Ulanowicz 1984, Ulanowicz 1997). The network approach had its origins in the economic Input-Output (IO) methods developed by Leontief in the 1930s and which form the basis of the life-cycle accounting methods now widely used to evaluate embodied carbon (Leontief 1986). However, the economists' methods largely focus on cumulative outputs like GDP, while ecologists are more interested in the organization of reinforcing flows within a network (Szyrmer and Ulanowicz 1987). A fundamental principle of the ecological analysis of networks is that the flow of energy, materials, or information within a network can reveal the structure and operation of an ecosystem.

The formulation of network complexity begins with Shannon's mathematical theory of communication, which is based on the uncertainty or entropy of information in a channel (Shannon 1948). In a thermodynamic system, such as a building, it characterizes the uncertainty of the distribution of energy or material, and it can be summed over the whole network to produce a cumulative entropy measure typically designated as H. Broadly speaking, the greater the uncertainty, the greater the potential information, though H reaches a maximum at an intermediate level of probability. The AMI involves a summation of all the channels in a network, taking the proportional distribution of flows as the measure of probability for the uncertainty measurement. The more determinate the network, meaning the fewer choices or pathways for resource flows, the higher the AMI, while a greater complexity of pathways increases the uncertainty and decreases the AMI. For the thermal behavior of a building, the AMI effectively measures the difference between a pile of building materials on the site (low AMI) and an assembled building (high AMI). They both have the same amount of materials but have very different effects. The ratio between AMI and H is an indication of network efficiency, of how much information has gone into its organization.

Self-organizing systems of all kinds exhibit maximizing behavior and though ecologists debate the best metric with which to capture it, they generally agree that systems seek to maximize some measure of useful power (Jorgensen 1992). In Ulanowicz's approach, self-organizing systems seek a trade-off between the gross consumption of resources and the complexity of the network. He developed a number of ways to capture that quality and the one that translates most directly to buildings is called Fitness, which is a normalized factor of the effective accumulation of useful energy. Ecosystems exhibit different degrees of Fitness through their lifecycle with greater Fitness in the earlier growth stages, tending toward greater AMI, and lower Fitness in the later, mature phases. The key point is that these stages of greatest power happen at intermediate levels of efficiency, with the actual maximum of Fitness occurring at an efficiency of 0.37. This is precisely the understanding of intelligence we are interested in for buildings—how they use information to minimize their use of energy and materials while maintaining comfort and utility for their occupants.

In evaluating the energy or environmental performance of a building, the usual measure is the consumption of energy purchased in the form of fuels or electricity, discounting environmental energies like sunlight as "free." In a recent dissertation, Hwang Yi used building information modeling to ask an important question. How do we compare two buildings that both minimize purchased energy (Yi 2016, Yi et al. 2017a)? He used two case studies, a reasonably efficient, conventional building using grid electricity and natural gas (Building A) and a net-zero energy building (NZEB) that uses photovoltaic (PV) panels to power its systems (Building B) (Figure 4.7.1). To clarify the value of the building envelope, he evaluated three versions of the normative building, one with a conventionally operated mechanical system, the second with the windows and a shading system actively managed by the occupants to optimize comfort, and a third with passive house levels of insulation and sealing added to the active management.

In the energy efficiency approach to sustainable design, the NZEB would be considered superior, even though there are considerable amounts of energy and materials used up in the production of PV panels and batteries. In order to account for the total life cycles costs of the energy and materials, including the work of the geobiosphere to prepare the materials and provide the renewable energies, he used the method of emergy (with an "m") synthesis to account for the throughput of the system (Odum 1996). One benefit of emergy synthesis is that it uses a common unit, the solar emjoule (sej), for all materials, services, and products, by accounting for the work required to deliver them to the building (Odum 1996). This makes it possible to compare the environmental costs of very different elements, for

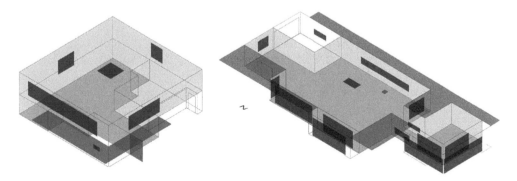

Figure 4.7.1   Test buildings A & B, a conventional and a Net-Zero Energy Building (NZEB) of similar size. Hwang Yi.

example, fresh water, electricity, concrete, or information, and to assess their contribution to the operation of a building.

To measure the information contained in the configuration of the building, he prepared an emergy flow diagram describing all the exchanges and interaction in the two buildings, including the work and resources embodied in the materials, in the purchased and environmental energies, and from the activities of the occupants (Figure 4.7.2). The embodied resources are included as depreciated values, using the expected lifespan of each component, so they are counted as annual costs comparable to resource flows such as energy. Information content can't be measured directly so is evaluated indirectly as the conditional probability associated with each exchange within the system, summarized in a network IO model. In a system with little uncertainty, resources would be dominated by a single pathway, think fuel-powered HVAC for example, but as channels are made differently

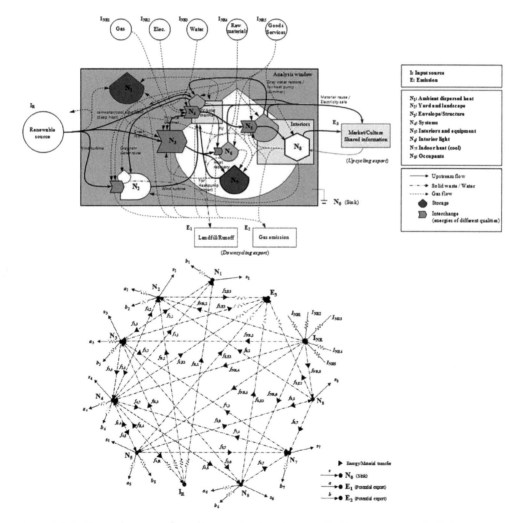

Figure 4.7.2 General emergy flow diagram (top) and network diagram (bottom) of the two test buildings. Hwang Yi.

selective (an operable window), the uncertainty of flows increases as does the effectiveness and complexity of the building.

Charts of the AMI, AMI/H, and Fitness of the buildings through a typical year show the variations in the complexity of the two buildings (Figure 4.7.3). The seasonal differences are largely the effect of the fuels and electricity used in building A and the intensive materials bound up in the PV panels and batteries of building B. Though the NZEB uses less purchased energy in its operation, it is not necessarily smarter or more resilient. The really useful insight can be discerned in the Spring and Fall when the Fitness of even the conventionally operated normative building exceeds that of the NZEB building. This is the period when the mechanical systems of the normative building generally don't operate, so comfort is provided by the thermal effects of the building envelope.

When that behavior is enhanced by smart occupants opening windows for ventilation and closing shades to reduce heat gain, then even more substantial building intelligence can be achieved. Across the year, the occupant-operated buildings have lower AMI/H's, approaching the optimum value of 0.37, with correspondingly higher fitness.

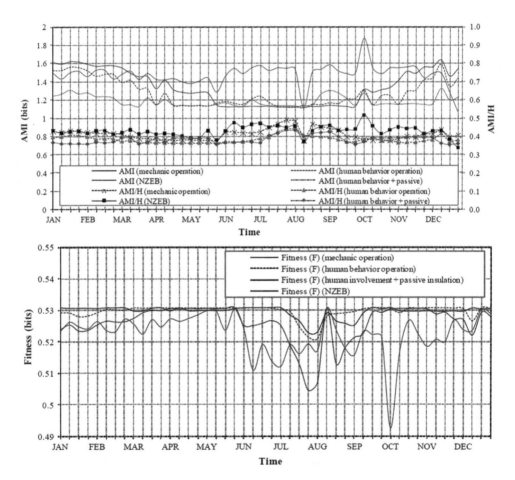

Figure 4.7.3   Average Mutual Information (AMI), Efficiency (AMI/H), and Fitness (F) of normative building (A) and NZEB building (B). Hwang Yi.

497

The occupant-controlled versions have the greatest Fitness because their actions adjust the channels of resource flow in the building in response to changing climatic conditions, leveraging the information content of the building as a system. For a clearer picture of the architecture of occupant adaptation, we can turn to the Esherick House.

Intelligence at the Esherick House

The Esherick house, completed by Louis Kahn in 1961, is one of his most studied buildings, admired for its simplicity and for the clear articulation of his distinction between served and service spaces (Marcus 2013). That distinction is somewhat contradicted by the occupant engagement involved in the operation of its windows when the "served" occupant has to do the "serving," but that contradiction is the secret of its intelligence. The building is rectangular with its long sides facing south to an open yard and north to a cul-de-sac. It shows influence from the solar experiments of the late 1940s when Kahn and Stonorov designed a "Pennsylvania Solar House" with large south-facing windows, roof overhangs, and a closed north façade (Simon 1947). That classically solar profile prefigures the distinctive features of the Esherick house, which includes a largely opaque north façade and four large south-facing windows flanked by groups of unglazed, shuttered openings that run from floor to ceiling. Kahn had visited Le Corbusier's convent at La Tourette the year before and was impressed with the shuttered ventilation openings and the way they directly connected the occupants to their environment (Figure 4.7.4).

Figure 4.7.4 South facade of the Esherick house showing the operable shutters and windows with valence for external shade. Photo: Y. Morishita.

Windows are among the most powerful bioclimatic elements of buildings. They can selectively control the heat of sunlight and the cooling effect of ventilation. In the Esherick house, Kahn separated the two functions, providing large, fixed glass windows for the sunlight and unglazed, shuttered openings for ventilation. Admitting sunlight can have a positive effect in cold weather, keeping the building warm, but is also the source of over-heating in warmer weather. Opening the shutters for ventilation can reduce that overheat-ing when outdoor temperatures are cooler. Passe and Battaglia prepared a detailed CFD model of the building and determined that the open shutters can completely change the air and temperature of the house in about ten minutes. In network terms, the occupant changes the interconnections of the envelope, shifting the energy flows between inside and outside according to the conditions (Passe and Battaglia 2015). When it is done well, they keep the building comfortable without turning on the furnace or air conditioner. They are activating the intelligence built into the envelope. An equally important aspect of cooling is to exclude the sun in warmer weather before the building actually overheats. There is evidence that Kahn planned a set of exterior louvers for the windows, but Margaret Esherick died shortly after moving into the house, so they were never installed. A subsequent owner-mounted roll-down blinds inside the glass can reduce glare but do little to reduce overheating.

In our analysis of the original Esherick house, with no shading and the shutters closed, the building was comfortable about 25% of the time. Without insulation, the building quickly loses whatever heat it captures from its large south windows, and it also overheats considerably in the summer. If we operate the shades and shutters according to indoor and outdoor temperatures, that amount of comfort can be increased. Opening the shutters whenever the interior is warm and the exterior is cooler, the building is comfortable 30% of the time, while shading windows whenever the indoor and outdoor temperatures pass about 20°C increases comfort to about 35%. When the two are combined, that increases comfort to about 36%, with most of the discomfort occurring in winter from underheat-ing. Neither shading nor ventilation help much when it is too cold inside, but sealing and insulating the building (the shutters were notoriously leaky and the wall was an uninsu-lated concrete block) increases the building's ability to retain the heat it captures from the sun, storing it in its plaster walls and substantial woodwork. In that better-insulated configuration, the managed shutters and exterior shades can achieve comfortable tempera-tures up to 80% of the time, simply by enhancing and effectively operating the building envelope.

Buildings already embody a great deal of intelligence—there is information written into the capacities of the envelope, which can be measured with AMI and Fitness, and there is information in the difference between inside and outside conditions, which can be used to decide when to adjust the building's interaction with those conditions. Effective bioclimatic buildings employ both kinds of information, so by contrast, most contemporary buildings would have to be considered developmentally challenged. Smart occupants or devices acti-vate bioclimatic potential, meaning the real intelligence is embodied in the building itself.

References

Banham, Reyner. 1984. *The Architecture of the Well-Tempered Environment.* The University of Chi-cago Press: Chicago.

Butler, S. 1872. *Erewhon, or Over the Range.* Trubner & Co: London.

Darwin, Charles. 1859. *The Origin of Species by Means of Natural Selection, or, The Preservation of Favored Races in the Struggle for Life,* John Wanamaker: Philadelphia.

Deleuze, G. and F. Guattari. 1983. *Anti-Oedipus: Capitalism and Schizophrenia*. University of Minnesota Press: Minneapolis.

Hirata, Hironori and Robert Ulanowicz. 1984. 'Information theoretical analysis of ecological networks.' *International Journal of Systems Science*, 15, 3: 261–270.

Jorgensen, S. E. 1992. *Integration of Ecosystem Theories: A pattern*, 3rd edition, Kluwer Academic Publishers: Dordrecht; Boston, c2002.

Kurzweil, Ray. 2005. *The singularity is Near: When Humans Transcend Biology*. Viking: New York.

Leontief, Wassily. 1986. *Input-Output Economics*. Oxford University Press.

Marcus, George H. 2013. *The Houses of Louis Kahn*. Yale University Press: New Haven.

Odum, Howard T. 1994. *Ecological and General Systems: An Introduction to Systems Ecology*. University of Colorado Press: Niwot.

Odum, Howard T. 1996. *Environmental Accounting: EMERGY and environmental Decision Making*. Wiley: New York.

Passe, U. and F. Battaglia. 2015. *Designing Spaces for Natural Ventilation: An Architect's Guide*. Routledge: New York.

Shannon, C. E. 1948. "A mathematical theory of communication." *Bell System Technical Journal*, 27 (July, October): 379–423, 623–656.

Simon, Maron J. 1947. *Your Solar House; A Book of Practical Homes for all Parts of the Country*. Simon and Schuster: New York.

Szyrmer, J. and R. E. Ulanowicz. 1987. "Total flows in ecosystems." *Ecological Modelling*, 35(1): 123–136.

Ulanowicz, Robert E. 1997. *Ecology: The Ascendent Perspective*. Columbia University Press: New York.

Vinge, Vernor. 1993. "Technological singularity." *Whole Earth Review*, 81: 88.

Yi, Hwang. 2016. *Information in Environmental Architecture: Ecological Network Analysis and New indices of Building Performance*, PhD dissertation, University of Pennsylvania, Philadelphia, PA.

Yi, Hwang, William W. Braham, David R. Tilley, and Ravi Srinivasan. 2017a. "A metabolic network approach to building performance: Information building modeling and simulation of biological indicators". *Journal of Cleaner Production*, 165: 1133–62.

Yi, Hwang, William W. Braham, David R. Tilley, and Ravi Srinivasan. 2017b. "Measuring ecological characteristics of environmental building performance: Suggestion of an information-network model and indices to quantify complexity, power, and sustainability of energetic organization." *Ecological Indicators*, 83: 201–17.

4.8

SMART ENERGY HARVESTING FROM NATURAL AND ARTIFICIAL AQUATIC SYSTEMS

Bastian Steudel

Abstract

This chapter explores the historical and contemporary integration of aquatic systems into urban environments, shedding light on the aesthetic and functional roles these systems have played over time. It discusses the primary production of biomass through photosynthesis in managed aquatic environments and highlights its potential for biofuel production. An overview of technical applications for energy harvesting from water bodies, including the use of kinetic energy from flowing water and the development of small-scale energy conversion devices, is given.

Furthermore, this chapter highlights the environmental, regulatory, social, and economic considerations associated with large-scale energy harvesting projects and offers insights into potential risks and mitigation measures. The environmental impact of hydroelectric dams, including the disruption of aquatic ecosystems and altered water flow patterns, along with the social and cultural impacts of large-scale energy projects, is examined. The economic viability of such projects is addressed, considering the costs of equipment, installation, operation, and maintenance, as well as electricity prices and government incentives.

In conclusion, this chapter emphasizes the significance of integrating a variety of small-scale energy harvesting methods to enable decentralized energy supply with a focus on primary production through plants and algae. The need for a complete infrastructure for processing algae biomass to replace fossil oil is underscored, calling for further research and development in this field. This chapter discusses the potential of aquatic systems as a renewable energy source and prompts readers to consider the complex interplay of ecological, social, and economic factors in the pursuit of sustainable energy solutions.

Aquatic systems have a high impact on the shape of urban and landscape environments. While urbanization is frequently reported as a threat to the ecology of natural water bodies like rivers and lakes (e.g., Booth and Jackson 1997, Alberti et al. 2007), integration into urban planning for aesthetical reasons reaches back to the Mesopotamian period 3000 BC (Stančius and Grecevičius 2021). It is thought that aesthetical integration into urban planning started with the utilization of water for agriculture. The early formal and geometric

DOI: 10.4324/9781003384113-56

artificial ponds, channels, and cascades later were changed to water bodies resembling natural habitats for aesthetical reasons representing the wish of integration of "natural beauties" into the living environment of human populations mid of the first millennium in China (Xiaoxiang 1994), while this concept was adopted much later in western countries. However, the "English gardens", first arranged in the early nineteenth century, are famous for their resembling natural landscapes, including artificial ponds and waterfalls. On the other hand, artificial cascades, ponds, springs, and fountains were used to create spectacular arrangements for the nobility (e.g., Versailles and its impact on other courts), or urban population (e.g., the Trevi fountain) and are often now considered world heritages.

Despite the ornamental use of water, it has been used for energy harvesting since millennia. As we all know, energy is never lost, it can only be converted into another form. However, all forms of energy can be converted into thermal energy. The technical conversion of energy is facing "energy lost" as not all energy can be converted into the aimed energy form without converting part of it to thermal energy or, in the case of mechanics, to friction, which is again thermal energy absorbed by the mechanics. Modern society uses a mixture of different energy sources (Figure 4.8.1).

While the use of traditional biomass changed only marginally, although the main source until the late nineteenth century, other sources of energy, namely, the fossil sources of natural gas, oil, and coal, are currently the main sources of energy. The increasing urge for energy in modern society now raises the question of whether aquatic systems can be integrated into energy harvesting concepts. In this chapter, I will divide this topic into three main paragraphs. Paragraph one will discuss possibilities to use aquatic organisms in managed environments to bind solar energy using photosynthesis, i.e., primary production of

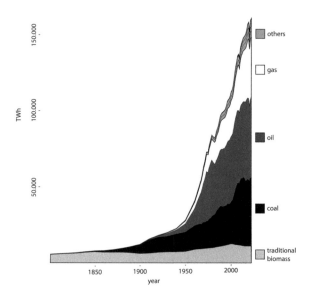

Figure 4.8.1 Overview of the global energy consumption by source. The data are taken from Ritchie, Roser, and Rosado (2020). Note that hydropower, nuclear power, and other renewable energies, including biofuels, solar, and wind energy, are combined with "others" but separated with thin lines. Hydropower and nuclear power contributed to about 50% each in the beginning, now with renewable energies, all contribute about one-third each. (Graph, courtesy of the author Bastian Steudel)

biomass. The second paragraph will deal with technical applications to harvest energy from water bodies. Further, a possible management scenario will be discussed and finally, I will conclude with paragraph three focusing on the risks of these techniques.

Primary Production

About half of the biological primary production (mainly photosynthesis) is done by algae, typically growing in aquatic systems (Ynalvez et al. 2018). This is much more than adding the photosynthesis ratio of all forests worldwide. In urban environments, often natural water bodies are removed or modulated for the construction of buildings. The lack of suitable habitats results in less biomass production and photosynthesis rates. By performing photosynthesis, plants and algae convert solar radiation into chemically bound energy, i.e., biomass. As a "byproduct", oxygen is produced and carbon dioxide (CO_2) as well as nutrients are taken up, resulting in cleaner air and water in the case of aquatic plants and algae.

A lot of our population is settled in rivers all over the world. In ancient times, rivers provided the most fertile soil for agriculture as the sediment deposited along the river sites contained a lot of nutrients. This changed in modern society as due to over-fertilization with nutrients in agriculture and by polluted industry wastewaters, downstream rivers, which catch up everything along their way to the ocean and often contain very high concentrations of nitrogen and phosphorus. These high concentrations of nutrients result in various ecological issues. However, such surface water could be used to grow aquatic plants, especially microalgae. The produced biomass could then be transformed into biofuel. This would result in various synergistic positive effects for the ecosystems and finally for human health and living conditions. Not only that the nutrients be reduced, which is beneficial for ecosystems, but the reduced CO_2 would contribute to a lower velocity in global change. Additionally, the bound nutrients could replace fertilizers in agriculture if the remaining parts of the microalgae were recycled.

In principle, such biomass production can be done by very versatile methods, including bioreactors or direct mechanical removal of biomass from semi-natural water bodies. However, the processing of biomass is challenging as the production processes to obtain biofuels are complex (Kumar, Korstad, and Singh 2015). Until now, algae production is limited due to several barriers (Araújo et al. 2021), including economic feasibility. However, facing the current energy crisis, we may need to re-evaluate the economic feasibility of algae-based biomass production. Unfortunately, additional aspects like CO_2 reduction or water- and air-cleaning services have been largely ignored in the economic calculations. Some countries developed a tax on CO_2 emissions, e.g., the European Union. The CO_2 uptake should be included in the calculations given that the future tax will be higher than now. The benefits to ecosystems due to nutrient uptake if nutrient-polluted water is used for algae production are as well neglected. Fossil oil is converted biomass of marine microalgae and other microbes which are directly dependent on microalgae. Those microbes sank to the bottom of the prehistoric ocean and were pressed by later overlaying sediment. Due to the application of high pressure, the biomass was eventually converted into raw oil. Hence, fossil oil was once as well microalgae which consumed and thereby stored big amounts of CO_2, a so-called carbon sink. If we now use this fossil energy, we release the CO_2 with the well-known consequences for the worldwide climatic conditions.

Natural or managed aquatic ecosystems in the urban environment can be divided into rivers, channels, lakes, and ponds. Dependent on the nutrient content and the velocity of water movement, there are big differences of naturally occurring algae and water plants in these systems. It would be beyond the limits of this contribution to mention all types of vegetation in such systems which could be used as an energy bounding system for energy harvesting. However, there is an increasing number of lakes and ponds which are heavily influenced by fast-growing algae. Those are typically situated at the lower stream regions of big rivers (often in the delta). The main contribution of algae growth in such lakes and ponds is nutrient input upstream of the river by agriculture and industries. As heavy algae growth can lead to ecological crises in the lake or pond, management measures often include the mechanical reduction of macro-algae with nets or combs. The harvested algae can then be used for biogas production. A systematic management and further use of such algae and other water plants is not proposed on a bigger scale yet. On the other hand, microalgae are difficult to harvest directly from the water body and are therefore often cultivated.

The use of microalgae as a source of energy has been of interest for a few years. This technique is CO_2 neutral as long as we use only energy harvested in the process, e.g., transport and maintenance of the facilities. Some single projects have been implemented, but there is no complete infrastructure built on algae energy yet.

A pilot project in Hamburg uses flat panels as bioreactors at the façade of a building, the so-called algae house (built in 2013) to produce microalgae (Figure 4.8.2a). In Mexico, the so-called artificial tree was developed which is a device containing a central bioreactor and light harvesting mirrors to ensure enough light input (Figure 4.8.2b). Similarly, in Serbia another type of artificial tree was built to be integrated as a bench into urban environment (Figure 4.8.2c). A great variety of bioreactors can be integrated into urban environment. In general, two main kinds of bioreactors can be built. The above-mentioned type of bioreactor is closed. In these bioreactors, microalgae are cultivated without direct contact with the environment. The other type of algae bioreactors are open pond systems, i.e., a basin where the microalga suspension is circulated for better sunlight and nutrient exposure. Open pond systems are often affected by infection of the algae by other organisms. To enable a cultivation of only the target algae, different management strategies can be applied. These include the cultivation of marine algae (e.g., *Spirulina/Arthrospira*) in a greater distance to the sea to prevent the introduction of marine organisms into the ponds. However, open pond systems are much more threatened by infection with other organisms than closed systems.

While open pond systems are limited in their design by the needs of the algae for growth (depth limits the exposure with light, the shape should be round or oval to enable a good mixture of the algae suspension), closed systems can be built with tubes. Such tubes can be used as a design element for attractive sculptures (Figure 4.8.2d). In general, the shape of microalgae bioreactors can vary greatly.

A sustainable integration of algae bioreactors into urban environments would only be possible if the harvested algae could be processed efficiently. This would need a complete new infrastructure, including a transport system and a processing plant. An overview of such a putative infrastructure is given in Figure 4.8.3. However, given that photosynthesis is considered a highly effective mechanism for converting solar energy into chemical-bound energy (Foyer et al. 2017), i.e., biomass such as carbohydrates, including fatty acids, it is worth to develop such an infrastructure. Up to about half of algae, biomass can be lipids (Vijayaraghavan and Hemanathan 2009), enabling high-energy harvest. The investment in a complete processing infrastructure would be high, but after a few years, the energy harvesting would reimburse for the investments.

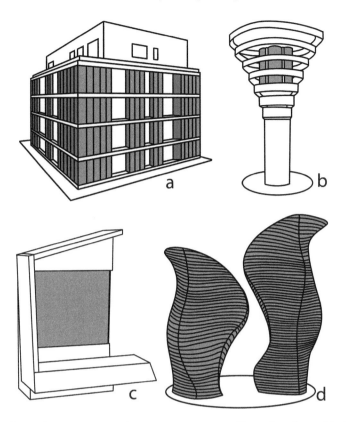

Figure 4.8.2   Different bioreactors in urban environments. (a) The "algae house" in Hamburg, Germany: part of the façade is covered with flat bioreactor panels. Microalgae are floating through the panels by air bubbling. (b) The artificial tree produced by the Mexican company BioUrban: light is reflected inside the upper area and concentrated in the cylindrical bioreactor in the middle of the "crown". (c) The artificial tree invented by Dr. Ivan Spasojevic, Serbia: the bioreactor is a simple basin for algae cultivation in combination with a bank. By pumping air through the system, CO_2 is taken up by the algae, and the air is cleaned from other particles. (d) A sketch of the PhotoBioReactor Sculpture by Charles Lee, 2008, part of the BIOS Design Collective working group. The tubes form the sculpture and algae circulate through the whole installation. Note: for all sketches, the gray parts are for algae cultivation. Drawings by Shidi Fu.

A future scenario could be that a variety of different photobioreactors produce microalgae throughout the city. Management of these reactors could be centralized, monitoring the concentration of algae in real-time. Then a collecting vehicle, similar to a garbage truck, could collect the produced microalgae for further processing. The microalgae used need to be selected for specific environmental conditions like temperature light availability, and nutrient content of the water, which is ideally taken from a nearby natural or artificial water resource. The algae species used likely need to be changed seasonally and they may differ for specific bioreactors. However, for energy harvesting, often microalgae need to face nutrient deficiency to switch their metabolism to fat production (Ferreira et al. 2019, Yaakob et al. 2021). Recently, some further algae strains were identified bearing high CO_2

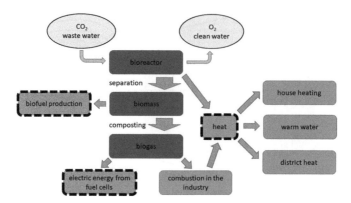

Figure 4.8.3 Schematic energy flow and putative energy harvesting processes by using bioreactors with microalgae. The produced alga biomass needs to be mechanically separated for further use. From the biomass, oil can be harvested for biofuel production. The remaining biomass can be composted, producing biogas which can be used for fuel cell electricity production o in the industries for combustion. The heat captured in the bioreactors or produced during these processes can be stored and used for heating or warm water production. Water and air is cleaned by the microalgae, facilitating improved conditions for the urban environment. (Diagram, courtesy of the author Bastian Steudel)

concentrations, possibly enabling the use of exhaust from industries for algae cultivation (Kryvenda et al. 2023). As the processing of the oil harvested from algae to fuels needs a big infrastructure, such a system would need a big investment.

Mechanical and Physical Methods

Kinetic energy from water has been used for thousands of years to harvest energy for moving heavy machines like mills or to elevate goods. Such machines were very complex and the engineers found efficient ways for the conversion of the energy provided by naturally moving water bodies like rivers or waterfalls. Some of these machine complexes included damming to get a more constant water flow, or management of whole mountain areas resulting in water management systems that shaped the ecosystems (Röhling et al. 2010). With the upcoming urge of electric power, hydroelectric power stations became more relevant than the direct mechanical use of water power. Two main areas need to be divided for hydroelectric power stations: ocean and freshwater systems.

Ocean energy conversion systems need to meet a bunch of requirements to be approved by US authorities. These criteria have been adopted worldwide since. They need to: (1) have high energy density, (2) not obstruct navigation, (3) not diminish the value of the expensive coastal real estate, (4) be friendly to marine life and the environment, (5) have low maintenance, (6) be robust, (7) meet life cycle cost targets, and (8) have a minimum life of 10–20 years (Bernitsas et al. 2008). Conversion of tidal kinetic energy has been used for about 50 years. Tidal power stations can be big projects with high investment costs but can provide constant energy harvests over decades (Wang and Wang 2019). Such tidal power stations can be implemented next to or inside of urban areas, e.g., harbors. However, most ocean energy conversion is situated well outside of populated areas.

Freshwater

Water dams are the leading infrastructure used to store water in artificial lakes to drive hydroelectric power stations. These complex buildings are well established and their functioning is stable. Most of these infrastructures are large-scale, and harvesting of up to 100 TWh of electricity per year (e.g., the Three Gorges Dam in Yichang, China (Seo and Seo 2021)) is technically possible. These large plants contribute locally significantly to the overall energy at present and are thought to contribute much more in the future (Zarfl et al. 2015, Seo and Seo 2021).

Recent developments focus more on smaller scale energy conversion devices. A new method to harvest energy from flowing water uses vortex-induced vibration (Bernitsas et al. 2008, Kong, Roussinova and Stoilov 2019). This system is of particular interest as it is a simple system which may be of low maintenance. Further, the use of vortex flow can be scaled depending on the energy required. Micro-scale energy harvesting by using rainwater (Zamora-Juárez et al. 2023) or water pipelines (Aqel et al. 2018, Ma et al. 2018) is not widely applied yet.

Whether the trend to smaller scale infrastructures, which have in general the advantage that decentralized energy harvesting leads to reduced newly built energy-transportation infrastructure like high voltage lines, will be implemented more in the future remains questionable. Similar to the discussion about other renewable energies, often big solutions are preferred by policymakers and stakeholders.

Energy Harvesting from Aquatic Systems and its Risks

While energy harvesting from aquatic systems offers several benefits, it is crucial to assess the risks and consider various aspects associated with this form of energy generation. I first reflect on the environmental, regulatory, social, and economic aspects of big infrastructures for energy harvesting from water systems, with a focus on the potential risks involved. Second, I describe how small-scale energy harvesting infrastructure can solve such risks.

One of the primary concerns with energy harvesting from water systems is its environmental impact. Hydroelectric dams, for instance, can disrupt aquatic habitats, block fish migration routes, and alter water flow patterns. This can lead to a decline in fish populations and negatively impact other aquatic organisms. Additionally, sedimentation in reservoirs due to energy harvesting systems can reduce water storage capacity and diminish system efficiency. Careful consideration and mitigation measures are necessary to balance energy production with environmental preservation. Dams represent probably one of the first engineering constructions ever, and their influence on natural habitats, including forests, wetlands, and aquatic ecosystems, has been known since decades (e.g., Baxter 1977, Dixon et al. 1989). Today, a lot of different measures are used to reduce the ecological risks of dams, including fish bypasses, construction of fish-friendly turbines, management of sediment accumulation, and environmental flow releases to provide sufficient nutrients and sediments for downstream ecosystems. However, research and innovations are still in progress. Dams, forming artificial lakes, thus negatively affect whole regions by the loss of natural habitats, including forests, wetlands, and aquatic ecosystems. On the other hand, these environments can provide new ecosystems by themselves (Kienert 1978, Mohammed, Ahmed, and El-Otify 1989, Gönülol and Obali 1998).

The potential power stored in artificial lakes bears as well another direct risk, namely, the break of the dam, which was assessed in a lot of economic and risk studies, resulting in highly efficient management measures (Baecher, Paté, and De Neufville 1980, Hariri-Ardebili 2018). Thus, energy harvesting projects from water systems often require permits and approvals from regulatory bodies. This process can be complex and time-consuming. Failure to comply with regulatory requirements can result in delays, fines, or project termination. Adequate planning, engagement with regulatory authorities, and adherence to environmental and safety regulations are essential to navigate the complex landscape of permits and approvals.

Large-scale energy harvesting projects, such as hydroelectric dams, can have significant social and cultural impacts. Displacement of communities, loss of livelihoods, and disruptions to cultural heritage and traditional practices can occur. It is crucial to engage with local communities, understand their concerns, and mitigate the adverse effects of these projects. Ensuring fair compensation, providing alternative livelihood opportunities, and preserving cultural heritage can foster social acceptance and minimize social disruptions.

While physical energy harvesting from water systems contributes to renewable energy conversion, economic viability needs to be addressed. The cost of equipment, installation, operation, and maintenance must be carefully evaluated. Additionally, electricity prices, government incentives, and payback periods must be considered to ensure that the investment is economically sustainable in the long term. A thorough economic analysis is necessary to assess the profitability and viability of big energy harvesting projects. Such analyses should include as well ecological consequences.

In opposite, small units to cultivate algae to harvest solar energy are relatively low-cost investments for the individual unit. One artificial tree of type "Mexico" (Figure 4.8.2b) costs about 12,000 $US, and I estimate one of the type "Serbia" (Figure 4.8.2c) at about 4,000 $US. However, the economic risk lies in small units in the infrastructure needed for the processing of the harvested algae. To overcome the first years of algae production, non-optimal processing could serve as an interim solution, even if it has lower energy transformation efficiency. For example, microalgae could be used as fertilizer in agriculture instead of artificial fertilizers, they could be fermented and used in biogas production plants, etc. If in a given community enough bioreactors produce algae, the building of processing plants can still be implemented. Small microalgae-producing units bear much lower ecological risks than big infrastructures. However, the introduction of alien species should be avoided. Hence, local algae strains need to be isolated and maintained for cultivation. This service is at least during the phase of microalgae isolation cost-intensive and needs to be estimated in the overall efficiency. However, the social acceptance of microalgae bioreactors is surprisingly high. It seems that the green color of the algae suspension leads to high acceptance, even if residents (e.g., in the algae house, Figure 4.8.2a) are in direct contact with the bioreactors. By integrating suitable sensors to measure algae density and fitness during cultivation, the risk of a total loss of a harvest can be minimized.

Small-scale physical techniques to harvest energy from water, e.g., vortex-induced vibration or from rain drainage or water pipelines, bear only the direct investment as a risk. Environmental, regulatory, or social risks are not known.

Conclusion

By enabling a variety of different small-scale energy harvesting methods, a decentralization of energy supply can be implemented. If microalgae are planned to be used, the processing of the biomass produced needs a centralized processing, however. A conversion of energy harvesting in the direction of renewable energies, however, should include aquatic systems to produce oil from (micro)algae to replace fossil oil as one of a variety of different sources of energy.

References

Alberti, M., Booth, D., Hill, K., Coburn, B., Avolio, C., Coe, S., & Spirandelli, D. (2007). The impact of urban patterns on aquatic ecosystems: An empirical analysis in Puget lowland sub-basins. *Landscape and Urban Planning*, *80*(4), 345–361.

Aqel, M. O., Issa, A., Qasem, E. & El-Khatib, W. (2018, October). Hydroelectric generation from water pipelines of buildings. In *2018 International Conference on Promising Electronic Technologies (ICPET)* (pp. 63–68). IEEE.

Araújo, R., Vázquez Calderón, F., Sánchez López, J., Azevedo, I. C., Bruhn, A., Fluch, S., ... & Ullmann, J. (2021). Current status of the algae production industry in Europe: an emerging sector of the blue bioeconomy. *Frontiers in Marine Science*, *7*, 626389.

Baecher, G. B., Paté, M. E., & De Neufville, R. (1980). Risk of dam failure in benefit-cost analysis. *Water Resources Research*, *16*(3), 449–456.

Baxter, R. M., (1977). Environmental effects of dams and impoundments. *Annual Review of Ecology and Systematics*, *8*(1), 255–283.

Bernitsas, M. M., Raghavan, K., Ben-Simon, Y., & Garcia, E. M. H. (2008). VIVACE (Vortex Induced Vibration Aquatic Clean Energy): A new concept in generation of clean and renewable energy from fluid flow. *Journal of Offshore Mechanics and Arctic Engeneering*, *130*(4), 041101.

Booth, D. B., & Jackson, C. R. (1997). Urbanization of aquatic systems: degradation thresholds, stormwater detection, and the limits of mitigation 1. *JAWRA Journal of the American Water Resources Association*, *33*(5), 1077–1090.

Dixon, J. A., Talbot, L. M., & Le Moigne, G. J. M. (1989). Dams and the Environment. *World Bank Technical Paper*, *110*.

Ferreira, G. F., Pinto, L. R., Maciel Filho, R., & Fregolente, L. V. (2019). A review on lipid production from microalgae: Association between cultivation using waste streams and fatty acid profiles. *Renewable and Sustainable Energy Reviews*, *109*, 448–466.

Foyer, C. H., Ruban, A. V., & Nixon, P. J. (2017). Photosynthesis solutions to enhance productivity. *Philosophical Transactions of the Royal Society B: Biological Sciences*, *372*(1730), 20160374.

Gönülol, A., & Obali, O. (1998). A study on the phytoplankton of hasan UĞURLU Dam Lake (Samsun-Turkey). *Turkish Journal of Biology*, *22*(4), 447–462.

Hariri-Ardebili, M. A. (2018). Risk, Reliability, Resilience (R3) and beyond in dam engineering: A state-of-the-art review. *International Journal of Disaster Risk Reduction*, *31*, 806–831.

Kienert, W. (1978). Ökologische Untersuchungen am Phytoplankton der Edertalsperre. PhD Thesis, Gesamthochschule Kassel, Germany.

Kong, H., Roussinova, V., & Stoilov, V. (2019). Renewable energy harvesting from water flow. *International Journal of Environmental Studies*, *76*(1), 84–101.

Kryvenda, A., Tischner, R., Steudel, B., Griehl, C., Armon, R., & Friedl, T. (2023). Testing for terrestrial and freshwater microalgae productivity under elevated CO2 conditions and nutrient limitation. *BMC Plant Biology*, *23*(1), 1–17.

Kumar, D., Korstad, J., & Singh, B. (2015). Life cycle assessment of algal biofuels. In *Algae and Environmental Sustainability*, Ed. Bhaskar Singh, Kuldeep Bauddh, & Faizal Bux, Springer, 165–181.

Ma, T., Yang, H., Guo, X., Lou, C., Shen, Z., Chen, J., & Du, J. (2018). Development of inline hydroelectric generation system from municipal water pipelines. *Energy*, *144*, 535–548.

Mohammed, A. A., Ahmed, A. M., & El-Otify, A. M. (1989). Field and laboratory studies on Nile phytoplankton in Egypt IV. Phytoplankton of Aswan High Dam Lake (Lake Nasser). *Internationale Revue der gesamten Hydrobiologie und Hydrographie*, *74*(5), 549–578.

Ritchie, H., Roser, M., & Rosado, P. (2020). "Energy". Published online at *OurWorldInData.org*. Retrieved from "hattp://ourworldindata.org/energy"

Röhling, H. G., Teicke, J., & Wellmer, F. W. (2010). The upper harz water regale. *Schriftenreihe der Deutschen Gesellschaft für Geowissenschaften*, *66*, 119–121.

Seo, S. N., & Seo, S. N., (2021). Energy revolutions: A story of the Three Gorges Dam in China. *Climate Change and Economics: Engaging with Future Generations with Action Plans*, Palgrave Macmillan, Cham, 113–129.

Stančius, A., & Grecevičius, P. (2021). *Influence of Ancient Mesopotamian Aesthetics of Gardens/ Parks and Water Installations on the Development of Landscape Architecture. Athens Journal of Architecture* 8(1), 9–34.

Vijayaraghavan, K., & Hemanathan, K. (2009). Biodiesel production from freshwater algae. *Energy & Fuels*, 23(11), 5448–5453.

Wang, Z. J., & Wang, Z. W. (2019, March). A review on tidal power utilization and operation optimization. In *IOP Conference Series: Earth and Environmental Science* (Vol. 240, No. 5, p. 052015). IOP Publishing.

Xiaoxiang, S. (1994). The city should be rich in the pleasures of wild nature—A traditional aesthetic concept of China for urban planning. *Ekistics*, 61(364/365), 22–28.

Yaakob, M. A., Mohamed, R. M. S. R., Al-Gheethi, A., Aswathnarayana Gokare, R., & Ambati, R. R. (2021). Influence of nitrogen and phosphorus on microalgal growth, biomass, lipid, and fatty acid production: an overview. *Cells*, 10(2), 393.

Ynalvez, R.A., Dinamarca, J. and Moroney, J.V., 2018. Algal photosynthesis. *eLS*, 1–9.

Zamora-Juárez, M. Á., Ortiz, C. R. F., Guerra-Cobián, V. H., López-Rebollar, B. M., Alarcón, I. G. & García-Pulido, D. (2023). Parametric assessment of a Pelton turbine within a rainwater harvesting system for micro hydro-power generation in urban zones. *Energy for Sustainable Development*, 73, 101–115.

Zarfl, C., Lumsdon, A. E., Berlekamp, J., Tydecks, L., Tockner, K. (2015). A global boom in hydropower dam construction. *Aquatic Sciences*, 77, 161–170.

4.9

AMPHIBIOUS STRUCTURES FOR SMART FLOOD RISK REDUCTION AND CLIMATE CHANGE ADAPTATION

Łukasz Piątek and Elizabeth C. English

Abstract

This chapter critically examines the shortcomings of traditional flood protection strategies and the need for innovative solutions to address the challenges posed by climate change. The conventional approach of separating buildings from floodwaters through raised dikes and barriers or elevated structures proves ineffective and unsustainable during severe floods that surpass predicted heights. Similarly, the alternative of retreat, involving the abandonment of high-risk settlements and relocation, incurs high economic and social costs in most contexts.

In response to this reality, this chapter advocates a paradigm shift toward SMART designs—innovative infrastructure and technical/structural solutions—capable of mitigating flood damage and adapting to extreme events. A groundbreaking solution explored in-depth is amphibious architecture, which enables structures to remain undisturbed on the ground during normal conditions but effortlessly float on the flood's surface when water levels rise, supported by buoyant foundations. This transformative approach offers versatile applications, serving as ordinary homes, public buildings, or other functions with developed surroundings, and settling back into their original positions as the water recedes.

This chapter investigates three main approaches in amphibious architecture: new buildings of moderate sizes, retrofits to existing structures, and purposefully designed neighborhoods for flood zones. These approaches differ in scale, level of intervention, response to flood risk, and environmental impact. The exploration delves into critical typologies defining the functionality of amphibious architecture, such as flotation type, flotation material, flotation position, implementation strategies, and anchoring methods.

Furthermore, this chapter provides a selected list of known amphibious buildings worldwide, showcasing diverse examples that illustrate the broad spectrum of this innovative approach. Through an in-depth analysis of these cases, this chapter underscores the varied applications of amphibious architecture and affirms its potential as a transformative technique in flood risk reduction and climate change adaptation within urban and rural contexts.

DOI: 10.4324/9781003384113-57

Climate change poses a formidable threat to the future world, with melting ice in the northern hemisphere and increased rainfall contributing to rising sea levels and more frequent floods. Coastal areas and deltas, home to three-quarters of the world's largest cities, are particularly vulnerable, as are riverine flood plains. With 70% of the global population projected to reside in urban areas by 2050, the exposure to floods is set to escalate dramatically. Existing conventional defenses are often insufficient, and despite ongoing climate change adaptation efforts, preventing flooding and storm damage in cities and rural settlements remains an elusive goal.

Traditional flood protection strategies based on the concept of separating the buildings from the flood waters, like raising dikes and barriers around the protected areas or using buildings elevated above the expected flood level, while familiar, prove ineffective and unsustainable when faced with severe floods surpassing predicted heights. Another option is retreat, meaning abandoning the settlements at the highest risk and relocating the people elsewhere, which in most contexts has unacceptably high economic and social costs.

This reality demands a paradigm shift and innovative solutions to coexist with the challenges posed by climate change. The imperative is clear: we need SMART designs—innovative infrastructures and technical/structural solutions—capable of not just mitigating flood damage but also adapting to extreme events. One such groundbreaking solution is amphibious architecture.

Definitions and Typologies

Amphibious architecture, in some sources also named "can-float" (Barker & Coutts, 2015) or "buoyant" buildings (English, 2009; Barsley, 2020), within the context of this chapter refers specifically to buildings permanently located on land but able to float when necessary. The clue to this concept lies in its unique foundation system, a truly SMART combination of low technical demands and high resilience capacity. It enables the structures to rest on the ground undisturbed until a flood occurs and meanwhile be used as ordinary homes, public buildings, and other functions with developed yards, gardens, and parking lots around them. But in case of flooding, as water levels rise, these buildings effortlessly float on the flood's surface, supported by buoyant foundations. Upon the water's receding, they settle back precisely into their original positions (English et al., 2016, 2018).

This chapter explores amphibious architecture comprehensively, delving into critical typologies that define its functionality. We examine the flotation type, flotation material, flotation position, implementation strategies, and anchoring methods employed in amphibious buildings. In addition, the discussion encompasses a selected list of known amphibious buildings worldwide, showcasing diverse examples that illustrate the broad spectrum of this innovative approach. Through an in-depth analysis of these cases, we aim to showcase the varied applications of amphibious architecture and affirm its potential as a transformative technique in flood risk reduction and climate change adaptation.

Notably, the use of the term "amphibious" excludes structures permanently floating on water lots, differentiating it from floating buildings. Despite some technical similarities, floating buildings are different in their relationships to ground and water, how they are accessed, and their legal status (Piątek, 2016).

According to Archimedes' principle, submerging an object in a fluid generates an uplift force proportional to the fluid volume displaced by the object acting on it. To achieve a stable floating condition, this force resulting from the displacement must equal the structure's weight (the floating platform and upper structure together). This can be provided if the flotation device under the building is non-absorbent and large enough to displace a sufficient volume of water. Since amphibious construction is an engineering solution that is, in essence, designing a buoyant platform upon which an otherwise ordinary building can float, a few technical features define the typologies of amphibious construction.

The most basic feature is the flotation type. There is a range of flotation types, each with unique structural elements (Figure 4.9.1). The oldest and the simplest of them is the raft, meaning a floating platform held above the surface of the water by elements made of non-absorbent materials lighter than water or by watertight containers holding air. In many cases, these containers are recycled or repurposed. The platform of the raft may, in some cases, be replaced by structural framing that holds the buoyancy elements in place and distributes the uplift force to carry the structure above. If the number of buoyancy elements is limited, they may be called pontoons. A pontoon structure is a more specific form of raft-type structure. It may employ watertight tanks filled with air in the form of prefabricated containers or those built especially for an amphibious or floating structure. Pontoons may also be fabricated from large blocks of low-density, non-absorbent materials. While small buildings may be set upon a single pontoon, larger structures may be supported by many modular units. Large, heavy pontoons may be structural, while the ones made of many small modules are likely to utilize a structural frame. The last flotation type, the hull, clearly refers to its waterborne counterparts, boats or ships. Unlike the raft and the pontoon, which lack internal access, the hull is characterized by its open-top design that allows for using its volume as an occupied part of the building. A hull always functions as a single structural element and, therefore, is the most vulnerable to leaks and structural breakdown. It requires the highest engineering and production skills. This is the most expensive and least common flotation type.

The materials used for amphibious foundations are related to the type of flotation to a large extent. Reinforced concrete, made in situ or prefabricated, is commonly employed for hulls. It provides good strength but is expensive and prone to production flaws. When combined with expanded polystyrene (EPS), concrete reinforced with steel mesh as the bearing and protective layer can form raft typologies. Steel may be the material selected for especially robust pontoons. When used as repurposed elements, steel drums may provide flotation for rafts, similar to plastic barrels and other containers. The plastic utilized for modular pontoons can also be new, manufactured in floating blocks. Wood, particularly bamboo in vernacular settings, is a cost-effective but less efficient choice of buoyancy material and is typically used only for rafts or framing systems. The use of wood for buoyancy is rare due to the poor mass-to-volume ratio. On the contrary, raft foundations built with EPS or XPS blocks held in wood or steel frames are quite popular due to their moderate cost and low maintenance.

From the architectural point of view, the positioning of flotation in relation to the terrain around the building is a critical consideration (Figure 4.9.2). "Above grade" placement involves the flotation structure resting on or slightly above the ground level, often with a concrete slab beneath it. This popular option requires the building to be slightly elevated, which, unless we are dealing with the retrofitting of a building with a crawl space, impacts the visual appearance and hampers access. "Below grade" positioning submerges the buoyant foundation into a pit, creating an elegant but costly solution with high maintenance demands, such as provision for the removal of water-borne debris. This high-end solution allows for keeping the ground floor close to ground level. The third option is an interesting

Figure 4.9.1 Three types of flotation: (a) Raft-type amphibious foundation in Old River Landing (*Source*: E. C. English); (b) Pontoon-type foundation in Warsaw (*Source*: Ł. Piątek); (c) Hull-type foundation in Marlow (*Source*: Baca Architects).

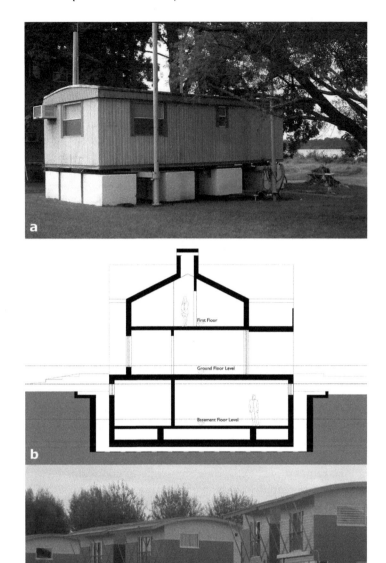

Figure 4.9.2 Three types of positioning the floating foundation: (a) Above grade—Old River Land-ing (*Source*: E. C. English); (b) Below grade—Henley upon Thames, UK (*Source*: Baca Architects); (c) Sloped—Maasbommel (*Source*: E. C. English).

compromise. The "sloped" setting, a hybrid approach, sets the building on an inclined terrain, usually along the bank of a water basin with the ground sloping down toward the water. This solution provides a good balance among cost, ease of access, and appearance.

The last distinctive technical feature of amphibious architecture is the anchoring to allow vertical movement while preventing lateral movement. Since the building while floating must be restrained horizontally and return to its original position as the water recedes, several types of anchoring devices have been invented, including static or telescopic poles, foldable arms, and spring chains. Although telescopic poles have yet to be fully developed, they are eagerly anticipated by architects interested in flush and concealed designs. Static guideposts, also known as vertical guidance posts or VGPs, are the only strategy that, to date, has proven its reliability. The VGPs are constructed from wooden posts, steel pipes, or concrete piles secured in the ground adjacent to the floatable base. The minimum number of posts capable of securing the building in place is two, but most of the structures have four, and in vernacular settings that use thinner pipes driven without heavy equipment, their number can rise to eight or more. Sleeves attached to the building's structure can slide up and down along the posts, while restraining it horizontally. VGPs can also prevent horizontal movement by penetrating an attached deck. Considerations of the visibility of the posts and their impact on the overall appearance of the structure are important issues. The solutions can range from raw visible placements next to the building to hidden positions inside the building or within its walls. Lateral restraint may also be provided by an adjacent static structure resistant to flood damage.

Three Approaches for Implementation

Amphibious architecture embraces three distinct approaches when integrated into the existing built environment, each contributing uniquely to flood risk reduction and climate adaptation.

Currently, the most conventional approach is the construction of new structures with built-in amphibious foundations, expanding the scope to complement existing urban and rural developments and potentially creating impact at a range of scales. Intervention levels vary, from individual houses in rural settings or as urban infills, to larger public buildings, to introducing the amphibious concept into new blocks or communities. One goal is to integrate flood-resilient structures seamlessly within established communities, ensuring a harmonious coexistence with the existing fabric.

The most traditional method involves retrofitting existing buildings, ranging from individual small houses to larger structures. This approach minimizes intervention in the fabric of the built environment, offering almost-invisible add-ins to enhance resilience. The primary focus is on preserving and adapting structures for individuals already residing in flood-prone areas who are unable or unwilling to relocate in the face of increasingly severe flooding. Amphibious retrofits reduce trauma by providing a homeowner with the choice of when to leave as conditions worsen rather than being forced out suddenly in the aftermath of a ruinous flood. It is also appropriate for the flood protection of heritage buildings. Retrofits involve modifying original foundations and adding buoyancy blocks, either within the existing crawl space or utilizing hydraulic jacking to install the new buoyant foundation.

The most progressive approach involves the urbanization of floodplains, addressing flood risk on a larger scale. This encompasses new urbanization projects that intentionally incorporate amphibious architecture. The intervention is extensive, ranging from new urban expansions on natural territories to the deliberate creation of communities in flood-prone areas. This strategy would be embraced in some countries and prohibited in others. Also, the environmental impact of new construction on wetland conservation may be an issue with such projects. Such a forward-thinking approach aims strategically to bring new populations to the floodplains and aspires to reverse the perception of water as a foe to water as a friend.

New buildings of moderate sizes that complement existing urban and rural developments, retrofits applied to existing structures, and new neighborhoods designed purposefully for flood zones are the three main approaches in amphibious architecture. They differ not only in scale but also in their level of intervention, response to flood risk, and impact on the environment. From subtle enhancements to the original building fabric in its original location to expansive urban growth on natural territories, each approach presents a unique perspective on how amphibious architecture can be integrated into diverse contexts.

Complementing Existing Urban and Rural Development

Within the realm of amphibious architecture, complementing existing urban and rural development through new construction constitutes the most extensive category. A prominent representative of this approach is the Amphibious House on the River Thames in Marlow, Buckinghamshire, UK (Figure 4.9.3). Designed by Baca Architects and popularized on the Discovery series Grand Designs, this house features a unique "basement" designed as a buoyant waterproof reinforced concrete hull (Figures 4.9.1c and 4.9.2b). The structure is placed in a "wet dock" comprising steel sheet piling walls, a permeable concrete bottom slab, and a reinforced concrete ring beam. During floods, rising groundwater fills the dock, lifting the 220-tonne structure (Barker & Coutts, 2015).

Another notable amphibious example is the FLOAT House in New Orleans, completed by Morphosis Architects in 2009 (Figure 4.9.4). Sponsored by the Make It Right Foundation after Hurricane Katrina, this house incorporates SMART design with prefabrication, enabling affordability through mass production. Featuring a raised base that integrates mechanical, electrical, plumbing, and sustainable systems, prefabricated as a single unit of EPS foam coated in glass fiber-reinforced concrete, the house is supposed to float in case of flooding (Morphosis Architects, n.d.; Watson & Adams, 2010). However, with no building codes available to look to for guidance, the designers specified sleeves that should slide smoothly up and down on the internal guideposts but were, in fact, constructed with insufficient tolerance (space between the post and the sleeve) to allow sliding and prevent binding (English, 2009).

A less explored but intriguing example in the existing urban environment is the Amphibious Boulevard Pavilions in Warsaw, Poland (Figure 4.9.5). Part of the winning entry in a competition for the Vistula Boulevard's revitalization, these non-residential buildings sit in a zone with a 5% annual risk of flooding along the Vistula, the largest Polish river, known for its semi-wild character. In 2017, eight prefabricated amphibious pavilions were completed, serving public functions such as lavatories, tourist information, and restaurants. Each pavilion comprises modular units, including a 0.7-meter-high steel watertight pontoon and a 3-meter-high steel container-like frame (Figure 4.9.1b). During floods, the pavilions are secured by four corner sleeves to slide vertically on large poles, capable of resisting the strong flood currents. While they remain untested due to the absence of major floods in Warsaw since their completion in 2018, these pavilions showcase the potential of

Figure 4.9.3 Amphibious house on the River Thames, Marlow.
Source: Baca Architects.

amphibious architecture in urban environments. These examples highlight the adaptability and innovation that new amphibious buildings bring to complement existing urban and rural development. They offer solutions that integrate seamlessly into diverse landscapes and urban contexts, especially when it comes to revitalizing neglected waterfronts and city ports where very often the high demand for public buildings cannot be met due to building restrictions resulting from the flood risk (Piątek & Wojnowska-Heciak, 2020).

Retrofitting Existing Buildings

Among the various approaches to introducing amphibious architecture, retrofitting existing buildings would be the most traditional. This method, in being visually unobtrusive, may be characterized by its discreet and incremental interventions as well as its low cost.

The Old River Landing (ORL) community in Louisiana provides one of the oldest and most enduring modern examples of amphibious retrofitting, dating back to the mid-1970s

Figure 4.9.4   The FLOAT House, New Orleans during construction. Elevation; inner guidepost and sleeve detail.

Source: E. C. English.

Figure 4.9.5   One of the Warsaw Pavilions.

Source: E.C. English.

Figure 4.9.6   Old River Landing.
Source: E. C. English.

(Figure 4.9.6). In rural areas like Raccourci Old River in Point Coupee Parish, where ORL is located, clusters of amphibious housing have been functioning reliably for almost five decades. Notably, local residents and recreational fishermen ingeniously devised an amphibious foundation system in the course of individual processes of trial and error. In most cases, large blocks of EPS were secured beneath the homes, raising them roughly 1 meter above the ground (Figures 4.9.1a and 4.9.2a). During floods, the blocks displace water to elevate the houses, which are prevented from moving laterally by long posts sunk into the ground, also known as VGPs or guideposts. Sliding sleeves around these guideposts allow the homes to rise and fall with the water level (English, 2009).

Other examples of amphibious retrofitting may be found in the work of the Buoyant Foundation Project (BFP). The BFP is a non-profit research organization that is dedicated to the development of amphibious architecture. The BFP was established by Elizabeth English in the aftermath of Hurricane Katrina in early 2006. It initially focused on safeguarding New Orleans' traditional cultures by proposing to retrofit traditional wooden shotgun houses with amphibious foundations. During 2006, the BFP developed several preliminary designs toward this end. Introduction to ORL in central Louisiana in late 2006 and collaboration with ORL homeowners contributed to the refinement of the BFP basic amphibious retrofit design and the 2007 construction of a prototype in Baton Rouge, Louisiana (English, 2009).

Over the years, the BFP has expanded its mission to address flood-sensitive locations globally. Notably, the BFP's amphibious retrofitting project in the Mekong River Delta, Vietnam, involved retrofitting the homes of four economically disadvantaged rural rice farmers and fishermen (Figure 4.9.7). Completed in 2018, all four of the retrofitted homes have successfully withstood the recurring monsoon floods, showcasing the effectiveness of the amphibious concept under real-world conditions (English et al., 2020).

Figure 4.9.7 Retrofits in the Mekong Delta.

Source: E. C. English and Pham D. T.

In exploring these examples, we witness the transformative power of retrofitting existing buildings with amphibious foundations, providing a glimpse into the potential of this traditional yet innovative approach for building resilience in flood-prone areas. Interestingly, amphibious retrofits as a strategy for incrementally improving community resilience are not only suitable for low-budget projects but are also aimed at preserving neighborhood character while preventing flood damage (English et al., 2021).

Urbanizing the Floodplains

Considered the oldest amphibious case built in modern Europe, the Gouden Kust Quarter in Maasbommel, the Netherlands, exemplifies the trend of urbanizing flood zones (Figure 4.9.8). Comprising 32 amphibious houses, each with 2 or 3 bedrooms, the neighborhood

Figure 4.9.8 Maasbommel.

Source: Ł. Piątek.

boasts a unified architecture characterized by distinctive barrel roofs. Positioned on the sloped bank of a lake fed by the Maas River, fenced lots with gardens and parking spaces create a typical residential appearance when viewed from the land. Hull-type buoyant bases, visible only from the water side, are made of site-cast waterproof reinforced concrete (Figure 4.9.2c). The hulls are 1.5 meters in depth, are open from the top, and are accessible from inside the house. They contain storage space at one end and living space at the other. Each hull carries a timber frame home. They are organized in pairs that share a common steel-framed platform. Tucked away between each pair of houses are two steel guideposts that pass through the platform to stabilize the houses and contribute to the overall resilience. In a location prone to flooding every few years, flexible pipes connect water, gas, electricity, and sewage to accommodate the rising house. Designed by Factor Architecten and Boiten Consulting Engineers and constructed by Dura Vermeer in 2005, this neighborhood stands as a testament to an experimental Dutch project of adaptable construction (Pötz et al., 2014; Boiten, Factor Architecten, 2011).

A paradigm of building outside the dikes is also apparent in the Arcadia Education Project, constructed in 2016, an amphibious school in Bangladesh founded by Razia Alam (Figure 4.9.9). Taking this approach was rather a necessity than a choice in this case due to the extensive annual flooding of the site. The school that caters to underprivileged children faces the challenge of being located on a river floodplain that is submerged up to 3 meters during a third of the year. Instead of trying to elevate the building, the architect of the project, Saif Ul Haque, proposed an amphibious structure anchored to the site that is capable of sitting on the ground or floating on water depending on seasonal flood conditions. The site was prepared with sandbags, sand, earth, and local brick infill, along

Figure 4.9.9 Arcadia.

Source: E. C. English.

with bamboo posts driven 2 meters into the ground as anchoring points. The amphibious school comprises a linear arrangement of rectangular blocks connected by a walkway, including classrooms, an office, a playground platform, a sanitary block, and a technical room. Built with three types of bamboo using rope-tied joints, the school utilizes recycled steel drums for flotation. The entire structure was coated with a preservative made from boiled local gaab fruit using a traditional method (Aga Khan Award for Architecture, 2019). While the project initially received acclaim, winning the 2019 Aga Khan Award for Architecture, it faced a serious challenge within a year. In 2020, floodwaters and heavy rains destroyed some parts of the project, leading to its current state of disrepair and abandonment (Mollard, 2023). The case of the Arcadia Education Project stands as an important example of both the potential of amphibious architecture for creating new affordable solutions for the underprivileged and the hurdles in implementation and upscaling in countries with limited availability of skilled workers and no building codes to specify adequately safe design for amphibious construction.

More information about the case studies presented here and other amphibious buildings around the world may be found on the resources page of the BFP website (Buoyant Foundation Project, n.d.).

Conclusions

This chapter presents a rich tapestry of design solutions within the amphibious concept encompassing three perspectives: new construction to complement existing fabric, retrofitting existing buildings, and expansion into flood zones. Through a detailed exploration of structural, spatial, and functional examples, we aim to provide a comprehensive understanding of the versatility and potential applications of amphibious architecture across varied scenarios. As we navigate the intricacies of each typology and case study, we hope this chapter will serve as a valuable resource for architects, urban planners, and researchers seeking insights into the practical implementation and potential advancements of amphibious design. By evaluating the strengths and limitations of this technique, we aim to promote a deeper understanding of its role in shaping resilient and adaptive built environments in the face of a changing climate and increasing flood risks.

Research on amphibious construction is ongoing. There remain many obstacles and unanswered questions. Three major impediments to the implementation of amphibious construction have been identified as (1) unsupportive government policies, (2) lack of acceptance from the insurance industry, and (3) the worldwide dearth of building codes or established standards of practice (English et al., 2016). To what level of safety should amphibious structures be designed? This is a question that has not been answered definitively, but we anticipate that the answers will be dramatically different in developing and industrialized countries due to different safety expectations. If the amphibious structure is small and lightweight with a narrow footprint, location in an environment with strong winds may cause concerns about buoyant stability. This is more of an issue for amphibious retrofits with low-density buoyancy elements than for new construction, where there is more often a heavy base structure. Also, the removal of water-borne debris that may have accumulated beneath the building while it was floating, or a means of preventing the debris from settling there, is another thorny issue that has not yet been broadly resolved.

Amphibious architecture emerges as a SMART design solution, revolutionizing the approach to regions characterized by extreme climates and susceptible to major climatic actions and changes. This innovative construction methodology introduces a paradigm shift, enabling the habitation of floodplains that were previously considered uncharted territories laden with geographical extremes, constraints, and challenges.

Amphibious architecture aligns with the principles of SMART solutions by operating as a flood mitigation strategy in harmony with a region's natural flooding cycles. Unlike traditional approaches that resist and control water through dikes and barriers, amphibious construction collaborates with water, allowing it to ebb and flow naturally. This approach prioritizes the protection of people, property, and belongings, allowing water to flow under and around buildings while minimizing flooding elsewhere—a concept referred to as "liv[ing] with the water" (Boiten, Factor Architecten, 2011).

One of the key strengths of amphibious architecture lies in its broad adaptability to a range of flood depths, with the necessary height and capacity of the guideposts serving as the primary limitation. In contrast to dikes and barriers, which will be overtopped in extreme flooding and are prohibitively expensive to heighten, well-engineered amphibious construction provides reliable and affordable flood resilience. This cost-effectiveness is especially needed in flood-prone low-income communities, where amphibious retrofits offer a solution to protect existing houses. In some places, these retrofits may allow residents to stay in their homes during floods, close to their belongings and property. Or if evacuation is required, the homeowner returns to an undamaged house allowing immediate reoccupancy. This fosters resilience and rapid recovery and reduces trauma within vulnerable populations.

Amphibious architecture addresses the psychological impact of trauma associated with disasters, mitigating threats to human life, property destruction, and the fear of recurring floods (English et al., 2018). By providing a low-tech SMART solution, amphibious architecture enhances users' experiences, capacities, and overall quality of life. It is an alternative that fosters smarter, cleaner, healthier, and more efficient living, showcasing its potential to reshape the future of resilient and sustainable built environments.

References

Aga Khan Award for Architecture. (2019). *Arcadia Education Project*. Retrieved January 2, 2024 from https://the.akdn/en/how-we-work/our-agencies/aga-khan-trust-culture/akaa/arcadia-education-project

Barker, R., Coutts, R. (2015). *Aquatecture: Buildings and Cities Designed to Live and Work with Water*. London: Royal Institute of British Architects, p. 214.

Barsley, E. (2020). *Retrofitting for Flood Resilience: A Guide to Building & Community Design*. London: Royal Institute of British Architects, p. 197.

Boiten, Factor Architecten. (2011). *Project Review: Floating Homes 'De Gouden Kust'. Maasbommel, the Netherlands, 1998–2005*. Retrieved January 2, 2024, from http://climate-adapt.eea.europa.eu/en/metadata/case-studies/amphibious-housing-in-maasbommel-the-netherlands/11310092.pdf.

English, E. (2009). "Amphibious foundations and the buoyant foundation project: innovative strategies for flood-resilient housing". In: *Presented at the International Conference on Urban Flood Management "Road Map Towards a Flood Resilient Urban Environment"*, November 25–27, 2009, Paris, France. Retrieved January 2, 2024, from www.buoyantfoundation.org/research.

English, E., Chan, L., Doberstein, B., Tran, T. (2020). *Development of Amphibious Homes for Marginalized and Vulnerable Populations in Vietnam. Ww216. Final Report – Executive Summary*. Waterloo: University of Waterloo. Retrieved January 2, 2024, from www.buoyantfoundation.org/research.

English, E., Chen, M., Zarins. R., Patange, P. Humenyuk, I. (2018). "An Innovative Strategy to Increase the Resilience of Flood-Vulnerable Communities while Reducing Risk of Population Displacement and Psychological Trauma". In *Presented at 8th International Conference on Building Resilience—ICBR Lisbon 2018, 14–16 November 2018—Lisbon, Portugal*. Retrieved January 2, 2024, from www.buoyantfoundation.org/research.

English, E., Chen, M., Zarins. R., Patange, P., Wiser, J. (2021). "Building Resilience through Flood Risk Reduction: The Benefits of Amphibious Foundation Retrofits to Heritage Structures". *International Journal of Architectural Heritage* 15(7): 976–984, DOI: 10.1080/15583058.2019.1695154.

English, E., Klink, N., Turner, S. (2016). "Thriving with Water: Developments in Amphibious Architecture in North America". *E3S Web of Conferences*, 7, 13009. DOI: https://doi.org/10.1051/e3sconf/20160713009.

Mollard, M. (2023). "Arcadia Education Project (2016–2020): Demolition Postcard". *The Architectural Review* [online]. Retrieved January 2, 2024, from www.architectural-review.com/essays/arcadia-education-project-2016-2020-demolition-postcard.

Morphosis Architects. (n.d.). FLOAT House. Retrieved January 2, 2024, from www.morphosis.com/architecture/126/

Piątek, Ł. (2016). "Displacing Architecture? From Floating Houses to Ocean Habitats: Expanding the Building Typology". In: Bezerra, L., Słyk, J., (Eds.) *Architecture for the Society of Knowledge; Education for Research, Research for Creativity*. Warsaw: Warsaw University of Technology, Volume 1, pp. 273–280.

Piątek, Ł., Wojnowska-Heciak, M. (2020). "Multicase Study Comparison of Different Types of Flood-Resilient Buildings (Elevated, Amphibious, and Floating) at the Vistula River in Warsaw, Poland". *Sustainability* 12(22): 9725, https://doi.org/10.3390/su12229725.

Pötz, H., Anholts, T., de Koning, M., (2014). *Multi-Level Safety. Water-Resilient Urban and Building Design*. Amersfoort: STOWA, Retrieved from https://www.stowa.nl/publicaties/ meerlaagsveiligheid-waterrobuust-bouwen-stedelijk-gebied-nl-en-english-version

Watson, D., Adams, M. (2010). *Design for Flooding*. Hoboken, NJ: Wiley, p. 244.

4.10

SMART OCEAN LIVING

Speculative Design of the North Atlantic Floating Archipelago

Łukasz Piątek

Abstract

In the twenty-first century, architects grappling with the challenges of rising sea levels, local overpopulation, and economic disparities have found inspiration in the realm of oceanic architecture. While a prevailing belief suggests the gradual extension of urbanized coasts with floating districts as the optimal approach for upscaling, this chapter contends that establishing an autonomous colony in the ocean could profoundly contribute to the popularization of floating architecture. Such a colony, serving as a living laboratory, showcases political commitment and fosters innovative technical and social solutions.

Employing speculative design, this chapter navigates future-oriented and critical solutions for ocean living. Taking a pragmatic stance, it meticulously examines the historical and tangible circumstances crucial for designing, constructing, and operating a human-built floating colony on the high seas. This analysis encompasses a broad spectrum of natural and cultural constraints, including security, climate, seabed conditions, winds, currents, ice range, marine life, sea routes, nutrition, and proximity to populated areas.

The proposed location for this ambitious endeavor is the Corner Rise Seamounts, a chain of submarine volcanoes in the North Atlantic strategically positioned between the US coast and the Azores. Envisioned as an artificial archipelago utilizing repurposed floating offshore rigs, this innovative concept serves as a potential starting point for the inaugural floating city. Notably, the design integrates a floating academic facility into the colony, drawing parallels with land-based campuses while offering elements of isolation and independence. This floating university not only adds prestige and media exposure to the project but also addresses a pivotal challenge in floating architecture – the lack of widespread public acceptance and market demand. By attracting individuals who may opt for permanent residence or return to land with firsthand insights into water-based living, the concept aims to revolutionize perceptions and pave the way for a sustainable future on the high seas.

The twenty-first century has witnessed a renaissance in the exploration of floating architecture. This dynamic field pushes the boundaries of traditional construction into the vast and

DOI: 10.4324/9781003384113-58

challenging realm of the high seas. Ocean cities, while presenting unique challenges, have captivated the imagination of successive generations of designers and planners who are compelled to transcend the limitations of building in more familiar inland or coastal waters (Piątek, 2023). Central to this exploration are pressing issues of our disruptive times, such as rising sea levels, local overpopulation, or economic inequalities.

Background

As we delve into this domain, it is essential to identify and understand the impediments that may hinder the realization of these visionary projects, paving the way for a comprehensive examination of the challenges and opportunities inherent in pursuing floating architecture. Two distinctive approaches emerge in the context of sea urbanization. The first one is the gradual extensions of urban areas with floating city blocks and districts adjacent to the coasts, like *Oceanix Busan* (Oceanix Ltd., 2023) or located in sheltered waters close to large cities, like *AT Floating City* (AT Design Office, 2015). The second approach, exemplified by *Shimizu Environmental Island* (Shimizu Corporation, 2014), is establishing entirely new built environments on the high seas.

Gradual extensions offer advantages such as organic growth, convenient access, coexistence with metropolises, and the ability to test small-scale initiatives before committing to larger endeavors, thus minimizing risks. However, this way may also have drawbacks, like increasing urban congestion or problems with inadequate regulations and codes. Moreover, it requires transforming the existing coastal built forms that may impact vital urban fronts, historic neighborhoods, leisure areas, or fishing grounds. Detached districts floating next to urbanized areas, free from some of these limitations, are strongly related to super-effective transportation as they aim at the functional expansion of the existing port city.

Building settlements in the ocean comes with even more severe challenges, including serious consequences of potential technical failure, the necessity for autonomy, lack of direct precedents, limited access to other populated regions, harsh environmental conditions, and the absence of proven government models. On the other hand, the floating colonies on high seas present some unique advantages beyond the reach of gradual extensions. Thanks to the effect of the novelty, they can gain public attention and become the catalysts for upscaling floating solutions worldwide even before they are built. When realized and occupied, acting as social laboratories that generate new conditions of floating living, they may contribute to developing new social models. According to the Seasteading movement, when set in international waters, offshore floating settlements with political independence would finally invent better ways of living (Quirk and Friedman, 2017).

As we navigate the complexities of these two approaches, a prevailing belief in the field advocates for a gradual transition, moving from low-risk endeavors like floating districts to higher-risk projects such as independent colonies. The rationale behind this approach asserts that floating cities will organically evolve once floating districts and coastal colonies are thoroughly tested (Czapiewski et al., 2013), assuming a linear continuum exists between them. This logical perspective is heavily anchored in the paradigm of the modern economy and free market orientation. It expects changing regulations allowing regular construction on the water will lead to cost decrease and widespread social acceptance (Lin et al., 2022). One of the basic assumptions of this approach is that the differences between land-based and water-based architecture are insignificant and that the technical problems may be overcome to the extent that living on land would be the same as living on water (Olthuis and Keuning, 2011).

Problem

With the focus on upscaling the floating development by gradually moving from shores to the high seas, it is easy to miss some essential multifaceted issues critical to urban growth. First, establishing a new city (whether on land or sea) requires more than just reasonable regulations. From Roman camps through funded medieval cities and overseas colonial ports to new capitols like Brasilia or Nusantara, it is a political commitment involving choosing the location, allocating resources, attracting inhabitants, and a substantial amount of time crucial to the successful process. However, governments may hesitate to embark on such endeavors in the neoliberal paradigm, pointing at businesses as potential investors. In turn, private companies could easily blame the governments for the lack of legal framework. But regulations, historically, need help to keep pace with innovation, as seen in cryptocurrency and artificial intelligence, which evolved despite the legal void, if not thanks to it. One could then raise a fundamental business issue of the demand for long-term water-based living. Why are people not actively seeking to live on the water amid a global housing crisis? Perhaps the low demand for living on the water stems from an attempt to replicate land-based living, a strategy that may not be fully realized?

Choosing a place to live is a fundamental decision driven by cultural context, living costs, career perspectives, available infrastructure, investment strategy, and many others. As with land-based counterparts, deciding to live in a floating city would also compromise aspirations and available resources. But in addition, it would require a significant expansion of understanding the meaning of the term "home". Convincing people to embrace water-based living requires not just more sophisticated technology and adjusting the costs but also a fundamental change in their perception: accepting the idea of taking root in the water. Numerous examples of people living on the water suggest that this transformation is possible for humankind. But they also prove that the floating lifestyle differs from the land-based one and that these differences grow with the distance to the firm shore. A *houseboat* in Amsterdam or a *péniche* in Paris (Gabor, 1979) could be comparable to the downtown apartment on the other side of the boulevard. At the same time, "Floatel Superior", an accommodation support vessel for a crew of 440 in the North Sea, is not a resort in the Caribbeans (Andersen et al., 2014). The challenge then becomes how to effectively communicate the bearable drawbacks and the unique advantages and allure of life on the water to a global populace deeply entrenched in traditional land-based living.

In light of the conventional approach advocating gradual progress from coastal to high-seas architecture, another idea of reaching the first floating city is still relevant: alongside this progression, there is a need to champion iconic developments in the vast ocean space that challenge social, economic, and legal barriers. The hypothesis posits that establishing and maintaining a colony in the ocean can serve as a potent symbol of political involvement in the floating architecture and become a living laboratory for technical and social solutions. Recognizing that permanent social changes are incremental, exploiting the ocean settlement should allow people to experiment with living on the water with minimal consequences. Paying tribute to the irreplaceable enthusiasts willing to venture into uncharted territory and move to the high seas for good, who are too few to make a reasonable social difference, the vision is based on the possibility of temporary living, with anticipated incentives for extending the stay. The notion of the temporary residence targets one of the main impediments to upscaling the floating development: the lack of public acceptance and market demand by attracting a large public who either choose permanent stay in the colony or decide to come back on land but would experience and understand living on the water. Realizing this endeavor by the international community in international waters addresses two other main problems in a new way: it fulfills the need for the political statement and surpasses the legal problems bound to national codes.

Speculative Design

This chapter embraces a pragmatic approach, bypassing utopian analyses to scrutinize the historical and tangible circumstances essential for designing, constructing, and operating a human-built floating colony on the high seas. Employing the method of speculative design allows for exploring the idea of living in the ocean in both future-oriented and critical ways. According to the classic definition, speculative design assumes implementing technologies or social concepts that still need to be created (Dunne and Raby, 2013). However, it must be clearly explained that the presented scheme is feasible without future solutions. A speculative approach is used here instead to propose a new arrangement of existing elements in the unique environmental and social contexts and, by doing so, to challenge the status quo of current floating development. From the architectural perspective, these new conditions are expected to generate attractive aesthetical, functional, and typological solutions focused on sustainability as a prime development factor while avoiding the tendency to repeat historical mistakes inevitable when expanding existing urban fabric.

With the political gesture of founding the new city being a crucial element of the endeavor's success, the issue of governance is essential. Historical examples of large national projects contracted and canceled by single governments like *Triton City* (Fuller, 2004) or *Hawaii's Floating City Development Program* (Craven and Hanson, 1972), as well as many individual private attempts to establish independent entities, like *Republic of Rose Island* (Hayward, 2014) or a prototype *Ocean Builders* floating house (Upholt, 2021), terminated by governments claiming rights to the occupied waters, show that creating a new ocean colony cannot happen without the political consensus. Bringing several states together on such a project, similar to scientific initiatives like the *International Space Station* or the *Large Hadron Collider*, would not only facilitate financing but, above all, also reduce diplomatic tensions on the grounds of the law of the sea. It seems reasonable to assume that several cooperating countries could govern the floating colony in international waters without arguing about expanding their exclusive economic zones (EEZ).

To consider the problem of location genuinely speculatively, one could start by questioning the idea of fixed location. There are already concepts of sea mega structures like *Lilypad* (Callebaut, 2014) or *Shimizu Environmental Island* (Shimizu Corporation, 2014) that envision drifting in the oceans. Here, a different approach was taken. Since any propulsion would need to be powered, it was assumed that anchoring the colony in a relatively fixed position would reduce energy consumption and increase sustainability.

Several interdependent factors must be considered when searching for the optimal location on international waters. First, security is strongly connected to the ownership and governance of the colony. Selected area needs to be free from the threat of piracy or military conflicts in a predictable future. Staying within close range of the navies of co-governing states would reduce possible security threats. Another consideration crucial for long-term resilience involves balancing the impact of the environmental forces resulting from winds, currents, and icebergs with the cost of raising and maintaining the structure. To lower the costs, the chosen area must be outside the hurricane paths and floating ice range and feature the lowest possible depths, allowing for the anchoring of the structures with standard techniques invented for offshore platforms. Next to these demands, ensuring proximity to existing marine routes and populated centers is paramount for accessibility and integration into global maritime networks. This facilitates transportation, trade, and connectivity, aligning the floating colony with established geostrategic flows. Finally, as the settlement is supposed to achieve a high level of autonomy, the availability of sea nutrition in the location must be considered. However, the construction and operation must not negatively influence the vulnerable marine ecosystems.

As a result, considering security, economic, and environmental factors, this speculative study strategically focuses on the North Atlantic – a dynamic water highway connecting Europe and North America, renowned for its robust ocean economy and relatively high political stability. The North Atlantic meets the demands for high geopolitical security. At the same time, its central and Southeastern portions are also free from floating ice and have low hurricane risk, making it an optimal area for an ocean settlement. Further delimitation of the possible location is driven by the ocean depths impacting the anchoring cost. Since the average depth of the world's ocean is 3,682 meters (NOAA, 2024), areas that are around 1,000 meters deep would be particularly interesting. The outcome of this analysis, presented in Figure 4.10.1, shows that these depths are available outside the EEZs only in the form of seamounts – large submarine volcanic islands.

The Corner Rise Seamounts, an area strategically located 700 nautical miles (NM) from Bermuda, 700 NM from Newfoundland, and 900 NM from the archipelago of Azores, emerges as the chosen site for potential oceanic settlement. This chain of extinct submarine volcanoes, stretching an impressive 300 NM with a minimum depth ranging from 800 to 900 meters, provides required anchoring feasibility, although sensitive local ecosystems

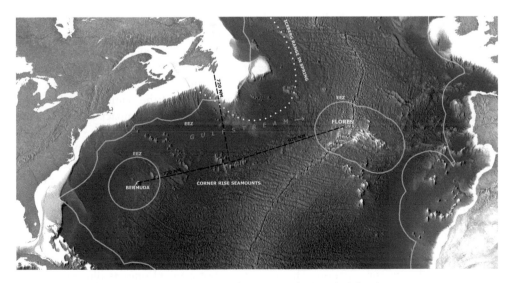

Figure 4.10.1   The Corner Rise Seamounts – location in the North Atlantic.

Source: Ł. Piątek.

need careful consideration. The site benefits from its position on the south edge of the Gulf-stream current, which enhances overall stability and moderates the climate, characterized by moderate-to-strong winds and waves, promising renewable energy production. Conveniently located on the West-East sailing route from Bermuda to the Azores, the Corner Rise Seamounts intersect crucial maritime pathways, fostering connectivity, trade opportunities, and potential collaborations with passing vessels. However, air access from the closest airports of the United States, Canada, Greenland, and the Azores poses a challenge due to the unlikelihood of constructing a full-scale runway on the floating structure in the open ocean. Therefore, learning from the case of Tristan da Cunha, one of the most remote populated islands in the world, it was assumed that the colony would be accessed more sustainably – primarily by the sea vessels that would require a three-day-long voyage. At the same time, emergency transportation would be provided by helicopters.

Selecting the most suitable technology for constructing the functional and resilient floating colony involves carefully considering several requirements, ensuring the successful realization of the vision. Robust anchoring systems are critical to securing the floating colony, providing stability and resilience against environmental forces like waves and wind. The seakeeping capabilities of the floating structure are the key to comfort onboard in severe sea conditions. Sufficient area and volume are essential for accommodating diverse activities, facilities, and communal spaces, as well as open areas, ensuring the well-being of the inhabitants. Provision for easy and safe access to the surrounding water is necessary for transport and recreational purposes, fostering a harmonious interaction between the community and the marine environment.

Since that colony would be placed in the open ocean at a depth of around 1,000 meters and where the wave height exceeds 10 meters, it was envisioned as a group of independent units capable of resisting the most severe storms on themselves. Attention was given to existing technologies for deep-sea platforms that align with the requirements of the high sea: the semisubmersible and the SPAR. Both technologies have already been used for ocean habitation in the offshore oil and gas production platforms. With their capacity to house hundreds of people in remote locations, they inform considerations of adaptability and functionality and provide lessons in modular construction, mobility, and infrastructure support on the water. Semisubmersible platforms are floating structures with sizeable rectangular operating decks elevated above the waves by columns resting on the submerged pontoons. Anchored by around a dozen chains, they offer adaptability to various water depths ranging from 200 to 2,000 m. The main advantage of the semisubmersible design is high seaworthiness thanks to the shape that minimizes the wave impact on the structure. The same idea was taken to the extreme in the second proper offshore type – a SPAR platform. SPAR, acting similarly to the fishing float, comprises a substantial single vertical cylinder tethered to the seafloor by cables facilitating operation in water depths up to 1,000 m, supporting a multistorey superstructure. It is characterized by a smaller footprint and more compact structure than semisubmersible.

In this speculative design process, it was envisioned to investigate repurposing decommissioned offshore semisubmersible or SPAR platforms rather than constructing a new structure. This strategy presents notable advantages such as cost-effectiveness and sustainability by minimizing CO_2 emissions, reducing material consumption, and lowering energy consumption during construction. This concept is not a novel one, as illustrated by the project *Sea Monster*, a creatively transformed North Sea rig (Newsubstance, 2024). Oil companies are already increasingly exploring the adaptation of platforms for renewable energy initiatives, encompassing wave energy converters, offshore wind farms, energy storage solutions, and carbon dioxide removal and storage. These purposes may be included next to the housing in the new colony project.

In the pursuit of sustainability, the design is centered around critical features that aim to minimize environmental impact and foster a harmonious relationship with the ocean. A crucial facet of the colony's sustainable practices lies in its diverse sources of green energy. By harnessing the power of waves, wind, and the sun, alongside exploring ocean thermal energy conversion, the colony seeks to establish a robust renewable energy portfolio. Sea water is desalinated locally, while a dedicated waste processing plant ensures responsible handling of generated waste. To go from the paradigm of being environmentally neutral to positive, the colony actively fosters the growth of an underwater reef on the structure's bottom, similarly to the *SeaManta* project (Baumeister, 2022). This intentional integration supports marine life and enhances the ocean ecosystem's health. The emphasis on aquatic reef development underscores the settlement's commitment to contributing positively to its marine environment.

After determining the governance model, location, and technology, envisioning the functional characteristics of the floating colony is another step in conceptualizing the idea. Here, the speculative approach can be fully exercised – contrary to the typical approach, where the purpose is the starting point of the design, the possible functions were proposed for a defined built environment set in an unusual context.

To match the isolated character of the colony and address the problem of creating possibilities for long-term but not necessarily permanent living, the target social group creating a future floating community was envisioned as young, mobile, open-minded, and international. As a result, a floating academic facility emerged as an optimal choice. Drawing an analogy to land-based academic campuses with elements of isolation and independence, a floating university offers high prestige and media exposure due to its public function. Its inherent mobility of the inhabitants, both in terms of students and staff with short- and long-term stays, aligns with the target demographic's characteristics.

This approach can contribute significantly to cultivating a diverse and resilient oceanic community by offering a unique opportunity for teachers and students to gain firsthand experience of living on the ocean. However, establishing and maintaining a thriving academic community on the high seas necessitates a critical mass of participants, presenting an initial hurdle to overcome, and bringing together a minimum initial number of students and staff remains challenging. To tackle this problem gradually, the first population of the facility that would rather be a research station than a university would comprise several hundreds of students and academics and some technical staff. The next step is a full-scale campus ranging from a population of 1,000 to 5,000 people, which would be comparable to the crew of an aircraft carrier. Most inhabitants would still be only temporary residents, willing to spend a semester or two on the ocean. But with adding new platforms and expanding the scope of services over the years, more academics and specialists would be attracted to join, and more students would be expected to stay after their graduation.

Research possibilities of the ocean station in fields such as marine biology, oceanology, ocean engineering, and others are promising, not to mention the potential of the living laboratory for social studies. The high internationality of such a facility and the positive attitude expected from the academic community provide a solid foundation for the floating campus's successful design, construction, and operation. Beyond academic pursuits, the research work conducted within the colony actively benefits the biosphere of the Corner Rise Seamounts. The colony becomes a proactive force in preserving and enhancing the local marine ecosystem by generating valuable insights and adopting eco-friendly practices. The research activities extend beyond the colony's confines, contributing to the broader conservation efforts of the Corner Rise Seamounts.

Next to these primary functions, the colony is conceptualized to serve secondary purposes. These include potential involvement in search and rescue operations and offering tourism activities. Sustainability is embedded in the colony's design, with urban farming, fishing, and aquaculture practices ensuring a self-sustaining source of fresh produce. Therefore, some parts of the colony would be dedicated to local food production. Other functions could evolve with the growth of the area and population of the settlement, and with the advancement of technology. Extracting green hydrogen from seawater with renewable energy can be one such solution, mainly due to the strategic location of the colony in the middle of the Atlantic, where hydrogen-propelled ships could refuel (Energy Observer, 2022). Another idea for diversifying the services of the new ocean city might be creating floating data centers cooled with seawater or participating in developing the new space sector by launching and landing space rockets on the floating platforms. This comprehensive approach reflects the vision of creating a self-sufficient and dynamic community that seamlessly merges academic excellence with sustainable ocean living and can gain economic independence in the long term.

The inception of a single platform marks just the commencement. Looking forward, a multitude of semisubmersibles and SPARs will collaboratively give rise to ocean urbanization, fostering diversity of the built forms grouped in visual distance. Instead of modular buoyant platforms surrounded by the floating breakwater, a solution popular among other coastal designs, giant buoyant megastructures will form an artificial archipelago of cooperating nuclei. This collective endeavor not only increases the safety of inhabitants by providing an emergency retreat but also aims to mitigate any sense of isolation by establishing a contextual relationship among the platforms that would naturally differ in size, purpose, and form. The envisioned archipelago will feature platforms of varying ages, ultimately necessitating the replacement of the oldest ones, akin to the ongoing renewal of buildings in a cityscape. The distribution of the population and density will be similar in a medieval setting, where densely populated towns with areas limited within city walls contrasted with the wild surroundings. As a result, new waterborne urban types will be created. Instead of traditional land-based urban typologies, like city center and outskirts, streets, and blocks, individual buildings on land plots, which are often replicated in case of floating extensions of coastal megacities, the floating archipelago would be built of independent super units connected by new means of water and air commuting fostering ideas of polycentricity and megastructures (Figure 4.10.2), recalling the ideas of Le Corbusier's *Unités* (Piątek and Słyk, 2017) and Archigram's *Walking City* (Jencks, 1973).

Architectural forms are expected to be diverse but highly influenced by the industrial character of the repurposed platforms and modularity, if not the containerization, of the superstructures. In envisioning the architectural characteristics of the floating colony, the primary challenge is to cultivate an expansive atmosphere, avoiding any sense of enclosure while prioritizing ample green spaces to harmonize with the surrounding seascape. Semisubmersibles, with their large decks, would be suitable for creating pocket parks or sports fields in the open air, serving as an equivalent of land. The SPAR platforms would instead transform into mega blocks isolated from the elements, featuring some internal public spaces in the form of covered plazas and halls. The structures would function as a thriving academic campus at their cores, seamlessly blending various components to

Figure 4.10.2   North Atlantic Floating Archipelago.

Source: Ł. Piątek.

curate a dynamic environment. A reference to creating such dense and vivid yet compact spaces may be an emerging concept of a vertical campus that, unlike traditional projects for academies, is purpose-built to accommodate multifunctional programs and layouts for various academic disciplines (Giovannini, 2002). Recognized as "high-performance urbanism," these campuses utilizing small sites to achieve commercial scale and grade developments within metropolitan areas may be role models for compact floating settlements (Figure 4.10.3).

Here, the main drawback of semisubmersible and SPAR structures would be their limited connection to the sea surface, which may complicate water commuting and leisure. To overcome this problem, new means of floating landing peers lowered on the water during good weather and risen back up during the storm must be developed.

Impact

The culmination of a critical thinking process reveals a confluence of circumstances that exert forces influencing the proposed design. The architectural concept emerges as a subjective response – an outcome of an investigative journey aimed at addressing tangible needs and enhancing existing solutions. However, a comprehensive evaluation of this idea's strengths and weaknesses provides a nuanced perspective.

Figure 4.10.3   Floating vertical campus.
Source: Ł. Piątek.

First, the potential for creating a substantial community of future seasteaders stands out as a notable strength of the vision. Still, despite the potential for settlement expansion, the idea of permanent residence faces challenges that must be addressed. In the current urban landscape, there is a growing trend of existing major cities expanding, while rural areas and small towns experience a population decline. Convincing individuals to relocate to a distant oceanic location may prove challenging in the face of this prevailing urban tendency. As the long-term solution to this issue, along with adding new functions to the settlement and financial incentives for the new citizens, the colony could become another destination for the climate, economic, and political migrants (Quirk and Friedman, 2017), boosting its growth. Although its small size and population, incomparable with megacities, cannot accommodate many refugees, moving from land to water to improve their lives would be precedent setting.

As long as the ocean settlement is a research and teaching facility, limited sea and air access is not a notable weakness. Nevertheless, overcoming the logistical hurdles of transportation poses a substantial challenge to the growth and prosperity of the colony. Hopefully, future transport solutions will increase connectivity more sustainably and flexibly than by constructing a floating international airport.

The long-term maintenance needs of the platforms in high seas, crucial for ensuring the viability and longevity of the floating university concept, introduce another significant challenge. The question of how to sustainably utilize the decommissioned platform for 50 or more years remains an open and pressing consideration. In the first operation phase, reliable technical conditions may be achieved by implementing mobile modular superstructures exchangeable between the platforms for local repairs or improvements. An empty floating base could then be towed to distant coast for refurbishment or scrapping or sink and turned into artificial reef. However, the ultimate smart solution would be to gain full technical autonomy and acquire the potential for decommissioning obsolete structures and building new ones in the ocean, contributing to the independence and diverse economy of the ocean city.

In conclusion, this paradigm shift envisions a floating development as an act of political will that captures attention and fosters a burgeoning need for water-based living. The underlying assumptions posit the creation of new, attractive conditions on the high seas, free from limitations and capable of generating innovative social solutions outside EEZ. Located over the Corner Rise Seamounts, characterized by unique geographical features and strategic maritime location, the colony represents an ideal frontier for exploring and establishing innovative oceanic architecture. Collectively implementing the arrangement of well-proven technologies and the expected ones results in a colony with a positive environmental impact. Through conscious design choices, eco-friendly practices, and a commitment to sustainable living, the floating community emerges as a model for demonstrating how human habitation can coexist with and contribute to the well-being of the surrounding natural environment.

While repurposing offshore platforms for academic purposes on the high seas demonstrates promise, discussing strengths and weaknesses underscores the importance of careful consideration and strategic planning in realizing this innovative vision. Expanding the discourse on the future of floating development necessitates a broader consideration of societal inclinations toward living on the water. Overcoming challenges related to population trends, accessibility, initial participation requirements, and long-term maintenance will be pivotal in shaping the success of this smart approach to oceanic living. Among various floating initiatives, an academic floating archipelago in the North Atlantic stands out with a high potential for upscaling the floating solutions by becoming a starting point for the first floating city. It is envisioned not merely as a structure but as a means to garner political attention and foster public acceptance by allowing the firsthand floating experience.

References

Andersen, T. L., Kvitrud, A., Jensen, J. E., and ASME (2014). "The floatel superior loose-anchor incident and its significance for design and operation of semi-submersibles," UNSP V04BT02A012.

AT Design Office (2015). *Floating City*, https://www.atdesignoffice.com/floating-city/. Accessed 3 January 2024.

Baumeister, J. (2022). "The evolution of aquatecture: SeaManta, a Floating Coral Reef," in *WCFS2020*, Ł. Piątek, S. H. Lim, C. M. Wang and R. de Graaf-van Dinther (eds.), Singapore: Springer Singapore, pp. 131–142.

Callebaut, V. (2014). "Lilypad: Floating ecopolis for climatical refugees," in *Large Floating Structures: Technological Advances*, C. M. Wang and B. T. Wang (eds.), Singapore: Springer Verlag, Singapore, pp. 303–327.

Craven, J. P., and Hanson, J. A. (1972). *Hawaii's Floating City Development Program First Annual Report - Fiscal Year 1972*. Honolulu: University of Hawaii and the Oceanic Institute. https://repository.library.noaa.gov/view/noaa/42324

Czapiewski, K. M., Roeffen, B., Dal Bo Zanon, B., and Graaf, R. de (2013). *Seasteading Implementation Plan*, Delft: DeltaSync.

Dunne, A., and Raby, F. (2013). *Speculative Everything*: *Design, Fiction, and Social Dreaming*, Cambridge, MA; London: The MIT Press.

Energy Observer (2022). *Energy Observer 2, a Demonstrator Vessel that Runs on Liquid Hydrogen*, https://www.energy-observer.org/resources/energy-observer-2-liquid-hydrogen. Accessed 12 January 2024.

Fuller, B. (2004). *A Study of a Prototype Floating Community*, Honolulu: University Press of the Pacific.

Gabor, M. (1979). *Houseboats*: *Living on the Water Around the World*, New York: Ballantine Books.

Giovannini, J. (2002). "The vertical campus—with Deft Strokes, Kohn-Pedersen-Fox builds a collegiate village in an urban tower (New Academic Complex, Baruch-College the City-University-of-New-York)," *Architecture*. Vol. 91, No. 10: pp. 62–67.

Hayward, P. (2014). "Islands and micronationality," *Shima: The International Journal of Research into Island Cultures*. Vol. 8, No. 1, pp. 1–8.

Jencks, C. (1973). *Modern Movements in Architecture*, Garden City: Anchor Press/Doubleday.

Lin, F.-Y., Spijkers, O., and van der Plank, P. (2022). "Legal framework for sustainable floating city development: A case study of the Netherlands," in *WCFS2020*, Ł. Piątek, S. H. Lim, C. M. Wang and R. de Graaf-van Dinther (eds.), Singapore: Springer Singapore, pp. 433–460.

Newsubstance. (2024). *Sea Monster*, https://seemonster.co.uk/. Accessed 12 January 2024.

NOAA. (2024). *How deep is the Ocean?: Ocean Exploration Facts. NOAA Office of Ocean Exploration and Research*, https://oceanexplorer.noaa.gov/facts/ocean-depth.html. Accessed 11 January 2024.

Oceanix Ltd. (2023). *Oceanix. Leading the Next Frontier for Human Habitation*. Accessed 3 January 2023.

Olthuis, K., and Keuning, D. (2011). *Float!: Building on Water to Combat Urban Congestion and Climate Change*, Amsterdam: Frame.

Piątek, Ł. (2023). "Amphibious buoyant architecture—designs for living with water: Floating futures," in *The Routledge Companion to Ecological Design Thinking*: *Healthful Ecotopian Visions for Architecture and Urbanism*, M. Kanaani (ed.), New York, London: Routledge, Taylor et Francis Group, pp. 413–423.

Piątek, Ł., and Słyk, J. (2017). "Jednostki—okrętowy rodowód modernistycznych koncepcji mieszkaniowych [Unités - marine origins of modernist housing concepts]," in *Architektura XX Wieku i jej Waloryzacja w Gdyni i w Europie*, Gdynia: Urząd Miasta Gdyni, pp. 245–250.

Quirk, J., and Friedman, P. (2017). *Seasteading*: *How Ocean Cities Will Restore the Environment, Enrich the Poor, Cure the Sick, and Liberate Humanity from Politicians*, New York: Simon & Schuster.

Shimizu Corporation (2014). *The Environmental Island, Green Float*, https://www.shimz.co.jp/en/topics/dream/content03/. Accessed 12 October 2021.

Upholt, B. (2021). The quest for a floating Utopia. *Hakai Magazine*, https://www.hakaimagazine.com/features/the-quest-for-a-floating-utopia/. Accessed 10 October 2021.

4.11

AQUATIC STRUCTURES
Designing Marine Futures

Joerg Baumeister

Abstract

The ocean's surface is becoming an increasingly crucial resource to support the expanding human population by providing both food and living space. Additionally, there is a need to establish designated compensation areas for regions affected by rising sea levels.

Currently, the use of aquatic structures is mostly confined to buildings on floating pontoons. This limitation may be also due to the absence of a well-established design typology for floating structures.

In this chapter, we aim to create a typology that employs design principles to enable aquatic structures to float. We propose three distinct types based on various buoyancy properties as a foundation for discussion, and we illustrate them with examples.

The example of the SeaManta incorporates air chambers within its artificial floating reef design. In contrast, the SeaOases uses air-filled membranes to create its overall shape. The third type exemplified by the SeaSurveyor utilizes external buoyancy bodies as flotation aids.

Using the typology together with drivers of design such as the natural environment, this study demonstrates how aquatic structures can help protect and revitalize marine ecosystems and ensure sustainable global food security. Further investigations will show which aquatic structures can be developed to design additional marine futures like for the expansion of humankind onto sea.

Marine versus Martian Research

Interestingly, there seems to be a greater focus on proposals for human settlement on Mars compared to efforts to establish structures on the sea. However, it is essential to give more consideration to the design of aquatic structures for several reasons. The emission of greenhouse gases is causing a minimum temperature rise of 2 degrees, leading to rising sea levels and displacing 250–400 million citizens who live in coastal cities (United Nations, 2023). Additional challenges include rapid subsidence caused by groundwater extraction (Setiadi et al., 2023) and the need for new habitats due to urbanization and population growth.

DOI: 10.4324/9781003384113-59

The latter significantly increases the demand for food. To address this, there is a growing emphasis on aquaculture, including the cultivation of fin fish and algae, as a response to the already industrially optimized agriculture (Baumeister and Giurgiu, 2022). Additionally, as clean drinking water becomes increasingly scarce worldwide, it can be produced locally at sea through processes like reverse osmosis. This method requires extra energy that can be harvested anyway more efficiently and cleanly from sources such as wind, waves, or algae fuel contributing to a reduction in greenhouse gas emissions.

In the article 'Technological Requirements for Terraforming Mars' (Zubrin and McKay, 1993), the authors seriously explored the opposite idea of generating a greenhouse gas effect on Mars through methods like mirrors, redirected ammonia asteroids, and other large-scale technological interventions. Their goal was to establish habitable environments with inflatable cities and residents equipped with life support systems to escape the climate catastrophe on Earth on an alternative planet.

Rather than indulging in technophilic dreams generously funded by government institutions such as NASA's Mars exploration program, which costs $300,000 per day (NASA), wouldn't it be smarter to focus on practical solutions, like introducing aquatic structures to prevent the earth from becoming more hostile to life?

In contrast to the idea of colonizing Mars, the concept of settling and utilizing the seas appears not only more sensible but also more effective in addressing and mitigating the human challenges posed by climate change.

In addition to coastal and offshore structures for the gas- and oil industry, there are plans for floating city extensions for wealthy citizens like in South Korea (BIG, 2022) and less wealthy residents in the Maldives (Waterstudio, 2023). However, these structures are typically conventional buildings, kept afloat using traditional concrete pontoons. These aquatic foundations not only generate significant CO_2 emissions during their production but are also costly, heavy, inflexible, and challenging to transport.

Similar to how Martian habitats consider a different atmosphere and gravity, we should inquire about the extent to which the design of aquatic structures is adapted to their water environment. How can we design aquatic structures that have learned to swim?

Aquatic Configurations

The positioning of buildings on floating foundations like pontoons doesn't make the building structures swim and will be therefore excluded, as well as vessels whose design is primarily used for transport and whose contact surfaces with the water consist of hydro-dynamically shaped hulls (Baumeister, 2021).

Aquatic structures have the unique ability to change their vertical position in the water by controlling the volume of their buoyancy bodies. This allows them to either "float" on the water's surface, "dive" in an equilibrium state within the water, or "stand" on the seabed (Baumeister, 2023).

The dive and stand configurations are thereby well-suited for specialized structures like undersea research bases, as they are not directly connected to the Earth's atmosphere and can handle increased pressure with greater water depth. On the other hand, the float configuration could be a favorable choice for extensive applications, thanks to its direct access to the atmosphere, including atmospheric pressure.

Unlike Martian structures, which share extreme limitations with the dive and stand configurations of marine habitats, the flexibility offered by floating marine structures may not only enhance the efficiency of the construction but also could make the design process more open due to the greater degree of creative freedom.

Typologies of Aquatic Structures

The definition of aquatic structures as places "in or near the water" (The Britannica Dictionary) where something "is built, arranged, or organised" (The Britannica Dictionary) includes devices in the marine environment for human beings, animals, and plants. Following the exclusion of floating pontoons and ships and the selection of the float configuration, the design of aquatic structures can explore various typologies demonstrated by the following thought experiment. Volumetric structures located on the water surface are thereby observed and interactions with the water researched.

Imagine a floating pumice stone and a soap bubble on the water's surface. In the first case, air is trapped within the pumice stone, providing buoyancy. In the second case, the soap bubble itself is the buoyant volume. A third thought experiment pictures a skeleton structure on the water's surface that would sink without additional buoyancy bodies to support it.

This leads to three distinct types of aquatic structures as illustrated in the top row of Figure 4.11.1. Due to its porous volume, the "sponge-type" floats in the water in the same way as the inflated "bladder-type", while the "frame-type" stays on the water surface due to supplementary buoyancy bodies.

The bottom row in Figure 4.11.1 demonstrates how each of the three types serves as a base for the development of various floating structures. Regardless of the chosen typology, the process of creating these structures is guided by design research, a method that involves research-based, goal-driven design iterations. This approach generates for different scales multiple design options, from which the most suitable is selected based on well-defined and logical selection criteria (Bayazit, 2004).

Applying this design process to aquatic structures, rather than terrestrial ones, results in significantly different outcomes. The contrast derives not solely from variations in "sponge-type, bladder-type, and frame-type" designs; it also results from the direct exposure to water, which amplifies the importance of factors such as wind and waves in influencing the design. Different types as well as different factors will be explored in the forthcoming examples, where the primary focus is on creating habitats for marine plants and animals, with humans assuming more a supporting role.

Each type of design has thereby a distinct interaction with the marine environment. The SeaManta's "sponge-type" body mitigates the effects of a deteriorating environment by

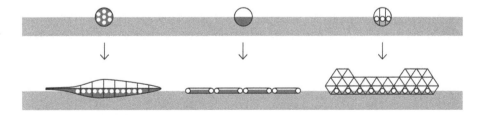

Figure 4.11.1   Three types (or species) of the aquatic structure presented in the top row as diagrams of the sponge-type, bladder-type, and frame-type (from left to right) leading to the three distinct concepts of the SeaManta, SeaOasis, and SeaSurveyor as demonstrated in the bottom row (copyright Joerg Baumeister).

creating an artificial coral reef. The "bladder-type" hydraulic membranes of the SeaOasis establish a closed marine environment customized for aquaculture, while the "frame-type" structure of the SeaSurveyor serves as a platform for monitoring Marine Protection Areas (MPAs).

The SeaManta

By Joerg Baumeister and Nikki Findlay (Baumeister, 2021) (Figure 4.11.2)

The significant decline in coral reefs worldwide has prompted numerous initiatives aimed at restoring coral populations and the overall health of reef ecosystems. The "sponge-type" 60-m long SeaManta demonstrates a novel technique to promote the underwater growth of porous limestone through low-voltage electrolysis of seawater. This allows the establishment of a floating coral reef habitat accommodating apart from corals a variety of other species required for a healthy ecosystem. The artificially grown limestone structure provides with feeding and breeding facilities to help populate the reef. Consequently, the design

Figure 4.11.2 SeaManta, a floating artificial reef (copyright Joerg Baumeister and Nikki Findlay).

incorporates features such as protected breeding areas, nursery aquariums, hiding spots, and integrated caves.

The shape of the aquatic structure is designed according to the principles of three key elements within the natural environment: water, wind, and sunlight. The underwater form has been optimized after a design iteration loop of physical and digital simulations to reduce drag by carefully considering the arrangement and size of the buoyancy elements and the placement of the chain for single-point mooring. Concerning aerodynamics, the structure above the water has been developed to minimize wind resistance and diminish vorticity, thereby preventing the deposition of desert sand.

To enhance the exposure of underwater reefs to sunlight, two key strategies were employed. Firstly, a longitudinal cut was made to facilitate central illumination, and secondly, lateral extensions were added to create underwater wing-like structures, which is the reason for the name "SeaManta".

In addition to its ecological function as a floating reef, the SeaManta is expected to attract two communities. The first is the scientific research community, which plays a crucial role in enhancing the efficiency and cost-effectiveness of the floating reef and managing associated risks. The second community is the tourism sector. To cater dive and non-dive tourists of all age groups, various additional attractions are suggested, including a glass bottom pool, event spaces, fish-attracting bubble rings, and underwater exhibitions.

The SeaOasis

By Joerg Baumeister and Ioana Giurgiu (Baumeister and Giurgiu, 2022) (Figure 4.11.3)

In many developing regions, the world is confronted with an escalating problem: the need to meet the rising global food requirements due to a growing population while facing constraints on the sustainable expansion of arable land. In response to this challenge, SeaOasis has been created to transition from land-based to aquatic surfaces.

To increase efficiency, reduce the use of fertilizers, and minimize environmental pollution, an aquatic food production system within a hybrid closed-loop framework has been developed that has been inspired by the traditional desert oases, hence the name "SeaOasis".

The innovative aqua-farming system combines hydroponics with a recirculation system resulting in freshwater aquaponics for saltwater or freshwater environments that can be adapted to specific climatic conditions. Small-scale farmers will be enabled to cultivate with the SeaOasis system high-value cash crops and gain access to global markets all while simultaneously producing essential fuel and food crops for local communities.

Affordability was the central focus during the design and development process. This began with the choice of "bladder-type" inflatable aqua-pods with a minimum diameter of 10m as modular, cost-effective system utilizing readily available components such as inner tubing from tractor tires. The aqua-pods are isolated from the surrounding environment by a bottom floor, enabling a closed-loop system. They can be combined as needed to meet specific requirements, and they are designed for simple installation and minimal maintenance.

Thanks to its cost-effective and adaptable construction, the Sea-Oasis system is expected to yield a return on investment within two to three years. Ideally, it will serve as a model of an economically viable and environment-friendly solution that generates food and income for smallholders.

SeaOasis © Joerg Baumeister + Ioana Giurgiu

Figure 4.11.3 SeaOasis, floating aquaculture for smallholders' global food security (copyright Joerg Baumeister and Ioana Giurgiu).

The SeaSurveyor

By Joerg Baumeister and Atiria Morrison (Baumeister and Morrison, 2023)

Following the presentation of the "sponge-type" by SeaManta and the "bladder type" by SeaOasis, we now introduce the "frame type" demonstrated by the SeaSurveyor. The SeaSurveyor utilizes a space frame structure in conjunction with externally attached buoyancy components. Its name derives from its purpose: it was designed for surveying MPAs established under the recently ratified UN High Seas Treaty. This treaty seeks to designate up to 30% of international waters as protected MPAs.

The success of the UN's treaty hinges on two critical factors: establishing a physical presence and implementing efficient monitoring. These are key indicators of effective protection for the remote MRAs. Some of the areas boasting exceptional marine biodiversity are found in submerged mountains within international waters. As a response to this, we suggest the installation of floating platforms above these sea mountains. The platforms will serve as monitoring and research centers for the MPAs and will be equipped with autonomous aerial and underwater vehicles capable of covering distances of up to 2000 kilometers.

Figure 4.11.4 SeaSurveyor, an innovative floating solution for establishing marine protection areas in shallow international waters (copyright Joerg Baumeister and Atiria Morrison).

The main emphasis in the development of SeaSurveyor's construction is on affordability. The more cost-effective it is, the greater the opportunity to establish a larger number. To achieve this goal, a lightweight space frame structure known from land-based building construction has been utilized.

It can be transported in standard containers and assembled on-site to accommodate the spatial requirements for autonomous aerial and underwater vehicles, workshops, training, and individual rooms. The size of the structure is adaptable. As an example, Figure 4.11.4 illustrates a structure measuring 70 meters by 35 meters which features a perforated aluminum mesh covering primarily designed for the protection of data.

Conclusion

Not all of the issues initially mentioned have been resolved, as separate research is currently underway to investigate the establishment of sea-based living spaces and the development of floating infrastructure for energy production.

But the examples SeaManta, SeaOasis, and SeaSurveyor validate already the idea that floating aquatic structures can be both efficiently built and exhibit a wide range of shapes. Various factors, including the natural environment, choice of materials, functionality, economic considerations, structural design, and safety requirements, can serve as determining parameters in their design.

For instance, SeaManta's design is primarily influenced by factors like water and wind and the creation of a marine environment. The SeaOasis, on the other hand, places a high priority on producing cost-effective aqua-pods to provide food and economic opportunities to poor communities. In the case of the SeaSurveyor, the central emphasis lies on its space-frame construction and the utilization of aluminum cladding to safeguard collected data.

The examples provided were developed using a particular typology that distinguishes between integrated, immanent, and external buoyancy. While these findings may not be generally applicable, they do showcase various aquatic solutions that differ significantly from their terrestrial counterparts.

It's also important to keep in mind that this chapter serves as an initial proposal for a typology of aquatic structures around the concept of buoyancy. The comprehensiveness of the types hasn't been confirmed, and it's not verified that buoyancy is the only logical basis for classification. Only with future efforts to develop a theoretical foundation for the design of aquatic structures can a comparison be made, enabling us to discuss and determine which typology is the most practical.

Finally, the question arises as to whether aquatic structures can be based on "smarter design thinking" leading to "sustainability", as suggested by the book's title. The application of design thinking has been described in the typologies chapter and the judgment of its smartness is left to the reader, whereas sustainability in its original definition of ecological sustainability will be discussed in the next closing paragraphs.

The implementation of aquatic structures poses of course also risks to the marine ecosystem by reducing sunlight exposure. However, given the structures' limited dimensions, their dynamic positions due to single-point mooring, and the inherent light filtering properties of water, any negative shadow effects are anticipated to be offset by the positive impact of these structures as fish-attracting devices.

In the SeaOasis project, a specific risk to the marine environment is the requirement for additional minerals boosting both productivity and marine pollution. To address this concern at a conceptual level, the entire system has been isolated from the natural environment. The project employs hydroponics and utilizes natural minerals to enhance food security, which proves to be an eco-friendly approach compared to conventional agriculture.

Regarding potential sustainable benefits of the three typologies, a clear conclusion can be drawn. The first type, illustrated by the SeaManta, offers ecologically advantageous opportunities due to its sponge-like volume, encouraging ecosystems to settle. The second type, exemplified by the SeaOasis, isolates itself from the marine environment through a membrane, making it suitable e.g. for aquaculture and marine nurseries. The final type, such as the SeaSurveyor, serves as a platform for monitoring and protecting existing marine ecosystems and may also accommodate facilities for tasks like cleaning sea water from plastic waste.

The suggested typology presents the opportunity for humanity to implement aquatic structures that are not harmful to the environment but actively contribute to the well-being of marine ecosystems. Instead of creating new problems on other planets such as Mars, it would be considerably wiser to direct investments toward developing marine solutions for Earth's health.

References

Baumeister, J. (2021). The evolution of Aquatecture: SeaManta, a floating coral reef. *Lecture Notes in Civil Engineering*, 131–142. https://doi.org/10.1007/978-981-16-2256-4_8

Baumeister, J. (2023). Developing aquatic urbanism: A taxonomy describing 7 strategies and 35 tactics. In: Baumeister, J., Giurgiu, I. C., Linaraki, D., Ottmann, D. A. (eds.), *SeaCities. Cities Research Series*. Springer, Singapore.

Baumeister, J., & Giurgiu, I. C. (2022*). SeaOasis: Floating Aquaculture for Smallholders' Global Food Security*. Springer Nature.

Baumeister, J., & Morrison, A. (2023*)*. SeaSurveyor: An innovative floating solution for establishing marine protection areas in shallow international waters. *Proceedings of the Third World Conference on Floating Solutions—WCFS2023 Tokyo*, Japan.

Bayazit, N. (2004). Investigating design: A review of forty years of design research. *Design Issues*, 20(1), 16–29. https://web-s-ebscohost-com.libraryproxy.griffith.edu.au/ehost/pdfviewer/pdfviewer?vid=0&sid=5f278d7f-1468-495f-8b36-0679bf5ae53e%40redis (accessed 3. November 2023).

BIG's Oceanix Busan. (2022). https://big.dk/#projects-ocxb (accessed 6. November 2023)

NASA's Mars Exploration Program. https://mars.nasa.gov/MPF/martianchronicle/martianchron6/mars300k.html (accessed 6. November 2023)

Setiadi, R., Baumeister, J., & Lo, A. (2023). Floating Jakarta: A human dimension. In: Baumeister, J., Giurgiu, I.C., Linaraki, D., Ottmann, D.A. (eds.), *SeaCities. Cities Research Series*. Springer, Singapore. https://doi.org/10.1007/978-981-99-2481-3_6.

The Britannica Dictionary's definition of 'aquatic'. https://www.britannica.com/dictionary/aquatic (accessed 6. November 2023)

The Britannica Dictionary's definition of 'structure'. https://www.britannica.com/dictionary/structure (accessed 6. November 2023)

United Nations. (2023). Climate change-induced sea-level rise direct threat to millions around World. https://press.un.org/en/2023/sc15199.doc.htm#:~:text=Rather%2C%20they%20are%20rising%2C%20and,new%20homes%20in%20new%20locations (accessed 6. November 2023)

Waterstudio. (2022). Maldives Floating City, a benchmark for vibrant communities. https://www.waterstudio.nl/projects/maldives-floating-city-a-benchmark-for-vibrant-communities-beyond-the-waterfront/ (accessed 6. November 2023)

Zubrin, R., & McKay, C. (1993). Technological requirements for terraforming Mars. In *29th Joint Propulsion Conference and Exhibit*. https://doi.org/10.2514/6.1993-2005

4.12

EXPANSION IN THE WATER

Growth and Design Processes to Grow Living Islands

Despina Linaraki, Joerg Baumeister, Tim Stevens and Paul Burton

Abstract

This research explores growth and design processes to address the challenges of coral island growth, including limited land resources, low elevation, and the adverse impacts of climate change. By the year 2050, it is projected that a significant proportion of these islands will become uninhabitable, necessitating the relocation of thousands of inhabitants and exacerbating ecosystem degradation.

Coral islands are dynamic and sustainable ecosystems that can self-grow, self-maintain, and self-adapt to environmental changes due to the living organisms that compose them. They are formed from sediments generated by corals, foraminifera, algae, and molluscs, and these organisms serve as protective agents for the islands, contributing to their growth, maintenance, and adaptation. However, climate change and anthropogenic pressures impact corals' survival, thereby affecting these islands' growth.

This study draws inspiration from these living ecosystems to propose growth and design processes for expansion methods in the water. The primary objective is to explore innovative approaches for creating "Living Islands", where living organisms, particularly corals, are integrated as fundamental components of the design process and contribute to the growth and maintenance of the islands. Specifically, this study explores eight growth processes for expanding land in aquatic environments, aiming to generate islands that promote sustainable coexistence among the natural environment, coral communities, and humans.

Keywords
Expansion in the water; Artificial islands; Coral islands; Nature-based solutions; Adaptation to the water.

Introduction

Coral islands (or cays) are dynamic landmasses in the water that grow only within a coral reef ecosystem and are formed by the remains of living organisms, such as corals, foraminifera, algae, and molluscs. Coral reefs, also formed by living organisms, such as corals and algae, act as protection barriers to the cays (Birkeland, 2015; Hubbard, 2015). Coral reefs exist mainly in tropical zones, where water temperature ranges between 18°C and 36°C, allowing corals to grow and produce the limestone that forms their "skeleton" and the reefs.

When corals attach to a hard surface, they start growing and producing calcium carbonate, a process known as calcification (Prathep et al., 2018). During calcification, calcium Ca^{2+} and carbonate CO_3^{2-} nutrients found in the water are converted to calcium carbonate ($CaCO_3$) in the form of $Ca^{2+} + CO_3^{2-} <\text{-}> CaCO_3$ (Done, 2011; Kench, Perry, & Spencer, 2009). This process creates robust structures that withstand extreme environmental conditions such as high waves and strong swells. Specifically, research on 255 coral reefs showed that forereefs dissipate 97% of the wave energy, while 86% is reduced (Ferrario et al., 2014). By preventing the waves, reefs provide essential protection to the coastlines as they mitigate coastal erosion. Furthermore, the waves break down corals and algae, creating sediments for the cay growth (Ramalho et al., 2013). Sediments also form when fish and molluscs consume corals and other hard-shelled organisms. The currents transport the sediments and accumulate them at the lagoon (Figure 4.12.1).

Thus, coral reefs are multifunctional ecosystems as they protect coastlines, increase local biodiversity, and produce biogenic sediments to grow coral islands. Moreover, coral reefs are self-grown and self-maintained living structures that grow in situ by corals without the need for funds, materials, or technological resources. Their significance in coastal areas is tremendous. However, they require years to develop and are susceptible to the impact of climate change and anthropogenic pressures.

On the other hand, significant funds, materials, and technological resources are used to expand land in the water and protect it from extreme events. Specifically, around 33,700 km² of land has been reclaimed in the last 30 years (Oppenheimer et al., 2019). Hong Kong and Seoul are expanding in the water to address overcrowding, as is Shanghai, which has reclaimed approximately 590 km² (Sengupta, Chen, & Meadows, 2018).

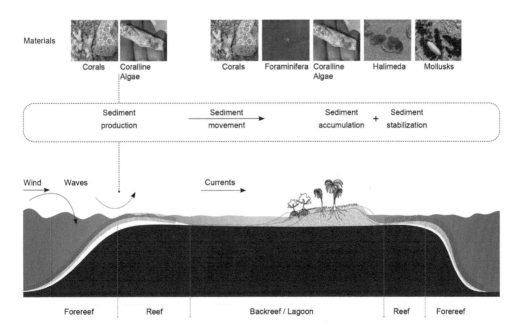

Figure 4.12.1 Coral Island growth and sediments. Images by D. Linaraki.

Kiribati is proposing the creation of artificial islands to relocate its population to safer areas due to sea-level rise (Linaraki, 2021; Lister & Muk-Pavic, 2015; Wyett, 2014). In the Persian Gulf, multiple artificial islands have been developed mainly for housing and recreation. Additionally, artificial islands have been constructed to accommodate airports such as Brisbane, Japan, and Hong Kong or for energy production in the Netherlands, Japan, China, Chile, and the UK (Girling, 2019).

The processes for expanding the land into the water include extraction and deposition of material such as in land reclamation, immersion of stilts underwater to act as foundations for structures above the sea level, extraction of water such as in polderisation, reformation of the existing landscape, or blending of floating vegetation (Linaraki, Baumeister, Stevens, & Burton, 2023). The expansion can be submerged or exposed above water, floating, or raised on stilts. The scale, morphology, and material used vary according to the environmental conditions, funds, material, technological and human resources, and the design brief. For example, coral sediments are mainly used for land expansion in coral islands. In the case of material shortage, they use debris as a landfill material, as happened with the construction of Thila Falhu in the Maldives (Naylor, 2015). Uros floating islands in Peru were made of local floating vegetation. Yet, contemporary structural methods mainly use concrete due to its structural integrity (Linaraki, Baumeister, Stevens, & Burton, 2023).

The construction method and design of the land expansion have a significant impact on the environment and on the effectiveness of the structure itself. For example, in Tarawa Atoll, the capital of Kiribati, people used land reclamation to connect or extend the islands. These solid-fill lands limit lagoonal flushing and cause erosion (Biribo & Woodroffe, 2013). Similarly, Dubai's palm islands were accused of pollution due to the stagnant waters that resulted from the enclosed shape of the construction (Gupta, 2015; Martín-Antón, Negro, José María del, López-Gutiérrez, & Esteban, 2016; Moussavi & Aghaei, 2013). Consequently, materials, construction methods, and morphology should be equally considered when designing for land expansion in the water.

Today, more artificial islands are being created due to overpopulation, economic benefits, and other needs. However, expanding into the sea has been accused of exacerbating erosion, compromising biodiversity, and working against environmental preservation. The materials and construction methods employed play an essential role in determining the effectiveness and adaptation of the structure.

This study incorporates the learning outcomes from exploring coral reefs to propose architectural design concepts for multifunctional artificial land expansion in the water that could self-grow, self-maintain, and be protected, up to a certain point, from extreme events by incorporating corals as fundamental elements in the design. At the same time, it could increase the local biodiversity and regenerate the coral reefs.

Growth Processes

Based on research by Linaraki et al., eight processes for growing artificial islands have been identified: deposition, consumption and disposal, extraction of water, extraction of land, growth in place, reformation, blending, and immersion (Figure 4.12.2; Linaraki, Baumeister, Stevens, & Burton, 2023). Each of these growth processes has been used to generate architectural design concepts for the growth of Living Islands. The concepts have been divided into four growth stages, starting with infrastructure development, then coral plantation, coral cultivation and infrastructure growth, and then human habitation.

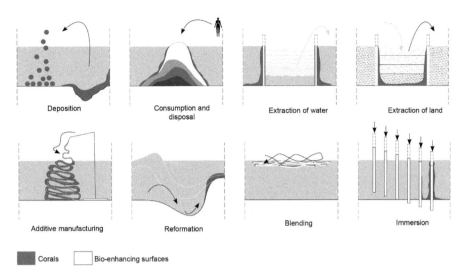

Figure 4.12.2 Artificial Island growth processes and the addition of corals. Images by D. Linaraki.

Growth and Deposition

Growth and deposition refer to the extraction of material (existing or growth of new) and then deposition of the filling material in a designated location until it penetrates the water surface. This material in a tropical environment derives from living organisms, mainly corals, but it can also derive from foraminifera, algae, Halimeda, or molluscs. This is the most common growth process of artificial islands in the tropics. Deposition can happen mechanically by dredging and depositing the material in the designated area or naturally through waves and currents. As mentioned above, this method is already used in the growth process of the coral islands. To promote natural growth, this process would require wave action to break the corals and strong currents to transport them. The design of the island should focus on the elements, such as curved walls, that would control the sediment movement (Figure 4.12.3). Simulations of movement in 3D software, such as Delft, are fundamental for this growth process to work.

Consumption and Disposal

Consumption and disposal refer to creating landmass in the water by consuming and declining unneeded products. This growth process has been observed in many coral islands as it is a way to deal with waste products. However, it has been linked to water pollution (Kapmeier & Gonçalves, 2018). Instead of industrial waste, disposals of biogenic materials such as oyster shells could be used. Oyster shells could provide a natural substrate for coral growth as they comprise $CaCO_3$. The design proposal should generate places for sediment deposition. Thus, designated modular crater morphologies would allow for sediment infill (Figure 4.12.3). The detailed design of the crater would be based on the infill material and the coral species. For example, if the infill material is oyster shells, a steel mesh could hold the oysters together as a contemporary solution, creating gabion-like structures. A waste treatment should be introduced before material deposition if other waste is used. In this case, solid perimetrical walls should divide the water from the infill area.

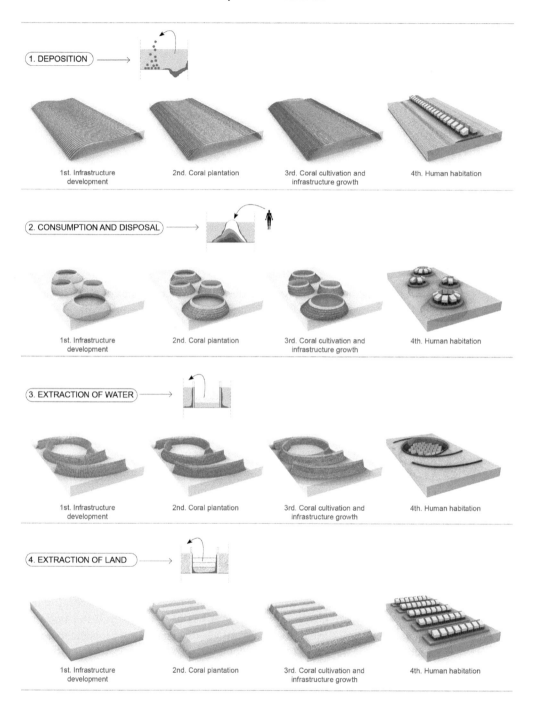

Figure 4.12.3   Concepts and stages for island growth. Images by D. Linaraki.

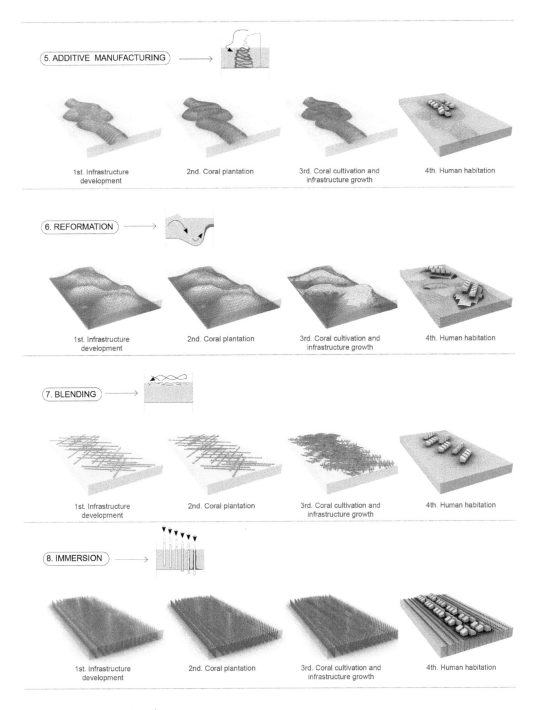

Figure 4.12.3 (Continued).

Extraction of Water

Water extraction involves developing artificial islands by creating dykes and extracting the water in designated areas. This method has been used extensively in European countries such as the Netherlands and France. However, it has not yet been used in the tropics. Evidence has shown that it requires a lot of maintenance and technological resources as the new land is always at a lower level than the sea level, which will require continuous water pumping and protection from flooding and overtopping (Linaraki, Baumeister, Stevens, & Burton, 2023). This concept could be placed on shallow lagoons, away from living corals in an atoll environment. Shallow waters would minimise the need for water extraction. High perimetrical walls (dykes) higher than the sea-level rise predictions should prevent water from flooding the structure (Figure 4.12.3). This design could also be used as a solution to protect existing low-lying islands from flooding.

Extraction of Land

Land extraction refers to creating channels on existing landmasses and allowing the water to flow through and form islands. This method has also been often observed in creating islands, mostly in areas with a lot of sand availability that want to increase the waterfront sites, such as Kuwait or at Sovereign Islands in Gold Coast (Linaraki, Baumeister, Stevens, & Burton, 2023). Also, in areas where they excavate underwater land to create harbours or channels and then use the material as a landfill to expand land in the water. This design requires a strong wall structure that holds the sediments together and prevents erosion (Figure 4.12.3). The island should be placed further away from living corals to avoid any covering from sedimentation during the construction.

Additive Manufacturing

Additive manufacturing refers to 3D printing structures in situ, with local material resources. It appears beneficial as it uses the material found on site, eliminating any transportation costs and CO_2 emissions related to the transport. This method is currently being extensively tested for structures above water. Although it has not been used for large-scale structures underwater, it has been used to create artificial reefs and design bio-enhancing surfaces to promote coral growth (Berman et al., 2023; Lange, Ratoi, & Co, 2020).

During the construction, floating barges should be developed to facilitate the 3D printers. Large pipes would dredge available sediments from the seabed. An environmental analysis should determine the extraction area to avoid destroying benthic biomes. Also, the dredging area should be in shallow water to decrease the construction cost. Following dredging, the sediment should go into further processing to refine it as much as possible. Fine sediments with binding agents could be added to the 3D printer to start printing the structure in situ. Robotic arms would be used to direct the material to the correct location as per design requirements. The design could be based on computer-aided design and provide optimised solutions that use minimum material resources (Figure 4.12.3). The 3D printers use the design from the computer and the GIS location to create the structure.

Reformation

Underwater landscape reformation refers to creating islands by rearranging the existing landscape. Understanding and enhancing natural processes such as swells, currents, and waves could promote the island's growth. MIT Media Lab is currently testing this process to create artificial islands in the Maldives (Self-Assembly Lab, 2019). The concept design should incorporate curved walls strategically to guide the sediments and enhance accumulation. Strong currents would transfer the sediments, and concave walls would guide the sediments to designated locations. The sediment should move away from existing corals, as increased sedimentation could cover them. Sediment movement stimulation programs like Delft could stimulate movement and inform the early design stages (Figure 4.12.3).

Blending

Blending refers to creating floating structures that could be used as a base for land expansion. This method has been observed primarily in enclosed protected environments by blending aquatic vegetation. However, a similar approach can grow living slabs by combining horizontal elements and attaching corals on top (Figure 4.12.3). Buoys should be attached to suspend the structure at least 1 m below the water surface to avoid coral exposure above water. A horizontal mesh could provide space for coral expansion over time, and the mesh surface would prevent sediment accumulation, which is essential for coral growth. The floating slab can then be used as a foundation to raise houses on stilts. It is crucial to notice that the floating structures cannot be placed in shallow waters, as they usually have deep bases.

Immersion

Immersion refers to the construction of islands by immersing piles in the water. The concept of immersion is currently the most used for temporary expansions at low-lying islands. This concept requires less material and technological resources than the others analysed above. However, it requires a good foundation system and a stable seabed to ensure that the piles will not sink over time. Adding corals to this growth process would enhance and strengthen the foundation system. The piles should be placed in a grid system that would allow for more efficient and controlled human and coral habitation development (Figure 4.12.3). The grid dimensions should be calculated to incorporate the needs for house development, coral growth, sediment, and water flow. The structure's development on top should allow maximum light penetration underneath the structures. Also, waste and water management would be mandatory to avoid water pollution. Developing the structures on piles allows for more controlled waste and water management underneath the structure.

Growth Stages

All the growth and design processes analysed above should incorporate four stages of development (as illustrated in Figure 4.12.3). The first stage would be to provide the minimum infrastructure for the growth of corals. The infrastructure should be designed to promote coral attachment and growth. To promote growth, it must consist of bio-enhancing surfaces utilising natural materials sourced from the site. Also, it should maximise the sunlight intake, an essential factor for coral growth. Sun path and radiation diagrams could assist in the placement of the structure to receive maximum sunlight.

Moreover, it should be structurally able to withstand extreme waves and strong currents and support corals in the early stages of development. The structure's foundation and design should consider the existing topographic and environmental conditions. Environmental and coastal engineer consultants should be deployed to survey the area and provide an analytic report of the site conditions that would be then used to design and place the infrastructure.

The second step would be to attach the corals. The coral species selection should be based on coral species existing in the local area and the design requirements. This research uses seven coral types distinguished based on their morphology: branching, massive, encrusting, columnar, foliose, mushroom/free-living, and laminar/table corals (Veron & Stafford-Smith, 2000). Each type can provide different opportunities for the design of the island. For example, branching corals grow fast and produce many sediments, whereas massive corals grow slowly but create solid structures that can act as wave breakers. Experienced divers should be employed to attach the corals to the structure as soon as the first step is complete.

The corals will start growing and expanding on top of the infrastructure while at the same time increasing sediment production. Community members, volunteers, and experts should monitor and maintain the growth during the growth period. After one to three years, they will grow stronger and enhance the stability of the structure. One of the challenges for this study is the slow growth rate, which is approximately 1 cm per year. However, the actual growth of corals depends on the type and the environmental conditions (Masselink, McCall, Beetham, Kench, & Storlazzi, 2021). Yet, examining the coral growth is not part of this chapter.

The fourth step examined in this project is the human habitation on top of the infrastructure. Land stabilisation techniques should take place when the land is above water level. The land should be compacted with artificial methods to ensure a stable base before human habitation. When the land is ready, houses could be raised on top. The island's design above water should consider the sea-level change predictions from the IPCC. Adaptation strategies such as accommodate, expansion, nature-based solutions, and protection should be considered when designing the island (Baumeister & Linaraki, 2023).

Design Process

The design process to grow living islands should be used to generate concepts in preliminary design phases (Figure 4.12.4). The first step is the site analysis. The analysis should be divided into geomorphology analysis, which will guide where to place the structure; benthic analysis, which will guide the design of bio-enhancing surfaces; and climate analysis to understand and adapt to the natural processes.

The geomorphic analysis should include satellite images to understand the context, size, and scale comparisons to understand the opportunities for urban development, bathymetric data to be used as a parameter for selecting the growth processes, and a geomorphic reef map to identify the reef zones that can be extracted from Coral Atlas.

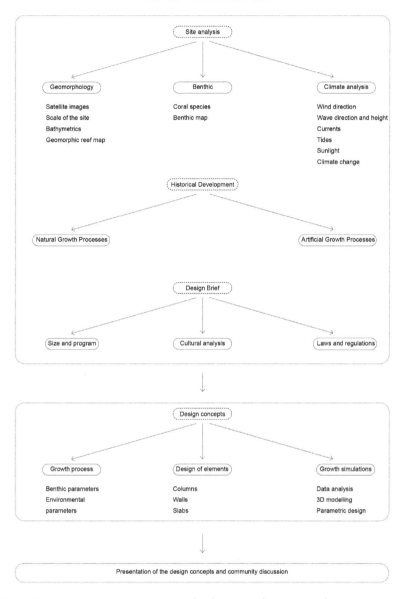

Figure 4.12.4   Design process to grow Living Islands. Images by D. Linaraki.

The benthic analysis should have a benthic map that can also be extracted from Coral Atlas and will help to identify the various substrate materials. Also, a coral species analysis of the existing corals will be used as a base to generate bio-enhancing structures for the particular species.

The climate analysis should include wind, wave, and current direction maps to predict the sediment movement. The tidal levels and sunlight availability data will be used for the

557

placement of the structure, as they could both affect the growth of corals. Also, it should include an analysis of the climate change predictions for at least the next 100 years, as the growth of living islands is a long-term investment that would be affected by rising sea levels and temperatures.

The second step of the design process should be a historical development analysis. This should include an analysis of the reef's natural growth processes and of any other islands in proximity to the site to understand, adapt, and enhance the natural growth. Also, it should include an analysis of the artificial island growth processes and any other anthropogenic impacts that could have affected the natural processes, such as harbour construction.

The third step would be the development of the design brief. That should include the size and program needs, a cultural analysis, and a compilation of the local laws and regulations. That would help to understand the design needs and sizes and create urban growth scenarios. Cultural analysis is significant as many designs have been developed on islands without considering the cultural needs and are not adaptable to the local culture.

The fourth and final step, for this preliminary stage, is generating living island growth design concepts. The selection of growth processes would be based on the existing benthic and environmental parameters as analysed above. Moving forward is the design of architectural elements that would be used to grow corals, guide sediments, and support the artificial islands. These elements include columns, slabs, and walls and should incorporate bio-enhancing surfaces to promote coral attachment and growth. Data analysis and parametric 3D modelling can help to simulate the growth stages and represent the design concepts. Following the concept design, there should be a community discussion to present and discuss the various ideas. Community engagement is essential for this design process.

Conclusion/Discussion

This research examined eight growth processes for growing land in the water. Adding corals as fundamental elements in the design would enhance the island's maintenance, growth, and adaptation while increasing biodiversity and promoting coral growth. However, many challenges should be considered, such as the time frame needed to grow the corals and the islands. As referred, this is a long-term investment requiring at least one to three years for coral establishment and then more years for coral growth.

Moreover, the design process cannot be fully controlled when designing with living organisms. Many parameters can affect the response of living organisms, which can significantly impact the design. Thus, various scenarios should be developed. Using parametric design could provide various design outcomes per parameters the designer sets. These should include the coral species and growth rates, the environmental conditions, and the climate change predictions.

Also, the proposed growth and design processes have been generated to adapt to coral types and can only be used in tropical zones where corals grow. However, similar scenarios could be developed to include other living organisms, such as algae or oysters. Living structures and islands made of oysters have already been developed in various locations worldwide. For example, the island of Mound Key in Florida was made of discarded oyster shells. Or, more recently, the proposal of SCAPE Architects to protect New York City's coastline by growing oysters around the bay.

Another important outcome is that the complexity of growing living islands requires a multidisciplinary approach. Environmental experts, along with coastal engineers, should survey the existing area and provide an analysis of the environmental and topographic conditions. Marine biologists specialising in corals should determine which coral species could be used for the growth of the structure. In collaboration with structural engineers and urban planners, architects should consider the surveys to propose various concept designs that respond to the design brief and the needs of the corals and the environment. A combination of growth processes could achieve maximum benefits for island and coral growth per the environmental and contextual conditions.

Last, it is essential to note that the design approach of this study primarily focuses on the environment and coral growth and is secondary to peoples' needs. The first step should be understanding the environment to enhance and adapt to the natural processes. Working against the environment has been proven to be detrimental in numerous projects. As the design and growth processes depend on the growth and survival of corals, the design should anticipate and promote coral growth.

References

Baumeister, J., & Linaraki, D. (2023). *Cities+1m, Urban Development Solutions for Sea Level Rise*. Singapore: Springer.

Berman, O., Weizman, M., Oren, A., Neri, R., Parnas, H., Shashar, N., & Tarazi, E. (2023). Design and application of a novel 3D printing method for bio-inspired artificial reefs. *Ecological Engineering, 188*, 106892. doi:https://doi.org/10.1016/j.ecoleng.2023.106892

Biribo, N., & Woodroffe, C. D. (2013). Historical area and shoreline change of reef islands around Tarawa Atoll, Kiribati. *Sustainability Science, 8*(3), 345–362. doi:10.1007/s11625-013-0210-z

Birkeland, C. (2015). *Coral Reefs in the Anthropocene* (1st ed.). Dordrecht: Springer Netherlands.

Done, T. (2011). *Corals: Environmental Controls on Growth* (pp. 281–293). In: Hopley, D. (ed) *Encyclopedia of Modern Coral Reefs. Encyclopedia of Earth Sciences Series*. Dordrecht: Springer. https://doi.org/10.1007/978-90-481-2639-2_10

Ferrario, F., Beck, M. W., Storlazzi, C. D., Micheli, F., Shepard, C. C., & Airoldi, L. (2014). The effectiveness of coral reefs for coastal hazard risk reduction and adaptation. *Nature Communications, 5*(1), 3794. doi:10.1038/ncomms4794.

Girling, M. (2019). The Netherlands is tackling climate change by making floating solar farms. Retrieved from https://www.weforum.org/agenda/2019/12/the-netherlands-is-building-solar-islands-to-fight-rising-sea-levels.

Gupta, P. (2015). Futures, fakes and discourses of the gigantic and miniature in 'the world' Islands, Dubai. *Island Studies Journal, 10*(2), 181–196.

Hubbard, D. K. (2015). Reef biology and geology - not just a matter of scale. In: Birkeland, C. (ed) *Coral Reefs in the Anthropocene*. Dordrecht: Springer. https://doi.org/10.1007/978-94-017-7249-5_3

Kapmeier, F., & Gonçalves, P. (2018). Wasted paradise? Policies for Small Island States to manage tourism-driven growth while controlling waste generation: the case of the Maldives. *System Dynamics Review, 34*(1–2), 172–221. doi:10.1002/sdr.1607

Kench, P., Perry, C., & Spencer, T. (2009). *Coral Reefs* (pp. 180–213). Cambridge University Press.

Lange, C., Ratoi, L., & Co, D. L. (2020). Reformative coral habitats. Rethinking Artificial Reef structures through a robotic 3D clay printing method. In *Paper Presented at the 25th International Conference of the Association for Computer-Aided Architectural Design Research in Asia*. Hong Kong.

Linaraki, D. (2021). *A comparison between alternative relocation options for the Pacific Islands based on a human-centred approach* (pp.253–269). In J. Baumeister, E. Bertone, & P. Burton (Eds.), *SeaCities*. Singapore: Springer.

Linaraki, D., Baumeister, J., Stevens, T., & Burton, P. (2023). An overview of artificial islands growth processes and their adaptation to sea-level rise (pp. 65–120). In J. Baumeister, I.C. Giurgiu, D. Linaraki, D.A. Ottmann (Eds.), *SeaCities*. Singapore: Springer.

Lister, N., & Muk-Pavic, E. (2015). Sustainable artificial island concept for the Republic of Kiribati. *Ocean Engineering, 98*, 78–87. doi:10.1016/j.oceaneng.2015.01.013

Martín-Antón, M., Negro, V., José María del, C., López-Gutiérrez, J. S., & Esteban, M. D. (2016). Review of coastal land reclamation situation in the world. *Journal of Coastal Research, 1*(75), 667–671. doi:10.2112/SI75–133.1

Masselink, G., McCall, R., Beetham, E., Kench, P., & Storlazzi, C. (2021). Role of future reef growth on morphological response of Coral Reef Islands to sea-level rise. *Journal of Geophysical Research. Earth Surface, 126*(2), n/a-n/a. doi:10.1029/2020JF005749

Moussavi, Z., & Aghaei, A. (2013). The environment, geopolitics and artificial islands of Dubai in the Persian Gulf. *Procedia - Social and Behavioral Sciences, 81*, 311–313. doi:10.1016/j.sbspro.2013.06.434

Naylor, A. K. (2015). Island morphology, reef resources, and development paths in the Maldives. *Progress in Physical Geography, 39*(6), 728–749. doi:10.1177/0309133315598269

Oppenheimer, M., Glavovic, B.C., Hinkel, J., van de Wal, R., Magnan, A.K., Abd-Elgawad, A., Cai, R., Cifuentes-Jara, M., DeConto, R.M., Ghosh, T., Hay, J., Isla, F., Marzeion, B., Meyssignac, B., & Sebesvari, Z. (2019). Sea level rise and implications for low-lying islands, coasts and communities. In: *IPCC Special Report on the Ocean and Cryosphere in a Changing Climate.* Monaco

Prathep, A., Prathep, A., Kaewsrikhaw, R., Kaewsrikhaw, R., Mayakun, J., Mayakun, J., . . . Darakrai, A. (2018). The effects of light intensity and temperature on the calcification rate of Halimeda macroloba. *Journal of Applied Phycology, 30*(6), 3405–3412. doi:10.1007/s10811-018-1534-y

Ramalho, R. S., Quartau, R., Trenhaile, A. S., Mitchell, N. C., Woodroffe, C. D., & Ávila, S. P. (2013). Coastal evolution on volcanic oceanic islands: A complex interplay between volcanism, erosion, sedimentation, sea-level change and biogenic production. *Earth-Science Reviews, 127*, 140–170. doi:10.1016/j.earscirev.2013.10.007

Sengupta, D., Chen, R., & Meadows, M. E. (2018). Building beyond land: An overview of coastal land reclamation in 16 global megacities. *Applied Geography, 90*, 229–238. doi:10.1016/j.apgeog.2017.12.015

Self-Assembly Lab (2019). Growing Islands. MIT. Retrieved https://selfassemblylab.mit.edu/growingislands

Veron, J. E. N., & Stafford-Smith, M. (2000). *Corals of the World.* Townsville, QLD: Australian Institute of Marine Science.

Wyett, K. (2014). Escaping a rising tide: Sea level rise and migration in Kiribati. *Asia and the Pacific Policy Studies, 1*(1), 171–185. doi:10.1002/app5.7

PARADIGMATIC CATEGORY 5

On Smart Design Mobility and in Defiance of Pollution

This Paradigmatic Category covers topics related to *Intelligent Mobility Systems* and their impact on the design of urban and built environments toward augmenting the space potentials within the buildings and cities – chapters include sustainable design mobility solutions and agendas that synthesize manufacturing, computing energy, and material, toward developing safer, cleaner, and more convenient means of transportations in and between future cities. This paradigm introduces eco-mobility, which prioritizes walking, cycling, public transportation, and shared light electric vehicles. It promotes travel through integrated socially inclusive and environmentally friendly options independent of privately owned vehicles. It gives priority to health, safety, low-emissions, and people-centered urban development encouraging circular and regional economies while limiting the impact of freight transport.

Chapters in this section expand on future visions of short distances, long-distance mobility systems, and breaking away from cultural attachments to cars and the infrastructure that supports them. It also introduces lessons learned from developments in Space Architecture.

DOI: 10.4324/9781003384113-61

5.1

SMART MOBILITY AND THE FUTURE OF CITIES

Jaymes Dunsmore

Abstract

It is essential for architects, designers, urban planners, and policymakers to understand how mobility shapes cities and impacts the physical, social, environmental, and economic well-being of urban residents in order to move toward smarter cities and a more sustainable planet. This chapter explores mobility through three lenses: (1) mobility as a function of transportation and access; (2) mobility as a system of paths, vehicles, and organization; and (3) mobility as a market with dynamic supply and demand.

This chapter explores how mobility has been a shaping force in cities throughout human history with a focus on Western Europe and North America and the impacts of our current mobility system. Drawing on the author's experience as an urban-planning practitioner and original research on mobility experience in those regions, this chapter illustrates how cities can move toward a smart, sustainable, and equitable mobility future with walkable neighborhoods, better transit, and smarter mobility. Finally, this chapter concludes with a discussion of how the principles outlined above provide a framework for understanding emerging and future mobility systems, including electric vehicles (EVs), autonomous vehicles (AVs), and electric vertical take-off and landing (EVTOL) vehicles.

What Is Smart Mobility?

What is smart mobility? When approaching an answer to this question, it is necessary to first ask: what is mobility, and what role does it play in urban development? Mobility is generally defined as the ability to move or be moved freely and easily (McKay, 2019). While mobility may be physical (the ability to move one's body), social, or economic (the ability to move between social groups or classes), within the context of urban planning and this chapter, mobility refers to the ability to move within and between cities. Mobility is closely related to the ideas of transportation and access: where mobility describes the *ability* to move, transportation is the *act* of moving something or someone, and access, defined as the ability to reach desired goods, services, or destinations, is generally the *purpose* of that

DOI: 10.4324/9781003384113-62

movement (McKay, 2019; Walker, 2011). Thus, smart mobility—here defined as the ability to move in a healthier, more equitable, sustainable, and efficient way—addresses the question of how to maximize access while minimizing the impacts of transportation on physical, social, environmental, and economic well-being.

Mobility as a System

Mobility operates as a system with three components: vehicles, paths, and rules. Within a mobility system, the vehicle is what moves, the path is the surface or substance along which or through which it moves, and rules are regulatory frameworks that govern and facilitate the vehicle's movement. Thus, cars are vehicles whose paths are roads, trains are vehicles whose paths are rails, ships are vehicles whose paths are waterways, and planes are vehicles whose path is the air. Rules include a range of regulations, such as vehicular codes, maritime laws, and airspace regulations, as well as insurance, operator licensing, and vehicle inspection requirements, all of which allow the safe and orderly use of limited paths by multiple vehicles. The characteristics of each of these components define how they impact urban development.

For ground-based mobility systems, paths require land and physical infrastructure and are therefore more expensive to construct and maintain than vehicles. In the preindustrial age, a single person could build a cart and care for a horse to pull it, but it would take an army (often literally) to build roads to every destination where you might want to drive it. Today, the average cost of a new passenger car is less than one hundredth the cost of a mile of urban roadway on which to drive it. For this reason, paths such as streets and highways tend to be publicly owned and maintained while most vehicles are privately owned and maintained. Likewise, paths tend to be more enduring but less technologically complex than vehicles. Vehicles can be replaced and upgraded technologically every few years or at most decades whereas paths established centuries, even millennia, ago remain in everyday use in cities around the world.

Mobility Supply and Demand

Mobility systems are subject to the same principles of supply and demand that govern other markets; however, because mobility infrastructure is often provided by cities and governments at a subsidized below-market price, the users generally pay with time rather than money. In the case of urban highways, supply is the roadway capacity, determined by the number of lanes and speed of traffic, expressed in vehicles per hour. Demand is dynamic and time-dependent. At night, for example, demand is generally low, and traffic may be free flowing. As the morning rush hour begins, demand increases, and congestion ensues. A trip that might take 30 minutes in light traffic at midnight could take twice as long or more at 8 am as the demand for travel outstrips the supply of roadway capacity. On urban roadways, supply is also dynamic. It may seem counterintuitive, but a congested freeway at rush hour moves fewer cars than the same roadway at night. Because capacity is a function of the number of lanes and travel speed, as congestion increases and the average vehicle speed slows, the capacity of the roadway drops exponentially.

The solution to traffic congestion may seem simple (even if not easy or inexpensive): just widen the road. However, by increasing the roadway capacity, the cost of driving to one's time is reduced, and more commuters decide to drive—a concept known as induced demand (Schneider, 2018). Some people who would have waited until later in the day, taken transit, or not traveled at all now decide to travel at peak times. Others who might have lived closer to their destinations may now decide to move farther away, believing that they can reduce their housing costs without increasing the cost of their commute. The phenomenon works the other way as well: reducing capacity by removing roadways reduces overall traffic. Thus, smarter solutions to increase mobility are needed—and can actually work.

Why Smart Mobility Matters

It is essential for architects, designers, urban planners, and policymakers to understand how mobility shapes cities and impacts the physical, social, environmental, and economic well-being of urban residents in order to move toward smarter cities and a more sustainable planet. These three principles—mobility as a function of transportation and access; mobility as a system of paths, vehicles, and rules; and mobility as a market with dynamic supply and demand—provide a basis for understanding mobility and its role in the urban environment.

The following sections of this chapter explore mobility as a shaping force in cities throughout human history with a focus on Western Europe and North America and the impacts of our current mobility system. Drawing on my experience as an urban-planning practitioner and original research on mobility experience in those regions, I will then share how cities can move toward a smart, sustainable, and equitable mobility future with walkable neighborhoods, better transit, and smarter mobility. Finally, this chapter concludes with a discussion of how the principles outlined above provide a framework for understanding emerging and future mobility systems.

Mobility as a Shaping Force in Cities

The location, size, and form of cities throughout history are direct results of the mobility systems in place at the time of their establishment. These mobility systems, particularly the paths established, continue to influence urban development for generations to come. From the dawn of the first cities, oriented toward water-based transportation and scaled to human mobility; to the industrial age, when cities expanded along with new technologies; to the modern age, defined by auto-oriented urban development, mobility has been a powerful shaping force in cities.

Mobility in Preindustrial Cities

Throughout the ancient world, cities were established along rivers, which served as the backbone of the mobility system of the day. The first cities emerged in Mesopotamia around 7500 BCE along the banks of the Tigris and Euphrates Rivers (National Geographic Society, 2022). Other early urban centers developed along the Nile River in Egypt, the Yellow River in China, and the Indus River in what is modern-day Pakistan and northwestern India (ibid.). Those cities best positioned for access grew in both size and importance. Two such ancient river cities, Rome and London, exemplify how mobility drove urban development in the preindustrial era.

Rome, founded along the Tiber River in 753 BCE, benefited from a location on the Italian peninsula near the center of the Mediterranean Sea, providing easy access by sea to the whole of the Mediterranean world (Foot et al., 2023). Rome became the largest city in the world and the first in human history to reach a population of over one million in the year 136 (ibid.). London, founded in the year 43 as the Roman outpost of Londinium, was sited at the point along the River Thames closest to the sea where the river was narrow enough to allow construction of a bridge but still deep and wide enough to allow navigation by ship (Ehrlich et al., 2023). From this strategic location, London grew to become the capital of a global maritime empire with a population of one million by the year 1800 (ibid.).

Despite the changes over nearly two millennia, Rome in the second century and London at the dawn of the nineteen century had a roughly similar size and urban form dictated by the limitations of the mobility system of the time. These cities were characterized by compact dense development along narrow streets, extending no farther than the distance a person could comfortably walk, which was the dominant form of intraurban transportation. Proximity to navigable waterways was essential as ships remained the primary mode of transportation beyond the city, notwithstanding the network of Roman roads connecting each city. Ground transportation in the preindustrial era was slow and expensive compared to the relative speed and ease of the sea, and cities reflected this reality.

Mobility in Industrializing Cities

Not until the industrial age did cities grow significantly in size as well as population, propelled by changes in mobility technology. Rail lines, first steam-powered and later electric, facilitated the movement of goods and people over greater distances at higher speeds and lower costs, allowing cities to grow exponentially and transforming urban life. During this period, the population in London increased nearly seven-fold from one million in 1800 to 6.7 million a century later while the United States underwent a similarly rapid period of urbanization (National Geographic Society, 2022). In 1800, less than 10% of the U.S. population lived in cities; by 1900, four in ten Americans were urban residents (ibid.).

This new mobility system was built over (as well as under) the existing mobility network. The first urban rail lines were laid along city streets. As traffic volumes increased, and conflicts between pedestrians, horse carts, and rail became apparent, urban leaders insisted that rail lines be separated from urban streets, leading to the advent of elevated and underground urban rail lines. In 1863, the world's first underground urban railway opened in London (Ehrlich et al., 2023). Other cities followed, and by the early 1900s urban railways, in the form of streetcars, elevated lines, and subways, could be found in most European and American cities.

These changes in mobility fundamentally reshaped how cities grew and the lives of urban residents. In preindustrial cities, most residents lived and worked in the same location, living above the shop or walking a short distance to their place of employment. With rail transportation, it was now possible for urban residents to live in one part of the city and work in another. In city centers, new rail terminals provided a concentration of potential workers and customers that led to the development of central business districts. On the urban edge, rail lines allowed cities from London to Los Angeles to sprawl across the surrounding countryside.

While most urban rail systems were originally built by private companies, as the cost of operating these networks grew, along with their importance to the cities they served, many were purchased by city governments forming the basis of public transit systems in London, New York, and San Francisco. In these cities, urban rail continued to shape urban development through the twentieth and into the twenty-first century. Other systems, such as the Pacific Electric in Los Angeles, once the largest interurban electric rail network in the country, fell into disrepair, unable to compete with an emerging mobility system: the automobile. With public investment in automobile infrastructure, the stage was set for this new mobility system to reshape cities.

Mobility in the Auto Age

The first automobiles were expensive and unreliable, but as the technology improved, one key advantage allowed autos to rapidly become the dominant form of urban transportation in major cities: unlike rail, which required extensive new infrastructure, autos could operate immediately on existing city streets. Once again, this new mobility system was built over the existing mobility network. In American cities, just as footpaths and wagon trails were replaced with rail lines and rail lines were developed into boulevards, with the rail lines eventually removed to make way for landscaped medians, dedicated turn lanes, and more space for private automobiles.

Automobility removed the limitations that previously constrained urban growth. While preindustrial cities were limited by the distance a person could walk and industrializing cities by the extent of rail infrastructure, automobiles allowed cities to grow in any and all directions simultaneously, constrained only by policy or physical geography. In the auto age, London grew to a diameter of over 30 miles with growth limited by the adoption of the Green Belt in the 1940s (Ehrlich et al., 2023), while Greater Los Angeles grew to an extent of more than 70 miles across and 90 miles long, limited only by the Pacific Ocean and surrounding mountains. With this, growth has come profound and interrelated social and environmental impacts.

The Social and Environmental Impacts of Our Current Mobility System

Air pollution in the form of "smog" was among the most immediate environmental impacts of widespread auto use. When one of the earliest recognized incidents of smog occurred in Los Angeles during World War II, the eye-watering and lung-searing pollution that descended on the city was so severe that it was first thought to be an enemy gas attack (Jacobs and Kelly, 2008). Not until the early 1950s was it understood that car-obsessed Angelenos had brought the crisis upon themselves: auto emissions combined with the region's abundant sunlight produced the smog for which Southern California had by then become infamous (ibid.). Despite remarkable progress over multiple decades in greatly reducing the incidence of hazardous air quality days, Los Angeles remains the smoggiest urban area in the country with significant impacts for the health and well-being of residents (American Lung Association, 2023), demonstrating both the potential and limitations of regulatory and technological responses to the impacts of automobility.

While smog-forming emissions remain a significant issue, their impact is largely regional; in contrast, greenhouse gas (GHG) emissions, in the form of carbon dioxide, have truly global impacts. According to the U.S. Environmental Protection Agency (n.d.), transportation is now the largest contributor of GHG emissions in the United States, accounting for approximately one-third of the U.S. GHG emissions. Cities are already at a higher risk from climate change due to the urban heat island effect whereby cities generate and retain more heat than surrounding areas, and auto use exacerbates that effect due to excessive waste heat from vehicles themselves and the heat-reflecting property of expansive asphalt parking lots and wide, car-focused roads (Wilson, 2021). With rising auto use in Asia, Africa, and Latin America, addressing the climate impacts of auto-oriented urban development is imperative for both urban residents and the global community.

Beyond the environmental impacts of automobiles, our auto-oriented mobility system has significant impacts on human health and well-being. The construction of urban freeways in American cities displaced residents, divided communities, and left a legacy of health impacts in freeway-adjacent neighborhoods that remain to this day (Loukaitou-Sideris et al., 2023). While these impacts disproportionally affect low-income and minority residents, automobility has negative consequences for all urban residents. Auto use is a driver of increasing rates of obesity with a 6% increase in the likelihood of obesity for each additional hour spent in a car per day (Frank et al., 2004). Finally, increased vehicle use is making city streets more dangerous for drivers and pedestrians, with pedestrian fatalities in U.S. cities reaching a 40-year high in 2022 (Governors Highway Safety Association, 2023).

While technological advancements, such as electric vehicles (EVs), address some of the environmental impacts of automobiles, such as smog and GHG emissions (assuming clean power is available for charging), they are not an environmental panacea. Issues remain with the mining, manufacturing, and disposal of EV batteries, as well as non-tailpipe pollution from tires. Additionally, even if all vehicles on the road had zero emissions, that would do nothing to address the social issues of divided neighborhoods and increasing obesity, while the higher average weight of EVs may make roadways more dangerous for pedestrians. The alternative is clear: smart mobility requires less dependence on driving.

The Covid-19 pandemic provided a glimpse of a less auto-dependent future. In the early days of the pandemic, as people stayed home, urban roadways cleared as did urban skies, with cities from Los Angeles to New Delhi reporting their best air quality in years (Saha et al., 2022). While lockdowns are not a viable solution to the ills of automobility, driving less and focusing on local neighborhoods to meet the daily needs of urban residents can be the basis for a smart mobility future.

Toward a Smart Mobility Future

How can cities move toward a smart, sustainable, and equitable mobility future? Understanding the needs, desires, and lived experiences of urban residents is one starting point. Global design firm Gensler is a leader in the field of experience-focused research and design. Drawing on a global survey of 15,000 residents in 30 cities around the world, Gensler's recent *Urban Mobility Report* offers insights into how the experience of mobility is changing post-pandemic and how cities can respond.

Walkable Neighborhoods

The primary finding of Gensler's research is simple: urban residents want walkable neighborhoods. Across all generations and user profiles included in the study, "living in a walkable neighborhood" was ranked as the most desired element of mobility, above access to a car, ease of commute, access to parking, and access to public transit (Gensler, 2022, 18).

> As downtowns and commercial districts emptied out in the first months of the pandemic, people began to engage with the public spaces, activities, and businesses in their local neighborhoods at increased rates. Outdoor activity increased by 20% in the U.S. alone, and the demand for bicycle infrastructure and pedestrian-friendly streets rose dramatically around the world. And though the public health crisis may be coming to an end, enthusiasm hasn't waned for walkable neighborhoods.
>
> *(ibid.)*

The key element of walkable neighborhoods and cities is the ability to get to goods and services without the need to drive. This principle, which has been popularized among urban planners as the "fifteen-minute city," is not a novel concept, but it is gaining increased appreciation among urban residents (Duany & Steuteville, 2021). Gensler found that urban residents today want to be located closer to work, shopping, and recreation and says that this has become more important post-pandemic (Gensler 20). In other words, city dwellers want greater access with less transportation—that's smart mobility (Figure 5.1.1).

Creating walkable neighborhoods requires a transition from auto-oriented urban planning. Walkable neighborhoods need meaningful density to make local businesses economically viable and mixed-use zoning to allow them to be located near their customers. Additionally, walkable neighborhoods need high-quality public spaces, such as tree-lined streets and sidewalks that are safe and comfortable to walk along. Finally, walkable neighborhoods need transit to provide access to social and economic opportunities at an urban scale.

Figure 5.1.1 Artist's interpretation of a walkable neighborhood with integrated housing, retail, recreation areas, and transit. Image © Gensler.

Better Transit

Transit is an essential component of walkable cities, yet around the world, transit is in crisis. Transit ridership in America was in a decade-long decline before 2020, and this trend was accelerated by the COVID-19 pandemic. Despite performing a heroic service throughout the pandemic for essential workers, transit systems are now facing declining revenue and ridership along with other serious challenges (Woodhouse, 2023). Despite these challenges, Gensler (2022, 27) found that most urban residents still value public transportation, with two out of three favoring new investments in transit infrastructure over highway expansions.

> Despite decreased usage, our data refutes the assumption that urban residents want to leave public transit behind. In fact, most respondents are in favor of expanding public transit, and nearly half are willing to pay more to have a better experience. But while most city dwellers feel positively about the reliability of their city's public transit system, and that it takes them where they need to go, fewer feel that it provides a great experience. This indicates that transit systems that fulfill basic functions are not doing enough—passengers need more.
>
> *(ibid.)*

To dig deeper, the Gensler Mobility Lab conducted a series of focus groups with riders in three American cities, Atlanta, Los Angeles, and Washington, D.C., to understand firsthand how riders' experiences and needs are changing post-pandemic.

We found that hybrid and remote work have resulted in former regular riders using transit less, but transit remains popular for social riders as urban residents seek to reconnect to activities in their cities. This change was summed up by one transit rider from Atlanta who said,

> I used to use MARTA a lot when I used to work in the city, but now due to the pandemic, I'm a teleworker. I don't have to go into the city as much anymore, so I just use MARTA for concerts and going out to eat.

In response, cities and transit providers need to rethink service patterns and fare structures to better serve riders other than traditional commuters.

Additionally, we found that, as riders have more choices, experience matters more. On all three systems, the in-station experience was rated lower than the onboard experience, with waiting and making connections identified as the low points in the typical transit journey. Rethinking station design, with a focus on enhancing passenger safety, comfort, and ease of use, represents an opportunity for transit providers to regain ridership and revenue (Figure 5.1.2).

Finally, when it comes to the experience of using transit, the age, race, and gender of passengers all have an impact. For example, younger passengers (age 18–24) expressed high levels of satisfaction with buying tickets—a task most do using mobile devices—while older passengers expressed greater difficulty with the ticket-buying process. Compared to other riders, Asian American and Pacific Islander (AAPI) passengers expressed the lowest level of satisfaction with the platforms, where well-publicized recent incidents of anti-Asian hate crimes contributed to concerns about violence. "I'm worried someone who is mentally

Figure 5.1.2 Artist's interpretation of transit station improvements to enhance passenger safety, comfort, and ease of use. Image © Gensler.

unstable could push me onto the tracks," said one AAPI rider, adding, "Police are few and far between." More equitable mobility requires cities, transit agencies, and designers to better engage diverse rider groups throughout the planning process.

Smarter Automobility

Even with walkable neighborhoods and high-quality transit, autos are likely to remain an important component of urban mobility. Gensler (2022, 38) found that half of urban residents are unwilling or unable to switch to public transportation to reduce their environmental impact. Smart mobility requires a better balancing of the costs and benefits of auto use with the goal of decreasing auto use in cities. Progressive jurisdictions are already moving in that direction. London's congestion charge, first introduced in 2003, has been largely successful in reducing vehicle use and congestion while increasing transit ridership (Intelligent Transport, 2023). American cities from New York to Los Angeles are now considering similar congestion pricing schemes. As electrification reduces gas-tax revenues, more cities will likely turn to a similar alternative funding mechanism. Done right, policy changes can make urban mobility cleaner, safer, and more efficient for everyone by making drivers pay their fair share.

New and Emerging Mobility

What is the future of mobility? From electrification and micro-mobility to autonomous vehicles (AVs) and urban air mobility, new and emerging technologies have the potential to

Figure 5.1.3 Artist's interpretation of potential future urban aerial mobility hub. Image © Gensler.

reshape cities and urban mobility. We can begin to evaluate the potential spread and impact of new and emerging mobility technologies with three questions:

1 Does this represent an innovation in vehicles, paths, or rules?
2 Does this increase or decrease the cost of mobility?
3 How will this change the balance of access, transportation, and mobility?

Innovative vehicles that use existing paths are more likely to be widely adopted than modes that require new vehicles and paths. For example, EVs are a recent innovation in vehicle technology. While EVs do require dedicated charging infrastructure, because they use existing paths and rules, they have the potential to quickly deploy across our transportation system. As a result, EV usage has increased dramatically over the last decade with significant growth projected (Brinley, 2023). Urban microgrids—small-scale electric grids that integrate solar photovoltaic generation, battery storage, and charging infrastructure—have the potential to further boost EV use, particularly for transit operators (Feller, 2021) (Figure 5.1.3).

Understanding how mobility systems function helps sort out science fact from science fiction. Visions of the future have long imagined city skies filled with flying cars and other aerial vehicles. Now, thanks to innovations in electric vertical take-off and landing (EVTOL) technology, this potential may soon be realized. Because EVTOLs can utilize existing paths (i.e. urban airspace) and regulatory structures (i.e. airspace regulations), they have the potential for widespread adoption if the economics of vehicle production and operation are made viable. In contrast, the notion of sealed pods transporting passengers through vacuum tubes (Elon Musk's so-called Hyperloop), which requires not just new vehicles but also cost-prohibitive new paths in the form of underground or elevated tubes, is likely to remain the stuff of fantasy. As the former vice president and chief engineer of

Hyperloop One put it: "[D]rawing straight lines through cities, it turns out, is challenging" (quoted in Garcia, 2018).

Since innovations in vehicle design or new types of paths take years or decades to design, test, and build, their potential is somewhat easier to anticipate; on the other hand, innovations in rules can bring the most impactful changes with surprising speed. Consider the rapid rise of Uber, Lyft, and other rideshare choices. Using existing vehicles, drivers, and roads, Uber created a new market for peer-to-peer ridesharing by providing rules and a platform for drivers and passengers to find each other. Where rideshare providers have to meet challenges is when their platform conflicts with existing rules and regulations, and the success of ridesharing as a mobility system is predicated on the resolution of those conflicts in favor of rideshare providers.

Rideshare platforms like Uber lowered the cost of private car use, contributing to an increase in vehicle use. Likewise, if AVs become widespread, thereby decreasing the cost of driving, we can expect them to contribute to more urban congestion. In contrast, policies that increase the cost of driving can have a real impact on decreasing auto use. As new technologies and mobility solutions emerge, asking how they will affect the cost of mobility is critical to assessing their impact.

Despite their potential for widespread adoption, innovations in vehicle technology, such as electrification or autonomous driving, aren't likely to fundamentally reshape cities: EVs and AVs provide the same transportation function and access as today's automobiles. While EVTOLs and hyperloops do have the potential to radically expand access and therefore the size of urban areas, the high cost of these systems, which makes them impractical for daily use by most people, means they won't turn Columbus, Ohio, into a suburb of Chicago just yet—despite headlines to the contrary (Davidson, 2019). However, there is one trend with the potential to sever the relationship of access and transportation, transforming cities in the process: virtual mobility.

With the rise of remote work, e-commerce, online dating, and social media, nearly all the social and commercial functions that drove humans to form cities can now be performed virtually. In other words, it is possible to have access to employment, goods, services, family, friends, and partners without transportation: what might be called virtual mobility. Within this new mobility system, what form will cities take? The walking city, rail city, and auto-oriented city were each defined by the distance and area those modes allowed urban residents to travel. With virtual mobility, distance is rendered meaningless, and access is potentially infinite. In this context, experience matters more. Beyond building the cities we need, we can build the cities we want.

As we look toward the future, one thing seems clear: mobility will remain a shaping force in cities. What form that takes is up to us.

References

American Lung Association. (2023). *State of the Air: 2023 Report*. Retrieved from https://www.lung.org/research/sota.

Brinley, S. (January 9, 2023). EV Chargers: How many do we need? *S&P Global Mobility*. Retrieved from https://www.spglobal.com/mobility/en/research-analysis/ev-chargers-how-many-do-we-need.html.

Davidson, J. (November 15, 2019). In 2029, a Hyperloop could turn Columbus, Ohio, into a Suburb of Chicago. *New York Magazine*. Retrieved October 22, 2023, from https://nymag.com/intelligencer/2019/11/by-2029-a-hyperloop-could-make-columbus-a-chicago-suburb.html.

Duany, A., & Steuteville, R. (February 8, 2021). Defining the 15-minute city. *CNU*. Retrieved from https://www.cnu.org/publicsquare/2021/02/08/defining-15-minute-city.

Ehrlich, B, Clout, H., & Hebbert, M. (2023). London. *Encyclopedia Britannica*. Retrieved November 5, 2023, from https://www.britannica.com/place/London.

Feller, G. (August 5, 2021). Microgrids + mass transit = resilient mobility in a future clouded by climate change. *Canary Media*. Retrieved from https://www.canarymedia.com/articles/mobility/microgrids-plus-mass-transit-equals-resilient-mobility-in-a-future-clouded-by-climate-change.

Foot, J., Ring, R., & Ehrlich, B. (2023). Rome. *Encyclopedia Britannica*. Retrieved November 5, 2023, from https://www.britannica.com/place/Rome.

Frank, L., Andresen, M., & Schmid, T. (August 27, 2004). Obesity relationships with community design, physical activity, and time spent in cars. *American Journal of Preventative Medicine*. Retrieved from https://pubmed.ncbi.nlm.nih.gov/15261894/.

Garcia, E. (May 24, 2018). Chicago to Pittsburgh in 45 minutes: A look at the high-speed hyperloop. *WTTW*. Retrieved from https://news.wttw.com/2018/05/24/chicago-pittsburgh-45-minutes-look-high-speed-hyperloop.

Gensler. (2022). *Urban Mobility Report*. Retrieved from https://www.gensler.com/gri/city-pulse-2022-urban-mobility-report.

Governors Highway Safety Association. (2023). *Pedestrian Traffic Fatalities by State: 2022 Preliminary Data*. Retrieved from https://www.ghsa.org/resources/Pedestrians23

Intelligent Transport. (February 17, 2023). London's congestion charge celebrates 20 years of success. Retrieved from https://www.intelligenttransport.com/transport-news/143883/londons-congestion-charge-celebrates-20-years-of-success/.

Jacobs, C., & Kelly, W. (2008). *Smogtown: The Lung-Burning History of Pollution in Los Angeles*. Abrams Press.

Loukaitou-Sideris, A., Handy, S., Ong, P., Barajas, J., Wasserman, J., Pech, C., Garcia Sanchez, J., Ramirez, A., Jain, A., Proussaloglou, E., Nguyen, A., Turner, K., Fitzgibbon, A., Kaeppelin, F., Ramirez, F., & Arenas, M. (2023). The implications of freeway siting in California: Four case studies on the effects of freeways on neighborhoods of color. *UCLA: Institute of Transportation Studies*. Retrieved from https://escholarship.org/uc/item/7mj2b24q.

McKay, J. (November 13, 2019). Transport or mobility: What's the difference and why does it matter? Retrieved from https://www.forumforthefuture.org/blog/transport-or-mobility#:~:text=Transportation%20(%E2%80%9Cacross%2Dcarry%E2%80%9D),mobility%20is%20something%20you%20have.

National Geographic Society. (2022). *The History of Cities*. Retrieved from https://education.nationalgeographic.org/resource/history-cities/.

Saha, L., Kumar, A., Kumar, S., Korstad, J., Srivastava, S., & Bauddh, K. (2022). The impact of the COVID-19 lockdown on global air quality: A review. *Environmental Sustainability* (Singapore). Retrieved from https://doi.org/10.1007/s42398-021-00213-6

Schneider, B. (September 6, 2018). CityLab University: Induced demand. *Bloomberg*. Retrieved from https://www.bloomberg.com/news/articles/2018-09-06/traffic-jam-blame-induced-demand.

Walker, J. (January 26, 2011). Transit's product: Mobility or access? *Human Transit*. Retrieved from https://humantransit.org/2011/01/transits-product-mobility-or-access.html.

Wilson, K. (September 20, 2021). Biden's 'Heat Island' strategy ignores cars. *Streetsblog USA*. Retrieved from https://usa.streetsblog.org/2021/09/20/bidens-heat-island-strategy-ignores-cars.

Woodhouse, S. (May 9, 2023). Commuters ditched public transit for work from home. Now there's a crisis. *Bloomberg*. Retrieved from https://www.bloomberg.com/news/articles/2023-05-09/us-public-transit-is-in-crisis-from-washington-to-san-francisco.

United States Environmental Protection Agency. (n.d.). *Transportation, Air Pollution, and Climate Change: Carbon Pollution from Transportation*. Retrieved September 17, 2023, from https://www.epa.gov/transportation-air-pollution-and-climate-change/carbon-pollution-transportation.

5.2

SMART AIRPORTS

Evolving Airports for a More Human-Focused Journey

Terence Young

Abstract

An airport is not a building. More so, it is a city. Regardless of size, these complicated projects experience planning and operational challenges beyond most buildings. Issues such as 24-hour energy production and management, cargo and baggage logistics, complicated pedestrian movements, roadways as well as automated transportation networks. Airports are required to provide public security and safety on top of passenger amenities and services. As cities, airports have both public (travelers) and private communities (tenants or employees). These two groups have vastly different expectations of the environment. One sees the airport as a journey experience, one sees it as a workplace. Airport operators and designers have been experimenting with the adoption of emerging technologies – to create more intelligent airports in service of both of these communities. In this chapter, the discussion will be on the opportunities and challenges we have seen as practitioners of airport design. This perspective may not be as far-flung as a Jules Verne "what if" thought exercise, but it is a description of how airports can become more resilient, serve their communities more fully, and bring enjoyment and delight. We define "smart airport" based on discussions and design work produced in our practice in the Airport Studio here at Gensler in 2024.

Design for air travel is a complicated design task that must take into consideration many complex systems: aircraft movement, roadway, and transit connections, and security protocols requiring inspection and verification of people and baggage supporting mixed-use public spaces. Often these projects take decades to plan and develop in conjunction with national and global authorities weighing in. But the goals of the airport journey have remained consistent: provide the safest, most pleasant journey possible while maximizing safety.

An airport is not a building. In my practice as an Architect of airports, I have come to think of these projects as city-making. Regardless of size, these complicated projects experience planning and operational challenges beyond most buildings (Figure 5.2.1). Issues such as 24-hour energy production and management, cargo and baggage logistics, complicated pedestrian movements, roadways as well as automated transportation networks. Airports

DOI: 10.4324/9781003384113-63

Figure 5.2.1 Architects and designers often use complex, digital tools to craft the design of airports. But what role does technology and artificial intelligence play in the making a "Smart Airport" journey? (Image courtesy of Gensler).

are required to provide public security and safety on top of passenger amenities and services. As cities, airports have both public (travelers) and private communities (tenants or employees). These two groups have vastly different expectations of the environment. One sees the airport as a journey experience, one sees it as a workplace. Airport operators and designers have been experimenting with the adoption of emerging technologies – to create more intelligent airports in service of both of these communities. In this chapter, I will limit the discussion to the opportunities and challenges I have seen as a practitioner of airport design for over 23 years. This perspective may not be as far-flung as a Jules Verne "what if" thought exercise, but it is a description of how airports can become more resilient, serve their communities more fully, and bring enjoyment and delight. I am defining the "smart airport" based on discussions and design work produced in our practice in the Airport Studio here at Gensler in 2024.

Design for air travel is a complicated design task that must take into consideration many complex systems: aircraft movement, roadway, and transit connections, and security protocols requiring inspection and verification of people and baggage supporting mixed-use public spaces. Often these projects take decades to plan and develop in conjunction with national and global authorities weighing in. But the goals of the airport journey have remained consistent: provide the safest, most pleasant journey possible while maximizing safety.

With this context in mind, we define "smart airports" as being predictive and adaptive through an active interface between the built environment and its occupants to maximize the comfort and enjoyment of journeys. We will also discuss next-generation advancements to create efficiencies and safety in operations. We will examine these topics in three categories:

1 Personalization and streamlining the customer journey
2 Predictive and adaptive building systems to manage resources and reduce building waste, increasing resilience and sustainability
3 Predictive and adaptive analytics in operations to increase revenue

Personalization and Streamlining the Customer Journey

Home to Curb to Gate

Within the air travel industry, the customer journey is often described as "curb to gate" – meaning from the departures curb to the aircraft boarding gate. With improvements in technology and the adoption by travel-related businesses, we have the opportunity to reframe the journey as "home (or hotel) to aircraft seat".

The integration of airport systems that are physically divorced from the airport is not new. Airlines – often seen as "part of the airport" – have allowed the printing of boarding passes, pre-processing checked luggage, and changing itineraries at home – remote from the airport check-in desk in the ticketing hall. These smart innovations are streamlining the ticket hall experience. Airports are increasingly eyeing the possibility of evolving other customer processes further away from the airport to reduce congestion. Customers often describe the most stressful part of the airport experience as a lack of agency. Redistributing customer processes reduces congestion at ticketing counters, giving more choices to travelers. Allowing customers to enter the secure areas through "enhanced portals" has become popular. CLEAR is a private company collecting biometric information and advertises shorter wait times through security and a "concierge" experience putting travelers at the head of the security checkpoint line. The notion of giving the customer choice for a congestion-free experience is a step toward relieving the stress of the security checkpoint.

Indeed, the banishment of congestion is the goal for a seamless customer journey. We define this as direct access to airports through a single mode of travel requiring no connections. A widely accepted strategy is to leverage the multiple positive aspects of public transit to connect to airports. Trains or buses can be powered by renewable energy and are more efficient at moving people by a magnitude compared to private vehicles. Today, there are airports with transit stations, but often it requires transferring from one train to another or a bus to the airport curb, then a separate process to check in baggage and identify and screen passengers. These mode transfers can be time-consuming and complicated for travelers and are a factor in deterring greater adoption of transit use to airports, even though they can cut through traffic efficiently and are a more efficient, resilient use of transportation energy. Passengers want direct, personalized access. The future smart airport might be able to accomplish this. What if the transportation system going to and from the airport was a seamless, enjoyable high-volume system that also happens to be powered by renewable energy and produces no waste?

A future such as this is not likely in the jurisdiction solely of the airport. Ideas such as this involve roadway planning and vehicle design partners. However, the opportunity to integrate the logistics into and out of the airport is an enticing opportunity to curate and personalize the journey.

The Evolved Security Checkpoint

Within the security protocols of airports, the traveler must be "known" and "safe" before boarding a commercial aircraft. The security and safety of air travel demands that contraband items be removed and that threats to others and to equipment be removed. In an age of evolving threats, modern security protocols are designed to respond typically after an incident has occurred. Airports across the world experienced this after the airborne terrorist attacks in the United States on 9/11. Immediately following that tragedy, new screening machines began to appear in airports everywhere. They were often shoehorned into awkward locations and long lines of frustrated, anxious passengers became the "modern traveler".

Innovations within the airport security developers seek to create systems that can be tuned to different threats with flexible sensors tied to a database shared with international law enforcement. This "hackable" airport security hopes to be predictive as threats evolve and so efficient as to be "invisible" to the passenger journey, making the transition from city to aircraft seamless.

We envision this system to be able to discern known and trusted people from those with a history of threatening behavior or who appear on law enforcement watch lists. Being quickly identified as "safe" will enhance commuters' and habitual traveler journeys by streamlining their travel through security. Enhancement to the SSCP equipment as well as its placement in the journey are an area being studied to eliminate human-caused air travel tragedies. Biometric screening matches a face scan or fingerprints previously stored in a government-issued record to positively identify a person.

These technologies are already becoming more common at checkpoints today. These systems largely can adapt to legacy equipment, with cameras being installed at many international arrival airports, as well as the previously mentioned CLEAR vendors for outbound domestic travel. The real innovation will be eliminating the checkpoint and moving the line of security or eliminating it.

This future model would use biometric technology communicating with a database to identify people and cross-analyze reference background information, and if necessary, detain an individual. In theory, the "checkpoint" could be a series of layers working synchronously beyond the airport boundary integrated into the fabric of the building rather than today's "corral" and "portal". For instance, if several technological advancements were made simultaneously such as personal vehicle automation, mobile baggage screening, and global adoption of self-baggage tagging, the security checkpoint we currently experience could disappear altogether. In such an example passengers would enter a trusted, secure, automated bus, train, or car. Such a vehicle would scan passengers and cargo autonomously, flag and identify any anomalies, and tag people or items for removal during travel but before reaching the airport. Passengers can be screened for contraband, weapons as well as health status. Once the airport has been reached, screened passengers continue to their gate as "known and safe". Meanwhile, their baggage and cargo have been screened, locked away, and sorted and are placed autonomously into the airports' baggage system with a secure chain of custody ensured. The airport trip could then become a truly seamless journey. A passenger is "airside" as soon as they step onto the sidewalk.

Integrating technology to screen passengers and scan baggage in a bus or a private car will need to engage and merge partners in the ground vehicle design, screening technology, and the law enforcement oversight required to ensure credibility (Figure 5.2.2).

The (curated) Airside Journey

A consistent goal among airports is to provide more variety to their customers, personalize amenities, and purchase offers to create a comfortable, enjoyable journey. Customer enjoyment has been shown to enhance passenger spending, as well as affect behaviors such as a desire to arrive at the airport early to experience a relaxed and personalized journey. These

Figure 5.2.2 This illustration speculates a train/airport interface with luggage and passengers being screened for security while in transit. Luggage is automatically conveyed to the aircraft and enplaning passengers arrive at the airport ready to explore, be entertained, or dine and meet. (Image courtesy of Gensler).

expenditures assist in the success of tenants but also the airport's financial performance as a whole by contributing to "non-aviation revenue". Increasingly, strategies that designers employ draw inspiration from the airport's surrounding culture and community to reflect local customs, art, natural ecosystems, and biomes. As designers, we seek to make the airport a component of the enjoyable journey.

The desire to "design a local experience" has arisen simultaneously with the desire to create a curated journey. A curated journey is mapped to the individual traveler and cross-references their needs and habits from home or hotel to aircraft. In a publication titled "The Principles of REACH", we defined five user types of travelers. In 2007, Gensler with SFO described different passenger journeys depending on the traveler's profile: business traveler, traveler with family, VIP traveler, etc. We noted how the journey was different for each traveler, with "needs and desires and pain points" customized to each profile. We have been working toward a responsive airport building that truly curates each journey and could be "tuned" to individual preferences and habits. Preferences and habits can be as simple as the "favorite hot beverage" location nearest to your gate in the concourse coinciding with "you've not hydrated for over 60 minutes" – for example. Personalized messages directing a passenger to a prayer room at a particular time of day might be as important as knowledge of which gate their aircraft is leaving. There is no technology more personal than one's mobile phone. This is a powerful tool that already knows the preferences and schedule of its owner. A journey that integrates and maps the location of desired amenities can make the first-time traveler's journey as seamless as that of a seasoned, weekly traveler. This information could come as an "itinerary" on a mobile device, collecting and conveying information about flight status, baggage status, gate location, preferred retail locations and sales promotions, medical information or reminders, and step-by-step navigation.

Innovations in dynamic signage and wayfinding technologies aim to eliminate language barriers between customers and airline agents.

In the past, air travel was designed for efficiency and speed: getting passengers to the gate was the primary goal. Now, we focus on providing a nurturing and pleasant journey throughout the airport and encourage greater dwell time and deeper engagement with the project's environment. This engagement has been evolving to better reflect awareness around Equity, Social Responsibility, and Good Governance (ESG goals). Amenity enhancement for marginalized communities is more available at the airport. We have already seen gender-neutral restrooms and adult care companion facilities, as well as mother's lactation rooms or sensory rooms. We have designed prayer and meditation rooms that aim to serve multiple faith groups simultaneously. As these communities of travelers become more vocal and visible, so too must our infrastructure respond. Smart Airport design can lend assistance with navigation aids and mobility assistance. As robotic intelligence advances beyond self-driving cars, wheelchairs with intelligent awareness will deliver customers through choice amenities and experiences at will, just like any other traveler. Primarily a mobility innovation, it could likely assist in communication, and translation and enable transactions for any number of scenarios.

Predictive and Adaptive Building Systems

Any building requires constant maintenance, cleaning, and replacement of components. A building that assists in "fixing itself" is the next generation of Smart Buildings. One that reports the physical condition, cleanliness, and lifespan of components (such as light fixtures, bathroom amenities, or mechanical filters for example) and allows the operator to focus energy on areas of heavy use, monitor replacement lifespan, and keep mechanical systems within their performance targets more efficiently utilizes staff.

Airports are complicated projects bringing together logistics, people, and transportation. The management system of the future could leverage the power of the "Digital Twin". The concept of a digital twin to a physical asset (building or system of buildings) pulls data from sensors embedded in physical space. This data could be occupancy flow or the processing speed of the baggage system for instance. It then reports on the physical state by mirroring received data on a dashboard or 3D visualization. It monitors mechanical systems, emergency systems, and security status as well as building maintenance and all airline operations. At present, many of these reporting systems are separate, being monitored in isolation from other systems, and therefore are not monitored in context. The power of the digital twin is to streamline the effort of staff and employees and bring efficiency to the overall system by reflecting the combined data streams into a high-resolution GIS or BIM digital model in real time. The power of the digital twin is to take each of the separate data streams and place operational conditions in context with each other. Baggage conflicts can be alerted due to a damaged belt system but diverted to an empty holding area due to a late arriving aircraft, for instance. Creating a balanced and comfortable passenger experience becomes the result of an intelligent airport being able to respond and model changes to the system.

Airports are investing in these integrated digital models. Hong Kong International Airport and Vancouver International Airport have reportedly commissioned and are operating digital twin technology to monitor and operate their airports. The system (Figure 5.2.3) reportedly alerts operations of maintenance issues and allows them to model solutions to

Figure 5.2.3   This digital twin dashboard at Vancouver International Airport reflects the real-time conditions of the airport to its operators. "Built as a people-first technology for the airport's front-line workers, designers, and community, YVR's digital twin leverages historical and real-time data and can present key information through 2D or 3D visualization, enabling better comprehension of complex operational systems, streamlined processes, and accelerated collaboration across the airport's key stakeholders". (Image courtesy of Vancouver International Airport).

problems and analyze possible performance before committing to physical changes. The area of building digital twins is a relatively new area of building management technology and promises better employee integration by unifying data, hopes to streamline changes to the buildings' operations and maintenance positively affect the cost of operations, and increase revenue. Vancouver Airport (YVR) discussed these innovations in a YouTube March 28, 2022 post titled: YVR's Digital Twin briefing – YouTube.

Efficiency in building systems, reduction in waste, and planning flexibility are the cornerstones of principles of sustainability and resilience. A typical airport campus includes terminal processors, parking facilities, transportation hubs, aircraft maintenance hangars, cargo facilities, energy plants, and waste processing operating 24 hours a day, 365 days a year. They can consume massive amounts of energy and produce mountains and rivers of waste. They are often publicly funded with long periods between renovations and improvements. An airport that grows incrementally or improves through smaller maintenance investments identified through a digital twin is a key to reducing environmental impacts.

An example of this is the development of the "all-electric-airside". This refers to the elimination of internal combustion engines for all vehicles servicing aircraft and passenger or staff transportation. This will dramatically reduce tailpipe emissions and improve the carbon footprint of the owners and operators.

The future of greater electrification requires a dependable capacity of electrical power from renewable resources. Whether an airport draws electricity from a regional grid or has its on-campus powerplant is a topic outside of this chapter and is a worthy subject for speculation in the topic of Smart Airports.

Predictive and Adaptive Analytics in Revenue

As previously stated, modern airports are planned and designed to provide a pleasant and memorable journey to travelers and an excellent work environment for staff and employees. We often state that our goal is for enplaning travelers to arrive early, and deplaning travelers to extend their journey at the airport before taking transportation away. There is much evidence that extending dwell time encourages greater spending at retail and concessions or revenue-generating amenities (enhanced Wi-Fi workspaces, showers, or transit hotels for instance). Today, predictive and adaptive revenue software airports monitor the circulation patterns and revenue performance of individual tenants. By integrating this data within the larger "digital twin" of the airport operational model, changes to increase performance could be modeled and analyzed. Solutions might be to model changes to customer circulation, signage location, store visibility or travel distance, product display placement, or lighting.

Another use of this predictive financial model could tie gate usage based on arrival or destination and create a changeable program for the amenities nearby. For instance, a morning peak of business travelers might trigger an enhanced workspace. If the same gate were being populated to a mid-afternoon distant family vacation destination, the space could morph into a play area themed to the destination to care for traveling children.

Conclusion

Much of the discussion around transportation connections relies on each regional attitudes toward mass transportation as well as cultural attitudes toward "opting in" to biometric information, personal information, and preferences. This innovation requires that people submit their information to governments (or corporations) and accept being monitored to receive these technological advancements. Today, this occurs almost invisibly with our mobile devices "listening in" to conversations and monitoring browser activity. This data is translated to targeted news and information or marketing. The future of air travel will bring this powerful two-way communication between information and customer to personalize the airport journey.

One might conclude that the smart airport is on the horizon, built upon the passenger and employee experiences that have been developing over several generations of air travel design. However, as the previous topics have discussed, there is often a multilayering of innovations upon which some of these developments must depend to be successful. Some of these innovations are being utilized today, while some may be far in the future. Security innovations depend not only on the security industry but upon the policies and politics of technology adoption across different states and countries, which may be an insurmountable goal. For example, if an airport utilizes "luggage scanning robot personal transit", the entire air travel system as a whole must agree to these security protocols as safe and acceptable. If not, passengers and their baggage would be required to rescreen at their destination, causing congestion and inconvenience. Another example – sensor-rich environments reporting the maintenance and repair data of mechanical equipment or the tracking of cellphone positions to reflect building status – is in use today. The questions of whether airport systems and city-contracted transportation data systems can be linked together persist.

Air travel continues to evolve, not only in how passengers and businesses use technology to ease travel pains but also in types of aircraft. Personal urban transportation is evolving toward an electric air mobility solution. Space tourism is becoming more feasible with private orbital vehicles being tested for commercial use. At the time of writing this chapter, our design practice is exploring spaceport planning, urban air mobility, and e-VTOL (electric, vertical take-off, and landing) air terminals, as well as domestic and international airports and related spaces. What we are discovering is surprising. We find that regardless of the vehicle (or the power source), designing for some basic human needs lies at the heart of any great travel project. We find that people want to feel connected to each other, but also to have a personalized, seamless, and private journey. People want to experience travel, but not feel inconvenienced. They want to explore while simultaneously needing the familiarity of home. They desire a human being to assist them in times of stress, and technology to replace human error. They want to fly above the clouds, but experience the plants and soil of a garden.

Being curious about the habits and psychology of people during a journey often leads to surprisingly simple solutions. Making these solutions work in the highly regimented constraints of an airport requires an evolution of how an airport operates. And despite all of the technology, the basics of human desire for safety, autonomy, and choice remain at the heart of the journey. With the rise of smarter buildings, intelligent transportation systems, and customer processing, we can make these journeys more seamless to more people. The tools we use both the design and to operate will evolve to streamline the journey, efficiently use resources, and reduce waste for greater environmental sustainability, enhanced profit, and resilience. Perhaps then, our airports will be the safest, most carefree destination in any city, and those who either work there or journey through them will feel that it was truly designed specifically with them in mind.

5.3

THE FUTURE OF ADVANCED AIR MOBILITY AND THE ROLE OF THE AIRPORTS

David Tomber

Abstract

As the world becomes more interconnected and technology advances at an unprecedented rate, the aviation industry is poised for a revolutionary transformation. One of the most exciting developments on the horizon is Advanced Air Mobility (AAM), a concept that promises to redefine the way we perceive air travel. In particular, the integration of AAM into airport operations holds immense potential for enhancing efficiency, reducing congestion, and ushering in a new era of seamless air transportation.

Although "flying taxis" are not yet part of our daily lives, the technology is advancing, regulators are developing certification pathways, and the public is intrigued. Airlines, airports, and aerospace companies are incorporating new types of passenger transport into their plans. Meanwhile, automotive OEMs and others in the broader mobility ecosystem are carefully following developments related to electric vertical take-off and landing (eVTOL) aircraft, knowing that they could provide a new sustainable option for passenger transport at the urban and regional level.

Investors sense the momentum behind passenger AAM and are directing more funding to the sector—$4.8 billion in 2021 and $1.2 billion in the first months of 2022 alone. In our lifetimes, we will likely see this new form of air transport emerge. Many companies hope to receive regulatory certification for their eVTOLs by the middle of the decade.

As the aviation industry braces for the era of AAM, airports stand at the forefront of this transformative wave. The integration of AAM vehicles into airport operations represents a paradigm shift, necessitating collaboration between airports, industry players, and regulators. Challenges notwithstanding, the potential benefits in terms of efficiency, sustainability, and economic growth make AAM integration a compelling avenue for the future of air travel. As the skies open up to new possibilities, the journey toward AAM at airports promises to be both exciting and revolutionary.

DOI: 10.4324/9781003384113-64

584

Introduction

As the world becomes more interconnected and technology advances at an unprecedented rate, the aviation industry is poised for a revolutionary transformation. One of the most exciting developments on the horizon is Advanced Air Mobility (AAM), a concept that promises to redefine the way we perceive air travel. In particular, the integration of AAM into airport operations holds immense potential for enhancing efficiency, reducing congestion, and ushering in a new era of seamless air transportation.

Although "flying taxis" are not yet part of our daily lives, the technology is advancing, regulators are developing certification pathways, and the public is intrigued. Airlines, airports, and aerospace companies are incorporating new types of passenger transport into their plans. Meanwhile, automotive OEMs and others in the broader mobility ecosystem are carefully following developments related to electric vertical take-off and landing (eVTOL) aircraft, knowing that they could provide a new sustainable option for passenger transport at the urban and regional levels.

Investors sense the momentum behind passenger AAM and are directing more funding to the sector—$4.8 billion in 2021 and $1.2 billion in the first months of 2022 alone. In our lifetimes, we will likely see this new form of air transport emerge. Many companies hope to receive regulatory certification for their eVTOLs by the middle of the decade. A future trip from San Francisco to Lake Tahoe could take under an hour by eVTOL, compared with almost four hours by car. Going from Zurich to St. Moritz would take about 30 minutes by air, compared with two-and-a-half hours by car (Figure 5.3.1).[1]

Figure 5.3.1   AI-generative-city-air-taxi-autonomous-high-speed- drone_32716104_Vecteezy_Created by Narinbg.

Understanding AAM

A system is being developed to make soaring over traffic in air taxis, providing public-good missions in the form of medical and emergency response by drone, receiving packages faster, and participating in a sustainable and safe mode of air transportation a reality. This new form of transportation is called AAM.[2]

Before delving into the future of AAM at airports, it's essential to establish a clear understanding of what AAM entails. AAM refers to the next generation of air transportation that goes beyond traditional commercial aviation. It encompasses a wide range of aerial vehicles, including eVTOL aircraft, drones, and other innovative flying machines designed for various purposes.

eVTOL aircraft are at the forefront of AAM. These electrically powered vehicles are designed to take off and land vertically, eliminating the need for traditional runways. Companies like Joby Aviation, Lilium, and Vertical Aerospace are pioneering the development of eVTOL aircraft for urban air mobility (UAM).

AAM extends beyond passenger transport to include the efficient movement of goods. Cargo drones are unmanned aerial vehicles (UAVs) designed to transport packages and supplies, offering a faster and more flexible alternative to traditional ground transportation.

Air taxis represent a promising solution to urban congestion. These small, piloted, or autonomous aircraft aim to transport passengers on short, intra-city routes, providing a quicker and more direct mode of transportation.

- **Emergency Response**—AAM has the potential to aid in disaster relief, assist in firefighting missions, and provide supplies to hard-to-reach areas during an emergency event. Several projects that support the AAM mission are working on elements to help make AAM a reality in emergency operations (NASA is Creating an AAM Playbook).
- **Healthcare**—AAM has the potential to provide medical transport for people and supplies around the world. Several projects under the mission are working on different elements to help make AAM a reality in medical operations (NASA is Creating an AAM Playbook).
- **Automation**—Automation software will perform airspace communication, flight path management, avoidance with other vehicles, and more skills needed to operate in a busy airspace (NASA is Creating an AAM Playbook).
- **Vertiports**—Many AAM aircraft designs will be eVTOLs so they will have the ability to take off and land vertically like helicopters. Research is being done where these vertiports or vertiplexes, which are multiple vertiports in proximity, will work into existing infrastructure (NASA is Creating an AAM Playbook).
- **Travel Time**—With the addition of AAM, another dimension of the sky is used for travel below traditional aircraft and above cars, buses, or trains below. Research is being done on how AAM could cut traffic commutes, make travel more sustainable, and make road trips shorter ((NASA is Creating an AAM Playbook).
- **Noise**—Design tools are being developed that manufacturers of AAM aircraft can use to reduce noise made by their aircraft. Data from testing will help define and optimize flight paths and assist the Federal Aviation Administration in creating policy (NASA is Creating an AAM Playbook).
- **Infrastructure**—Research is being done on how adding new aviation capabilities will affect communities. This includes physical areas of focus—including adding vertiports to existing airports and creating charging stations—and digital areas of focus, how aircraft will communicate with one another and with air traffic control.[2]

- **Future Airspace**—Industry and government partners must develop new air traffic management technologies so new types of aircraft can fly safely with existing aircraft. Research on new automated navigation systems that will improve airspace coordination.[2]
- **Safety**—Before new types of aircraft can fly in the airspace, the FAA needs to ensure they are safe. Evaluating how the addition of advanced automation systems and improved vehicle design can guarantee this new class of aircraft is safe to operate.[2]
- **Ride Quality**—In order to create a viable market for eVTOLs, designers will have to create a comfortable passenger experience. Research will provide design guidance to industry manufacturers, ensuring passengers will have a smooth ride.[2]
- **Cargo Delivery**—AAM has the potential to revolutionize the cargo transportation industry by providing faster and cleaner modes of moving packages. This will include both large cargo delivery aircraft and small package delivery drones.[2]
- **Accessibility**—AAM will connect both urban dwellers and rural residents by adding a new way to travel by air. Like commercial air travel today, accommodation will need to be made to these aircraft to cater to all levels of ability. This could include installing ramps for wheelchair access, specialized seats and seatbelts, and added visual and auditory aids to make the aircraft ADA compliant.[2]

The Role of Airports in AAM

Airports as AAM Hubs

As AAM technologies mature, airports are positioned to become central hubs for the integration and operation of these innovative vehicles. The following factors highlight the pivotal role airports will play in the future of AAM:

- **Infrastructure Development**—Airports will need to adapt their infrastructure to accommodate the unique requirements of AAM vehicles. This includes dedicated vertiports for eVTOLs, charging stations, and advanced air traffic management systems.
- **Collaboration with AAM Industry Players**—Airports will need to collaborate closely with AAM manufacturers, service providers, and regulators to establish standardized protocols and ensure the safe and efficient integration of these new vehicles into existing airspace.

Groupe ADP and Volocopter, alongside the French Civil Aviation Authority (DGAC) and Paris Region, have confirmed that the launch of the first eVTOL aircraft services over Paris Region skies for the 2024 Olympic and Paralympic Games is on track. Insights of 1.5 years of testing (safety, airspace integration, acceptability, passenger experience) at the Pontoise testbed are coming to fruition by bringing UAM to life in Paris (Groupe ADP).

AAM is a new form of sustainable aviation that will provide regions and cities with an additional form of transportation. Groupe ADP and Volocopter have collaborated to bring UAM to Paris, conducting flight tests with new electric air taxis, or eVTOLs at the Pontoise testbed, and bringing all regulators and stakeholders together since 2020. Volocopter has more than ten years of electric aircraft development experience and is currently the only eVTOL company on track to achieve certification in 2024 from the European Union Aviation Safety Agency. Electric air taxis are certified to the same strict safety standards as airliners and create safety through redundant aircraft features that have been tested in over 1,500 test flights (Groupe ADP).

In Paris, partners will start with three connection routes and two tourist round-trip flights, with several aircraft. The three connection routes will serve:

- Paris-Charles de Gaulle Airport and Paris-Le Bourget Airport: integrating successfully into the skies of Europe's busiest airport.
- Vertiport of Austerlitz barge and Paris Heliport: integrating into the skies over the densely populated urban area of Paris.
- Paris Heliport <> Airfield of Saint-Cyr-l'École (Versailles): validating the route potential for tourism use cases.

Tourist round-trip flights will be offered from Paris-Heliport and Paris-Le Bourget.

Operations in Paris will begin from five vertiports and will gradually grow to cover the whole Paris region over the next decade. Volocopter aircraft, which have the capacity for one pilot and one passenger, will be flying at heights below 500 meters and will not be audible from ground level in urban environments.

Challenges and Opportunities for Airports in AAM

- **Infrastructure Challenges**—Adapting existing airports to accommodate AAM vehicles poses significant infrastructure challenges. However, these challenges also present opportunities for innovation in airport design and development
- **Regulatory Framework**—The regulatory landscape for AAM is still evolving. Airports will need to work with aviation authorities to establish clear guidelines for AAM operations, addressing issues such as air traffic management, safety standards, and noise regulations.
- **Economic Opportunities**—The integration of AAM at airports opens up new economic opportunities. From providing maintenance services for AAM vehicles to offering charging infrastructure, airports can diversify their revenue streams and contribute to the growth of the AAM industry.

Technological Advancements Driving AAM Integration

Electric Propulsion and Sustainable Aviation

The shift toward electric propulsion is a cornerstone of AAM development. As environmental concerns continue to shape the aviation industry, AAM presents an opportunity to reduce carbon emissions and make air travel more sustainable.

A key aspect of AAM sustainability lies in the electrification of aircraft. Unlike traditional helicopters that rely on fossil fuels, eVTOL aircraft are powered by electric propulsion systems. This shift not only reduces greenhouse gas emissions but also minimizes noise pollution, making AAM a more environmentally friendly option for urban transportation.

Furthermore, the source of electricity is a critical factor in determining the overall sustainability of AAM. Integration with renewable energy sources such as solar, wind, or hydroelectric power ensures that the entire ecosystem is aligned with the goals of environmental conservation.

eVTOLs stand out for their zero-emission operations, as they are fully battery-powered. A week-long test campaign by Groupe ADP has also shown that Volocopter aircraft are so quiet that they will not be heard against the Paris city soundscape: Volocopter aircraft are four times quieter than helicopters while in flight.[3]

In addition, the construction and maintenance of these vertiports should adhere to eco-friendly standards, incorporating sustainable materials and energy-efficient designs. This approach ensures that the overall ecological footprint of AAM infrastructure remains as minimal as possible.

The success of AAM in promoting sustainability hinges on intentional planning, investment, and collaboration among stakeholders. By prioritizing electrification, green energy integration, eco-friendly infrastructure, lifecycle assessments, and seamless integration with public transportation, the aviation industry can pave the way for a sustainable and connected urban mobility ecosystem. As technology continues to advance, the ongoing commitment to environmental stewardship will be vital in realizing the full potential of AAM.

Autonomous and Semi-Autonomous Systems

The integration of autonomous and semi-autonomous systems is a key driver of AAM's potential. These systems enhance the safety and efficiency of air travel, reducing the reliance on human pilots and opening the door to new possibilities for on-demand aerial transportation (Figure 5.3.2).

Figure 5.3.2 AI-generative-city-air-taxi-autonomous-high-speed -drone_Vecteezy_created by Yuliya. esina.85668435.

Advanced Air Traffic Management Systems

Traditional air traffic management systems are ill-equipped to handle the complexities of AAM. Advanced systems that can dynamically manage the movements of diverse aerial vehicles in real time are essential for the safe and efficient operation of AAM at airports.

Global Initiatives and Case Studies in AAM Integration

Several cities around the world are actively pursuing AAM initiatives to alleviate urban congestion and enhance transportation options. Case studies of UAM projects, such as those in Paris, Dubai, Singapore, and Los Angeles, provide valuable insights into the challenges and successes of integrating AAM into urban environments.

Companies in the AAM space are conducting trials and forming strategic partnerships to test and refine their technologies. Examining these trials and partnerships sheds light on the progress being made in AAM development and its potential impact on airport operations.

Wisk Aero has conducted Los Angeles' first public air taxi flights and held discussions with local and city officials about implementing AAM within the region.

In October 2023, Wisk Aero became the first eVTOL air taxi company to fly in the greater Los Angeles area with the launch of test flights at Long Beach airport. The test flights provided the opportunity to conduct autonomous flight operations in a complex, real-world commercial airport environment, alongside other passenger airline operations.

The company concluded its flight program with the first public demonstration of an eVTOL air taxi flight in the Los Angeles region during Long Beach's Festival of Flight. The multi-transition flight was conducted using Wisk's fifth-generation Cora autonomous, eVTOL aircraft, demonstrating the safety and reality of autonomous passenger flight.[4]

The Los Angeles Department of Transportation (LADOT), The Los Angeles Department of City Planning, and the Los Angeles Mayor's office are collectively and proactively developing the policies and procedures to regulate UAM operations in anticipation of greater adoption. These efforts align with the City's broader vision for safety and sustainability and specifically aim to use UAM and its infrastructure as new tools for equity through choice of mobility.[5]

Los Angeles' approach to UAM implementation considers privacy, workforce development, data, and economic growth while developing policies for site and operation permitting. Achieving equitable access, acceptable noise and emission levels, multimodal transportation integration, and understanding UAM impact on land use, density, and safety all require a careful and considerate evaluation of land use policies, permitting, planning, public engagement, and interagency coordination.[5]

UAM services must simultaneously consider the natural and built environment as well as civilian-use airspace. Regulatory gaps between land and air authorities and the varying context affecting vertiports are requiring new types of dialogue and collaboration between City stakeholders, the FAA, developers, and UAM service providers.[5]

UAM has the potential to facilitate movement across the LA area in minutes. Evaluating UAM's perceived benefits of greater goods access, enhanced medical, emergency, and public safety trips, air-taxi, as well as new and emerging use cases will take years. Many challenges remain ahead with little about UAM in the air or on the ground being certain.[7]

AAM Vertiport Design for Deconstruction

Designing vertiports for deconstruction is a forward-thinking approach that aligns with the principles of sustainability and circularity. As the AAM industry continues to grow, prioritizing environmentally conscious design strategies for vertiports is essential. By considering material lifecycle, adopting modular construction methods, implementing smart technology, and engaging with local communities, we can build a future where vertiports are not only efficient and innovative but also leave a minimal environmental footprint as they gracefully transition from active service to the next phase of their lifecycle.

The first step in designing a vertiport for deconstruction is the careful selection of materials. Opting for sustainable and recyclable materials ensures that the vertiport's environmental impact is minimized from the outset. Additionally, considering the entire lifecycle of these materials, from extraction and manufacturing to use and eventual disposal, is essential for making informed decisions about the facility's long-term sustainability.

Embracing a modular and prefabricated construction approach facilitates both construction and deconstruction processes. Prefabricated components not only speed up the construction phase but also allow for easy disassembly when the vertiport reaches the end of its operational life. This approach promotes resource efficiency and reduces the amount of waste generated during both construction and decommissioning.

Designing vertiports with connective infrastructure in mind is vital for their adaptability and ease of deconstruction. Interconnected modules and systems should be designed with standardized interfaces, allowing for efficient disassembly without compromising the structural integrity of the entire vertiport. This modular connectivity also supports scalability, enabling vertiports to be easily expanded or downsized based on changing transportation needs.

The foundations of a vertiport are a critical aspect of its structural stability. Designing demountable foundations allows for the easy removal of support structures when decommissioning the vertiport. This approach minimizes the disturbance to the surrounding environment and provides the flexibility to relocate or repurpose the vertiport infrastructure as needed.

Incorporating smart technology into vertiport design not only enhances operational efficiency but also aids in the deconstruction process. Sensors and monitoring systems can provide real-time data on the condition of materials, allowing for proactive maintenance and facilitating targeted disassembly when necessary. Intelligent systems can also assist in the identification of salvageable materials for reuse or recycling.

Engaging with local communities and considering their input in the design process is crucial for creating vertiports that harmonize with the surrounding environment. An adaptive design approach, which takes into account the evolving needs of the community and the aviation industry, ensures that vertiports can be repurposed or deconstructed without causing disruption or resistance.

Security and Safety Considerations in AAM

The integration of AAM vehicles introduces new security challenges, including the potential for unauthorized access and the need for robust cybersecurity measures to protect air traffic management systems.

Establishing safety standards and certification processes for AAM vehicles is crucial for ensuring the public's confidence in these innovative transportation modes. Collaboration between aviation authorities and AAM industry stakeholders is essential to develop and enforce these standards.

The technological advancements driving AAM also necessitate the establishment of cutting-edge safety standards. Traditional aviation safety protocols are being reevaluated and adapted to accommodate the unique challenges posed by eVTOL aircraft. The integration of automation, artificial intelligence, and advanced sensors requires a comprehensive approach to ensure the reliability and resilience of AAM systems.

To guarantee the safety of AAM, rigorous certification processes and robust regulatory oversight are imperative. Aviation authorities worldwide must collaborate with industry stakeholders to establish clear and standardized certification criteria for eVTOL aircraft. These criteria should encompass not only the physical design and manufacturing standards but also the software and control systems that govern these aerial vehicles.

A fundamental principle for AAM safety is adopting a safety-by-design philosophy. This entails incorporating safety considerations at every stage of the development process, from initial design concepts to the manufacturing and operational phases. By instilling a safety culture in the industry, manufacturers and operators can proactively address potential risks and vulnerabilities.

A key challenge in integrating AAM into existing airspace is the development of effective collision avoidance systems and robust traffic management solutions. As the skies become more crowded with eVTOL aircraft, sophisticated technologies such as sensors, radars, and communication systems must work in unison to prevent collisions and ensure safe navigation.

Human factors remain a critical element in aviation safety. As AAM introduces new cockpit designs and operational procedures, pilot training programs must evolve to equip aviators with the skills necessary to operate these advanced aircraft safely. Additionally, ongoing professional development and recurrent training will be essential to keep pilots abreast of the latest technological advancements and safety protocols.

Preparation for unforeseen circumstances is a cornerstone of aviation safety. AAM operators and relevant authorities must establish robust emergency response plans that encompass a range of scenarios, including system failures, adverse weather conditions, and unforeseen events. Collaborative efforts between the aviation industry and emergency services will be vital in ensuring a swift and effective response to any incident.

The Socioeconomic Impact of AAM Integration

The AAM industry has the potential to create a significant number of jobs across various sectors, including manufacturing, maintenance, and operations. Examining the socioeconomic impact of AAM integration provides a comprehensive understanding of its potential benefits for communities and economies.

AAM has the potential to enhance accessibility and inclusivity in transportation. By providing faster and more direct routes, AAM can reduce travel times and improve connectivity, benefiting individuals and communities that may have been underserved by traditional transportation modes.

Conclusion

As the aviation industry braces for the era of AAM, airports stand at the forefront of this transformative wave. The integration of AAM vehicles into airport operations represents a paradigm shift, necessitating collaboration between airports, industry players, and regulators. Challenges notwithstanding, the potential benefits in terms of efficiency, sustainability, and economic growth make AAM integration a compelling avenue for the future of air travel. As the skies open up to new possibilities, the journey toward AAM at airports promises to be both exciting and revolutionary.

References

1 McKinsey and Company, perspectives on advanced air mobility airmobilitypdf.pdf (mckinsey.com).
2 NASA is creating an advanced air mobility playbook NASA is creating an advanced air mobility playbook—NASA.
3 Groupe ADP, *Volocopter and Groupe ADP at Forefront of Electric Urban Air Mobility (UAM): A World First in Summer 2024*. Groupe ADP—Service Presse.
4 *Business Air News*, October 26, 2023, Wisk expands AAM influence in Los Angeles. *Business Air News*.
5 *Los Angeles DOT*, Urban air mobility aligns department vision & tactics to design our most preferred future aerial mobility report. *LADOT* (lacity.gov).

5.4

SPACE STATION ARCHITECTURE PRECURSOR FOR A COMPREHENSIVE SMARTER ARCHITECTURAL DESIGN STUDY

The Triangular-Tetrahedral (Tri-Tet) Space Station

Marc M. Cohen

Abstract

The architectural design of the International Space Station has features that can be considered as the smartest examples for the future of architectural constructs on the Planet Earth, as well. The usage of modular design, as an example of the largest conceivable architectural robot, contains features that can become a model for advancement of technological studies for design of the smartest built environments on Earth. The architectural design of the space station includes advancement in ease of assembly in weightlessness, in addition to considerations for design concepts guided by four specific principles of modularity, maintainability reconfigurability as well as accessibility. Interior hardware racks and utilities could be replaced easily, standardized so that they could be plugged into a slot in any module made of massive triangular prismatic truss structure, and swung away for easy access to utility lines of the pressure hull. This chapter includes the tangible experiences of Marc Cohen the former architect of NASA involved in development of the new concept and design of the multimodule space station.

Introduction

In 1973, NASA launched Skylab, the United States' first crewed space station. Skylab was occupied by three crews in 1973–1974. In 1979, Skylab reentered the Earth's atmosphere. That same year, NASA began a new internal study for a second-generation space station (Livingston, 1979).

During the same decade, the Soviet Union coordinated the development and launch of its Salyut series of space stations with its five-year economic plans. Thus, they launched their major space stations at five-year intervals: Salyut 1 in 1971, Salyut 6 in 1976, and Salyut

DOI: 10.4324/9781003384113-65

7 in 1981. The Salyuts eventually supported three crewmembers, with occasional visits from other crews, notably from the Soviet's international cosmonaut program. Because the Salyuts were intended to serve in orbit for only five years, it appeared that the Soviets had developed a complete space station assembly line that would enable them to produce, launch, and operate progressively larger and more complex space stations twice per decade.

The United States had launched the Skylab space station in 1973 using components from the Apollo program. For lack of a Saturn launch vehicle, the second, backup Skylab unit remains in the Smithsonian Air and Space Museum. Because the Skylab depended upon surplus Apollo program hardware — and production of Apollo systems had come to a screeching halt under the Nixon administration — the United States had no ready means to respond to the growing Soviet Salyut program. Instead, NASA focused upon developing the Space Shuttle.

In the early 1980s, the Reagan administration developed the speculation that the 1986 launch of "Salyut 8" would be capable of supporting six cosmonauts. In 1986, the Soviets launched the first module of the *Mir* (Peace) space station. The administration established the Space Station Task Force at NASA HQ in 1982, headed by John Hodge, a veteran of the Apollo and Space Shuttle programs. They proposed that if the Soviets were going to deploy a space station for six crewmembers, then the United States should deploy a space station for at least eight crew members. In April, 1983, NASA established the Space Station Concept Development Group (CDG) with offices in the GAO building in Washington, DC.

The CDG completed its work in 1984, and President Reagan promptly christened its CDG-1 construct as *Space Station Freedom* (SSF). Eventually, the SSF evolved into the *International Space Station* (ISS) with Russian participation. The "Mir 2 core" serves now as the *Zvezda* core module of the ISS.

The author was appointed to the CDG as a "commuting member," with a monthly schedule of travel. He spent one week in Washington, one week at a NASA center or aerospace company, and the intervening time back at NASA Ames, his "home center" between trips. This assignment provided a profound, in-depth education. It was not just "drinking from the fire hose," but it was bathing in the fire hose, too. This essay describes the role of one Space Architect in contributing to the design of the Space Station and to the theory and practice of space station design.

Preface

In January, 1983, Louis Polaski, the Deputy Division Chief in the Systems Engineering Division at the NASA Ames Research Center put out a "call for volunteers" to work on the nascent space station program. I volunteered. Lou provided me with a set of documents to study and asked that I come back with a proposal for something we could do in the Division.

Lou provided me with this set of documents and a caveat. The caveat was that while Marshall Space Flight Center (MSFC) had been generous in sharing their documents, Johnson Space Center (JSC) was not sharing. The only way he could obtain data on the JSC concept or concepts was to ask NASA HQ and MSFC. The documents provided to me were:

NASA HQ (1981, Sept. 29). "Space Station Program Overview" including the JSC SOC and the MSFC SAMSP. Washington, DC: NASA.
MSFC (1981, Oct). "Science and Applications Manned Space Platform: Conceptual Design and Analysis Study Program Development." Huntsville, Alabama: MSFC.

Unknown (1981). "Space Platform Applicability for Manned Space Station, including SAMSP Inhouse Concept: MDAC—Evolutionary Science and Applications Space Platform and JSC—SOC."
Brady (1983, March 2016).

The tasks that Mr. Polaski assigned me were:

1 Study the above concept documents and identify salient architectural features. Also survey relevant reference literature.
2 Consider and recommend methods or techniques of architectural design analysis appropriate for application to a space station.
3 Consider and evaluate architectural geometric systems as appropriate for space station construction.
4 Attempt to indicate how the application of these methods might contribute to space station concept design and design development.

I developed this outline and the following approach in response to my reading of this paucity of data.

Space Station Architecture Study Objective

Explore alternative concepts to conventional space station designs.
Review of Current Concepts and the Fundamental Questions Raised:

1 Why assume Cartesian (X-Y-Z) coordinates for a space station structure in micro-g where there is no "up" and "down"?
2 Do Apollo or Apollo-Soyuz-type plug-in docking joints that align with the modules' longitudinal axes determine the entire space station structure?
3 Why should an alignment with docking of an active, propulsive vehicle be used for the berthing of a passive, non-propulsive payload?
4 Can space station function dictate geometry (as opposed to structural geometry dictating everything else)?
5 How can we use geometry to plan for unpredictable growth?
6 Why baseline a rectangular configuration that makes it difficult or impossible to install the "last side" of the rectangle and equally makes it impossible to change out or replace a module?
7 How do connecting elements serve as structural determinants?

Space Station Architecture Issues to Be Addressed

This review of NASA's current manned space station concepts (circa 1983) indicates the need for a basic architectural design study. The existing concepts appear to transfer numerous terrestrial assumptions to the space station/micro-g environment, but without fully considering terrestrial architectural analysis and design techniques. At the same time, other Earth precedents for long-term habitation and functional organization appear to have been overlooked.

This architectural design study applies a variety of analytical and design methods to the Space Station Project, focusing on questions raised in a review of the JSC/Boeing Space Operations Center (SOC) and the MSFC/McDonnell Douglas Science and Applications Manned Space Platform (SAMSP). Among these concerns about these current space station concepts are:

- Selection of an appropriate geometric system
- Structural rigidity and stability
- Planning for Growth
- Safety and internal circulation, and
- Standardization of interfaces at connecting elements.

These factors are all interrelated. The connections and interactions between them shall be examined. This study leads to proposing an alternate space station concept and geometry.

Summary of Review of Current Concepts (January 1983)

The two principal concepts submitted for architectural design review are the SAMSP proposed by MSFC with their contractor McDonnell-Douglas Astronautics Corporation (MDAC) and the SOC proposed by JSC and their contractor the Boeing Company. Please refer to Figure 5.4.1.

Each concept develops from its own clearly formulated philosophical basis, which is described in the concept documents. The differences in design solution appear to derive

Figure 5.4.1   View of the two space station concepts under review in 1983, (upper image) the JSC/Boeing SOC and (lower image) the MSFC/McDonnell Douglas SAMSP. (Courtesy of Author Marc M. Cohen).

largely from these differences in philosophy. These philosophies appear to grow from deployment criteria for "reduced peak funding" or "lower design and manufacturing costs," but they do not posit incompatible differences in the function of the fully assembled space station. After reading the several sets of design criteria, one is a little surprised to find that the architectural similarities between the two concepts appear to overshadow their differences.

Each space station concept comprises three key elements:

1 A solar power unit
2 Cylindrical modules for human activity and habitation, and
3 One or more kinds of linking or docking element.

Each station concept would house about four people in the initial, modest phases and fully assembled would support about 12 people for periods of 90 days or more. As the space station expanded, a variety of secondary detachable elements would proliferate, as would the number and type of connecting or adapting elements. The definition and function of each of these three primary elements seemed to vary in clarity.

The solar power units seemed most clearly defined, being identified precisely and consistently in all concepts. It is always designated for deployment on the first launch. The only ambiguity concerned to what extent the power unit or "energy section" could be accessed or served from inside the space station.

The cylindrical modules for human habitation and activity were also fairly well defined. The cylinder dimensions are limited by the interior of the Shuttle cargo bay, but it was apparent that within the approximately 14 m (46 ft) length available in the cargo bay while the EVA airlock is in place, some variation is possible within each concept.

SAMSP suggests the use of the basic ESA Spacelab module and indicates a diversity of possible lengths and functional combinations, all within the 4.25 m (14 ft) maximum diameter. However, there is no variation in the diameter and very little experimentation with the overall form of this module. The central corridor runs the length of the module, just as it does on Spacelab.

SOC incorporates the Spacelab-type module only as a detachable "science module," while developing several new types of cylindrical modules. The SOC "command" and "service" modules would have diameters of either 2.4 m (8.0 ft) or 3.45 m (11.5 ft), with lengths varying from 9 m (30 ft) to 15 m (50 ft). The SOC habitation module would be a 4.25 m (14 ft) diameter cylinder divided across the long axis by floors or bulkheads into approximately four compartments reminiscent of the crew deck in the Skylab Saturn Workshop.

SOC puts a major emphasis on a primary command module adjacent to the "energy section," and incorporates science modules only as temporary, secondary components. In contrast, the SAMSP does not appear to require a "command module" type of function, but each module would presumably act more self-sufficiently in regulating utilities and life support systems than the SOC modules. These distinctions in cylindrical module design seem to be the most significant manifestations of the differences in basic design philosophy.

Both concepts include one or two habitation modules as major components. During this review, a pair of analogies arose to the two methods of subdividing the cylindrical modules: the SAMSP to the "hot dog" model and the SOC to the "salami" model. Neither model appeared to have a significant effect to determining the external assemblage of space station modules.

Each space station concept appears to propose two or more kinds of linking elements in the completed assemblies. These linking elements were given a number of names: airlock adapter, pressurized tunnel adapter, orbiter interface, berthing interface, berthing ports, tunnel module, and tunnel airlock. This proliferation of names for the same type of function suggests a degree of indecision as to the particular functions of these connecting elements, both in terms of connections between space station modules and for the interface with external elements such as the space shuttle or science lab modules. These connecting elements appear to be of critical importance both structurally and functionally and appear to want further study.

Each concept shows the ability to accept a multitude of secondary elements such as a reboost module (RM), science module, space tug hangar, and logistics rack. Each proposal recognizes implicitly an aspect of randomness or unpredictability about when and where these secondary components or payloads might attach or detach.

This problem of unpredictability runs as an unarticulated theme through all the space station concept options. It encompasses both the addition of secondary components to the core modules and the expansion or replication of the core modules themselves. The pervasiveness of this uncertainty leads to a difficult question: Do these proposals simply show how many ways it may be possible to assemble modules into a space station OR do they show how we *want* to assemble them? The questions arising from this uncertainty lead to the suggestion that architectural design analysis techniques might be applied to help find better answers about the functional organization of a space station.

The leading question that stood unanswered was why both station concepts applied a Cartesian system of x-y-z coordinates to a structure in an environment where *there is no up or down*. A careful reading of the Skylab Experience Bulletins and Mission Reports indicated these reasons for up-down design in the interior of the habitable modules: fabrication and simulation on the ground and astronaut orientation and convenience within a specific workspace or module. However, no definitive reason was found why the configuration of assembled modules should be based on Cartesian coordinates, much less make all element-to-element connections orthogonally at 90° angles.

The Role of Geometry

A common factor in all the space station concepts comprises the selection of a geometric pattern or system. All the existing concept proposals subject to review assume a Cartesian/orthogonal x-y-x geometry for the placement and connection of space station modules. A further common, unexamined practice presumes that all connections must occur by "plugging-in" the module along its longitudinal axis. While this geometry appears simple and straightforward, the role that function plays is not in evidence. This rectangular geometry presents problems of structural rigidity insofar as the module-to-module connecting joint must resist moments, racking, and torques in an orthogonal system. Planning for control of the Center of Gravity (CG) emerges as an issue throughout the configuration growth process. This study evaluates the configuration geometry as a structural logic that unites all the other aspects of the space station.

The problem of structural rigidity and control of CG led to the consideration of a variety of polyhedrals, particularly the five "Platonic Solids." Traditionally, these five three-dimensional solids have been ordered they their number of faces (hedra). That ordering subsumes a complex set of assumptions about the nature of construction geometry as practiced on Earth. However, the space station is not terrestrial; it should be open to nonterrestrial geometry.

As an example of such a nonterrestrial geometry, Buckminster Fuller revised the ordering of the Platonic polyhedral based on the number of vertices (Fuller, 1963; Cohen, 2012). This revision recognized that in the construction of a spherical polyhedral, the vertices or joints are more important than the number of sides (hedra). This approach offers insight into the vertex/joint/connection problems of a space station. Fuller states further that the tetrahedron (4 vertices, 4 sides, 6 edges), the octahedron (6 vertices, 8 sides, 12 edges), the icosahedron (12 vertices, 20 sides, 30 edges), and the *vector equilibrium solid* of his invention (eight triangular sides, and six squares) are the only self-rigidizing or self-stabilizing polyhedral in the universe (Fuller, 1975). Fuller's revision suggests two things. First, it excludes the cube and other rectangular, right-angle-based polyhedrals and the dodecahedron from consideration for space station configurations. Second, it suggests an investigation into the replication and extension properties of these four self-rigidizing polyhedrals.

This geometric exercise indicates that the tetrahedron offers particular advantages of structural rigidity, control of CG, and replication of a stable structure. As the tetrahedron comprises triangular faces, each face of three edges is also self-stabilizing. This self-stabilizing property compares favorably to rectilinear forms of configuration that are not self-stabilizing. These orthogonal configurations demand that the structural joints be strengthened to resist bending moments, racking, torques, and other loads that do not generally pose problems for a triangulated structure, also known as a *space truss*.

Orthogonal structures pose a set of problems that reflect all the terrestrial assumptions brought into the space station design process that impose serious limitations on what is admissible. To sum up the problems of rectangular structural configurations in space:

1 They assume that all configurations must deploy at right angles or straight lines from module to module.
2 The modules must join together by plugging them together along the longitudinal axis of the module being connected.
3 The joint unit, whether is described as an adapter, a berthing or docking module, a hub, or a node must resist structural moments and other stresses by providing "short arm" moment resistance across the opening or diameter of the joint unit.
4 Although orthogonal modules may lend themselves to "up-down" local orientation, that does not change the Skylab results where two astronauts were disoriented by "translating" from the Skylab airlock to the Skylab Saturn Workshop. And those two modules were aligned along the same longitudinal axis. However, it is not correct to equate the *LOCAL VERTICAL* in a module with the *GLOBAL VERTICAL* of the entire space station. To make the pseudo-ergonomic assertion that astronauts need the entire space station at the same vertical vector orientation is to assume that astronauts cannot learn their way around the space station despite varying local verticals in different modules.

In Fuller's lexicon, triangles and tetrahedra are "omnidirectional symmetric" (Fuller, 1975). They are not bound by the terrestrial shibboleths of up/down, left/right, and x-y-z. This study evaluates the applicability for the triangular-tetrahedral (Tri-Tet) unity for a space station configuration. The accompanying tables describe some of the properties of the self-rigidizing polyhedral.

Alternative Geometry Space Station

The application of architectural design analysis coordinated with geometric observations indicates the criticality of inter-module connecting elements on both the functional and structural levels. This concern about the primacy of connections leads to the consideration of an entirely difference geometric configuration. As shown in the following diagrams, this alternative approach presents the following advantages for solutions to several problems in space station design. Please refer to Figure 5.4.2.

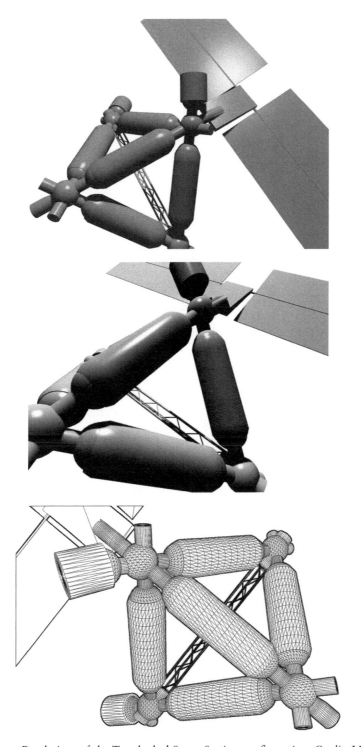

Figure 5.4.2   a–c Renderings of the Tetrahedral Space Station configuration, Credit: LEK, Courtesy of the author, produced by the office of James Stewart Polshek, Architect.

601

Structural Stability

A square/cube system would collapse except for the rigidity of the joints. In order to prevent collapse, the joints between modules must take substantial stress. These stresses store energy in the intermodular joint. Jack Stokes of NASA MSFC concluded that:

> A design goal should be that no stored energy shall exist in any of the components prior to, during, or following mating of the components. If stored energy components do exist, the energy level should be kept to a minimum.
>
> *(Stokes, pp. 198–199)*

The same principle applies to connections between space station modules. A self-stabilizing triangle or tetrahedron will minimize stresses at the joints while still affording transfer of forces because each basic unit of structure is self-rigidizing.

Sequence of Assembly and Migration of Center of Gravity (CG)

The *principle* for sequence of assembly is that the configuration can handle greater asymmetries when the mass is smaller, but as the mass increases, the configuration must grow toward greater symmetry to balance the mass in two or three axes/vectors. For the space station, in the initial phase of assembly, the configuration consists of one module, one connective unit, and one power unit. If a linear assembly, the sequence will be essentially similar to the conventional current concepts. However, there are many possible reasons to make the initial configuration asymmetric, such as hanging the power module or logistics module off the side of the connecting element. But, once the first triangle is completed, the assembly process will take on a different character, with efficiency and stability increasing as the sequence progresses as shown in Figure 5.4.3.

Figure 5.4.3 shows this assembly sequence as forming a two-dimensional, planar configuration of two triangles. However, the Tri-Tet system enables extending the configuration into three dimensions while forming an infinite variety of module connection patterns. Figure 5.4.4 displays a 3D model that projects its triangles at 120° apart, with three perimeter connecting beams.

Symmetry/Control of the CG

The CG represents the center of mass factoring in the moment arms around that center to the various elements such as modules and connecting units. Beyond their initial phases of deployment, all existing space station proposals appear to encounter problems with the control of CG. The Tri-Tet system will afford more precise control of the CG because of configuration symmetries that can be maintained and enhanced as the system grows as demonstrated in Figure 5.4.3. Structural stability is also maintained with cantilevered modules kept to a minimum.

Planning for Unpredictable Growth

Existing space station proposals assume an almost random, linear/incremental approach to growth, starting from the most minimal possible initial core. The Tri-Tet space station would require a slightly more complex starting investment but would benefit from an

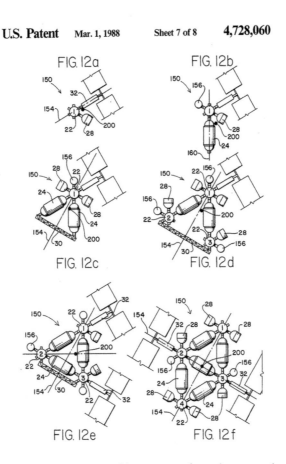

Figure 5.4.3   Triangular Space Station Assembly Sequence from the patent drawings. The center of mass appears as callout No. 200. (Courtesy of Author Marc M. Cohen).

increasingly stable geometry and the economies of agglomeration and scale. As the station expands, costs for each new increment would probably decrease because of multiple uses of connecting hubs, while providing the same level of services or better.

Circulation

Existing space station proposals show unclear circulation patterns, where either people must circulate through a central command module, pass inappropriately through an experiment of habitation module, or go well out of their way to avoid such an "invasion of privacy." Tri-Tet system can solve this set of problems—allow adjacency for all modules and allow people to bypass the command module.

Standardization of Docking/Interface/Connector Conditions

The existing space station proposals all show at least two and sometimes three of four different interface/docking/fabrication conditions (e.g., end and side of cylindrical modules,

Figure 5.4.4 Views of a model of the Tri-Tet Space Station in 3-triangle Configuration. Hair curlers by Fabregé. (Courtesy of Author Marc M. Cohen).

end and side of docking tunnels, service modules, or airlock/adapters). The Tri-Tet system will provide a single, universal, and omnidirectional docking hub adapter. These spherical hubs would provide an omnidirectional docking hub adapter. These spherical hubs would provide circulation, communications, logistics, life support, and utility links between all modules. The hubs also provide space shuttle docking ports.

This spherical/hemispherical system would provide both the connecting hubs and the docking ends for module cylinders, all shaped from a single basic 3.6 m (12 ft) spherical diameter template. This singularity of purpose should help hold down manufacturing costs compared to three or four diversified interface units. These docking hubs would further have the capability of containing airlocks, EVA suit storage and prep, and all the functions designated for the "airlock adapter/safe haven." If such functions are deemed appropriate for specific locations in the configuration. The problems and requirements for the actual hatch connections with pneumatic and communications interfaces are essentially aligned with the needs for the hatches or ports proposed in the SOC and the SAMSP. The main potential divergence of Tri-Tet from the other proposals is that the hub would need docking capability with a lateral vector across two hubs.

Space Shuttle Navigation Approach Cone

The existing proposals for rectangular geometries present potential difficulties that may make docking a space shuttle to the space station more ticklish than necessary. Nearly all the proposed shuttle docking ports occur at or close to the center of a cylindrical assembly, creating a somewhat tight approach cone. On Skylab, the multiple docking adapter (MDA) was located at the distal end of the configuration. Docking by Apollo spacecraft was accomplished without difficulties in maneuvering. In the Tri-Tet station, all docking ports would be located at a distal "corner" presenting a "reverse" approach cone and making docking less difficult.

RM Location

The existing space station concepts locate the RM at or near the end of one axis of the space station, possibly posing problems of attitude control and stabilization upon reboost. As the rectangular type of station grows, the RM becomes more remote from the system symmetry. In contrast, the Tri-Tet docking hubs will allow the location of the RM upon at least two major structural axes of the space station. Combined with the inherent symmetry of the Tri-Tet, this location for the RM will result in less problems of attitude control and stabilization.

Redundancy

Redundancy is the first pillar of reliability, provided there are not too many diverse parts. In the existing proposals, redundancy appears to require an extra effort, with multiple different repetitive elements and duplication of many diverse items. In contrast, in the Tri-Tet closed-loop system, redundancy becomes intrinsic to the space station geometry. Every module can incorporate two access points for circulation and all logistics, pneumatics, utilities, communications, etc., through a docking hub at each end. As the configuration grows, proportionally fewer hubs are required to support the space station. Please see the configuration growth table (Table 5.4.1). Theoretically, the tetrahedral space station could grow indefinitely—if not infinitely—while conserving control of CG, dual access to every module, dual remote egress from every module, structural stability, and symmetry.

Table 5.4.1 Properties of the Platonic Solids for Selecting a Space Station Configuration Geometry Where the Edges Become Cylindrical Modules and the Vertices Become Nodes

Solid	Vertices (V)	Faces	Edges (E)	Ratio of V/E	Self-Rigidizing?
Tetrahedron	4	4	4	0.67	YES
Octahedron	6	8	12	0.50	YES
Cube	8	6	12	0.67	NO
Icosahedron	12	20	30	0.40	YES
Dodecahedron	20	12	30	0.67	NO

Habitable Cylindrical Modules

Although the SOC favors the "salami" module and the SAMSP favors the "hot dog" module, the Tri-Tet station can accept either model for a habitat interior. In order to make the module more compatible with the 60° joints around the hubs, it would be necessary to apply the hemispheres as end-caps at the same diameter as the spherical hubs. The maximum diameter for the module cylinder is the 4.25 m (14 ft) dictated by interior fairing clearance of the space shuttle cargo bay. One interesting variation would be the inclusion of an airlock for EVA at one end of a "workshop" module, within a hemispherical end cap. Such a large airlock could accommodate a fairly large EVA work team at the same time—up to four or five fully suited space walkers pre breathing pure O_2 at the same time. This EVA airlock function could also be located in part of a spherical docking hub, but within a cylindrical module endcap, it may offer better access to work tools. The use of this airlock would not block access through the hub or hemisphere for extended periods of time.

Interchangeability/Replaceability of Modules

The existing space station concepts do not appear to address the issues of interchangeability or replacement. At best, they can create some kind of workaround to use a flexible tunnel to tie in an extra module as shown in Figure 5.4.2. Boeing sketch by Brand Griffin. The basic problem with all these rectangular configurations is that once the square or rectangle is formed and closed, it becomes impossible to change out a module without pulling apart the whole configuration to remove the old module and install the new one. In comparison, the Tri-Tet is designed to accommodate the removal of modules and their replacement. The key to this interchangeability is that the berthing mechanism is not dependent upon a longitudinal plug-in. On the contrary, it operates laterally, allowing modules to be slipped out or slipped in sideways. This approach neither stresses nor endangers the structural stability of the configuration. The Tri-Tet employs a new lateral vector docking mechanism that obviates all the problems with rectangular/orthogonal configurations for changing out modules.

Tri-Tet Lateral Berthing Mechanism

The existing space station concepts use the plug-in type docking mechanism developed for the Apollo Program. NASA used this method successfully for Apollo-LM, Apollo-Skylab, and Apollo-Soyuz rendezvous and docking. It made the docking approach as simple as possible by aligning both vehicles on their longitudinal axes before closing straight in and docking. This docking joint consisted of a structural connection and pressure seal, accomplished through a simultaneous alignment for roll, pitch, and yaw in this single vector plug-in system. Both concepts advanced for the SOC and SAMSP use this conventional aligned plug-in approach.

For the Space Station, the docking mechanism will be required to carry a considerable number of additional functions besides the longitudinal alignment and pressure seal. Computer data links, electrical power, intercom, life support system, pneumatics, video links, etc. The addition of these functions to the single vector simultaneous plug-in joint imposes a level of complexity that exceeds the original intent of that design. Current efforts at designing a single vector simultaneous alignment joint for all utilities have encountered considerable obstacles in trying to force all the space station functions into a plug-in joint or mechanism. The other problems inherent in the plug-in joint for a rectangular/cube-type station concern the structural strength and assembly sequence. These rectangular joints must take much greater moments and torques than intended for Apollo docking. Given a rectangular assembly of a space station, once a module is installed, it becomes impossible to remove or replace it without disassembling much of the module structure that closes it. Figure 5.4.4 illustrates the multifunctionality of these berthing connectors.

An analysis of the plug-in/simultaneous alignment joint suggests that there are simply too many functions to deploy on the single vector. However, if we separate the functions by vector or degree of freedom, it becomes no longer necessary to make a simultaneous alignment of all pipes, pins, and other connections. Thus, instead of a simultaneous alignment and plug-in of all utilities, an alternative appears as a multiple vector/sequential alignment lateral slip-in joint for the Tri-Tet space station.

To explain the Tri-Tet docking joint as shown in Figure 5.4.5, it is necessary to describe briefly the process by which it was designed. The design starts from two premises:

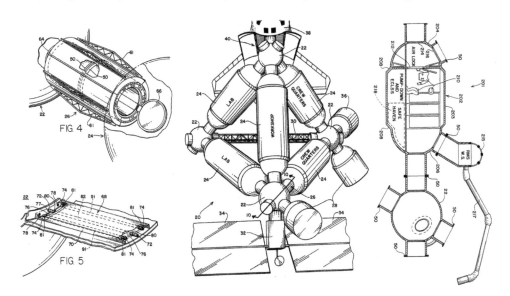

Figure 5.4.5 A triptych of patent drawings for the Tri-Tet Space Station. In the center panel is a view of the Tri-Tet space station with a Space Shuttle docked to it. On the left are details of the berthing mechanism connecting a module to a hub (or node) plus the utility connection channel that would line the tunnel. The panel on the right shows a module and a hub berthed to it. The module has a cupola attached to a berthing port. This patent is the origin of the cupola on the ISS. (Courtesy of Author Marc M. Cohen).

1 There is a universal/omnidirectional docking hub that harkens to Fuller's description of the tetrahedron as omnisymmetrical, to support the docking mechanism.
2 There is a module that acts as an edge or struts in the tetrahedron that can slip laterally into a pair of geometrically opposite docking hubs.

The initial assumption was that since the spherical docking hub was a specialized unit to support docking, it should carry any active docking mechanism. However, it soon became apparent that a hub with active docking mechanisms presents difficulties. If the active clamping mechanism is mounted on the hub itself, it limits the approach path of modules to a narrow window and the mechanisms would create congestion around the hub itself.

Eventually, the author built a study model that placed the active docking mechanism on the ends of each module, around the docking tunnel. The spherical hub assumes the role of a passive recipient of the active docking module. This model represents a significant philosophical step forward; it defines a basic principle: the more omnidirectional a structural/mechanical element is, the more passive it must be. Conversely, the more active a structural element is, the more unidirectional it becomes. Therefore, for the docking hub to be truly omnidirectional within the omnisymmetrical tetrahedron, it must be passive. The complementary module must carry the active docking mechanism(s). This module appears in Figure 5.4.6.

The combination of the active module docking mechanism and the passive hub receiving system makes it possible to add a module between hubs or to remove a module from between hubs without disrupting the rest of the space station structure.

Lessons Learned from Tri-Tet

1 Because the reliability strategy for modules is design for minimum risk, the modules are very robust with a safety facto on the order of 3 or 4. Therefore, the design of the joints or hubs to handle moments and other loads and stresses is not an issue; the design for minimum risk handles this amount of load and stress easily. This reliability factor diminishes one of the key arguments for triangulated geometry.
2 At the time I did this project, the assumption was that the space station would incorporate a docking connector about the same size as the 1.0 m diameter mid-deck hatch on the space shuttle. However, as we developed the space station program, it became obvious we needed a much larger clear passage to pass full-size Space Station Freedom racks through the entry and docking hatches. The dimensions of these racks are 1.05 m wide, 2.10 m tall, and 0.9 m. deep. They could not possibly pass through a 1.0 m circular hatch. The station hatch is 1.25 m square; we had one hell of a fight to establish those dimensions, and the envelope around it is even larger—approaching 2 m in diameter.
3 The consequence of this change in hatch size means that the 3.6 m diameter spherical hub is not large enough to hold all the berthing ports required for the Tri-Tet module connections. That means that the hub must become larger, possibly equal to the 4.25 diameter of the module itself. However, it should be possible to make a 4.25 m diameter hemispherical endcap and hub. The circumference of the spherical hub would be 14.18 m. That would allow 6 × 2 m perimeter berthing ports with 0.36 m between them.

Figure 5.4.6 View of the model of the lateral berthing mechanism to bring modules into the Tri-Tet configuration and to change them out or replace them. From the top image, the module lines up in parallel with the axis between the berthing ports. The middle image shows the module lining up axially with the berthing ports on the hubs. The lower image shows the berthing mechanism closing around the berthing ports on the hubs. Crafted by the author. (Courtesy of Author Marc M. Cohen).

Bibliography

Cohen, Marc M. (2012). The Continuum of Space Architecture from Earth to Orbit (AIAA 2012–3575). *42nd International Conference on Environmental Systems (ICES)*. Reston, VI: American Institute of Aeronautics and Astronautics.

Fuller, R. Buckminster. (1963). *Ideas and Integrities*. Englewood Cliffs, NJ: Prentice-Hall, Inc.

Fuller, R. Buckminster. (1975). *Synergetics*. New York: Macmillan Publishing Co.

MSFC. (1974, July). *Skylab Lessons Learned* (NASA TMX-64860). Huntsville, AL: NASA.

MSFC. (1974, Oct). *Skylab Mission Report—Saturn Workshop*, NASA TMX-64814). Huntsville, AL: NASA.

Schneider, William & Hanes, Thomas [Editors] (1975). *The Skylab Results. Advances in the Astronautical Sciences, Vol 31, Parts 1 & 2*. Tarzana, CA: American Astronautica Society.

Stokes, Jack W. (1981, May). Comparative Evaluation of Operability of Large Space Structure Connectors, *15th Aerospace Mechanisms Symposium* (NASA CP-2181). Washington, DC: NASA.

Ter Haar, G. H. (1978, April). Hatch Latch Mechanism for Spacelab Scientific Airlock, *12th Aerospace Mechanisms Symposium* (NASA CP-2080). Washington, DC: NASA.

5.5

MOBILE ARCHITECTURE FOR, WITH, AND BY THE PEOPLE

Smart Design Responses to Climate Change Challenges

Eric Farr and Poorang Piroozfar

Abstract

The denotation of mobile architecture has evolved due to the turns, shifts, and variations it has gone through since the 1950s. The concept of semantic extension/ shift has been adopted – from its context of origin, logic, and linguistics – and epitomized to shed light on what the concept of mobile architecture and mobility in/or architecture have sustained in the course of their evolution.

The notion of motion and place (as opposed to space) will be looked into to investigate the bearings these may have on our discourse. Environmentality will follow to help us lead the discussion into how mobile architecture may be re-framed concerning climate change/crises.

This chapter concludes by drawing a comprehensive picture of (smart) technological advancements that can be utilized to devise a smart platform for mobile architecture to incorporate a higher degree of intelligence and sustainability. This will allow for a new genre of mobile architecture that is all-inclusive, accommodating, agile, and adaptable. It delivers smart, future-proof, responsible, fit-for-purpose, environmentally concerned solutions that recognize and respect the "One Planet" philosophy at its core. Finally, we propose three different alternative typologies that mobile architecture can develop into, in the future.

Introduction

The process of adoption of a concept from one discipline and its adaption/adaptation and application to another discipline has proven beneficial especially when x-disciplinarity is intended, and/or inevitable. What happens through such a process is "semantic extension". In logic and semantics, extension (and intension) is referred to as a correlative word that indicates the reference of a term or concept. "Intension" indicates the internal content of a term or concept that constitutes its formal definition, whereas "extension" shows its range of applicability by naming the particular objects that it denotes (The Editors of Encyclopaedia Britannica, Invalid Date). Extension is usually quite risk-free when it takes

DOI: 10.4324/9781003384113-66

place at a certain time – synchronically – within a particular discipline. It is, however, more sensitive when it happens across two or more disciplines synchronically or within one discipline diachronically (as an inter-generational involuntary permeation or deliberate handover of a concept) and entails different extents and degrees of evolution of the technical concepts and/or jargons, varying from semantic drift, semantic shift, semantic extension, right up to semantic change.

An important attempt at the coinage of "Mobile Architecture" is Yona Friedman's account in the 1950s which was based on the idea that everyone can do architecture (Friedman, 1970, 2020). The concept was about a liberal, all-inclusive, and enabling approach to the design of, and, in architecture as much as it was about the concept of flexibility, adaptability, and customizability of the space by its end users while provisioning underlying tectonic layers, which are less prominent in the formation of design, are centralized and procured by the design teams/experts. Heathcote (2022) tells us that for Friedman, while the architect's job is to provide the superstructure and the elements, it is the dweller's job to build their own life within it. "Meuble plus", Friedman's solution for architecture, which he further developed in the latter part of his life, was initiated through his work with migrants as he believed that cities were always built by migration. It took the surface area of pieces of furniture as well as the surface needed to use them as a "living unit", a box, a building block or component, a small moveable room; or a new suburban style to build up the architecture with or around them. However, Friedman admits that when he came up with the concept of "mobile architecture" in the 1950s, he thought we were limited by networks, be the phone networks or electric grids; "but we aren't dependent on them anymore", he asserts[1] (PCA, 2017).

"Mobile Architecture" with its overtly declared or naturally evolved developments over the past half a century is a classic example of how semantic change can take place, intentionally or unintentionally, knowingly or unknowingly, and decisively or indecisively; in some cases, including this one, with limited if any owing to the main concept as it was.[2] If the purpose of architecture, for Corbusier, is "to move us", for Friedman, mobile architecture is not about its capability to move or be moved but more about the freedom of change and liberating architecture from the exclusive and time-locked role of the architect at the time of the creation of architecture. Almost without any exception, the first impression many experts in the built environment will have had of mobile architecture ever since is moveable architecture.[3]

Locus Standi

In a bibliographic review of Space and Place for Oxford Bibliographies,[4] Lawrence-Zuniga (2017) tells us that space is often defined by an abstract scientific, mathematical, or measurable conception while place refers to the elaborated cultural meanings people invest in or attach to a specific site or locale. She continues to assert that in coping with mobility and displacement, studies on space and place now consider migration, place-making, and identity construction. The review suggests that notions of hegemony, surveillance, and the actions of the state interpenetrate local ethnographic sites that now must consider context in more complex ways than simply adapting to the physical environment. Although architecture is not free from politics and most specifically land politics, and although space and place are two utterly different but not mutually exclusive concepts and can potentially play an instrumental role in a discourse on mobility, we would intentionally and decisively keep our owning to the concept limited to *locus standi*. The denotation of *locus standi* is "the right to have a stand [and be heard] in the court [of law]". Nonetheless, we use our prerogative regarding the semantic extension to use a more liberal connotation of it as "the right (of architecture) to stand on (or occupy) a piece of land". That is regardless of whether this right is primarily over space to create a place on/within the land or the right of the place itself (immediately as a sole property on land, or intermediately as the right over land through land lease agreements for flats and apartments) to create a secondary intended, ultimate and individually occupiable place of/for living.

For mobile architecture, not only is the issue of place (location) – or their lack of – what matters but the notion of motion embedded in architecture's capability of movability (or simply its mobility) is another important matter. Recounted by Aristotle, Zeno's Paradoxes of motion and place go hand in hand back to the C 5th BCE. Out of Zeno's three paradoxes of motion, two[5] – the Paradox of Achilles and the tortoise and the Dichotomy Paradox which are not mutually inclusive – are both probably the closest geometric interpretation of the algebraic notion of "limit" in differential mathematics. Regardless of the usefulness and perceived or proven usability of the concept of "limit" in modern science and engineering, its applicability to our discussion here remains purely at a theoretical level. Zeno's Paradox of place which states: "everything that exists occupies a place, and so does place itself, *ad infinitum*" is another stimulating concept that can add some new dimensions to our discourse on mobile architecture. Whether the mobility of architecture is enforced by the lack of a permanent place for it to locate itself as a "thing" or it is an intentional decision to avoid such an earthly attachment to the land – probably to get closer to the idealistic view of immortality even if that is in its algebraic sense of "limit" – is a debate which can steer our discussion as will follow. Suffice it to say that architecture if and when it moves and either decidedly or forcefully leaves its place, cannot take away its place – the piece of land or even the right to that piece of land – with itself even if we assume that its place has a place of its own. The nature of the place for a (mobile) architecture is in essence different from the nature of the place of the place of that architecture (supposing Zeno's Paradox of Place holds up). This said if and when architecture moves, it will inevitably take away with itself the memories that it has created in association with its occupied land – its place – and neither of the two will possess those memories fully, completely, and independently from one another and from the time they have been bodily associated with each other. The contemporary implication of "mobile architecture", however, goes way beyond that point. In a *sensu stricto*, it may plainly and directly denote mobile parks (mobile homes or homes on wheels), floating homes (on water e.g. permanent moorings), shipping containers, RVs, flatpack homes (flatpack architecture), caravans, tents, temporary shelters, deployable structures, foldable structures. In a rather *sensu lato*, it may indirectly connotate concepts such as DIY, tiny homes, citizen designer, prefab, personalization, co-creation (which, as a more modern concept, is probably the closest of all to Friedman's original concept), Buckminster Fuller's Dymaxion[6] House, Jan Kaplický's Neofuturistic projects, The Situationist City,[7] Archigram's "The Plug-in City", "The Walking City", and "The Instant City" (among other Megastructuralist's visionary ideas), submersible and underwater habitats, and even Rudofsky's concept of "architecture without architects"[8] (which shares some bases with Friedman's concept of mobility, albeit distantly).

Some of the aforementioned concepts, approaches, and movements are by nature deemed mobile architecture exclusively "for", "with", or "by" the people whereas the status of some others remain contingent on the context, policy, decision, and collaborative working processes, funding mechanisms as well as stakeholders group's nature and extent of involvement and may be classified under more than one category or may change from one to another throughout the project as it develops and evolves.

Inexorability and Mobility

We start this section with a title that may well look like an oxymoron. According to Merriam-Webster, the Latin antecedent of inexorable is inexorabilis, formed of the prefix "in-", meaning "not", and "exorabilis", meaning "pliant" or "capable of being moved by entreaty" which in essence makes inexorable in a dialectic – if not an existentialist – contradiction – if not an impasse – with mobile (architecture). However, the cause, root, context, and implication of the two are not quite the same, and neither are the direction and nature of their causal-effect relationships with human agents.

Inexorability imposed on the vulnerable, the unprivileged, the deprived, the neglected, less-heard voices, and those who could receive a better share of environmental justice may have its roots in geopolitical conditions, socioeconomic dynamics, as well as ethical, gender, health, age differences among, or together with, other sociocultural challenges.[9] The inflexibility of unyielding societies to accommodate people of diverse *proprium* will impose a demand for higher levels of temporality and flexibility of those diverse social classes if they seek to integrate in their host communities or with the majority in the society. No longer is migration limited to its narrow traditional definition. In a broader sense, migration entails disassociation from a relatively stable or at least known – but not necessarily desirable – status quo, proceeding through a state of transformation in the hope of association with and probably integration into a better (or allegedly better) and more longed for but not necessarily known new status; a journey which may or may not warrant the intended outcome. For Gonzalez (2020), migration is a means of reparation as a response to climate change which she sees as an injustice caused primarily by the world's most affluent populations rather than a misfortune for the vulnerable groups at the receiving end of it. Sassen (2016: 204) believes that "the categories we use to understand and describe migrations – that is, the notion of people in search of a better life, who leave behind a family and home that they want to support from afar and possibly return to" is not quite "enough to capture the specificity of these emergent flows" (in migration). She goes on to conclude that the three extreme flows of refuge seekers she explores in her article "are just a sort of first indication of a process that is likely to escalate. They may be the most visible and extreme case of a much larger history in the making"; in search of what she calls "bare life" (Sassen, 2016: 224).

Placement and Displacement in "War and Peace", … and Climate Change

Together with migrants and Romanis/Romas, the modern urban nomads – the city-dwellers,[10] the rough sleepers, and the homeless – are the perfect resident candidates for the concept of mobile architecture in the residential sector. Their needs, experiences, and wants are an enriched source of collective knowledgebase for developing a new genre of mobile architecture that needs to be welcoming, succinct, compact, agile, flexible, efficient, effective, affective, adaptable, and above all movable. There is a wealth of knowledge in mobile architecture endorsed by developments in the caravan, campervan, and RV industry but such knowledge needs embedment of the characteristics, needs, wants, and priorities of their intended new user groups with all emotional, traumatic, and even tantalizing feelings of a utopian life such user groups may have lived with or been seeking.

The world pandemic in 2019 gave an unprecedented angle to migration as it alienated many mainstream people by detaching them from their pre-pandemic routines into an unknown realm of "digitality"; an area not quite explored proportionate to the extent it was to be utilized ending up with some expected consequences some still persistent five years on. This modern recurrence of *nomadity*[11] – both pre- and post-pandemic – has introduced new dimensions of which uncertainty and lack of the warranted intended or promised future are the ones not to be taken lightly. This has added a new dimension to what already was a semantic change to Friedman's original idea of mobility.

The harsh contextual conditions of human-induced disasters – e.g. conflicts or wars – or natural disasters – e.g. floods or earthquakes – usually lead to major displacements which require makeshift solutions for quick and temporary mass resettlement. This in essence is a less glorious, less planned, and less wished-for form of mobile architecture. This is hardly because this is the lower level of what Friedman aimed to achieve working with migrants but because this is the byproduct of torturous/traumatic incidents that almost all involved parties should (and probably would) long for to come to an end sooner rather than later. Any mass shelter of such nature, although represents a perfect category of mobile architecture due to its intrinsically temporary nature, is what has been least researched and worked on for all the aforementioned reasons. With the world experiencing more and more of such natural and human-made disasters and an unprecedented rise in the number of displaced across the world, it is probably time to put an end to this collective emotional reaction of "ignoring it and hoping it all goes away" and start working on this front of mobility in architecture in a more organized and systemic manner. This will provide a new collaborative working platform where the environmental credentials can be integrated form as early as the "point of beginning".[12]

The Parody of Environmentality: Foucault vs. …

For Foucault "Environmentality" has an "indivisible and inseparable"[13] element of politics and governing bodies, hence its sister terminology "Ecogovernmentality" which was built on the concept of governmentality[14] developed by Foucault in 1970–1980s. Environmentality in its mutual discourse with governmentality has been used as a way to explore changing environmental identities and actions broadly, including those related to waste (Harris, 2011), and for exploring power dynamics, changing attitudes and actions regarding waste, waste management, waste disposal, (Leonard, 2013, Moore, 2012) and probably more recently for waste elimination; some implicit references to it can be traced even in the circular economy movement. However, more recently the definition of environmentality has found its way more toward a literal reading of the term as awareness of environmental issues and sense of responsibility to the natural world, or another word for environmentability (Colman, 2009). In both its definitions – from the Foucauldian discourse in which power and more specifically biopower have a major role to play, to a more recent reading of it focusing more on the environment at its core – environmentality has a significant bearing at the least, and a major impact at the most, on mobile architecture and mobility in architecture and how it can and should evolve. Scarcity of land (even in developed countries such as the Netherlands) has led to adopting construction methods and technologies that need to adapt to their geographical and geological contexts. Building on water or floating architecture, which has mobility as an inherent characteristic, is not a solution merely for the deprived or underprivileged as it used to be in some developing countries but rather one and sometimes the only feasible solution to take up on. Epitomizing floating architecture, permanent moorings is a form of mobile architecture whose mobility can hypothetically be operationalized anytime needed.

Climate change is an undebatable fact and the action against it has already started finding its way into the "business-as-usual" models, changing many established practices throughout the life cycle of products, processes, and projects in the Architecture, Engineering, and Construction (AEC) industry and beyond. In some cases, nonetheless, the fear of climate change has caused some severe distractions resulting in actions whose environmental benefits, although well exhibited thanks to the broad publicity campaigns and marketing propaganda, are subject to fundamental concerns. As climate change and its detrimental environmental impacts become more prevailing, we should be expecting more severe weather conditions, more unexpected, skewed, or asymmetric patterns of precipitation, rising sea and ocean levels, more flood incidents, and longer and more extreme hot and cold seasons all of which can be responded to more effectively and more efficiently by a fully equipped mobile architecture which can be relocated and repositioned out of the temporary climate danger zones and back to their usual "place" once the threat is over.

Mobility in the Modes of Fabrication, Manufacturing and Assembly

Mobility in/architecture can benefit from proportionate modes of fabrication, manufacturing, and assembly. American construction methods (Balloon Frame Construction and Western Frame Construction), Copper House, and Packaged House (Wachsmann et al., 1930, in Piroozfar and Farr, 2013) are just but a few flatpack factory-made systems that were well developed and utilized for family houses in the United States in early C20th and later in Canada. Kurokawa's Nakagin Capsule Tower (a.k.a. Sony Tower)[15] in Tokyo was a case example of what we call "PnP (Plug & Play) technology" in the AEC industry. Although its potential for the replacement of prefabricated capsules was not fully put into practical application beyond the point of its completion, it had all the technical capacity and technological substructure to make it an exemplary case of mobility in architecture and mobile architecture. With the advent of new technologies, the modes of fabrication, manufacturing, and assembly can get even more aligned with the advanced and more sophisticated offerings that mobile architecture can be expected to deliver in the future.

The Way Forward

Underneath the current global threats – imposed either by climate change, or incidents such as wars, pandemics, droughts and famines, food shortage, and water scarcity among many others – and sector-specific growing restrictions on the use of raw materials, excessive construction and demolition waste, shortage of construction general, skilled and highly skilled labor, endless demand for change, novelty, and innovation in design and construction as well as the fast pace of change in the nature of construction market and supply chain structure to name but a few – lies an undeniable necessity and a great opportunity for a systemic, evidence-based, and continuous development of mobile architecture. Although it can be argued that the concept is backed by up to seven decades of a solid and enriched wealth of collective knowledge and experience, much more timely, effective, and context-specific outcomes can be expected if we decisively choose to unlearn/delearn and relearn part, if not all, of what we have already learned about the mobility of architecture and mobile architecture. This is due to the fact that we are facing unprecedented contextual and background conditions like never before and adjustment of what we already know requires a colossal amount of time, effort, and coordination and might not warrant a just-in-time reply to ever-evolving localized global (or globalized local) conditions we are facing in case-based design scenarios across the world. This indeed is totally and utterly different from ignoring or undermining the lessons that are there to be learned from as if we do that, we will be destined to repeat history and go through the same paths and take the same steps/actions that could and should have taken differently.

Mobile architecture and mobility in/of architecture – as a movement, school, style, or even as trivial as it may sound as an approach – are in a unique position to utilize smart technologies, IoT/IoP/IoE (Internet of Things/Places/Everything),[16] 5G/6G, APU/CPU/GPU (future of local processing), and e-living and Industry 4.0 and 5.0 implications, AI (along with ML and DL) to benefit from the mobile production, novel and smart fabrication technologies (new material technologies, smart, vertical and mobile factories, agile/mobile robotics, UAV robotics, 3D printing and additive manufacturing), to produce a new genre of architecture – mobile architecture – which is either: (i) instantaneously movable (architecture on wheels),[17] or (ii) occasionally movable (craneable architecture),[18] or (iii) deployable architecture[19] (Figure 5.5.1).

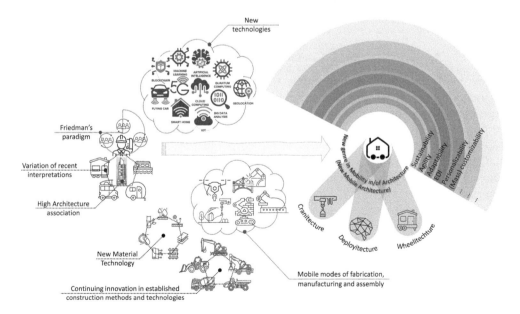

Figure 5.5.1   Potential future directions of mobile architecture (Image courtesy of author, Eric FARR).

Revisioning, reinterpretation, and readjustment of our approach to mobility in architecture facilitate not only the development of a smart platform that incorporates a higher degree of intelligence and sustainability,[20] but also offers unparalleled opportunities to promote and enable EDI (equality/equity, diversity, and inclusivity),[21] to give way to an architecture which is more accommodating, agile, flexible, adaptable to human, society, ecosystem, environment, and global musts, needs and necessities as well as personal wants, community preferences, and corporate responsibilities. Suffice it to say that economies of scale in such an approach are key but should not be mistaken with Fordism. In addition to their documented and proven benefits in the AEC, manufacturing, and service industries, (mass) customizability and personalizability at the service of such architecture will not only help reduce waste generation and decrease resource depletion but also create a platform for circularity which will significantly extend the life cycle of the built environment and architecture on different fronts (from material and component levels up to city and regional levels by redefining a new context-specific for the concept of circularity in the building and construction industry). To that end, mobile architecture, to be able to survive and thrive, will require a robust, modularized, and standardized network of urban and rural utilities for water, wastewater, power (electricity and gas), and last but not least data (airborne, fiber optics or cable). Such support networks might or might not be as mobile as the architecture itself can be but need to be highly standardized and modularized so they can be commonly used by/for the end products of the mobile architecture using a PnP system and regardless of the producers, the building and construction systems, and the data architecture/structure or even the geographical location. The unique standing point we are in provides an unprecedented opportunity to embed "smartness" in this new genre of mobile architecture which will be proactively interacting with its environment, and users, through its power and data networks to constantly update/upgrade its soft/firmware, enhance its performance to best serve, and protect its users and to lower or diminish its/their detrimental impacts on its immediate and wider environmental and ecological contexts.

Concluding Comments

Today, mobile architecture is appealing to many including its new clientele for different reasons the least of which – among many other noble humanitarian and necessitating reasons – is due to its potential environmental credentials and added personal, social, and corporate values. More than ever before – in addition to international aid organizations, NGOs, and charities – the affluent class and corporates are showing interest in mobility and agility in their quest for contemporary architecture to showcase their care for the environment and commitment to climate change. Avoiding the usual pitfalls that such a sudden rise of interest may bring along, architects and technologists are in a unique position to use such opportunities as testbeds to explore the extent to which mobile architecture may be able to offer to wider and potentially less privileged user groups. Through such unique opportunities, building upon the current technologies, using smart thinking that can be incorporated to create a real-time smart design, the designers can stretch the existing boundaries of application, acceptance, and affordability of mobility of/in architecture both in its original sense, in the capacities associated with more current readings of it and beyond, exploring new territories in unprecedented ways facilitated by the application of high-end and novel digital, material, and manufacturing technologies inside and out of the AEC industry.

Notes

1 This was around 2017–2019 when he was working on a new version of his book, *L'architecture mobile*, first published in 1970. The new version was published in 2020 under the title of: *L'architecture mobile (1958–2020): Vers une cité conçue par ses habitants eux-mêmes*

2 See as an example: Seonwook, K. & Pyo, M. Y. 2012. *Mobile Architecture*, Dom Publishers.

3 Based on authors' experience in pedagogical contexts in the UK and the United States, some digital natives (millennials) take the semantic drift to the next level to associate the concept of mobile architecture to architecture of smartphones.

4 Oxford Bibliographies are available at: https://www.oxfordbibliographies.com/

5 Zeno's third paradox of motion, the Arrow Paradox, is more concerned about the relativity of time and how motion is perceived or can be defined in a segment of time or time as a continuum.

6 Dymaxion was an acronym created by Bucky himself, out of his three favorite terms: DY (dynamic), MAX (maximum), and ION (tension).

7 Simon Sadler's quest for The Situationist City in the manifestos, tracts and artworks of the Situationist International political and artistic movement (1957–1972) has been documented in his book: Sadler, S. 1998. *The Situationist City*, MIT Press.

8 See: Rudofsky, B. 1987. *Architecture Without Architects: A Short Introduction to Non-pedigreed Architecture*, University of New Mexico Press.

9 e.g. Cultural Barriers, Social Inequities, Cultural Disparities, Societal Issues, Cultural Sensitivity Challenges, Social Justice Issues, Cultural Diversity Challenges, Sociocultural Disparities, Intersectionality Issues, Ethnic Disparities, Cultural Competency Issues, Social Bias, Cultural Insensitivity, Social Exclusion, etc. which may materialize in form of discrimination, pretense, fear, pretext, prejudice, ignorance, oblivion, insensitivity, and illiteracy to name but a few.

10 City dwellers (or urban dwellers) vs desert dwellers (or Bedouins).

11 Traditional nomadity associated with the desert dwellers' (or Bedouins') lifestyle entailed a form of mobility (in life and shelter but not necessarily architecture) that is more restricted, administered and predictable due to its repetitive seasonal cycles of wandering and sometimes – in ancient times – rambling, but definitely not of roaming nature.

12 In surveying practice, the point of beginning is a mark at the beginning location for the surveying of a land where the ending point should exactly end up at. This is to denote closing the circle in the environmental discourse associated with this new approach to mobile architecture which we would like to emphasize; an embedded life cycle approach and/or the circularity incorporated in this new attempt.

13 After Indivisibiliter ac Inseparabiliter (German) or oszthatatlan és elválaszthatatlan (Hungarian); The Austro-Hungarian Empire motto.

14 According to Barnhart (2016), "Governmentality argues that a governing body manages a complex web of people and objects with the purported intent to improve the welfare and condition of the population through changing the relationship between the governing body and those it governs, mediated through objects of concern such as waste. This is achieved through scaled relationships of power, technologies of government, knowledge production, and discourse which results in individuals changing their thoughts and actions such that they then self-regulate and further the goals of the governing body (Foucault 1991a, 1991b)".

15 Built between 1972 and 1976 and demolished in 2022.

16 Cisco defines the Internet of Everything (IoE) as the networked connection of people, process, data, and things (Cisco, 2013).

17 Or "Wheely Architecture" or "Wheelitecture"

18 Or "Cranitecture"

19 Currently the concept of "Deployability" in the AEC industry remains very much limited to "deployable structures". Our proposal is to push the boundaries of deployability beyond the limited structural tectonic to architecture which – in addition to the structural elements – comprises external envelope systems, internal partitioning systems, MEP systems and ideally also furniture and white goods, hence the proposed term "Deployitecture".

20 Sustainability in its broadest possible sense including but not limited to Net-/Near-Zero Energy/Carbon, Circular Economy, Decarbonization, Greening, waste elimination, etc.

21 It is of paramount importance that increasing the mobility of architecture must not decrease the mobility in architecture by disadvantaging the physically- or mentally disabled, and the visually- or hearing-impaired.

References

Barnhart, S. 2016. Environmentality. *Discard Studies* [Online]. Available: https://discardstudies.com/2016/07/27/environmentality/ [Accessed 17 Jan 2024].

CISCO. 2013. *The Internet of Everything—Global Public Sector Economic Analysis* [Online]. Available: https://www.cisco.com/c/dam/en_us/about/business-insights/docs/ioe-value-at-stake-public-sector-analysis-faq.pdf [Accessed 19 Jan 2024].

Colman, A. M. 2009. *Environmentality*. Oxford University Press.

Foucault, M. 1991a. Governmentality. *In*: Burchell, G., Gordon, C. & Miller, P. (eds.), *The Foucault Effect: Studies in Governmentality*. Chicago: University of Chicago Press.

Foucault, M. 1991b. Politics and the study of discourse. *In*: Burchell, G., Gordon, C. & Miller, P. (eds.), *The Foucault Effect: Studies in Governmentality*. Chicago: University of Chicago Press.

Friedman, Y. 1970. *L' Architecture Mobile*, Centre d'Etudes Architecturales.

Friedman, Y. 2020. *L'Architecture Mobile (1958–2020): Vers une cité Conçue par ses Habitants Eux-Mêmes*, Eclat (De l').

Gonzalez, C. G. 2020. Migration as reparation: Climate change and the disruption of borders. *Loyota Law Review*, 16, 401–444.

Harris, L. 2011. Neo(liberal) Citizens of Europe: Politics, scales, and visibilities of environmental citizenship in contemporary Turkey. *Citizenship Studies*, 15, 837–859.

Heathcote, E. 2022. *Yona Friedman (1923–2020)* [Online]. EMAP Publishing Limited (The Architectural Review). Available: https://www.architectural-review.com/essays/reputations/yona-friedman-1923-2020 [Accessed 14 Jan 2024].

Lawrence-Zuniga, D. 2017. *Space and Place* [Online]. Available: https://www.oxfordbibliographies.com/view/document/obo-9780199766567/obo-9780199766567-0170.xml [Accessed 15 Jan 2024].

Leonard, L. 2013. Ecomodern discourse and localized narratives: Waste policy, community mobilization and governmentality in Ireland. In: Campos, M. J. Z. & Hall, C. M. (eds.) *Organising Waste in the City: International Perspectives on Narratives and Practices*. Bristol: Policy Press.

Moore, S. A. 2012. Garbage matters: Concepts in new geographies of waste. *Progress in Human Geography*, 36, 780–799.

PCA. 2017. *Exploiting the Revolutionary Potential of Technology?* [Online]. PCA-Stream. Available: https://www.pca-stream.com/en/articles/yona-friedman-architecture-for-the-living-122 [Accessed 14 Jan 2024].

Piroozfar, P. & Farr, E. R. P. 2013. Evolution of nontraditional methods of construction: 21st century pragmatic viewpoint. *Journal of Architectural Engineering*, 19, 119–133.

Rudofsky, B. 1987. *Architecture Without Architects: A Short Introduction to Non-pedigreed Architecture*, University of New Mexico Press.

Sadler, S. 1998. *The Situationist City*, MIT Press.

Sassen, S. 2016. A massive loss of habitat: New drivers for migration. *Sociology of Development*, 2, 204–233.

Seonwook, K. & Pyo, M. Y. 2012. *Mobile Architecture*, Dom Publishers.

The Editors of Encyclopaedia Britannica. Invalid Date. *Intension and Extension* [Online]. Encyclopedia Britannica. Available: https://www.britannica.com/topic/intension [Accessed 14 Jan 2024].

Wachsmann, K., Grüning, M. & Sumi, C. 1930. *Building the Wooden House: Technique and Design*. Birkhäuser.

PARADIGMATIC CATEGORY 6

Simulation and Advancements in Digital Technologies and Data-Driven Smart Designs

This Paradigmatic Category focuses on the technology of design production and the impact of *Smart Design Productions* on the direction of today's design methodology. This paradigmatic realm looks into new technology and tools utilized in architectural design focused on efficiency, sustainability, and optimization goals. It considers smart methodologies for the production and manufacturing of design constructs. Chapters in this realm reflect on creative advancement in integrative design and construction processes of smart buildings, and how new technologies inform and improve the design process and production. This final section focuses on the idea that buildings are increasingly considered smart self-sufficient structures that are automated and networked, as intelligent machines for living.

DOI: 10.4324/9781003384113-67

6.1

SIMULATION-DRIVEN ECO-SOCIAL DESIGN

Towards Creating Smart Designs

Robert R. Neumayr

Abstract

Today's pressing eco-social and environmental questions have changed architecture's role from that of a passive reflection of societal conditions to that of an active agent of change.

This chapter explains how architects and engineers have adjusted, updated, and re-organised their digital design techniques and technologies along with their concepts and ideas to respond to the societal and environmental challenges contemporary architecture is subjected to and lists and describes the most impactful ones. It argues that these procedural changes can be best illustrated by examining their impact on the typology of the skyscraper, a building type otherwise well known for its resistance to change.

It introduces the strategy of Tectonic Articulation as a means of negotiating architectural expression and structural necessities and investigates how this concept might lead to the introduction of multi-scalar green spaces with interlocking eco-systems inside high-rise buildings illustrating possible outcomes with an academic studio design project.

It describes the concept of artificial intelligence (AI) and machine learning in architecture, explaining their use as creative machines by architects as a combination of human imagination and machinic capacities and how the designer retains control over his creative process by curating input data and results to create smart design solutions, illustrating these points by discussing an AI project for social housing high-rise typologies.

It describes contemporary computational approaches within the building and construction industry which are about to turn a trade once well known for its labour-intensive processes into a business increasingly relying on algorithms and AI to optimise their production and assembly processes, exemplifying in more detail contemporary computational form-finding and large-scale vertical robotic assembly strategies.

It finally concludes with a brief outlook on how evolving digital tools and technologies might enable architects and designers to more deeply engage in the design challenges to come.

DOI: 10.4324/9781003384113-68

Keywords
Simulation-Driven Design; Digitalism; Social Design Strategies; Architectural Semiology

Introduction

Arguably, the role of contemporary architecture has changed considerably over recent years. For a long time considered mere reification of prevailing societal and economic conditions, nowadays pressing socio-cultural questions as well as the urgent need to reduce the built environment's impact on global climate in general have forced architecture to redefine its position as an active agent of change, shifting the profession's perspective in search of more socially and environmentally sustainable design strategies. Rising to the challenge, architects and engineers have responded by developing their computational tools and techniques to engage the crucial social, economic, and ecological problems at hand. While earlier parametric digital tools were typically used to playfully explore vast design spaces in search of unprecedented shapes and forms, algorithms have now become smart, assisting designers in simulating, assessing, and optimising buildings and their components according to various socio-cultural and environmental performance criteria. Their capacity to quantify and, thereby, computationally process ecological and social parameters as well as material and structural properties has enabled designers to formulate, devise and test novel approaches to today's architectural and urbanistic challenges.

Throughout the last decades of computational revolution, increasingly sophisticated digital form-finding processes have been developed by engineers and architects alike, albeit with different objectives. From early contributions by Paul Coates with his physical computation models and pioneering work by John Frazer in the field of algorithmic design (Coates and Derix, 2014: 34), these technologies have evolved into advanced applications such as parametric design programs, evolutionary design solving algorithms and machine learning processes. However, while engineers tend to use these tools to optimise a building's performance strictly in terms of its technological aspects, such as structure or energy consumption, architects and designers were quick to discover the creative potential of computational power. Nowadays, architects are free to experiment with creative processes that go beyond traditional design methodologies while still being able to incorporate robust scientific data obtained from parallel simulation processes. A conventional design process is largely characterised by a number of discrete deterministic decisions based on a designer's intuition and previous experience and, therefore, allows for the reliable development of "satisficing" (Simon, 1956) solutions to a specific problem within well-known parameters. Innovative solutions to contemporary design challenges, however, arguably require less linear and directed approaches, well outside established design parameters. Based on an iteratively changing set of parametric values, computational design strategies assist the architect in systematically generating considerable numbers of complex shapes and forms which are no longer limited by experience or imagination and subsequently can be evaluated, selected, and optimised according to set performance criteria in order to ensure that design solutions adhere to contemporary standards of efficiency, sustainability, or spatial, social, and ecological quality.

The convergence of these design trajectories within a new paradigm of socio-ecological design responsibility has resulted in their imminent potential to effectively transform all contemporary building typologies, including those considered to be most resistant to change. Of all current building typologies, I would argue, the typology of the high-rise exhibits the strongest inertia. It is, therefore, instructive to understand the mechanisms behind the typology's unresponsiveness to contextual and environmental change and to analyse which of today's smart design strategies have successfully instilled overdue transformation into this building category.

Engaging Robust Architectural Typologies

More than any other contemporary building type, the high-rise building has always been widely regarded, by the public as well as within the profession itself, as a symbol for technological innovation, advancement, and socio-economic success. Consequently, any discourse about the typology's apparent development has predominantly been conducted along two major narratives. The first account is strictly chronological, understanding the skyscraper as a shapeless commercial function space that – through socio-cultural imprint – adapts to and represents the styles and ideologies of the time it was built in. The second reading focuses on mechanisation, identifying continuous innovation in building and construction technology as the main driver behind any typological changes.

Only recently attention has been given to the question of how the principles of capitalism and financial speculation have affected the skyscraper's historic and typological development. In her book *Form Follows Finance*, Carol Willis (1995), for example, shows that high-rise buildings, especially in Chicago and New York, have always been speculative developments, and that their form, location, and distribution throughout the city are the result of complex interactions of parameters such as plot sizes, local or regional building patterns, cost-effective construction technologies, fluctuating real estate cycles, building codes, and zoning laws, rather than the product of aesthetic or technological considerations. She concludes that the skyscraper as a symbol of modern financial capitalism reflects the economic and social forces it is shaped by. Matthew Soules (2021) even suggests that high-rise buildings in their current shape and form are not merely a passive reflection of capitalism, but rather play an active role in its perpetuation, as their conception and realisation serve as financial instruments to generate profit for the wealthy, thus altering not only architectural forms but also the very nature of our built environment. Current tower typologies such as the very thin condominium towers increasingly common in major cities around the world, Soules argues, are no longer designed as residences but optimised and serialised as speculative capitalist investments.

In a similar way to product design which John Thackara argues, "[...] is thoroughly integrated in capitalist production [...]" and, therefore, "[...] bereft of an independent critical tradition on which to base an alternative" (Thackara, 1988: 21), the typology of the skyscraper is interwoven so intricately with its financial background, technological context, and material constraints, that it needs to be considered a type of architectural hegemonic system in which, as Manfredo Tafuri states, true ideological alternatives cannot exist (Tafuri, 1974). Consequently, it has become almost impossible to formulate typological alternatives outside the predominant academic discourse.

As a result, the typology of the high rise has remained remarkably stable since its beginnings in the late nineteenth century. For a long time, towers were basically maximised volumes, extruded along site boundaries with office spaces located along the building perimeter around a central core, vertically staggered in accordance with local zoning laws. In the 1950s, two new typologies emerged. Lever House by SOM combined an open public ground floor underneath a 2nd-floor podium with a thin vertical slab for office space on top, and Mies van der

Rohe set back his Seagram Building off Park Avenue kerbside to create a large public space in front of the building, in exchange for the city's permission to considerably increase the building's height. These three volumetric types, then, went on to define the morphology of the skyscraper throughout the decades to follow, albeit with one recent addition: Nowadays, pencil towers, extremely slender and tall residential high-rise buildings, have started to sprout all over the world's most expensive cities, operating mainly as financial investment instruments. Alternative architectural or typological concepts, such as Peter Eisenman's Max Reinhard House high-rise project in Berlin Altona, whose design parameters were well within the existing technological and material boundaries set by the building and construction industry of that time, have remained sparse and, at the time of their conception, largely unrealised.

Recently, however, the need for typological (rather than technological) innovation in the organisation of vertical space has moved back into the focus of international architectural research. Economic considerations, standardised engineering solutions, and mass-market production with its repetitive programmatic solutions had increasingly resulted in poor urban and spatial standards leading to a lack of spatial variety and, consequently, social quality. At the same time, growing ecological considerations underlined the need for the development of quality-oriented high-density urbanisation with its reduction of land consumption and soil sealing. These prospects have shifted the discourse back towards a more socially and environmentally biased research agenda, foregrounding the sustainability-based responsibilities of future high-rise building typologies.

Tectonic Articulation

In general, complex buildings can be understood to be composed of a series of interconnected systems and subsystems (such as, for example, facade, structure, circulation, or infrastructure) which are negotiated to form one coherent spatial organisation. Throughout the architectural history of the skyscraper, various building systems have shown different degrees of resistance to innovation and change, in particular in the 1950s, when the skyscraper as a building type was briefly evolving and building systems adapted to the typological changes that occurred. More recently, as technological advancement resulted in more elevated constructions, the necessity to cope with exponentially increasing structural loads put a stronger emphasis on a buildings' structural system. As a consequence, various structural systems were developed, assessed for structural efficiency and correlated with existing high-rise topologies. Engineers were among the first to capitalise on the then emerging computational techniques for advanced calculation, iteratively driving structural systems towards optimisation, thus locking modernist high-rise typologies into their current configuration.

But if a building's structure and, therefore, its optimisation is assumed to be only one layer of its multi-layered organisation of systems, then structural design can no longer be understood only as an end in itself but rather as a means to reflect a spatial organisation's environmental and societal complexities and communicative and semiological framework through tectonic composition. Socially responsible buildings should not be designed predominantly to the concerns of technical, economic, or structural efficiency, which would be a structural engineer's approach, but with the clear aim to articulate a building's various elements and components to form one comprehensive spatial envelope in accordance with its societal and environmental context. This design strategy based on a well-balanced relationship between a building's technical and articulatory dimensions is known as Tectonic

Articulation, a term coined by Patrik Schumacher. "If we define tectonics as the strategic detournement of an element's technically induced morphology in order to address substantial functions in the articulatory dimension, then tectonics can be redeemed and integrated within contemporary notions of handling form-function relationships", Schumacher (2012: 21) explains. Tectonic articulation, then, can be understood as a conceptual tool to navigate a multi-dimensional design solution space which is constrained by structural considerations in order to assemble a geometric repertoire that is able to spatially frame contemporary human interactions within the built environment. Resulting structural and spatial articulations, however, always remain tectonic. Aesthetic and semiotic forms and shapes are inherently structurally and technically motivated, as the field of possible novel design solutions is constrained by previously conducted structural research.

A well-known example of tectonic articulation in practice is Zaha Hadid Architects' One Thousand Museum residential tower whose parametrically differentiated tectonic morphology sharply contrasts with the neighbouring standardised modernist high-rise buildings it happens to form an architectural ensemble with along Miami's Biscayne Boulevard. Rather than relying on traditional rectilinear composition strategies with their repetitive floor plans and normative facade patterns, the structure's design features a curvilinear exoskeleton designed to accommodate the flow of structural forces along the building's envelope, thus minimising the number of columns in the interior space. At the same time, as described by the architects, the exposure of the primary building structure is used to visually order and articulate "[...] the diverse offering [of] the complexity of dense urban sites and contemporary [design] briefs". (Schumacher, 2014: 46) on a phenomenological and semiological level. Making use of contemporary computational technology such as physics engines or generative engineering tools, which have become readily available to the entire profession, architects "[...] are enabled to explore this more disciplined universe of possibilities with the eyes and intuition of a designer, while simultaneously keeping engineering constraints in play" (Schumacher, 2014: 49), developing morphological building features that allow them to articulate social and semiotic functions that need to be visually coded and organised.

Interlocking Ecologies

While the architects themselves tend to emphasise One Thousand Museum's eloquent parametric design "[standing] out against the mute, monotonous seriality of the modernist context" (Schumacher, 2023: 94), upon closer examination the building, more interestingly, also reveals the concept's potential to subtly integrate programmatic shifts into the skyscraper's design, such as, for example, in the case of the building's corner columns whose thickening horizontal bracing elements form massive balcony slabs towards the bottom but split towards the top to allow for gradually increasing corner windows. The capacity of Tectonic Articulation to induce programmatic and – as a consequence – typological shifts to previously long-standing building typologies is more clearly visible when looking at Zaha Hadid Architects' LeeZa Tower in Beijing where the parametric negotiation between tectonic necessities, internal and external constraints and design ambition resulted in the creation of a rotating atrium space vertically stretching throughout the entire building and directly connecting to public transportation network, intended to serve as a novel type of differentiated interior public space for the city. Although the concept of the atrium tower has its precedents dating back to the twentieth century, most notably probably John C. Portman's hotel and office buildings with their multi-storied interior atrium spaces such as the

1967 Hyatt Regency Atlanta or, maybe more famously, his more expressive 1985 Atlanta Marriot Marquis, the tectonic differentiation of a building's interior space and its constituent building systems marks a profound change of typology, moving away from Portman's representational and normative grand spaces towards multiscalar interiorities that allow for the accommodation of various interlocking social and environmental ecologies.

This design technique comes to fruition at a time, when concerns about climate change and urban microclimatic conditions intensify, calling for the implementation of differentiated interior green spaces into high-rise designs which no longer predominantly emphasise the emotional affects such vast interior spaces might evoke but much rather focus on the environmental and sustainable effects these interiorities can exert on their built environment. The concept of interior green spaces dates back to the twentieth century as well when, in an attempt to contrast commonplace mid-century International Style New York tower schemes, which positioned their public plaza in front of their respective buildings, Kevin Roche and John Dinkeloo, both just recently appointed heads of the late Eero Saarinen's architectural office, completed the design and construction of the first vertical indoor garden as early as in 1968, developing a 49 metres high public atrium at the centre of Manhattan's Ford Foundation building with a multi-level landscaped garden layout. Mainly designed and intended as an informal and low-threshold meeting area for the neighbouring communities, however, the atrium's climatic conditions proved to be difficult and only few of the original plants survived (Pelkonen, 2011: 133). Departing from these initial attempts to bring nature into urban environments, vertical gardens and green walls have now become customary, however, rarely evolving into complex ecosystems. Contemporary digital design techniques with their renunciation of simple Cartesian construction and surface logics in favour of more dynamic yet structurally sustainable and parametrically controllable building configurations show the potential to utilise biophilic design principles in order to give shape to differentiated surface morphologies that are able to sustain numerous interdependent animal and plant species in various scales and sizes within one coherent yet meaningfully differentiated spatial envelope (Figure 6.1.1).

Such built environments, then, can create seamless connections between the indoors and the outdoors as well as between different interlocking social and environmental ecologies, enhancing their functionality beyond energy efficiency, water retention, or air quality to become self-sustaining biodiverse ecosystems woven into the surrounding city fabric with the capacity to transform their urban environments.

Machine Learning, Creative Artificial Intelligence, and Social Spaces

The rapid development of artificial intelligence (AI) has revolutionised various industries, and art, architecture, design, and construction are no exceptions. Not unlike any other tool in use within the fields of architecture and engineering, two distinct areas of application have started to form: For one, AI is most notably being employed by engineers to optimise the performance of various building systems and components. Architects and designers, however, who are mainly concerned with design of the built environment have also started to harness AI's generative potential. In the same way that AI-driven art can be understood as just "[...] another turn in the entangled history of humans and technology" (Zylinska, 2020: 65) as art production has always been emerging from the artefacts and instruments of its time, architects have consistently relied on the latest tools and technologies available, physical as well as digital, to explore architecture's design space. Gradually

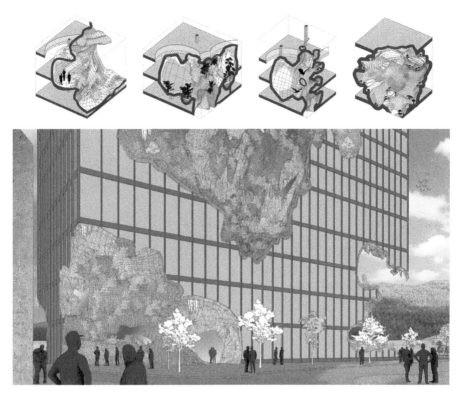

Figure 6.1.1   Lamp & Hofer, University of Innsbruck: Syntactic skyscrapers - The symbiotic spot. Spaces of interlocking ecologies structure the high-rise building.

Source: Theresa Lamp & Jan Hofer, Institute of Structure and Design, University of Innsbruck.

replacing parametric design and genetic algorithms, machine learning processes have now become efficient tools to develop, assess, and select architectural morphologies. Within this fast-moving field of research, various programs and algorithms based on different concepts have emerged. A concise summary of current techniques is, for example, provided by Del Campo and Leach (2022).

In AI-driven design processes, human inspiration is not replaced by machine creativity. At this point, discussions still revolve around questions such as whether machines can even exhibit creativity in their own right (yet). Daniel Bolojan (2022: 25) points out that while "similarities between machines and humans can be drawn […] the two should not be equated". As the way they understand and respond to the environment are notably different. Much rather, the task is to combine human imagination and machinic capacities. While machine learning algorithms learn from given sets of training data and statistical models in order to generate compositions not limited by human imagination, they are themselves conceived, optimised, and controlled by the designer who selects the input data and identifies successful design proposals. Architects maintain their design agency, strategically exploiting the machinic algorithms' speed at processing data and producing potentially novel architectural solutions. In such design setups, various scripts and algorithms are concatenated and

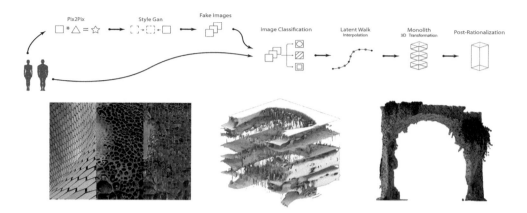

Figure 6.1.2 Czarnecka & Schwägerl, University of Innsbruck: Cyberphysical towers - Neo renaissance. Sequence of machine learning processes applied during design phase.

Source: Lucyna Czarnecka & Leonard Schwägerl, Institute of Structure and Design, University of Innsbruck.

combined to form complex digital procedures where each consecutive step processes previous results curated and altered by the designer. The artful development of the procedure as such, therefore, becomes an important part of the creative process itself (Figure 6.1.2).

By now, creative AI has left its academic environment and started to contribute to the improvement of our built environment. Cities like Singapore or Vienna, for example, which are well known for their long and successful histories of realised social housing schemes and can, therefore, rely on a rich source of useful input data, have fostered research projects to innovate their social housing typologies. Immanuel Koh, Director of Artificial-Architecture at the Singapore University of Technology and Design (SUTD), has collaborated with the municipality of Singapore to investigate innovative forms of social housing by pushing machine learning systems towards "incorporating more complex architectural notions of spatial interiority, programmatic semantics and contextual bias:" (Koh, 2022: 93). Machine learning algorithms were trained on thousands of the city's high-rise public housing buildings in the search for potentially believable housing typologies. To harvest original results, it is critical to avoid computational overfitting and constrain the computational output to an area of the digital design space where the algorithm still produces a wide range of formal, spatial, and semiological geometric solutions, but with a clear notion of fitness for habitation, which can later be assessed and developed into novel social housing ecologies.

Innovative Construction and Realisation Strategies

In quite the same way in which the high-rise building as architecture is known to be resistant to typological change, building and construction as an industry, despite its economic importance, has been notorious for its slow pace of innovation and adaptation, mainly due to fragmented standards and complex regulations, but also because of resistance to change within the industry itself (Woudhuysen and Abley, 2004). However, AI and machine learning have recently started to percolate through every stage of the construction process injecting much-needed intelligence and precision into an industry for a long time dominated by tradition and manual calculations. Algorithms are now processing vast datasets, tailoring material systems to their specific environment, fully utilising their non-linear material properties and optimising their structural performance and integrity. But also, construction itself is affected. AI-powered machineries have started taking over repetitive or dangerous tasks such as bricklaying and welding, improving accuracy, productivity, and safety. Sensors and connected devices collect data on site conditions, equipment performance, construction progress, and worker activity, providing real-time information for better decision-making.

But not only AI has contributed significantly to recent advancements in the building and construction industry. In the field of structural engineering, innovative computational form-finding and fabrication strategies allow for more integrative design approaches, cohering programmatic requirements, architectural expression, and structural necessities into one digital process of multi-criteria optimisation. "The terms 'expressive' and 'structurally efficient' are no longer oxymorons". as explained by Philippe Block (2016: 70) who – in the face of architecture's rediscovered predilection for expressively curved shapes – leads a research programme on curvilinear surface structures at the Block Research Group (BRG) at the ETH Zurich. At the same time, industrial robots, which were introduced to building and construction some time ago for mass-customised production processes and large-scale 3D printing, become increasingly subjected to architectural experiments pushing the scale of robotic intervention and, thereby, exploring the potentials of robotic design and materialisation processes at a larger building scale. Fabio Gramazio and Matthias Kohler, for example, have pioneered this field of research by developing robotic construction strategies for residential high-rise buildings and researching the use of flocks of flying robots to collectively assemble building modules into vertical structures as a "tectonic inquiry into high-rise typologies through digital design and fabrication processes" (Gramazio, Kohler and Willmann, 2014: 18) which puts a new perspective on the transformative potential of robotic operations for architectural and urban morphologies.

Conclusion and Outlook

Recent years saw a general shift of contemporary architectural theory and practice towards a more social, economic, and environmental agenda. Reconsidering conventional modernist and capitalist concepts, architects and designers have been increasingly able to define conceptual positions outside of traditional notions of design and production, moving novel concepts and strategies towards realisation. Innovative digital tools and technologies assist them in materialising these ideas and ambitions. In the light of contemporary challenges to collaborate towards a more social and human-centred global built environment, these innovative concepts and strategies can be understood as instruments "[n]ot only for improving design as 'problem-solving', but in creating a space for designers to reflect upon the ideas, theories, logics, and implications of design in and through practice" (Mazé and Redström, 2007: 32). As the digital tools and technologies that help shape our built environment today continue to evolve, we can expect even more transformative changes in the way we design, plan, and build the world around us to generate the materials, forms, and spatiality necessary to frame our future social interactions.

References

Block, P. (2016). "Parametricism's structural congeniality". *Parametricism 2.0. Rethinking Architecture's Agenda for the 21st Century. AD Vol. 86, 02/2016.* pp. 68–75.

Bolojan, D. (2022). "Creative AI. Augmenting design potency". *Machine Hallucinations. Architecture and Artificial Intelligence. AD Vol. 92, 03/2022.* pp. 22–27.

Coates, P. and Derix, C. (2014). "The deep structure of the picturesque". *Emphatic Spaces. The Computation of Human-Centric Architecture. AD Vol. 84*, 05/2014. pp 32–37.

Del Campo, M. and Leach, N. (2022). "Can machines hallucinate architecture? AI as design method". *Machine Hallucinations. Architecture and Artificial Intelligence. AD Vol. 92*, 03/2022. pp. 6–13.

Gramazio, F., Kohler, M. and Willmann, J. (2014). "Authoring robotic processes". *Made by Robots. Challenging Architecture at a Larger Scale. AD Vol. 84*, 03/2014. pp. 14–21.

Koh, I. (2022). "Architectural plasticity. The aesthetics of neural sampling". *Machine Hallucinations. Architecture and Artificial Intelligence. AD Vol. 92*, 03/2022. pp. 86–93.

Mazé, R. and Redström, J. (2007). "Difficult forms. Critical practices of design and research". *Research Design Journal. Vol. 1/09*, pp. 28–39.

Pelkonen, E. *et al* (2011). *Kevin Roche: Architecture as environment.* New Haven: Yale University Press with Yale School of Architecture.

Schumacher, P. (2012). *The autopoiesis of architecture Vol. II. A New agenda for architecture.* Chichester: Wiley & Sons Ltd.

Schumacher, P. (2014). "Tectonic articulation. Making engineering logics speak". *Future Details. AD Vol. 84*, 04.2014, pp. 44–51.

Schumacher, P. (2023). *Tectonism. Architecture for the twenty-first century.* Melbourne: The Images Publishing Group Pty Ltd.

Simon, H. A. (1956). "Rational choice and the structure of the environment". *Psychological Review, Vol. 63*(2), pp. 129–138.

Soules, M. (2021). *Icebergs, zombies, and the ultra thin—architecture and capitalism in the twenty-first century.* New York: Princeton Architectural Press.

Tafuri, M. (1974). "L'Architecture dans le Boudoir: The Language of Criticism and the Criticism of Language". *Oppositions, Vol. 3*, pp. 291–316.

Thackara, J. (1988). "Beyond the object in design". *Design after modernism.* New York: Thames and Hudson, pp. 11–34.

Willis, C. (1995). *Form follows finance. Skyscrapers and skylines in New York and Chicago.* New York: Princeton Architectural Press.

Woudhuysen, J. and Abley, I. (2004). *Why is construction so backward?* Chichester: John Wiley & Sons Ltd.

Zylinska, J. (2020). *AI art. Machine visions and warped dreams.* London: Open Humanities Press.

6.2

SMART PROTOTYPING: FROM DATA-DRIVEN MASS-CUSTOMIZATION TO COMMUNITY-ENABLED CO-PRODUCTION

*Sina Mostafavi, Bahar Bagheri, Ding Wen Bao
and Asma Mehan*

Abstract

Materialization practices in the architecture and building industry have evolved with the advancement of manufacturing and information technologies. This evolution is evident across various design and production phases, with a pronounced impact on prototyping. Advances in design and fabrication tools have empowered prototypes, integral in any production cycle, to furnish a growing array of information and feedback for designers and manufacturers. In this context, prototypes have transformed from merely showcasing data-driven building solutions to presenting socio-environmentally conscious systems. Innovation in prototyping connects the initial design and construction stages to the operational phase, creating a seamless transition throughout the project lifecycle. This chapter provides a range of definitions and prototypical case studies for smart prototyping by identifying practiced approaches in integrated design to production workflows. This chapter introduces three paradigms for smart prototyping: Digital prototyping focuses on data-driven design for mass customization, phygital prototyping involves mixed-reality-enabled design and assembly, and thirdly collaborative prototyping explores human-machine hybrid intelligence and co-production in architectural and urban contexts. The chosen case studies in this chapter and how they are categorized aim to provide a comprehensive overview of smart prototyping, covering projects conducted in both research and practice. This chapter concludes with potential future trends and the role of emerging and evolving mediums of prototyping for smart design and construction.

Introduction and Background

Architects and designers used physical models and prototypes to present and test their ideas and to communicate their design intent (Eissen, 1990). As architectural design and production methods evolve with technological advancements, prototypes have shifted from mere presentational tools to invaluable sources of feedback and catalysts for innovation. While

DOI: 10.4324/9781003384113-69

physical models sometimes were representational supplements to drawings (Frampton et al., 1981), architects like Antonio Gaudi have utilized models like hanging chains as tangible examples of prototypes driving the design process. Michelangelo used physical prototypes to communicate construction details and for marketing to investors. Palladio used full-scale wooden prototypes of architectural elements to plan costly stone works (Sass & Oxman, 2006). While its historical role remains, the function of prototyping is evolving. This chapter explores what makes a prototyping process smart by emphasizing the intelligent integration of data-driven and context-aware design and production processes.

Beaudouin-Lafon et al. identified a prototype as a "tangible artifact" representing a solid example of part or all an interactive system (Beaudouin-Lafon et al., 2007). Prototyping is a powerful tool for designers as a feedback source to communicate form and functionality and to evaluate their materiality, feasibility, manufacturability, cost, appearance, and maintenance regarding their desired specifications (Virzi, Sokolov, & Karis, 1996; Sauer, Seibel, & Rüttinger, 2010; Scharge, 2010). In contemporary contexts, prototypes have been described as a "physical or digital embodiment of critical elements in the design" that can be used "at any point in the design process" (Lauff, Kotys-Schwartz, & Rentschler, 2018).

With the advent of the digital age, prototyping has adapted emerging technologies, evolving into new formats that efficiently incorporate sets of information to optimize time and resource utilization in the production process. By entering the age of mass customization, prototyping became a critical tool for the manufacturer to ensure the quality and desirability of their target market and how they needed to manage the resources in the demand-supply chain. Laser cutting, 3D printing, computer numerically controlled (CNC) manufacturing, and even printed circuit board (PCB) manufacturing are some of the commonly used tools that provide the capability to produce parts in a variety of forms and building materials for functional interactive mechatronic components (Chang, Hsiao, Chen, & Huang, 2020). Rapid prototyping by utilizing these tools allowed the designers to promptly receive feedback on their designs, making the design process much more efficient and effective. In the transition to the era of big data and cyber-physical systems (CPSs), intelligent information systems have significantly influenced the industry. Serving as sources interpretable by both humans and machines, these systems introduce novel modes of materialization, facilitating the development of smart products.

The early advent of CAD tools rose to prominence, and Scharge foresaw the emergence of "virtual prototypes" alongside conventional "palpable prototypes," recognizing their mutually enhancing potential (Scharge, 2010). Recent developments in the manufacturing industry focus on integrating artificial intelligence (AI) into smart products, defined as those leveraging advanced technology and incorporating intelligent features (Li et al., 2017). These products consist of two integral components: a physical aspect (related to tangible bodies) and a data aspect (associated with intangible intelligence). Typically, the intangible aspect of a smart product is embedded within its tangible components (Hoffman & Novak 2018). Smart prototyping in the built environment entails the design of context-aware production systems utilizing emerging digital design and manufacturing technologies. Context awareness involves systematically incorporating data related to the natural, built, and socio-economic environment. Emerging technologies include computational, fabrication, and material technologies integrated into the prototyping process.

This chapter introduces smart prototyping systems as seamlessly integrated intelligent mediums within design processes, offering transformative opportunities in manufacturing. The integration of these systems marks a paradigm shift from traditional prototyping methods, highlighting a dynamic synergy between tangible and virtual representations in the data and resource-driven design and manufacturing landscape. The exploration of emerging mediums of prototyping systems further delves into their evolving nature, contributing to innovative approaches in the architecture, engineering, and construction (AEC) sectors.

Emerging Mediums of Prototyping Systems

This chapter identifies three paradigms in smart prototyping, considering systems' capabilities in data processing and interaction with users and contexts: digital, phygital, and collaborative prototyping. Digital prototyping focuses on data-driven design for mass customization, phygital prototyping involves mixed -reality-enabled design and assembly, and thirdly collaborative prototyping explores human-machine hybrid intelligence and co-production in architectural and urban contexts. The chosen case studies in this chapter and how they are categorized aim to provide a comprehensive overview of smart prototyping, covering projects conducted in both research and practice. the chapter concludes with potential future trends and the role of emerging and evolving mediums of prototyping for smart design and construction.

Digital Prototyping: Data-Driven Design for Mass Customization

The programmability and flexibility of digital prototyping systems facilitate advanced data integration across multiple levels and scales in design-to-production workflows, resulting in distinctive modes of intelligence. Design intelligence involves systematically applying integrated computational workflows to generate data-driven and performance-oriented architectural solutions. Production intelligence incorporates programmable robotic fabrication routines, enabling automation and materialization to inform design through iterative feed-forward and feedback loops (Mostafavi, 2021). Within this framework, digital prototyping facilitates mass customization of building components, yielding higher precision and purposeful differentiation in the design. It illustrates how patterns and tectonics may significantly enhance quantitative aspects of structural integrity and environmental responsiveness, along with qualitative and functional considerations.

The digitalization of design and fabrication in the manufacturing industry enhances product design and decision-making by providing data on resource consumption. This addresses sustainability goals, extending product life cycles, promoting circularity, and offering precise information, including product location and compatibility, facilitating the tracking of material life cycles and identification of potential failures.

Therefore, the integration of data-driven design and prototyping empowers designers to purposefully access diverse datasets extracted and processed from customer preferences or simulations. Computational simulations forecast structural and environmental performances within the simulated design context, enabling designers to make decisions based on multiple criteria. In this scenario, CPSs, Internet of Things (IoT), Internet of Services (IoS), cloud-based solutions, AI, big data analytics, and real-time production data are recognized as pivotal facilitators of smart manufacturing, supporting swift and precise decision-making (Zheng et al., 2018). Cloud storage services, collaborative workspaces, and social networks present opportunities in the transformative landscape of manufacturing and prototyping, aiming to enhance customized requirements, improve quality, and reduce time to market (Rittinghouse et al., 2016). This transformative impact extends to manufacturing processes, where sensors empower machines to seamlessly detect, act, and communicate (Zhang et al., 2014), introducing another dimension to smart customization.

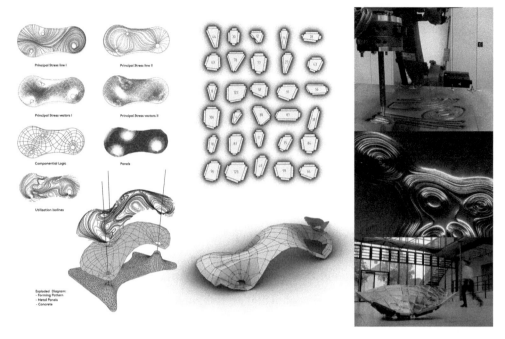

Figure 6.2.1 Digital prototyping: Left – Data-driven design materialization within integrated computational design workflows, Middle – Mass-customization through the programmability of robotic production, Right – Robotic prototyping employing incremental sheet forming to enhance the structural performance of planar metal material. Credit: Authors, Project conducted at DARS lab, Dessau Institute of Architecture at Bauhaus.

Robot-assisted construction has become pivotal in contemporary architecture in the Fourth Industrial Revolution era. By leveraging industrial robots, digital fabrication simulations, and tailored tool designs for diverse building materials, factories can efficiently and cost-effectively mass-customize non-standardized prefabricated building components, facilitating both on-site and off-site construction (Barberio et al., 2023). This growing field has attracted significant attention from renowned architectural institutions, academic trailblazers, and disruptors in the building industry. Digital fabrication technologies such as 3D printing, CNC, and robotic manufacturing enable data-driven rapid prototyping to empower designers, makers, and builders to actively participate in the production process, anticipate potential challenges, strategic planning of assembly and resource consumption, and enhancement of material properties through purposeful application of informed tectonics and mass customization facilitated by adaptable and programmable modalities of robotic fabrication, as illustrated in Figure 6.2.1.

Phygital Prototyping: Mixed-Reality–Enabled Design and Assembly

Cyber-physical production systems are advanced production mediums that result from the heightened integration of intelligence and manufacturing technology, offering phygital mediums for prototyping. The term "phygital" implies the fusion of digital and physical elements, encompassing spaces where digital functionalities seamlessly integrate into the tangible experience. In a phygital prototyping system, various sensors digitally process environmental data, including cameras, scanners, and motion detectors, enabling a hybrid experience where digital and physical realms coexist interactively. These settings can be provisioned through immersive technologies exemplified by holographic drawings, including augmented reality (AR) gadgets, which have the potential to bridge the gap between the digital and physical world, offering a contextual, scaled, and palpable experience in real-world surroundings (Mann et al., 2015; Jahn et al., 2019).

Several institutions and companies have developed mixed reality (MR)-enabled devices and frameworks across construction, engineering, healthcare, and education. A commonly used tool in the AEC sectors is the Microsoft HoloLens headset, which exemplifies an interactive hybrid space featuring a head-mounted AR device with a close-to-real-world interface and improved precision (Taylor, 2016). The Fologram company, which began experimenting with MR fabrication at RMIT University, utilizes AR glasses like Hololens to transform three-dimensional models into full-sized construction guides. This technology overlaps digital guidance in the workspace, assisting in the measurement, verification, and targeted management required for complex project assembly. It facilitates step-by-step guidance for prototype assembly during construction, streamlining intricate structures and installations. Projects that are realized using the Fologram technology range from the building of cemented curved brick walls (Jahn et al., 2020), as illustrated in the top part of Figure 6.2.2, to complex pavilion structures in the design and assembly of the Tallinn Biennale project, Steampunk pavilion, with the support of AR (Jahn et al., 2022).

AR applications in digital fabrication within architecture can be classified into various approaches, including AR holographic instruction, AR data sharing, and AR human-computer interaction (Song et al., 2021). Phygitally prototyping extends from generating an entity from scratch to modifying the digital twin of an existing object (Kent et al., 2021). MR demonstrates notable utility in on-site assembly scenarios, particularly in situations where robots face challenges in unpredictable conditions, unexpected locations, and uncontrolled environments (Jahn, 2020). This is particularly relevant in architectural and urban production, characterized by production machines smaller than the objects they produce (Mostafavi, 2021). MR platforms for personal manufacturing, as presented by Wiechel et al. (2014), enable users to interact directly with virtual items using body motions, offering potential benefits in human resource training and construction time reduction.

Phygital platforms provide opportunities for multi-agent, multi-location interactive collaboration between humans and machines in linked personalized environments. In this context, the mapped and interactive annotated digital twin in the physical environment enables users to navigate through the sequence of fabrication and assembly. Computer vision technology and connected sensors have the potential to facilitate communication across the physical and digital worlds. Therefore, a larger spectrum of clients and users can engage in the design and prototyping process through phygital prototyping, supporting the growing localization and community-enabled culture (Mehan et al., 2023). The digital dimension of phygital prototyping that enables a hybrid experience can transcend the limits of an on-site human presence and allow for an online presence as well. This allows for machine or human collaboration at various interaction scales throughout the design to the production process using a range of tools and machines (Figure 6.2.2).

Figure 6.2.2   Phygital prototyping: Top: Bricklaying in AR by construction team (Jahn et al., 2020). Credit Fologram, Bottom left: Collaborative AR-enabled assembly of a prototype, Bottom right: MR environment of the final product and its digital twin. Credit: Project conducted at Hi-DARS lab, Texas Tech University by Authors.

Collaborative Prototyping: Hybrid Intelligence and Co-Production in Urban Social Contexts

Outreach and impact in collaborative prototyping delves into the dynamics of human-machine interactions, particularly in urban contexts, orchestrating the involvement of diverse communities through the utilization of digital tools and platforms. This approach engages the network of stakeholders, such as builders, designers, users, machines, suppliers, and policymakers, yielding a multifaceted impact on urban ecosystems (Varış Husar et al., 2023; Kolarevic, 2003). The network contributes to co-design and co-production processes (Mehan & Mostafavi, 2023a; 2022). The paradigms of situatedness and connected ecosystems in collaborative prototyping refer to urban environments' specific, localized needs and conditions. The ecosystem of the human, machine, and built environment forms the core of collaborative prototyping, where human intelligence, machine capabilities, and the built environment interact seamlessly (Sanchez, 2021; Mostafavi & Mehan, 2023)

Employing digital and phygital prototyping facilitates Open-Source Architecture and offers a participatory approach on larger urban and community scales by democratizing the design and production processes (Ratti, 2012; Mehan, 2023). In this context, distributed building systems such as FAB labs, in situ systems, and connected virtual spaces are crucial for experimentation and innovation in architecture and urban planning, fostering collaborative learning and making (Kolarevic, 2003). Furthermore, exploring co-design and production within the metaverse underscores the transformative influence of virtual spaces in enhancing collaboration across geographical boundaries, highlighting the importance of phygital platforms in facilitating design and planning collaborations in multiple locations (Khasraghi & Mehan, 2023; Wojtowicz, 1995).

Illustrated in the left and upper sections of Figure 6.2.3, FabriCity XR, a phygital immersive installation at Venice Architecture Biennale, 2023, demonstrates the potential of phygital mapping by developing a web-based AR platform. Here, users without any need for additional applications can actively explore the immersive environment on their smart devices and compare the mapped and processed data related to socio-environmental justice in the two port cities of Amsterdam and Houston (Mehan & Mostafavi, 2024; Tedeschi & Rochielle Sievert, 2024). This showcases the practical application of phygital concepts, emphasizing the co-productions of liminal spaces, and demonstrates the feasibility of these ideas in diverse urban settings (Mostafavi et al., 2024). Here, the modifiable and interactive MR layers become an integral part of the spatial constructs to be accessed, perceived, and personalized by and for public users (Mehan & Mostafavi, 2023b). In addition to the interdisciplinary collaboration necessary to advance software applications for interactive phygital platforms, such as cloud-based networks connecting people, ideas, data, and applications, the progression of hardware in collaborative prototyping requires the development of frameworks for human-robot collaboration (Mehan & Mostafavi, 2023c). This transition involves incorporating intelligent cobots to replace industrial robotic arms, resulting in a hybrid collaboration that enhances the capabilities of both humans and machines in manufacturing and assembly processes. As illustrated in the bottom right section of Figure 6.2.3, these systems provide a softer and safer approach to direct interaction, facilitating the co-production of the physical environment across various scales, contexts, and agents.

Conclusion and Discussion

Smart prototyping systems, as delineated in this chapter, are data-driven and context-aware procedures that leverage advanced technologies in the design, production, and operation of the built and natural environment. Additionally, the three categories of smart prototyping – digital, phygital, and collaborative – function as feedback loops for decision-makers and users to conceive informed design solutions and facilitate the transition to more efficient use of resources. Therefore, the development of a smart prototyping system is crucial in community-enabled design, on-demand production, and the imperative shift toward glocalization – a key challenge for communities transitioning to a circular economy.

With the widespread growth of open-source data sets, software, and hardware, the mediums of prototyping in AEC sectors are poised to experience advancements on multiple fronts. These improvements, combined with progress in what is referred to as hybrid intelligence, are anticipated to foster greater interconnectedness among places, people, and processes. Consequently, prototyping is anticipated to evolve toward being

Figure 6.2.3 Hybrid intelligence and collaborative prototyping in socio-environmental contexts. Left and Top-right: FabriCity XR in ECC Venice Architecture Biennale 2023, an immersive environment with embedded phygital trails and interactions (Hi-DARS lab and AHU lab, TTU). Bottom-Right: Human-robot collaborative prototyping with a robotic arm (Mostafavi et al., 2023, DARS lab, DIA Bauhaus, and Materiality Research Group, DDD).

more performance-driven, immersive, and collaborative. This indicates a transformative phase where smart prototyping significantly contributes to shaping the future of co-design, co-production, and collective operation.

References

Barberio, M., Colella, M., Figliola, A., & Battisti, A. (Eds.). (2023). *Architecture and Design for Industry 4.0: Theory and Practice*. Springer Cham. https://doi.org/10.1007/978-3-031-36922-3

Beaudouin-Lafon, Michel, & Mackay, Wendy E. (2007). Prototyping tools and techniques. In *The Human-Computer Interaction Handbook* (pp. 1043–1066). CRC Press.

Chang, T.-W., Hsiao, C.-F., Chen, C.-Y., & Huang, H.-Y. (2020, Jan 1). CoFabs: An interactive fabrication process framework. In P. F. Yuan, M. Xie, N. Leach, J. Yao, & X. Wang (Eds.), *Architectural Intelligence*,(pp. 271–292). Singapore: Springer Nature Singapore Pte Ltdhttps://doi.org/10.1007/978-981-15-6568-7_17

Eissen, K. (1990). *Presenting Architectural Designs: Three-Dimensional Visualization Techniques*. London: Architecture Design and Technology Press.

Frampton, K., Kolbowski, S., & Studies, I. F. (1981). *Idea as Model*. New York: Institute for Architecture and Urban Studies: Rizzoli International Publications.

Hoffman, D. L., & Novak, T. P. (2018) Consumer and object experience in the internet of things: An assemblage theory approach. *Journal of Consumer Research*, 44(6), 1178–1204.

Jahn, G., Newnham, C., & van den Berg, N. (2022). Augmented reality for construction from steam-bent timber. In: *CAADRIA Proceedings*. CAADRIA 2022: Post-Carbon. CAADRIA. https://doi.org/10.52842/conf.caadria.2022.2.191.

Jahn, G., Newnham, C., van den Berg, N., Iraheta, M., & Wells, J. (2020). Holographic construction. In: C. Gengnagel, O. Baverel, J. Burry, M. Ramsgaard Thomsen & S. Weinzierl (Eds.), *Impact: Design with All Senses. DMSB 2019*. Cham: Springer. https://doi.org/10.1007/978-3-030-29829-6_25.

Kent, L., Snider, C., Gopsill, J., & Hicks, B. (2021). Mixed reality in design prototyping: A systematic review. *Design Studies*, 77, 101046. https://doi.org/10.1016/j.destud.2021.101046

Khasraghi, S. S., & Mehan, A. (2023). Glocalization challenges and the contemporary architecture: Systematic review of common global indicators in Aga Khan Award's winners. *Journal of Architecture and Urbanism*, 47(2), 135–145.

Kolarevic, B. (2003). *Architecture in the Digital Age: Design and Manufacturing*. New York: Spon Press.

Lauff, C. A., Kotys-Schwartz, D., & Rentschler, M. E. (2018). What is a prototype? What are the roles of prototypes in companies? *Journal of Mechanical Design*, 140(60). https://doi.org/10.1115/1.4039340

Li, B., Hou, B., Yu, W., Lu, X., & Yang, C. (2017). Applications of artificial intelligence in intelligent manufacturing: A review. *Frontiers of Information Technology & Electronic Engineering*, 18(1), 86–96. https://doi.org/10.1631/fitee.1601885

Mann, S., Feiner, S., Harner, S., Ali, M. A., Janzen, R., Hansen, J., & Baldassi, S. (2015, January). Wearable computing, 3D aug* reality, photographic/videographic gesture sensing, and veillance. In *Proceedings of the Ninth International Conference on Tangible, Embedded, and Embodied Interaction*. Association for Computing Machinery, New York, NY, USA (pp. 497–500). https://doi.org/10.1145/2677199.2683590

Mehan, A., & Mostafavi, S. (2024). Spatial justice through immersive art: an interdisciplinary approach, in Gray, C., Ciliotta Chehade, E., Hekkert, P., Forlano, L., Ciuccarelli, P., Lloyd, P. (eds.), *DRS2024: Boston*, 23–28 June, Boston, USA. https://doi.org/10.21606/drs.2024.302

Mehan, A., Odour, N., & Mostafavi, S. (2023). Socio-spatial micro-networks: Building community resilience in Kenya. In: Cheshmehzangi, A., Sedrez, M., Zhao, H., Li, T., Heath, T., Dawodu, A. (eds) *Resilience vs Pandemics. Urban Sustainability*. Singapore: Springer. https://doi.org/10.1007/978-981-99-7996-7_9

Mehan, A. (2023). The role of digital technologies in building resilient communities. *Bhumi, The Planning Research Journal*, 10(1), 33–40. https://doi.org/10.4038/bhumi.v10i1.92

Mehan, A., & Mostafavi, S. (2023a). Portcityscapes as liminal spaces: Building resilient communities through parasitic architecture in port cities. In *ARCC 2023 Conference Proceeding* (pp. 631–639). Architectural Research Centers Consortium, Inc.

Mehan, A., & Mostafavi, S. (2023b). Navigating AI-enabled modalities of representation and materialization in architecture: Visual tropes, verbal biases, and geo-specificity. *Plan Journal*, 8(2), 1–16. https://www.doi.org/10.15274/tpj.2023.08.02.6

Mehan, A., & Mostafavi, S. (2023c). Temporalities and the urban fabric. Co-producing liminal spaces in transitional epochs. *UOU Scientific Journal*. https://doi.org/10.14198/UOU.2023.6.12

Mehan, A., & Mostafavi, S. S. (2022). Building resilient communities over time. In *Building Resilient Communities Over Time* (pp. 1–4). Springer International Publishing. https://doi.org/10.1007/978-3-030-51812-7_322-1

Mostafavi, S. (2021). Hybrid intelligence in architectural robotic materialization (HI-ARM): Computational, fabrication and material intelligence for multi-mode robotic production of multi-scale and multi-material systems. *A+ BE| Architecture and the Built Environment*, 12, 1–266. https://doi.org/10.7480/abe.2021.12.5799

Mostafavi, S., Kemper, B. N., Kretzer, M., Etemadi, A., Mahmoud, H. A., Yaseen, A., Nabizadeh, M., Balazadeh, T., & Chatterjee, S. (2023). Cobotic matters – collaborative robots and discrete assembly design: From stacking to self-interlocking of reciprocal components. In *Proceedings of the 28th*

Conference on Computer Aided Architectural Design Research in Asia (CAADRIA) [Volume 2]. CAADRIA 2023: Human-Centric. CAADRIA. https://doi.org/10.52842/conf.caadria.2023.2.241

Mostafavi, S., & Mehan, A. (2023). De-coding visual cliches and verbal biases: Hybrid intelligence and data justice. In Diffusions in Architecture: Artificial Intelligence and Image Generators (pp. 150–159). Wiley.

Mostafavi, S., Mehan, A., Howell, C., Montejano, E., & Stuckemeyer, J. (2024). FabriCity-XR: A phygital lattice structure mapping spatial justice–Integrated design to AR-enabled assembly workflow. In *112th ACSA Annual Meeting Proceedings*, Disruptors on the Edge (pp. 180–187). Vancouver, Canada: ACSA Press. https://doi.org/10.35483/ACSA.AM.112.25

Ratti, C. (2012). Open-source architecture (OSArc). *Domus Magazine*, 961, 1–5.

Sanchez, J. (2021). *Architecture for the Commons: Participatory Systems in the Age of Platforms.* Routledge.

Sass, L., & Oxman, R. (May 2006). Materializing design: The implications of rapid prototyping in digital design. *Design Studies*, 27(3), 325–355.

Sauer, J., Seibel, K., & Rüttinger, B. (2010). The influence of user expertise and prototype fidelity in usability tests. *Applied Ergonomics*, 41(1), 130–140. https://doi.org/10.1016/j.apergo.2009.06.003

Song, Y., Koeck, R., & Luo, S. (2021). Review and analysis of augmented reality (AR) literature for digital architectural fabrication. *Automation in Construction*, 128, 103762. https://doi.org/10.1016/j.autcon.2021.103762.

Taylor, A. G. (2016). *Develop Microsoft HoloLens Apps Now* (1st ed.). Berkeley, CA: Apress. https://doi.org/10.1007/978-1-4842-2202-7

Tedeschi, M., & Rochielle Sievert, J. (2024). Spatial justice in design research: A transdisciplinary discourse, in Gray, C., Ciliotta Chehade, E., Hekkert, P., Forlano, L., Ciuccarelli, P., Lloyd, P. (eds.), *DRS2024: Boston*, 23–28 June, Boston, USA. https://doi.org/10.21606/drs.2024.116

Varış Husar, S. C., Mehan, A., Erkan, R., Gall, T., Allkja, L., Husar, M., & Hendawy, M. (2023). What's next? Some priorities for young planning scholars to tackle tomorrow's complex challenges. *European Planning Studies*, 1–17. https://doi.org/10.1080/09654313.2023.2218417

Virzi, R. A., Sokolov, J. L., & Karis, D. (1996). Usability problem identification using both low- and high-fidelity prototypes. In *Proceedings of the SIGCHI Conference on Human Factors in Computing Systems Common Ground - CHI '96*. https://doi.org/10.1145/238386.238516

Weichel, C., Lau, M., K. D., Villar, N., & Gellersen, H.-W. (2014). MixFab: A mixed-reality environment for personal fabrication. In *CHI '14: Proceedings of the SIGCHI Conference on Human Factors in Computing Systems*, Association for Computing Machinery, 3855–3864. https://doi.org/10.1145/2556288.2557090

Wojtowicz, J. (Ed.) (1995). *Virtual Design Studio.* Hong Kong University Press.

Zhang, Y., Zhang, G., Wang, J., Sun, S., Si, S., & Yang, T. (2014). Real-time information capturing and integration framework of the internet of manufacturing things. *International Journal of Computer Integrated Manufacturing*, 28(8), 811–822. https://doi.org/10.1080/0951192x.2014.900874

Zheng, P., Wang, H., Sang, Z., Zhong, R. Y., Liu, Y., Liu, C., Mubarok, K., Yu, S., & Xu, X. (2018). Smart manufacturing systems for industry 4.0: Conceptual framework, scenarios, and future perspectives. *Frontiers of Mechanical Engineering*, 13(2), 137–150. https://doi.org/10.1007/s11465-018-0499-5

6.3

ARCHITECTURE, ENGINEERING, AND CONSTRUCTION (AEC) INDUSTRY 4.0 AND BEYOND

Building Construction Automation through 3D Printing and Additive Manufacturing Toward Lower Environmental Impacts

Poorang Piroozfar and Eric Farr

Abstract

Global efforts and sector-wide commitments to reducing the contribution of the Architecture, Engineering, and Construction (AEC) industry to climate change have started showing positive impacts. Automation enabled by smart and autonomous technologies contributes to the efficacy and efficiency of the process and product, thereby paving the way toward an N-Z society.

While Industry 4.0 frees up time to focus more on planning, strategizing, innovation, and technology-based creativity and development, Industry 5.0 will be concentrating, more at meta-levels, on prosperity beyond jobs and growth, on the well-being of employees, and the holistic health of/in the built and natural environments.

Multi-level perspective (MLP) and disruptive innovation theory will be employed as the theoretical underpinning for a prominent transition framework to envision potential shifts toward automation in construction through advancements in large-scale 3D printing and additive manufacturing in a post-Industry 4.0 era. Enabled by smart technologies, the future scenarios of 3D printing and additive manufacturing will be drawn upon; the futures which would either intervene, disrupt, improve, or revolutionize the status quo of the common practice in the AEC industry with a main focus on their ecological impacts.

Introduction

Global efforts and sector-wide commitments to reducing the contribution of the Architecture, Engineering, and Construction (AEC) industry to climate change (e.g. moving toward nationwide N-Z (Net-/Near-Zero) targets in some construction economies) have started

DOI: 10.4324/9781003384113-70

showing some positive outcomes. However, the contribution of the sector to GHG emissions and energy consumption remains high at a 40% sector average.

Depending on the ways 3D printing – as a definite example of automation – is introduced to the industry on a large scale as a technological/innovation intervention, it can potentially contribute to the efficacy and efficiency of activities and procedures thereby paving the way toward a more environmentally concerned sector. Industry 4.0 and its envisaged successor Industry 5.0 pave the way toward liberating the workforce more on planning, strategizing, innovation, and technology-based creativity and development (Industry 4.0) and further toward prosperity beyond jobs and growth, freeing up some further capacities to concentrate on the well-being of employees and beyond, on the holistic health of the built and natural environments (Industry 5.0).

Multi-level perspective (MLP) as a middle range theory (MRT) and disruptive innovation theory have been deployed to lay the foundation for our argument for the possibilities and potentials that can arise with respect to improving our sector's traditionally high environmental impacts (EIs) if large-scale 3D printing is adopted and transitioned to as one of the future scenarios in the AEC industry.

This chapter focuses on the future scenarios of large-scale 3D printing and the innovation traits it can take which would either intervene, disrupt, improve, or revolutionize the status quo of the common practice in the AEC industry. Possible future developments of large-scale 3D will be envisaged to respond to possible, probable, or likely future scenarios with a main focus on their ecological impacts.

Industry 4.0 and Beyond

According to MathsWorks (2021), Industry 4.0 is "the automation of traditional manufacturing and industrial processes using technologies such as Industrial IoT, [virtualization], big data analytics, artificial intelligence [and machine learning], robotics [and automation], and autonomous [and smart] systems". European Commission (2021) asserts that:

> *Industry 5.0 provides a vision of an industry that aims beyond efficiency and productivity as the sole goals, and reinforces the role and the contribution of industry to society... It places the wellbeing of the worker at the center of the production process and uses new technologies to provide prosperity beyond jobs and growth while respecting the production limits of the planet.*

Industry 4.0 aims to increase manufacturing capability, productivity, and efficiency while enabling flexible, customer-centric production, and reducing operation and maintenance costs (MathsWorks, 2021). Industry 5.0 complements Industry 4.0 by "specifically putting research and innovation at the service of the transition to a sustainable, human-centric and resilient European industry" (European Commission, 2021).

An "i" for Evolution: From Automaton to Automation

Whether we assume that robotics – as one of the outstanding insignia of automation – root back to Goerge C. Devol's "Unimate" in the 1950s or its commercially developed version by Joseph Engleberger in the 1960s or Charles Rosen's "Shakey" developed in the Stanford Research Institute in the 1950s, the yearning for devolving repetitive, dreary, and tedious tasks to some inferior beings with no power to complain and no sense of getting tired or bored has been next to an obsession for our ancestors for centuries. It is suggested that some of the earliest examples of such attempts date back to 1415–1380 BCE when water clocks were made using human figurine to strike a bell in ancient Egypt.[1] Archytas's flying wooden pigeon[2] in 400 BCE, hydraulically operated statues that could speak in Hellenic Egypt during the second century BCE, a doll that could move like a human being made by Petronius Arbiter in the first century CE and a wooden robot that could fetch the emperor's daily bread from the store made by Giovanni Torriani in 1557 are just to name but a few other examples[3]. Referring to the *Canard Digérateur*, or the "Digesting Duck" – an automaton in the form of a duck, created by Jacques de Vaucanson, unveiled on 30 May 1739 in France – Voltaire wrote in 1741: "sans la voix de la le Maure, & le canard de Vaucanson, vous n'auriez rien qui fit ressouvenir de la gloire de la France" (Without the voice of le Maure – Catherine-Nicole Lemaure, an C18th French soprano – and Vaucanson's duck, you would have nothing to remind you of the glory of France) (Voltaire, 1819:491). The Jaquet-Droz Writer (circa 1774) who was a little boy, 70 cm tall, carved from wood, and composed of a very complicated mechanism still works. It can write "I do not think, therefore I will never be".

In *"The Architecture Machine"*[4] (1970), Negroponte draws our attention to a matter of paramount importance in automation where he suggests that machines should be able to work with missing or incomplete information exactly the way human beings do[5]. However, with the advent and prevalence of machine learning and AI, this does not seem to be the case anymore as "the machine" can learn and educate itself to best facilitate the automation task it is tasked to do, if not exceed the initial intent, job specification or requirements.

Additive Manufacturing and 3D Printing

Additive manufacturing was probably first introduced to the built environment in form of large-scale 3D printing by Khoshnevis in 2004; what he called contour crafting (CC). He suggested that "CC will most probably be one of the very few feasible approaches for building structures on other planets, such as Moon and Mars, which are being targeted for human colonization before the end of the new century" (Khoshnevis, 2004:5). This preposition is probably right if we exclude off-site, prefabricated, assembly-based unitized, panelized or volumetric systems for outer space/celestial construction. Regardless of the material – whether it is cementitious material, welded steel, plastic-based, or clay-based, and regardless of the system – whether it is a three-axis gantry system or six-axis robotic system at the very best, large-scale 3D printing is the most widely used additive manufacturing method which has been as an on-site modern method of construction.

Multi-level Perspective

Although it is not in particular in this chapter's scope, it is still useful to draw our attention to some potential underpinning theoretical frame of reference. Efficacious introduction of new technologies is dependent on many contextual success factors – related to the environment, people, societies, culture, hard and soft technological infrastructures, and methods and sequences of introduction or application of those technologies to name but a few. "Technological diffusion" or diffusion of innovation – the process through which technology or technological innovations spread to different users, or permeate into distinct uses or applications, societies or regions – has been theorized and modeled extensively to help understand and improve the process of technology acceptance, its efficacy and overall success. Technology Acceptance Model (TAM, TAM2, TAM3), Theory of Reasoned Action (TRA), Theory of Planned Behavior (TPB), Information Diffusion (ID), Information System Success Model (ISSM), Task Technology Fit (TTF), the Unified Theory of Acceptance and Use of Technology (UTAUT, UTAUT2), and the MLP are theoretical models either exclusively developed to study technological/information/ innovation diffusion or have been borrowed from other fields or disciplines (e.g. education, social sciences, health sciences, etc.) to help to do so. MLP is deemed the most relevant model to explain, understand, and facilitate the technological innovation diffusion associated with large-scale 3D printing in the AEC industry. This, on the one hand, is due to MLP's concept, structure and the way in which it has been used to explain and relate various concepts using empirical research to identify recurring patterns and generalizable inductions. It is, on the other hand, because of the inherent nature of large-scale 3D printing as a technological diffusion which entails socio-technological transition to different extents depending on its context, the process intents, and the targeted deliverables and intended goals. MLP is an MRT[6] that aims to conceptualize dynamic patterns in socio-technical transitions (Geels, 2011:26).

Such transition processes entail a non-linear structure which arises from the interplay of developments at three analytical levels: the niches that is the locus for radical innovations, the socio-technical regime(s) that are the locus/loci of established practices and associated rules that stabilize the existing systems, and, last but not the least, an exogenous socio-technical landscape (Rip & Kemp, 1998, Geels, 2002, Geels, 2005). Figure 6.3.1 depicts the MLP originally conceptualized as an MRT and here applied to investigate the capabilities and expand the capacities of large-scale 3D printing in AEC industry, facilitate its uptake, and improve their EIs.

Disruptive Innovation Theory

This approach to innovation in industry and business has been studied from different vantage points. Earlier research suggests that technical innovation can be classified into two categories (Bower & Christensen, 1995): sustaining innovation – which happens when better-performing products are created by a company to sell to its best customers for higher profits (Cote, 2022) – and disruptive innovation, which is subsequently divided

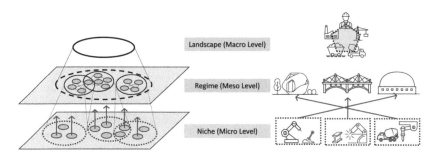

Figure 6.3.1 MLP model applied to large-scale 3D printing as an MRT technology acceptance model (Image courtesy of authors).

into two sub-categories: "low-end disruption" – in which a low-cost business model is used by a company to enter at the bottom of an existing market and claim a share of the market – and "new-market disruption" – where a new segment in an existing market is created and claimed by a company aiming at catering to an underserved customer base (Cote, 2022). Low-end disruption is when businesses come in at the bottom of the market with a "good enough" product at a cheaper cost (Landry, 2020) or products with characteristics or advantages that those of incumbents' do not possess. Christensen et al. (2015)[7] describe this as "disruptive innovation," which is the process by which a smaller company – usually with fewer resources – moves upmarket and challenges larger, established businesses (Cote, 2020). Disruptive theory of innovation is a theory that elucidates how innovation transforms an existing market or sector by introducing new advantages or characteristics such as ease of use, simplicity, convenience, accessibility, affordability, and, in our argument, more environmentally aware approach. More consented view, however, is that low-end disruption and new-market disruption can sometimes grow in difference to the extent that they find totally different trajectories hence three categories of innovation are suggested as:

- Sustaining (or incremental) innovation is where a company creates better-performing products to sell for higher profits to its best customers. Typically, it is used by companies already successful in their industries (Cote, 2022).
- Disruptive innovation improves existing markets by exceeding the needs of a customer base, eventually displacing the old market (Cote, 2022, Big Think+, 2018, McKinney, 2022). Disruptive innovation focuses on long-term impact and may involve displacing current products, altering the relationship between customers and suppliers, and creating completely new product categories (Cote, 2022).
- Radical (or destructive) innovation focuses on long-term impact and may involve displacing current products, altering the relationship between customers and suppliers, and creating completely new product categories (Hopp et al., 2018).

The introduction of CC concept to the AEC industry in form of large-scale 3D printing has all characteristics, requisites and potentials – endogenously and exogenously – to be further looked into with more details, applied and developed/envisaged to develop in the future as a disruptive innovation in construction capable of introducing a fundamentally different approach with environmental concerns at its center of focus.

Possible Future Trends

3D-printing fabrication method consists of a processing phase where the material is prepared, cured, or stabilized. Processing can take place prior to printing (pre-processing), during the printing (thru-processing), or after printing (post-processing). The fabrication method is usually mutually intertwined with the type of printing material. In pre-processing where the material is processed prior to printing stage, usually concrete is the most common material, whereas in thru-processing where the material is processed throughout the printing, a common example will be steel welding and for post-processing where the material is processed after printing some plastics or clay/adobe which may require chemical curing post-printing stage are typical examples. Suffice to say that both gantry and robotic systems can be used in automation of more conventional methods of construction such as bricklaying or in established

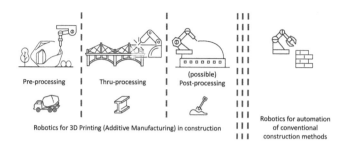

Figure 6.3.2 Robotics for pre-, thru-, and post-processing 3D-printing fabrication methods (and far right: for automation of conventional construction methods) (Image courtesy of authors).

practices in the design or construction such as restoration and refurbishment projects, interior design project, production of building furniture or urban furniture, etc. (Figure 6.3.2).

Depending on the choice of the fabrication method and the material, the procurement strategy, the technology, level of specialized workforce and machinery/equipment, printing form, size and speed, accuracy and flexibility, efficiency and efficacy of the process, project lead time, cost and cashflow, return on investment as well as the EIs of the process vary significantly. Almost all aforesaid aspects have been studied to some different extents. Research on the EI of large-scale 3D printing, however, remains few and far between.

If large-scale 3D printing is to achieve a major breakthrough with regard to the construction industry's EI, it should follow the disruptive innovation theory as a model. To do so and to avoid what Christensen et al. (2015) warn us against where they point out that "The problem with conflating a disruptive innovation with any breakthrough that changes an industry's competitive patterns is that different types of innovation require different strategic approaches", if large-scale 3D is aimed at as a proper and genuine disruptive innovation trait, it should de-learn and re-learn the common, conventional and established trends, exercises and practices in the construction industry by taking an alternative strategic approach to all activities involved in the design, production/fabrication, construction and assembly processes in the AEC industry. Only in such situation may large-scale 3D printing be able to set out to radically change the high EI traditionally associated with and inherent in the building and construction industry. Figure 6.3.3 depicts future directions that the AEC industry can take with reference to large-scale 3D printing and the potentials for meeting bottom-line sustainability targets and lowering the sector's EIs and contribution to climate change potentials through three innovation scenarios.

Concluding Comments

It is an irrefutable fact that the AEC industry can do more to alleviate its impact on climate change. There are certain actions with proven or some with disputable impacts, but some moves which will potentially have some positive impacts depending on how they are introduced to and throughout the AEC industry. CC or large-scale 3D printing (using robotic or gantry systems) is an area where automation can be introduced to the sector with some potential inter- and intra-sector – local or universal – benefits. 3D printing, although established in other manufacturing industries with proven benefits, is still in its infancy in building and construction industry.

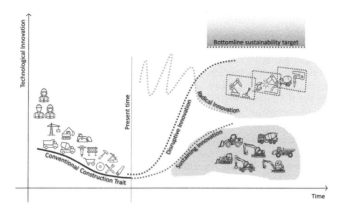

Figure 6.3.3   Future directions the AEC industry can take with reference to large-scale 3D printing and the potential for meeting bottom-line sustainability targets through three innovation scenarios (Image courtesy of authors).

There are, however, concerns that the way or ways in which automation through 3D printing can be applied to the AEC industry may end up more wasteful and resource-intensive with potentially higher EIs than the conventional construction methods and technologies. AEC has a tactical advantage to observe and learn from the experience and expertise in other industries where automation, robotics, and 3D printing have been gestated, evolved, and excelled. This, however, may require a partially or fully de-learning/re-learning process for such novel technologies to be effective and able to offer their full potential to the building and construction industry.

Based on these premises, we laid an underpinning foundation for our argument using two theoretical streaks: MLP as an MRT to explain how a socio-technical transition as the diffusion of large-scale 3D printing in the context of the building and construction industry is can be understood and embedded in an effective yet realistic way and disruptive innovation theory (as one of the three different streams new technological innovation – that is additive manufacturing – can be facilitated in the context of its destination: AEC industry).

This chapter presented this original idea for the first time and drew attention to this transition process with the EI at its main core. We argued that if a disruptive innovation approach – as opposed to its alternatives at either end of the spectrum, namely a sustaining or a radical innovation approach – is taken, it would be a much more profound chance for improving the sector's overall EI through the application of large-scale 3D printing to the building and construction industry.

Notes

1 https://collection.sciencemuseumgroup.org.uk/objects/co454/egyptian-water-clock-water-clock-model-representation
2 https://weird-history-facts.com/the-flying-pigeon-of-archytas-of-tarentum/
3 https://cs.stanford.edu/people/eroberts/courses/soco/projects/robotics/history.html
4 "It is reasonable to assume that the presence of machines, of automation in general, will provide for some of the omitted and difficult-to-acquire information. However, it would appear foolish to suppose that, when machines know how to design, there will be no missing information or that a single designer can give the machine all it needs. Consequently, we, the Architecture Machine Group at M.I.T., are embarking on the construction of a machine that can work with missing

information. To do this, an architecture machine must understand our metaphors, must solicit Information on its own, must acquire experiences, must talk to a wide variety of people, must improve over time, and must be intelligent. It must recognize context, particularly changes in goals and meaning brought about by changes in context" (Negroponte, 1970:119–120).

5 The proposition that human beings can work with missing or incomplete information is through but the proposition that they always do choose to work with missing or incomplete information is subject to debate from different angles and can indeed take two trajectories one for and the other one against it. It can be argued that with the pervasiveness of the World Wide Web, humans are fully capable and entitled – in theory – to choose not to work with missing information. At the other end of the spectrum and acknowledging that we, human beings, have always been working that way, developing methods and processes to assist us in making complex decisions with partial or missing information (e.g. Analytic Hierarchy Process or AHP, etc.).

6 MRT was designed as "theories that lie between the minor but necessary working hypotheses that evolve in abundance during day-to-day research and the all-inclusive systematic efforts to develop a unified theory that will explain all the observed uniformities of social behavior, social organization and social change" (Merton, 1968:39). It aims to wed pure empiricism, which focuses only on data-collection and data-analysis with the extremes of grand theory (e.g. in Parson's structural functionalism). Merton suggested that "An array of concepts does not constitute theory... It is only when such concepts are interrelated in the form of a scheme that a theory begins to emerge" (1968:143). MRTs comprise three main characteristics that are: (a) MRT is not about broad, abstract entities such as 'society' or 'social system', but about concrete phenomena (such as socio-technical transitions), (b) MRT differs from grand theory because it emphasizes interactions between theory and empirical research. So, MRT does not consist of elaborate frameworks with endless conceptual distinctions and limited linkages to empirical research, (c) MRT specifies relationships between concepts into analytical models (Geels, 2007).

7 Although some believe or claim that the term, "disruptive innovation" was coined by Harvard professor Clayton Christensen in 1995, some others assert that the concept was previously described in the book "*Innovation: The Attacker's Advantage*" by Foster (1986) and in an earlier academic paper by Cooper and Schedel (1976).

References

Big Think+. 2018. *Radical vs. disruptive innovation: What they mean for organizations* [Online]. Big Think Available: https://bigthink.com/plus/radical-vs-disruptive-innovation-what-they-mean-for-organizations/ [Accessed 3 Nov 2023].

Bower, J. L. & Christensen, C. M. 1995. *Disruptive technologies: Catching the wave*. Harvard Business Review. Boston, MA: Harvard Business School.

Christensen, C. M., Raynor, M. E. & Mcdonald, R. 2015. *What is disruptive innovation?* Harvard Business Review. Boston, MA: Harvard Business School.

Cooper, A. C. & Schendel, D. 1976. Strategic responses to technological threats. *Business Horizons*, 19, 61–69.

Cote, C. 2020. *What is disruptive innovation?* [Online]. Harvard Business School. Available: https://online.hbs.edu/blog/post/what-is-disruptive-innovation [Accessed 5 Nov 2023].

Cote, C. 2022. *Sustaining vs. Disruptive innovation: What's the difference?* [Online]. Harvard Business School. Available: https://online.hbs.edu/blog/post/sustaining-vs-disruptive-innovation [Accessed 4 Nov 2023].

European Commission. 2021. *Industry 5.0* [Online]. European Commission Directorate-General for Research and Innovation, Publications Office. Available: https://research-and-innovation.ec.europa.eu/research-area/industrial-research-and-innovation/industry-50_en [Accessed 1 Nov 2023].

Foster, R. N. 1986. *Innovation: The attacker's advantage*. Summit Books.

Geels, F. W. 2002. Technological transitions as evolutionary reconfiguration processes: A multi-level perspective and a case-study. *Research Policy*, 31, 1257–1274.

Geels, F. W. 2005. The dynamics of transitions in socio-technical systems: A multi-level analysis of the transition pathway from horse-drawn carriages to automobiles (1860–1930). *Technology Analysis & Strategic Management*, 17, 445–476.

Geels, F. W. 2011. The multi-level perspective on sustainability transitions: Responses to seven criticisms. *Environmental Innovation and Societal Transitions*, 1, 24–40.

Hopp, C., Antons, D., Kaminski, J. & Salge, T. O. 2018. *What 40 years of research reveals about the difference between disruptive and radical innovation*. Harvard Business Review. Harvard Business School.

Khoshnevis, B. 2004. Automated construction by contour crafting—related robotics and information technologies. *Automation in Construction*, 13, 5–19.

Landry, L. 2020. *3 Types of innovation you should know* [Online]. Harvard Business School. Available: https://online.hbs.edu/blog/post/3-types-of-innovation-you-should-know [Accessed 5 Nov 2023].

MathsWorks. 2021. *Demystifying industry 4.0* [Online]. Available: https://www.mathworks.com/content/dam/mathworks/white-paper/demystifying-industry-4-0.pdf [Accessed 8 Nov 2023].

Mckinney, P. 2022. *Disruptive innovation vs radical innovation: What's the difference?* [Online]. Killer Innovation. [Accessed 1 Nov 2023].

Negroponte, N. 1970. *The architecture machine*, Cambridge, MA, M.I.T. Press.

Rip, A. & Kemp, R. 1998. Technological change. *Human Choice and Climate Change*, 2, 327–399.

Voltaire, P. V. F.-M. A. 1819. *Ouvres Complètes de Voltaire (in French)*, Paris, P. Plancher.

6.4

NESTING FABRICATION

An Integrated Approach Using Existing Tools to Minimize Waste in Large-Scale Freeform Construction

Alireza Borhani and Negar Kalantar

Abstract

The increasing waste produced by both conventional and digitally driven building practices underscores the urgent need for dedicated research on and investment in finding more efficient ways of preserving our resources. This chapter encourages the exploration and adoption of a method called "Nesting Fabrication" in the pursuit of sustainable construction, emphasizing its capacity to contribute to a resource-efficient and environmentally conscientious future. Here, the authors present Nesting Fabrication as an innovative strategy for addressing the challenge of waste creation in large-scale freeform construction. Nesting Fabrication involves a geometric method for dividing complex freeform surfaces into nested and stackable pieces that consider fabrication tool limitations early on in the design process. This chapter explores three distinct approaches: 2D, 2.5D, and 3D nesting. Each is tailored to accommodate specific fabrication tools, materials availability, and the complexity of the given geometry.

This chapter explains the multifaceted benefits of Nesting Fabrication, highlighting its capacity to minimize materials waste, reduce production time, lower transportation costs, and decrease storage space requirements. Beyond waste reduction, Nesting Fabrication is proven to be a viable solution for addressing challenges posed by larger fabrication tools, instead of employing existing tools to produce smaller nested components for use in the construction of large, tessellated building shells.

Reflecting on the Current Construction Industry Landscape

Contributing nearly USD$10 trillion USD (about 6% of the global GDP), the construction sector accounts for 40% of global energy consumption and 12% of potable water usage, while also generating 40% of solid waste and 39% of global greenhouse gas emissions (Meng et al. 2023; Kongboon et al. 2022; Resch et al. 2020; Ferriss 2020; IPCC 2021; European Commission 2019; IEA and UNEP 2018; Agustí-Juan et al. 2017). The need for immediate action to address the industry's inefficiency and significant environmental impact

DOI: 10.4324/9781003384113-71

is more evident than ever. To lessen the harm to our planet caused by the AEC industry and accommodate rapid urban population growth, urgent changes must be made to how we design and construct new buildings. This pressing need to alter our approach is undeniable, as the construction of 13,000 urban buildings is required every day to house the extra 200,000 people being added to cities (Bertollini 2018). The immediacy of the need for change is intensified by the projection that two-thirds of the anticipated 9.8 billion global population in 2050 will reside in urban areas (United Nations 2017).

To address the environmental crisis resulting from the materials-based demands of the building sector and its associated waste, it is essential to challenge conventional norms in the construction process that have outlived their usefulness (Bock 2015). Doing so requires engaging in a transformative journey wherein technology, creativity, and sustainability seamlessly intersect in the construction process. The integration of digital technology into construction has the potential to significantly enhance speed, accuracy, efficiency, and output quality by reducing materials, manpower, human error, and time. However, the main challenge lies in this traditional, fragmented, and risk-averse sector adopting this technology and overcoming its resistance to change (Giesekam et al. 2016; Arora et al. 2014; Pinkse & Dommisse 2009). To meet the challenge of incorporating unfamiliar technology into this project-based industry, practitioners should underscore its adaptability and versatility. This emphasis will produce tangible outcomes, especially in assisting small construction firms with managing various complexities across different sites and effectively addressing specific project challenges.

Digital Fabrication: At the Intersection of Progress and Complexity

Digital fabrication technologies are numerous and have various applications. Considered computer-aided design and manufacturing (CAD/CAM), digital fabrication involves controlling machines with computers to directly translate digital models into physical artifacts (Iwamoto 2013). While digital fabrication enables the creation of a series of distinct, complex, curving forms with nearly the same effort as mass-producing identical ones, its primary benefit lies in managing the construction process of buildings and their components by extracting the required information from a set of design documents (Kolarevic 2003). This digitally driven process liberates both designers and builders from repetitive tasks, instead providing them with sufficient control to implement desired modifications. Therefore, the potential consequences of these changes can be predicted and tracked throughout the remaining construction steps.

Despite a significant need for effective, expeditious, and materials-efficient construction approaches, there is currently insufficient demand from clients in the AEC industry to fully leverage the potential of digital technologies and motivate the construction industry to evolve. The transition from analog to digital drawing, along with the longstanding use of CAD/CAM processes in architecture (e.g., Gehry's office adopting CATIA in 1989) has not caused a dramatic shift in the appearance of our buildings. They continue to be designed and constructed in a manner that reflects the pre-digital era. Despite advances in computer-controlled processes and technologies, a significant gap remains between our design capabilities and construction practices, or in other words, what we draw and what we can bring into existence.

In the relatively limited number of buildings capable of showcasing the integration of digitally driven design and fabrication, the primary focus has been on sophisticated iconic structures demonstrating expressive architecture. Many of these structures have been one-off projects such as pavilions or museums, setting them apart from day-to-day projects such as housing and commercial development (that deal with regular client challenges) (Agustí-Juan et al. 2017; Agustí-Juan and Habert 2017). Besides that limited number of full-scale projects, the potential for and application of digital fabrication in architecture remain largely untapped (de Soto et al. 2018). It is primarily used to produce building elements, components, and furniture (Bock 2015) and accelerate model-making and prototyping processes.

Navigating Barriers in Digital Fabrication for Construction

Architects have been employing digital drawing for over 40 years. Throughout this extended period, numerous robust CAD software options in the AEC industry have facilitated digital form-finding to model advanced geometries with double curvatures. By employing these software tools, the processes for designing and analyzing buildings with sophisticated performative forms are not inherently challenging and can be completed in a relatively short period of time. However, the presence of such buildings remains surprisingly limited, even in prosperous cities worldwide. Several factors contribute to the scarcity of buildings with non-orthogonal forms, including the associated fabrication costs, which are influenced by the availability of the materials and tools required to bring such designs into reality. For example, in the US, construction supply stores predominantly offer materials that are flat and confined to one or two dimensions, such as lumber and plywood sheets. These non-stretchable and comparatively rigid materials are better suited for constructing boxy buildings with basic geometric designs comprised of straight lines. It seems that the dominance of orthogonal forms with developable flat faces is likely the result of the preference of local contractors to align with existing codes (which were established to accommodate readily available materials). Conversely, numerous common digital fabrication tools on the market are tailored to 2D materials such as laser cutters, plasma arcs, and waterjet machines. Also, most commercial flatbed three-axis CNC routers often have limited Z-axes, as compared to their X- and Y-axes. This restriction limits their ability to work primarily on sheet materials or relatively thin blocks. Such constraints hinder these machines from efficiently carving deep double-curvature forms out of thick material in a single operation. Fabricating such forms comes with added constraints, such as the expense of the material block and considerable waste generated when removing material to achieve a desired 3D shape. Moreover, utilizing a workshop equipped with a large CNC machine with a high Z-axis may be challenging and cost-prohibitive, especially for smaller projects.

In architecture, digitally crafted projects constructed in the 21st century commonly share certain characteristics such as higher costs and substantial fabrication time. Additionally, in many cases, waste reduction plays a role secondary to that of the designer's desire to create freeform architecture. While some publications underscore the potential sustainability benefits of employing digital technologies in small-scale processes, a literature review revealed the lack of environmental assessment in current large-scale digital fabrication strategies, particularly concrete construction, resulting to excessive materials waste (Liebringshausen et al. 2023; Agustí-Juan and Habert 2017). In practice, for the construction of geometrically complex concrete elements ranging from iconic buildings like Gehry's Zollhof Tower in Düsseldorf to SANAA's Rolex Learning Center in Lausanne, de Portzamparc's House of Dior in Seoul, and Matsys's Confluence Park Pavilion in San Antonio, large disposable formworks are either CNC-milled from Styrofoam or crafted from plywood. Such labor-intensive projects are indeed constructed twice: first with Styrofoam or plywood as formwork, and then with concrete. In rare instances such as the Confluence Park Pavilion, distinguishable by its repetitive modules, gigantic formworks are used to cast multiple identical pieces.

Construction-Informed Design for Waste Reduction

As discussed, traditional construction is notably wasteful and inefficient in its use of resources. Compared to conventional construction, digital fabrication has significant potential to minimize its environmental impact by strategically distributing materials where structurally needed and effectively managing the allocation of time, tools, and human resources. Despite the potential of digitally driven design and fabrication for form-finding, simulation, optimization, and contributing to more sustainable and resource-efficient construction practices, the available capacity remains underutilized. While digital technologies empower designers to more comprehensively consider different aspects of their buildings, the priority often rests on creating freeform architecture with a distinctive visual presence, overshadowing the consideration of other critical aspects in the proposed design. Consequently, the role of waste minimization in guiding the design and construction processes is secondary (Abdelmohsen and Hassab 2020; Craveiro et al. 2019; Lavery 2013).

A deeper reflection on the issue of waste in both conventional construction and digital fabrication raises the following question: What if we could produce complex buildings with minimal or no waste? The authors fully agree with the statement of the European Commission: "More than 80% of the environmental impact of a product is determined at the design stage" (European Union 2012). From this perspective, the authors' scholarly and practical focus for the past several years has been on exploring opportunities to bridge the gap between design and construction. By identifying potential challenges and impacts emerging early on in the design process and working to integrate them into a viable fabrication solution, the authors believe it is feasible to develop practical approaches for optimizing materials usage, improving fabrication efficiency, and streamlining logistics and assembly processes.

Taking into account the constraints and opportunities presented by fabrication tools, coupled with the geometry arising from particular materials' behavior, the authors have navigated various form-finding strategies to meet project requirements. These strategies necessitate a nuanced understanding of the intelligence embedded in tools, materials, and contextual factors to adeptly translate them into a performative form. Essentially, the constructed form is regarded as a medium for addressing technical, functional, structural, and environmental considerations, seamlessly incorporating them into the building's aesthetic and tectonic qualities.

Nesting Fabrication: Geometric Solutions for Sustainable Construction

One strategy developed by the authors to address the issue of waste in the construction of large-scale freeform surfaces is called "Nesting Fabrication." This approach involves integrating construction constraints into the early stages of the design process. This novel construction-informed geometric system relies on the optimization of materials usage and fabrication time, with the goal of achieving nearly zero-waste construction and assembly processes. Conceptually, the suggested method resembles a set of Russian dolls, where each doll fits snugly inside another. Despite the considerable potential for applying Nesting

Fabrication and its adaptability to various tools and materials, finding precedents that embody the governing principles of this method is difficult. Notable instances include Kudless's Zero/Fold Screen, Zuuk's Re-Settle Studio, the work of Povilas, Enrique Ordoñez, and Piles from AA School of Architecture, as well as Enrique's research at ETH Zurich (Kudless 2010; Kristen and Taron 2019; Enrique et al. 2016; Povilas et al. 2011; Zuuk 2016).

The term "nesting" diverges from the industry terminology often used to describe cost-effective methods for creating compact clusters with some gaps between 2D and 3D drawings, commonly applied to laser cutting, CNC routing, and 3D printing. Within the context of the authors' work, nesting is a geometric procedure tailored to the limitations of a chosen fabrication tool. In this method, a freeform surface is subdivided into multiple identical yet interconnected pieces for sequential production. These subdivided pieces are nested successively with minimal gaps, creating the least number of stacks needed for fabrication. In every stack, each piece is part of a larger whole, either horizontally nestled alongside another piece or vertically arranged on top of a lower piece. In both stack types, the front or top side of one piece matches the back or bottom of its neighboring piece. This geometric strategy of subdividing the original surface and rearranging the pieces in a stack minimizes waste in the fabrication process. Upon assembly, the nested pieces come together to shape the intended freeform surface. The resulting compartmentalized assembly showcases a unique geometric relationship between the front (or top) side of certain pieces and the back (or bottom) side of others within the final structure (Figure 6.4.1).

As mentioned above, Nesting Fabrication is a systematic process used to translate certain constraints of freeform construction into geometric principles. Depending on the selected fabrication tool, materials availability, assembly preferences, and most importantly, complexity of the given surface, the Nesting Fabrication method can be implemented through three approaches: 2D, 2.5D, and 3D. In each, regardless of the formal complexity of the components in a stack, the first piece shapes the form of the second. To achieve each of these methods, it is important to create a volume of a given surface geometry in a certain way. Then, such volume is subdivided with cutting planes through a specified process.

A Methodical Approach to Creating Nested Stacks

The following outlines a basic process for transforming a curved surface into a stackable volume by using cutting planes. Imagine a surface positioned vertically on the ground. Three parallel evenly spaced cutting planes horizontally intersect this surface, dividing it into four equal segments. Overall, the number of cutting planes and gaps between them determine the count and height of the nested pieces in the stack. The following steps describe the creation of a nested stack.

- To ensure the creation of a volume with nested pieces, it is crucial that the geometries of the volume's front and back sides are interrelated before the volume is divided with cutting planes. To transform the given surface into a volume with nested components, the surface is considered the front side of the volume. This surface is then duplicated at a specified distance to create the backside. The gap between the two surfaces depends on the desired thickness of the final volume and its structural characteristics.
- Before connecting the front and back sides with additional side surfaces, the back surface is raised in a direction perpendicular to that of the normal cutting planes. The amount of this upward shift corresponds to the distance between the existing cutting planes.

Figure 6.4.1   Light Pavilion showcases an intricate shell construction created via Nesting Fabrication, minimizing waste and optimizing efficiency. Designed by Venessa Davidenko in CCA's Advanced Studio, Fall 2020, taught by the authors.

- The excess area is then trimmed off the back surface above the front side and back surface extended downward to meet the ground.
- Four additional side surfaces are then made to connect the front and back. Next, the front, back, and side surfaces are joined to form a closed or solid volume.
- The horizontal planes are then used to cut the volume into four sub-volumes. These sub-volumes can be rearranged to create a nested stack. All sub-volumes except the first can be relocated simultaneously in two directions: downward and upward.
- Following the suggested steps ensures that the back side of each successive sub-volume aligns with the front side of the preceding one. As a result, a nested stack is created with each sub-volume seamlessly connected to the ones adjacent.

In the above example, the entire front surface is duplicated and repositioned at the back to maintain the relationship between the volume's front and back. Instead of using the entire front surface, it is possible to divide it into several segments. Then, each of these subdivided segments can be duplicated and relocated to the back. When employing the front segments in the back, they can either be extended or partially used. While the front segment can be used in different sizes and orientations at the back, it is essential to adhere to a defined order to regulate their arrangement at the back. Having front segments in random sizes and arbitrary angles at the back will not result in acceptable nested pieces with a desirable stacking order.

The orientation of the cutting planes significantly influences both the nesting of the volume and orientation of the pieces within the stack. These cutting planes intersect the volume where subdivided segments are positioned, establishing a mutually dependent relationship between the cutting planes and subdivided segments. This reciprocal and inseparable connection has a profound impact on how the volume can be nested. For instance, maintaining parallel cutting planes or adjusting the angles to create non-parallel planes determines how the pieces stack in 2D, 2.5D, or 3D configurations. When dividing a volume with parallel cutting planes, the result is 2D and 2.5D nesting, whereas the use of non-parallel planes yields a 3D nested stack. In 3D nesting, the cutting planes can progressively change their angles along the X-, Y-, or Z-axes, or a combination thereof. The angles of these cuts are contingent on the geometrical relationship between the volume's front and back sides.

2D NESTING

2D nesting is the optimal strategy when working with sheet materials and a 2D or 2.5D subtractive tool such as a laser cutter or three-axis CNC router, as altering the tool's head to cut at an angle is not possible. To fabricate from thin sheets an undulated volume designed based on nesting principles, the geometry can be sliced with parallel cutting planes to create numerous sections or ribs. The back of the upper ribs aligns with the front parts of the lower ribs, allowing all to be laid out without gaps, side by side on a flat surface. After a slight shifting of the ribs to accommodate the subtractive tool's thickness, the ribs can be cut with minimal waste (except for the cutoff width). The cut ribs are then assembled alongside one another to form the undulated volume. As all ribs share edges with their neighbors, a significant reduction in machining time can be achieved. When each cut creates the front and back of neighboring pieces, only "N+1" cuts are needed to produce "N" number of ribs.

2.5D NESTING

Like 2D nesting, in 2.5D nesting, parallel cutting planes are employed to create nested stacks. This method accommodates both subtractive and additive three-axis tools. Unlike the previous method, when using a subtractive tool in the 2.5D approach, there is no limitation to working solely with thin sheet materials or employing a tool that exclusively cuts materials vertically. This method can be applied to thicker materials to maintain a precise volume profile and geometry when cutting materials at various angles. Ideal subtractive tools for this purpose are those capable of cutting material in a linear form, such as a waterjet, diamond wire saw, wire EDM, chainsaw, plasma arc, or hotwire cutter. The 2.5D nesting method can easily be employed by 3D printers to minimize the need for temporary supports or scaffolding. Whether utilizing subtractive or additive fabrication tools, the tops and bottoms of stacked pieces remain parallel. The sides of nested pieces can incorporate projected and protruded parts, facilitating the creation of an interlocked assembly with male and female connectors.

In the 2.5D nesting method, it is important to quickly analyze the overall volume geometry to determine whether it is closed or open. A closed volume such as a cone, cylinder, or sphere is fully enclosed, comprised of an unbroken surface with a continuous boundary. In contrast, an open volume such as a shell has free border edges that do not shape an enclosed space. Within a closed volume, nested components can configure a compact centric stack, where the outer side of one component shapes the inner side of its adjacent counterpart. In an open volume, however, the stacks are no longer centric and the components are positioned side by side.

In a closed volume, it is crucial to focus on the Gaussian curvature (Wikipedia: Gaussian curvature 2024) or surface curvature at a given point. When the Gaussian curvature of the volume shifts from positive to negative or the surface transforms from concave to convex in a specific area, it becomes essential to divide the volume at that area of change. This division creates separate nested stacks for each sub-volume. Without this division, a proper thickness will not remain for the nested components located in the changing area. When dealing with a closed volume, it is crucial to design the nested pieces for easy slicing, without any collisions. Paying attention to the overall volume geometry will assure that all components can be moved smoothly out of the stack.

3D NESTING

As explained above, in both the 2D and 2.5D nesting methods, parallel cutting planes are utilized to slice a volume and create stackable components for fabrication, transportation, and storage. However, in the 3D nesting method, the cutting planes deviate from a parallel positioning. These cutting planes can be rotated along the X-, Y-, and Z-axes, and combinations thereof. As a result, the components are arranged consecutively, forming stacks without parallel sides. Depending on the angles of the cutting planes, the top and bottom sides of the stack may exhibit similar or different angles. Moreover, the height and orientation of the nested components in the stacks will vary based on the angles of the cutting planes.

The 3D nested pieces have at least one tapered and wedge-like side. By strategically positioning the cutting planes to enhance the structural stability of the geometry, these tapered sides can be tailored to fit together and create a curved surface, reflecting the characteristics of voussoirs in arch structures. The nested pieces being of adequate thickness is crucial for effectively dispersing forces and allowing for the efficient transfer of the vertical load to adjacent pieces. The intentional arrangement and angles of these tapered sides play a pivotal role, not just in improving structural integrity but also in enhancing the aesthetics of the final form.

Exploring Fabrication Possibilities in a Nested Assembly

Nesting Fabrication is a strategy for creating the primary components of a building or generating substrates for casting such elements. To accomplish this objective, both subtractive and additive fabrication processes can be employed to craft nested pieces for double-curved geometry.

Subtraction

The use of subtractive digital fabrication tools has become common in the last two decades (de Soto et al 2018). When using a subtractive tool with a line-form cutting device, instead of individually carving out each piece and generating substantial waste, a single block of material can be sliced through sequential cuts in predefined directions, thus creating a nested assembly. In contrast to a CNC router, which generates a significant amount of waste and dust to achieve a desired form, the use of tools such as waterjets, plasma arcs, hotwires, wire EDMs, diamond wire saws, and chainsaws can result in cutting less material, almost equal to the width of the cutting kerf. Additionally, these tools contribute to faster and more efficient production of required pieces as compared to CNC milling, which typically requires considerable time to achieve refined surface finishes. Whether employing electro-, chemically-, or mechanically-reductive processes, the linearity of the cutting device results in fabricated pieces characterized by ruled surfaces generated by multiple straight lines. Depending on the fabrication tool, the use of a non-linear cutting device with a specific curvature can be viable. Another option is the development of a cutting device with the ability to alter its geometry through pushing or pulling, thereby extending beyond ruled surfaces.

Moreover, there is no need to provide a massive block to create larger nested pieces. Smaller blocks can be used to produce portions of the nested pieces. Preserving the geometry of these smaller blocks during subtractive processes allows for easy connection and the formation of larger nested pieces. Instead of using subtractive tools to make entire nested pieces from a block of material, an alternative approach is to create only the shared surfaces between two adjacent pieces. These surfaces can be placed inside a box to make a formwork for casting the required pieces that use the appropriate material. Post-casting, these surfaces can either be detached from the pieces or retained on one or both sides.

Addition

Additive manufacturing processes offer significant potential for sustainable construction. Beyond waste reduction, these processes typically require equipment smaller in size than that which is used in subtractive manufacturing. One drawback of using subtractive tools in Nesting Fabrication is the necessity of working on a block of material, ranging from a thin plywood sheet in 2D nesting to a thick 4'–8' polystyrene foam block in 2.5D and 3D nesting. Handling such blocks can be challenging. In contrast, additive processes eliminate the need to manage block materials and fabrication tools larger than the block itself.

Nesting Fabrication facilitates the printing of intricate, large-scale geometries that feature significant overhangs, eliminating the need for temporary scaffolds or supports during the printing phase. This innovative approach enhances the sustainability of 3D printing by optimizing materials use and minimizing waste. The principles underlying Nesting Fabrication expand the application of fresh cementitious or clay materials beyond paste printing, such that pieces within a nested stack support one another throughout the printing process. This interdependency enables lower pieces to support upper ones and side pieces to uphold those adjacent, thereby minimizing waste and reducing the need for post-processing to clean up the final product. This inherent mutual support in the nested arrangement facilitates the creation of more complex geometries in the following ways.

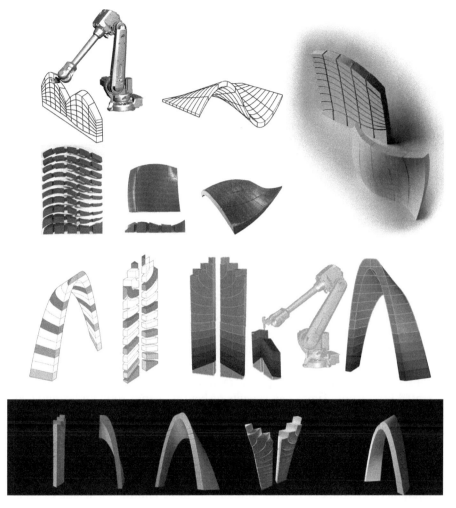

Figure 6.4.2   PRINT on PRINT: 3D-printed freeform building components in concrete or clay without temporary support, using lower pieces for upper fabrication. (Credit to Alireza Borhani).

PRINT on PRINT:

This method involves creating nested pieces in a vertical stack, where the lower pieces support the upper ones during printing. In such a nested stack, the relationship between the lower sides of the upper pieces and the upper sides of the lower pieces makes it easy to use the lower printed pieces as a substrate for depositing layers of the upper pieces. Depending on the geometry of the first piece in the stack, it may be necessary to also print temporary supports to hold the stack in place (Figure 6.4.2).

PRINT in PRINT:

Having nested components arranged horizontally side by side presents an opportunity for the inner parts of the left pieces in the stack to support the outer parts of the right pieces. To achieve a more successful outcome and minimize the necessity for any additional printed support for the stack's beginning or end pieces, it is beneficial to pay attention to the overall slope of the nested pieces. The direction and extent of overhangs determine whether printing from the inside to the outside or the outside to the inside will provide better support via the adjacent printed pieces.

Benefits of Nesting Fabrication

There are several noteworthy advantages to 2D, 2.5D, and 3D nesting, the three approaches that can be used to create stacked nested pieces. Such advantages include the reduction of materials waste, decreased production time, lower transportation costs, and minimal storage space requirements.

1 **Reduced Materials Waste:** As all constituent components of the original volume are stacked in a nested fashion, they inherently support themselves during fabrication. Whether using subtractive or additive methods, working on pieces with unusual overhangs or vulnerable features becomes more feasible because the back side of one piece is either partially or entirely in contact with the front of its neighboring piece. When employing a 3D-printing technique, the neighboring pieces can serve as temporary scaffolding to support the printed layers, eliminating the demanding task of removing breakable or dissolvable scaffolding parts. Moreover, preserving the temporary scaffolding material used in large 3D-printed pieces is a step toward more sustainability. Utilizing neighboring pieces as scaffolding is particularly advantageous in paste printing with clay or concrete, where the challenge of removing scaffolded parts is not comparable to the ease of removing relatively weak plastic materials from typical desktop printers.

2 **Decreased Production Time:** The benefits of Nesting Fabrication go beyond conserving materials during the production of individual pieces.

2.1- In subtractive methods, Nesting Fabrication not only saves substantial material but also significantly reduces machining time, as well as the time required for loading, setup, unloading, and handling. When employing a CNC router for 2D nesting or a waterjet, chainsaw, or hotwire for 2.5D or 3D nesting, each cutting operation simultaneously shapes the front side of one piece and the back side of its adjacent counterpart. In other words, each set of three cuts results in two completed pieces. When compared to the production of non-nested pieces, where more cutting operations are necessary to manufacture each piece, the adoption of Nesting Fabrication accelerates the production pace, leading to a notable reduction in overall project expense.

2.2- In additive methods, the approach avoids the need to print temporary scaffolding parts, saving time and enhancing efficiency. By printing multiple pieces in a stacked fashion and eliminating scaffolded parts, wear and tear on the printer is reduced and its lifespan is increased. This not only reduces maintenance costs but also decreases the number of printers required and their overall footprint.

5 **Lower Transportation Costs:** Compared to pieces manufactured using other fabrication methods, nested stacks can be shipped more economically, requiring fewer logistical trips to transport pieces from one place to another. Shipping pieces in their stacked configuration reduces the risk of loss during transportation. The stacked arrangement also assists the assembly crew in recognizing the order of pieces, making it easier to locate them without constant reference to labels.

6 **Minimal Storage Space Requirements:** In addition to reducing fabrication waste and machining time through the creation of compact stacks, Nesting Fabrication offers another advantage: a decrease in the storage space required. As the pieces are produced side by side, they naturally occupy less space before assembly. If the nested pieces are designed for disassembly, they can easily return to their original stacked configuration, avoiding the need for extra storage space.

Nested Structures in Practice

To examine how the principle of nesting operates, three structures were made using subtractive and additive tools: two nested vaults and one nested column.

NESTED VAULTS

During their residency at the Autodesk Technology Center in Boston, faculty from Texas A&M University created two self-standing interlocking vaults with 3D nested components (Borhani and Kalantar 2020, 2021). The objective was to explore the feasibility of constructing a lightweight disaster relief structure that could quickly be assembled and disassembled without the need for tools and scaffolding. Using two single blocks of expanded Polystyrene measuring 4' × 4' × 3', two 18' tall arches were produced that featured both circular and oval sections. These two shapes were selected to investigate how their geometry influences the fabrication process and final structural integrity. To enhance stability and expand the structures' footprint, the arches' geometry transitioned from a V-shaped piece at their bottom to a flat piece at the highest point. Employing a track-mounted ABB 4600 industrial robot arm equipped with a hotwire end effector, each single block underwent 16 successive cuts. The result was 15 nested pieces and minimal waste, as all side edges aligned within the block boundary. Leveraging the interlocking features of the nested pieces, each structure was assembled in approximately 20 minutes by five people, without the need for scaffolding or tools. Since all pieces were created from a single block, the assembly process was straightforward and did not require the use of labels to identify the pieces. Each of these 18' arches transformed into a compact 4' × 4' × 3' block, easily loaded into a FedEx truck. Thanks to the compact nature of the disassembled pieces, they could be stored on the Texas A&M campus before being reassembled (Figure 6.4.3).

NESTED COLUMN

Another project that exemplifies the potential of Nesting Fabrication was a tower-like column created by a robotic 3D printer. Based on the principles of 2.5D nesting, the column was constructed from cone-like ring pieces that formed a centric stack. Employing the PRINT in PRINT method, the nested pieces were designed such that the inner parts of the wider pieces were supported by the outer sides of their narrower neighboring pieces. Developed by Mehdi Farahbakhsh during his doctoral work at Texas A&M, this project offered the opportunity to create removable and sustainable formwork for casting nested pieces out of concrete (Farahbakhsh et al. 2021). After finalizing the geometry of the nested pieces, only the outer layers were printed with clay as formworks. Subsequently, once the clay skins set, the space between them was filled with concrete. Then, the concrete solidified and the clay layers were dissolved in water. At that time, the nested pieces were ready for the final assembly. To achieve

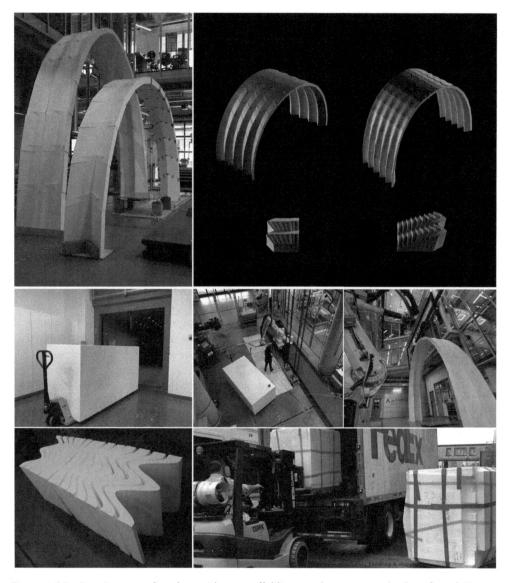

Figure 6.4.3 Erecting nested arches without scaffolding to demonstrate the benefits of Nesting Fabrication. (Credit to Alireza Borhani).

more precise nested pieces and a continuous structure, the clay skin layers were printed in two separate sets. This project showcases how a small fabrication tool such as the ABB IRB 1200 robot can be used to produce a structure four times larger than itself. Additionally, the pieces could be returned to a nested stack and transported by an SUV in a single trip. Utilizing clay as a reusable material for formwork introduces endless possibilities for creating nested pieces from robust and homogeneous materials such as concrete, ceramic, plaster, etc. These structures can be post-tensioned after assembly, with the option of being detached and recycled when needed (Figure 6.4.4).

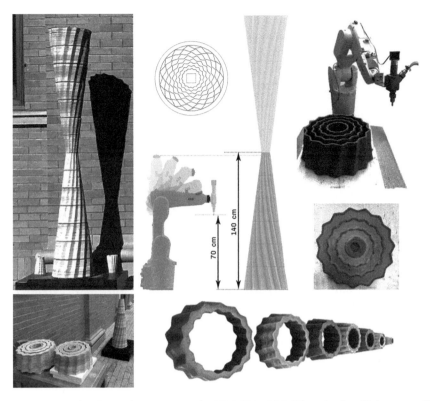

Figure 6.4.4 A nested column demonstrates the PRINT in PRINT method, utilizing a smaller tool for making larger elements. Designed by Mehdi Farahbakhsh.

Discussion

In addition to minimizing materials waste, reducing fabrication time, optimizing storage space, and decreasing the frequency of transportation trips required for shipping, Nesting Fabrication makes significant contributions to construction in two ways:

1 Using existing tools to minimize the need for larger machines.
2 Producing smaller nested components for larger tessellated building shells.
   Using Existing Tools to Minimize the Need for Larger Machines: Historically, most digital fabrication methods in construction have drawn inspiration from manufacturing processes in which the size of the production tool typically exceeds that of the product. In manufacturing, tool tolerance, accuracy, and speed all align with expected outcomes. However, when these tools are employed in construction, their sizes and operational speeds often fail to meet the demands of the project's scale and delivery timeframe. Recent advancements in construction technologies, including robotics and 3D printing, have fueled a competition to develop increasingly larger tools capable of operating on a building scale. For example, in the field of concrete printing, there is a growing trend of enlarging printers to print entire building structures. An example of such a machine is the large-scale gantry 3D printer,

which typically surpasses the size of a massive building to enable outside-in printing. Nevertheless, creating such gigantic tools with the necessary level of tolerance for acceptable surface finish requires substantial capital investment and engineering effort. Moreover, the inability to easily disassemble such a large machine at one construction site and set it up in another location, along with the associated time, manpower, and cost, present significant challenges. While recognizing the considerable time and energy invested in the creation of these machines and addressing numerous challenges, these printers currently can only print buildings of two or three stories. Thus, a key question arises: how much larger should these printers be made to accommodate the construction of 5-, 10-, or 15-story buildings? Moreover, could we explore the possibility of printing a building inside-out and using a smaller tool, rather than defaulting to making ever-larger and bulkier machines? Alternatively, what if we utilized existing precise fabrication tools to construct non-monolithic buildings from assembled pieces, rather than investing significant resources in creating a potentially less accurate but larger tool? Nesting Fabrication is a method that uses smaller equipment to fabricate larger objects, while also making use of existing subtractive or additive tools. Since a building shell comprises tessellated pieces nested together, with this approach, the need to manufacture more extensive fabrication equipment is significantly reduced.

Producing Smaller Nested Components for Larger Tessellated Building Shells: Buildings have traditionally been assembled from numerous pieces arranged to meet specific expectations. Even in so-called monolithic structures, practical constraints such as material size, the limitations of fabrication tools, and transportation capabilities necessitate constructing these structures from multiple parts. Along with addressing the required tolerance and precision, the concept of assembly has been integral to establishing centuries of construction practices. Technological advancements and the ability to produce prefab components offsite allow for larger component sizes with fewer joints. As discussed above, the advent of large-scale 3D printers has enabled the creation of entire building shells as monolithic pieces. While this offers several advantages to the construction industry, challenges may arise in repairing large, defective pieces and transporting them back to the site for replacement. While larger pieces facilitate faster building construction and require fewer joints vulnerable to external and internal forces, careful thought should be given to the adaptability of such construction processes and the ultimate expense. Scaling up the size of building components requires careful consideration of the dimensions of fabrication tools and their designated spaces. In the context of offsite fabrication, attention must be directed toward factors such as the frequency of trips required to transport components to the site, facilities for loading and unloading, storage space, and the development of a secure method for handling and transporting elements to the final assembly location. Nesting Fabrication is a versatile method capable of generating a building shell from a variable number of tessellated pieces. The most appropriate and desirable size of these nested pieces is determined by subdividing the shell based on the material, tools, and space provided for production, transportation, and installation. Even with the creation of large components, there is no need to ship individually or dedicate a truck to transport limited oversized pieces. The ability to transport a stack of fabricated pieces in a single trip will reduce overall project cost and promote more sustainable construction practices.

Conclusion

For over two decades, the increasing adoption of digital technology in the AEC industry has shown that digital fabrication is more complex than creating a CAD drawing file and sending it to a production machine (Hnin 2022). Both in terms of quantity and quality, the construction of digitally driven buildings underscores the need for ongoing demand, research development, and capital investment. This is essential to the production of large-scale geometrically complex pieces at a reasonable cost and efficient use of resources. Unfortunately, this is one area in which the AEC industry has been lacking.

When encouraging the use of digital fabrication in construction, beyond asking how fast, how well, or at what cost a building can be made, we need to emphasize how wasteless construction can be. The authors hope that this research contributes to the introduction of more resources dedicated to this cause. By dividing the global geometry of a freeform surface into stackable pieces, Nesting Fabrication serves as a means of seamless integration of appearance with the performance of the final construction. Nesting Fabrication is a pioneering effort toward establishing more sustainable construction practices that minimize waste while also addressing various factors such as formal complexity, fabrication techniques, materials preferences, assembly and disassembly methods, and transportation and storage considerations. This approach is shaped by both the constraints and opportunities inherent in these various elements.

References

Abdelmohsen, S., & Hassab, A. (2020). A computational approach for the mass customization of materially informed double curved façade panels. In 25th International Conference on Computer-Aided Architectural Design Research in Asia, CAADRIA 2020. The Association for Computer-Aided Architectural Design Research in Asia (CAADRIA), Chulalongkorn University, Bangkok, Thailand, 163–172.

Agustí-Juan, I., & Habert, G. (2017). Environmental design guidelines for digital fabrication. *Journal of Cleaner Production*, 142, 2780–2791.

Agustí-Juan, I., Müller, F., Hack, N., Wangler, T., & Habert, G. (2017). Potential benefits of digital fabrication for complex structures: Environmental assessment of a robotically fabricated concrete wall. *Journal of Cleaner Production*, 154, 330–340.

Arora, S. K., Foley, R. W., Youtie, J., Shapira, P., & Wiek, A. (2014). Drivers of technology adoption—The case of nanomaterials in building construction. *Technological Forecasting and Social Change*, 87, 232–244.

Bertollini, V. (2018) Here's what building the future looks like for a 10-billion-person planet. https://www.autodesk.com/design-make/infographics/building-the-future

Bock, T. (2015). The future of construction automation: Technological disruption and the upcoming ubiquity of robotics. *Automation in Construction*, 59, 113–121.

Borhani, A. & Kalantar, N. (2020). *Interlocking Shell, Transforming a Block of Material into a Self-Standing Structure with No Waste*. ACADIA, 226–231.

Borhani, A. & Kalantar, N. (2021). *Nesting Fabrication, Using Minimum Material & Production Time to Deliver Nearly Zero-Waste Construction of Freeform Assemblies*. ACADIA, 318–327.

Craveiro, F., Duarte, J. P., Bartolo, H., & Bartolo, P. J. (2019). Additive manufacturing as an enabling technology for digital construction: A perspective on Construction 4.0. *Automation in Construction*, 103, 251–267.

de Soto, B. G., Agustí-Juan, I., Hunhevicz, J., Joss, S., Graser, K., Habert, G., & Adey, B. T. (2018). Productivity of digital fabrication in construction: Cost and time analysis of a robotically built wall. *Automation in Construction*, 92, 297–311.

Enrique, L., Cepaitis, P., Ordoñez, D., & Piles, C. (2016). CASTonCAST: Architectural freeform shapes from precast stackable components. *VLC Arquitectura. Research Journal*, 3(1), 85–102.

European Commission (2019). Clean energy for all Europeans package. https://energy.ec.europa. eu/topics/energy-strategy/clean-energy-all-europeans-package_en#:~:text=The%20package%20 includes%20a%20robust,NECPs)%20for%202021%2D30.

European Union (2012). Ecodesign your future - Publications Office of the European Union. https:// op.europa.eu/en/publication-detail/-/publication/4d42d597-4f92-4498-8e1d-857cc157e6db

Farahbakhsh, M., Borhani, A., Kalantar, N., & Rybkowski, Z. (2021). PRINT in PRINT: A nested robotic fabrication strategy for 3D printing dissolvable formwork of a stackable column. In *International Conference on Computer-Aided Architectural Design Futures* (pp. 317–328). Singapore: Springer Singapore.

Ferriss, L. (2020). *The New Net Zero*. Boston Society for Architecture. https://www.architects.org/ news/the-new-net-zero

Giesekam, J., Barrett, J. R., & Taylor, P. (2016). Construction sector views on low carbon building materials. *Building Research & Information*, 44(4), 423–444.

Hnin, T. (2022). The role of fabrication in construction industry and its significance. https://www. novatr.com/blog/fabrication-in-construction-industry

IEA and UNEP (2018). *Global Status Report 2018: Towards a Zero-Emission, Efficient and Resilient Buildings and Construction Sector*. http://www. ren21.net/status-of-renewables/ global-status-report/.

Iwamoto, L. (2013). *Digital Fabrications: Architectural and Material Techniques*. Princeton Architectural Press.

Kolarevic, B. (2003). *Architecture in the Digital Age: Design and Manufacturing*, London: Taylor & Francis Group, 59.

Kongboon, R., Gheewala, S. H., & Sampattagul, S. (2022). Greenhouse gas emissions inventory data acquisition and analytics for low carbon cities. *Journal of Cleaner Production*, 343, 130711.

Kristen, F. & Taron, J. (2019). *Waste Ornament: Augmenting the Visual Potency of Sustainable Facade Designs*. ACADIA, 90–99.

Kudless, A. (2010). *Zero/Fold Screen*. https://www.matsys.design/zero-fold-screen/

Lavery, C. (2013). Spencer dock bridge. *Concrete International*, 35(6), 28–31.

Liebringshausen, A., Eversmann, P., & Göbert, A. (2023). Circular, zero waste formwork-Sustainable and reusable systems for complex concrete elements. *Journal of Building Engineering*, 80, 107696.

Meng, Q., Hu, L., Li, M., & Qi, X. (2023). Assessing the environmental impact of building life cycle: A carbon reduction strategy through innovative design, intelligent construction, and secondary utilization. *Developments in the Built Environment*, 16, 100230.

Pinkse, J. & Dommisse, M. (2009). Overcoming barriers to sustainability: an explanation of residential 673 builders' reluctance to adopt clean technologies. *Business Strategy and the Environment*, 18, 515–527.

Povilas, C., Enrique, L., Ordoñez, D. & Piles, C. (2011). *Towards Waste-Free Concrete Fabrication Without Conventional Molds*. Holcim Foundation. https://www.holcimfoundation.org/about/ news/awards/towards-waste-free-concrete-fabrication-without-conventional-mol

Resch, E., Lausselet, C., Brattebø, H., & Andresen, I. (2020). An analytical method for evaluating and visualizing embodied carbon emissions of buildings. *Building and Environment*, 168, 106476.

United Nations, Department of Economic and Social Affairs (2017). *World Population Prospects 2050*. https://www.un.org/en/desa/world-population-projected-reach-98-billion-2050-and-112-billion-2100.

Wikipedia (2024). *Gaussian Curvature*. Wikimedia Foundation, last modified 13 March, 2024. https://en.wikipedia.org/wiki/Gaussian_curvature

Zuuk, R. (2016). *Re-Settle Studio*. https://www.renevanzuuk.nl/re-settlestudio

6.5

HUMAN-ROBOT RECONFIGURATIONS

Advancing Feminist Technoscience Perspectives for Human-Robot-Collaboration in Architecture and Construction

Gili Ron, Thomas Wortmann,
Cordula Kropp and Achim Menges

Abstract

The integration of robots in the construction industry is an important requirement for urgently needed improvements in productivity and sustainability. This integration requires new perspectives on human-robot collaboration (HRC) to retain skilled staff and support skills and decision-making while considering conditions on-site. This chapter reflects on HRC for prefabrication and construction from the perspective of feminist technoscience, a transdisciplinary field offering distinct ways of thinking about society, technologies, bodies, power, and the environment. Specifically, the chapter proposes new perspectives on agents, agency, and collaboration. Applied to HRC, these perspectives can for example imply (1) situated interfaces supporting multi-agent collaborations of skilled workers and robots, (2) human training of robots on how to adapt to changing conditions and uncertainties on-site enabled by machine learning, and (3) collaborative prefabrication and construction processes supporting on-the-fly design decisions. Such approaches reconsider "agency" as a collaborative unit of human and non-human agents and foster trust and sensible task distribution for improved efficiency in fabrication.

Introduction

The construction industry suffers from a significant and persistent shortage of skilled workers and a high employee turnover, resulting in low productivity and quality. This problem is exacerbated by supply-chain vulnerabilities: rising material and energy costs, escalating inflation, transport bottlenecks, and geopolitical uncertainties. Consequently, the industry fails to meet an ever-growing demand in the building sector (United Nations Environment Programme, 2022).

DOI: 10.4324/9781003384113-72

These disruptions advance an embracing of cyber-physical systems, specifically robotic arms and cobots ("collaborative robots"): to optimize production chains (Liao et al., 2017), increase productivity, and improve worker safety (Hermann et al., 2016).

Robotic fabrication in prefabrication and construction has been researched for two decades, advancing design-customization, bespoke fabrication methodologies, and accessible interfaces for novice users (Knippers et al., 2021). Despite its accord in academic research, robotic fabrications' adoption in prefabrication and construction is sluggish. Reported challenges include inaccessibility, low resilience to uncertainties, lack in worker safety, and lack of trust in automation (Weiss et al., 2021), resulting in overall decreased productivity (Kumar et al., 2021).

In light of the preceding, robotic fabrication in prefabrication and construction is transforming from fully automated to collaborative processes, where human intelligence works alongside advanced technology and artificial intelligence (AI). Similarly, academic research sees a rise in interest in human-robot collaboration (HRC) processes and a paradigm shift from "Industry 4.0" to "Industry 5.0" (Machado & Davim, 2023).

HRC aims to improve automations' implementation by combining complementary strengths of humans and robots, namely, knowledge, agility, ingenuity, and communication skills; and precision, stamina, and digital interconnectivity, respectively (Javaid et al., 2021). To face a growing employee shortage and rising market demands in the prefabrication and construction industry, HRC design must improve efficiency, reduce costs, and support current and future employees employed demographics. This includes supporting tasks, work routine, decision-making, and matching the needs of new and diverse demographics (Müller et al., 2018). But, how?

Feminist technoscience perspectives (FTS) merit engaging with the needs of a diverse demographic when designing technologies. Fields like architecture and design, but also computer science, human-computer interaction, and critical data studies use FTS perspectives to manifest an ethical practice and an activist research and design stance. FTS for HRC in prefabrication and construction has potential to animate an inclusive, diverse, and democratic use of technology.

In this chapter we ask: can FTS critique retain skilled staff and introduce new and diverse demographics into the industry, considering the relationship between productivity to safety, trust and accessibility? Furthermore, what conceptual framework should be considered to promote: (1) feelings of trust and safety with technology, (2) adaptation to tasks and site conditions, (3) inclusive and sensible task distribution, and (4) user feedback?

This chapter lays the foundations of FTS critique to support the design of HRC in contemporary architectural research. Our aim is to raise questions about the decisions we make as designers: design digital technologies in tune with users' needs, raise awareness of the inclusivity of our designs and our own biases, and advance equitable futures. The chapter commences presenting FTS and its relevance for design practices. It proceeds with a theoretical framework for FTS, encompassing four key concepts: Embodiment, Reconfiguration, Interrelations, and Participation. Each concept includes reflexive questions to raise designers' attention to issues of inclusivity and design bias in HRC for prefabrication and construction. The subsequent section outlines how ongoing research at the Cluster of Excellence "Integrative Computational Design and Construction" (IntCDC) contributes to these objectives. We culminate with a description of our ongoing research in HRC design, for a diverse demographic (Figure 6.5.1).

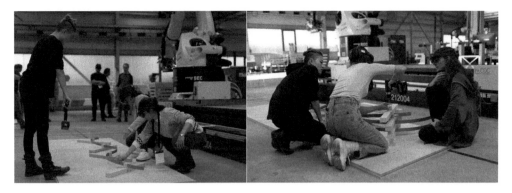

Figure 6.5.1   Instructive HRC and multi-actor task sharing in timber prefabrication. A user study in multiple-agent collaboration with head-mounted AR-devices in the prefabrication environment, conducted by ICD researchers Aimée Sousa Calepso and Xiliu Yang (RP04). The user study was part of the IntCDC Cluster of Excellence Advance AEC Autumn School, at the University of Stuttgart, 2022. Integrating human craft, industrial robots, and augmented reality as collaborative actors and create a highly adaptive prefabrication setup, suitable for the demands of project-based building elements production in the AEC environment.

Source: Aimée Sousa Calepso (2022).

Theoretical Framework

In this section, we present feminist technoscience (FTS), and the role of FTS critique in HRC design. We then elaborate on four FTS and their reflexive questions, namely, Embodiment, Reconfiguration, Interrelations, and Participation. Importantly, the method of reflexive questions is perceived as an assisting instrument for design practices: aimed to raise awareness during the design process and to navigate HRC design toward equitable futures.

FTS is a transdisciplinary field that offers distinct ways of thinking about society, technologies, bodies, power, and the environment (Åsberg, 2010). Evolving from feminist critiques, it concerns the entanglements of gender and society with science and technology. FTS critique reflects on equal access to technology (Wajcman, 2004), inclusivity, and biases in design (Suchman, 2006), accounting for the mal-effects of technology and its ethical accountabilities (Rosner, 2020; D'Ignazio & Klein, 2020).

FTS critiques' relevance to HRC is firstly as a domain concerned with human aspects, and secondly as an established paradigm already employed in related fields such as design and architecture human-computer interaction, human-robot interaction (Bardzell, 2010), and AI design (Zimmerman et al., 2022). FTS critique is used in the aforementioned fields, to account for systemic power and bias, bias in datasets, design inclusivity, and participatory design processes (Young, 2020; D'Ignazio & Klein, 2020; Winkle et al., 2023).

Employing FTS critique in HRC is a straightforward shift from human-computer and human-robot interaction fields. But how can FTS inform HRC in the construction industry, where tacit knowledge prevails, and experience in working with digital tools isn't common?

Alongside a successful, accurate, and efficient fabrication process in HRC, how can FTS relieve worker shortage, and improve workers' feelings of safety and trust with robots?

The following sections extend FTS to facilitate a shift toward unbiased, diverse, and inclusive HRC in the construction industry. Specifically, it proposes new viewpoints on agents, agency, and collaboration to retain skilled staff (support skills and decision-making), consider on-site conditions, endorse sociocultural diversity, and foster trust and safety. The four key concepts discussed are Embodiment, Reconfiguration, Interrelations, and Participation. Chosen from a selection of FTS critique, these concepts are relevant for advancing: (1) adaptation to worker's bodies, senses, and feelings; (2) adapting to worker's needs on-site; (3) agency's redistribution for inclusivity and a sensible task distribution; (4) user-inclusivity in the design process. The key concepts connect and overlap, to promote a diverse, democratic, and inclusive use of technology.

2.1 Embodiment

Embodiment prompts the shaping and modulating of innovations to better fit users' needs and considers their bodies, senses, and feelings relevant to design decisions. Embodiment promotes inclusivity in design by pivoting from a "Universal User" notion and instead seeking to serve people who are well served, current users and future users alike.

> *A timeless and universal stance in cross-cultural design is dangerous because it demotes cultural, social, regional, and national differences in user experiences and outlooks.*
> *(Bardzell, 2010)*

Embodiment – reflexive questions:
1 Who are the users? What are their strengths and viewpoints?
2 What are their barriers, problems, concerns, and needs?
3 How to fit their bodies and perceptions?
4 How to foster their sense of safety and trust?

The reflexive questions' relevance is in sensitizing designers to: users' preferences relating to skill, tasks, and work routine; and also to their bodies, perceptions, and feelings. As HRC primarily involves the body, it draws attention to diverse bodies and their needs when designing interaction, collaboration, and any supporting interfaces, for example, adjusted displays (text size), adjusted auditory tools, size-suited hand-held devices, and adjusted wearables. Embodiment also draws attention to feelings of safety and trust, for example: distances from the body, duration of interaction (related to concentration and fatigue), and responsiveness to the users and their preferences. HRC should relieve stress and difficulties from the process, and not add to them.

Applying *Embodiment* for HRC in prefabrication and construction means supporting a demographic that has much tacit knowledge and know-how in craft and material but can differ in its levels of technology-affinity. HRC tools and interfaces should enable equal access to varied demographics, providing them control over the process and also over parameters that support their comfort.

Reconfigurations

Reconfiguration examines how technology is used, and how its design and deployment shape the experiences of people who use it. This means to inspect tools, interfaces, and procedures for the actions they enable and disable, and to question their adequacy for users, the task at hand and the work environment.

Technologies take part of our activities and practices and materialize them
(Suchman, 2007)

Reconfiguration-reflexive questions:
1 What are the interfaces, tools, and procedures proposed? Which actions and choices do they enable and disable?
2 Do they fit with the task, environment, routine, and users?
3 Do they augment users and assist in solving challenges? Are we solving an existing or an assumed challenge?
4 Can they adapt to changing conditions?

Reconfiguration-reflexive questions highlight connections between tools, interfaces, and procedures and their effects on task-results and HRC success, worker routine and needs, site-conditions, change, and uncertainty. Importantly, it allows a scrutinized view of technology's necessity, adequacy, and side effects. Unlike human-computer interaction, HRC employs more tools (computer, robot, interface, software, sensors, cameras) making it more difficult to pinpoint factors to success and failure.

Reviewing HRC in prefabrication and construction not only means reviewing tools, interfaces, and processes for increased or decreased efficiency but also relates to what a procedure or tool allows you to do thinking about design fabrication and assembly. To use fabrication as an example means asking: are the tools of HRC supporting an accurate, fast, and clean production of X units, in due time? Can manufacturing take place if: lighting conditions change, a component is missing, a machine breaks down? Are users augmented? Is their routine improved? Is communication, control, supervision satisfactory? What other effects emerge? (Figure 6.5.2).

Figure 6.5.2 Human-guided robotic training for assembly tasks in construction. ITECH Master Dissertation exploring deep reinforcement learning and haptic teaching, to enhance the cobot's autonomous performance for wood joint assembly. Students: Sarvenaz Sardari, Selin Sevim, Pengfei Zhang. Tutors: Samuel Leder, Gili Ron.

Source: Gili Ron (2023).

Interrelations

Interrelations focus on the relationships, interactions, and co-constitutions between different users to inspect tools, interfaces, and procedures. Inspired by Actor-Network Theory (ANT, by Akrich, Callon & Latour; Latour, 2005), it accounts for all humans and non-humans participating in HRC ("agents"), and for their ability for action ("agency"), to evaluate actions, processes, and results and illuminate tendencies, challenges, and responsibilities.

Interrelations-reflexive questions:
1 Are all agents considered for their characteristics, tasks, and needs? Co-productive strengths in a collaboration?
2 Do agents augment each other?
3 Does the task distribution fit with the agent's characteristics, strengths, needs, and co-productive potentials?
4 What relationships and power structures emerge as a result of using the new interfaces, tools, and procedures?

Interrelations' reflexive questions focus on agents' qualities, potentials, and challenges. It is beneficial in illuminating power relations between agents: collaboration, augmentation, dependency, control, etc., and reviewing for beneficial or harmful consequences.

Interrelations relevance for the assessment of HRC in prefabrication and construction is manifold: first, accounting for all existing agents (code, simulative environments, machines, materials, procedures, environment, and people) is helpful in analysing their effects and contributions to successes and failures in a task. Second, in designing new extended agencies for inclusivity: reimagining new agents, agencies, and their collaborations. Linking new demographics previously excluded with tools and interfaces that would match and augment them can increase the number of potential users in fabrication and construction and accommodate varied ages, genders, body types, intelligences, and technological affinities.

Third, accounting for new agents, human and non-human, allows a more sensible task distribution that would cater to the well-being of human workers in workload, fatigue, and safety.

Participation

Participation helps reflect on HRC design decisions taken in the context of inclusivity, stereotypes, and discrimination. It emphasizes the importance of user feedback guiding the design and designing to answer an actual as opposed to an assumed need (Rosner, 2020).

Participation-reflexive questions:
1 How to include people in a participatory design?
2 How to account for their expertise and needs?
3 How can their feedback affect the design process and improve the design?
4 How to protect people's data?

Interrelation relevance for the assessment of HRC in prefabrication and construction is in properly responding to employee shortage and understanding the difficulties of the practice from within: what are the reasons that push people away from the industry? What are the current challenges in workers' routine and the task at hand? What are the difficulties that workers face in the work environment? And how can design solutions better cater to

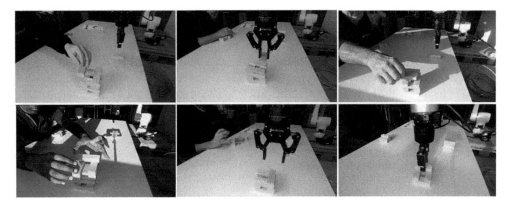

Figure 6.5.3   Human robot collaboration user study with industry partner Müller-Blaustein GmbH, at the IntCDC Large-Scale Robotics Lab (LCRL). A user study of user experience in human robot collaboration empowered with machine learning, studying human' response to close collaboration. Employees of construction company Müller-Blaustein HolzBauWerke GmbH are documented practicing collaborative timber assembly with a cobot.

Source: Gili Ron (2023).

these difficulties? Once these questions are addressed, a new set of questions relating to participatory processes commences, namely, how to cultivate participatory processes in a convenient environment that allows employees access and evaluation of design solutions (Figure 6.5.3).

HRC Research at the Cluster of Excellence IntCDC

This section outlines recent research in HRC at the "Integrative Computational Design and Construction for Architecture" (IntCDC) Cluster of Excellence, at the University of Stuttgart. The IntCDC's research mission explores "co-design as a comprehensive approach for the computational design and construction of buildings, aiming to enhance the efficiency of these processes and minimize material usage" (Knippers et al., 2021). HRC expands this mission in efficient building methodologies using responsive digital design-to-production workflows, while promoting worker's safety and reducing their workload (Weiss et al., 2021). HRC research at the IntCDC focuses on design, fabrication, and assembly tasks, using robotic arms and robots, computers, sensors, displays, tracking, live updates, and feedback. The tools augment skilled workers, technology natives, and novice users. The research encompasses multi-agent collaborations (Vasey et al., 2016; Kyjanek et al., 2019), robotic control with interactive interfaces, and augmented reality (Amtsberg et al., 2021; Amtsberg et al., 2023; Yang et al., 2022), task sharing of heterogeneous agents (Sousa Calepso et al., 2023; Yang et al., 2023; Lauer et al., 2023), and their support with a bespoke data framework (Skoury et al., 2022), and a model-based simulator (Kaiser et al., 2022).

To further link the vast research with current stresses of the fabrication and construction industry, there is room to extend exploration in computational design and construction beyond a focus on process and material efficiency (Boeva et al., 2022). The FTS framework previously introduced begs asking new questions about the necessity of proposed design solutions: do they alleviate existing challenges? Do they foster a positive work environment?

What is their effect on employees over time? Are they endorsed by skilled staff? Can they support future employees and new demographics?

This calls for an in-depth inspection of HRC design not only for stakeholders at current but also potential new users varying in experience, age, and gender; non-human entities like materials and the environment, and technological devices such as computers and robots. As designers in the field of HRC for prefabrication and construction, we challenge ourselves: is the way we conduct research and experimentation inclusive enough to hold and answer these questions?

Designing Inclusive Research in HRC: Thoughts for the Future

Contemplating this, we aim for a future practice where a discourse shared by academia and the industry leads to worldly changes in architecture making, to foster inclusivity in design, design for well-being, avoid biases and potential harms, and bring forth equitable futures. We believe concepts of FTS can lead HRC designers in an ethical, democratic, and inclusive path toward making for the better. Importantly, a careful study of how HRC designs are made and tested is called for. The framework presented highlights a need for stakeholder participation, to discuss feelings of safety and trust with automation, answer existing needs, design for accessibility and diversity, and confront factors yet unknown. This and more, stakeholders' inclusion in the design process preferably starts at an early stage of the design process, to better steer design decisions, and avoid biases from the designers' side that may perpetuate regressive and harmful practices. This leads to new questions about representation in participation and the need to include not only current workers but also consider the demographic of tomorrow. With new technologies constantly emerging, new demographics could participate in prefabrication and construction and contribute in new and meaningful ways. To assess HRC case studies, we ask: what is a task distribution that supports professional knowledge and leads to meaningful contribution? Another aspect illuminated is the length of experimentation in HRC. There is room to consider user studies that continue beyond a single interaction or experimentation, and instead focus on aspects of fatigue and stress – known factors of working with technology. These questions help see the responsibility designers have in making work environments and work conditions satisfying, and future works worth having. Finally, in speculation on future designs, we must leave room for the unknown: inspect interactions and collaboration as they happen to make room for what emerges.

Acknowledgment

This research was supported by the Deutsche Forschungsgemeinschaft (DFG, German Research Foundation) under Germany's Excellence Strategy - EXC 2120/1 - 390831618, and the Stuttgart Research Focus "Interchange Forum for Reflection on Intelligent Systems (IRIS)," funded by the Ministry of Science, Research and Arts Baden-Wuerttemberg Az. 33-7533-9-19/54/5. We thank Dr. Yana Boeva for her involvement at the begining of this research.

References

Amtsberg, F., Yang, X., Skoury, L., Ron, G., Kaiser, B., Sousa Calepso, A., Sedlmair, M., Verl, A., Wortmann, T., Menges, A. (2023) *Multi-Akteur-Fabrikation im Bauwesen: Co-Design-Methoden für eine anpassungsfähigere Vorfabrikation.* Bautechnik. https://doi.org/10.1002/bate.202300070

Amtsberg, F., Yang, X., Skoury, L., Wagner, H., Menges, A. (2021) iHRC: An AR-based interface for intuitive, interactive and coordinated task sharing between humans and robots in building construction. In *Proceedings of the 38th International Association for Automation and Robotics in Construction Conference (ISARC)*, Dubai, UAE. 25–32 https://doi.org/10.22260/ISARC2021/0006

Åsberg, C., Lykke, N. (2010) Feminist technoscience studies. *European Journal of Women's Studies*, 17(4), 299–305.

Bardzell, S. (2010) Feminist HCI: Taking Stock and outlining an agenda for design. In *CHI '10: Proceedings of the SIGCHI Conference on Human Factors in Computing Systems, April 2010*. 1301–1310. https://doi.org/10.1145/1753326.1753521

Boeva, Y., Wortmann, T., Kropp, C., Menges, A. (2022) Architectural computing and design optimization for healthful Ecotopian built environments? In Kanaani, M. (Ed.), *The Routledge Companion on Intelligent Design Paradigms for a Smart Planet: Visions for the Future of Design Culture in Architecture & Urbanism*. New York: Routledge. https://doi.org/10.4324/9781003183181-33

D'Ignazio, C., Klein, L. F. (2020) *Data Feminism*. Boston: The MIT Press. ISBN: 9780262547185

Hermann, M., Pentek, T. and Otto, B. (2016) Design Principles for Industrie 4.0 Scenarios. *Proceedings of 49th Hawaii International Conference on System Sciences HICSS*, Koloa, 5-8 January 2016, 3928–3937. https://doi.org/10.1109/HICSS.2016.488

Javaid, M., Haleem, A., Singh, R. P., Suman, R. (2021) Substantial capabilities of robotics in enhancing industry 4.0 implementation. *Cognitive Robotics*, 1, 58–75. https://doi.org/10.1016/j.cogr.2021.06.001

Kaiser, B., Reichle, A., Verl, A. (2022) Model-based automatic generation of digital twin models for the simulation of reconfigurable manufacturing systems for timber construction. In *Proceedings of the 55th CIRP Conference on Manufacturing Systems*, pp. 387–392. https://doi.org/10.1016/j.procir.2022.04.063

Knippers, J., Kropp, C., Menges, A., Sawodny, O., Weiskopf, D. (2021) Integrative computational design and construction: Rethinking architecture digitally. *Civil Engineering Design*, 3, 123–135. https://doi.org/10.1002/cend.202100027

Kumar, S., Savur, C., Sahin, F. (2021) Survey of human–robot collaboration in industrial settings: Awareness, intelligence, and compliance. *IEEE Transactions on Systems, Man, and Cybernetics: Systems*, 51(1), 280–297. https://doi.org/10.1109/TSMC.2020.3041231

Kyjanek, O., Al Bahar, B., & Vasey, L., Wannemacher, B., Menges, A. (2019). "Implementation of an Augmented Reality AR Workflow for Human Robot Collaboration in Timber Prefabrication." *2019 Proceedings of the 36th ISARC. Banff: The International Association for Automation and Robotics in Construction*. 1223–1230. https://doi.org/10.22260/ISARC2019/0164

Latour, B. (2005) *Reassembling the Social: An Introduction to Actor-Network-Theory*. Oxford and New York: Oxford University Press. ISBN: 9780199256051.

Lauer, A. P. R., Benner, E., Stark, T., Klassen, S., Abolhasani, S., Schroth, L., Gienger, A., Wagner, H. J., Schwieger, V., Menges, A., Sawodny, O. (2023) Automated on-site assembly of timber buildings on the example of a biomimetic shell. *Automation in Construction*, 156, 105118. ISSN 0926–5805, https://doi.org/10.1016/j.autcon.2023.105118.

Liao, Y., Loures, E. R., Deschamps, F., Brezinski, G., Venâncio, A. (2017) The impact of the fourth industrial revolution: A cross-country/region comparison. *Production*, 28, e20180061. https://doi.org/10.1590/0103-6513.20180061

Machado, C. F., Davim, J. P. (2023) *Industry 5.0: Creative and Innovative Organizations*. Ed. Machado, C. F., Davim, J. P., Cham: Springer Nature. pp: v–vii. ISBN 3031262328

Müller, S. L., Shehadeh, M. A., Schröder, S., Richert, A., Jeschke, S. (2018) An overview of work analysis instruments for hybrid production workplaces. *AI & Society*, 33(3), 425–432.

Rosner, D. (2020) *Critical Fabulations: Reworking the Methods and Margins of Design* (1st ed.). Boston, MA: MIT Press. ISBN 9780262542685.

Skoury, L., Amtsberg, F., Yang, X., Wagner, H.J., Menges, A., Wortmann, T. (2022) A framework for managing data in multi-actor fabrication processes. In: Gengnagel, C., Baverel, O., Betti, G., Popescu, M., Thomsen, M.R., Wurm, J. (Eds.), *Towards Radical Regeneration. DMS 2022*. Cham: Springer. https://doi.org/10.1007/978-3-031-13249-0_47

Sousa Calepso, A., Fleck, P., Schmalstieg, D., Sedlmair, M. (2023) Exploring Augmented Reality for Situated Analytics with Many Movable Physical Referents. In *Proceedings of the 29th ACM Symposium on Virtual Reality Software and Technology*. pp 1–12. https://dl.acm.org/doi/pdf/10.1145/3611659.3615700

Suchman, L. (2007) *Human-Machine Reconfigurations: Plans and Situated Actions* (2nd ed.) Cambridge: Cambridge University Press. https://doi.org/10.4018/978-1-61520-813-5

United Nations Environment Programme (2022) *2022 Global Status Report for Buildings and Construction: Towards a Zeroemission, Efficient and Resilient Buildings and Construction Sector.* Nairobi. ISBN: 978–92–807–3984–8

Vasey, L. & Grossman, T., Kerrick, H., Nagy, D. (2016) *The Hive: A Human and Robot Collaborative Building Process.* ACM SIGGRAPH 2016 Talks (SIGGRAPH '16), 1–2. https://doi.org/10.1145/2897839.2927404

Wajcman, J. (2004) *Technofeminism.* Cambridge: Cambridge University Press. Doi: ISBN-13978–0745630441.

Weiss, A., Wortmeier, A. K., Kubicek, B. (2021) Cobots in industry 4.0: A roadmap for future practice studies on human–robot collaboration. *IEEE Transactions on Human-Machine Systems, 51,* 335–345. https://doi.org/10.1109/THMS.2021.3092684

Winkle, K., McMillan, D., Arnelid, M., Harrison, K., Balaam, M., Johnson, I. (2023) Feminist human-robot interaction: Disentangling power, principles and practice for better, more ethical HRI. In *Proceedings of the Conference on Human-Robot Interaction (HRI '23)*, March 13–16, 2023, Stockholm, Sweden. New York: ACM, 11 pages. https://doi.org/10.1145/3568162.3576973

Yang, X., Amstberg, F., Skoury, L., Wagner, H. J., Menges, A. (2022) VIZOR: Facilitating cyber-physical workflows in prefabrication through augmented reality. In *"POST-CARBO": Proceedings of the 27th International Conference of the Association for Computer Aided Architectural Design Research in Asia (CAADRIA)*, Hong Kong, Vol. 2, 141–150. https://doi.org/10.52842/conf.caadria.2022.2.141

Yang, X., Sousa Calepso, A., Amtsberg, F., Menges, A., Sedlmair, M. (2023) Usability Evaluation of an Augmented Reality System for Collaborative Fabrication between Multiple Humans and Industrial Robots. In: *Proceedings of the 2023 ACM Symposium on Spatial User Interaction (SUI '23).* pp. 1–10. https://doi.org/10.1145/3607822.3614528

Young, J (2020) Feminist design tool: Defensible decision making for interaction design and AI. https://ugc.futurelearn.com/uploads/files/16/b0/16b088ad-6145-45eb-b5d8-3753a41b4b88/2-10_FeministDesignTool_2.0.pdf

Zimmerman, M., Bagchi, S., Marvel, J., Nguyen, V. (2022) An analysis of metrics and methods in research from human-robot interaction conferences, 2015–2021. In *Proceedings of the 2022 ACM/IEEE International Conference on Human-Robot Interaction* (HRI '22). Sapporo, Hokkaido, Japan: IEEE Press, 644–648.

CONTRIBUTORS BIO

Michael A. Arbib, FAAAS and FAAAI, building on the development of diverse computational brain models, studied language evolution (*How the Brain Got Language,* OUP 2012) and the role of brains in the experience and design of architecture (*When Brains Meet Buildings*, OUP 2021). He was the founding coordinator of the Advisory Council of the Academy of Neuroscience for Architecture.

Bahar Bagheri is an architect and a researcher. She earned her Master of Digital Architecture in Architectural Technologies and Bachelor of Architectural Engineering both from the University of Tehran. She started doing research and working in the domains of digital fabrication and computational design in 2018. As a tutor and participant, she has contributed to research-based design workshops and design projects. Architectural robotics and material system manufacturing are the main areas of her PhD studies at Texas Tech University.

Ding Wen Bao (Nic), PhD, is a senior lecturer in Architecture and Architecture Technology Course Coordinator at the School of Architecture and Urban Design, RMIT University, where he directs the FormX Research Lab. His research focuses on advanced architecture, computational design, topology optimization, behavioral algorithms, robotic fabrication, and additive manufacturing. Bao is also a practicing registered architect in Australia, the UK, and the US, who is the director of B.W (BWA) Architects and Wonderform Studio and a partner at Ameba Technology.

Hansel Bauman, is the past Campus Architect for Gallaudet University, where he developed the DeafSpace Design Guidelines --a groundbreaking catalog of architectural principles attuned to deaf sensibilities receiving the International Association of Universal Design Gold Award in 2015, published in major design journals and displayed at Smithsonian's Cooper Hewitt Museum, New York.

Joerg Baumeister, Prof. Dr.-Ing. is the director of SeaCities Lab situated at CRI, Griffith University developing water-adapted cities and floating structures as a world-first, highly inter-disciplinary initiative, building on synergies between established disciplines including architecture and design, urban planning, marine biology and engineering, tourism, and data science. He has been a practitioner, educator, researcher, and consultant for Architecture and Urban Design for more than 20 years throughout Europe, Africa, the Arabian Peninsula, Asia, and Australia.

Sander Løkkegaard Benner works within architectural practice, research, and teaching. He is trained as a carpenter, has a bachelor's degree in Architectural Technology, and graduated from the master's program in Architectural Technology at the Royal Danish Academy in June 2023. His focus areas include architectural technology, bio-based materials, design for disassembly, etc.

Frederick Besançon is a licensed architect, landscape architect, and a contributing faculty member at the NewSchool of Architecture and Design. He founded the firm, Connected Studio, with his wife to explore multi-disciplinary topics based out of the San Diego region.

Shajay Bhooshan is an associate director at Zaha Hadid Architects where he co-founded and heads the Computation and Design research group (ZHACODE, 2007). He is an alumnus and a studio master at the post-graduate course of Design Research Laboratory at the Architectural Association, London (AADRL, 2006). Shajay pursued his scientific interests in digital design and robotic fabrication during his doctoral studies at the Block Research Group (BRG, 2022) at the ETH, Zurich, and previously as an M.Phil. graduate from the University of Bath (2016).

Alireza Borhani is an innovator, architect, educator, and co-principal of transLAB. His interdisciplinary experience has broadened his career across a diverse range of projects at the intersection of design computation, emerging material systems, additive manufacturing workflows, and robotics. Leading in kinematic and lightweight structures, ranging from architectural-scale shelters to small products, he has been actively engaged in the field of transformable and adaptive design for the past two decades. At the California College of the Arts and Texas A&M, Alireza has taught architecture studios while simultaneously engaging in research and practice.

William W. Braham, PhD, FAIA, is a professor of Architecture at the University of Pennsylvania where he is Director of the programs in Environmental Building Design. He has worked on energy and architecture for over 40 years as a designer, consultant, researcher, and author of numerous articles and books. His latest book is *Architecture and Systems Ecology: Thermodynamic Principles for Environmental Building Design, in three parts.*

Paul Burton is a professor of Urban Management and Planning and a member of the Cities Research Institute at Griffith University. He trained and worked as a planner in London before joining the University of Bristol and then moving to Griffith University in 2007, where he is currently researching the popularity and regulation of tiny houses.

Silvio Carta is a professor of Architecture at the University of Greenwich, London. Silvio's recent publications include *Big Data, Code and the Discrete City: Shaping Public Realms – Routledge Studies in Urbanism and the City* (Routledge 2019), *Machine Learning* *and the City. Applications in Architecture and Urban Design* (Wiley 2022), and *How Computers Create Social Structure: Accidental Collectives* (Palgrave MacMillan 2024).

Miquel Casals is a full professor and the head of the Department of Project and Construction Engineering at the Technological University of Catalonia (UPC). He is also the leader of the Group of Research and Innovation in Construction (www.gric.upc.edu) and holds wide expertise in RTD activities in buildings and energy-related fields, including a vast number of projects and publications.

Brian Cody is a professor and head of the Institute of Buildings and Energy at Graz University of Technology, founder and CEO of the consulting firm Energy Design Cody, and visiting professor at the University of Applied Arts in Vienna. His focus in research, teaching, and practice is on maximizing the energy performance of buildings and cities.

Marc M. Cohen is a licensed architect who has devoted his career to founding and developing the field of Space Architecture. He has worked for NASA at Ames Research Center as an Aerospace Engineer (26 years), Northrop Grumman Aerospace Systems, and his businesses, Astrotecture®, and Marc M. Cohen, Architect. Marc holds degrees in Architecture from Princeton (A.B.), Columbia (MArch), and Michigan (DArch). He holds eight NASA patents.

Karolina Czumaj is Architect, Lead Architect, and BIM Manager. She holds a master's degree in Architecture at Warsaw University of Technology in 2018. Associated with Kuryłowicz & Associates since 2018, she is coauthor of Polish Antarctic Station, East, Ochota, and Solec Railway Stations on the Warsaw Cross-City Line, office Building "Swobodna Spot" in Wrocław.

James Allen (Jim) Dator, PhD, is Professor Emeritus and former Director of the Hawaii Research Center for Futures Studies, Department of Political Science, University of Hawaii at Manoa; Core Lecturer, Space Humanities, International Space University, Strasbourg, France; Adjunct Professor, Graduate School of Futures Strategy, Korean Advanced Institute of Science and Technology, Daejeon, Korea; and former President, World Futures Studies Federation.

Matias Del Campo, PhD, is a registered architect, designer, and educator. He is an associate professor at the University of Michigan, Director of the AR2IL, the Architecture and Artificial Intelligence Laboratory at UoM, and an affiliate faculty member of Michigan Robotics and MIDAS. He is the cofounder of the architecture practice SPAN, best known for its pioneering efforts in the application of AI in architecture design.

Julia Del Rio is an architect at Gapont Atelier, Liechtenstein, and part of ANFA (Academy of Neuroscience For Architecture)'s Advisory Council, currently pursuing a PhD on the disciplines of Neuroscience and Architecture, focused on how the design of the built environment can be used as a brain training tool to fight cognitive decline associated with dementia (Polytechnic University of Valencia, Spain).

Chris Downey, AIA, is President of Architecture for the Blind. Chris has 20 years of architectural practice. In 2008, he emerged from rehabilitation for total sight loss with unique insights now leveraged in projects for the blind and disabled community. He speaks internationally about disability, teaches with the UCB Department of Architecture, and chairs the California Commission on Disability Access.

Jaymes Dunsmore, AICP, is a senior associate with Gensler. He leads the Gensler Mobility Lab, focusing on transforming the future of cities through design innovation. Jaymes has a master's degree in City Planning from the Massachusetts Institute of Technology and a Bachelor of Arts in History from the University of California, Berkeley.

Elizabeth English, PhD, is Professor of Architecture at the University of Waterloo. Her education, practice, teaching, and research are interdisciplinary, with degrees in Architecture from Princeton and Penn and in Civil Engineering from MIT. She founded and directs the Buoyant Foundation Project (BFP), a non-profit research organization that develops amphibious foundation systems as sustainable low-cost flood mitigation and climate adaptation strategies. The BFP focuses on amphibious retrofit construction. The website is www.buoyantfoundation.org.

Keith Evan Green is a professor of design and mechanical engineering at Cornell University (USA). He addresses the problems and opportunities of an increasingly digital society by developing meticulous, artfully designed, robotic artifacts at a larger scale. For Green, the built environment – furniture to metropolis – is the next frontier of human-machine interaction.

Sue Fairburn is a design educator/researcher focusing on design for/with the body in extreme environments. Her research informs our understanding of how the changing climate yields extreme contexts that challenge our response and inform our resilience. Raised on the dry prairies, Sue now lives in a rainforest.

Ali Farajmandi is an architect who completed a Master's in Advanced Architectural Design from the California College of the Arts (CCA). Specializing in kinetic and transformable design, Ali's passion is creative problem-solving through computational design and digital craft, providing innovative solutions at the intersection of architecture and technology.

Eric Farr, PhD, is currently dedicated to a professorship in architecture and design, with the University of Liverpool, and the academic advisory board of the Design Institute of San Diego. Having undertaken research projects at the intersection of technology and sustainability, his multi- and cross-disciplinary approach is based on the concept of a multi-agent "nature-human-city-architecture-interior-machine" model of collaborative environmental intervention. He believes that every attempt must become nature- and environment-aware, context-, community-, people- and equity-aware, information- and technology-aware, and very soon droids- and virtuality-aware. He has named it "the pillars of our time."

Thomas Fisher is a professor in the School of Architecture and the director of the Minnesota Design Center at the University of Minnesota. He has written 12 books and over 75 book chapters and over 600 journal articles. His newest book, *Space, Structures and Design in a Post-Pandemic World* (Routledge, 2022) addresses the impact that pandemics have had on the built environment.

Harrison Fraker is FAIA Emeritus. After receiving his MArch from Princeton and Cambridge Universities and taught for 15 years at Princeton, he was the founding dean of a new College of Architecture and Landscape Architecture at the University of Minnesota and became the 5th Dean of the College of Environmental Design at UC Berkeley. He is considered a pioneer in climate-responsive architecture and sustainable urban design, an award-winning practitioner, author, and committed teacher. He won the 2014 Topaz Medallion, the highest award in architectural education.

Kristi Gaines, PhD, serves as the Associate Dean in the Graduate School and Professor and Chair in the Department of Design at Texas Tech University. She received her PhD in Environmental Design with collaterals in Architecture and has a combined 20 years of professional design and teaching experience. She is an internationally recognized researcher in designing for autism spectrum and developmental disorders.

Sergei Gepshtein, PhD, is a scientist working in the areas of perceptual psychology and computational neuroscience. He is a member of the Center for the Neurobiology of Vision at the Salk Institute for Biological Studies, where he directs research on Adaptive Sensory Technologies aiming to translate results of basic science for applications in visual technologies, forensic science, and architectural design. In 2018, he established the Center for Spatial Perception and Concrete Experience at the University of Southern California in Los Angeles. He is the Vice President of the Academy of Neuroscience for Architecture.

Carlo Giovannella is Physicist, Expert in complex systems, and Designer for the experience. As President of ASLERD, Giovannella works on the development and benchmarking of Smart Learning Ecosystems, as drivers of social innovation and regional development, together with the dissemination of design literacy. At the University of Tor Vergata for 25 years chaired the ISIM garage, a research lab devoted to the design and development of educational tools and methods, integrated community-based environments for TEL, and smart communities. Carlo Giovannella is Editor-in-Chief of *Interaction Design and Architecture(s) Journal*.

Henry Gordon-Smith is a sustainability strategist with a BA from UBC, and an MSc from Columbia University. Henry specializes in urban agriculture and water. In 2014, he founded Agritecture Consulting, advising on 250+ urban agriculture projects across 40 countries, addressing global needs for technology-agnostic guidance.

Shari G. Grant, DArch, ARA, is an award-winning architect, artist, engineer, and financial analyst. Grant is also Board Member of CA Council SARA American Registered Architects, Recipient of AIA National Award Architecture: Doctor of Architecture, MArch II, AA Engineering: MS, BS, AA (incomplete PhD Operations Research, Finance).

Christiane Margerita Herr is a researcher and educator focusing on intersections of the natural and the artificial in high-density, high-rise urban environments. She is Professor at the School of Design, Southern University of Science and Technology, Shenzhen, and Past President of CAADRIA (Association for Computer-Aided Architectural Design Research in Asia).

Ying Huang received a PhD degree from the Missouri University of Science and Technology in 2012. She is currently Professor at the Department of Civil and Environmental Engineering, at North Dakota State University. Her research interests include intelligent transportation systems, corrosion mitigation and assessment, smart structures, and structural health monitoring.

Margaret Ikeda is an associate professor of Architecture at California College of the Arts (CCA) in San Francisco, California. She is the co-founder and co-director of the CCA Architectural Ecologies Lab that serves as a platform for collaborative research between designers, scientists, and manufacturers.

Barbara Imhof is an internationally recognized space architect, design researcher, and educator. She specializes in architecture for resource-constrained environments. Her diverse work spans from minimal and transformable space design to integrating biological systems into architecture. With a background in architecture and space studies, she collaborates across disciplines, from arts to science and engineering.

Shabtai Isaac is a senior lecturer at the Department of Civil and Environmental Engineering, Ben Gurion University of the Negev, Israel. His research focuses on the development of digital models and tools for planning, constructing, and managing buildings and cities. He is Member of the board of the International Association for Automation and Robotics in Construction and Chair of the Committee for Data Sensing and Analysis at the European Council on Computing in Construction.

Evan Jones is a senior adjunct professor of Architecture at California College of Arts (CCA) and a practicing architect. As Co-Founder and Principal of Assembly, an architecture firm located in Berkeley California, Evan has worked on many scales of projects from furniture and museum installations to landscape planning and multi-story housing projects.

Negar Kalantar, PhD, is an associate professor of Architecture and the co-director of the Digital Craft Lab at California College of the Arts (CCA) in San Francisco. Her research focuses on materials exploration, robotic and additive manufacturing technologies, and the integration of architecture, science, and engineering to address pivotal global issues in the built environment, such as carbon emissions and waste.

Mitra Kanaani is a Fellow of the American Institute of Architects (FAIA) and a Fellow and Distinguished Professor of the Association Collegiate Schools of Architecture (DPACSA). Mitra holds a DArch, with a focus on Performative Architecture, and an MArch, with a minor in Structural Engineering, as well as a Master of Urban Planning and a BA in Musicology. She is the former chair of the NewSchool of Architecture and an active researcher, author, and editor. She is currently on the California Architect Board, a Global Associate faculty with the BIHE, and their liaison with the UIA.

Branko Kolarević is a professor and former dean at the New Jersey Institute of Technology in Newark, USA. He has taught architecture at several universities in North America and Asia and has lectured worldwide on the use of digital technologies in design and production.

His most recent book is *Mass Customization and Design Democratization* (co-edited with Jose Duarte).

Cordula Kropp, Prof. PhD, holds the chair of Sociology of Technology, Risk and Environment at the Institute for Social Sciences and is the director of the Centre for Interdisciplinary Risk and Innovation Research at the University of Stuttgart (ZIRIUS). She is a member of the board of directors at the Cluster of Excellence Integrative Computational Design and Construction for Architecture (IntCDC).

Piotr Kuczyński is an architect associated with Kuryłowicz & Associates since the beginning of his professional activity in 1983, and served as Vice-President, Associate, and Project Manager. Piotr Kuczyński holds a Master's degree in Architecture from the Warsaw University of Technology and is the co-author of major projects including Polish Antarctic Station, Focus Filtrowa Office Centre, Hotel Marriot Courtyard on Chopin Warsaw Airport, Warsaw Underground Station A-17, Department Store Wolf-Bracka "VitKac," Office building "Prosta Tower" in Warsaw, Modlin Airport Terminal near Warsaw, and City Stadium in Białystok.

Ewa Maria Kuryłowicz, PhD and DSC, is an architect and professor of Architectural Studies (1972–1977) at WTU Warsaw, Poland, as well as Iowa State University, USA. Ewa has been a Designer at Kuryłowicz & Associates since 1990, and from 2011–2023; and a General Designer of the Studio from 2011–2023. Ema's selected projects are: Foreign Language Faculties Bldg., University of Warsaw, 2022; Arctowski Polar Station, Antarctica, under construction (2024), National Music Forum in Wroclaw (2016), Sports Stadium in Bialystok (2014), commercial and residential bldgs, and many others. Her research is devoted to universal design, environmental and climatic problems and generally to the issues related to the theory of architecture. She is a member of Polish Academy of Science Architecture and Urban Planning Committee. www.apaka.com.pl

Olga Popovic Larsen is a Professor of Structures and Materials and Head of the Architectural Technology master's program at the Royal Danish Academy in Copenhagen. Her research is applied and explores the crossover between aesthetics and structural/material efficiency, bridging artistic and technological approaches, and contributing to a more sustainable building practice.

Neil Leach is a professor of Architecture at FIU, where he directs the doctor of Design Program. He has also taught at the Architectural Association, Harvard GSD, Columbia GSAPP, Cornell, IaaC, and SCI-Arc. He is the co-founder of DigitalFUTURES, an online educational platform that operates in ten languages; a former researcher for NASA, where he developed 3D printing technologies for the Moon and Mars. He has published over 40 books on architectural theory and digital design and is currently working in artificial intelligence.

Despina Linaraki, PhD, is a Greek/Australian architect engineer, and a lecturer in Architecture at Griffith University. Her research interests lie in the symbiosis between Architecture and Ecology, focusing on climate change adaptation. She holds degrees from Columbia Griffith University, University and the Technical University of Crete.

Eduardo Macagno, Late Professor, was a neuroscientist and Distinguished Professor at the University of California San Diego (UCSD). He was the founding dean of the Division of Biological Sciences in 2001. He was involved in the development of an interface between Neuroscience and Architecture engaged with the Academy of Neuroscience for Architecture and developed courses at UCSD on "Brains and Buildings." His research projects employed biometric devices and virtual reality environments and the interaction of normal and neurologically impaired subjects with the built environment, particularly in the areas of navigation, wayfinding, and spatial memory.

Sandra Manninger, is an architect, researcher, and educator. Born and educated in Austria, she co-founded SPAN Architecture with Matias del Campo in 2003. Her award-winning projects have been published and exhibited internationally, including at La Biennale di Venezia, MAK, and Autodesk Pier 1, and have been included in the permanent collections of the FRAC, Design Museum in Munich, and the Albertina in Vienna. Sandra has taught internationally at TU Vienna, University for Applied Arts, DIA Bauhaus in Dessau, UPenn, Tongji and Tsinghua Universities, the University of Michigan, and the Royal Melbourne Institute of Architecture.

Maryam Mansoori, PhD, is an assistant professor at the School of Design and Construction, at Washington State University. Her interdisciplinary scholarship lies at the nexus of architectural design, and emerging technology to explore innovative design approaches. She specializes in applying advanced materials and geometries to create adaptive architecture – surfaces designed to interact with and respond to their environments.

Asma Mehan, PhD, is a researcher, educator, and architect working on the intersection of architectural humanities and critical urban studies. She is an assistant at Texas Tech University Huckabee College of Architecture and the director of the Architectural Humanities and Urbanism Lab (AHU Lab). Her Publications are *Tehran: From Sacred to Radical* (Routledge, 2022); and *Kuala Lumpur: Community, Infrastructure, and Urban Inclusivity* (Routledge, 2020). She has authored numerous articles on critical urban studies, architecture, urban planning, and heritage studies in scholarly books and journals in multiple languages.

Achim Menges, Prof. AA Dipl. (Hons.) RIBA II, Architect BDA, AKH, is a registered architect in Frankfurt and a full professor at the University of Stuttgart, where he is the founding director of the Institute for Computational Design and Construction (ICD) and the director of the Cluster of Excellence Integrative Computational Design and Construction for Architecture (IntCDC).

Susmita Mohanty is a serial space entrepreneur and space diplomat. She co-founded three space companies between 2001 and 2021. Prior to that, she worked at NASA and Boeing. She now serves as the director general of Spaceport SARABHAI. She is a member of the World Economic Forum Global Future Council for Space Technologies.

Edgar Montejano Hernandez, currently a PhD fellow at Texas Tech University, possesses a master's degree in Architecture. His expertise lies in digital design and robotic fabrication, with a specific focus on advancing the design and manufacturing of lattice structures.

Demonstrating proficiency in various tools, Edgar adeptly integrates academic research with practical experience, fostering interdisciplinary approaches within the architectural domain.

Sina Mostafavi, PhD, is an associate professor at Texas Tech University's Huckabee College of Architecture, focusing on innovative applications of emerging materials and technologies, where he is the director of the Hi-DARS lab. Sina is the founder of the award-winning SETUParchitecture studio. Mostafavi has authored the book *Hybrid Intelligence in Architectural Robotic Materialization*. His projects have been exhibited at global venues, including the Venice Architecture Biennale and Centre Pompidou in Paris. He has held research and faculty positions in the Netherlands, Germany, and the UK.

Stephen Mueller is an associate professor in the Huckabee College of Architecture (HCOA) at Texas Tech University in El Paso, where he is the founding director of POST-Project for Operative Spatial Technologies. Mueller is coeditor of the *Journal of Architectural Education* issue on Deserts and coauthor of *Fronts: Military Urbanisms and the Developing World*.

Anastasia H. Muliana, PhD, is a Linda and Ralph Schmidt Professor of Mechanical Engineering at Texas A&M University. She received her PhD degree in Civil Engineering from Georgia Tech. in 2004. Her research focuses on modeling mechanical responses of hierarchical structures, active materials, and flexible structures.

Dyche Mullins is a professor and chair of the Department of Cellular and Molecular Pharmacology at the University of California San Francisco (UCSF). Work in the Mullins Lab focuses on the assembly and regulation of cytoskeletal networks – collections of molecules that self-assemble into complex structures that enable cells to transport molecular cargoes, change their shape, and propel themselves from place to place.

Robert R. Neumayr, Arch. Dipl.-Ing. Dr. techn. MArch AA Dist., is an architect, researcher, and educator. He studied architecture in Vienna and London and holds a doctoral degree from the University of Applied Arts Vienna. Since 2000 Robert has been researching contemporary digital design practice, focusing on the simulation and optimization of architecture's social performativity. Robert has been teaching and lecturing in Austria and internationally and is currently a lecturer at the Institute of Structure and Design at the University of Innsbruck.

Ibrahim Odeh, PhD, MBA, is a professor and the founding director of the GLCM program at Columbia University. He is a unique combination of a strategist, academic, innovator, and entrepreneur. Odeh provides leading AEC firms with unique market insights, growth strategies, and advice on digital transformation and technological trends that are reshaping the construction industry.

Victor Olgyay, FAIA, is a principal in RMI's buildings practice promoting the adoption of net zero district developments, low embodied carbon materials, and comprehensive building energy retrofits. He is a professor, architect, writer, researcher, daylighting designer, and environmental consultant. His work creates buildings to be part of our climate solution.

Łukasz Piątek, PhD, Arch, is an assistant professor at the Faculty of Architecture, Warsaw University of Technology, and the owner of Kilson Design. He has been reviewing the project of the Rules for the Classification and Construction of Stationary Floating Objects for the Polish Register of Shipping. He co-chaired the International Conference on Amphibious Architecture, Design and Engineering 2019 and 2023 and the World Conference on Floating Solutions 2020. He is a member of the Society of Floating Solutions (Singapore).

Poorang Piroozfar, PhD, is a reader (Senior Associate Professor) in Architectural Technology and Digital Construction at the School of Architecture, Technology and Engineering, University of Brighton where he leads the Digital Construction Lab and BSc (Hons) Architectural Technology and MSc Digital Construction. Informed by systems thinking, Poorang's research is on and around digitality and the digital transformations in the built environment at the intersection of people, information, technology, and the environment.

Tiziana Proietti, PhD, is an architect and educator. She is a professor at the Gibbs College of Architecture of the University of Oklahoma and Director of the Sense-Base Laboratory. Together with Sergei Gepshtein (Salk Institute for Biological Studies), she is developing an interdisciplinary program of research to bridge neuroscience and architecture and to test human response to architectural proportions.

Pierce Reynoldson, AIA, is an AEC technologist and the Vice President of Technology & Innovation at Entech Engineering, PC. He lectures on technology and digital practice across the industry. He also developed and taught the Yale School of Architecture's first fully BIM-enabled class.

Iasef Md Rian is an associate professor of Architecture and member of the Design and Fabrication Lab at Xi'an Jiaotong-Liverpool University in Suzhou, China. His research focuses on fractal geometry, materials exploration, robotic and additive manufacturing technologies, and the integration of architecture, science, and engineering to develop sustainable design through lightweight structures and materials-by-design in the built environment.

Giuseppe Roccasalva, is a chartered architect and engineer, and a professional consultant for different public authorities and municipalities dealing with environmental and landscape assessment design. He was appointed as research manager for supporting the development of EU-funded projects and is an expert evaluator of Solar Impulse Foundation for sustainable concepts and prototypes. He has been a research advisor at Polytechnic of Turin – Faculty of Architecture/Urban Studies, and a consultant for two research centers, SiTI (Higher Institute on Territorial Systems for Innovation) and LAQ-Tip (High-Quality Lab- Territorial Integrated Projects).

Raquel Rodrigues is a graduate of Texas Tech University, where she received her undergraduate and graduate degrees in Interior and Environmental Design. She is currently an MArch graduate student at Boston Architectural College, expected to graduate in December 2026. Her research interests include sustainability, vulnerable populations, and environmental planning.

Gili Ron, MArch, BArch, is a research associate and a doctoral candidate at the Institute for Computational Design and Construction (ICD) and the International Max Planck Research School for Intelligent Systems (IMPRS-IS). Her research interests center on human-robot collaboration and machine learning in co-design and fabrication, and their review from feminist techno-science perspectives.

Nasim Rowshan, (illustrator) has a BArch from BIHE and an MArch from Yale. She is the recipient of the James Gamble Prize, Yale Drawing Prize 2017 as well as the Soan Foundation Fellowship 2018. She worked at Kent Bloomer Studio and Newman Architects in New Haven, Grimshaw Architects in NYC, and Gensler in DC. She is a Global Faculty teaching remote design studio at the Baha'i Institute for Higher Education (BIHE).

Carmina Sánchez-del-Valle is a professor of Architecture in the School of Engineering, Architecture and Aviation at Hampton University. Her efforts have been focused on architectural education with an interest in collaborative creative approaches and cross-disciplinary projects. She has worked on graphic interactive databases mapping historical areas and on kinetic adaptive transformable structures.

Patrik Schumacher is the principal of Zaha Hadid Architects. He studied philosophy, mathematics, and architecture in Bonn, Stuttgart, and London and received his PhD at the Institute for Cultural Science in Klagenfurt. In 1996, he founded the Design Research Laboratory at the AA in London where he continues to teach. Since 2007 he has been promoting Parametricism as an epochal style. In 2010/12, he published *The Autopoiesis of Architecture* in two Volumes theorizing architecture's societal function. His latest book, *Tectonism – Architecture for the 21st Century*, was released in 2023.

Brett Steele is an architect. He was a founder and director of the Design Research Lab and later director of the Architectural Association School of Architecture, in London. He's currently Dean of the UCLA School of the Arts and Architecture. He has been appointed the Della & Harry Macdonald Dean's Chair at the University of Southern California School of Architecture, in Los Angeles. He begins work there in 2024.

Michael Stepner, FAIA FAICP, is a professor emeritus of Architecture and Urban Design and Former dean of the NewSchool of Architecture & Design in San Diego. His professional career spans academia and the public and private sectors. He is the former City Architect and Acting Planning Director for the City of San Diego.

Melissa Sterry, PhD, CSci, FIScT, FDRS, FRSA, is a transdisciplinary design scientist, complex systems theorist, biofuturist, and multi-award-winning serial entrepreneur and innovator. Melissa is known for creating projects that chart unprecedented conceptual, creative, and commercial potentialities. Her current activities include Founder/Director of biofuturism consultancy Bioratorium®, and of Biodesign research and publishing projects Bionic City® and Panarchic Codex®

Bastian Steudel, PhD, studied biology in Goettingen and did his PhD at the universities of Goettingen and Zurich about increasing biomass production in species-rich communities under stress in model experiments using swamp plants and microalgae. Employed as an Assistant Professor at Xi'an Jiaotong-Liverpool University, China, he leads a team performing laboratory experiments with microalgae to disentangle the mechanisms of how species interact.

Tim Stevens, PhD, is a benthic ecologist and senior lecturer at Griffith University. His research focus is the dynamics of reefal systems and habitat mapping for marine conservation planning. He has worked closely with government and NGO agencies in marine protected area design.

Anna Strøe completed her BSc in Cognitive and Brain Sciences from Tufts University in 2018, and her MA in Art and Science from Central Saint Martins, University of the Arts London in 2021. She is currently pursuing a PhD at the Queen Square Institute of Neurology and the Bartlett School of Architecture, UCL, where she is researching and developing eXtended Reality applications for neurorehabilitation of brain injury.

Blanca Tejedor is an assistant professor at the Department of Project and Construction Engineering of the Polytechnic University of Catalunya from since 2021. Her research expertise is focused on the implementation of quantitative infrared thermography for building diagnosis, the assessment of indoor thermal comfort, and the smart management of building facilities. Dr. Tejedor is an officer of the Data Sensing & Analysis (DSA) Committee of the European Council on Computing in Construction (EC3).

Madhu Thangavelu has a background education in Civil Architecture and Astronautical Engineering. He conducts the graduate Space Exploration Architecture Studio in the Department of Astronautical Engineering within the Viterbi School of Engineering and teaches Space Architecture in the School of Architecture at the University of Southern California. He is the author or coauthor of several publications relating to Space Architecture and human space activities. Madhu is on the faculty of the International Space University and an active member of the American Institute of Aeronautics and Astronautics, and on the Board of Directors of the National Space Society and Vice President for NSS India region.

Mark Tholen has been teaching architecture and building technology and has worked as an architect with various award-winning offices in Germany, Canada, the US, and China, involved in large-scale museums to mini-home designs. His teaching and practice are based on a tectonic philosophy with a design-build education focus, embracing thousands of years of traditions in the use of materials and methods of analog construction, from felt making to Japanese wood joinery to current parametric tools and robotic manufacturing.

David Tomber, FAIA, is a recognized expert in the aviation industry with 40 years of public and private sector experience in planning, design, construction, and asset management at over 100 airports worldwide. David Tomber authored over 150 articles and presentations at industry events on various aspects of airport development. As a member of the American Institute of Architects, David Tomber was elected to the College of Fellows FAIA.

Paul Toyne, PhD, C Env., FIMEA, leads the global architecture and design practice Grimshaw on sustainability, overseeing their goals of net zero carbon-ready designs by the end of 2025 and truly sustainable and regenerative designs by 2030. Paul's project experience covers all elements of the built environment, from flagship buildings/developments to infrastructure. He has a PhD in Ecology from Imperial College and has a butterfly named after him.

Hafiz Usman Ahmed received his MS student in Civil and Environmental Engineering at North Dakota State University in 2020. His research interests include intelligent transport systems, traffic modeling, and simulations.

Luis Othón Villegas-Solis has a master's in design studies from Harvard University. He is the director of LVS Architecture in Guadalajara Mexico, and an Advisory Council member of the ANFA Academy of Neuroscience for Architecture. Mr. Villegas-Solis cofounded the Institute of Neuroscience for Architecture and Design in Mexico (INPAD).

Nick Ward is a professor of Clinical Neurology & Neurorehabilitation at UCL Queen Square Institute of Neurology and The National Hospital for Neurology and Neurosurgery, Queen Square. He is the lead of the first dedicated upper limb neurorehabilitation program in the UK. He is Coeditor of the Oxford Textbook of Neurorehabilitation, Deputy Editor of the *Journal for Neurology, Neurosurgery and Psychiatry*, and Associate Editor of *Neurorehabilitation and Neural Repair*. He is Chair of the International Stroke Rehabilitation and Recovery Alliance.

Andy Watts is the director of Design Technology at Grimshaw and leads the practice's global Design Technology team, overseeing digital disciplines such as computational design, BIM, extended reality, urban computation, applications development, and environmental performance. As an architect with a background in computational design, Andy is interested in the problem-solving, regardless of scale or platform. From low-key computational tinkering to digital transformation on a practice scale, his passion lies in making the lives of architects and designers easier through the use of technology.

Andrew Whalley, OBE, BArch (Mackintosh) AA Dipl D.Litt. RIBA FAIA FRSA, has been an instrumental part of Grimshaw since the earliest days of the practice and has been a partner in charge of projects in diverse sectors including education, performing arts, transportation, and workplace. Throughout his career, Andrew has had a passionate interest in Sustainability. Andrew was appointed as Deputy Chairman in 2011 and succeeded Sir Nicholas Grimshaw as Chairman in June 2019; the Chairman's Office is responsible for managing the practices' core design ethos and long-term strategies.

Tim Williams, PhD, is head of cities for Grimshaw, the international architecture and design practice. Tim has for many years advised leaders in several countries in governments, councils, and the private sector on urban strategies and development. Tim was the special advisor to five successive UK planning and housing ministers. Now in Australia, he was CEO of the Committee for Sydney, the nation's prime urban think tank, where he published several reports on Smart Cities. Tim is an adjunct professor at Western Sydney University and is a qualified barrister.

Thomas Wortmann, PhD, Dipl.-Ing., MSc, is a tenure-track professor of Computing in Architecture at the Institute for Computational Design and Construction (ICD) and a

PI at the Cluster of Excellence Integrative Computational Design and Construction for Architecture (IntCDC).

Xinyi Yang received BS and MS degrees in Statistics and Civil Engineering from North Dakota State University in 2018 and 2020. Xinyi Yang is currently pursuing a PhD in Civil and Environmental Engineering and Computer Science at NDSU. Her research interests include intelligent transport systems, deep learning, traffic modeling, and simulations.

Terence Young, with more than 25 years of experience in aviation and transportation, has designed an impressive range of world-class projects, both in the US and internationally. As a principal and design director for Gensler Los Angeles, he guides teams in the design of pioneering projects such as Incheon International Airport Terminal 2; and San Francisco International Airport Terminals 1, 2, and 3, on multiple projects at the Los Angeles International Airport. He approaches each commission with a desire to express the cultural heritage and pride of the cities and communities.

Mengni Zhang is an assistant professor of Design Studies at the University of Wisconsin–Madison. As a licensed architect with a focus on healthcare, his practice and research work focuses on creating and evaluating spatial designs to understand the impact of the built environment on human behavior to improve life qualities.

Fiona Zisch, PhD, is the program director of the Bartlett School of Architecture's transdisciplinary M.Arch Design for Performance and Interaction at University College London. She works across architecture and cognitive science, where her research explores cognitive ecologies with a focus on intuition and radical (4EA) embodiment, as well as how Neuroarchitecture as a transdisciplinary threshold might develop more wicked thinking. Fiona also collaborates on healthcare research, for example, neurorehabilitation spaces in physical and virtual – and eXtended – environments.

INDEX

Note: **Bold** page numbers refer to tables; *italic* page numbers refer to figures and page numbers followed by "n" denote endnotes.

693

T - #0121 - 221024 - C0 - 246/174/34 [36] - CB - 9781032469904 - Matt Lamination